ZAGAT®

New York City Gourmet Shopping & Entertaining

2009

EDITOR
Carol Diuguid

Published and distributed by
Zagat Survey, LLC
4 Columbus Circle
New York, NY 10019
T: 212.977.6000
E: nycgourmetshopping@zagat.com
www.zagat.com

ACKNOWLEDGMENTS

We thank Betsy Andrews, Siobhan Burns, Caren Weiner Campbell, Mikola De Roo, Margot P. Ernst, Lynn Hazlewood, George Louis Jr., Gerard Miller, Bernie Onken, Patty Tang, Alexandria Tara, Miranda Van Gelder and Laura J. Vogel, as well as the following members of our staff: Josh Rogers (associate editor), Sean Beachell, Maryanne Bertollo, Sandy Cheng, Reni Chin, Larry Cohn, Alison Flick, Jeff Freier, Michelle Golden, Roy Jacob, Natalie Lebert, Mike Liao, Dave Makulec, Andre Pilette, Kimberly Rosado, Becky Ruthenburg, Sharon Yates, Yoji Yamaguchi, Anna Zappia and Kyle Zolner.

Maps © 2008 GeoNova Publishing, Inc., except for p. 8, provided by Steven Shukow.

Contents

Ratings & Symbols

	Zagat Top Spot	Name	Symbols		Category		Zagat Ratings			
							QUALITY	DISPLAY	SERVICE	COST

Area, Address & Contact

Z Tim & Nina's ◐ *Seafood*

W 50s | 4 Columbus Circle (8th Ave.), 1/A/B/C/D to 59th St./Columbus Circle | 212-977-6000 | www.zagat.com

∇ 23 | 9 | 13 | I

Review, surveyor comments in quotes

Fanatical fish fanciers find that the fastest route to "fairly fared fin fare" is a foray to this "grungy grotto" below Columbus Circle, where the catch is "never more than a day old" and "the price is always net"; still, sensitive shoppers say the "surly staffers should be used as fish-bait"; P.S. check out the "daily East River specials" and Tim and Nina's catering service on the A train.

Ratings

Quality, Display and **Service** are rated on the Zagat 0 to 30 scale.

0	–	9	poor to fair
10	–	15	fair to good
16	–	19	good to very good
20	–	25	very good to excellent
26	–	30	extraordinary to perfection
	∇		low response	less reliable

Cost

Reflects our surveyors' average estimate of the price range, indicated as follows:

I Inexpensive

M Moderate

E Expensive

VE Very Expensive

Symbols

Z Zagat Top Spot (highest ratings, popularity and importance)

◐ open until 8:30 PM or later

☷ mail order available via catalog, phone or web

⌿ no credit cards accepted

About This Survey

This **2009 New York City Gourmet Shopping & Entertaining Survey** is an update reflecting significant developments since our last Survey was published. It covers 1,801 establishments in New York City, including 72 important additions and 343 party sites, plus 75 outstanding online sources. We've also indicated new addresses, phone numbers and other major alterations, and surveyed recent arrivals as well as last year's unrated properties to bring this guide up to the minute.

WHO PARTICIPATED: Input from 6,807 avid customers forms the basis for the ratings and reviews in this guide (their comments are shown in quotation marks within the reviews). Of these surveyors, 60% are women, 40% men; the breakdown by age is 12% in their 20s; 28%, 30s; 22%, 40s; 22%, 50s; and 16%, 60s or above. Their collective experience adds up to over 650,000 transactions a year. We sincerely thank each of these participants – this book is really "theirs."

HELPFUL LISTS: Whether you're looking for food, flowers, wine or liquor, caterers or locations or whether you want to save money or splurge, our lists can help you find exactly the right place. See Best Overall (page 9), Top Ratings (pages 10–18) and Best Buys (page 19). We've also provided 57 handy indexes and included an Online Sources section to help guide you to the best websites for everything from fresh flowers, fish and meat to candy, baked goods and even hard-to-find party accessories. (See Best Overall and Top Quality Ratings pages 324–325).

ABOUT ZAGAT: This marks our 29th year reporting on the shared experiences of consumers like you. What started in 1979 as a hobby involving 200 of our friends has come a long way. Today we have over 325,000 surveyors and now cover airlines, bars, clubs, dining, entertaining, golf, hotels, lounges, movies, music, resorts, shopping, spas, theater and tourist attractions worldwide.

VOTE AND COMMENT: We invite you to join any of our upcoming surveys at **ZAGAT.com**. There you can rate and review establishments year-round without charge. In fact, in exchange for participating you will receive a free copy of the resulting guide when published.

AVAILABILITY: Zagat guides are available in all major bookstores as well as on **ZAGAT.com, ZAGAT.mobi** (for web-enabled mobile phones) and **ZAGAT TO GO** (for smartphones). All of these products allow you to reserve at thousands of places with just one click.

FEEDBACK: There is always room for improvement, thus we invite your comments and suggestions about any aspect of our performance. Is there something more you would like us to include in our guides? Did we get anything wrong? We really need your input! Just contact us at **nycgourmetshopping@zagat.com**.

New York, NY
July 17, 2008

Nina and Tim Zagat

What's New

Though the national economy may be struggling, NYC's gourmet shopping scene continues to flourish, especially in Brooklyn, where a full third of our Noteworthy Newcomers have set up shop. Here's a look at what's been happening:

GOING GREEN: Last year 82% of our surveyors told us that they were willing to pay more for organic food, so it's no surprise that shops and services offering organic, locally sourced and/or sustainably produced goods are proliferating. Gourmet shops specializing in such provender are cropping up all over town – and with their design-conscious aesthetics and sophisticated wares they're a far cry from the sprouts-and-wheat-germ health fooders of yore. The most recent arrivals include the locavore-oriented **Urban Rustic Market** in Williamsburg, **Greene Grape Provisions** in Fort Greene and **Organic Heights** in Park Slope, where **Get Fresh,** an eco-conscious market/ready-to-cook meals service also set up shop. Midtown Manhattan saw the debut of **FreeFoods,** a take-out place catering to office workers with mostly organic items, while the city's first organic florist, **Gardenia Organic,** blossomed in the West Village. Three different organic frozen dessert purveyors made their debuts, and each has already begat a second location: **Blue Marble Ice Cream** (in Boerum Hill and Prospect Heights), **Öko Frozen Yogurt & Tea** (Park Slope, the East Village) and **/eks/** (Williamsburg, the East Village).

FROZEN FRENZY: Speaking of frozen yogurt, the craze that **pinkberry** ignited when it came East from LA – inspiring lines out the doors of its splashily decorated storefronts with its real milk-based, fresh-fruit topped product – shows no signs of cooling off. For the first time in this guide we provide a ranking of the top-rated fro-yo purveyors, and, surprisingly, the one that started it all has been outstripped by those who arrived in its wake: the aforementioned Öko, the mini-chain **Red Mango** and the Gramercy newcomer **Flurt** all

received higher Quality ratings than pinkberry. Other new arrivals to the scene include Murray Hill's **Berrywild,** the East Village's **Very Berry** and the West Village's **Yogurtland** – the latter brings a novel concept to the genre: self-service.

CAFFEINE HIGH: Just as upscale frozen yogurt places seem to be popping up on every corner, so too do connoisseur-quality coffee shops, whose pedigreed beans and sophisticated brewing technology place them miles above the corner Starbucks. Notably, NYC has finally scored an outlet of the legendary Philadelphia roaster **La Colombe,** in TriBeCa, while the East Village gained **Abraço Espresso,** an upstart that out-rated many seasoned veterans in the field, as well as **Mercury Dime,** from cocktail guru Sasha Petraske. **Joe** rolled out two new branches, in Chelsea and in Grand Central Terminal, as did the venerable **Porto Rico Importing Co.,** which opened a stall in the Essex Street Market and a shop in Williamsburg. Two Brooklyn arrivals opened for business with coveted, ultra-high-end Clover coffee machines:

Williamsburg's **El Beit** and Park Slope's **Root Hill Cafe.** Meanwhile, the seriously high-tech Lower Eastsider **Roasting Plant** has been generating lots of buzz since it opened a little more than a year ago, and has in the works a second, even more impressive West Village location. Also, legendary Portland, OR, roaster Stumptown Coffee has set up a facility in Brooklyn from which it is supplying **Ninth Street Espresso** as well as several restaurants; its first NYC retail store will be inside the Ace Hotel near Macy's, set to open in late 2008.

GOODBYE, HELLO: But just as a multitude of exciting businesses entered the scene, three of its cherished, long-running players made their exit. Kielbasa king Kurowycky Meat Products closed its doors after serving its East Village community for 52 years; Queens legend Jahn's Ice Cream Parlor in Richmond Hills – first scoop served in 1900! – dished up its last Kitchen Sink sundae earlier this year; and Midtown cookware store extraordinaire, Bridge Kitchenware, announced plans to move to East Hanover, NJ, this month. Still, nostalgists can take heart at a handful of this year's arrivals that nod to the city's rich past: they include **Friedman's Delicatessen** in Chelsea, modeled after NYC delis of the 1940s; Prospect Heights' **Old Brooklyn Parlor,** a perfect replica of an old-fashioned neighborhood soda fountain, and two Williamsburg entries, **Spuyten Duyvil Grocery** and the aforementioned Urban Rustic, both of which, while the epitome of hip, possess an old-general-store aesthetic and a back-to-basics approach.

RANDOM NOTES: The city gained its first store dedicated exclusively to Japanese sake and spirits this year in the elegant East Village arrival **Sakaya,** while two new shops specializing in Japanese tea and sweets opened, Gramercy's **Amai** and East Midtown's **Tafu** . . . Essex Street Market on the Lower East Side continues its revival, with new stalls debuting including artisanal confectioner **Roni-Sue's Chocolates, Paradou Marché,** a sandwich offshoot of the Meatpacking District eatery Paradou, and the aforementioned branch of Porto Rico Importing Co. . . . The city's passion for cupcakes never seems to wane, but another sweet morsel seems to be coming to the fore: the French-style macaron. Venerable Gallic spots like **Payard** and **La Maison du Chocolat** have long carried them, but recently some newer players have entered the field, offering novel flavors, including **Kee's Chocolates** (kaffir lime, rose-lychee), **Bouchon Bakery** (yuzu, peaches 'n' cream) and newcomers **How Sweet It Is** (black sesame) and **Madeleine Patisserie** (an ever-changing array of more than 20 flavors) . . . On the Major Gourmet Market front, **Trader Joe's** debuted an outlet in Rego Park, Queens, and has announced plans for another in Brooklyn Heights, Brooklyn upstart **Union Market** opened its second location in Park Slope and is at work on a third in Fort Greene, while **Whole Foods** has broken ground on locations in TriBeCa and Park Slope . . . And sweet tooths take note: Park Slope's **Chocolate Room** has a Cobble Hill offshoot in the works, while **Chocolate Bar,** currently with just one outlet in Midtown, is expected to open an East Village branch in mid-summer 2008.

New York, NY
July 17, 2008

Carol Diuguid

W. 86th St.
Dean & DeLuca*
E. 86th St.

UPPER WEST SIDE
Zabar's
W. 79th St.

American Museum of Natural History

Metropolitan Museum of Art

E. 83rd St.
UPPER EAST SIDE
Lobel's Prime Meats

E. 79th St.

La Maison du Chocolat

William Poll

Citarella
E. 75th St.

Citarella
W. 74th St.
Levain Bakery
W. 72nd St.
Grandaisy Bakery
W. 70th St.

The Lake

CENTRAL PARK

Payard Pâtisserie & Bistro
E. 72nd St.

Ito En
E. 69th St.

W. 66th St.

Borgatti's Ravioli & Egg Noodles

N.J.

Absolute Bagels

BRONX

Citarella

Top detail

La Guardia Airport

MAN.

Bottom detail

Artopolis Bakery

Ralph's Famous Italian Ices*

QUEENS

Lemon Ice King of Corona

Sahadi's Two for the Pot

Blue Apron

D'Amico Foods

BROOKLYN

Kennedy International Airport

Coluccio & Sons

Villabate Pasticceria

Time Warner Center
Bouchon Bakery
Whole Foods

Central Park South
Columbus Circle
Petrossian Boutique & Cafe

Westerly Natural Market

The Pond

E. 61st St.
Sherry-Lehmann
E. 59th St.
Queensborough Bridge

E. 57th St.

MIDTOWN
E. 55th St.

Rockefeller Center

La Maison du Chocolat

E. 52nd St.
Pisacane Midtown
Zezé
E. 49th St.

E. 47th St.
United Nations

Sullivan St. Bakery

Grand Central Terminal

Murray's Cheese Shop
Penzeys Spices

W. 42nd St.

BRYANT PARK

New York Public Library

Original SoupMan

Burgundy Wine Company
W. 26th St.

East River

Whole Foods
W. 23rd St.

MADISON SQ. PARK

CHELSEA

W. 20th St.

GRAMERCY PARK
E. 21st St.

GRAMERCY PARK

E. 23rd St.

L'Arte del Gelato
W. 18th St.

Moore Brothers Wine Co.
E. 18th St.

Amy's Bread
Chelsea Market

Belle Fleur
W. 16th St.

UNION SQ.

W. 14th St.
Whole Foods
E. 14th St.

MEAT-PACKING DIST.

W. 12th St.
E. 12th St.

EAST VILLAGE

Citarella
W. 10th St.

E. 10th St.

TOMPKINS SQ. PARK

WEST VILLAGE

Patisserie Claude

WASHINGTON SQ. PARK

Abraço Espresso
E. 7th St.

E. 4th St.

L'Arte del Gelato
Florence Meat

GREENWICH VILLAGE

Whole Foods
Russ & Daughters
Sugar Sweet Sunshine

Colette's Cakes
Murray's Cheese Shop

Dean & DeLuca*

Il Laboratorio del Gelato

LOWER EAST SIDE

Raffetto's Olive's

Alessi

NOLITA

Kee's Chocolates
Grandaisy Bakery

DiPalo Dairy

Pickle Guys

Kossar's Bialys

SOHO

Divalicious

Viet-Nam Bánh Mì So #1

LITTLE ITALY

Hudson River

TRIBECA

Bazzini, A.L.

CHINATOWN

Manhattan Bridge

Korin Japanese Trading Co.

City Hall

Brooklyn Bridge

FDR Dr.

East River

* Check for other locations

Best Overall

Averaging Quality, Display & Service ratings.

28 | Zezé | *Flowers*
Moore Brothers | *Wines*
Colette's Cakes | *Bakery*

27 | Lobel's Meats | *Meat*
Belle Fleur | *Flowers*
Ito En | *Coffee/Tea*
Minamoto Kitchoan | *Candy*
Bottlerocket Wine | *Wine*
Petrossian | *Caviar*

26 | Takashimaya | *Flowers*
Pierre Marcolini | *Candy*
La Maison Chocolat | *Candy*
Vino | *Wines*
Dessert Delivery | *Bakery*
Murray's Cheese | *Cheese*
Sylvia Weinstock | *Bakery*
Nespresso | *Coffee/Tea*
Le Dû's Wines | *Wine*
Artisanal | *Cheese*
East Village Meat | *Meat*
Russ & Daughters | *Smoked Fish*
Sherry-Lehmann | *Wine*
Artopolis Bakery | *Bakery*
LeNell's | *Wines**
Jacques Torres | *Candy*
Staubitz Market | *Meat*

25 | Abigail Kirsch | *Caterer*
Payard Pâtisserie | *Bakery*
Williams-Sonoma | *Cookware*
Burgundy Wine | *Wine*

Bloom | *Flowers*
Faicco's Pork | *Meat*
DiPalo Dairy | *Cheese*
Lady M | *Bakery*
Italian Wine | *Wine*
Bedford Cheese | *Cheese*
Blue Apron | *Specialty*
Teuscher Chocolates | *Candy*
Manhattan Fruitier | *Specialty*
Crush Wine | *Wine*
Florence Meat | *Meat*
Kee's Chocolates | *Candy*
Morrell | *Wine*
Despaña Foods | *Specialty*
Martine's Chocolates | *Candy*
Red, White & Bubbly | *Wine*
Glorious Food | *Caterer*
Villabate | *Bakery*
Korin Japanese | *Cookware*
Almondine Bakery | *Bakery*
Bouley Bakery | *Bakery*
Biancardi Meats | *Meat*
Vosges | *Candy*
Black Hound | *Bakery*
Confetti Cakes | *Bakery*
Financier Pâtisserie | *Bakery*
Bay Ridge Bakery | *Bakery*
Ladybird | *Bakery*
Bierkraft | *Beer*
Ariston | *Flowers*

KEY NEWCOMERS

Our take on some of the year's main arrivals. See page 280 for a full list.

Abraço Espresso | *Coffee/Tea*
applewares | *Cookware*
Batch | *Baked Goods*
Blue Marble | *Ice Cream*
ChikaLicious Puddin' | *Baked Goods*
D.O.C. Wine Shop | *Wine/Liquor*
Friedman's Deli | *Deli/Sandwich*
Gardenia Organic | *Flowers*

How Sweet It Is | *Baked Goods*
La Colombe | *Coffee/Tea*
Madeleine Patisserie | *Baked Goods*
Oro Bakery and Bar | *Baked Goods*
Pappabubble | *Candy/Nuts*
Sakaya | *Wine/Liquor*
Urban Rustic Mkt. | *Specialty Shop*
Zucker's Bagels | *Bagels*

---

* Indicates a tie with property above

Top Quality Ratings

Excludes places with low votes, unless indicated by a ▽. Major Gourmet Markets are listed by the scores they received for the applicable department.

29 | Colette's Cakes
Lobel's Meats
Zezé
Florence Meat
Grandaisy Bakery*
Kee's Chocolates
Salumeria Biellese
Burgundy Wine
DiPalo Dairy
La Maison Chocolat
Staubitz Market | Bklyn
Borgatti's Ravioli | Bx
Martine's Chocolates
Moore Brothers
Sherry-Lehmann

28 | Petrossian
Dessert Delivery
Belle Fleur
Murray's Cheese
Ladybird Bakery | Bklyn
Vino*
Il Laboratorio/Gelato
Artisanal
Russ & Daughters
Kossar's Bialys

Ito En
Korin Japanese*
Villabate | Bklyn*
Artopolis Bakery | Qns
Pierre Marcolini
Levain Bakery
Sullivan St. Bakery
Almondine Bakery | Bklyn
Calabria Pork | Bx*
East Village Meat*
Faicco's Pork | multi
Takashimaya
Pisacane
Bierkraft | Bklyn
Simchick, L.
Payard Pâtisserie
Randazzo's | Bx
Blue Ribbon Market
Jacques Torres | multi
Madonia Bakery | Bx
Ronnybrook Milk Bar
Coluccio & Sons | Bklyn
Raffetto's
Lady M
Joe's Dairy

BY CATEGORY

BAGELS/BIALYS

28 | Kossar's Bialys
26 | Absolute Bagels
Ess-a-Bagel
Bagel Oasis | Qns
Murray's Bagels
H & H Bagels
25 | Terrace Bagels | Bklyn
Hot Bialys | Qns

BREAD

29 | Grandaisy Bakery
28 | Sullivan St. Bakery
Blue Ribbon Market
Madonia Bakery | Bx
27 | Balthazar Bakery
Bouley Bakery
Falai Panetteria
Addeo Bakery | Bx

CAKES

29 | Colette's Cakes
28 | Dessert Delivery
Ladybird Bakery | Bklyn
Payard Pâtisserie
Lady M
27 | Soutine
S&S Cheesecake | Bx
26 | Black Hound

CANDY

29 | Kee's Chocolates
La Maison Chocolat
Martine's Chocolates
28 | Pierre Marcolini
Jacques Torres | multi
Minamoto Kitchoan
27 | Teuscher Chocolates
26 | Vosges

CATERERS/EVENTS

26 Abigail Kirsch | *multi*
25 Glorious Food
   Blue Smoke
   Cleaver Co.
24 Foremost
   Great Performances
23 David Burke
   Movable Feast | *Bklyn*

CAVIAR/SMOKED FISH

28 Petrossian
   Russ & Daughters
   Zabar's
27 Paramount Caviar | *Qns*
   Barney Greengrass
   Murray's Sturgeon
   Sable's
26 Caviar Russe

CHEESE/DAIRY

29 DiPalo Dairy
28 Murray's Cheese
   Artisanal
   Ronnybrook Milk Bar
   Zabar's
   Joe's Dairy
27 Alleva Dairy
   Dean & DeLuca

COFFEE

27 D'Amico Foods | *Bklyn*
   Abraço Espresso
   Jack's Stir Brew
   McNulty's Tea
26 Porto Rico Import | *multi*
   Mudspot
   Joe
25 Nespresso

COOKIES

28 Levain Bakery
27 Patisserie Claude
   Stork's Pastry | *Qns*
26 Black Hound
   Duane Park
25 City Bakery
   Veniero's
24 One Girl Cookies | *Bklyn*

COOKWARE/SUPPLIES

28 Korin Japanese
27 Zabar's
   Williams-Sonoma
   Alessi
   Dean & DeLuca
26 Cook's Companion | *Bklyn*

   Broadway Panhandler
   Sur La Table

CUPCAKES

27 Sugar Sweet
26 Amy's Bread
25 Baked | *Bklyn*
   Billy's Bakery*
   Make My Cake*
24 BabyCakes
   Sweet Melissa | *Bklyn*
23 Magnolia Bakery

DELIS/SANDWICHES

(See also Sandwich Shops)
27 Dean & DeLuca
   Zabar's
26 William Poll
   Agata & Valentina
25 E.A.T.
   Whole Foods
24 Katz's Deli
   Fairway | *multi*

FLOWERS

29 Zezé
28 Belle Fleur
   Takashimaya
27 Ariston
   Bloom
26 Dahlia
25 Surroundings
   Plaza Flowers

GIFT BASKETS

29 Sherry-Lehmann
28 Dessert Delivery
   Artisanal
27 Orchard | *Bklyn*
   Manhattan Fruitier
26 Black Hound
   Wild Edibles
24 Chelsea Baskets

GREENMARKET VENDORS

29 Bulich Mushroom
   Violet Hill Farm
   Blue Moon Fish
   Yuno's Farm
28 Keith's Farm
   Flying Pigs
   Cherry Lane Farms
   Berried Treasures

HEALTH/NATURAL FOODS

27 Whole Foods
25 Westerly Natural

Gary Null's
Commodities Natural
Fairway | *multi*
24 LifeThyme Mkt.
Perelandra Natural | *Bklyn*
Bell Bates Natural

HERBS/SPICES

27 Penzeys Spices
Dean & DeLuca
Kalustyan's
26 Aphrodisia
24 Spice Corner
House of Spices | *Qns*
23 Angelica's Herbs
Foods of India*

ICE CREAM

28 Il Laboratorio/Gelato
27 L'Arte del Gelato
Grom
26 Sant Ambroeus
Cones
25 Brooklyn Ice Cream | *Bklyn*
Ciao Bella Gelato
Chinatown Ice Cream

ICES/FROZEN YOGURT

27 Lemon Ice King | *Qns*
24 Ralph's Ices | *multi*
Öko | *Bklyn*
22 Red Mango | *multi*
21 Flurt
pinkberry | *multi*
Rita's Ices | *SI*
20 Yolato

MAJOR GOURMET MKTS.

27 Zabar's
Dean & DeLuca
26 Whole Foods
Citarella
Agata & Valentina
Fairway | *multi*
25 Eli's Manhattan
Eli's Vinegar

MEATS/POULTRY

29 Lobel's Meats
Florence Meat
Salumeria Biellese
Staubitz Market | *Bklyn*
28 Calabria Pork | *Bx*
East Village Meat*
Faicco's Pork | *multi*
Agata & Valentina

NEWCOMERS (RATED)

27 Abraço Espresso
24 ChikaLicious Puddin'
applewares | *Bklyn*
Madeleine Patisserie
Old Brooklyn Parlor | *Bklyn*
23 Think Coffee
22 Red Mango | *multi*
D.O.C. Wine Shop | *Bklyn*

NUTS/DRIED FRUITS

29 Bazzini, A.L.
27 Sahadi's | *Bklyn*
Kalustyan's
26 Dean & DeLuca
25 Zabar's
24 Economy Candy
23 Sweet Life
21 Aji Ichiban

PARTY RENTALS

24 Divalicious Fountains
23 Atlas Party Rentals
22 Party Rental Ltd.
20 Party Time
Props for Today*
19 Broadway Party

PASTAS

29 Borgatti's Ravioli | *Bx*
28 Raffetto's
27 Agata & Valentina
Queen Ann Ravioli | *Bklyn*
Piemonte Ravioli
26 Pastosa Ravioli | *multi*
Durso's Pasta Co. | *Qns*
24 Bruno

PASTRIES

28 Villabate | *Bklyn*
Artopolis Bakery | *Qns*
Almondine Bakery | *Bklyn*
Payard Pâtisserie
27 Financier Pâtisserie
Bouley Bakery
Bouchon Bakery
Margot Pâtisserie

PIES/TARTS

28 Payard Pâtisserie
27 Bouchon Bakery
26 Silver Moon
La Bergamote
Duane Park
25 Steve's/Pies | *Bklyn*
City Bakery
Once Upon A Tart

PREPARED FOODS

26 Dean & DeLuca
   William Poll
   Remi to Go
   Pepe
25 Bottega/Via
   Lorenzo & Maria's
   Zabar's
   E.A.T.

PRODUCE

27 Dean & DeLuca
   Whole Foods
26 Greenmarket
   Eli's Manhattan
25 Fairway | *multi*
   Garden of Eden | *multi*
   Greenwich Produce
24 Manhattan Fruit Ex.

SANDWICH SHOPS

(See also Delis/Sandwiches)
25 Olive's
   Bánh Mì Saigon
24 'wichcraft
   Nicky's Vietnamese | *multi*
23 Carve
   Viet-Nam Bánh*
   Starwich
   sNice

SEAFOOD

28 Citarella
   Pisacane
   Randazzo's | *Bx*
27 Cosenza's Fish | *Bx*
26 Leonard's
   Lobster Place
   Rainbo's Essex
   Wild Edibles

SINGULAR FOCUS

27 Pickle Guys (*pickles*)
   Stonehouse (*olive oil*)

25 O&CO. (*olive oil*)
23 Dale & Thomas (*popcorn*)
   Pickles, Olives (*pickles*)
   Rice to Riches (*rice pudding*)

SOUPS

25 Zabar's
   E.A.T.
24 Dishes
23 Soup Spot
   Original SoupMan | *multi*
22 Hale & Hearty | *multi*
   Fairway | *multi*
22 Fashion Soup

SPECIALTY SHOPS

28 Coluccio & Sons | *Bklyn*
27 Blue Apron | *Bklyn*
   Bangkok Grocery
   Despaña | *multi*
   Sahadi's | *Bklyn*
   Kalustyan's
26 Titan Foods | *Qns*
   Teitel Bros. | *Bx*

TEA

28 Ito En
27 Two for the Pot | *Bklyn*
   Tea Box
   McNulty's Tea
26 Porto Rico Import | *multi*
   T Salon
25 Ten Ren Tea | *multi*
24 Dean & DeLuca

WINES/LIQUOR

29 Burgundy Wine
   Moore Brothers
   Sherry-Lehmann
28 Vino
   Bierkraft | *Bklyn*
27 Morrell
   Italian Wine
   Le Dû's Wines

BY ETHNIC FOCUS

AMERICAN

28 Ladybird Bakery | *Bklyn*
26 Two Little Red Hens
   Cake Man Raven | *Bklyn*
25 City Bakery
   Make My Cake
   Eddie's Sweet | *Qns*
   Shake Shack

CENTRAL EUROPEAN

27 Schaller & Weber
   Stork's Pastry | *Qns*
26 Oppenheimer Meats
   Duane Park
23 Yorkville Meat
   Andre's | *multi*
22 Andrew & Alan's | *SI*

CHINESE

25	Ten Ren Tea	*multi*
23	May May
	Bayard St. Meat
	Flor de Mayo
22	Hong Keung
21	Kam Man Food
	Asia Market

EASTERN EUROPEAN

28	East Village Meat
26	Caviar Russe
25	Astoria Meat∇	*Qns*
	First Ave. Pierogi∇
24	Eagle Provisions	*Bklyn*
	M & I Foods	*Bklyn*

FRENCH/BELGIAN

29	Burgundy Wine
	La Maison Chocolat
	Martine's Chocolates
28	Petrossian
	Pierre Marcolini
	Payard Pâtisserie
	Jacques Torres	*multi*

GREEK/MED.

28	Artopolis Bakery	*Qns*
26	Titan Foods	*Qns*
	Poseidon Bakery
25	O&CO.
24	Todaro Brothers
	Mangia
23	Ninth Ave. Int'l

INDIAN/MIDEASTERN

27	Sahadi's	*Bklyn*
	Kalustyan's
25	Damascus Bakery	*Bklyn*
	D'Vine Taste	*Bklyn*
24	Spice Corner
	Tamarind Tea
23	Hampton Chutney

ITALIAN

29	Florence Meat
	Grandaisy Bakery
	Salumeria Biellese
	DiPalo Dairy
	Borgatti's Ravioli	*Bx*
28	Vino
	Villabate	*Bklyn*

JAPANESE

28	Ito En
	Takashimaya
	Minamoto Kitchoan
27	Tea Box
24	Beard Papa
23	Katagiri
	Sunrise Mart

JEWISH (KOSHER‡)

28	Russ & Daughters
	Kossar's Bialys‡
27	Fischer Bros.‡
	Pickle Guys‡
	Barney Greengrass
	Murray's Sturgeon‡
26	Oppenheimer Meats

BY LOCATION

CHELSEA

29	Salumeria Biellese
	Burgundy Wine
28	Ronnybrook Milk Bar
27	Williams-Sonoma
	Ariston
	L'Arte del Gelato
26	Lobster Place
	T Salon

CHINATOWN/LITTLE ITALY

29	DiPalo Dairy
27	Bangkok Grocery
	Alleva Dairy
	Despaña
	Piemonte Ravioli
25	Ten Ren Tea

| | Bánh Mì Saigon |
| | Chinatown Ice Cream |

EAST VILLAGE

28	East Village Meat
27	Abraço Espresso
26	Porto Rico Import
	Black Hound
	Mudspot
	Russo Mozzarella
	Chocolate Bar
	Joe

FLATIRON/UNION SQ.

29	Moore Brothers
28	Belle Fleur
27	Italian Wine
26	Whole Foods
	Bottlerocket Wine

25 City Bakery
Union Sq. Wines
Shake Shack

GARMENT DISTRICT
28 Artisanal
25 Esposito Meat
24 Ben & Jerry's
Häagen Dazs
Manganaro Foods
23 Starwich
Soup Spot
22 Hale & Hearty

GREENWICH VILLAGE
29 Florence Meat
28 Murray's Cheese
Faicco's Pork
Blue Ribbon Market
Raffetto's
27 Dean & DeLuca
Jack's Stir Brew
Patisserie Claude

LOWER EAST SIDE
28 Il Laboratorio/Gelato
Russ & Daughters
Kossar's Bialys
27 Falai Panetteria
Pickle Guys
Sugar Sweet
26 Porto Rico Import
Clinton St. Baking

MIDTOWN
29 Zezé
La Maison Chocolat
Martine's Chocolates
28 Petrossian
Dessert Delivery
Pierre Marcolini
Sullivan St. Bakery
Takashimaya

MURRAY HILL/GRAMERCY
28 Vino
Artisanal
27 Manhattan Fruitier
Kalustyan's
26 Les Halles
Wild Edibles
Ess-a-Bagel
25 Milano Gourmet

NOHO/NOLITA
26 Eileen's Cheesecake
25 Astor Wines

24 Ciao Bella
Häagen Dazs
Café Habana
23 Parisi Bakery
Rice to Riches
Think Coffee

SOHO
29 Grandaisy Bakery
Kee's Chocolates
28 Jacques Torres
Joe's Dairy
27 Balthazar Bakery
Dean & DeLuca
Alessi
26 Vosges

TRIBECA/DOWNTOWN
28 Korin Japanese
27 Financier Pâtisserie
Bouley Bakery
Dean & DeLuca
Jack's Stir Brew
Stonehouse
26 Sylvia Weinstock
Chambers St. Wines

UPPER EAST SIDE
29 Lobel's Meats
La Maison Chocolat
Martine's Chocolates
Sherry-Lehmann
28 Ito En
Payard Pâtisserie
Lady M
27 Teuscher Chocolates

UPPER WEST SIDE
29 Grandaisy Bakery
28 Levain Bakery
Jacques Torres
27 Soutine
Fischer Bros.
Zabar's
Bouchon Bakery
Barney Greengrass

WEST VILLAGE
29 Colette's Cakes
27 Le Dû's Wines
McNulty's Tea
26 Sant Ambroeus
Li-Lac Chocolates
Pepe
24 Integral Yoga
Milk & Cookies

OUTER BOROUGHS

BRONX

- 29 Borgatti's Ravioli
- 28 Calabria Pork
- Randazzo's
- Madonia Bakery
- 27 Vincent's Meat
- S&S Cheesecake
- Addeo Bakery
- Biancardi Meats

BROOKLYN: CARROLL GARDENS/ COBBLE HILL

- 29 Staubitz Market
- 27 D'Amico Foods
- 26 Esposito's Pork
- American Beer
- 25 Fish Tales
- Court Pastry
- Mazzola Bakery
- 24 One Girl Cookies

BROOKLYN: HEIGHTS/DUMBO

- 28 Almondine Bakery
- Jacques Torres
- 27 Sahadi's
- Two for the Pot
- 26 Cook's Companion
- 25 Brooklyn Ice Cream
- Heights Chateau
- Damascus Bakery

BROOKLYN: PARK SLOPE

- 28 Ladybird Bakery
- Bierkraft
- 27 Blue Apron
- 26 Russo Mozzarella
- Red, White & Bubbly
- Cocoa Bar
- Prospect Wine
- 25 Chocolate Room

QUEENS

- 28 Artopolis Bakery
- 27 Ottomanelli's Meats
- Paramount Caviar
- Despaña
- Lemon Ice King
- Ottomanelli & Sons
- Stork's Pastry
- 26 Titan Foods

STATEN ISLAND

- 26 Pastosa Ravioli
- Royal Crown
- Mother Mousse
- 25 Eggers Ice Cream
- 24 Bari Pork
- Ralph's Ices
- Sedutto's
- 23 Original SoupMan

Top Display Ratings

28
Zezé
Takashimaya
Payard Pâtisserie
Colette's Cakes
Bloom
La Maison Chocolat

27
Ito En
Bottlerocket Wine
Minamoto Kitchoan
Belle Fleur
Nespresso
Petrossian
Williams-Sonoma
Dylan's Candy
Moore Brothers
Pierre Marcolini

26
Sylvia Weinstock
MarieBelle's
Terence Conran
Jacques Torres | *multi*
Plaza Flowers*
Black Hound
Artopolis Bakery | *Qns*
Alessi
Lady M
Dean & DeLuca
Abigail Kirsch | *multi*
Teuscher Chocolates
Rice to Riches
Vosges

25
Artisanal
Crush Wine
Financier Pâtisserie
Murray's Cheese
Lobel's Meats
Vino
Crate & Barrel
Discovery Wines
Confetti Cakes
Sant Ambroeus
O&CO.
Glorious Food
Whole Foods
Bouley Bakery
Pescatore
Chocolate Bar
Bouchon Bakery
Blue Apron | *Bklyn*
Wild Edibles
Manhattan Fruitier
East Village Meat

24
Eleni's Cookies
Martha's Bakery | *Qns*
Tea Box
Godiva
Bedford Cheese | *Bklyn*
La Bergamote
Astor Wines
Dessert Delivery
Max Brenner

Top Service Ratings

29 Moore Brothers	Staubitz Market | *Bklyn**
	Confetti Cakes
28 Zezé	Borgatti's Ravioli | *Bx*
Florence Meat	Big Nose Full Body | *Bklyn*
	Ito En
27 Colette's Cakes	Italian Wine
Lobel's Meats	Burgundy Wine
Jeffrey's	Fish Tales | *Bklyn**
Bottlerocket Wine	Petrossian
	Esposito's Pork | *Bklyn*
26 Cleaver Co.	Esposito Meat
Le Dû's Wines	Murray's Cheese
Ottomanelli & Sons | *multi*	Sundaes & Cones
Dessert Delivery	Bierkraft | *Bklyn*
Bay Ridge Bakery | *Bklyn*	Chambers St. Wines
Dorian's Seafood*	DiPalo Dairy
LeNell's | *Bklyn*	East Village Meat
Pisacane	
Prospect Wine | *Bklyn*	**24** Smith & Vine | *Bklyn*
	Despaña | *multi*
25 Simchick, L.	Glorious Food
Sylvia Weinstock*	Michael-Towne Wines | *Bklyn**
Minamoto Kitchoan	Russ & Daughters
Vino	Pierre Marcolini
Two for the Pot | *Bklyn*	Bedford Cheese | *Bklyn*
applewares | *Bklyn*	Sherry-Lehmann
Abigail Kirsch | *multi*	Kee's Chocolates
Faicco's Pork | *multi*	West Side Wine
D'Vine Taste | *Bklyn*	William Poll*
Nespresso*	Oppenheimer Meats
Red, White & Bubbly | *Bklyn**	Leonard's
Tavalon Tea*	Is Wine
Belle Fleur	
Biancardi Meats | *Bx*	

Best Buys

In order of Bang for the Buck rating.

1. Moore Brothers
2. Bottlerocket Wine
3. Borgatti's Ravioli | *Bx*
4. Madonia Bakery | *Bx*
5. LeNell's | *Bklyn*
6. Villabate | *Bklyn*
7. Artopolis Bakery | *Qns*
8. Bay Ridge Bakery | *Bklyn*
9. Pickle Guys
10. Delillo Pastry | *Bx*
11. East Village Meat
12. DiPalo Dairy
13. Raffetto's
14. Sugar Sweet
15. Faicco's Pork | *multi*
16. Jack's Stir Brew
17. Eddie's Sweet | *Qns*
18. Red, White & Bubbly | *Bklyn*
19. Sahadi's | *Bklyn*
20. Bangkok Grocery
21. Sundaes & Cones
22. Greenmarket | *multi*
23. Porto Rico Import
24. Skyview Discount | *Bx*
25. Addeo Bakery | *Bx*
26. Penzeys Spices
27. Calabria Pork | *Bx*
28. Prospect Wine | *Bklyn*
29. Murray's Cheese
30. D'Amico Foods | *Bklyn*
31. Java Girl
32. Smith & Vine | *Bklyn*
33. Biancardi Meats | *Bx*
34. Almondine Bakery | *Bklyn*
35. Harlem Tea
36. Vino
37. Dahlia
38. Jeffrey's
39. Coluccio & Sons | *Bklyn*
40. Florence Meat
41. Titan Foods | *Qns*
42. Best Cellars
43. Salumeria Biellese
44. Grandaisy Bakery
45. Artuso Pastry | *Bx*
46. Mudspot
47. Esposito's Pork | *Bklyn*
48. Astor Wines
49. Dessert Delivery
50. Greene Grape | *multi*

OTHER GOOD VALUES

Alleva Dairy
American Beer | *Bklyn*
Aphrodisia
Bedford Cheese
Bierkraft
Billy's Bakery
Chambers St. Wines
Cosenza's Fish | *Bx*
Court Pastry | *Bklyn*
Damascus Bakery | *Bklyn*
Despaña | *multi*
D'Vine Taste | *Bklyn*
Egidio Pastry | *Bx*
Esposito Meat
Financier Pâtisserie
Heights Chateau | *Bklyn*
Joe
Kossar's Bialys
L'Arte del Gelato
McNulty's Tea
Michael-Towne Wines | *Bklyn*
Mister Wright
Piemonte Ravioli
PJ Wine
Poseidon Bakery
Queen Ann Ravioli | *Bklyn*
Randazzo's | *Bx*
Rocco's Pastry
Royal Crown | *multi*
Russ & Daughters
Staubitz Market | *Bklyn*
Sullivan St. Bakery
Sweet Life
Teitel Brothers | *Bx*
Terrace Bagels | *Bklyn*
Trader Joe's | *multi*
Two for the Pot | *Bklyn*
Vincent's Meat | *Bx*
Vintage New York
West Side Wine

NYC SOURCES
DIRECTORY

NYC Sources

Abbey Rent-All *Party Rentals*　　`- | - | - | M`

Bayside | 203-16 Northern Blvd. (204th St.) | Queens | 718-428-8899 | 800-924-0428 | www.abbeyrent.com

For nearly 50 years, this Bayside rental outfit has been keeping parties going with a full range of tents, canopies, chairs, tables, linens and – summertime hosts, take note – even ice cream carts and portable air conditioners; N.B. delivery rates vary from borough to borough: $150 to the Bronx and Brooklyn, $125 to Manhattan, and $25 to Queens and LI.

Z Abigail Kirsch *Caterer*　　`26 | 26 | 25 | VE`

Chelsea | 71 W. 23rd St. (6th Ave.) | F/V to 23rd St. | 212-696-4076

Chelsea | Chelsea Piers | Pier 60 (Hudson River & 23rd St.) | C/E to 23rd St. | 212-336-6060

Chelsea | Chelsea Piers Lighthouse | Pier 61 (Hudson River & 23rd St.) | C/E to 23rd St. | 212-336-6144

Bronx | Botanical Garden | 200th St. (Southern Blvd.) | B/D to Fordham Rd. | 718-220-0300

Tarrytown | Tappan Hill | 81 Highland Ave. (bet. Benedict Ave. & Gunpowder Ln.), NY | 914-631-3030

www.abigailkirsch.com

"Everyone should be lucky enough to have an event – or go to one – run by Abigail Kirsch" according to acolytes of this reigning deity of catering and her "wonderful" operation voted NYC's "absolute best"; whether off-site or in one of her "memorable venues", "fabulous food" and "professional", "courteous" service "turn special occasions into something extraordinary", though keep in mind this is "champagne living on a champagne budget."

Z NEW Abraço Espresso ⊘ *Coffee/Tea*　　`27 | 19 | 23 | M`

E Village | 86 E. Seventh St. (bet. 1st & 2nd Aves.) | 6 to Astor Pl. | 212-388-9731 | www.abraconyc.com

Hailed as a "coffee-lover's dream" in a "sea of Charbucks", this "new-kid-on-the-block" East Villager is garnering raves for its "delicious, strong" espresso pulled "the way God intended"; it's also appreciated for its "excellent pastries" and "friendly" staff, while its standing-only coffee bar setup and absence of decaf can be chalked up as part of the "truly European experience."

Z Absolute Bagels ●⊘ *Bagels*　　`26 | 14 | 20 | I`

W 100s | 2788 Broadway (bet. 107th & 108th Sts.) | 1 to 110th St. | 212-932-2052

"It's the real deal" declare the "students carbo-packing" at this "hole-in-the-wall" near Columbia, which honors the "old-fashioned" "art of bagel-making" with "doughy" hand-rolled "spheres" sporting a "perfect" "crunchy" crust; with an "imaginative" "multitude of toppings" and "cheery" service that ensures the "lines move quickly", it's hailed by "those in-the-know" as the "absolute best" in the area.

	QUALITY	DISPLAY	SERVICE	COST

Academy Floral Co. ▣ *Flowers*   23 | 19 | 23 | M

W 100s | 2780 Broadway (107th St.) | 1 to 110th St. | 212-222-0771 |
800-231-7592 | www.academyfloral.com
Appreciated as a "classic florist", this "reliable" family-owned blooms
biz near Columbia has been making arrangements "for all occasions"
for almost a century now; though its specialty is flowers from Holland
and South America, often arrayed in signature fishbowl vessels, they
can also produce gift baskets with fruit, candy, plants and balloons.

Acker Merrall &   26 | 21 | 22 | E
Condit Co. ◑▣ *Wine/Liquor*

W 70s | 160 W. 72nd St. (bet. B'way & Columbus Ave.) | 1/2/3 to
72nd St. | 212-787-1700 | www.ackerwines.com
It's "first-class all the way" at this veteran UWS "wine haven" offering a "good balance of prices" and a "great range" of choices, with
particular strengths in California Cabernets, Bordeaux, Burgundys
and Super Tuscans; add to that a staff that "really knows how to help
customers" and its "famed" auctions (live or online), regular tasting
events, monthly specials and an "excellent" assortment of single-
malts, and it's easy to see why it's "been here for nearly 200 years."

Ackerson, T.B.,   - | - | - | M
Wine Merchants ◑ *Wine/Liquor*

Ditmas Park | 1205 Cortelyou Rd. (Westminster Rd.) | Brooklyn | Q to
Cortelyou Rd. | 718-826-6600 | www.tbackersonwine.com
Brooklyn's latest neighborhood-to-watch, Ditmas Park, gets its
first wine boutique with the arrival of this slim, husband-and-wife-
run shop, whose attractively arranged "great selection" is limited
but slowly expanding; its labels from around the globe are mostly
from small production vineyards, including some hard-to-find
bottlings, with an emphasis on organic, bio-dynamic and kosher
selections, many of them priced under $20; N.B. it hosts regular
tastings and seminars.

Acme Smoked Fish ⊭ *Caviar/Smoked Fish*   24 | 13 | 18 | M

Greenpoint | 30 Gem St. (N. 15th St.) | Brooklyn | G to Nassau Ave. |
718-383-8585 | www.acmesmokedfish.com
"Get to the source" advise afishionados of this "family-owned"
Greenpoint wholesaler, which "supplies the best" smoked fish to
outlets like Zabar's and Citarella; on Fridays from 8 AM-1 PM anyone can snag "top-flight" lox, Nova, sable, whitefish, herring and
sturgeon straight from the on-site smokehouse – if you're willing to
"schlep" for "fresher" goods "at bargain-basement prices", "you
won't be disappointed."

Addeo Bakery ⊭ *Baked Goods*   27 | 18 | 22 | I

Bronx | 2352 Arthur Ave. (bet. Crescent Ave. & 186th St.) | 2/5 to
Pelham Pkwy. | 718-367-8316
Bronx | 2372 Hughes Ave. (186th St.) | 2/5 to Pelham Pkwy. |
718-367-8316
"Old-world products do still exist" sigh supporters of this family-run
"step-back-in-time" Arthur Avenue bakery and its nearby offshoot,

whose *pane di casa* and other "top-notch" "rustic" loaves continue to make it a "staple" of "the Bronx's Little Italy"; though the staff of life is the thing here, it also bakes savory biscotti and "love-'em" hand-rolled seeded breadsticks that could be "NYC's best."

Z Agata & Valentina ●◗⎗ *Major Gourmet Mkt.*

26	23	20	E

E 70s | 1505 First Ave. (79th St.) | 6 to 77th St. | 212-452-0690 | www.agatavalentina.com

Its East Side champions claim this "culinary godsend" "should be the template" for "superior" Italian-style gourmandizing everywhere given its "go-to" status for "flavorful" prepared foods, "excellent" "fresh" pastas, meats "like buttah" from a "fantastic butcher", "wonderful" seafood, "fab cheeses" featuring "unusual choices" and "beautiful" baked goods, all backed by "accommodating" "staffers who know their products"; though the setup's a "congested" "labyrinth" that "can be daunting" "to maneuver", everyone in the area "tolerates it willingly" given that it's a proven "lifesaver" for a "premium" "mangia."

Ah Wong Bakery ⊘ *Baked Goods* (fka Maria's Bakery)

20	15	16	I

Chinatown | 42 Mott St. (bet. Bayard & Pell Sts.) | 6/J/M/N/Q/R/W/Z to Canal St. | 212-732-3888

It changed names not long ago, but this Chinatown bakery continues to turn out the same "high-quality", "low-priced" "typical Chinese pastries" (rice balls, stuffed buns, mooncakes, egg tarts) it's been making for more than 20 years; it's "nothing fancy", but "if you want something authentic" you can "surely get it here" – and at "a really good deal."

Aji Ichiban ⎗ *Candy/Nuts*

21	20	17	M

Chinatown | 167 Hester St. (bet. Elizabeth & Mott Sts.) | 6/J/M/N/Q/R/W/Z to Canal St. | 212-925-1133
Chinatown | 23 E. Broadway (bet. Catherine & Market Sts.) | F to E. B'way | 212-571-3755
Chinatown | 37 Mott St. (bet. Bayard & Pell Sts.) | A/C/E to Canal St. | 212-233-7650
Little Italy | 188 Lafayette St. (Grand St.) | B/D to Grand St. | 212-219-0808

Like a "Candy Land from the other side of the world", these Chinatown–Little Italy "snack-food boutiques" (links of a Hong Kong chain) boast "a myriad" of "delightful" "bite-size oddities" – "colorful sweets", "excellent, exotic dried fruits", beef jerky, dried fish, etc. – to "feed your taste for adventure"; it's "not cheap", but the stock is "unique" and for those "unidentifiable" items, "free tastings" "make it easier to decide."

Albert & Sons Prime Meats ⎗ *Meat/Poultry*

26	21	23	E

E 60s | 836 Lexington Ave. (bet. 63rd & 64th Sts.) | F to Lexington Ave./63rd St. | 212-751-3169 | www.albertandsons.net

"Yeah, baby – let me sink my teeth into one of those rib-eyes" roar carnivores of the "excellent" steaks and other meat, poultry and game (including organic selections) cut with care at this family-owned, 45-year-old UES butcher; some say it's "cheaper to dine out", but those who can stomach the "expensive" tabs swear "you really can taste the difference in every bite"; N.B. it also offers seafood and prepared foods.

✓ Alessi ⌨ *Cookware*   27 | 26 | 20 | E

SoHo | 130 Greene St. (bet. Houston & Prince Sts.) | N/R to Prince St. | 212-941-7300 | www.alessi.com

"Eye candy" abounds at this "cool" "museumlike" SoHo store showcasing Alessi's brand of "well-designed" "high-end" stainless-steel cookware, appliances and "avant-garde" tabletop items from Italy; though some surveyors quip the "esoteric" gadgets work best as an "IQ test", most find the wares "fabulous", "if you can afford them"; P.S. "savor a true cappuccino after shopping" at the in-store branch of Joe coffee bar.

Alice's Tea Cup *Coffee/Tea*   24 | 23 | 20 | M

W 70s | 102 W. 73rd St. (bet. Amsterdam & Columbus Aves.) | 1/2/3 to 72nd St. | 212-799-3006

Alice's Tea Cup, Chapter II *Coffee/Tea*

E 60s | 156 E. 64th St. (bet. Lexington & 3rd Aves.) | 6 to 68th St. | 212-486-9200

Alice's Tea Cup, Chapter III *Coffee/Tea*

E 80s | 220 E. 81st St. (bet. 2nd & 3rd Aves.) | 6 to 77th St. | 212-734-4832
www.alicesteacup.com

"A trip to Wonderland" for "discriminating tea lovers", this "super-cute" Upper Westsider (with two East Side sequels) pairs its "countless" types of "tea-licious" brews with "scrumptious" scones, finger sandwiches and "fairy-tale desserts"; the "whimsical", Lewis Carroll-inspired setting is "popular to a fault" for "mom-and-daughter" confabs or "light lunch with the girlfriends", "intimate bridal showers" or children's parties; P.S. the front shop vends bulk teas, pots, books and more.

Alidoro ⊄ *Deli/Sandwich*   ∇ 27 | 18 | 22 | M

SoHo | 105 Sullivan St. (bet. Prince & Spring Sts.) | C/E to Spring St. | 212-334-5179

"Let the maestro do his work and you won't be disappointed" say regulars of this SoHo storefront where the "huge" "quality" sandwiches with an Italian bent (many featuring fresh mozzarella) are best when "made by the proprietor" and enjoyed on a bench in one of the nearby parks; though a few find "the long waits amongst pretentious hipsters" hard to bear, most are happy to "tune out" the surroundings for what they call "the best in the city, period."

Alleva Dairy ⌨ *Cheese/Dairy*   27 | 20 | 23 | M

Little Italy | 188 Grand St. (Mulberry St.) | 6/J/M/N/Q/R/W/Z to Canal St. | 212-226-7990 | 800-425-5382 | www.allevadairy.com
The "real deal" "for all your Italian cheese" needs, this "family-owned" Little Italy vet (established 1892) is "committed" to supply-

	QUALITY	DISPLAY	SERVICE	COST

ing the "highest quality" in "mouthwatering" mozzarella, ricotta and assorted imports; also featuring a sideline in salami, prosciutto, olive oils and the like, it's a "nice surprise" "that hasn't compromised", with "good prices" to boot.

☑ Almondine Bakery ⊘ *Baked Goods* 28 | 23 | 23 | M

Dumbo | 85 Water St. (bet. Dock & Main Sts.) | Brooklyn | A/C to High St. | 718-797-5027 | www.almondinebakery.buzz

It's "the real stuff" rave Francophiles of this little shop's "superlative" French bakery staples – notably the "finest" croissants and baguettes and "jewellike" pastries – considered "the closest thing to Paris" this side of the East River; "master" baker (and Le Bernardin alum) Hervé Poussot is the man behind this operation touted by locals as "one more reason to move to Dumbo."

NEW Amai Tea & 20 | 19 | 18 | M
Bake House ◐ ▤ *Baked Goods*

Gramercy | 171 Third Ave. (bet. 16th & 17th Sts.) | 4/5/6/L/N/ Q/R/W to 14th St./Union Square | 212-863-9630 | www.amainyc.com

In addition to a tea menu whose length rivals many a wine list's, this "relaxed" Gramercy bakery/teahouse with a Zen-like aura ('amai' is Japanese for 'sweet') offers an array of "fresh", all-natural baked treats featuring "clever flavors that definitely work", such as cookies tinged with Earl Grey tea and brownies filled with exotic fruit; N.B. their wares are also available on their website and at stores around town like Takashimaya.

A Matter of Health ◐ ▤ *Health Food* 21 | 16 | 19 | M

E 70s | 1478 First Ave. (77th St.) | 6 to 77th St. | 212-288-8280 | www.amatterofhealth.net

Really it's a matter of space at this health food store, a "cramped" but much-appreciated source in the underserved neighborhood bordering Yorkville carrying a "broad selection" of natural products at "reasonable prices"; yes, "crowded shelves" and "narrow aisles" can be claustrophobic, but luckily there's a "friendly" staff you can "ask for what you're looking for."

Ambassador Wines & Spirits ◐ *Wine/Liquor* 24 | 18 | 20 | E

E 50s | 1020 Second Ave. (54th St.) | E/V to Lexington Ave./53rd St. | 212-421-5078 | www.ambassadorwines.com

This "reliable" East Side wine shop "always has a little something tucked away for the experimental customer", with different areas displaying Burgundies, dessert wines, half-bottles and magnums, as well as a "walk-in refrigerated case" holding its "excellent range of sake"; the "helpful" staff "knows its stuff", and regulars can purchase Bordeaux and Burgundy futures with no deposit required.

American Beer Distributing *Beer* 26 | 18 | 23 | M

Cobble Hill | 256 Court St. (bet. Butler & Kane Sts.) | Brooklyn | F/G to Bergen St. | 718-875-0226 | www.americanbeerbuzz.com

From "cheap" "macro swill" to pricier "exotic brews from far and wide", the beer "flows like bottled water" at this "longtime"

	QUALITY	DISPLAY	SERVICE	COST

Cobble Hill "institution", which also offers snacks and other beverages; the staff "bends over backwards" to help you "shop easily" in the "bare-bones" but "well-organized" 4,000-sq.-ft. space, and it also delivers.

Amish Market ❶ *Major Gourmet Mkt.*   23 | 21 | 17 | M

E 40s | 240 E. 45th St. (bet. 2nd & 3rd Aves.) | 4/5/6/7/S to 42nd St./ Grand Central | 212-370-1761
Financial District | 53 Park Pl. (bet. Church St. & W. B'way) | 2/3/A/ C/E to Park Pl. | 212-608-3863
W 40s | 731 Ninth Ave. (bet. 49th & 50th Sts.) | C/E to 50th St. | 212-245-2360
Glendale | 8000 Cooper Ave. (80th St.) | Queens | L/M to Myrtle/ Wyckoff Aves. | 718-894-1199
www.amishfinefood.com

Maybe the "name is disingenuous" ("where are the Amish?"), but this "fast, convenient" gourmet grocer quartet is still "good for the soul" given the "bounty" of its "wide array of cheeses", "beautifully displayed produce", "great mix of prepared foods" (including "appetizing" pizza) and extras like "vats of olives"; nonbelievers contend it's "more a wannabe" where "service is often spotty", but it's always "useful in a pinch", especially at the Park Place location, which is among the area's few "reliable" "meal savers."

☑ Amy's Bread *Baked Goods*   26 | 22 | 20 | M

Chelsea | Chelsea Mkt. | 75 Ninth Ave. (bet. 15th & 16th Sts.) | A/ C/E/L to 14th St./8th Ave. | 212-462-4338
G Village | 250 Bleecker St. (Morton St.) | A/B/C/D/E/F/V to W. 4th St. | 212-675-7802 ❶
W 40s | 672 Ninth Ave. (bet. 46th & 47th Sts.) | C/E to 50th St. | 212-977-2670 ❶
www.amysbread.com

Carbophiles "sing the praises" of the "heavenly" "artisan" goods at Amy Scherber's bakery trio, now considered a NYC "classic"; reknowned for its "fantastic" handmade breads (including signatures like the semolina-raisin-fennel), it also traffics in sweets from "out-of-this-world" sticky buns to "awesome cupcakes", as well as "delicious sandwiches" and other "good lunchables" – perfect for "eating at one of the few tables" if you can snag one.

Andre's Cafe ▣ *Baked Goods*   23 | 18 | 19 | M

E 80s | 1631 Second Ave. (bet. 84th & 85th sts.) | 4/5/6 to 86th st. | 212-327-1105 | www.andrescafenyc.com

Andre's Hungarian ▣⊅ *Baked Goods*

Forest Hills | 100-28 Queens Blvd. (67th Ave.) | Queens | G/R/V to 67th Ave. | 718-830-0266 | www.andresbakery.com

"Where else can you buy cabbage strudel in this day and age?" wonder grateful groupies of this "old-school", family-run bakery/cafe pair proffering "delicious", "moderately priced" babka, rugalach and other Hungarian specialties "just like you remember"; the 30-plus-year-old Forest Hills original recently "received a fresh look", while the newer UES outpost offers Budapest-worthy savory fare in addition to the sweets.

	QUALITY	DISPLAY	SERVICE	COST

Andrew & Alan's Bakery & Chocolate Factory ⌨ *Baked Goods*

22 | 22 | 22 | M

Staten Island | 61 New Dorp Plaza (bet. New Dorp Ln. & Rose Ave.) | 718-667-9696 | www.andrewandalansbakery.com

"If you're ever in Staten Island", supporters suggest you "stop in" at this veteran German-American bakery/chocolate shop and "try any" of the treats, including "old-world" favorites (babka, strudel), special-occasion cakes and chocolate-covered strawberries and pretzels that alone are "worth the trip"; as the "long lines on holidays" attest, it's considered the "closest to homemade you'll find" in these parts.

Angelica's Herbs, Spices & Oils ⊄ *Herbs/Spices*

23 | 18 | 20 | M

E Village | 147 First Ave. (9th St.) | 6 to Astor Pl. | 212-677-1549

"Excellence and temptation abound" in this "treasure trove" of herbs and spices in the East Village, where you might feel a bit "dizzy" to be surrounded by the "earthy, medicinal, exotic, intriguing" selection; the "very informative" staff will help you find what you need, whether it's the ingredients for your own curry powder, or advice on how to cure what ails you.

Annie's *Produce*

21 | 17 | 18 | M

E 80s | 1204 Lexington Ave. (bet. 81st & 82nd Sts.) | 4/5/6 to 86th St. | 212-861-6078

E 80s | 1330 Lexington Ave. (bet. 88th & 89th Sts.) | 4/5/6 to 86th St. | 212-427-8800 ◑

There's "something for everyone" at this East Side duo known for its "good-looking and good-tasting produce" (including organic options at comparatively "lower prices") as well as for its flowers; still, a few naysayers note they "have everything you need – but nothing special"; N.B. the 88th Street location is open 24/7 with free delivery.

Anopoli Ice Cream Parlor ⊄ *Ice Cream*

22 | 17 | 21 | I

Bay Ridge | 6920 Third Ave. (bet. Ovington & Bay Ridge Ave.) | Brooklyn | R to Bay Ridge Ave. | 718-748-3863

Paying a visit to this 100-year-old ice cream parlor in Bay Ridge is "like going back in time", given the "fantastic old-school ambiance" featuring ornate wood trim, large mirrors and "friendly" service; all the soda fountain classics – "delicious" floats, malts and banana splits – are based on housemade ice cream, and you can "get a whole meal there too" thanks to the full "Greek diner" menu.

Anstice Carroll Catering ⊄ *Caterer/Events*

∇ 26 | 26 | 26 | M

G Village | 622 Greenwich St. (bet. Leroy & Morton Sts.) | 212-242-1498 | www.ansticecarrollcatering.com

By appointment only

Admirers "love working with" this West Village caterer who's "in a class of her own", demonstrating "elegance in performance and spirit" as she coordinates events with the "finest attention to detail"; from the "delicious and beautiful food" to the "flowers, staff, rentals and location", she's "as good as it gets."

	QUALITY	DISPLAY	SERVICE	COST

Anthony Garden Boutique Ltd. *Flowers*

| – | – | – | E |

E 70s | 1027 Lexington Ave. (bet. 73rd & 74th Sts.) | 6 to 77th St. | 212-737-3303

Whether patrons are in pursuit of a landscaped terrace complete with vintage ornaments, flowers in abundance for a "large-scale gala or wedding" or simply a "beautiful, classy arrangement", they'll receive "something appropriate" from this UES floral boutique; its "creative" owner, trained in the 17th-century style, displays "a discriminating eye for fabulous finds" and pays "attention to the smallest detail" – no wonder he's been "in business for years."

Antony Todd *Events/Flowers*

| – | – | – | VE |

E Village | 44 E. 11th St. (bet. B'way & University Pl.) | 4/5/6/L/N/Q/R/W to 14th St./Union Sq. | 212-529-3252 | www.antonytodd.com

There's absolutely "nothing cutesy" about the work of this East Village event designer known for his "edgy, contemporary" mix of "beautiful flowers" and fabrics; big corporate bashes, weddings and private parties all get gussied up in high style, so naturally he comes "highly recommended", but "be prepared to spend a pretty penny" for such sensational work.

Aphrodisia *Herbs/Spices*

| 26 | 22 | 22 | M |

G Village | 264 Bleecker St. (bet. 6th & 7th Aves.) | A/B/C/D/E/F/V to W. 4th St. | 212-989-6440 | www.aphrodisiaherbshoppe.com

"Dusty and cluttered but fun", this "warm, sensual shop" that's been on Bleecker since "way back when" is "crammed" full of "every earthly spice" imaginable; there's also "a nice selection of teas, small gifts and jewelry", but it's the "exotic, mystical, intoxicating, bewitching" selection of herbs and seasonings that distinguishes this "excellent gem in the heart of the Village."

Appellation Wine & Spirits ● 🖃 *Wine/Liquor*

| ▽ 25 | 23 | 25 | M |

Chelsea | 156 10th Ave. (bet. 19th & 20th Sts.) | A/C/E/L to 14th St./8th Ave. | 212-741-9474 | www.appellationnyc.com

The "well-chosen" stock at this eco-minded "boutique wine store" in Chelsea is a sign that organic, biodynamic and sustainable wineries are becoming "mainstream", but for the uninitiated there's "personal service" as well as weekly tastings and a handy reference bookcase to help "wine geeks and the curious" explore this "under-represented" market segment; the setup of its "stark", "amazing"-looking space has bottles organized in order from light to full-bodied.

NEW appletwares *Cookware*

| 24 | 23 | 25 | E |

Park Slope | 548 10th St. (7th Ave.) | Brooklyn | F to 7th Ave. | 718-576-2484

From the owners of the nearby eatery applewood comes this "cute new" Park Slope shop stocking a "beautifully selected" mix of cook's tools from the mainstream (Le Creuset, Cuisinart) to the professional (chef's whites, Lamson Sharp cutlery), from the affordable to the high-end; it's considered a "great addition to the neighborhood"

	QUALITY	DISPLAY	SERVICE	COST

for its line of locally made pottery alone, although a few wish it carried a little "more product."

Areo Ristorante *Caterer*

∇ 21 | 17 | 17 | E

Bay Ridge | 8424 Third Ave. (85th St.) | Brooklyn | R to 86th St. | 718-238-0079

If you want to spice up your event with "deliciously fresh" traditional Italian fare served by a "friendly" crew (with a side of "Brooklyn attitude") and even entertainment, this popular Bay Ridge restaurant can deliver; it's also possible to hold a party in its 65-seat space, though planners should note that it can get "very noisy."

Ariston Floral Boutique ⌧ *Flowers*

27 | 24 | 23 | E

Chelsea | 110 West 17th St. (bet. 6th & 7th Aves.) | 4/5/6/L/N/Q/R/W to 14th St./Union Sq. | 212-929-4226 | 800-422-2747 | www.aristonflorist.com

E 40s | 425 Lexington Ave. (bet. 43rd & 44th Sts.) | 4/5/6/7/S to 42nd St./Grand Central | 212-867-8880 | www.aristonfloralboutique.com

With a Chelsea location a few blocks from its old Union Square digs and an East Side seedling too, business seems to be flourishing for the "flower experts" at this family-run operation creating bouquets of "exquisite" blooms and providing "excellent service"; surveyors say they can be "creative" or do just "exactly what you want" and the result will be "stunning", albeit with "prices to match."

Arte Around the Corner *Baked Goods*

24 | 20 | 20 | M

W 70s | 274 Columbus Ave. (bet. 72nd & 73rd Sts.) | 1/2/3 to 72nd St. | 212-875-2195 | www.artearoundthecorner.com

Touted as a "hidden treasure" by locals who "love getting their morning espresso and muffin" here, this UWS coffee bar/bakery around the bend from its parent, Arté Cafe, vends "excellent" baked goods, Italian specialty products (including fresh and dried pastas) and prepared foods; there are a few seats, but "cramped quarters" have most placing it in the best-for-takeout category.

Arthur Avenue Caterers *Caterer*

∇ 24 | 18 | 20 | M

Bronx | Arthur Avenue Retail Mkt. | 2344 Arthur Ave. (186th St.) | B/D to Fordham Rd. | 718-295-5033 | 866-272-5264 | www.arthuravenue.com

"For Italian specialties", there's "nothing like" the catering arm of the Arthur Avenue Retail Market, affiliated with the Bronx institution Mike's Deli; providing "primo" homestyle *cucina* for large and small events and even offering mozzarella-making demos, it has catered for the likes of Martin Scorsese, the Mayor of NY and the Yankees.

Artie's Deli ●⌧ *Deli/Sandwich*

21 | 17 | 18 | M

W 80s | 2290 Broadway (bet. 82nd & 83rd Sts.) | 1 to 79th St. | 212-579-5959 | www.arties.com

"Fantastically fresh", "colossal" sandwiches, matzo ball soup, smoked fish and other kosher-style specialties are "pure comfort" "for the soul" say surveyors smitten with this "solid" "old-fashioned" UWS deli; though some kvetch it's a "pale alternative" to the city's stalwart nosheries, even critics concede "you could do much worse if you're stuck Uptown."

☑ Artisanal 🖃 *Cheese/Dairy* | 28 | 25 | 23 | E |

Garment District | 500 W. 37th St., 2nd fl. (10th Ave.) | 1/2/3/A/C/E to 34th St./Penn Station | 212-239-1200 | www.artisanalcheese.com
Murray Hill | 2 Park Ave. (32nd St.) | 6 to 33rd St. | 212-532-4033 | www.artisanalbistro.com ◑
877-797-1200

"If you're a turophile", "paradise" awaits at Terrence Brennan's Murray Hill bistro, where the "bountiful" retail counter is "the ultimate" "showcase" of "fragrant", "scary-delicious" fromage in a 250-strong "worldwide assortment" that's stocked on-site in carefully calibrated caves; if the "phenomenal selection" "makes your head spin", a "true-believer staff" of "cheese masters" will assist with "queries and discoveries", helping to justify the "lofty prices"; P.S. the Garment District wholesale/mail-order location, now separately owned, hosts "very informative" classes toward cheese degrees.

☑ Artopolis Bakery ◑ *Baked Goods* | 28 | 26 | 23 | M |

Astoria | Agora Plaza | 23-18 31st St. (23rd Ave.) | Queens | N/W to Astoria/Ditmars Blvd. | 718-728-8484 | 800-553-2270 | www.artopolis.net

"Transcends" what you'll find in a "neighborhood full of Greek bakeries" rave connoisseurs of this Astoria Hellenic's baked goods touted as some of the "best variety and quality outside of Athens"; its offerings, both traditional and with French leanings, include "outstanding" pastries and cakes, "peasant" breads and some savories ("go for the tiropites and spanakopites"), all arrayed in a "beautiful" space whose marble-and-lacquered pine fittings were imported from Greece.

Artuso Pastry Shop *Baked Goods* | 26 | 22 | 22 | M |

Bronx | 670 E. 187th St. (Cambreleng Ave.) | 2/5 to Pelham Pkwy. | 718-367-2515 | www.artusopastry.com

A bona fide "neighborhood favorite", this Bronx mainstay boasts a rich "history" (since 1946) to go with its "wonderful" Italian pastries including "fresh, quality" cakes, cookies, cannoli, sfogliatelle and the like; with "Artuso family" members still at the helm, supporters say it's the "ultimate in Arthur Avenue-area" pasticcerias.

A Salt & Battery ◑ *Prepared Food* | 22 | 15 | 18 | M |

W Village | 112 Greenwich Ave. (bet. 12th & 13th Sts.) | A/C/E/L to 14th St./8th Ave. | 212-691-2713 | www.asaltandbattery.com

"Real-deal" "fresh fish 'n' chips", "done right" and dished up by "helpful, quick-witted" authentic Brit "blokes" make this West Village chippy "a must for Anglophiles", expats or anyone fostering "fantasies of living in the East End"; other "guilty, fattening pleasures" include "wonderful" battered sausage and pot pie – and "if you're feeling naughty" go for the "deep-fried Mars bar."

	QUALITY	DISPLAY	SERVICE	COST

Asia Market *Specialty Shop*
21 | 12 | 13 | I

Chinatown | 71½ Mulberry St. (bet. Bayard & Canal Sts.) | 6/J/M/N/Q/R/W/Z to Canal St. | 212-962-2020

Your "complete one-stop shop for Asian cooking", this market in Chinatown carries "quality", "reasonably priced herbs, dried goods", produce, sauces and teas as well as "all the spices for Indonesian, Malaysian and other Southeast Asian" cuisines; despite the "hordes" of shoppers and a "nonexistent staff", it's well "worth a visit."

Astoria Meat Products ⊄ *Meat/Poultry*
▽ 25 | 19 | 22 | M

Astoria | 35-09 Broadway (bet. 35th & 36th Sts.) | Queens | N/W to B'way | 718-726-5663

After more than 40 years in business, this old-fashioned emporium in Astoria specializing in cured and smoked Eastern European meats remains a family-run operation; it can be counted on not only for its "great selection" of hams, sausages, kielbasa, meatloaf and cold cuts, but also "personal service", "fair prices" and a relaxed shopping experience that "sure beats the frenzy at all-inclusive" butchers.

Astor Wines & Spirits ◑ ▣ *Wine/Liquor*
25 | 24 | 22 | M

NoHo | 399 Lafayette St. (E. 4th St.) | 6 to Astor Pl. | 212-674-7500 | www.astorwines.com

"Bigger and better" than ever in its "snazzy" 11,000-sq.-ft. digs, NoHo's "heavyweight champion of booze" continues to knock out customers with its "mind-boggling array" of liquors, sake and "quality" vinos, both "known and unknown vintages"; "friendly service", "free tastings", a "dog-friendly" setup and a range of choices "to fit all budgets" add up to a "terrific adult candy store"; N.B. a varied roster of wine and food classes are on tap at the Astor Center, its new "upstairs classroom" division.

Ⓩ Atlas Party Rentals *Party Rentals*
23 | 18 | 20 | M

Mt. Vernon | 554 S. Columbus Ave. (Sandford Blvd.), NY | 212-929-8888 | 800-695-6565 | www.partyrenter.com

A "large assortment of rentals" from tents and dance floors to tables, chairs and dishes can be delivered to party-throwers in the five boroughs (plus LI, Westchester and Connecticut) by this two-pronged team, a merger of Atlas and AAA Best Chair Rentals, with showrooms in Mount Vernon, NY, and Westport CT; respondents cite as points in their favor "reliable" service and decent prices, comparatively speaking, and a willingness to take on last-minute jobs; N.B. $150 minimum order for delivery.

Au Bon Pain *Baked Goods*
16 | 16 | 14 | I

E 40s | 16 E. 44th St. (bet. 5th & Madison Aves.) | 4/5/6/7/S to 42nd St./Grand Central | 212-867-6356
E 40s | 600 Third Ave. (40th St.) | 4/5/6/7/S to 42nd St./Grand Central | 212-370-9823
Financial District | 80 Pine St. (Water St.) | 2/3 to Wall St. | 212-952-9007
Garment District | Macy's | 151 W. 34th St. (bet. 6th & 7th Aves.) | 1/2/3/A/C/E to 34th St./Penn Station | 212-494-1091 ◑

(continued)

Au Bon Pain

Garment District | 420 Fifth Ave. (37th St.) | 7/B/D/F/V to 42nd St./ Bryant Park | 212-730-5401 ☻

G Village | 58 E. Eighth St. (Mercer St.) | R/W to 8th St. | 212-475-8546 ☻

NoHo | 684 Broadway (W. 3rd St.) | A/B/C/D/E/F/V to W. 4th St. | 212-420-1694 ☻

Union Sq | 73 Fifth Ave. (15th St.) | 4/5/6/L/N/Q/R/W to 14th St./ Union Sq. | 212-242-9836 ☻

W 50s | 1251 Sixth Ave. (50th St.) | B/D/F/V to 47-50th Sts./ Rockefeller Ctr. | 212-921-5908 ☻

Downtown | 1 Metrotech Ctr. (Myrtle Ave.) | Brooklyn | A/C/F to Jay St./Borough Hall | 718-624-9598

800-825-5227 | www.aubonpain.com

Additional locations throughout the NY area

"Nine-to-fivers" and other "on-the-go" types "depend" on this "ubiquitous" bakery/sandwich shop chain that "serves its purpose" as a "quick, cheap snack" haven and "lunchtime staple" supplying muffins, sandwiches, soups and such that are "perfectly accept-able", especially "in a pinch"; just remember that "mass-produced" quality and "spotty service" are part of the deal – "behind the French name" is a "typical" "American" "franchise."

Australian Homemade ☻ *Ice Cream*   `23` `21` `21` `M`

E Village | 115 St. Marks Pl. (bet. Ave. A & 1st Ave.) | 6 to Astor Pl. | 212-228-5439

G Village | 33 E. Eighth St. (bet. B'way & University Pl.) | R/W to 8th St. | 212-477-7787

www.australianhomemade.com

"Ice cream addicts" always "have a g'day" at this East Village purveyor of "super-rich and creamy" concoctions, offering plenty of "interesting flavors", including the popular Belgian chocolate, in "cute, modern" digs; if you "don't get enough calories" from your cone or cup, there's also a line of "delicious" chocolates that are almost "too pretty to eat"; N.B. the Greenwich Village branch opened post-Survey.

BabyCakes NYC ☻▣ *Baked Goods*   `24` `21` `22` `M`

LES | 248 Broome St. (bet. Ludlow & Orchard Sts.) | F/J/M/Z to Delancey/Essex Sts. | 212-677-5047 | www.babycakesnyc.com

"Who knew wheat-free, dairy-free could be so delicious?" marvel converts to this "cute", "'50s-ish little" Lower East Side bakery "offer-ing alternatives" for the food-sensitive with its "delicious" cupcakes, cakes, pastries, cookies and other "vegan goodies" they manage to make without gluten, refined sugar or other problem ingredients for the "allergic" and "health-conscious"; completing the picture is an overall "happy vibe" that has groupies gushing "I'm in love!"

Bacchus Wine
Made Simple ☻▣ *Wine/Liquor*   `19` `21` `21` `E`

W 70s | 2056 Broadway (bet. 70th & 71st Sts.) | 1/2/3 to 72nd St. | 212-875-1200 | www.bacchusnyc.com

The focus at this "easy-to-navigate" Upper West Side wine purveyor is on "carefully chosen" bottles from small-production vineyards, all

	QUALITY	DISPLAY	SERVICE	COST

of which are arranged and displayed according to style/taste categories (juicy, bold, premium, etc.); cynics pan the minimalist approach as a "gimmick", but most agree it works well for "beginners" and the "indecisive."

Back to the Land ◑ *Health Food* | 23 | 21 | 20 | M |

Park Slope | 142 Seventh Ave. (bet. Carroll St. & Garfield Pl.) | Brooklyn | F to 7th Ave. | 718-768-5654 | www.backtothelandnaturalfoods.com

Park Slopers who aren't "members of the Food Coop" turn to this "well-stocked" neighborhood "legend" for "high-quality" organic products and health foods; its "thorough" selection makes it "convenient" and the "checkout lines move quickly", but "chichi" price points explain why many "locals call it 'Back to the Bank.'"

Bagel Bob's *Bagels* | 22 | 15 | 18 | I |

E 80s | 1638 York Ave. (bet. 86th & 87th Sts.) | 4/5/6 to 86th St. | 212-535-3838
G Village | 51 University Pl. (bet. 9th & 10th Sts.) | R/W to 8th St. | 212-533-2627 ⬡

"Convenient" outlets for "fresh" bagels, this Yorkville–Greenwich Village twosome "does the trick" for a "cheap carb fix", especially "Mondays from 4 to 7" PM when the "half-price" deal "can't be beat"; the "efficient" "assembly-line" setups may seem like "nothing special", but hey, this could be "the best reason to go to NYU" – "nice job, Bob."

Bagel Buffet ◑ *Bagels* | 17 | 14 | 16 | I |

G Village | 406 Sixth Ave. (bet. 8th & 9th Sts.) | A/B/C/D/E/F/V to W. 4th St. | 212-477-0448

After more than 30 years in business, this 24/7 "Village institution" remains a "cheap" resource for "decent bagels" and deli fare served in "old"-school "cafeteria-style" digs; though it "looks a little tired" and "crusty", it's "always open" for a "quick" day-or-night bite "in the heart of" Downtown.

Bagel Hole ⬡ *Bagels* | 22 | 14 | 18 | I |

Park Slope | 400 Seventh Ave. (bet. 12th & 13th Sts.) | Brooklyn | F to 7th Ave. | 718-788-4014 | www.bagelhole.net

"All bagels are not created equal", and the "smaller", "chewy" rounds with a "blistery crust" at this "handy" "Park Slope favorite" earn a hole lotta love from "traditional" types for demonstrating the way they're "supposed to be"; but if the goods "aren't oversized and full of air", neither is the "cramped" space.

Bagel Oasis ◑ ▭ *Bagels* | 26 | 15 | 20 | I |

Fresh Meadows | 183-12 Horace Harding Expwy. (L.I. Expwy.) | Queens | 718-359-9245 | 888-224-3561 | www.bageloasis.com

The "Hamptons"-bound attest "traffic won't seem so bad" after an "easy stop" at this Fresh Meadows vet (since 1961), which "should be a landmark" given its "amazing" handmade bagels made to "old-fashioned" standards: crisp outside, "heavenly inside" and "baked fresh" "all day and night long"; it's open round the clock, so once "hooked" you'll never have to "pass it without going in."

	QUALITY	DISPLAY	SERVICE	COST

Bagels & Co. ⊄ *Bagels* | 22 | 18 | 18 | I |

E 70s | 1428 York Ave. (76th St.) | 6 to 77th St. | 212-717-0505 ◗
W 70s | 393 Amsterdam Ave. (79th St.) | 1 to 79th St. |
212-496-9400 ◗ 🖃
Hillcrest | 188-02 Union Tpke. (Saul Weprin St.) | Queens | 718-217-7755
"If you need kosher", this "traditional" threesome's "big, fluffy bagels" and "delicious" bialys fit the bill, as do the other "reliable" fare and the "efficient" staff; and for company of your own, the catering service offers "good quality" at some of the "cheapest" prices around; N.B. it closes at 3 PM on Friday and all day Saturday.

Bagels on the Square ◗ *Bagels* | 21 | 18 | 19 | I |

G Village | 7 Carmine St. (bet. Bleecker St. & 6th Ave.) | A/B/C/D/E/F/V to W. 4th St. | 212-691-3041
Put away "enough calories for a week" at this 24/7 Village "staple", where "chewy" bagels "the size of your head" come in a "really unique" range of flavors (like "the French toast one") and slathered with "mounds" of "delicious spreads"; perhaps it's "not for purists", but given the "speedy", "cheerful" service and square deal, "what's not to love?"

Bagelworks, Inc. ◗ *Bagels* | 23 | 14 | 18 | I |

E 60s | 1229 First Ave. (bet. 66th & 67th Sts.) | 6 to 68th St. | 212-744-6444
It's definitely "not flashy", but Upper Eastsiders "swear by" this "tiny" "neighborhood" joint's "flavorful (and not excessively doughy)" bagels, "made on-premises" and topped with a "toothsome" lineup of "interesting spreads"; despite the "no-frills" space and service "without the hoo-ha", worked-up fans find that "waiting in line" here is "worth your while."

Baked 🖃 *Baked Goods* | 25 | 21 | 21 | M |

Red Hook | 359 Van Brunt St. (bet. Dikeman & Wolcott Sts.) |
Brooklyn | F/G to Smith/9th Sts. | 718-222-0345 | www.bakednyc.com
"Delicious" "twists on old American favorites" produced by this Red Hook "hipster" bakery – "homey, delicate", "amazing" cakes and cupcakes, muffins, scones, the "best" brownies – lead many to moon "wish it were in Manhattan"; its "funky" modern digs make a "nice place to sit with your coffee and something sweet" (and there are also panini and a few other prepared items at lunchtime) – meaning it's perfect for "fortifying yourself" pre-"Fairway."

Baked Ideas 🖃 *Baked Goods* | - | - | - | M |

SoHo | 450 Broadway (bet. Grand & Howard Sts.) | 212-925-9097 |
www.bakedideas.com
By appointment only
The likenesses of celebrities and politicians often turn up on the "lovely" handiworks of SoHo baker/designer Patti Paige, whose whimsical edible specialties include hand-decorated novelty cookies in shapes ranging from the expected (a NYC taxicab) to the esoteric (10 different yoga poses, from Downward Dog to Lotus); not surprisingly, she does a big business in customized edible favors for corporate events and weddings, and also bakes cakes.

	QUALITY	DISPLAY	SERVICE	COST

ⓩ Balducci's ◐ ⌧ *Major Gourmet Mkt.*

| 25 | 24 | 20 | E |

Chelsea | 81 Eighth Ave. (14th St.) | A/C/E/L to 14th St./8th Ave. | 212-741-3700
W 60s | 155 W. 66th St. (bet. Amsterdam Ave. & B'way) | 1 to 66th St./Lincoln Ctr. | 212-653-8320
www.balduccis.com

Maybe "this ain't the old Balducci's", but even nostalgists who miss the defunct Greenwich Village original give the nod to this "beautiful" Chelsea megamart (with a less impressive Lincoln Center–area branch) for its "wealth of" gourmet goods, including a "rich assortment of meats", "well-crafted" prepared foods, "luscious" produce displayed "like art", "delicious" deli, "irresistible" bakery items and "seafood so fresh it'll slap you"; it continues to "tantalize" with imports "you can't find anywhere else" and quality that remains "exceptional in its class", and even those stymied by "wildly expensive" price tags find it "fun to browse"; P.S. the extras Downtown include a coffee bar and "secret seating" upstairs.

Balthazar Bakery ◐ *Baked Goods*

| 27 | 24 | 21 | E |

SoHo | 80 Spring St. (bet. B'way & Crosby St.) | 6 to Spring St. | 212-965-1785 | www.balthazarny.com

"Voilà – a little bit of Paris when you can't jump on a plane" is the refrain of those who "squeeze" into this wildly "popular", "way-too-crowded" French bakery (sidecar to SoHo's famed brasserie) vending "terrific", "crunchy" baguettes and other "can't-be-beat" breads, "fabulous" croissants and tarts "worth every calorie"; no, this level of "culinary craftsmanship" doesn't come cheap, but then its legions of devotees declare they'd "pay anything" for the "ethereal" goods here.

Banchet Flowers ⌧ *Flowers*

| - | - | - | VE |

Meatpacking | 809 Washington St. (bet. Gansevoort & Horatio Sts.) | A/C/E/L to 14th St./8th Ave. | 212-989-1088 | www.banchetflowers.com

Although they're "never too ornate", the "avant-garde" "luxury arrangements" from the "talented florists" at this "wonderful" Meatpacking District shop are "meant to impress" according to surveyors who also cite its "incredible orchids" – not to mention seriously "expensive" tabs; the chic quarters double as an event space for weddings, fashion shows and parties, while the adjacent Flower Bar includes a drinks counter where bouquet buyers can wait for their posies.

ⓩ Bangkok Center Grocery *Specialty Shop*

| 27 | 17 | 23 | I |

Chinatown | 104 Mosco St. (bet. Mott & Mulberry Sts.) | 6/J/M/N/Q/R/W/Z to Canal St. | 212-349-1979 | www.bangkokcentergrocery.com

Hidden away on a Chinatown backstreet, this "gem" of a market is "small but well-stocked" with "hard-to-find ingredients" – from housemade curry pastes to fresh coconut milk – that will enhance "your Thai dinner at home"; regulars report you "can always rely on them" to dispense "friendly cooking advice" and, really, "where else can you buy fresh kaffir lime leaves?"

Bánh Mì Saigon Bakery 🚫 *Deli/Sandwich* | 25 | 11 | 16 | I |

Chinatown | 138-01 Mott St. (bet. Grand & Hester Sts.) | 6/J/M/N/ Q/R/W/Z to Canal St. | 212-941-1541

One of the "best-kept secrets in Chinatown", this Vietnamese hide-away at the back of a Mott Street jewelry store sells what supporters say is the "perfect" *bahn mi* sandwich – roast pork, cilantro, pickled carrots, cucumber and hot peppers loaded up on "crusty" French bread – amounting to a "salty, sweet, spicy, crunchy, delicious" meal for "practically pennies"; seating is limited and "ambiance" nil, but its "filling" "quick fixes" always "satisfy"; N.B. it now offers meat-ball, chicken and veggie options.

Barbarini Alimentari *Prepared Food* | - | - | - | M |

Financial District | 225 Front St. (bet. Beekman St. & Peck Slip) | A/C/ J/M/Z/2/3/4/5 to Fulton St. | 212-227-8890 | www.barbarini.net

"Delicious", "authentic-as-it gets" Italiana abounds at this "tiny" Financial District "gem" of a deli/cafe, where "lovingly assembled sandwiches", pastas and other prepared foods, as well as pastries and baked goods, share space with staples imported from The Boot (olive oils, vinegars, cheeses, sauces, jams, coffee, etc.); there are a few cafe tables for eating on-premises, and it also specializes in ca-tering business lunches and other office affairs.

Bari Pork Store *Meat/Poultry* | 24 | 21 | 22 | M |

Bensonhurst | 6319 18th Ave. (64th St.) | Brooklyn | N to 18th Ave. | 718-837-9773

Gravesend | 158 Ave. U (W. 7th St.) | Brooklyn | N to Ave. U | 718-372-6405

Staten Island | 1755 Richmond Rd. (bet. Dogan Hills & Seaver Aves.) | 718-667-7780

www.barigourmet.com

"It's hard to choose" among the housemade Italian sausages and other pig-licious products at these individually owned "real-deal" Italian meat shops in Brooklyn and Staten Island, which also carry imported cured meats and pantry goods; made-on-the-premises mozzarella, *arancini* (fried rice balls) and all manner of antipasti round out the offerings.

Bari Restaurant Equipment *Cookware* | 24 | 15 | 17 | M |

LES | 240 Bowery (bet. Houston & Prince Sts.) | F/V to Lower East Side/ 2nd Ave. | 212-925-3845 | www.bariequipment.com

When you "aspire to culinary greatness, this is the place" cheer cham-pions of this "crowded" no-frills LES restaurant supply shop where the "pro-grade" inventory spanning "everything *including* the kitchen sink" – from walk-in freezers to esoteric utensils – appeals to pros and amateurs alike; service may be variable, but the "good" prices make up for any shortcomings.

Ⓩ Barney Greengrass 🖃 *Caviar/Smoked Fish* | 27 | 18 | 19 | E |

W 80s | 541 Amsterdam Ave. (bet. 86th & 87th Sts.) | 1 to 86th St. | 212-724-4707 | www.barneygreengrass.com

"If it's smoked, you want Greengrass" is the word on this West Side "old-world wonder" with a "lofty reputation" as "the most authentic" purveyor of "sturgeon extraordinaire", "sable like butter", "delectable fresh whitefish" and caviar; the "classic" '20s-era setup is a "true NY experience" with "sporadic" service and "chaotic" conditions when the "line outside for brunch" forms on weekends, but "it's been there forever for a reason" and remains "the gold standard" (but just "bring your gold card").

Basket Shop of NY *Specialty Shop* ▽ 23 | 21 | 18 | M

Borough Park | 1368 39th St. (bet. 13th & 14th Aves.) | Brooklyn | F to Church Ave. | 718-853-8535 | www.thebasketshopny.com

It's gift basket heaven at this "fun" 65-plus-year-old Borough Park shop that has an assortment for every conceivable – or inconceivable – occasion imaginable (e.g. "for the neighbor who slipped on your walk and isn't suing you"); in person or via its website, customers can choose premade or custom baskets, browse more than 2,500 types of candy, including kosher, low-fat and sugar-free options.

Baskin-Robbins ● *Ice Cream* 17 | 15 | 14 | I

Chelsea | 269 Eighth Ave. (bet. 23rd & 24th Sts.) | C/E to 23rd St. | 212-229-2622

Chelsea | 289 Seventh Ave. (bet. 26th & 27th Sts.) | 1 to 28th St. | 212-229-4799

E 60s | 1225 First Ave. (66th St.) | 6 to 68th St. | 212-734-5465

Flatiron | 536 Sixth Ave. (bet. 14th & 15th Sts.) | F/L/V to 14th St./6th Ave. | 212-727-0444

Gramercy | 218 E. 14th St. (bet. 2nd & 3rd Aves.) | 4/5/6/L/N/Q/R/W to 14th St./Union Sq. | 212-388-9992

Murray Hill | 302 Fifth Ave. (31st St.) | B/D/F/N/Q/R/V/W to 34th St./Herald Sq. | 212-268-0686

Murray Hill | 601 Second Ave. (33rd St.) | 6 to 33rd St. | 212-532-5083

TriBeCa | 100 Chambers St. (bet. B'way & Church Sts.) | 1/2/3/A/C to Chambers St. | 212-619-1222

TriBeCa | 321 Broadway (bet. Thomas & Worth Sts.) | R/W to City Hall | 212-577-7550

Greenpoint | 892 Manhattan Ave. (Greenpoint Ave.) | Brooklyn | G to Greenpoint Ave. | 718-349-2930

800-859-5339 | www.baskinrobbins.com

Additional locations throughout the NY area

If you've got an "ice cream urge" and don't like the "fancy", "high-butterfat" choices at other places, this "inexpensive", "reliable" "American classic" is "good in a pinch", offering one of the "biggest selection" of flavors around ("more than 31"); the less-enthralled say the "chemical" "aftertaste" and "surly" service aren't so sweet, but parents find it hard to beat their "amazing" cakes when it's time for a birthday party.

NEW Batch ●♢ *Baked Goods* - | - | - | M

G Village | 150B W. 10th St. (bet. Greenwich Ave. & Waverly Pl.) | 1 to Christopher St. | 212-929-0250

Sugar maestro Pichet Ong has opened this diminutive new sweets shop next door to his Greenwich Village dessert bar, P*ong, but its storefront space with a few seats is moody and romantic (scarlet walls, crystal chandeliers) where its older sibling is ultramodern; the goods are American classics with an Asian twist – think yuzu-shortbread sandwiches, Thai-tea tiramisu pudding – many of them made with organic ingredients.

Bayard Street Meat Market *Meat/Poultry* | 23 | 17 | 13 | I |
(aka Deluxe Food Market)

Chinatown | 57 Bayard St. (Elizabeth St.) | 6/J/M/N/Q/R/W/Z to Canal St. | 212-619-6206 🖻
Little Italy | 79 Elizabeth St. (bet. Grand & Hester Sts.) | B/D to Grand St. | 212-925-5766 ◗

A bastion of fresh beef, pork, poultry and just about any animal part you can imagine ("*the* place to get duck's tongue"), these Chinatown–Little Italy meat retailers are justly appreciated for their "large variety" and fair prices that "will always beat the supermarket's"; insiders note the shopping experience is even better if "you know Mandarin or Cantonese"; N.B. the vast Elizabeth Street location also features fish counters and a food court offering sushi, fresh juices, pastries, ice cream and more.

Bay Ridge Bakery *Baked Goods* | 25 | 23 | 26 | M |

Bay Ridge | 7805 Fifth Ave. (78th St.) | Brooklyn | R to 77th St. | 718-238-0014 | www.bayridgebakery.com

"You want great pastries?" – Bay Ridge locals suggest this longtime bake shop turning out "elegant" "European-style" specialties including cakes, pies and tarts, Danish and a few Greek classics like baklava; it's a family-owned operation that's rated among the "best" in the area, with the added appeal of an open kitchen allowing customers to watch the chef in action; N.B. it specializes in wedding and other special-occasion cakes.

🖬 Bazzini, A.L., Co. 🍴 *Major Gourmet Mkt.* | ▽ 27 | 20 | 21 | E |

TriBeCa | 339 Greenwich St. (Jay St.) | 1 to Franklin St. | 212-334-1280 | www.bazzininuts.com

It's "well known" that this 1880s-vintage TriBeCa fixture "shines" as an "established" source of "delicious nuts" – the "freshest" "A+ quality" with "fantastic" choices from almonds to walnuts – but these days it also "comes up big" as an "excellent gourmet shop" where the "very inviting" draws include "fresh produce" and meats, "tasty" prepared foods, "Italian delicacies" like imported pasta and olive oils, and an "excellent assortment" of dried fruits and candy; yes, it's on the "expensive" side, but it's "def worth it" for anyone driven nutty by the area's "sorely lacking" options.

Beacon Wines & Spirits ◗🍴 *Wine/Liquor* | 21 | 18 | 16 | M |

W 70s | 2120 Broadway (74th St.) | 1/2/3 to 72nd St. | 212-877-0028 | www.beaconwine.com

A "respectable" purveyor of "fine wines and spirits" located right "across the street from Citarella" and Fairway, this Upper West Side shop boasts a "wide-ranging" selection of "attractively priced" and "easy-to-find" bottles; sure, it lacks "ambiance" and "helpful" staffers can be "hard to find", but "if you know your wines and what you want", "you'll surely find something."

	QUALITY	DISPLAY	SERVICE	COST

Beard Papa Sweets *Baked Goods* | 24 | 17 | 20 | I |

E 40s | Cafe Zaiya | 18 E. 41 St. (bet. 5th & Madison Aves.) | 4/5/6/
7/S to 42nd St./Grand Central | 212-779-0600
E Village | 740 Broadway (Astor Pl.) | 6 to Astor Pl. |
212-353-8888 ◐
W 70s | 2167 Broadway (bet. 76th & 77th Sts.) | 1/2/3 to 72nd St. |
212-799-3770
www.beardpapas.com

Find "little pockets of heaven" within these brightly lit outposts of a
Japanese chain "devoted to the cream puff" – "amazingly delicious",
"crispy-on-the-outside" cream-filled babies in weekly changing flavors from "rich vanilla" to "exquisite green tea and chocolate"; addicts "hooked from the very first bite" say its "indulgent" treats
"should be classified as a controlled substance", though a skeptical
few shrug this "one-trick pony" "doesn't live up to the hype."

Bed Bath & Beyond ◐ ▣ *Cookware* | 20 | 19 | 15 | M |

Chelsea | 620 Sixth Ave. (bet. 18th & 19th Sts.) | 1 to 18th St. |
212-255-3550
E 60s | 410 E. 61st St. (1st Ave.) | 4/5/6/N/R/W to 59th St./
Lexington Ave. | 646-215-4702
NEW **TriBeCa** | 270 Greenwich St. (bet. Murray & Warren Sts.) | 1/
2/3 to Chambers St. | 212-233-8450
W 60s | 1932 Broadway (Columbus Ave.) | 1 to 66th St./Lincoln Ctr. |
917-441-9391
Canarsie | 459 Gateway Dr. (Fountain Ave.) | Brooklyn | A/C to
Euclid Ave. | 718-235-2049
Elmhurst | 72-15 25th Ave. (bet. 72nd & 73rd Sts.) | Queens | G/R/
V to Elmhurst Ave. | 718-429-9438
Rego Park | 96-05 Queens Blvd. (63rd Dr.) | Queens | G/R/V to
Woodhaven Blvd. | 718-459-0868
Staten Island | Staten Island Mall | 2795 Richmond Ave. (Platinum Ave.) |
718-982-0071
800-462-3966 | www.bedbathandbeyond.com

"It's all about convenience" at this "reliable" "one-stop" franchise
whose kitchen departments boast a "staggering" array of "mainstream" pots and pans, utensils, cutlery and appliances, as well as a
"limited" selection of "high-end" brands; though it's a "zoo" on
weekends and the staffers can be "clueless", its "amazing return
policy", "reasonable prices" and frequent "20% off coupons in the
mail" mean that even those who swear they "hate chain stores" consider it a "necessary evil" for "stocking up" city apartments.

☑ Bedford Cheese Shop ◐ ▣ *Cheese/Dairy* | 27 | 24 | 24 | E |

Williamsburg | 229 Bedford Ave. (N. 4th St.) | Brooklyn | L to Bedford Ave. |
718-599-7588 | 888-484-3243 | www.bedfordcheeseshop.com

Ensconced in a "lovely" corner space, this Williamsburg "pioneer"
proves that the "hip can do dairy" with "by far" the neighborhood's
"best selection" of "unique cheeses" (150-plus varieties) tended by
"knowledgeable" staffers who dole out samples and "make everything sound interesting"; it also "abounds" with "hard-to-find gourmet" goods and bread from leading bakeries, resulting in "really fun"
shopping for "expensive" tastes.

	QUALITY	DISPLAY	SERVICE	COST

Beekman Liquors ◑ 🖃 *Wine/Liquor* | 24 | 19 | 24 | M |

E 40s | 500 Lexington Ave. (bet. 47th & 48th Sts.) | 4/5/6/7/S to 42nd St./ Grand Central | 212-759-5857 | www.beekmanliquors.com

"Packed full" with 3,500 wines (most from California and France) as well as a "wide range of spirits", in particular single-malts, "rare" whiskeys and sake, this "small", "solid" Midtown store near Grand Central is ideal for a "quick pickup"; it's been "around for decades" and "looks it" quip some, but the service still "makes the grade."

Beekman Marketplace 🖃 *Meat/Poultry* | ▽ 22 | 19 | 22 | M |
(aka Empire Purveyors)

E 40s | 883 First Ave. (bet. 49th & 50th Sts.) | 6 to 51st St. | 212-755-7756 | www.beekmanmarketplace.com

Since relocating from its original shop on the same block, this Sutton Place butcher and grocer has been expanding its offerings, providing patrons not only with the "finest quality" prime meat, poultry and game, but also breads and pastries, comfort-oriented prepared foods and even a line of gift baskets, all overseen by second-generation owners who provide a wonderful "family touch."

Belfiore Meats *Meat/Poultry* | ▽ 25 | 19 | 22 | M |

Staten Island | 2500 Victory Blvd. (Willowbrook Rd.) | 718-983-0440

Known to regulars for its "high-quality" "always-fresh" meats, this Italian butcher–cum–specialty foods shop–cum–caterer also purveys prepared foods (roast chicken, roast pork) and baked goods; surveyors say the "expert" service is generally "friendly", if occasionally undercut by a little "Staten Island 'charm.'"

Bell Bates Natural Food Market *Health Food* | 24 | 20 | 20 | M |

TriBeCa | 97 Reade St. (bet. Church St. & W. B'way) | 1/2/3/A/C to Chambers St. | 212-267-4300 | www.bellbates.com

"They have everything" at this "Downtown pioneer" of natural foods, offering TriBeCa residents and workers a "wide variety" of "healthy choices", including a "large selection of spices", coffee and other bulk items; service can vary between "knowledgeable" and "indifferent", but the salad bar and prepared foods are always "quite good."

🆉 Belle Fleur *Flowers* | 28 | 27 | 25 | VE |

Flatiron | 134 Fifth Ave., 4th fl. (bet. 18th & 19th Sts.) | N/R/W to 23rd St. | 212-254-8703 | www.bellefleurny.com

"The name says it all" at this Flatiron District florist where "exquisite", "chic blooms" arranged by a "mother-daughter duo" that shares a "gorgeous sense of color" result in "flawless", "artful" ensembles; "exceptional one-on-one service" means "lucky recipients are always thrilled", so even though "price tags are high", it's "the perfect way to say 'I love you – and I'm really rich.'"

Ben & Jerry's *Ice Cream* | 24 | 18 | 18 | M |

E 40s | Grand Central Terminal | main concourse (42nd St. & Vanderbilt Ave.) | 4/5/6/7/S to 42nd St./Grand Central | 212-953-1028 ◑

(continued)

(continued)

Ben & Jerry's

E Village | 41 Third Ave. (bet. 9th & 10th Sts.) | 6 to Astor Pl. | 212-995-0109 ❶
Garment District | Macy's | 151 W. 34th St. (bet. 6th & 7th Aves.) | B/D/F/N/Q/R/V/W to 34th St./Herald Sq. | 212-594-0018 ❶
W 40s | 30 Rockefeller Plaza, concourse level (bet. 49th & 50th Sts.) | B/D/F/V to 47-50th Sts./Rockefeller Ctr. | 212-218-7843
W 40s | 680 Eighth Ave. (43rd St.) | A/C/E to 42nd St./Port Authority | 212-221-1001 ❶
W 100s | 2722 Broadway (104th St.) | 1 to 103rd St. | 212-866-6237 ❶
www.benandjerrys.com

"Simply the best" exclaim enthusiasts of this "goofy and wonderful" Vermont-based chain with outposts throughout the city scooping "over-the-top flavors" of "all-natural" ice cream; while some claim it's "too sweet", "too rich" and "long past its prime", most others insist it'll "leave you craving more."

Ben's Best ⊟ *Deli/Sandwich* | 23 | 16 | 18 | M |

Rego Park | 96-40 Queens Blvd. (63rd Dr.) | Queens | R/V to 63rd Dr. | 718-897-1700 | www.bensbest.com

This "unabashed original" with a "long history" (since 1947) in Rego Park is "everything" a Jewish deli "should be", satisfying "cravings" for "juicy" sandwiches heaped with "mounds" of the "tastiest" pastrami and other "quality" meats in "nothing-fancy" environs that happily "haven't changed in years"; go with "a huge appetite and several friends" – and consider the "heartburn-inducing service" part of the "authentic" experience; P.S. "their catered platters are terrific."

Ben's Kosher Deli ❶⊟ *Deli/Sandwich* | 21 | 17 | 17 | M |

Garment District | 209 W. 38th St. (7th Ave.) | 1/2/3/7/N/Q/R/S/W to 42nd St./Times Sq. | 212-398-2367
Bayside | Bay Terrace | 211-37 26th Ave. (Bell Blvd.) | Queens | LIRR to Bayside | 718-229-2367
800-344-2367 | www.bensdeli.net

The "monster sammies" made with "amazing" house-cured pastrami and corned beef are more than worth the "artery clog" according to advocates of this "reasonably priced", "old-fashioned" Garment District–Bayside kosher deli duo, whose "flaky knishes" and "can't-miss matzo-ball soup" also "hold their own"; however, a few find it a bit "watered-down" compared to other "Jewish-style" spots – maybe "if the waiters were ruder, it would be perfect."

Bergen Bagels ❶⇴ *Bagels* | 22 | 17 | 18 | I |

Boerum Hill | 473 Bergen St. (Flatbush Ave.) | Brooklyn | 2/3 to Bergen St. | 718-789-7600 | www.bergenbagel.com

Neighbors have a soft spot for this Boerum Hill hole-in-the-wall that offers lots of "local appeal" along with its "big, fluffy", "fresh" bagels and bialys and "wonderful", ever-changing selection of flavored cream cheeses; it's "fast", "friendly", open late and located "right by the train" – now if they could only get "a little more seating and atmosphere."

	QUALITY	DISPLAY	SERVICE	COST

Berger's On The Go *Deli/Sandwich*

▽ 21 | 11 | 20 | M

(fka Berger's Delicatessen)

Murray Hill | 2 E. 39th St. (bet. 5th & Madison Aves.) | 7/B/D/F/V to 42nd St./Bryant Park | 212-719-4173

A longtime Diamond District "favorite", this deli moved to Murray Hill in 2006 and modernized its offerings, adding more health-conscious and to-go items; supporters say it's a "consistent" contender with "great corned beef" and "fast" service, though sentimental sorts say it's "not what it used to be."

Berkshire Berries ▣⊘ *Produce*

27 | 22 | 24 | M

See Greenmarket; for more information, call 413-623-5779 or 800-523-7797 | www.berkshireberries.com

Gooseberry and wild blueberry–ginger are among the flavors offered by this Berkshires-based Greenmarket vendor offering "excellent preserves" made from "ripe and luscious" fruit; loyalists also "love the NYC rooftop honey" (from apiaries atop city buildings) and "the best maple syrup", and note that while the "service is fine", the ratio of "quality to price" is even better.

Berried Treasures ⊘ *Produce*

28 | 22 | 24 | M

See Greenmarket; for more information, call 646-391-3162

"Justifiably known for her strawberries", "friendly" nutritionist-turned-farmer Franca Tantillo brings "small, fragrant, flavorful, juicy" specimens from her Catskills farm to grateful NYC Greenmarket shoppers; "in recent years, she's been branching out", growing other types of berries along with a "broad selection of potatoes", several kinds of beans, garlic and shallots – "superior produce" that fans "always" find "worth a try."

🆕 Berrywild *Ice Cream*

▽ 22 | 19 | 19 | M

Murray Hill | 427 Third Ave. (30th St.) | 6 to 33rd St. | 212-686-5848 | www.berrywildyogurt.com

One of the latest arrivals on the city's burgeoning fro-yo scene, this Murray Hiller crowns its "delish" frozen yogurt with a multitude of "very fresh" toppings, and it also swirls a line of smoothies; early visitors rank it among the "best of the pinkberry knockoffs"; N.B. delivery and online ordering are on the horizon.

Best Cellars ●◗▣ *Wine/Liquor*

21 | 24 | 23 | I

E 80s | 1291 Lexington Ave. (87th St.) | 4/5/6 to 86th St. | 212-426-4200
W 80s | 2246 Broadway (bet. 80th & 81st Sts.) | 1 to 79th St. | 212-362-8730
www.bestcellars.com

"Always on the cutting edge" with a "fabulous" "rotating selection" and "knowledgeable" staff, this "unintimidating" pair of independently owned vintners "proves cheap wine doesn't have to be bad", and while "experienced oenophiles" may cringe at the categorization of labels by taste ('juicy', 'smooth', 'big', etc.), the system is "accessible" to "novices"; the East Side store offers "frequent" tastings, while the Broadway location hosts educational dinners and other programs.

	QUALITY	DISPLAY	SERVICE	COST

Beth's Farm Kitchen 🖳 *Specialty Shop* | 27 | 24 | 26 | M |

See Greenmarket; for more information, call 800-331-5267 |
www.bethsfarmkitchen.com

Hudson Valley–based preserves purveyor Beth Linskey buys produce from area farmers to go into her "diverse" assortment of "delectable" jams and jellies, "superb chutneys" and pickles sold at the Greenmarket; regulars rave about "the absolute best" raspberry jam "known to man" and "addictive" red-pepper jelly, and appreciate the "cheery", "informative" booth workers' usage suggestions for the more unusual products; P.S. "beautifully wrapped" gift boxes are "ready for giving year-round."

Better Burger ● *Prepared Food* | 19 | 15 | 17 | M |

Chelsea | 178 Eighth Ave. (19th St.) | C/E to 23rd St. |
212-989-6688
Murray Hill | 561 Third Ave. (37th St.) | 6 to 33rd St. | 212-949-7528
W 40s | 587 Ninth Ave. (bet. 42nd & 43rd Sts.) | A/C/E to 42nd St./
Port Authority | 212-629-6622
www.betterburgernyc.com

When healthy-minded sorts want to "satisfy the burger 'n' fries craving" "without guilt", they say this "earth-conscious" mini-chain is "much appreciated", offering organic "tasty alternatives" ("where else can you get an ostrich burger with air-baked fries and wasabi ketchup?"); fat-free "delicious smoothies" are another plus, though a few who "don't get the hubbub" want to know "better than what?"

Betty Bakery *Baked Goods* | 23 | 19 | 22 | M |

Boerum Hill | 448 Atlantic Ave. (bet. Bond & Nevins Sts.) | Brooklyn |
A/C/G to Hoyt/Schermerhorn Sts. | 718-246-2402
An "absolute fave" in Boerum Hill after only a year in business, this "reasonably priced" bakery from exclusive wedding-cake crafters Cheryl Kleinman and Ellen Baumwoll (the latter of Bijoux Doux) focuses on "amazing" cupcakes, "beautiful" petit fours and, yes, full-size cakes too; its snug "grandma's kitchen"–like quarters, centered around a pastel-green 1930s-era stove, include a few seats in which to savor the treats, along with coffee and tea poured by a "friendly" crew.

Between the Bread *Caterer* | 21 | 18 | 18 | M |

W 50s | 145 W. 55th St. (bet. 6th & 7th Aves.) | N/Q/R/W to 57th St. |
212-765-1840 | www.betweenthebread.com
"Business meetings" and "office parties" "look easy" in the hands of this Midtown "corporate-catering" specialist and prepared foods shop that provides a "wonderful variety" of "seasonal" New American fare in "creative presentations"; some pan its offerings as "pedestrian", but many others hail it as a "dependable" option for "no-fuss" planning.

Biancardi Meats ⇗ *Meat/Poultry* | 27 | 23 | 25 | M |

Bronx | 2350 Arthur Ave. (bet. Crescent Ave. & 187th St.) | B/D to
Fordham Rd. | 718-733-4058
This family-owned, Italian-oriented Arthur Avenue butcher has been taking meat "seriously" since 1932 and continues to "reign su-

preme" with "excellent-quality", "value"-priced cuts of all kinds, as well as sausages and more esoteric offerings (baby goat, game birds, rabbit and more – "just ask and it will appear"); given that "great traditional" places like this are "losing popularity to supermarkets and gourmet shops", far-flung fans say it's more than "worth the trip" to the Bronx.

⛁ Bierkraft ●▣ *Beer*　　　　28 | 21 | 25 | M

Park Slope | 191 Fifth Ave. (bet. Berkeley Pl. & Union St.) | Brooklyn | M/R to Union St. | 718-230-7600 | www.bierkraft.com

For "one-stop gourmet shopping", regulars recommend this Park Slope beer expert that offers not only a "vast" (more than 1,000), "well-curated" selection of suds, including drafts you can take home in "reusable growler jugs", but also "tasty" "delights" such as 200–300 varieties of "wonderful" cheeses, "mouthwatering cold cuts", "gift-worthy" condiments, "handmade chocolates" and more; an "approachable" staff will guide you along this "dangerous but delicious route", which is "costly", but hey, still "cheaper than going to Belgium."

Big Apple Florist ▣ *Flowers*　　　∇ 24 | 24 | 25 | M

E 40s | 228 E. 45th St. (bet. 2nd & 3rd Aves.) | 4/5/6/7/S to 42nd St./Grand Central | 212-687-3434 | 800-554-0001 | www.bigappleflorist.com

"Too bad about the deli"-esque name, because this East Midtown florist's "designer-looking" arrangements are "haute level" according to aficionados; the staff is "personable" and willing to design "something custom, even over the phone", resulting in posies that are "pleasing to the eye", and, better still, come "without the big-bucks price tag."

Big Nose Full Body ●▣ *Wine/Liquor*　　24 | 21 | 25 | M

Park Slope | 382 Seventh Ave. (bet. 11th & 12th Sts.) | Brooklyn | F to 7th Ave. | 718-369-4030 | www.bignosefullbody.com

It's a "pleasure to spend time" at this "wonderful", "quaint" Park Slope shop where oenophiles can sniff out "smart choices" "for every budget" from the "limited", but "interesting" selection of 350 labels, "hand selected by the owner" and "beautifully displayed"; with "knowledgeable service", a "fabulous website" and weekly tastings, it's "what a neighborhood wine store should be."

Bijoux Doux Specialty Cakes ⊄ *Baked Goods*　– | – | – | M

Boerum Hill | 448 Atlantic Ave. (bet. Bond & Nevins Sts.) | Brooklyn | 718-237-2271 | www.bijouxdoux.com

By appointment only

"Beautiful, delicious cakes with imaginative designs" distinguish pastry chef Ellen Baumwoll's Boerum Hill–based boutique bakery, which caters to brides-to-be and high-end party planners; her signature flavors are hazelnut-almond and Valrhona-chocolate, in layers that stack up in "wonderful" designs both classic and contemporary; N.B. Baumwoll's bespoke business shares space with Betty Bakery, the retail bake shop she runs together with fellow gâteau great Cheryl Kleinman.

	QUALITY	DISPLAY	SERVICE	COST

Billy's Bakery ● *Baked Goods*

	25	23	22	M

Chelsea | 184 Ninth Ave. (bet. 21st & 22nd Sts.) | C/E to 23rd St. |
212-647-9956 | www.billysbakerynyc.com

"Bless Billy!" enthuse admirers of this Chelsea bakery known for its
"moist, buttery" cupcakes topped with "to-die for" icing, as well as
for "tasty" full-size cakes, pies and other "homespun" "American-
style" sweets, all "beautifully displayed" in "hip" "retro"-'40s digs;
the "friendly" counter folk only "add to the sugar high", and while
"lines out the door" are not uncommon, at least they're "not as long"
as at that higher-profile cupcakery to the south; N.B. it now runs a
kiosk in the Javitz Center, open during conventions only.

Birdbath *Baked Goods*

	23	22	23	M

G Village | 145 Seventh Ave. S. (Charles St.) | 1 to Christopher St. |
646-722-6570

Build a Green Bakery ●⊟ *Baked Goods*

E Village | 223 First Ave. (bet. 13th & 14th Sts.) | 646-722-6565
www.buildagreenbakery.com

"Indulge while you save the earth" could be the motto of this East
Village–West Village pair of eco-conscious bakeries/coffee shops
from the City Bakery's Maury Rubin, the interiors of which are made
from environmentally sound materials, right down to the counter
crew's hemp jackets; its "fabulous" cookies, "flaky pastries" and
such made with wholesome, all-organic ingredients have reviewers
raving "political correctness" "never tasted so good"; P.S. there's a
25% discount for those who "arrive by bicycle."

BJ's Wholesale

	17	10	8	I

Club ●☰ *Major Gourmet Mkt.*

Starrett City | Gateway Ctr. | 339 Gateway Dr. (Erskine St.) | Brooklyn |
3 to Van Siclen Ave. | 718-942-2090

College Point | 137-05 20th Ave. (Whitestone Expwy., exit 15) |
Queens | 718-359-9703

Middle Village | Metro Mall | 66-26 Metropolitan Ave. (69th St.) |
Queens | M to Middle Vill./Metropolitan Ave. | 718-326-9080
www.bjs.com

For "Super Bowl parties and such" this outer-borough wholesaler
chain is a bonanza of "bargains" sold "in bulk", with "warehouse"
aisles lined with "prepackaged deli items", frozen prepared foods
that make "acceptable side dishes", "cheap bakery products"
and "generic" housewares like "crock pots and snow-cone machines"; conditions are basic and "disorganized" and the "run-of-
the-mill" goods "leave taste in the mind of the beholder", but if
you need "5 lbs of anything" it's "quick and inexpensive" – "what
do you expect?"

☑ Black Hound New York ●☰ *Baked Goods*

	26	26	22	E

E Village | 170 Second Ave. (bet. 10th & 11th Sts.) | L to 1st Ave. |
212-979-9505 | 800-344-4417 | www.blackhoundny.com

"Stunning" works of art that are as "beautiful to behold as they are
delicious to eat" are the trademark of this "lovely little" East Village
bakery prized for "wicked", "wonderfully rich" cakes – including

	QUALITY	DISPLAY	SERVICE	COST

"mini" versions "perfect for two" – as well as "fancy" cookies, tarts and truffles sure "to set your diet back centuries"; a "disappointed" minority claims that the taste of some items "doesn't lives up to" their "perfect looks", but most find the goods "top-notch" – and "you pay for it"; N.B. gift baskets are also a specialty.

Blanc & Rouge ●□ *Wine/Liquor* ▽ 25 | 21 | 23 | M

Dumbo | 81 Washington St. (bet. Front & York Sts.) | Brooklyn | F to York St. | 718-858-9463 | www.brwine.com

A "friendly", "quaint secret", this Dumbo locals' "favorite" housed in an old factory space "isn't huge" as wine stores go (it stocks some 150 labels), but it still features a "good selection" of "affordable" and unusual bottles from the New World (Chile, Argentina, Australia, New Zealand, etc.) as well as the traditional Burgundies and Bordeaux; other pluses are a "helpful, knowledgeable" staff that "treats you like a good neighbor" and tastings on Wednesday evenings.

☑ Bloom *Flowers* 27 | 28 | 22 | VE

E 50s | 541 Lexington Ave. (50th St.) | 6 to 51st St. | 212-832-8094 | www.bloomflowers.com

Its "gorgeous", "work-of-art" arrangements "receive raves from everyone" say customers of this "beautiful" Midtown shop, which offers "not just flowers" but home furnishings and accessories too, meaning "there's plenty to look at while you wait for your creation"; given such "simple" yet "over-the-top" bouquets, its near-"extortionate" prices are "a given", but happily "the blooms last long enough" that most are able to "forget the cost"; N.B. they also offer event-planning and interior design services.

Bloomingdale's Cookware ●□ *Cookware* 24 | 22 | 16 | E

E 50s | 1000 Third Ave. (bet. 59th & 60th Sts.) | 4/5/6/N/R/W to 59th St./Lexington Ave. | 212-705-2237 | 800-472-0788 | www.bloomingdales.com

"Watch for sales!" advise insiders of this famed East Side department store's kitchen section, whose "well-organized" selection of "top" "consumer" brands ("All-Clad, Calphalon", etc.) and "terrific" variety of utensils and gadgets are priced on the "high end" but become "bargains" if you can "wait" for a reduction; service runs the gamut from "extremely knowledgeable" to "nonexistent", but still this stalwart wins raves for its wedding registry service and "exquisite gift-wrapping."

☑ Blue Apron Foods *Specialty Shop* 27 | 25 | 24 | E

Park Slope | 814 Union St. (7th Ave.) | Brooklyn | B/Q to 7th Ave. | 718-230-3180

"An oasis in the borough", this pint-size Park Slope specialty shop is an epicurean "favorite" for its locally "unparalleled" cheese and charcuterie selection and well-edited lineup of "fine foods", from imported pastas to Jacques Torres chocolates, including some of "the most obscure ingredients, with advice on how to use them"; "knowledgeable" staffers and "lovely displays" "make up for" the "cramped" quarters and "steep prices."

	QUALITY	DISPLAY	SERVICE	COST

NEW Blue Marble Ice Cream ● *Ice Cream* | ▽ 24 | 20 | 22 | M |

Boerum Hill | 420 Atlantic Ave. (bet. Bond & Nevins Sts.) | Brooklyn | A/C/G to Hoyt/Schermerhorn Sts. | 718-858-1100
Prospect Heights | 186 Underhill Ave. (St. Johns Pl.) | Brooklyn | 2/3 to Grand Army Plaza | 718-399-6926 ⊞
www.bluemarbleicecream.com

Filling a neglected niche along Boerum Hill's Atlantic Avenue strip is this charming, eco-conscious ice cream shop whose whitewashed wood accents lend it a rural feel, while a play area stocked with toys earn it "kid-friendly haven" status; its "oh-my-god-yum" organic scoops come in two sizes (mini and regular), and it also pours quality brews from Irving Farm Coffee and In Pursuit of Tea; N.B. the Prospect Heights location opened post-Survey.

Blue Meadow Flowers *Flowers* | - | - | - | E |

E Village | 336 E. 13th St. (bet. 1st & 2nd Aves.) | L to 1st Ave. | 212-979-8618

"Classy, tightly wrapped bouquets with flowers that last for weeks" come in unusual vases and terra-cotta containers at this East Village floral boutique; its "innovative designs" based on classic European and Victorian styles are deemed "just beautiful" and (no surprise) "expensive" too; N.B. open weekdays only.

Blue Moon Fish ⊞ *Seafood* | 29 | 20 | 26 | M |

See Greenmarket; for more information, call phone number unavailable | www.bluemoonfish.com

A "Greenmarket staple" since 1987, this North Fork fishmonger has seafood lovers "over the moon" with its "pristine local" offerings that are nearly "as fresh as if you caught them yourself"; the fish comes filleted or whole, or even smoked, and accompanied by "loads of knowledge and suggestions" about how to cook it courtesy of "charming", "skillful" staffers – given the "great vibe" and "fair prices", it's no wonder there are always "long lines" ("get there early").

Blue Pig ● *Ice Cream* | 21 | 17 | 20 | M |

Brooklyn Heights | 60B Henry St. (bet. Cranberry & Orange Sts.) | Brooklyn | 2/3 to Clark St. | 718-596-6301 | www.bluepigicecream.com

"Be a piggie" at this "cute", "charming" Brooklyn Heights ice cream parlor, a spin-off of a Croton, NY, favorite, where the "fabulous" flavors are "unusual" without being "too unusual" and the ingredients are "fresh"; it's just the kind of "fun" place to hit "on a summer night" before "walking the promenade" – happily, cones for pint-size customers come with "plastic holders to catch the drips."

☑ Blue Ribbon Market *Baked Goods* | 28 | 22 | 23 | E |

G Village | 14 Bedford St. (bet. Downing & W. Houston Sts.) | 1 to Houston St. | 212-647-0408 | www.blueribbonrestaurants.com

Acclaimed as a "wonderful addition" to the Bromberg brothers' "empire", this "tiny" Greenwich Village storefront allows fans of the famously "fresh, homey" and "delicious" breads baked in the 150-year-old oven of its nearby restaurant sibling, Blue Ribbon Bakery, to "take them home"; it also sells a small selection of spreads, cheeses, smoked fish, oils and condiments to go with the loaves, as well as "superb" 'toasts' (open-faced sandwiches) and soups, all dispensed by a "friendly" low-key crew.

Blue Smoke Catering *Caterer*

25 | 20 | 23 | E

Gramercy | 116 E. 27th St. (bet. Lexington & Park Aves.) | 6 to 28th St. | 212-447-6058 | www.bluesmoke.com

For an "alternative party idea", 'cuennoisseurs recommend the catering arm of Danny Meyer's upscale Gramercy smokehouse, which supplies "yum" "country-style food" including "oh, yeah" barbecue and the "best mac 'n' cheese in the world"; there's also "helpful" pro service whether the event's held at the restaurant, downstairs jazz club or off-site, and while it's true that the fare's mostly "limited to carnivores", c'mon – "who doesn't love good BBQ?"

Blue Water Flowers *Flowers*

– | – | – | E

SoHo | 265 Lafayette St. (bet. Prince & Spring Sts.) | 6 to Spring St. | 212-226-0587 | 800-964-7108 | www.bluewaterflowers.com

A striped awning and antique shutters give an old-fashioned feel to this "tasteful" SoHo shop, but the flowers are up-to-the-minute, unusual blooms arranged in ginger jars; those in search of something longer lasting will find orchids planted in ceramic or terra-cotta pots, as well as topiaries of rosemary, myrtle, ivy and azalea and dried-flower wreaths; N.B. gourmet gift baskets are also available.

Boerum Hill Food Company *Prepared Food*

22 | 18 | 21 | M

Boerum Hill | 134 Smith St. (bet. Bergen & Dean Sts.) | Brooklyn | F/G to Bergen St. | 718-222-0140

At this "cozy little" Boerum Hill cafe/prepared foods shop/catering biz (an offshoot of the down-the-block eatery Saul), the "delicious" homemade lures range from fresh-baked muffins for breakfast to soups and "mac 'n' cheese to die for" for lunch or "monster egg sandwiches" that are "satisfying any time of day"; there's also coffee from Gorilla and sweets like brownies, which satisfy those on-the-run as well as those opting to linger in its "pleasant" space.

Bonsignour ❶ *Prepared Food*

▽ 26 | 18 | 23 | M

W Village | 35 Jane St. (8th Ave.) | A/C/E/L to 14th St./8th Ave. | 212-229-9700

A "friendly, neighborhood kitchen" in the West Village, this "casual", "charming" shop is "a real winner" avow aficionados who mention "the best muffins baked every morning" ("get there while they're still warm") as well as "great salads", "good sandwiches" and diverse daily dinners-to-go like chili, lasagna or jambalaya, best followed by one of the cupcakes and other sweets; some take out just as far as the "appealing bench" outside on the sidewalk.

☒ Borgatti's Ravioli & Egg Noodles ⌧ *Pasta*

29 | 19 | 25 | I

Bronx | 632 E. 187th St. (bet. Belmont & Hughes Aves.) | B/D to Fordham Rd. | 718-367-3799 | www.borgattis.com

You'd think they'd been "waiting for you all day" given the warm welcomes you get at this more than 70-year-old pasta purveyor on

QUALITY · DISPLAY · SERVICE · COST

Arthur Avenue, where buyers can watch the goods being made by the "third generation of Borgattis", a family whose "passion for their product" "comes across" in "superlative fresh" noodles (some "cut to order") and ravioli made with "the most exquisite silken, salty ricotta"; even though the old-time "rolling machines" have been retired, the entire experience is still "wonderfully nostalgic" right down to the "bargain" prices.

Bottega del Vino ●◖▣ *Prepared Food* | 25 | 21 | 20 | E |

E 50s | 7 E. 59th St. (bet. 5th & Madison Aves.) | N/R/W to 5th Ave./ 59th St. | 212-223-3028 | www.bottegadelvinonyc.com

Via Quadronno ●◖▣ *Prepared Food*

E 70s | 25 E. 73rd St. (bet. 5th & Madison Aves.) | 6 to 77th St. | 212-650-9880 | www.viaquadronno.com

At this "festive" East Side Italian-style duo, "Euro-types" mingle with "movers and shakers" to nibble "tiny servings of fabulous food", sip "outstanding cappuccino" and stock up on oils, vinegars and coffees; "panini are the real bargain" among the "delicious" if "ultra-expensive" offerings (the Uptown branch is famous for them), while wines (natch) are highlighted at the roomy Midtown spot with its signature risotto Amarone and its own special glassware to sip from or buy.

Bottino *Prepared Food* | 22 | 21 | 18 | M |

Chelsea | 248 10th Ave. (bet. 24th & 25th Sts.) | C/E to 23rd St. | 212-206-6766 | www.bottinonyc.com

The take-out adjunct of the same-name Italian restaurant next door, this West Chelsea "gem" is just the place for meals on-the-go, or for snack breaks while gallery-hopping; among the many offerings are "a good selection of creative sandwiches, salads" and soups, as well as baked-on-premises pies, tarts and cookies, all for "a good price."

☒ Bottlerocket Wine & Spirit *Wine/Liquor* | 26 | 27 | 27 | M |

Flatiron | 5 W. 19th St. (bet. 5th & 6th Aves.) | 1 to 18th St. | 212-929-2323 | www.bottlerocketwine.com

An "innovator" among vintners, this Flatiron shop gets an "A+ in creativity" for the "eye-catching" themed displays for its 365 labels, with such categories as 'takeout' and 'gifts', that are a "godsend" for novices and "fun for the initiated"; "printed descriptions" for each bottle and a "friendly" staff help "make shopping unintimidating and enjoyable" at this "terrific addition to the winescape of Manhattan."

Bottle Shoppe *Wine/Liquor* | - | - | - | M |

Williamsburg | 301 Bedford Ave. (bet. S. 1st & S. 2nd Sts.) | Brooklyn | L to Bedford Ave. | 718-302-3433 | www.myspace.com/bottleshoppe

"Cool displays based on what you're looking for" ("gift for the boss, hot date", etc.) endear this little Williamsburg wine shop to the locals, as do the "fair prices" ($8–$15 a bottle) and well-edited selection of labels that are "not the typical, run-of-the-mill" stuff; free tastings on Friday nights boost the overall "friendly" vibe.

	QUALITY	DISPLAY	SERVICE	COST

☑ Bouchon Bakery ● *Baked Goods* — 27 | 25 | 21 | E

W 60s | Time Warner Ctr. | 10 Columbus Circle, 3rd fl. (bet. 58th & 60th Sts.) | 1/A/B/C/D to 59th St./Columbus Circle | 212-823-9366 | www.bouchonbakery.com

"Perfectly decadent" say the swarms buzzing around Thomas Keller's perpetually packed ("be prepared to wait") French-inspired bakery/take-out counter in the Time Warner Center, adjacent to his casual cafe of the same name, providing "magical" pastries, cakes, cookies, breads and other baked goods as well as "delicious" sandwiches, quiches, salads, soups and even housemade chocolates, all on view in "gorgeous display cases"; neither the sometimes "overwhelmed" staff nor the "high-rent" prices (if "cheap compared to per se" upstairs) dissuade the "masses"; P.S. there's a small seating area for on-the-spot "indulging."

☑ Bouley Bakery & Market *Baked Goods* — 27 | 25 | 22 | E

TriBeCa | 130 W. Broadway (Duane St.) | 1 to Franklin St. | 212-608-5829 | www.davidbouley.com

You just might "want to move to TriBeCa" after visiting chef David Bouley's tri-level destination for "uniformly superb", "splurge"-worthy French-style baked goods – "heavenly" brick-oven breads, croissants, tarts, macarons – all "displayed like precious jewelry" on the first floor, along with "excellent sandwiches" and other prepared foods; in the cellar are cheeses, fish, meats, olives, oils and such, while the second story houses the eatery Upstairs.

Bowery & Vine ● *Wine/Liquor* — - | - | - | M
(fka Elizabeth & Vine)

LES | 269 Bowery St. (bet. E. Houston & Stanton Sts.) | 212-941-7943 | www.boweryandvine.com

Formerly named for the intersection where it was located, this LES wine shop has just moved (and changed its name accordingly) into the airy space that in the 1930s was the bustling Bowery Cafeteria; fitted with a marble tasting table in back, a temperature-controlled fine wine room and two 'liquor library' rooms, it aims to please – as does its staff of self-proclaimed 'wine nerds.'

Bowery Kitchen Supplies ▭ *Cookware* — 22 | 14 | 15 | M

Chelsea | Chelsea Mkt. | 75 Ninth Ave. (bet. 15th & 16th Sts.) | A/C/E/L to 14th St./8th Ave. | 212-376-4982

Bowery Kitchen East ▭ *Cookware*

LES | 5 Rivington St. (Bowery) | F/V to Lower East Side/2nd Ave. | 212-477-8681
www.shopbowery.com

A "cook's haven" tucked into the back of Chelsea Market (with an offshoot on the LES), this "incredibly cluttered" kitchenware shop has earned a rep for being one of the "best" for "hard-to-find items" like "ramekins, small whisks and other strange things" as well as cookware, cutlery, appliances, professional-grade stainless-steel work tables and storage racks, all at "reasonable" prices; despite "uneven" service, all agree it's fun for "browsing."

	QUALITY	DISPLAY	SERVICE	COST

Brasil Coffee House 🖭🚭 *Coffee/Tea* | 21 | 18 | 21 | I |

Murray Hill | Ramada Hotel | 161 Lexington Ave. (30th St.) | 6 to 28th St. | 212-213-9725 ◑

LIC | 45-02 23rd St. (45th Ave.) | Queens | E/V to 23rd St./Ely Ave. | 718-729-7424

LIC | 48-19 Vernon Blvd. (49th Ave.) | Queens | 7 to Vernon Blvd. | 718-729-5969 ◑

877-327-2745 | www.brasilcoffeehouse.com

Considered a "change of pace" for a caffeine "boost", this "charming" Murray Hill–Long Island City cafe trio dispenses "decent Brazilian coffee" along with "delish" Amazonian nibbles like *coxinha* (chicken croquettes), cheesebread, coconut muffins and other "rare finds"; being "unpretentious" "places to chill", they're somewhat "neglected" but always a "pleasant" "reprieve" from the megachains.

Bread Alone 🖭 *Baked Goods* | 27 | 20 | 22 | M |

See Greenmarket; for more information, call 845-657-3328 or 800-769-3328 | www.breadalone.com

"Addicts" aver the array of "rich, nutritious", "chewy" whole-grain artisanal loaves – not to mention "delicious muffins", "must" scones and handrolled croissants – from this Ulster County organic bakery is "worth a trip" to the Catskills; fortunately, carbophiles without cars can get their fix at the year-round Greenmarket booth, where "friendly" staffers are anything but crusty.

Bread Stuy 🚭 *Baked Goods* | – | – | – | M |

Bed-Stuy | 403 Lewis Ave. (bet. Decatur & Macdonough Sts.) | Brooklyn | A/C to Utica Ave. | 718-771-0633 | www.breadstuy.com

This funky Bed-Stuy bakery/cafe run by a husband-and-wife team is appreciated for its housemade breads, red velvet cake and other sweets, as well as panini; its warm, wood-accented space serves as something of a local gathering spot, a venue for kids' art classes and a place for local artists to display their works.

Broadway Panhandler 🖭 *Cookware* | 26 | 20 | 19 | M |

G Village | 65 E. Eighth St. (bet. B'way & University Pl.) | R/W to 8th St. | 212-966-3434 | 866-266-5927 | www.broadwaypanhandler.com

"Long before the chains moved in", cooks counted on this kitchenware "favorite" for its "inspiring", "expansive" assortment of "moderate to upscale" wares including "one of the best selections of Le Creuset in the city", as well as for its "well-informed" staff and "decent prices"; its move in 2006 to the Village has brought it "closer to its Broadway roots" and all agree it remains a "great resource" for both "serious cooks" and amateurs.

Broadway Party Rentals *Party Rentals* | 19 | 17 | 17 | M |

Union Sq | 200 Park Ave. S., Suite 1610 (17th St.) | 4/5/6/L/N/Q/R/W to 14th St./Union Sq. | 212-269-2666

Williamsburg | 134 Morgan Ave. (bet. Johnson Ave. & Meserole St.) | Brooklyn | L to Morgan Ave. | 718-821-4000

www.broadwaypartyrentals.com

With a 60,000-sq.-ft. warehouse in Williamsburg and a 2,000-sq.-ft. Union Square showroom, this party-rentals outfit "always has enough in stock", making it a "no-nonsense supplier that always comes through" with tables, chairs, dinnerware and dance floors (though no tents) at "moderate prices"; it has a tendency to be a "very busy place", so the initiated advise it's "best if you know what you want before calling"; N.B. the minimum order ranges from $250–$1,000 depending on the time of year, with a $45 delivery fee.

Brooklyn Ice Cream Factory ⬤⊅ *Ice Cream*

| 25 | 18 | 20 | M |

Dumbo | Fulton Ferry Landing Pier | Old Fulton St. (Water St.) | Brooklyn | A/C to High St. | 718-246-3963
Greenpoint | 97 Commercial St. (Manhattan Ave.) | Brooklyn | G to Greenpoint Ave. | 718-349-2506

A "purist's delight", this "old-school" Dumbo destination on the Fulton Ferry Pier (with a newer Greenpoint offshoot) dishes out eight "classic" and "really, really creamy", "made-on-premises" flavors, "each one a winner", including the "rich, dark" chocolate and "to-die-for" peach; you may have to stand in a "line going out the door", but at least the "spectacular view is free."

Brooklyn Kitchen ▣ *Cookware*

| 23 | 19 | 23 | M |

Williamsburg | 616 Lorimer St. (Skillman Ave.) | Brooklyn | L to Lorimer St. | 718-389-2982 | www.thebrooklynkitchen.com

This "adorable", "affordable" Williamsburg kitchenware shop has a retro feel owing perhaps to its stock of "vintage Pyrex" and refurbished cast-iron pans, which round out its "broad range of kitchen tools" and "top-quality" cookware from the likes of Le Creuset and All-Clad; factor in an "über-friendly" staff that "knows all" and classes offered in a "small" on-site kitchen, and it's no wonder it's considered a "terrific resource for Brooklyn cooks."

Brooklyn Liquors ⬤ *Wine/Liquor*

| 23 | 15 | 19 | I |

Sunset Park | Costco | 976 Third Ave. (bet. 37th & 38th Sts.) | Brooklyn | D/M/N/R to 36th St. | 718-499-2257 | www.brooklynliquors.com

"Perfect party planning" for a song can be yours at this "friendly" "Costco neighbor under the Gowanus Expressway" in Sunset Park, where you can shop for "discount Dom Perignon" and other "fine wines" and spirits priced "cheap"; the choices are "limited", but there's "free parking" and "you can't beat" the "weekly specials."

Bruno Bakery ⬤▣ *Baked Goods*

| 23 | 22 | 18 | M |

G Village | 506 La Guardia Pl. (bet. Bleecker & Houston Sts.) | B/D/F/V to B'way/Lafayette St. | 212-982-5854 | www.pasticceriabruno.com

The "gorgeous" cases at this "busy" "old-time" Village Italian bakery and its NYU-area offshoot are filled with "everything for the sweet tooth" from master baker Biagio Settepani's "wonderful" cakes, biscotti and cannoli to "delicious" gelato; "helpful" service, "fair" prices and espresso bars ensure they're "always worth a stop."

Bruno the King of Ravioli ⬤ *Pasta*

| 24 | 18 | 20 | M |

Gramercy | 282 First Ave. (bet. 16th & 17th Sts.) | L to 1st Ave. | 212-254-2156

(continued)

(continued)

Bruno the King of Ravioli

Gramercy | 387 Second Ave. (bet. 22nd & 23rd Sts.) | 6 to 23rd St. |
212-685-7666

W 70s | 2204 Broadway (bet. 78th & 79th Sts.) | 1 to 79th St. |
212-580-8150

888-652-7866 | www.brunoravioli.com

Boasting three fiefdoms in Manhattan, this Hoboken-based noodle slinger rewards loyal subjects with pastas that are "fit for a
king" but better suited to a "peasant's budget", including a "multitude" of ravioli ("seasonal choices are the best!") and other shapes;
there are also sauces and prepared dishes that will "convince anyone that you are an Italian chef"; P.S. "stock up and put the rest
in the freezer."

Bulich Mushroom Co., Inc. ✍ *Produce*

| 29 | 23 | 27 | M |

See Greenmarket; for more information, call 518-943-3089

One of the last mushroom growers left in NY State, this third-
generation Hudson Valley fungus farmer pops up on Saturdays at
the Greenmarket; surveyors feel "sooo lucky" to get the "incredibly
fresh" portabello, crimini, shiitake, oyster and white table varieties,
all with "excellent concentrated flavor" ("they smell just like
earth"), and are also grateful for the "reasonable" rates and
"friendly", "helpful" staffers who let you "choose as small an
amount as you desire."

BuonItalia 🖃 *Specialty Shop*

| 26 | 18 | 16 | M |

Chelsea | Chelsea Mkt. | 75 Ninth Ave. (bet. 15th & 16th Sts.) |
A/C/E/L to 14th St./8th Ave. | 212-633-9090 |
www.buonitalia.com

Offering "every Italian item you could ever need", this specialty
grocer "conveniently located in the Chelsea Market" stocks "top-
quality" "treasures" – "from Parmesan to black truffles" to a "wonderful supply of pastas" – that include "some interesting imports";
still, a few fret that the "staff seems indifferent" and the goods
"overpriced", although they admit shopping here is "definitely
cheaper than flying to Italy"; N.B. the back counter and cafe
serve prepared foods.

☒ Burgundy Wine Company 🖃 *Wine/Liquor*

| 29 | 23 | 25 | E |

Chelsea | 143 W. 26th St. (bet. 6th & 7th Aves.) | 1 to 28th St. |
212-691-9092 | 888-898-8448 |
www.burgundywinecompany.com

"Focus" has its rewards, as this "brilliant" Chelsea "pro" demon-
strates with its "reliable", "top-notch" selection of Rhônes,
Oregonians and, "of course", wines from the namesake French region, all shown off by a staff of "enthusiastic" "experts willing to
share their knowledge"; the "prices go with the territory", but it's
"simply heaven" for "serious buyers", and "regular folk" "will feel
welcome" also; P.S. the tastings every day are simply "amazing" –
and on Wednesday evenings there's live jazz too.

	QUALITY	DISPLAY	SERVICE	COST

Busy Chef, The *Prepared Food* | 21 | 18 | 21 | M |

Brooklyn Heights | 60 Henry St. (Market St.) | Brooklyn | B/D to Grand St. | 718-624-3182

Brooklyn Heights denizens too harried to cook head to this storefront for "better-than-average" packaged prepared foods that are "ready to heat and eat"; it's a "great concept" pulled off by "accommodating" staffers, even if the bright-white setup strikes some as "somewhat clinical"; P.S. insiders say the "end-of-day specials" are "so affordable it's crazy."

Buttercup Bake Shop *Baked Goods* | 23 | 21 | 20 | M |

E 50s | 973 Second Ave. (bet. 51st & 52nd Sts.) | 6 to 51st St. | 212-350-4144 ◐

W 70s | 141 W. 72nd St. (bet. Amsterdam & Columbus Aves.) | 1/2/3 to 72nd St. | 212-787-3800
www.buttercupbakeshop.com

This East Side–West Side twosome specializes in "beautiful and delicious" cupcakes crowned with a "colorful" range of "creamy, light" frostings, not to mention "classic" layer cakes, "incredible" banana pudding and other sweet Americana; "friendly" and "kitschy", it gets "pretty packed", especially "around the holidays"; N.B. separately owned.

Butterfield Market ▣ *Specialty Shop* | 23 | 21 | 19 | E |

E 70s | 1114 Lexington Ave. (bet. 77th & 78th Sts.) | 6 to 77th St. | 212-288-7800 | www.butterfieldmarket.com

Infused with that "old New York feeling" (it dates to 1915), this "gourmet" grocer and caterer on the Upper East Side is a "heaven for the kitchen-challenged", "covering all the bases" with its "wonderful prepared entrees and side dishes", "tasty sandwiches" and "museum-quality produce"; all in all, surveyors are "never disappointed, except when paying the bill" – "this is one expensive market."

Café Grumpy ◑ *Coffee/Tea* ∇ | 26 | 13 | 19 | M |

Chelsea | 224 West 20th St. (bet. 7th & 8th Aves.) | 1 to 18th St. | 212-255-5511

Greenpoint | 193 Meserole Ave. (Diamond St.) | Brooklyn | G to Nassau Ave. | 718-349-7623
www.cafegrumpy.com

Promoting java "snobbery at its finest", these Chelsea-Greenpoint cafes "treat coffee like wine", listing "beans by region" on an exotic international menu (new brews are highlighted monthly) and grinding each cup fresh on state-of-the-art "drip" equipment; the "unique" "fix" "might be the best" in town, and with a "knowledgeable staff" also serving sandwiches (Brooklyn only) and "real espresso", even "purists" find nothing to grouse about.

Café Habana To Go ◑ *Prepared Food* | 24 | 14 | 16 | I |

NoLita | 229 Elizabeth St. (bet. Houston & Prince Sts.) | N/R to Prince St. | 212-625-2002 | www.ecoeatery.com

"When the wait's too long" for "delicious" Cuban eats at the NoLita restaurant next door ("and when isn't it?"), fans know "plan B" is takeout from this offshoot, where "curt service is worth putting up with" for "fabulous sandwiches", trademark "amazing" grilled corn, "giant burritos" and other "tasty", "authentic" grub; "prices are easy to digest" too, making it clear "this place sure knows how to do to-go."

Cafe Regular ⊄ *Coffee/Tea*

▽ 24 | 22 | 22 | M

Park Slope | 318A 11th St. (bet. 4th & 5th Aves.) | Brooklyn | F/M/R to 4th Ave./9th St. | 718-768-4170

Park Slopers "love the European feel" of this "tiny" coffeehouse, an "adorable" nook with a Parisian-style marble-top bar and a bench-lined wall where the regular crowd cozies up for "great coffee, espresso and repartee" with the staffers; featuring "amazing" beans blended by La Colombe and baked goods from the Sullivan Street Bakery, it has its "hip" clientele saying "Manhattanites will be jealous."

Cafe Spice Express ◗ *Prepared Food*

19 | 16 | 17 | M

E 40s | Grand Central Terminal | dining concourse (42nd St. & Vanderbilt Ave.) | 4/5/6/7/S to 42nd St./Grand Central | 646-227-1300 | www.cafespice.com

"Savory" subcontinental dishes for those on-the-go is the deal at this take-out arm of the Indian mini-chain on Grand Central's dining concourse; the less-than-impressed shrug "unremarkable", but commuters who rely on its convenience call it "quick, easy" and "pretty tasty" – especially given the "food-court" milieu.

Caffé Roma Pastry ◗⊄ *Baked Goods*

23 | 21 | 18 | M

Little Italy | 385 Broome St. (Mulberry St.) | 6/J/M/N/Q/R/W/Z to Canal St. | 212-226-8413

"Low-key" but long on history and "atmosphere", this Little Italy "old-timer" (since 1918) is a guardian of "classic" Italian *dolces* such as "tasty" ricotta cheesecake, cannoli, gelati and tiramisu that are often washed down with a cup of espresso; nostalgists note that tasting the treats here "seems like old times."

Cake Chef Inc. ⊄ *Baked Goods*

▽ 22 | 18 | 23 | I

Staten Island | 957 Jewett Ave. (Victory Blvd.) | 718-448-1290

"The quality" is "unsurpassed" rave reviewers of this Staten Island bake shop beloved for its cakes, pastries and a "cheese crumb ring that's to die for" as well as its collection of vintage cookie jars, which can be bought and filled with "home-baked" treats; one caution: the selection is "small", so "order ahead" because "if you go after 2 PM on a Sunday, you can forget it."

Cakeline *Baked Goods*

- | - | - | E

Rockaway Beach | 220 Beach 132nd St., Belle Harbor | Queens | 718-634-5063 | www.cakeline.com

By appointment only

Once a pastry chef for über-caterer Glorious Food, Cynthia Peithman now heads her own cakery in Rockaway Beach, turning out custom-crafted multi-tier confections (including her signature Autumn Leaf style) for weddings and other special occasions; customers who "don't mind the cost" can choose from seven flavors of cake and more than two dozen buttercream, ganache and mousse fillings.

	QUALITY	DISPLAY	SERVICE	COST

⊠ Cake Man Raven
Confectionery ● *Baked Goods* | 26 | 15 | 14 | M |

Fort Greene | 708 Fulton St. (bet. Oxford St. & Portland Ave.) | Brooklyn |
C to Lafayette Ave. | 718-694-2253 | www.cakemanraven.com

The "best red velvet cake this side of the Mason-Dixon" results in
"lines out the door" at this unassuming Fort Greene sweets spot run
by a South Carolina–bred baker, whose other "moist, rich and tasty"
variations include carrot, mocha-peanut butter and pineapple-
cream cheese; walk-ins can purchase up to four "mammoth" slices
at a time (whole cakes must be ordered a week in advance), and
though some say service "has been lacking recently", most shrug
"the product is so good, who cares?"

Cakes 'N Shapes *Baked Goods* ▽ 22 | 17 | 22 | M |

W 50s | 466 W. 51st St. (bet. 9th & 10th Sts.) | 212-629-5512 |
www.cakesnshapes.com
By appointment only

"Custom photo cakes" are the calling card of "easy-to-deal-with"
bespoke baker Edie Connolly, who at her Hell's Kitchen shop produces faux magazine and book cover gateaux that look so lifelike,
guests might be tempted to try a flip-through; supporters swear her
"terrific-quality" creations "taste even better" than they look, and,
sweetest of all, they come at a surprisingly "reasonable" price;
N.B. she also does free-form sculpted cakes and decorated cookies.

⊠ Calabria Pork Store ▭▱ *Meat/Poultry* 28 | 21 | 24 | M |

Bronx | 2338 Arthur Ave. (bet. 183rd & 187th Sts.) | B/D to Fordham Rd. |
718-367-5145 | www.calabriaporkstore.com

"Pork, pork and more pork" is the deal at this Arthur Avenue Italian
deli, where shoppers find aromatic sausages dangling from the ceiling
and an "old-fashioned" butcher counter boasting a "fair-priced",
porcine-oriented "great selection", manned by a "knowledgeable"
crew – all of which "takes you back 40 years"; among its other
"delicious" products are housemade mozz and lots of imported goods.

Calandra Cheese Co. ▱ *Cheese/Dairy* ▽ 26 | 18 | 22 | M |

Bronx | 2314 Arthur Ave. (bet. Crescent Ave. & 186th St.) | B/D to
Fordham Rd. | 718-365-7572

Since 1952, this "simple" Arthur Avenue shop has been a "find" for
"authentic Italian cheese", notably its homemade specialties: "creamy
mozzarella", "ricotta that melts on your tongue" and the enriched
mozz variants scamorza and caciocavallo; add a hoard of imports,
"old-world hospitality" and "real value", and "it's a must" on the strip.

Callahan Catering ▱ *Caterer/Events* - | - | - | VE |

Garment District | 37 W. 39th St., Suite 406 (bet. 5th & 6th Aves.) |
212-327-1144 | www.callahancatering.com
By appointment only

This "exclusive" off-site caterer based in the Garment District delivers the "best, most creative" party ideas to a well-heeled clientele,
which applauds its "gorgeous" food-and-drink offerings that "never
cease to entertain the eye"; no task seems too big, be it flying

	QUALITY	DISPLAY	SERVICE	COST

European chefs into the Hamptons or organizing acrobats in tents, and admirers insist it's "worth every penny" – "if you can afford it."

Call Cuisine Caterers *Prepared Food*

24	20	20	E

E 50s | 1032 First Ave. (bet. 56th & 57th Sts.) | E/V to Lexington Ave./ 53rd St. | 212-752-7070 | www.callcuisinecaterers.com

"Fabulous takeout" meals from this Sutton Place standby please "older", well-heeled locals "when their chef is off", but regular folk – or "anyone who wants to be praised for cooking they haven't done" – can find a "top-quality" selection of prepared dishes here; though "snooty" counter help can annoy, the business, which specializes in hors d'ouevres, has been catering to clients like the U.N. since 1980.

Caputo Bakery ▣⧷ *Baked Goods*

23	17	18	I

Carroll Gardens | 329 Court St. (bet. Sackett & Union Sts.) | Brooklyn | F/G to Carroll St. | 718-875-6871 | www.caputobakery.com

"Don't miss the lard bread, especially if it's just coming out of the oven" urge regulars who revere this "excellent old-time" Carroll Gardens institution for its "crusty, not mushy" loaves, including "wonderful" semolina, olive, prosciutto, brioche and "seasonal specialties" all at "low prices"; the "teenage counter girls" take their time, so it helps if you "know what you want when you walk in."

Carmine's Takeout ❶ *Prepared Food*

23	16	18	M

W 40s | 200 W. 44th St. (bet. 7th & 8th Aves.) | 1/2/3/7/N/Q/R/ S/W to 42nd St./Times Sq. | 212-221-3800
W 90s | 2450 Broadway (bet. 90th & 91st Sts.) | 1/2/3 to 96th St. | 212-721-5493
www.carminesnyc.com

"A boon for the harried" and those who "need a red-sauce fix" without the "headache" of a noisy dining room, these adjuncts to the famed West Side eateries offer the same "hearty, delicious" Italian fare for takeout or delivery; though service is on the "slow" side, its portions "gigantic" enough to last "for three days" ("don't even try to eat the whole thing") ensure "lots of bang for the buck" and make it an apt choice when feeding "a crowd."

☒ Carnegie Deli ❶▣⧷ *Deli/Sandwich*

23	16	15	E

W 50s | 854 Seventh Ave. (55th St.) | N/Q/R/W to 57th St. | 212-757-2245 | 800-334-5606 | www.carnegiedeli.com

"Blue collars", "blue bloods" and everyone in between come with "mouths open wide" for the "ridiculously" "overstuffed" brisket, corned beef and pastrami sandwiches ("just try to finish one") that are the hallmark of this NYC deli "icon"–cum–"tourist" attraction; no surprise it's perpetually "overrun", while the "delightfully brusque" service seems like it "hasn't changed for generations"; P.S. "you gotta have the cheesecake."

Carol's Cafe ❶ *Caterer*

-	-	-	E

Staten Island | 1571 Richmond Rd. (Four Corners Rd.) | 718-979-5600 | www.carolscafe.com

At her SI cafe and cooking school, Carol Frazzetta is a "perfectionist" and it shows in her "excellent food" and ability to make celebratory affairs "effortless and beautiful"; whether on the premises of her restaurant or off-site, she "always tries to give an above-board event", which explains why she's "been around for years – and we hope years to come."

Carrot Top Pastries *Baked Goods*   23 | 18 | 20 | I

Washington Heights | 3931 Broadway (bet. 164th & 165th Sts.) | 1/A/C to 168th St./B'way | 212-927-4800 ◗
Washington Heights | 5025 Broadway (214th St.) | 1 to 215th St. | 212-569-1532
www.carrottoppastries.com
The "excellent" namesake cake has made this toothsome twosome a "neighborhood favorite" in Washington Heights (and a "must-visit" for "Columbia" types) – but its offerings, all baked at the 165th Street location, now encompass cheesecake, pies, muffins, cookies and even breakfast and lunch entrees; "accommodating service" is the icing on the cake.

Carry On Tea & Sympathy ◗ ▱ *Coffee/Tea*   23 | 20 | 20 | M

W Village | 110 Greenwich Ave. (bet. 12th & 13th Sts.) | A/C/E/L to 14th St./8th Ave. | 212-989-9735 | www.teaandsympathynewyork.com
"Exiles and Anglophiles alike" are keen on "one-stop shopping" for "real British" goods like "you'd get in Sainsbury's" at this "teeny" carry-out store appended to the West Village's Tea & Sympathy; stocked with "loose teas", condiments, sweets, teapots and heaps more, it's a "sure bet" for a "proper English" spread that's "authentic" down to the "expat staff's" "lurvely accents"; P.S. they can also arrange for a "London black cab" to convey catering to your door.

Carve ◗ *Deli/Sandwich*   23 | 16 | 16 | M

W 40s | 760 Eighth Ave. (47th St.) | C/E to 50th St. | 212-730-4949
Choice carved-to-order meats help explain why followers find this shop to be the "best" of its kind in Midtown; yes, seats are sometimes "scarce" and the tabs "expensive", but most maintain it's an obvious pick when you're seeking something other than "the usual tuna on rye."

Casa Cupcake *Baked Goods*   22 | 19 | 19 | M

W 40s | 545 Ninth Ave. (bet. 40th & 41st Sts.) | A/C/E to 42nd St./Port Authority | 212-268-9975

Cupcake Cafe *Baked Goods*

Flatiron | Books of Wonder | 18 W. 18th St. (bet. 5th & 6th Aves.) | 1 to 18th St. | 212-465-1530
www.cupcakecafe.com
"Buttercream babes line up" for this Flatiron–Hell's Kitchen duo's "intensely colored", "piped flower"–adorned cupcakes, "a real wow" at "office parties" and other festive occasions; "eye-popping custom-made cakes", "fresh" muffins, pecan pie and doughnuts also please proponents, even as a "disappointed" minority murmurs the cupcakes' "taste and texture definitely do not live up to" their "decadent" look; N.B. the Flatiron offshoot is located inside Books of Wonder.

	QUALITY	DISPLAY	SERVICE	COST

Casa Della Mozzarella *Cheese/Dairy*   ▽ 29 | 21 | 25 | M

Bronx | 604 E. 187th St. (Arthur Ave.) | B/D to Fordham Rd. | 718-364-3867
"The best fresh mozzarella" "this side of heaven" is plenty of incentive to "schlep" to this Arthur Avenue stalwart, where patrons can "watch it being made" before requesting a standard ball or an order of bocconcini (their "life-altering" mini-mozzes); it's also "a real Bronx deli experience" for "old-time Italian" "staples" including "excellent" "sliced meats" and house-brand olive oil, and everything comes with "the friendliest" "banter" on the side.

Cassinelli Food Products 🏷 *Pasta*   ▽ 25 | 18 | 22 | M

Astoria | 31-12 23rd Ave. (31st St.) | Queens | N/W to Astoria/Ditmars Blvd. | 718-274-4881
For more than 50 years, this Astoria pasta purveyor has been a favorite among carb connoisseurs thanks to its "better-than-homemade" pastas; the offerings include ravioli, a whole line of meat tortellini as well as the usual suspects like fettuccine and linguine, which lauders label "everything you want them to be."

Castle & Pierpont *Flowers*   ▽ 24 | 22 | 21 | VE

Garment District | 353 W. 39th St. (bet. 8th & 9th Aves.) | 212-244-8668 | www.castlepierpont.com
By appointment only
The "easy-to-work-with" proprietors at this Garment District floral studio show "great artistic talent in arranging" "the freshest" "exotic flowers" according to smitten surveyors who say the results are "always lovely"; the "fun" staff can also orchestrate details (tableware, lighting, decor) for high-style events ranging from intimate parties to Broadway openings and corporate extravaganzas, whether beneath chandeliered ceilings or in garlanded gazebos.

Catering by
Restaurant Associates *Caterer*   20 | 19 | 20 | E

Garment District | 330 Fifth Ave. (bet. 32nd & 33rd sts.) | B/D/F/N/Q/R/V/W to 34th St./Herald Sq. | 212-613-5500 | www.restaurantassociates.com
Arguably the "largest player in town", with exclusive rights to parties at local major venues, including the Guggenheim and Met, this mammoth Garment District–based operation "handles large parties with ease", offering "solid food preparation and presentation"; while some feel this "corporate" giant may have "stretched itself too thin", to many others it's an "institution" and "one of the best values around."

Catering Company, The 🏷 *Events*   - | - | - | E

Chelsea | 215 W. 29th St. (bet. 7th & 8th Aves.) | 1 to 28th St. | 212-564-5370 | www.thecateringcompanynyc.com
"Extremely professional" staffers at this hip Chelsea-based caterer are "wonderful to work with" and pull off "perfect events" with "creative" cuisine and "excellent service" for "nonprofits" and "corporate clients" alike, including film and stage premieres, fund-raisers and book launches; it's on the "expensive" side, but "worth the money" for the "fantastic" "personal attention."

	QUALITY	DISPLAY	SERVICE	COST

Cato Corner Farm ▣✍ *Cheese/Dairy*   27 | 19 | 24 | E

See Greenmarket; for more information, call 860-537-3884 | www.catocornerfarm.com

"Very popular" for its raw-milk and hormone-free cheeses created by a "dedicated" Colchester, CT, producer, this Greenmarket vendor's "exceptional" artisanal fromages include "breathtakingly lovely cheddar", "tangy blue", "pungent, flavorful" washed-rind 'hooligan' and "earthy" 'womanchego', all dispensed by a "knowledgeable" crew; though there are a few grumbles about "uneven" selection and "high prices", most don't mind given such "glorious" products from a "real family farm."

Caviar Russe ◑▣ *Caviar*   26 | 22 | 23 | VE

E 50s | 538 Madison Ave., 2nd fl. (bet. 54th & 55th Sts.) | E/V to 5th Ave./53rd St. | 212-980-5908 | 800-692-2842 | www.caviarrusse.com

"Serious caviar lovers" jonesing for a "fix" of "the best Russian product" head for this Midtown restaurant and its "extraordinary selection" of "very fresh" eggs to take out, along with "high-end appetizers" like smoked salmon and foie gras; the "solicitous service", opulent digs and "top-notch" "little touches" like mother-of-pearl spoons and silver tureens on sale will make you "feel like the rich and famous", but "expect to pay the cost."

CBK Cookies ▣ *Baked Goods*   ▽ 23 | 22 | 20 | E

E 80s | 337 E. 81st St. (bet. 1st & 2nd Aves.) | 212-794-3383 | www.cbkcookies.com
By appointment only

Befitting this "cute" "hole-in-the-wall" bake shop's UES milieu, its "pretty" sugar cookies and "top-quality" character birthday cakes are all bespoke; customers who consider Cynthia Bruce Kramer's decorative tins of custom cookies "great for client gifts" or wedding showers willingly place orders and keep the necessary appointments (no walk-ins); N.B. it also offers cookie-decorating classes.

Ceci-Cela *Baked Goods*   24 | 19 | 16 | M

Little Italy | 55 Spring St. (bet. Lafayette & Mulberry Sts.) | 6 to Spring St. | 212-274-9179 | www.ceci-celapatisserie.com

"Ooh-la-la", "you can smell the fabulous pastries from down the block" assert *amis* who love to "grab treats" at this "small" Little Italy patisserie whose wares include "great almond brioche", pain au chocolat and "the best tarts"; a faction frets that its "French style" extends to "uneven service" ("can't beat this place for a croissant and a snub"); N.B. they also do wedding cakes.

Cellar 72 ◑▣ *Wine/Liquor*   ▽ 26 | 26 | 23 | E

E 70s | 1355 Second Ave. (bet. 71st & 72nd Sts.) | 6 to 68th St. | 212-639-9463 | www.cellar72.com

Led by vino expert Guy Goldstein of the Tour de France restaurant group (Nice Matin, Marseille), this "classy" Upper East Side boutique boasts "real sommeliers" who will gladly help a customer choose from the "outstanding" array of 3,000 labels in the "cool wine cellar" that's visible through the glass floor; it's "expensive", but surveyors find the scene a "refreshing change", and a computer to help pair bottles with food is a nice plus.

Ceriello Fine Foods ⌑ *Specialty Shop* — 24 | 22 | 20 | E

E 40s | Grand Central Mkt. | Lexington Ave. (43rd St.) | 4/5/6/7/S to 42nd St./Grand Central | 212-972-4266 ◐
Douglaston | 4435 Douglaston Pkwy. (Northern Blvd.) | Queens | 718-428-2494
877-613-6637 | www.ceriellofinefoods.com

"It's like a sausage museum!" marvel commuters who "love the convenience" of this Grand Central Market stall stocking "quality" links as well as dry-aged porterhouses, stuffed pork roasts and other "fantastic meats"; you "pay a premium for the location", however, so head for the Queens original, which is also "nirvana for Italian foodstuffs."

Certé *Caterer/Events* — ▽ 26 | 21 | 22 | M

W 50s | 20 W. 55th St. (bet. 5th & 6th Aves.) | E/V to 5th Ave./53rd St. | 212-397-2020 | www.certenyc.com

"Specializing in catering and order-at-the-counter lunch", this Midtown eatery provides "gorgeous, delicious" global-inspired cuisine for off-site affairs small and large, all staffed by an "excellent" crew; among the neighborhood office set, it's also a popular choice for "quick", "reasonably priced" "business lunch deliveries."

Chambers Street Wines ◑⌑ *Wine/Liquor* — 26 | 21 | 25 | M

TriBeCa | 160 Chambers St. (bet. Greenwich St. & W. B'way) | 1/2/3/A/C to Chambers St. | 212-227-1434 | www.chambersstwines.com

"Quality" is key at this "terrific" TriBeCa wine shop whose many "treasures" include an "impressive" inventory of small production *vins* (especially from the Loire Valley) offered at modest prices; the "knowledgeable" staffers do their utmost to please, "walking visitors through" the selections and helping them "pick out something great" they might "never have tried otherwise."

Charbonnel et Walker *Candy/Nuts* — 22 | 22 | 19 | E

E 40s | Saks Fifth Ave. | 611 Fifth Ave., 8th fl. (bet. 49th & 50th Sts.) | E/V to 5th Ave./53rd St. | 212-940-4024 | www.charbonnel.co.uk

"You'll never eat another M&M" after a stop at this "premium" English confectioner's Saks Fifth Avenue showcase, where Yanks can now indulge in the "finest-quality Mayfair chocolates", notably "sublime" truffles, in an attractive cafe/espresso bar setting; add a tasting counter with a conveyor belt showcasing brownies, toffee cupcakes and other "decadent" desserts, and it's enough to get the majority "hooked" even if some shrug the "staid offerings" are "not exciting."

Charles, Sally & Charles Catering ⌗ *Caterer/Events* — ▽ 25 | 24 | 25 | E

Park Slope | Brooklyn Botanic Garden | 1000 Washington Ave. (Montgomery St.) | Brooklyn | Q to Prospect Park | 718-398-2400 | www.palmhouse.com

As the exclusive caterer for the Brooklyn Botanic Garden, this "top-notch" Park Slope outfit can set your event in a "beautiful" 52-acre "garden oasis" complete with Victorian greenhouse; still, it's the food "better than most restaurants'" and "friendly" staff striving to ensure "every detail is perfect" that really makes it "something special."

Cheeks Bakery ⊟ *Baked Goods* | - | - | - | M |

Williamsburg | 378 Metropolitan Ave. (bet. Havemeyer & Marcy Sts.) | Brooklyn | L to Bedford Ave. | 718-599-3583 | www.cheeksbakery.com
On a heavily trafficked stretch of Metropolitan Avenue, this small Williamsburg bakery is fast becoming a local standby; owner-baker Melanie Schrimpe takes an artisanal approach, using all-natural and local ingredients to concoct inventively flavored scones and homey "old-fashioned" desserts like red velvet cake with boiled icing, cupcakes, quick breads and cookies.

Cheese of the World *Cheese/Dairy* | 25 | 21 | 23 | M |

Forest Hills | 71-48 Austin St. (Queens Blvd.) | Queens | E/F/G/R/V to Forest Hills/71st Ave. | 718-263-1933
"Try a taste of something new" at this "amazing" "neighborhood cheese joint" in Forest Hills, whose "tiny" space is chock-a-block with 400-odd "value-adjusted" wheels, including "interesting types" you "can't even find in the city"; with an "energetic staff" that "knows its cheese" and a sideline in "cured meats" and "specialty goods", it's the type of local "landmark" that "makes it difficult to move."

Chef & Company *Caterer/Events* | ∇ 25 | 25 | 24 | E |

Flatiron | 8 W. 18th St. (bet. 5th & 6th Aves.) | 646-336-1980 | www.chefandco.com
By appointment only
"Their forte is corporate" say businesslike backers of this Flatiron caterer/cafe, commended for its "professional" style and the "creative and chic" twists on International favorites that result in some "amazing" menus; they're equally "accommodating" for workplace gatherings or full-service events at their various venues, though surveyors part company on the cost ("reasonable" vs. "too expensive").

Chelsea Market Baskets ▣ *Specialty Shop* | 24 | 23 | 21 | E |

Chelsea | Chelsea Mkt. | 75 Ninth Ave. (bet. 15th & 16th Sts.) | A/C/E/L to 14th St./8th Ave. | 212-727-1484 | 888-727-7887 | www.chelseamarketbaskets.com
"It's more than just baskets" at this Chelsea Market "wonderland" where you can "make your own" "customized, specialty gift basket", choosing from an "endless" selection of baby toys, books, "chocolates, cookies, popcorn and all things gourmet" (including "imported goodies" "with a British twist"); in short, this shop has "something for everyone" – and "every budget"; N.B. it does a mostly mail-order business.

Chelsea Wine Vault ▣ *Wine/Liquor* | 23 | 23 | 22 | M |

Chelsea | Chelsea Mkt. | 75 Ninth Ave. (bet. 15th & 16th Sts.) | A/C/E/L to 14th St./8th Ave. | 212-462-4244 | www.chelseawinevault.com
A "willing and able" staff guides vinophiles through this "spacious" cellar-esque wine shop with a "convenient" location inside Chelsea

	QUALITY	DISPLAY	SERVICE	COST

Market and an "eclectic" selection strong on labels from California and France; "fun" tastings four nights a week, classes and an overall "friendly, unpretentious" vibe have most saying "it's a pleasure to shop" here.

Cherry Lane Farms ⊘ Produce | 28 | 24 | 26 | M |

See Greenmarket; for more information, call 856-455-7043

Aficionados "wait all year for the fabulous asparagus" at the Greenmarket stall of this second-generation South Jersey farm, whose 30 types of "high-quality", "wonderfully robust produce" also include tomatoes, okra, zucchini, baby lettuces, eggplant, cauliflower and a growing array of herbs; the colorful, fresh vegetables and "service with a smile" make this "one of the nicest stands in the market, from every point of view"; N.B. though the name would suggest otherwise, the only fruit it offers is strawberries.

Cheryl Kleinman Cakes ⊘ Baked Goods | ▽ 28 | 25 | 25 | E |

Boerum Hill | 448 Atlantic Ave. (bet. Bond & Nevins Sts.) | Brooklyn | 718-237-2271
By appointment only

"Easy to work with" and incorporating designs both traditional and modern, this Boerum Hill baker of special-occasion cakes has patrons pledging undying love for her nuptial creations, which are not only "delicious" ("lemon pound cake every bit as good as they say") but are also "so beautiful" that surveyors "almost want to plan another wedding"; if "expensive for Brooklyn", boosters say it's still "half the price" of its Manhattan "equals"; N.B. there's also a retail shop on the premises, Betty Bakery.

Chestnuts in the Tuileries Flowers | - | - | - | VE |

TriBeCa | 55 Van Dam St., Ste. 801 (bet. Hudson & Varick Sts.) | 212-367-8151 | www.chestnutsnyc.com
By appointment only

Inspired by gardens in Paris, floral and special events designer Emily Weaver (a former City of Lights denizen) brings a dash of Gallic flair to her TriBeCa studio, producing "unique" tailored arrangements known for their monochromatic color schemes, textured foliage and use of rare orchids; though some wilt at the "sky-high prices", the few surveyors who know her work say she's among the "best in the area."

🆕 ChikaLicious Puddin' Baked Goods | 24 | 22 | 23 | E |

E Village | 204 E. 10th St. (bet. 1st & 2nd Aves.) | 6 to Astor Pl. | 212-475-0929 | www.chikalicious.com

When you can't get into the "mother ship", this "fun and funky" "across-the-street" adjunct of the East Village's popular dessert bar ChikaLicious picks up the slack with its puddings, cakes and other "delectable" sweets to go – unless you're lucky enough to score one of the "few seats" in its "precious" little cafe area; it can sometimes get "crowded" and "chaotic", and prices are on the "Chika-spensive" side, but nevertheless devotees declare it "*the* place to go for cupcakes."

	QUALITY	DISPLAY	SERVICE	COST

Chinatown Ice Cream Factory ◑ ▣ ✒ *Ice Cream*

25 | 15 | 19 | I

Chinatown | 65 Bayard St. (bet. Elizabeth & Mott Sts.) | 6/J/M/N/Q/R/W/Z to Canal St. | 212-608-4170 | www.chinatownicecreamfactory.com

A "scrumptious selection of exotic Asian flavors" "call out to your wild side" at this Chinatown ice cream parlor where the "friendly, helpful" staff is generous with samples, which help you choose between such offerings as the "incredible" lychee and "yummy" black sesame; although there's "no seating", most agree it's the perfect spot for a "post-dim sum sweet."

Choc-Oh! Lot Plus *Candy/Nuts*

▽ 25 | 21 | 23 | M

Bay Ridge | 7911 Fifth Ave. (bet. 79th & 80th Sts.) | Brooklyn | R to 77th St. | 718-748-2100

With 1,000-plus chocolate molds for sale, this Bay Ridge "supply store for candy-making" provides "all the fixings for chocoholics" to cast their own stash, along with "lots of" other paraphernalia for creating and decorating cakes and confections – and they also offer cookie and cake decorating classes; for faster gratification, they stock ready-made candies, truffles and holiday cookies too.

Chocolate Bar ▣ *Candy/Nuts*

26 | 25 | 22 | E

W 50s | Henri Bendel | 712 Fifth Ave., 3rd fl. atrium (56th St.) | F to 57th St. | 212-582-8283 | www.chocolatebarnyc.com

Its original location closed recently, but this offshoot inside Midtown's famed Henri Bendel department store still "lives up to its rep" with a "delectable" lineup of chocolates (both bars and bon-bons), and also boasts a full-service eatery; another branch is in the works for the East Village, at 127 East Seventh Street, which is expected to be a coffee nook/gourmet candy store along the lines of its erstwhile West Village progenitor.

Chocolate Girl ▣ *Candy/Nuts*

23 | 19 | 20 | E

Park Slope | 383 Seventh Ave. (bet. 11th & 12th Sts.) | Brooklyn | F to 7th Ave. | 718-788-4475

"Original, cute" and all-kosher, this pink-hued newcomer along Park Slope's Seventh Avenue strip offers "quality" hand-dipped chocolates, non-dairy soft-serve ice cream and some 18 flavors of hot cocoa, with the added bonus of being able to watch the candy being made in a back work area; with its attractive back garden and paint-with-chocolate concept, it could become a favored local birthday party venue; N.B. store hours are in keeping with Shabbat.

Chocolate Room, The ◑ ▣ *Candy/Nuts*

25 | 21 | 21 | M

Park Slope | 86 Fifth Ave. (bet. St. Marks Pl. & Warren St.) | Brooklyn | 2/3 to Bergen St. | 718-783-2900 | www.thechocolateroombrooklyn.com

Now there's room for "indulging" in Park Slope thanks to this "cozy" cafe and sweets boutique, which will "rock your world" with "killer" specialty desserts and a line of "divine" chocolates from renowned confectioner Fritz Knipschildt, not to mention dessert wines and "real-deal" "hot cocoa"; it's a "great" after-dinner drop-by with "a date" ("if you're lucky"), but be forewarned that "the word is out" and the crowds are coming in; N.B. a roomier offshoot at 269 Court Street in Cobble Hill is expected to open in July 2008.

Chocolat Moderne ▣ *Candy/Nuts* ▽ 26 | 25 | 22 | E
Chelsea | 27 W. 20th St., Suite 904 (bet. 5th & 6th Aves.) | 212-229-4797 | www.chocolatmoderne.com
By appointment only

Banker-turned-chocolatier Joan Coukos has gained something of a cult following for her "rich", dark chocolate–covered bonbons with sophisticated flavorings, sold at "high-end" outlets around town like the City Bakery, Murray's Bakery and Russ & Daughters (as well as at her Chelsea factory, if you make an appointment); "heaven for chocoholics", her "beautiful", intensely flavored creations include a line made with traditional Japanese ingredients, as well as filled 'bistro bars' and grapefruit caramels covered in dark chocolate.

Choice Market ●⇟ *Prepared Food* ▽ 23 | 20 | 14 | M
Clinton Hill | 318 Lafayette Ave. (Grand Ave.) | Brooklyn | G to Classon Ave. | 718-230-5234

Locals consider this take-out spot a Clinton Hill "jewel" thanks to its pastries, pies and other "gorgeous sweets", as well as "excellent" prepared foods like mac 'n' cheese, pasta salads and sandwiches, all at "reasonable prices"; service can be "disorganized", but this place is usually "packed" nonetheless.

Choux Factory *Baked Goods* 23 | 17 | 21 | I
E 40s | 865 First Ave. (bet. 48th & 49th Sts.) | 6 to 51st St. | 212-223-0730
E 80s | 1685 First Ave. (bet. 87th & 88th Sts.) | 4/5/6 to 86th St. | 212-289-2023 ●

Ok, they may be "costly" and "cholesterol-boosting", but otherwise "what's not to like?" wonder worshipers of the "scrumptious" cream-filled pastry puffs in "unique flavors" (green tea, strawberry) turned out by this Japan-based chainlet; there's also "rich, tasty Kona coffee" to go with 'em, poured by a staff that remains "gracious" "no matter how busy" things get.

Christie's Jamaican ▽ 21 | 14 | 18 | I
Patties ●⇟ *Prepared Food*
Prospect Heights | 387 Flatbush Ave. (bet. 8th Ave. & Sterling Pl.) | Brooklyn | Q to 7th Ave. | 718-636-9746

"There's nothing else like" the West Indian–style curries, jerk chicken and other island specialties at this Prospect Heights purveyor where the "coco bread is the best on the planet", and the beef and veggie patties are popular too; the bright yellow digs are "not the most appealing" to some, but most agree the fare's "worth closing your eyes for."

Christopher Norman 23 | 23 | 23 | E
Chocolates ▣ *Candy/Nuts*
Financial District | 60 New St. (bet. Beaver St. & Exchange Pl.) | 4/5 to Bowling Green | 212-402-1243 | www.christophernormanchocolates.com
"A little piece of heaven" "tucked away" in the Financial District, this "modest shop" and chocolate factory is the fiefdom of "artistic"

	QUALITY	DISPLAY	SERVICE	COST

confectioner John Down, who "rivals" "top-tier chocolatiers" with his handmade truffles and bars, notably those sculpted into "amazing" designs; the goods are "expensive" but "hard to resist", and though the store is "worth finding" for the freshest possible product, you can also "get it at Whole Foods" and Dean & DeLuca.

Christos Steak House ◑ *Meat/Poultry* 　　23 | 21 | 21 | E

Astoria | 41-08 23rd Ave. (bet. 41st & 42nd Sts.) | Queens | N/W to Astoria/Ditmars Blvd. | 718-726-5195 | www.christossteakhouse.com
This two-for-one spot in Astoria – it's both a Greek restaurant and a butcher shop – has been under new ownership since 2006, but continues to gratify carnivores with its "nicely displayed", expensive selection of "quality" prime aged meats, sausages, poultry and game; don't forget to "order early" for that "Easter baby lamb!"

Ciao Bella Gelato ▣ *Ice Cream* 　　25 | 20 | 18 | M

E 40s | Grand Central Terminal | lower level (42nd St. & Vanderbilt Ave.) | 4/5/6/7/S to 42nd St./Grand Central | 212-867-5311 ◑
E 90s | 27 E. 92nd St. (bet. 5th & Madison Aves.) | 4/5/6 to 86th St. | 212-831-5555
Financial District | World Financial Ctr. | 225 Liberty St. (bet. S. End Ave. & West St.) | 1/2/3/A/C to Chambers St. | 212-786-4707
NoLita | 285 Mott St. (bet. Houston & Prince Sts.) | B/D/F/V to B'way/Lafayette St. | 212-431-3591 ◑⇚
800-435-2863 | www.ciaobellagelato.com
"Italy must be jealous" of this mini-chain of "sublime", high-end gelaterias given its "rich palette" of "luscious", "incredibly creamy" flavors, including "creative" seasonal specialties and sorbets "saturated with fruit"; while a few sniff that it's "not quite as special as it used to be" (save for the "extraordinary prices"), they're outvoted by those who consider it the "crème de la crème of ice cream."

Cipriani Le Specialità ▣ *Baked Goods* 　　26 | 24 | 20 | E

E 40s | 110 E. 42nd St. (bet. Lexington & Park Aves.) | 4/5/6/7/S to 42nd St./Grand Central | 212-557-5088 | www.cipriani.com
Gourmets are gleeful about this Grand Central–area bakery/take-out chip off the Cipriani block proffering high-end Italian baked goods and prepared foods including fresh-made breadsticks, pastries and sandwiches; there are also house-label imported comestibles such as olive oils, pastas, sauces and vinegars; P.S. those who feel it's a tad "overpriced" just "wait for the rush hour specials."

☑ Citarella ▣ *Major Gourmet Mkt.* 　　26 | 23 | 22 | E

E 70s | 1313 Third Ave. (75th St.) | 6 to 77th St. | 212-874-0383 ◑
G Village | 424 Sixth Ave. (9th St.) | A/B/C/D/E/F/V to W. 4th St. | 212-874-0383 ◑
Harlem | 461 W. 125th St. (bet. Amsterdam & Morningside Aves.) | 1 to 125th St. | 212-874-0383
W 70s | 2135 Broadway (75th St.) | 1/2/3 to 72nd St. | 212-874-0383 ◑
866-248-2735 | www.citarella.com
Go "upscale without the attitude" at this famed mini-chain of "one-stop" shops for "the refined gourmet", which "built its reputation" by supplying an "abundant variety" of "impeccable" seafood so "ex-

QUALITY DISPLAY SERVICE COST

ceptionally fresh" it's practically "still quivering", along with "top-of-the-line meats" from "cheerful" "old-fashioned butchers"; they're also "incredibly helpful" sources of "hearty" prepared foods likened to "edible art", "high-end" deli items, a "super" "array of cheeses", "gorgeous" produce "staples" and "top-drawer" smoked fish and caviar, and though "prices are pretty steep", legions of "happy shoppers" confirm quality is "never an issue."

☑ City Bakery *Baked Goods* | 25 | 22 | 18 | E |

Flatiron | 3 W. 18th St. (bet. 5th & 6th Aves.) | 4/5/6/L/N/Q/R/W to 14th St./Union Sq. | 212-366-1414 | www.thecitybakery.com
Maury Rubin's legendary Flatiron bakery/cafeteria specializes in "decadent" sweets "to diet for": "perfect pretzel croissants", "outstanding tarts", "platonic-ideal" cookies, "famously" "unbeatable hot chocolate" and now even a "selection of vegan baked goods"; the "heavenly" prepared foods (including some of the "best mac 'n' cheese in the city") made with "top-notch ingredients" add up to "magic in your mouth" as well, so despite "ditzy help" and "stratospheric prices", it's no surprise this NYC "classic" is "always crowded."

☑ Cleaver Company ❂ *Caterer/Events* | 25 | 20 | 26 | E |

Chelsea | Chelsea Mkt. | 75 Ninth Ave. (bet. 15th & 16th Sts.) | A/C/E/L to 14th St./8th Ave. | 212-741-9174 | www.cleaverco.com
"You had me at first bite" enthuse fans of Mary Cleaver's "high-quality" Chelsea Market caterer, which shows off "brilliant" chops in concocting the "freshest", most "innovative" dishes with a "commitment" to local, "organic, sustainable suppliers" (including many Greenmarket regulars); covering details from venue to menu, the "imaginative" event planning service features "excellent" "responsive" staffers who "definitely set them apart"; P.S. its seasonal "munchies" are also served at the neighboring eatery The Green Table.

Clinton St. Baking
Company ❂⊘⇲ *Baked Goods* | 26 | 20 | 20 | M |

LES | 4 Clinton St. (bet. Houston & Stanton Sts.) | F/J/M/Z to Delancey/Essex Sts. | 646-602-6263 | www.clintonstreetbaking.com
"Moist and tender" muffins "as big as a city pothole", "fabulous" scones and "fluffy" biscuits that may be "the best" in town are among the unimpeachable wares of this tiny Lower East Side bakery/cafe; meanwhile, "dinner plate-size" blueberry pancakes and the like draw "multitudes" of "students, hipsters and other Downtown characters" for weekend brunches that "feel so NYC"; P.S. it also offers "wonderful special-order birthday cakes."

Cobblestone Foods *Specialty Shop* | 21 | 20 | 19 | E |

Carroll Gardens | 199 Court St. (bet. Bergen & Wyckoff Sts.) | Brooklyn | F/G to Bergen St. | 718-222-1661 | www.cobblestonefoods.com
"Just what the neighborhood needed", this "warm, inviting" Carroll Gardens specialty shop is "tiny" but well-stocked with "quality" products, including "delicious" prepared foods, baked goods and a "carefully" chosen selection of artisanal cheeses; service is "friendly and helpful", and best of all "samples are given"; N.B. it also caters.

	QUALITY	DISPLAY	SERVICE	COST

Cocoa Bar ◑ *Candy/Nuts* — 26 | 22 | 19 | M

LES | 21 Clinton St. (bet. Houston & Stanton Sts.) | F/J/M/Z to Delancey/Essex Sts. | 212-677-7417
Park Slope | 228 Seventh Ave. (bet. 3rd & 4th Sts.) | Brooklyn | F to 7th Ave. | 718-499-4080
www.cocoabarnyc.com

A "comfortable" "place to meet" and "while away" some time, this Park Slope coffee/wine bar's "carefully curated variety" of goodies includes "first-class chocolates" that inspire "delicious" pairings with vino, plus "excellent" desserts, java and hot cocoa; with its "hipster staff", "free Internet access" and "gorgeous" "outdoor seating", it earns its standing as a "neighborhood staple"; N.B. the more expansive LES location opened post-Survey.

Cold Stone Creamery ◑ *Ice Cream* — 20 | 20 | 19 | M

E 80s | 1651 Second Ave. (bet. 85th & 86th Sts.) | 4/5/6 to 86th St. | 212-249-7085
G Village | 2 Astor Pl. (bet. B'way & Lafayette St.) | 6 to Astor Pl. | 212-228-4600
G Village | 349 Sixth Ave. (bet. Washington Pl. & W. 4th St.) | A/B/C/D/E/F/V to W. 4th St. | 212-741-0077
W 40s | 253 W. 42nd St. (bet. 7th & 8th Aves.) | 1/2/3/7/N/Q/R/S/W to 42nd St./Times Sq. | 212-398-1882
NEW W 50s | 750 Ninth Ave. (bet. 50th & 51st Sts.) | C/E to 50th St. | 212-757-7570
W 70s | 162 W. 72nd St. (bet. Amsterdam & Columbus Aves.) | 212-877-7800
Downtown | Atlantic Terminal Mall | 139 Flatbush Ave. (Atlantic Ave.) | Brooklyn | D/M/N/R to Pacific St. | 718-230-1562
Astoria | 34-20 Broadway (bet. 34th & 35th Sts.) | Queens | G/R/V to Steinway St. | 718-204-7298
Elmhurst | 88-01 Queens Blvd. (B'way) | Queens | G/R/V to Grand Ave. | 718-760-0800
Fresh Meadows | 176-60 Union Tpke. (Utopia Tpke.) | Queens | E/F to Kew Gardens/Union Tpke. | 718-591-5800
www.coldstonecreamery.com
Additional locations throughout the NY area

"Be prepared for sugar coma" at this "kitschy" ice cream chain, where the concept is pick-your-own "decadent" add-ins to be "smashed" into "super-creamy" concoctions; while the jaded grumble about paying "a lot of money for some frozen milk" and "annoying" singing servers pandering to "children and tourists", for many the "massive servings" of "sinful" treats are "worth every extra lap to burn off the calories."

☑ Colette's Cakes ✄ *Baked Goods* — 29 | 28 | 27 | VE

W Village | 681 Washington St. (bet. Charles & W. 10th Sts.) | 212-366-6530 | www.colettescakes.com
By appointment only

West Village wedding and special-occasion cake baker Colette Peters excels at sculptured, "inventive" and "simply exquisite" multilayer creations that are "almost too pretty to eat" – but happily taste "marvelous"; Peters is sweet with the customers as well ("she sat with us for over an hour"), and while naturally "you pay for" such "unbeatable" quality – voted Tops in this Survey – and service, acolytes attest it's "worth every penny."

Colin Cowie Lifestyle ⊄ *Events*   ▽ 28 | 29 | 25 | VE

SoHo | 568 Broadway, Ste. 705 (bet. Houston & Prince Sts.) | 212-396-9007 | www.colincowie.com
By appointment only

With its "over-the-top" orchestration, this ultra-exclusive SoHo-based event planner "puts the wow factor" into "fabulous" fetes produced on the chicest sites (eateries, museums, homes of the rich and famous) for a boldface-name clientele that includes Jerry Seinfeld, John Travolta and Oprah; niceties like theme coordination and fashion design ensure "guests feel like Hollywood royalty", and though impresario Cowie is notoriously "full of himself", "anything you wish for, you will get."

Colson Patisserie *Baked Goods*   ▽ 25 | 21 | 22 | M

Park Slope | 374 Ninth St. (6th Ave.) | Brooklyn | F to 7th Ave. | 718-965-6400 | www.colsonpastries.com

Park Slope "needed this place" sigh surveyors smitten with this "small" "standout", a French-Belgian "patisserie that really deserves its European" descriptor given its expertly rendered, "*delicieux*" output including "lovely small pastries" ("excellent" financiers, brioche, croissants, etc.), cakes, tarts, housemade gelato and sandwiches; despite its ambitious output, however, the vibe is strictly laid-back "neighborhood place", another reason locals only wish it had "more tables."

⚡ Coluccio & Sons *Specialty Shop*   28 | 21 | 22 | M

Borough Park | 1214 60th St. (bet. 12th & 13th Aves.) | Brooklyn | N/B to New Utrecht Ave. | 718-436-6700

"You'll feel like you're in Italy" "the second you walk in" to this "old-school", family-owned "king of Italian specialty products" in Borough Park that "has anything you can imagine" when it comes to "high-quality" imported and local products – cheeses, meat, olives, oils, vinegars and some 80 different kinds of pasta – all at "hard-to-beat prices"; "it's loyal to its customers and its customers are loyal in return."

Columbus Circle Wine & Liquor ◐ ▣ *Wine/Liquor*   22 | 17 | 20 | M

W 50s | 1802 Broadway (bet. CPS & 58th St.) | 1/A/B/C/D to 59th St./Columbus Circle | 212-247-0764 | www.columbuscirclewine.com

Everyone down to the "cash-register guy knows his wine" at this "welcoming" Columbus Circle wine shop that offers "surprisingly good" selections that are "priced competitively"; it moved a block up Broadway post-Survey to a smart, wood cabinet–lined space that's equipped with an enomatic tasting system that allows customers to sample several different labels at any given time; N.B. a back room for finer vintages is in the works.

	QUALITY	DISPLAY	SERVICE	COST

Commodities Natural
Market ● *Health Food*

25	20	19	M

E Village | 165 First Ave. (bet. 10th & 11th Sts.) | 6 to Astor Pl. | 212-260-2600 | www.commoditiesnaturalmarket.com

"If you know what you want", this "neighborhood health food store" in the East Village is a solid "standby", offering a "very good selection" and a juice bar that's the "perfect place for a healthful snack", all presided over by a "helpful" staff; the "small space" can often get "too crowded", however, and persnickety shoppers complain about its sometimes "unkempt" appearance.

Cones, Ice Cream Artisans ●⊄ *Ice Cream*

26	21	21	M

G Village | 272 Bleecker St. (bet. Morton St. & 7th Ave. S.) | 1 to Christopher St. | 212-414-1795

"Even in the dead of winter, there's always a crowd" at this Greenwich Village ice cream shop owned by a pair of Argentinean brothers, where the "creative" flavors are handmade employing the "freshest real ingredients"; the cones can be "pricey", but groupies say it's "worth it" for "pure, rich" ice cream that's "truly a step above", if not "bordering on the sublime."

Confetti Cakes ⊄ *Baked Goods*

24	25	25	E

W 80s | 102 W. 87th St. (bet. Amsterdam & Columbus Aves.) | 212-877-9580 | www.confetticakes.com
By appointment only

Former fashionista Elisa Strauss produces "painstakingly beautiful" wedding and special-event cakes at her Upper West Side bespoke bakery, creating hand-sculpted shapes and designs that range from cartoon characters and handbags to yachts and cases of wine, offering a wide variety of flavors and fillings; just remember that while here you can "have your icing and eat it too", you may have to "pay an arm and a leg"; N.B. she also teaches classes.

Connecticut Muffin ⊄ *Baked Goods*

17	16	17	M

Brooklyn Heights | 115 Montague St. (bet. Henry & Hicks Sts.) | Brooklyn | 2/3/4/5/M/N/R/W to Borough Hall/Court St. | 718-875-3912 ●
NEW **Ditmas Park** | 1106 Cortelyou Rd. (Stratford Rd.) | Brooklyn | Q to Cortelyou Rd. | 718-287-7900 ●
Fort Greene | 423 Myrtle Ave. (Clinton St.) | Brooklyn | G to Clinton/Washington Aves. | 718-935-0087
Fort Greene | 59 Lafayette St. (bet. Lafayette & Fulton) | Brooklyn | 718-254-9350
Park Slope | 171 Seventh Ave. (1st St.) | Brooklyn | F to 7th Ave. | 718-768-2022 ●
Park Slope | 206 Prospect Park W. (bet. 15th & 16th Sts.) | Brooklyn | F to 15th St. | 718-965-2067 ●

This "cute" Brooklyn chain remains a "reliable" "standby" for "neighborhood" types to "chat" over "good-tasting muffins", scones and the like along with cups of "great coffee", all for "very little dough"; still, foes fed up with its "mediocre" output grumble "I wish they'd go back to Connecticut."

	QUALITY	DISPLAY	SERVICE	COST

Cook's Companion, A *Cookware*　　26 | 21 | 23 | M

Brooklyn Heights | 197 Atlantic Ave. (bet. Clinton & Court Sts.) | Brooklyn | 2/3/4/5/M/N/R/W to Borough Hall/Court St. | 718-852-6901

A "well-chosen selection" of pots and pans, "quality knives", cookbooks and other kitchen accessories "from A (All-Clad) to Z (Zyliss)" "pack" this "charming little" Brooklyn Heights shop where "reasonable prices", "helpful salespeople" and "two congenial cats" boost the "charm" factor; it's a "neighborhood asset" according to locals who say it's a "wonderful place to just browse" but essential when those "last-minute entertaining binds" arise.

Corner Bagel Market, The *Bagels*　　22 | 16 | 20 | I

E 80s | 1324 Lexington Ave. (88th St.) | 4/5/6 to 86th St. | 212-996-0567
"Consistent" quality proves they don't cut corners at this Upper Eastsider, a "favorite local" source for "darned good" housemade bagels that have a "delicious" thin crust but are "not huge and pillowy"; nostalgists claim the results are "almost as good as" the classic rounds of "memory."

Corner Café & Bakery *Deli/Sandwich*　　- | - | - | E

E 90s | 1645 Third Ave. (92nd St.) | 6 to 96th St. | 212-860-8060
E 90s | 1659 Third Ave. (92nd St) | 6 to 96th St. | 212-860-8060
www.cornercafe-bakery.com

Following an ownership split, these two branches of the former Yura triumvirate have a new name but otherwise produce the same baked goods and prepared foods that have gained it such a passionate following in its Upper East Side neighborhood and beyond; the 1645 Third Avenue location has an attached full-service cafe where the goods can be sampled on-site.

Corrado Bread & Pastry *Baked Goods*　　21 | 18 | 18 | M

E 40s | Grand Central Mkt. | Lexington Ave. (43rd St.) | 4/5/6/7/S to 42nd St./Grand Central | 212-599-4321 ◐
E 70s | 960 Lexington Ave. (70th St.) | 6 to 68th St. | 212-774-1904
E 90s | 1361 Lexington Ave. (bet. 90th & 91st Sts.) | 4/5/6 to 86th St. | 212-348-8943
www.corradobread.com

These flour-power brokers gather breads and pastries from the area's finest bakeries "all under one roof" to sell from their UES storefronts (plus a "convenient" stall at Grand Central), saving carb-lovers some steps; the "kudos" that go to their "excellent baguettes", brioches, cakes, muffins, scones and sandwiches are slightly offset by gripes about variable service and a feeling among some that prices are a "little high."

Cosenza's Fish Market *Seafood*　　27 | 21 | 23 | M

Bronx | 2354 Arthur Ave. (186th St.) | B/D to Fordham Rd. | 718-364-8510
"The clams and oysters are begging to be gobbled right up" at this Bronx seafood "favorite" where the *vongole, scungilli* and other "amazing" delights are always gloriously "fresh"; run by a third-generation fishmonger and his "helpful" staff, this "old-Italy" vet-

eran is "well worth the trip" to Arthur Avenue; N.B. the oyster bar is located in front of the main market.

Così *Deli/Sandwich* | 18 | 17 | 15 | M |

E 50s | 60 E. 56th St. (bet. Madison & Park Aves.) | 4/5/6/N/R/W to 59th St./Lexington Ave. | 212-588-1225

Financial District | 3 World Financial Ctr. | 200 Vesey St. (Church St.) | R/W to Cortlandt St. | 212-571-2001

Financial District | 55 Broad St. (bet. Beaver & Exchange Sts.) | J/M/Z to Broad St. | 212-344-5000

Gramercy | 257 Park Ave. S. (21st St.) | 6 to 23rd St. | 212-598-4070 ◐

G Village | 504 Sixth Ave. (13th St.) | F/L/V to 14th Ave./6th Ave. | 212-462-4188 ◐

G Village | 841 Broadway (13th St.) | 4/5/6/L/N/Q/R/W to 14th St./Union Sq. | 212-614-8544 ◐

Murray Hill | 461 Park Ave. S. (31st St.) | 6 to 33rd St. | 212-634-3467

W 40s | 11 W. 42nd St. (bet. 5th & 6th Aves.) | 1/2/3/7/N/Q/R/S/W to 42nd St./Times Sq. | 212-398-6662 ◐

W 50s | Paramount Plaza | 1633 Broadway (51st St.) | 1 to 50th St. | 212-397-9838 ◐

W 70s | 2186 Broadway (bet. 77th & 78th Sts.) | 1 to 79th St. | 212-595-5616 ◐

www.getcosi.com

Additional locations throughout the NY area

"You can't beat" the "delicious", "fresh"-baked flatbread that's "the main event" at this "solid" all-over-town sandwich chain, which many deem all the more "deelish" given its "myriad" healthy options and "reasonable prices"; however, the less-content cite "just-ok" offerings, "spotty" service and not-so-cosi interiors.

Costco Wholesale ◐ ▣ *Major Gourmet Mkt.* | 21 | 13 | 10 | I |

Sunset Park | 976 Third Ave. (bet. 37th & 39th Sts.) | Brooklyn | D/M/N/R to 36th St. | 718-965-7603

Astoria | 32-50 Vernon Blvd. (bet. B'way & 33rd Rd.) | Queens | N/W to B'way | 718-267-3680

Staten Island | 2975 Richmond Ave. (Independence Ave.) | 718-982-9000 800-774-2678 | www.costco.com

"If bigger is better", this warehouse-chain "juggernaut" is "the greatest" at furnishing the "suburban hordes" with "in-bulk" quantities of "well-known brands" at "deep discounts", making it an apt choice for a "lifetime supply" of "surprisingly" "edible" fare like "prepacked" seafood, "nice fruits and veggies", "cheap meats" ("one package lasts a year") and "everyday baked goods", along with "whole sets" of cookware; "don't expect service", but if you're "feeding a crowd" and "have the space" for storage, "the price is very right."

County Chair Party Rentals *Party Rentals* | - | - | - | M |

Mt. Vernon | 25 Oak St. (West Lincoln Ave.), NY | 914-664-5700 | www.countychair.com

In business since 1934, this Mt. Vernon–based party rentals enterprise makes its "nice assortment" of tents, tables, chairs, grills and countless other wares and furnishings available to the five boroughs and satisfies hosts and hostesses with "usually reliable" "easy-to-deal with" service; in sum, "no complaints here."

Court Pastry Shop ⇪ *Baked Goods*

25 | 19 | 21 | I

Cobble Hill | 298 Court St. (bet. Degraw & Douglass Sts.) | Brooklyn | F/G to Carroll St. | 718-875-4820

Once you "inhale the wonderful aroma" it's hard to "resist buying one of everything" report regulars at this Cobble Hill Sicilian institution (since 1948) where the "top-notch" treats include "addictive" cannoli, "delightful" traditional cookies, "excellent ices in the summer" and perhaps the "best biscotti west of Genoa"; its "old-neighborhood feel" and staffers straight "out of *Moonstruck*" give fans even more reason to "love this place."

Cousin John's Bakery ● *Baked Goods*

21 | 19 | 20 | M

Park Slope | 70 Seventh Ave. (bet. Berkeley & Lincoln Pls.) | Brooklyn | B/Q to 7th Ave. | 718-622-7333

"Still a neighborhood favorite" after nearly 20 years in business, this "funky little" Park Slope bakery turns out "delicious" treats – strawberry shortcake, tarts, croissants, muffins, cookies and the like – as well as "great coffee" to wash it all down; N.B. eat in the open kitchen upstairs and you can watch the bakers at work.

Cozy Soup & Burger ● *Prepared Food*

17 | 10 | 14 | I

G Village | 739 Broadway (Astor Pl.) | R/W to 8th St. | 212-477-5566 | www.cozysoupnburger.com

Some of the "biggest", "juiciest" burgers around and a "surprising variety of comfort foods" draw "NYU students" and others to this veteran Village "retreat" that's open 'round the clock; fashionistas fuss that it's "not much to look at", but fans hardly care as long as their "appetite's sated" and the grub's this "cheap."

Crate & Barrel ▱ *Cookware*

22 | 25 | 20 | M

E 50s | 650 Madison Ave. (59th St.) | N/R/W to 5th Ave./59th St. | 212-308-0011

NoHo | Cable Bldg. | 611 Broadway (Houston St.) | N/R to Prince St. | 212-780-0004 ●

800-967-6696 | www.crateandbarrel.com

"From soup bowls to nut jars", these "clean-lined" East Side and NoHo chain outposts stock a "vast" selection of "young and zippy" cookware, cutlery, gadgets and accessories, as well as tableware and barware, at "reasonable prices"; while the "enticing" displays are "fun to browse", surveyors split on quality ("excellent" vs. "will only last one season") and the service that some find "knowledge-able" and others wish were "better."

Creative Cakes ⇪ *Baked Goods*

25 | 23 | 23 | E

E 70s | 400 E. 74th St. (bet. 1st & York Aves.) | 6 to 77th St. | 212-794-9811 | www.creativecakesny.com

Since 1979 UES sugarmeister Bill Schutz has been concocting "gorgeous", "wonderfully imaginative" custom cakes "for every occasion", available in two dimensions (personalized magazine covers, Monopoly boards) as well as sculpted 3-D shapes ("want a Rubik's Cube cake, a piano, a train?"); only one element never changes: all cakes are chocolate fudge with buttercream icing.

	QUALITY	DISPLAY	SERVICE	COST

Creative Edge Parties *Caterer* ▽ 25 | 28 | 27 | E

W Village | 110 Barrow St. (bet. Greenwich & Washington Sts.) |
212-741-3000 | www.creativeedgeparties.com
By appointment only

Those keen on this West Village caterer/event planner cite its
"amazing" gourmet New American eats, custom-crafted with skill
worthy of a fine restaurant to give it the edge in "quality"; it lives up
to its name with "truly creative presentations", and though the cost
is steep, many consider it "reasonable" given the expertise – and
"great service" from "the nicest" folks.

Crossroads ◐ ▤ *Wine/Liquor* 25 | 10 | 22 | M

Union Sq | 55 W. 14th St. (bet. 5th & 6th Aves.) | 4/5/6/L/N/Q/R/
W to 14th St./Union Sq. | 212-924-3060 |
www.crossroadswines.com

Some call this "unpretentious" Union Square store a "lovably cluttered" "treasure trove" of wines, while others disparage the "poor"
layout that has "bottles crammed into every nook", creating a
"claustrophobic" impasse; either way, "there's quality behind the
stacked boxes", and if you can navigate the aisles, you'll find some
"incredible buys" – and if you can't, "just ask" the "patient" staff.

Crumbs Bake Shop *Baked Goods* 22 | 21 | 21 | M

E 70s | 1371 Third Ave. (bet. 78th & 79th Sts.) | 6 to 77th St. |
212-794-9800 ◐
NEW **Financial District** | 87 Beaver St. (bet. Hanover & Pearl Sts.) |
2/3 to Wall St. | 212-480-7500
G Village | 37 E. Eighth St. (University Pl.) | R/W to 8th St. |
212-673-1500 ◐
W 40s | 43 W. 42nd St. (bet. 5th & 6th Aves.) | 7/B/D/F/V to 42nd St./
Bryant Park. | 212-221-1500 ◐
W 70s | 321½ Amsterdam Ave. (bet. 75th & 76th Sts.) | 1 to 79th St. |
212-712-9800 ◐
www.crumbsbakeshop.com

Best known for its "huge, decadent" specialty cupcakes in "scrumptious" flavors like Oreo, Reese's, red velvet and tiramisu, this rapidly
expanding chainlet should "please the sweet tooth in anyone" –
small wonder you'll often "spot celebrities cheating on their
Hollywood diets" here; all of its products, from cookies, muffins and
brownies to even wedding cakes, are kosher.

Ⓩ Crush Wine & Spirits ◐ ▤ *Wine/Liquor* 26 | 25 | 24 | E

E 50s | 153 E. 57th St. (bet. Lexington & 3rd Aves.) | 4/5/6/N/R/W to
59th St./Lexington Ave. | 212-980-9463 | 877-980-9463 |
www.crushwineco.com

It's no mere crush – more like "love at first sight" for novices and "serious" oenophiles who visit this chic Midtown boutique stocking a
"fabulous", "diverse" selection of wines mainly from small growers; of
course, with 3,000 labels comprised of "everyday drinking" vintages,
collectible "rarities" (the latter stored in 'The Cube', the temperature-
controlled room at the back of the store) and an "expert" staff, this
"one-stop shop" is "easy to get passionate" about.

	QUALITY	DISPLAY	SERVICE	COST

Cucina & Co. *Prepared Food* | 21 | 20 | 16 | M |

E 40s | MetLife Bldg. | 200 Park Ave. (45th St.) | 4/5/6/7/S to 42nd St./
Grand Central | 212-682-2700 ◑
Garment District | Macy's Cellar | 151 W. 34th St. (bet. 6th & 7th Aves.) |
B/D/F/N/Q/R/V/W to 34th St./Herald Sq. | 212-868-2388 ◑
W 40s | 30 Rockefeller Plaza, north concourse level (bet. 49th & 50th Sts.) |
B/D/F/V to 47-50th Sts./Rockefeller Ctr. | 212-332-7630
www.patinagroup.com

A "solid bet" for an "above-average lunch" or a bite "before getting
on the train home", this trio housed in Macy's, Rockefeller Center
and the MetLife Building offers a "variety" of "well-prepared"
dishes, including the "best rotisserie chicken", "imaginative salads"
and "outstanding cookies"; there's "something for every taste" –
and it's "not expensive", either.

Cucina Vivolo *Prepared Food* | ▽ 23 | 17 | 21 | M |

E 50s | 222 E. 58th St. (bet. 2nd & 3rd Aves.) | 4/5/6/N/R/W to
59th St./Lexington Ave. | 212-308-0222
E 70s | 138 E. 74th St. (bet. Lexington & Park Aves.) | 6 to 77th St. |
212-717-4700 ◑
www.vivolonyc.com

Either for "good" Italian takeout or "a light meal", Upper Eastsiders
turn to this "nice" cafe duo (spin-offs of the restaurant Vivolo) for
"good-size servings" of "dependable" panini at lunch, pastas at dinner and homemade desserts anytime of day; delivery is "prompt",
while the "homey ambiance" and "great-deal" prix fixe offerings
make it a "favorite hangout" of many.

Dahlia *Flowers* | 26 | 22 | 23 | M |

E 40s | Grand Central Terminal | dining concourse (42nd St. &
Vanderbilt Ave.) | 4/5/6/7/S to 42nd St./Grand Central | 212-697-5090
E 40s | Grand Central Terminal | main concourse (42nd St. &
Vanderbilt Ave.) | 4/5/6/7/S to 42nd St./Grand Central | 212-697-5090
W 40s | 30 Rockefeller Ctr., concourse level (bet. 49th & 50th Sts.) |
B/D/F/V to 47-50th Sts./Rockefeller Ctr. | 212-247-2288
Glendale | Atlas Pk., Building H-101 | 7119 80th St. (71st Ave.) |
Queens | 718-417-4700 ◑

For flowers that last "so long you start to question if they're real",
folks "hurrying" through Grand Central or Rockefeller Center hit
these "convenient" petal purveyors whose "robust bunches" and
"cute vases" are perfect for "that quick bouquet"; gilding the lily are
the "corner-deli prices" – no wonder it's a "madhouse during the
holidays"; N.B. the Glenadale branch opened post-Survey.

Daisy May's BBQ USA ◑ *Prepared Food* | 24 | 12 | 18 | M |

W 40s | 623 11th Ave. (46th St.) | A/C/E to 42nd St./Port Authority |
212-977-1500 | www.daisymaysbbq.com

There's "no better cure for the 'cue craving" than this Hell's Kitchen
storefront's BBQ rated "worth the trek" to "outer Mongolia" (aka 11th
Avenue) – though its "convenient street carts" save Midtown and
Wall Street office workers the trip; "portions are generous" and
"cheap" and it delivers anywhere below 110th Street, so you can "invite the neighbors for a party."

Dale & Thomas Popcorn ◗ ▣ *Specialty Shop* | 23 | 20 | 20 | M |
W 40s | 1592 Broadway (48th St.) | N/R/W to 49th St. | 212-581-1872 |
800-679-6677 | www.daleandthomaspopcorn.com
Definitely "not your mother's popcorn", the many "amazing, inventive flavors" featured at this "cute" if "touristy" Times Square chain outpost are both "exotic" and "delicious", even if regulars recommend "sticking to the basics" (i.e. the "to-die-for kettle corn"); given its "friendly staff" and "generous portions", "the only problem is if you check the calorie count" before diving into the "chocolate-covered popcorn."

Damascus Bakery ▣ *Baked Goods* | 25 | 16 | 22 | I |
Brooklyn Heights | 195 Atlantic Ave. (bet. Clinton & Court Sts.) |
Brooklyn | 2/3/4/5/M/N/R/W to Borough Hall/Court St. |
718-625-7070 | www.damascusbakery.com
A "jewel in the crown of Mideastern Atlantic Avenue", this Brooklyn Heights Syrian bakery turns out "divine" baked "delicacies" from "fresh" flatbreads "in every possible iteration" to "high-quality" pastries ("excellent spinach pies" and some of the "best baklava" going) to dips and spreads; "friendly owners" and evocative "old-school" surroundings make patrons' hearts go pita-pat.

Z D'Amico Foods ▣ *Coffee/Tea* | 27 | 19 | 23 | I |
Carroll Gardens | 309 Court St. (bet. Degraw & Sackett Sts.) |
Brooklyn | F/G to Carroll St. | 718-875-5403 | 888-814-7979 |
www.damicofoods.com
Wake up and "smell the coffee roasting" at this "old-school" Carroll Gardens java merchant, a "real neighborhood" stalwart (since 1948) where an "incredible" selection of beans are roasted daily and scooped straight from the sack to guarantee "the freshest" brews around; it's also an affordable "Italian specialties" grocer and sandwich maker, and locals "love" that "nothing changes" here since it's already "as good as it gets."

Daniel's Bagels ◗ *Bagels* | 24 | 18 | 18 | I |
Murray Hill | 569 Third Ave. (bet. 37th & 38th Sts.) | 4/5/6/7/S to 42nd St./Grand Central | 212-972-9733
For "Murray Hillers" and those "on the way to Grand Central", this "busy" "neighborhood fave" is among the few options for "mouth-watering" "homemade" bagels "that still have holes" topped with "yum-o" spreads; the "pallid" surroundings are easily forgiven, but "be prepared" for "long lines" and "lacking" service that make it "unwieldy on weekends."

David Beahm Designs *Flowers* | - | - | - | VE |
Chelsea | 631 W. 27th St. (bet. 11th & 12th Aves.) | 212-279-1344 |
www.davidbeahm.com
By appointment only
"Jaws drop" at the "absolute beauty" of the "artful" bouquets that come out of David Beahm's Chelsea floral studio, where he also designs events and custom celebrations such as Catherine Zeta-Jones' opulent wedding to Michael Douglas; those lacking a superstar's

budget can choose à la carte arrangements and still get the "amazing service and attention to detail" that make him "a joy to work with."

David Burke at Bloomingdale's *Caterer/Events*

| 23 | 21 | 20 | E |

E 50s | Bloomingdale's | 150 E. 59th St. (bet. Lexington & 3rd Aves.) | 4/5/6/N/R/W to 59th St./Lexington Ave. | 212-705-3800 | www.burkeinthebox.com

The "funky" style of celeb chef David Burke's "busy" New American cafe (located right "inside Bloomie's") extends to its catering arm, which brings his "signature elegance" to an imaginative array of "fresh" and "delish" edibles from hors d'oeuvres to desserts, with a "friendly" team to tend to events either in-store or off-site; doubters say despite "much hoopla" it's "good but not incredible."

David's Bagels *Bagels*

| 23 | 12 | 18 | I |

E Village | 228 First Ave. (bet. 13th & 14th Sts.) | L to 1st Ave. | 212-533-8766 ●
Gramercy | 331 First Ave. (bet. 19th & 20th Sts.) | L to 1st Ave. | 212-780-2308

Boosters boast this "underrated" East Village and Gramercy duo "can rival any" for "exceptional" bagels featuring a "crusty outside" with a "good crunch" and a "fluffy" center that's "not too doughy"; some say the "standard" setups "could use a bit of an upgrade", but given rounds this "cheap" and "reliable", "who wants frills?"

David Stark Design & Production *Caterer/Events*

| - | - | - | VE |

Carroll Gardens | 87 Luquer St. (Clinton St.) | Brooklyn | 718-534-6777 | www.davidstarkdesign.com
By appointment only

Taking the maximal approach to event planning and production, this Carroll Gardens–based studio works on a showstopping scale to re-shape whole venues with lighting effects, oversize stage props and wildly creative backdrops while integrating everything from invitation design to floral arrangements; the one-of-a-kind results have secured a high-rolling corporate, media and private clientele as well as institutions like the NYC Opera and MoMA.

David Ziff Cooking *Caterer*

| ▽ 22 | 19 | 21 | E |

E 90s | 184 E. 93rd St. (bet. Lexington & 3rd Aves.) | 6 to 96th St. | 212-289-6199 | www.davidziffcooking.com

They "make it all so easy" gush admirers of this full-service Upper East Side caterer co-owned by chef David Ziff and Alan Bell, which draws on global gastronomy to cook up "excellent and interesting" menus that "guests rave about"; with a "caring" crew to provide the service, it's a "great experience from start to finish" that's "worth every penny" of the considerable cost.

☑ Dean & DeLuca *Major Gourmet Mkt.*

| 27 | 26 | 20 | VE |

E 80s | 1150 Madison Ave. (85th St.) | 4/5/6 to 86th St. | 212-717-0800
Financial District | Borders Books & Music | 100 Broadway (Pine St.) | 4/5 to Wall St. | 212-577-2153

(continued)

Dean & DeLuca

G Village | 75 University Pl. (11th St.) | 4/5/6/L/N/Q/R/W to 14th St./
Union Sq. | 212-473-1908
Murray Hill | Borders Books & Music | 562 Second Ave. (32nd St.) |
6 to 33rd St. | 212-696-1369 ◗
SoHo | 560 Broadway (Prince St.) | N/R to Prince St. |
212-226-6800
NEW **W 40s** | 1 Rockefeller Plaza (on 48th St., bet. 5th & 6th Aves.) |
212-664-1372
W 40s | Paramount Hotel | 235 W. 46th St. (bet. B'way &
8th Ave.) | 1/2/3/7/N/Q/R/S/W to 42nd St./Times Sq. |
212-869-6890 ◗
W 40s | 9 Rockefeller Plaza (49th St., bet. 5th & 6th Aves.) | B/D/F/V to
47-50th Sts./Rockefeller Ctr. | 212-664-1363 ◗
W 50s | Time Warner Ctr. | 10 Columbus Circle, 2nd fl. (bet. 58th &
60th Sts.) | 1/A/B/C/D to 59th St./Columbus Circle |
212-765-4400 ◗
800-221-7714 | www.deandeluca.com

"The Tiffany's of gourmet groceries", this ever-"fashionable" "fancy food" chain remains "the benchmark" "for the discriminating" with its "exquisite" presentation of "anything your heart desires" in the way of "museum"-grade produce, "exceptional" prepared foods, "scrumptious" baked goods, an "excellent range" of "rare" and "exciting" cheeses, "imaginative" specialty items, "high-quality spices" "you aren't even sure how to spell" and "fantastic kitchenware"; "top-dollar" prices that some deem "prohibitive" "bordering on the outlandish" mean it's "not practical for everyday", but those who go to "shop selectively" or "just to browse" are in for a "true experience"; N.B. the SoHo and Madison Avenue sites stock the full lineup, with the other outlets limited to coffee, prepared foods and baked goods.

Debauve & Gallais ▣ *Candy/Nuts*   ∇ 27 | 25 | 26 | VE

E 60s | 20 E. 69th St. (bet. 5th & Madison Aves.) | 6 to 68th St. |
212-734-8880 | www.debauveandgallais.com
Imported "from Paris with love", this "very fine, very French" Upper East Side chocolatier boasts more than two centuries of history in its native land, where it supplied the court at Versailles and still ranks among "the world's best"; the "elegant", chandelier-lit boutique stocks "regal-looking" handmade bonbons and truffles that are undeniably "good enough for kings", but watch out for price tags so "expensive" they'd shock Marie Antoinette.

Delillo Pastry Shop ▣ *Baked Goods*   26 | 22 | 23 | I

Bronx | 606 E. 187th St. (bet. Arthur & Hughes Aves.) | B/D to
Fordham Rd. | 718-367-8198
"Some things just never change, thank goodness" sigh smitten surveyors who come to this Bronx institution (since 1925) for the "freshest" "traditional Italian pastries", including "delicious" cannoli that's been handmade by the owner's uncle for the past 40 years; no wonder the "small seating area" can't accommodate the

many *amici* seeking to "complete their trip to Arthur Avenue" with "a latte and Napoleon" here.

Deli Masters Kosher Deli ◑ *Deli/Sandwich* | 21 | 16 | 17 | M |

Fresh Meadows | 184-02 Horace Harding Expwy. (184th St.) | Queens | 718-353-3030 | www.delimasterskosher.com

Sure, it may have "less flash" than other places, but this circa-1950 Fresh Meadows kosher deli legend is still a "good rest stop if you're stuck on the LIE" thanks to "high-quality" offerings including the "best" pastrami sandwiches; naturally, it's advised to "bring a big appetite."

Delmonico Gourmet Food ◑ *Specialty Shop* | 21 | 19 | 18 | E |

E 40s | 375 Lexington Ave. (bet. 41st & 42nd Sts.) | 4/5/6/7/S to 42nd St./Grand Central | 212-661-0150

E 50s | 55 E. 59th St. (bet. Madison & Park Aves.) | 4/5/6/N/R/W to 59th St./Lexington Ave. | 212-751-5559

Get "in and out fast" with the lunchtime crowd at this Midtown food market pair, where the "service counters are tops for sandwiches" and the "fresh", "well-monitored" "buffet offerings" are generally "worth" the "high prices"; given the "great variety" and 24/7 accessibility, regulars find them "convenient and better than the delis", "but 'gourmet' is pushing it."

Deluxe Food Market ◑ *Specialty Shop* | ▽ 21 | 13 | 9 | I |

Chinatown | 79 Elizabeth St. (bet. Grand & Hester Sts.) | B/D to Grand St. | 212-925-5766

"You'll find exactly what you want" at this Chinatown market that's a "favorite source" for Asian products (it "has everything") as well as "fresh fish", meats, baked goods, sandwiches and prepared foods; sensitive shoppers report it can be "a bit chaotic", but "superior quality" and "cheap prices" prevail.

DeRobertis Pasticceria & Caffe ◑◱ *Baked Goods* | 22 | 21 | 21 | I |

E Village | 176 First Ave. (bet. 10th & 11th Sts.) | L to 1st Ave. | 212-674-7137 | www.derobertiscaffe.com

"Step back in time" to the "days when the East Village had an Italian contingent" at this "old-fashioned", "New Yawky" pastry shop where the "decor is 1923" and the fourth generation of DeRobertises "purveys the treats of yore"; most notable are the "gold-standard" pignoli cookies, "great cannoli", ices and "delicious coffee."

☑ Despaña Foods ◱ *Specialty Shop* | 27 | 23 | 24 | E |

Little Italy | 408 Broome St. (bet. Cleveland Pl. & Lafayette St.) | 6 to Spring St. | 212-219-5050

Jackson Heights | 86-17 Northern Blvd. (bet. 86th & 87th Sts.) | Queens | 7 to 90th St. | 718-779-4971
www.despananyc.com

An "unbelievable resource for Spanish foods", this Jackson Heights import store and its newer Little Italy offshoot are "chock-full" of "amazing" Iberian items, from "delectable sausages" and house-made chorizo to some 55 varieties of cheese and plenty of bottled, jarred and canned imported goods; plus, the staff is "very informative about their products and provide generous samples", making it "a great place to explore and discover new treats"; P.S. "don't miss the sandwiches prepared at the back counter."

☑ Dessert Delivery ⌨ *Baked Goods*   28 | 24 | 26 | E

E 50s | 360 E. 55th St. (bet. 1st & 2nd Aves.) | E/V to Lexington Ave./ 53rd St. | 212-838-5411 | www.dessertdeliveryny.com

This little shop in East Midtown "can get anyone off their diet" confide cookie connoisseurs citing a clever and "well-edited" selection of sweet treats the likes of "beautiful" cakes that also taste "really delicious", "apple pie that's about the best there is" and what may be "the city's finest black-and-white cookie"; "first-class" owners oversee the "fast, friendly service", assuring that customers get their just desserts; N.B. the Say It With Flour division makes gift baskets.

De Vino ●⌨ *Wine/Liquor*   ▽ 25 | 24 | 23 | E

LES | 30 Clinton St. (bet. Houston & Stanton Sts.) | F/J/M/Z to Delancey/Essex Sts. | 212-228-0073 | www.de-vino.com

Owner Gabrio Tosti di Valminuta (who hails from a family of winemakers) shares his passion for vinos at his small Lower East Side boutique; there's "no attitude, just good service" and primo advice on the "wonderful", well-displayed wines that are mostly Italian in origin.

Devon & Blakely *Prepared Food*   22 | 20 | 18 | M

E 40s | 140 E. 45th St. (bet. Lexington & 3rd Aves.) | 4/5/6/7/S to 42nd St./Grand Central | 212-338-0606
E 40s | 250 Park Ave. (bet. 46th & 47th Sts.) | 4/5/6/7/S to 42nd St./ Grand Central | 212-661-0101
E 40s | 461 Fifth Ave. (bet. 40th & 41st Sts.) | 7/B/D/F/V to 42nd St./ Bryant Park | 212-684-4321
E 40s | 780 Third Ave. (49th St.) | 6 to 51st St. | 212-826-0212
E 50s | 650 Fifth Ave., lower level (52nd St.) | B/D/F/V to 47-50th Sts./ Rockefeller Ctr. | 212-489-0990
www.devonandblakely.com

"Freshly made" soups, "amazing" salads and "reliable" sandwiches served up in locations dotted "all over Midtown" make this chain a "convenient" "lunch standby" for many; however, critics warn that service "can be slow", while its "gourmet" aspirations translate to somewhat "steep" tabs.

Di Fiore Marquet ● *Baked Goods*   - | - | - | E
(fka Marquet Patisserie)

G Village | 15 E. 12th St. (bet. 5th Ave. & University Pl.) | 4/5/6/L/ N/Q/R/W to 14th St./Union Sq. | 212-229-9313

Formerly a branch of Marquet Patisserie, this "comfortable" NYU area bakery/cafe still offers "great French pastries" (brioche, croissants), breads from Balthazar and other "wonderful" baked goods, but it's now making a name for itself with ambitious prepared foods (think filet mignon and roasted fish), including many dishes with a Brazilian or French twist.

	QUALITY	DISPLAY	SERVICE	COST

☒ DiPalo Dairy   *Cheese/Dairy* | 29 | 23 | 25 | M |

Little Italy | 200 Grand St. (Mott St.) | 6 to Spring St. | 212-226-1033
A "shrine" to "the gospel of cheese", this "family-run" Little Italy "institution" is "legendary" for its "exhaustive" selection of formaggio, voted No. 1 in NYC, featuring "unbeatable" "fresh mozzarella" and ricotta plus a "wide range" of "real Italian" imports from parmigiano to pecorino; also a source of "old-country" "delights" like pasta and olive oil, it's operated "with love" by "chatty" "experts" who "won't rush you" "once your number is up", and though there are often "long lines", that only confirms it's "one of the greats."

DiPaola Turkeys   ✍ *Meat/Poultry* | 27 | 16 | 24 | M |

See Greenmarket; for more information, call 609-587-9311
It's "all turkey, all the time" at this Hamilton, NJ–based Greenmarket poultry provider whose devoted fans "gobble up" its "luscious", "moist" farm-raised birds year-round; "fresh, not frozen", the meat comes in the form of "superior" tenderloins, breasts and burgers, as well as "addictive" Italian sausage (try the spicy for a "wild pasta sauce"); there may be "no deals" here – aside from the "free samples" – but all agree "you get what you pay for."

Dirty Bird to-go   ◑ *Prepared Food* | 20 | 15 | 16 | M |

W Village | 204 W. 14th St. (bet. 7th & 8th Aves.) | A/C/E/L to 14th St./8th Ave. | 212-620-4836 | www.dirtybirdtogo.com
The "soul-satisfying" "free-range chicken is a real treat" at this small Village takeout dishing up "delicious" brined birds rotisserie-style or in a "heavenly fried" version, with roasted potatoes, garlic kale, cornbread, sandwiches and wraps rounding out the menu; "fast, efficient delivery" is a plus, but some "wish the sides were better", given that "it's not cheap."

Discovery Wines   ◑☖ *Wine/Liquor* | 22 | 25 | 21 | M |

E Village | 10 Ave. A (bet. Houston & 2nd Sts.) | F/V to Lower East Side/2nd Ave. | 212-674-7833 | www.discoverywines.com
Service-with-a-swipe is the hook at this "cool" gallerylike East Village wine store, whose "high-tech information portals" enable customers to scan bar-coded picks for pricing, tasting info, food suggestions and images of vineyards; the kiosks are "entertaining", but Luddites can always look to "human help" if need be.

Dishes   *Prepared Food* | 24 | 23 | 17 | E |

E 40s | 6 E. 45th St. (bet. 5th & Madison Aves.) | 4/5/6/7/S to 42nd St./Grand Central | 212-687-5511
E 40s | Grand Central Terminal | dining concourse, 42nd St. & Vanderbilt Ave. | 4/5/6/7/S to 42nd St./Grand Central | 212-808-5511 ◑
NEW **E 40s** | Grand Central Terminal | main fl., 42nd St. & Vanderbilt Ave. | 212-808-5511 ◑
E 50s | Citigroup Ctr. | 399 Park Ave. (54th St.) | E/V to 5th Ave./53rd St. | 212-421-5511
www.dishestogo.com
"When you're on the run" in the Grand Central area, this "upscale" mini-chain is a "convenient" option for "spot-on salads", "wonderful

	QUALITY	DISPLAY	SERVICE	COST

soups" and other "quality lunchtime fare"; "be careful not to take too much" from the "beautifully presented" buffet, however, for everything's a "bit pricey"; N.B. only the dining concourse location is open on weekends.

Divalicious Chocolate Fountains *Candy/Nuts*

	24	24	24	M

Little Italy | 365 Broome St. (bet. Elizabeth & Mott Sts.) | 6 to Spring St. | 212-343-1243 | www.divaliciouschocolate.com

Its shelves are stocked with a "gift-worthy" selection of "delicious" chocolate bark, bonbons, etc., but this "friendly, unpretentious" Little Italy dessert shop is best known as the place to "rent chocolate fountains" for parties; its elaborate tabletop machines come in three sizes (serving from 100–600 people, at a cost of about $350–$700 for a three-hour rental), and are accompanied by a uniformed attendant as well as, yes, lots of melted chocolate and dried fruits, marshmallows, etc. for guests to dip – "how can you go wrong?"

NEW D.O.C. Wine Shop *Wine/Liquor*

	22	21	23	M

Williamsburg | 147 Broadway (bet. Bedford & Driggs Aves.) | Brooklyn | J/M/Z to Marcy Ave. | 718-388-0087

From the "D.O.C. Wine Bar folks", this Williamsburg newcomer with an "old-world feel" is a "wine-lover's delight" given its "well-chosen", Italian-focused selection that includes a few hard-to-find vintages and spirits too; locals who "could get lost for hours" browsing the bottles housed in "funky" 19th-century credenzas (you "expect a séance to start at any moment") feel they already "couldn't live without" this shop; N.B. wine tastings are held on Wednesdays and Saturdays, and delivery service is in the works.

Doma Cafe & Gallery ●⊅ *Coffee/Tea*

	▽ 25	25	20	M

W Village | 17 Perry St. (7th Ave.) | 1/2/3 to 14th St. | 212-929-4339

Every boho hangout "should aspire to" be like this "very West Village" coffeehouse/wine bar, a "relaxed" retreat for "watching the world go by" over "wonderful coffee" and "yummy" "snacks", including pastries, panini, soups and such; it's the favored domain of "screenwriters" and other "loafers" with "laptops", many of whom seem to "live there."

Dorian's Seafood Market ▣ *Seafood*

	25	20	26	E

E 80s | 1580 York Ave. (83rd St.) | 4/5/6 to 86th St. | 212-535-2256

UES denizens were delighted when the "knowledgeable staff" from the dearly departed Rosedale Fishmarket opened this similarly "top-quality" market dealing in "amazingly" "fresh" seafood and prepared items – smoked fish, clam chowder and the like – "delivered with total assurance" (and at no charge, citywide); yes, it's "expensive", but you can expect to "get what you ordered in perfect condition", and the counter folk will even shuck your bivalves while you wait.

	QUALITY	DISPLAY	SERVICE	COST

Ⓩ Doughnut Plant ⊘ *Baked Goods* — 26 | 15 | 19 | M

LES | 379 Grand St. (bet. Essex & Norfolk Sts.) | F/J/M/Z to Delancey/Essex Sts. | 212-505-3700 | www.doughnutplant.com

Living up to its name with a "bare-bones" industrial interior and minimal seating, this LES factory turns out "artisanal doughnuts" so "addictive" they "should have a warning label" (think "Homer Simpson's wildest dreams come to life"); the owner's "infectious enthusiasm" for seasonal ingredients inspires "flavors you couldn't imagine" – chestnut, banana pecan, tres leches – and ensures his "high-end" product is "worth the extra dough."

Downtown Atlantic ❶ *Prepared Food* — ▽ 21 | 20 | 21 | M

Boerum Hill | 364 Atlantic Ave. (bet. Bond & Hoyt Sts.) | Brooklyn | A/C/G to Hoyt/Schermerhorn Sts. | 718-596-1827 | www.downtownatlantic.com

"You'd never guess there's a world-class bakery hidden in the basement" of this family-owned Boerum Hill restaurant, where pastry chef Fran Sippel's "huge, out-of-this-world" cupcakes and other "treats" are "sold from a small counter at the front"; it also serves simple soups, salads and sandwiches to go at lunchtime.

Dual Specialty Store, Inc. ❶ *Herbs/Spices* — ▽ 22 | 18 | 19 | I
(fka Dowel Quality Products)

E Village | 91 First Ave. (bet. 5th & 6th Sts.) | F/V to Lower East Side/ 2nd Ave. | 212-979-6045

Anything you might need to cook up an Indian feast can be found at this East Village spice heaven, where the "vast selection" of Indian grocery items, dried and preserved fruits, spices and herbs, teas, breads and sweets will make an "addict" of any wandering foodie; it's "inexpensive", "the people are friendly" and there's a "terrific beer selection" (over 400 labels) – no wonder devotees gush "these guys are the greatest in the neighborhood."

Duane Park Patisserie *Baked Goods* — 26 | 17 | 20 | E

TriBeCa | 179 Duane St. (bet. Greenwich & Hudson Sts.) | 1/2/3/A/ C to Chambers St. | 212-274-8447 | www.madelines.net

"A real place in TriBeCa, as opposed to a scene-maker" is the general consensus on this longtime patisserie that pleases patrons with "wonderful" Austrian, French and German specialties spanning "truly magical" cupcakes, "exquisite" pastries, "traditional cookies" and "beautiful, delicious" custom cakes; though service gets mixed reviews and the prices are "expensive", most take it in stride because clearly "much love and expertise goes into the work."

DUB Pies ❶ ⊟ *Prepared Food* — ▽ 24 | 15 | 24 | I

Carroll Gardens | 193 Columbia St. (bet. Degraw & Sackett Sts.) | Brooklyn | F/G to Carroll St. | 646-202-9412

NEW Windsor Terrace | 211 Prospect Park W. (16th St.) | Brooklyn | F to 15th St. | 718-788-2448 ⊘
www.dubpies.com

Traditional Australian and New Zealander "savory pies" "make meat lovers happy" at this West Carroll Gardens (i.e. Navy Yard) takeaway shop and its newer Windsor Terrace offshoot, but there are also "solid vegetarian" dishes and "sweet dessert pies" among the "fantastic cheap eats" on offer; the moniker stands for 'Down Under Bakery', but also names the style of reggae that often fills the air here.

Dumpling Man ● *Prepared Food* | 20 | 16 | 17 | I |

E Village | 100 St. Marks Pl. (bet. Ave. A & 1st Ave.) | L to 1st Ave. | 212-505-2121 | www.dumplingman.com
For "awesomeness in one bite", East Villagers head to this tiny eat-in/takeaway spot where you can watch the kitchen staff's "craftsmanship" in packing the "thin, delicate" wrappers with "inventive" fillings, including a hearty veggie version; even though it's "cheap", purists pooh-pooh it as "yuppie Americanized fusion cuisine" and recommend you "save your money for Chinatown."

Durso's Pasta & Ravioli Co. ▣ *Pasta* | 26 | 20 | 23 | M |

Flushing | 189-01 Crocheron Ave. (Utopia Pkwy.) | Queens | 7 to Flushing-Main St. | 718-358-1311 | www.dursos.com
"Phenomenal pastas" and "great sauces to go with them" earn endorsements from shoppers at this Flushing specialty-foods store with an Italian accent, which also serves more than 50 kinds of prepared dishes, fresh meat and poultry, lotsa bakery items, imported treats and an extensive selection of cheeses – "lines are long at times" but it's "worth it."

☑ D'Vine Taste ● *Specialty Shop* | 25 | 21 | 25 | M |

Park Slope | 150 Seventh Ave. (bet. Carroll St. & Garfield Pl.) | Brooklyn | 2/3 to Grand Army Plaza | 718-369-9548
The "fabulous selection of cheeses, olives", spreads and other "gourmet groceries" keeps Park Slope residents coming back to this Middle Eastern specialty store whose bifurcated space also houses "interesting, delicious prepared foods" including sandwiches at lunchtime; the housemade "fig cakes are addictive" here, as are the "well-stocked" shelves, affordable prices and "friendly, warm and genuinely helpful service."

☑ Dylan's Candy Bar ●▣ *Candy/Nuts* | 21 | 27 | 17 | E |

E 60s | 1011 Third Ave. (60th St.) | 4/5/6/N/R/W to 59th St./Lexington Ave. | 646-735-0078 | www.dylanscandybar.com
A "cornucopia of candies", this "fantastical" East Side "playground" "for ages 10–110" offers its "bazillion" varieties of sweets (including "vintage stuff" like Dubble Bubble and Dots) in an "eye-popping" setting complete with a coffee/ice cream bar; sure, it's a "bedlam" of "tourists and tweens" and the "inflated prices" will bust your "entire piggy bank", but "just try to resist" "the fun factor"; N.B. it underwent a renovation and expansion (now three floors!) post-Survey.

Dynasty Supermarket ● *Specialty Shop* | 19 | 13 | 12 | I |

Chinatown | 68 Elizabeth St. (Hester St.) | 6/J/M/N/Q/R/W/Z to Canal St. | 212-966-4943 | www.dynastysuper.qpg.com
Considered the "mother of all Manhattan Asian markets", this Chinatown superstore is "about as authentic as it gets", offering an "incredible selection" of "live fish, octopi and eels" plus meats, pro-

duce, condiments, rice and "every comestible possible in dessicated form"; "there's even a sushi bar, jewelry store" and herbal medicine counter, so although "service is nonexistent", shoppers "keep coming back for the incredible bargains."

Eagle Provisions   *Meat/Poultry* | 24 | 13 | 19 | M |

Park Slope | 628 Fifth Ave. (18th St.) | Brooklyn | M/R to Prospect Ave. | 718-499-0026

The "incredible aroma of kielbasa" will have you "salivating" upon entry to this enormous Park Slope food market, a "terrific" resource for house-smoked meats and other "authentic" Polish specialties as well as "great gourmet products" from all over ("surprisingly good lox"); perhaps most "impressive" is the "massive" beer selection comprising 1,000 labels, "imported and microbrew."

Earthmatters ● *Health Food*   ∇ | 21 | 15 | 12 | M |

LES | 177 Ludlow St. (bet. Houston & Stanton Sts.) | F/V to Lower East Side/2nd Ave. | 212-475-4180 | www.earthmatters.com

A healthful oasis on the Lower East Side, this organic market and cafe has a lounge where (mainly vegetarian) homemade snacks and sandwiches are served, along with organic wines or beers; while it boasts a large selection of teas, most rely on it more as a source for wholesome prepared foods than as a place to "shop for groceries."

East Coast Beer Co.   *Beer*   ∇ | 22 | 16 | 19 | M |

Sunset Park | 316 37th St. (3rd Ave.) | Brooklyn | D/M/N/R to 36th St. | 718-788-8000

Suds for all seasons and from all regions is the specialty of this "awesome" Brooklyn brew expert; for most it's a haul to Sunset Park, but it's "worth the trip" on account of the "huge selection" (700 varieties) that's genuinely "international", and what's more, the eclectic stock is reasonably priced – though budget-watchers note you "shouldn't expect to get off on the cheap."

East Side Bagel ● *Bagels* | 21 | 16 | 19 | I |

E 70s | 1496 First Ave. (78th St.) | 6 to 77th St. | 212-794-1403

Upper Eastsiders salute this "simple" local shop for the "huge and delicious bagels" that lead a lineup of "brunch essentials" including sandwiches, salads and housemade black-and-white cookies; holdouts shrug it's "only so-so", but those in the market for "old-fashioned" "value" "can't complain."

East Village Cheese Store ⊟ *Cheese/Dairy* | 22 | 17 | 19 | I |

E Village | 40 Third Ave. (bet. 9th & 10th Sts.) | 6 to Astor Pl. | 212-477-2601

"How do they do it?" wonder "bargain"-hunters at this "busy" East Village retailer, loaded "wall to wall" with "cheese, wonderful cheese" at "unbelievably low" prices (check out those "$2.99 specials"), along with spreads, cold cuts and breads; it's "nothing fancy" and "freshness can be hit-or-miss", but "if you know what's good" and "need to stock up", "there's no better" deal; P.S. it's "cash only."

	QUALITY	DISPLAY	SERVICE	COST

East Village Ice Cream ●⊘ *Ice Cream* | 22 | 19 | 21 | M |

E Village | 218 Avenue B (bet. 13th & 14th Sts.) | L to 1st Ave. |
212-673-6030

Some of the "most satisfying ice cream" for blocks is produced by
this tiny, mango-hued East Village parlor peddling "delicious"
housemade, small-batch scoops that come in an "inventive", ever-
changing array of flavors – though enduring favorites like vanilla-
chocolate-chunk and pistachio are usually on hand; there are jars of
toppings on the counter to complete the treat, as well as a few seats
in which to savor it.

☑ East Village | 28 | 25 | 25 | M |
Meat Market ▣ *Meat/Poultry*

E Village | 139 Second Ave. (bet. 9th St. & St. Marks Pl.) | 6 to Astor Pl. |
212-228-5590

Admirers of this "old-school" East Village meat market "in the classic East European/Polish tradition" "hope it never changes" given
that the house-smoked hams, "beautiful" cold cuts and sausages
("the best kielbasa") and fresh meats on display can "provoke drool-
ing on sight"; moderate prices and "old-fashioned, personal service"
at the counter are the crowning touches.

☑ E.A.T. ●▣ *Prepared Food* | 25 | 21 | 17 | VE |

E 80s | 1064 Madison Ave. (bet. 80th & 81st Sts.) | 4/5/6 to 86th St. |
212-772-0022 | www.elizabar.com

"Everything is delicious" at Eli Zabar's Upper East Side cafe-cum-
prepared foods shop, from the "fabulous crusty breads" to the
"fresh", "high-quality" sandwiches, soups and varied hot dishes; the
scene can be "chaotic" and the service "grumpy", and while your
chances of spotting "famous people" aren't bad, you're more likely
to "see stars when you get the bill."

Eckerton Hill Farm ⊘ *Produce* | 26 | 23 | 23 | E |

See Greenmarket; for more information, call 610-562-2591

"The godfather of heirloom tomatoes" since 1996, Greenmarket
stalwart Tim Stark also harvests "exceptionally good peppers of all
sizes and heat gradients" in late summer from his bucolic
Pennsylvania farm; these two "superlative" crops are proffered in
"interesting and unusual" varieties, along with colorful clusters of
"wonderful" sweet peas to "make you smile."

Economy Candy ▣ *Candy/Nuts* | 24 | 17 | 18 | I |

LES | 108 Rivington St. (bet. Essex & Ludlow Sts.) | F/J/M/Z to Delancey/
Essex Sts. | 212-254-1531 | 800-352-4544 | www.economycandy.com

"You name it, they have it" at this "Lower East Side landmark" where
"every inch" of the "old-school" space is "crammed full" with "every
imaginable" candy, both "retro and modern", as well as nuts and
dried fruits, offered individually or in "bulk" "at rock-bottom prices";
it's a "time warp to sweeter" days where your "inner child" can re-
discover the "classics" ("keep digging, you'll find it"), and despite
"cluttered" conditions, penny-pinchers and nostalgists alike will
think they "went to heaven."

	QUALITY	DISPLAY	SERVICE	COST

Eddie's Sweet Shop ●⊄ *Ice Cream* | 25 | 24 | 22 | I |

Forest Hills | 105-29 Metropolitan Ave. (72nd Rd.) | Queens | E/F/G/R/V to Forest Hills/71st Ave. | 718-520-8514

"Go for nostalgia's sake" but stay for the "heavenly" ice cream at this "vintage" Forest Hills "throwback" where the "fresh whipped cream" and "unbelievable" hot fudge make for a mean sundae; while the "old-time parlor" setting, complete with "counter", "tin ceilings" and "tall glasses", is a "blast from the past", it's the "homemade" frozen stuff that is "not to be missed."

Edible Arrangements ▭ *Caterer* | 22 | 24 | 22 | E |

E 50s | Food Court of 875 3rd Ave. | 875 Third Ave. (53rd St.) | E/V to Lexington Ave./53rd St. | 212-644-0455

G Village | 29 Seventh Ave. S. (bet. Bedford & Morton Sts.) | 1 to Houston St. | 212-741-0069

W 100s | 239 W. 105th St. (bet. Amsterdam Ave. & B'way) | 1 to 103rd St. | 212-665-8800

Bronx | 2021 Williamsbridge Rd. (bet. Lydig & Neill Aves.) | 2/5 to Pelham Pkwy. | 718-823-4646

Park Slope | 500A Fifth Ave. (12th St.) | Brooklyn | F to 4th Ave./9th St. | 718-832-0100

Sheepshead Bay | 1736 Sheepshead Bay Rd. (bet. Voorhies Ave. & Shore Pkwy.) | Brooklyn | B/Q to Sheepshead Bay Rd. | 718-535-7909

Williamsburg | 601 Lorimer St. (bet. Conselyea St. & Skillman Ave.) | Brooklyn | L to Lorimer St. | 718-389-0700

Bayside | 213-02 42nd Ave. (Bell Blvd.) | Queens | 718-819-0911

Forest Hills | 104-16 Metropolitan Ave. (72nd Ave.) | Queens | E/F/R/W to Forest Hills | 718-575-4124

Staten Island | Woodrow Shopping Plaza | 655 Rossville Ave. (Woodrow Rd.) | 718-227-4422

www.ediblearrangements.com

Additional locations throughout the NY area

The "clever idea" behind this ubiquitous chain – you've "seen the trucks, advertisements and flyers" – is "cutting and arranging fresh fruit" "like a floral bouquet", and delivering it to "baby showers, wakes" and other affairs all over town; enthusiasts gush about its "sweet", "whimsical" arrangements that make a "delicious alternative to the usual", but critics call them "kitschy" ("the fruit equivalent of sending carnations") and "pricey" too; either way, "eat it quick before it wilts."

Egg Custard King Café ● *Baked Goods* | 21 | 16 | 13 | I |

Chinatown | 76 Mott St. (bet. Canal & Bayard Sts.) | J/M/Z to Canal St. | 212-226-8208

"The name says it all" about this "tiny" Chinatowner that's beloved for its "cheap", "delicious" egg custard tarts offered in a "variety of flavors" (honeydew, strawberry, almond, etc.), though it also vends a "wide array" of other Asian pastries, plus buns and Hong Kong–style 'cafe food' such as sandwiches, noodles and rice dishes; no wonder most are willing to shrug off the "assembly-line" setup and "no-warmth" service.

	QUALITY	DISPLAY	SERVICE	COST

Eggers Ice Cream Parlor ●⌀⇆ *Ice Cream* | 25 | 19 | 21 | M |

Staten Island | 1194 Forest Ave. (bet. Jewett Ave. & Manor Rd.) |
718-981-2110

Staten Island | 7437 Amboy Rd. (Yetman Ave.) | 718-605-9335

The "old-fashioned creamy treats", including "the best hot fudge,
hands down", on top of "always fresh-tasting" ice cream, are "off the
charts" at this "classic" ice cream parlor on Staten Island, which also
boasts a nostalgia-inducing candy selection; cakes and pies are
made on the premises, and it's available for birthday parties;
N.B. the Forest Avenue location is independently owned.

Egidio Pastry Shop ▭ *Baked Goods* | 24 | 23 | 22 | M |

Bronx | 622 E. 187th St. (Hughes Ave.) | 2/5 to Pelham Pkwy. |
718-295-6077

"Visit the old country" without leaving the city at this "real-deal"
Bronx pasticceria (since 1912) where owner-baker Carmela
Lucciola whips up "mouthwatering" "traditional Italian pastries"
("full-size or miniature"), "the best biscotti", "great cappuccino"
and summertime ices; N.B. wedding cakes and gingerbread houses
are also specialties.

Eileen's Special | 26 | 18 | 19 | M |
Cheesecake ●▭ *Baked Goods*

NoLita | 17 Cleveland Pl. (Kenmare St.) | 6 to Spring St. | 212-966-5585 |
800-521-2253 | www.eileenscheesecake.com

This NoLita "old-timer" still specializes in "creamy", "dreamy"
cheesecakes "so light" a person could almost "eat an entire 10-inch
cake" report respondents who rhapsodize about the "blissful" array
of sizes and "innovative flavors" (e.g. mango and dulce de leche)
that make for a "smashing smorgasbord"; despite occasional
"crankiness", service is "generally good"; N.B. low-carb and sugar-
free versions available.

Eisenberg's Sandwich Shop *Deli/Sandwich* | 20 | 13 | 18 | I |

Flatiron | 174 Fifth Ave. (bet. 22nd & 23rd Sts.) | N/R/W to 23rd St. |
212-675-5096 | www.eisenbergsnyc.com

Serving up "the real deal" since 1929, this "glorious NY institution"
"takes you back in time" with its "overstuffed sandwiches" ("try the
chopped liver" or "to-die-for tuna" salad) and "great egg creams";
although some say the "vintage" Flatiron setting "has seen better
days", most consider that to be "a nostalgic virtue."

NEW /eks/ ● *Ice Cream* | - | - | - | M |

E Village | Beard Papa Sweets | 740 Broadway (Astor Pl.) | 6 to Astor Pl. |
212-353-8888

Williamsburg | 488 Driggs Ave. (10th St.) | Brooklyn | L to Bedford St. |
718-599-1706

Its name is pronounced 'X', and this Williamsburg newcomer is
marking its spot on the frozen yogurt scene with organic, low-
sugar fro-yo made in-house and topped with the customary fresh
fruit; it also distinguishes itself with an enormous subterranean
space affording plentiful seating, though if the bold red-and-

white design scheme doesn't suit, local delivery is also an option; N.B. a second location opened inside the East Village branch of Beard Papa recently.

NEW El Beit � Coffee/Tea | - | - | - | M |

Williamsburg | 158 Bedford Ave. (bet. 8th & 9th Sts.) | Brooklyn | L to Bedford Ave. | 718-302-1810

Possessing a much-touted, ultradeluxe Clover coffee machine – one of only a handful in the city – this new Williamsburg coffee house is aimed at the serious javaphile; it offers a choice of beans from Vancouver's 49th Parallel, priced at market rates (in the neighborhood of $3–$6), which are pre-portioned in glass jars and ground to order; N.B. it recently added a few tables out back.

Eleni's Cookies ▭ Baked Goods | 22 | 24 | 20 | E |

Chelsea | Chelsea Mkt. | 75 Ninth Ave. (bet. 15th & 16th Sts.) | A/C/E/L to 14th St./8th Ave. | 212-255-7990 | 888.435.3647 | www.elenis.com

"The crème de la crème of illustrated cookies" may well be this Chelsea Market storefront's "elaborate" "little works of art" customizable "for every conceivable occasion and theme" (e.g. "actor-face cookies for your Oscar party"); while some say the confections "look better than they taste", most maintain the "amazing workmanship" and "original presentation" make these "truly special" (if "pricey") gifts; N.B. there are now cupcakes, cakes and candy by the pound.

☑ Eli's Manhattan ☽▭ Major Gourmet Mkt. | 25 | 24 | 16 | VE |

E 80s | 1411 Third Ave. (80th St.) | 4/5/6 to 86th St. | 212-717-8100 | www.elizabar.com

A "great comfort" to Upper Eastsiders, Eli Zabar's "fabulous" "all-around" gourmet market ensures "young professional" types stay well fed on "outstanding" breads and baked goods ("always a crowd-pleaser"), a "wide-ranging selection" of "beautiful" cheeses, "awe-inspiring" specialty items, "picturesque produce" of "exceptional quality", "superior" prepared foods featuring a "wall of soups" and a "rather small" but "incredible" meat and seafood department; of course, "excellence has its price", and with tabs tailored to "hedge-fund owners", regular folk must "choose wisely" here.

Eli's Vinegar Factory ☽▭ Major Gourmet Mkt. | 25 | 21 | 16 | VE |

E 90s | 431 E. 91st St. (bet. 1st & York Aves.) | 4/5/6 to 86th St. | 212-987-0885 | www.elizabar.com

It's so far over on the East Side you might think you "somehow left the island", but the intrepid can "count on" Eli Zabar's original emporium for "anything gourmet", starting with "bountiful", "always-fresh" produce that "looks like it should be in a gallery" and following through with "beautiful" "crusty breads" and "first-rate" prepared foods, cheeses, meat, seafood and specialty items; even if the "extreme" pricing strikes some as "way out of whack", it's always a "likable" place to splurge on a "special dinner" or a "once-in-a-while treat."

	QUALITY	DISPLAY	SERVICE	COST

Elizabeth Ryan Floral Design *Flowers*   ▽ 28 | 24 | 26 | E

LES | 178 Norfolk St. (bet. Houston & Stanton Sts.) | F/V to 2nd Ave. |
212-995-1111 | 800-260-1486 | www.erflowers.com

"What an eye" Elizabeth Ryan has declare devotees of the "spectacular, unusual flowers" arranged in "fabulous containers" that
emerge from her roomy new (post-Survey) Lower East Side emporium; the "finished products are so glorious" they "always draw high
praise" and help make any celebration or "party a smash success";
N.B. tablecloths and lighting are also available.

Emack & Bolio's ● *Ice Cream*   25 | 18 | 20 | M

E 80s | 1564 First Ave. (bet. 81st & 82nd Sts.) | 4/5/6 to 86th St. |
212-734-0105 ⊘
SoHo | 73 W. Houston St. (W. B'way) | 1 to Houston St. | 212-533-5610
W 70s | 389 Amsterdam Ave. (bet. 78th & 79th Sts.) | 1 to 79th St. |
212-362-2747 ⊘
www.emackandbolios.com

Even rabid Sox haters are "so glad" this "creative" mini-chain "made
its way from Boston" given its "awesome array" of "decadent",
"well-crafted" ice cream in "totally addictive" flavors; cynics find it
"vastly overrated" and "too expensive", but for most its "spoonable
magic" is "worth the calories and the price."

Embassy Wines & Spirits ●▣ *Wine/Liquor*   ▽ 19 | 16 | 15 | E

E 60s | 796 Lexington Ave. (bet. 61st & 62nd Sts.) | 4/5/6/N/R/
W to 59th St./Lexington Ave. | 212-838-6551 |
www.embassywinesandspirits.com

True to its name, this East Side store displays wines and liquors from
around the globe, including 100 kosher vintages; it's "convenient"
for busy shoppers who "need something quickly", and the 'bargain
basement' yields some nice windfalls (all wines there are under
$10), otherwise, some gripe that it caters to those "who don't care
what they pay."

Empire Coffee & Tea Co. ▣ *Coffee/Tea*   23 | 19 | 22 | M

W 40s | 568 Ninth Ave. (bet. 41st & 42nd Sts.) | 1/2/3/7/N/Q/R/
S/W to 42nd St./Times Sq. | 212-268-1220 | 800-262-5908 |
www.empirecoffeetea.com

"Ask and they'll probably have it" at this "old-style" (circa 1908)
Hell's Kitchen shop, a "funky little" space chock-full of "wonderful"
fresh-roasted coffees and "interesting teas" as well as cookies, candies and paraphernalia like grinders, coffeemakers and kettles; it's a
somewhat "hidden" resource, but the "sweet", "dedicated" service
gets a "thumbs-up" and "you can't beat the prices."

Empire Market *Meat/Poultry*   ▽ 16 | 14 | 16 | M

College Point | 14-26 College Point Blvd. (bet. 14th Ave. & 14th Rd.) |
Queens | 718-359-0209 | www.empire-market.com

This tin-ceilinged German meat-and-poultry shop in College Point,
a fourth-generation family business that dates from the 1850s,
proves that what's old can be new again with its lineup of all-natural,

organic, no-nitrate meats, including a broad selection of items prepped in their own smokehouse (bacon, knockwurst, kielbasa and 10 kinds of chicken sausage); in sum, this is a "place you can trust."

Esposito Meat Market *Meat/Poultry*

25	19	25	M

Garment District | 500 Ninth Ave. (38th St.) | A/C/E to 42nd St./ Port Authority | 212-279-3298

For the "best pork and sausage" dispensed with a side of "old-Italian-NY" atmosphere, take a "highly recommended" visit to this West 30s butcher shop, a third-generation family business purveying the "freshest meats" and game (including venison, quail and rabbit); customers appreciate the "expertise" of its "old-school" staffers, who also happen to be "very friendly."

Esposito's Pork Store ⊅ *Meat/Poultry*

26	21	25	M

Carroll Gardens | 357 Court St. (bet. President & Union Sts.) | Brooklyn | F/G to Carroll St. | 718-875-6863

One of the last "holdouts" in gentrified Carroll Gardens, this third-generation Italian meat market has been supplying Brooklynites with "outstanding pork products" since 1971; it's especially known for its "vast assortment" of house-cured and dried sausages (salami, hot and sweet soppresata, pepperoni), but it also offers imports like prosciutto as well as made-on-premises mozz and prepared foods like arancini, lasagna and sandwiches.

Ess-a-Bagel ●◗▭ *Bagels*

26	17	18	I

E 50s | 831 Third Ave. (bet. 50th & 51st Sts.) | 6 to 51st St. | 212-980-1010
Gramercy | 359 First Ave. (21st St.) | 6 to 23rd St. | 212-260-2252
www.ess-a-bagel.com

"Nothing beats" these Eastsiders for "hilariously huge" bagels that "can double as flotation devices" but still achieve a "blend of chewiness and crustiness" that's "among the best" and "heartiest" in town; only the "joshing" "countermen are fresher" than the "loads of spreads", making this a "ritual" dose of "moxie" "you can only get in the Big Apple", complete with "madhouse" conditions on weekends.

Euro Shop ▭ *Specialty Shop*

-	-	-	M

Sunnyside | 42-07 Queens Blvd. (bet. 42nd & 43rd Sts.) | Queens | 7 to 40th St. | 718-786-6026

With an E.U. flag incorporated into its logo, this pocket-size Sunnyside grocery store bills itself as a "European gourmet deli" and stocks an "eclectic mix" of imported goods from "various countries" on the Continent; however, it places special emphasis on all things Hungarian, from sundries, pastries, and candies to a "great smoked meat selection" at the butcher counter brimming with link after link of housemade sausage.

Evelyn's Hand-Dipped Chocolates ▭ *Candy/Nuts*

25	20	22	M

Financial District | 4 John St. (bet. B'way & Nassau St.) | A/C to B'way/Nassau | 212-267-5170

Dipping since 1963, this "tiny shop" is a "Wall Street standby" for "handmade (really) chocolates" that are "always fresh" and "just

	QUALITY	DISPLAY	SERVICE	COST

the right amount of sweet"; "simply" "fabulous" goods at prices "less expensive than the big names" make it a "mecca" "around the holidays", and for followers it's a pleasure "to see Evelyn there" any time.

Fabiane's Cafe & Pastry ◑⇗ *Baked Goods* — | — | — | I

Williamsburg | 142 N. Fifth St. (Bedford Ave.) | Brooklyn | L to Bedford Ave. | 718-218-9632

At this "laid-back" Williamsburger, a French Culinary Institute-trained chef offers a mix of Brazilian, French and American fare, much of it organic; the menu ranges from "delicious desserts" and baked goods (the "best" croissants", passion-fruit mousse, vegan tofu-almond pistachio cake, etc.) to chicken pot pie and other prepared foods; there's also a cafe that's prime for "hipster-watching."

☑ Faicco's Pork Store *Meat/Poultry* 28 | 23 | 25 | M

G Village | 260 Bleecker St. (bet. 6th & 7th Aves.) | A/B/C/D/E/F/V to W. 4th St. | 212-243-1974

Bay Ridge | 6511 11th Ave. (bet. 65th & 66th Sts.) | Brooklyn | N to Fort Hamilton Pkwy. | 718-236-0119

Specializing in "all parts of the pig but the oink", these traditional Italian meat markets/salumerias and their offerings including "hard-to-find cuts" are the "real deal", as is its "wonderful selection" of "housemade sausages" (fresh as well as dried and cured); there's also fresh mozzarella, housemade sauces, oils, vinegars and other imported comestibles, all rung up by "friendly" counter folk; N.B. the Village branch is the original (circa 1940), while the Bay Ridge sibling is newer and bigger.

☑ Fairway ◑ *Major Gourmet Mkt.* 26 | 19 | 17 | M

Harlem | 2328 12th Ave. (bet. 132nd & 133rd Sts.) | 1 to 125th St. | 212-234-3883

W 70s | 2127 Broadway (74th St.) | 1/2/3 to 72nd St. | 212-595-1888

Red Hook | 480-500 Van Brunt St. (Reed St.) | Brooklyn | F/G to Smith/9th Sts. | 718-694-6868

www.fairwaymarket.com

All that "your heart desires" from "staples" "to the exotic" awaits "under one rooftop" at this "competitively priced" UWS gourmet market "workhorse" and its "gargantuan" Harlem and Red Hook outposts; it's a "consummate" shopping "experience" with an "encyclopedic" selection of "beautifully presented" produce, a "cornucopia" of "sublime" smoked fish, a "terrific cheese counter" tended by "well-informed" folks, a "great choice of organic" goods, "hard-to-beat" specialty items ("they've got it somewhere"), "yummy" prepared foods and a "diverse fresh selection" of seafood and "perfectly aged prime beef"; sure, "navigating" the "hectic" "scrum" "is an acquired skill", but those whose perseverance is "rewarded" confirm this is "the way to go."

Falai Panetteria ◑▣ *Baked Goods* 27 | 21 | 21 | M

LES | 79 Clinton St. (bet. Delancey & Rivington Sts.) | F/J/M/Z to Delancey/Essex Sts. | 212-777-8956 | www.falainyc.com

Pastry chef-turned-restaurateur Iacopo Falai opened this "tiny", sunlit Lower East Side panetteria/cafe to purvey his "excruciatingly

QUALITY | DISPLAY | SERVICE | COST

fresh and subtly flavored breads" and "fantastic pastries"; among the "wonderful" sweets on display are cream-filled Italian doughnuts, almond croissants, fruit tarts, and cocoa-dusted nuts and raisins, while savories span *salumi*, homemade pastas and hot panini.

Family Store, The *Specialty Shop*
- | - | - | M

Bay Ridge | 6905 Third Ave. (bet. Ovington Ave. & 69th St.) | Brooklyn | R to Bay Ridge Ave. | 718-748-0207

Living up to its name, this "quaint shop" in Bay Ridge is run by a "friendly" family that "goes out of its way to make you feel welcome" as you browse the store's "authentic" selection of dry goods and "housemade" Middle Eastern and Mediterranean prepared foods; the "delicious" items "vary daily", so "whether you're cooking or letting them do it", this is a "wonderful" option.

Famous Wines & Spirits *Wine/Liquor*
∇ 22 | 17 | 23 | M

Financial District | 40 Exchange Pl. (William St.) | 2/3 to Wall St. | 212-422-4743 | www.famouswines.com

"Convenience is the key to the success" of this "friendly" family-run "sleeper" of a wine shop in the Financial District that proves "reliable vintages" can be found in "unexpected locations"; its "excellent" inventory – and "free tastings every Friday" evening – is a surefire investment for the stockbroker–heavy clientele.

F&B ● *Prepared Food*
20 | 17 | 17 | I

Chelsea | 269 W. 23rd St. (bet. 7th & 8th Aves.) | C/E to 23rd St. | 646-486-4441 | www.gudtfood.com

"Hot dogs with flair" are the main attraction of this "cool" cafe/takeaway joint in Chelsea where Danish franks and brockwurst with "spectacular toppings" make for "wonderful combos", the smoked tofu dog is "veggie heaven" and the frites should trigger an "addiction alert."

Fashion Soup *Soup*
22 | 14 | 18 | M

W 40s | 124 W. 41 St. (bet B'way & 6th Ave.) | 1/2/3/9 to 42nd St. | 212-704-0909 | www.fashionsoup.com

"Lines out the door during lunch hour" tell you "you've hit upon something good" at this Midtown standout for "delicious soup" in flavors that change daily but always include something "for everyone", from "vegetarian to carnivorous", "healthy to not-so-healthy"; for most, the "bread, fruit and cookie" thrown in with each order "somewhat justifies" what would otherwise be a "stylishly high" tab; P.S. local office workers know to "steer clear" when the Bryant Park fashion "tents invade."

Fat Witch Bakery *Baked Goods*
25 | 21 | 21 | M

Chelsea | Chelsea Mkt. | 75 Ninth Ave. (bet. 15th & 16th Sts.) | A/C/E/L to 14th St./8th Ave. | 212-807-1335 | 888-419-4824 | www.fatwitch.com

"Moist", "fudgey", "seriously dangerous brownies" in a variety of flavors (caramel, cherry, cappuccino) cast a spell on Muggles seeking "chocolate fixes" at this Chelsea Market shop, while waistwatchers opt for the three-bite Witch Babies so as not to "eat too many and fall off the broomstick"; yes, prices may be "a bit steep", but "go later in the afternoon" for "goodies at a discount."

Fay Da Bakery ≠ Baked Goods | 19 | 17 | 13 | I |

Chinatown | 191 Center St. (Hester St.) | 6/J/M/N/Q/R/W/Z to Canal St. | 212-966-8934
Chinatown | 82 Elizabeth St. (bet. Grand & Hester Sts.) | B/D to Grand St. | 212-966-8206
Chinatown | 83 Mott St. (Canal St.) | 6/J/M/N/Q/R/W/Z to Canal St. | 212-791-3884
Elmhurst | 86-12 Justice Ave. (B'way) | Queens | B/V to Grand Ave./Newton | 718-205-5835
Flushing | 37-11 Main St. (37th Ave.) | Queens | 7 to Flushing-Main St. | 718-888-9890
Flushing | 41-60 Main St. (Sanford Ave.) | Queens | 7 to Flushing-Main St. | 718-886-4568
Flushing | 46-15 Kissena Blvd. (Juniper Ave.) | Queens | 718-353-0730
www.fayda.com

This Chinese bakery chain satisfies with "fresh" delights from "the best" steamed buns to the "lightest, spongiest cakes", some with "fresh fruit and cream" (a "nice change" from "rich" European desserts), and other "delicacies" "tonged out of the bins by the staff"; service that's "not too attentive" and "no-nonsense" environs don't deter regulars, who confess they "always wind up with bags and bags."

Feast & Fêtes ≠ Caterer | ∇ 27 | 27 | 26 | VE |

E 60s | 20 E. 76th St. (bet. 5th & Madison Aves.) | 212-737-2224 | www.danielnyc.com
By appointment only

It's no surprise that this Upper East Side outfit "knows how to do upscale events" since it's the catering arm of *très* tony eatery Daniel, with chef Daniel Boulud and event planner Jean-Christophe Le Picart heading off-premises to take any fete "over the top"; they match the same "superb" fare served in the restaurant with "impeccable service" that's just as "impressive", and though the pedigree comes "at a cost", fat wallets call it "surprisingly affordable for the quality."

Fellan Florist Flora Galleria ▭ Flowers | ∇ 24 | 23 | 26 | E |

E 60s | 1243 Second Ave. (65th St.) | 6 to 68th St. | 212-421-3567 | 800-335-5267 | www.fellan.com

"Superior service" is a signature of this "reliable" family-owned Upper East Side florist that's been serving the carriage trade for 80 years; "absolutely fresh flowers" imported from around the world "tell the story" of their continued popularity, and if it's a gift basket that's needed, those are available too.

Fermented Grapes ◐▭ Wine/Liquor | 22 | 21 | 24 | M |

Prospect Heights | 651 Vanderbilt Ave. (bet. Park & Prospect Pls.) | Brooklyn | 2/3 to Grand Army Plaza | 718-230-3216 | www.fermentedgrapes.net

You "can't go wrong with any bottle" here vouch Prospect Heights vinophiles of this "neighborhood" wine shop whose "quality-over-quantity" approach results in a "limited but interesting" selection; its "helpful", "down-to-earth" staff and "frequent" tastings with "generous pours" have locals toasting it as a "favorite."

Ferrara Cafe ⦿ ▱ *Baked Goods*

22	23	18	M

Little Italy | 195 Grand St. (bet. Mott & Mulberry Sts.) | 6/J/M/N/Q/R/W/Z to Canal St. | 212-226-6150 | 800-533-6910 | www.ferraracafe.com

"You can smell it blocks away" so fans can't resist a stop at this Little Italy "landmark" offering "nearly every" "old-fashioned" Italian sweet imaginable – "consistently fresh" pastries from "delicious" Napoleons and cannoli to "don't-miss" lobster tails and tiramisu "that never goes wrong" – plus "sodas in every flavor" and "great gelato"; more modern touches are the "tourist lines and high prices", as well as a few gripes that its confections with a "commercial" feel are "more hype than hypnotic."

Fifth Avenue Chocolatiere ▱ *Candy/Nuts*

20	17	20	E

E 40s | 693 Third Ave. (bet. 43rd & 44th Sts.) | 4/5/6/7/S to 42nd St./Grand Central | 212-935-5454

E 50s | 969 Third Ave. (bet. 57th & 58th Sts.) | 4/5/6/N/R/W to 59th St./Lexington Ave. | 212-230-0065

Financial District | 1 NY Plaza (Broad & Water Sts.) | 4/5/6 to 63rd St. | 212-514-8426

800-958-8474 | www.1800chocolate.net

For more than 30 years, this East Side chocolate bastion (with outposts in the East 40s and the Financial District) has been enticing with its "soft, melty" truffles and other all-kosher confections; "fun novelty shapes" are a specialty – think "vampire-bat lollipops" at Halloween, baby bottles for a new arrival, etc. – and they can be customized for parties and office events.

Fifth Avenue Epicure ⦿ *Prepared Food*

▽ 19	21	20	M

Flatiron | 144 Fifth Ave. (bet. 19th & 20th Sts.) | N/R/W to 23rd St. | 212-929-3399

When "home-cooked meals without the hassle" are needed, this Flatiron prepared foods shop is a "popular" option offering a "wide selection" of goods that includes the "best soup" (10 varieties) and "nicely displayed" baked-in-house brownies, pastries and more; even better, it's "not too expensive, despite the neighborhood."

Fika *Coffee/Tea*

▽ 22	16	21	M

W 50s | 41 W. 58th St. (bet. 5th & 6th Aves.) | N/Q/R/W to 57th St. | 212-832-0022 | www.fikanyc.com

"Still a relative secret", this Midtown espresso bar/cafe is a "little Scandinavian" surprise specializing in "amazing coffee" imported from Sweden ("who knew?") along with "delicious" sweet "treats" and a sandwich board featuring gravlax and Swedish meatballs; the streamlined space is too compact for kicking back, but it beats a "trek out to Ikea" for your next lingonberry fix.

Financier Pâtisserie *Baked Goods*

27	25	21	E

Financial District | Winter Garden | 3-4 World Financial Ctr. (Vesey St.) | 1/2/3/A/C to Chambers St. | 212-786-3220

(continued)

Financier Pâtisserie
Financial District | 35 Cedar St. (bet. Pearl & William Sts.) | 2/3 to Wall St. | 212-952-3838 ◐
Financial District | 62 Stone St. (bet. Mill Ln. & William St.) | 2/3 to Wall St. | 212-344-5600 ◐
www.financierpastries.com

Wall Streeters are sweet on this threesome of Financial District patisseries boasting an "amazing selection" of "impeccable" Parisian confections so "gorgeous" it almost "seems wrong to eat them"; among the "delicious delights" are well-known favorites (croissants, éclairs, Napoleons) "done to perfection" plus some "hard-to-find" specialties, a growing menu of savories and "incredible coffee"; prices called "steep" by some are justifiable to others "given the high quality."

Fine & Schapiro ◐ *Deli/Sandwich* | 20 | 15 | 17 | M |
W 70s | 138 W. 72nd St. (bet. B'way & Columbus Ave.) | 1/2/3 to 72nd St. | 212-877-2874 | www.fineandschapiro.com

Noshers crown this "convenient" UWS "old-time deli" (celebrating its 80th year) as a "jewel for kosher dining" thanks to its "large menu" of "fresh, fabulous" "overstuffed sandwiches" and other "classic" offerings that mark it as "one of a dying breed"; maybe "the surroundings are tired" and service is with "an attitude", but it's a treasured "survivor" nonetheless.

First Avenue Wines & Spirits ◐ *Wine/Liquor* | 23 | 19 | 23 | M |
Gramercy | 383 First Ave. (bet. 22nd & 23rd Sts.) | 6 to 23rd St. | 212-673-3600

Oenophiles make a run on the "great buys" at this Gramercy wine shop that stocks "name brands" along with lesser-known labels, including strong showings in California boutique wines as well as producers from Australia, New Zealand and Long Island, all presided over by staffers brimming with "helpful information"; the back room, with its "excellent assortment of fine" vintages, helps bear out the store's reputation as an "out-of-the-way" "gem."

First Ave. Pierogi & Deli Co. ⊄ *Prepared Food* | ▽ 25 | 13 | 19 | I |
E Village | 130 First Ave. (bet. 7th St. & St. Marks Pl.) | L to 1st Ave. | 212-420-9690

"Pierogi and blintz heaven" awaits at this East Village deli that, in addition to the "fantastic" namesake, dishes out "stuffed cabbage, barley mushroom soup" and other stick-to-your-ribs "Ukrainian specialties" deemed "well-worth a trip Downtown"; just ignore the "Soviet-era setting" advise apparatchiks, and focus instead on the "bang for the buck."

Fischer Bros. & Leslie ▭⊄ *Meat/Poultry* | 27 | 19 | 22 | VE |
W 70s | 230 W. 72nd St. (bet. B'way & West End Ave.) | 1/2/3 to 72nd St. | 212-787-1715 | www.fischerbros.com

The "Tiffany's" of glatt butchers is how devotees describe this meat shop/deli that "serves an important Upper West Side niche" with its kosher meats ranked among "the best in the city", as well as its "great" prepared foods; it doesn't take credit cards, so, given the premium pricing, you may want to "cash your paycheck" first; N.B. there's weekly delivery service to Connecticut and New Jersey, as well as the Hamptons in summertime.

Fish Tales *Seafood*   25 | 22 | 25 | M

Cobble Hill | 191A Court St. (bet. Bergen & Wyckoff Sts.) | Brooklyn | F/G to Bergen St. | 718-246-1346 | www.fishtalesonline.com
"It's like the fishing boat is docked in front" of this "small", "outstanding" Cobble Hill market where the "first-class" catches "from the briny deep" are "so fresh" and the staff "super-helpful" and "knowledgeable"; it also offers a "nice selection" of "ready-to-eat specialties", along with "free lemons" and recipes – but just "go early", because the "top-quality" offerings are "limited."

Floralies *Flowers*   ▽ 26 | 23 | 24 | E

E 50s | 122 E. 55th St. (bet. Lexington & Park Aves.) | E/V to Lexington Ave./53rd St. | 212-755-3990 | www.floraliesinc.com
Swank clients like Cartier and Le Bernardin attest to the success of this Murray Hill florist, where owner Kostas creates "unusual" arrangements that are "elegant and stunning without being over-the-top"; he's been in business for more than a quarter-century now, bringing his "reliably beautiful" touch to parties, weddings and big corporate bashes alike.

Flor de Mayo ◗ *Prepared Food*   23 | 14 | 18 | I

W 80s | 484 Amsterdam Ave. (bet. 83rd & 84th Sts.) | 1 to 86th St. | 212-787-3388
W 100s | 2651 Broadway (101st St.) | 1 to 103rd St. | 212-595-2525
"Moist", "tender" rotisserie chicken is the "flavorful" favorite at these "no-frills" Upper West Side takeouts serving an "interesting" array of Peruvian, Chinese and Cuban fare, though while everything's "well cooked", many just "stick with the Latin food"; it all comes "for a song" and the service is "friendly."

Z Florence Meat Market ▣ *Meat/Poultry*   29 | 19 | 28 | M

G Village | 5 Jones St. (bet. Bleecker & W. 4th Sts.) | 1 to Christopher St. | 212-242-6531
Satisfied surveyors consider this "old-time" (circa 1936), sawdust-sprinkled Village butcher among the "best and nicest in the business", known for "exceptional quality", "unparalleled service" and "some terrific bargains" – especially on "their famous Newport steak" – along with more "pricey cuts" and game too; "if you need to rustle up an amazing dinner, start here"; N.B. call ahead and pre-order – you may be spared a long "wait."

Flowers by Reuven *Flowers*   ▽ 27 | 26 | 23 | E

Garment District | 255 West 36th St., 2nd fl. (bet. 7th & 8th Sts.) | 212-564-4740 | www.flowersbyreuven.net
By appointment only
Now ensconced in a second-floor Garment District studio, floral and event designer Reuven and his staff continue to create "drop-dead"

	QUALITY	DISPLAY	SERVICE	COST

tailor-made arrangements and displays for weddings and dinner parties that have garnered them rave reviews "for many years" now (more than three decades); you simply "can't go wrong" according to admirers – who include a sprinkling of celebs and actors – especially given the relatively "fair prices."

Flowers of the World ▭ *Flowers* | ▽ 28 | 29 | 24 | VE |

Financial District | 80 Pine St. (bet. Pearl & Water Sts.) | 2/3 to Wall St. | 212-425-2234
W 50s | 150 W. 55th St. (bet. 6th & 7th Aves.) | N/Q/R/W to 57th St. | 212-582-1850
800-582-0428 | www.flowersoftheworld.com

"Walk by and see" the "truly divine displays" of "superb" flowers in the windows of this "innovative" Financial District bloomery and its West 50s offshoot, known for their "breathtaking arrangements"; those who droop over the "insane prices" perk up at the thought of ready-to-go "inexpensive mini-bouquets that are a lifesaver" for the forgetful.

NEW Flurt *Ice Cream* | 21 | 19 | 18 | M |

Gramercy | 284 Third Ave. (22nd St.) | 6 to 23rd St. | 212-777-6177

One of the "new breed" of "pinkberry doppelgangers" sweeping the city, this "adorable" new Gramercy Park frozen yogurt stop "delivers" on its promise of "fresh" product crowned with "high-quality fruit" and other toppings; wallet-watchers note it's a bit "expensive for what you get", but those seeking to "satisfy a craving" "without major guilt" don't seem to mind.

Flying Pigs Farm ▭ *Meat/Poultry* | 28 | 19 | 25 | E |

See Greenmarket; for more information, call 518-854-3844 | www.flyingpigsfarm.com

Pigs do fly – off the shelves of a Greenmarket booth – in the form of "consistently outstanding pork" from this upstate farm; among the "high-quality, natural" "porcine products" are "flavorful" roasts, bacon and sausage ("love the smoked shanks", "superb liverwurst") while poultry lovers crow FPF's chickens and eggs are "the best they've ever eaten"; the wares are "certainly not cheap", but "approachable employees" can provide "great recipes" along with the meat; N.B. open seasonally.

Fong Inn Too Inc. ●⊅ *Specialty Shop* | ▽ 18 | 8 | 10 | I |

Chinatown | 46 Mott St. (bet. Bayard & Pell Sts.) | 6/J/M/N/Q/R/W/Z to Canal St. | 212-962-5196

Talk about specialization: this Chinatown food shop sells only 27 products, including "excellent bean curd", soy milk, "fresh rice noodles", "fried taro cakes" and egg roll skins, all at "cheap" prices and "made on-site"; it's mainly a restaurant supplier, which might explain the sometimes "nonexistent service."

Food Emporium ● *Major Gourmet Mkt.* | 16 | 14 | 12 | M |

E 50s | 405 E. 59th St. (1st Ave.) | 4/5/6/N/R/W to 59th St./Lexington Ave. | 212-752-5836
E 50s | 969 Second Ave. (51st St.) | 6 to 51st St. | 212-593-2224

(continued)

(continued)

Food Emporium

E 60s | 1175 Third Ave. (68th St.) | 6 to 68th St. | 212-249-6778
E 80s | 1450 Third Ave. (82nd St.) | 4/5/6 to 86th St. | 212-628-1125
Murray Hill | 200 E. 32nd St. (3rd Ave.) | 6 to 33rd St. |
212-686-0260
TriBeCa | 316 Greenwich St. (Duane St.) | 1 to Franklin St. |
212-766-4598
Union Sq | 10 Union Sq. E. (14th St.) | 4/5/6/L/N/Q/R/W to 14th St./
Union Sq. | 212-353-3840
W 40s | 452 W. 43rd St. (bet. 9th & 10th Aves.) | A/C/E to 42nd St./
Port Authority | 212-714-1414
W 60s | 2008 Broadway (68th St.) | 1/2/3 to 66th St./Lincoln Ctr. |
212-787-0012
W 90s | 2430 Broadway (90th St.) | 1/2/3 to 96th St. | 212-873-4031
www.thefoodemporium.com
Additional locations throughout the NY area

"If the cupboard is bare", this Manhattan-wide franchise serves as an "all-purpose" "convenience" stocked with a "utilitarian selection" of "standard supermarket" goods; there are efforts afoot for this chain to go more "gourmet", with the more "upscale" Bridgemarket emporium below the Queensboro Bridge leading the way, but fulminating foes still feel they "leave much to be desired" and come off as "pricey for fairly basic stuff."

Food For Thought   *Prepared Food*   ▽ 21 | 16 | 15 | M

Chelsea | 130 W. 25th St. (bet. 6th & 7th Aves.) | F/V to 23rd St. |
212-929-4689 | www.foodforthoughtnyc.com

Whether it's for a wedding, cocktail party or corporate gala, this "easy to work with" event planner/caterer is the choice for those looking for an affordable option; the 7,000-sq.-ft. Chelsea headquarters showcases a cafe and tasting room where potential clients can peruse the possibilities.

Foods of India   *Herbs/Spices*   23 | 16 | 17 | I

Murray Hill | 121 Lexington Ave. (bet. 28th & 29th Sts.) | 6 to 28th St. |
212-683-4419

Chances are you'll find "something wonderful that you have never tried before" at this Murray Hill spice emporium that's a "must-visit" if you're cooking Indian food at home; it's a "very inexpensive" source of a "more than impressive" variety of curry pastes and powders, and "always worth a look" if you're a fan of South Asian flavors.

Foragers Market ▣ *Specialty Shop*   22 | 22 | 22 | E

Dumbo | 56 Adams St. (Front St.) | Brooklyn | F to York St. | 718-801-8400 |
www.foragersmarket.com

A "well-edited", "high-quality" selection "makes it a pleasure to shop" at this Dumbo market whose "pricey" "gourmet" goodies – everything from artisanal cheeses and charcuterie to produce and sandwiches – are in keeping with the store's mantra of 'Seasonal, Regional, Organic'; it also strives to be as green as possible in its packaging and operations, so although some dismiss it as "trendy", others say it's a "splendid" choice.

Foremost Caterers *Caterer*

| 24 | 22 | 22 | VE |

Moonachie | 65 Anderson Ave. (Romeo St.), NJ | 201-664-2465 | www.foremostcaterers.com

For "strictly" glatt kosher catering, consensus calls this firm "the absolute best" at providing "interesting ideas" and food so "fine" you may not "believe that it's kosher"; it's considered "reliable" for events of "any size", from personal gatherings to large-scale dos at the Waldorf-Astoria or the United Nations, and boasts a "top-shelf staff" so "attentive" it's "like having your mother plan the party – without the baggage."

Formaggio Essex *Cheese/Dairy*

| ▽ 26 | 22 | 22 | E |

LES | Essex Street Market | 120 Essex St. (bet. Delancey & Rivington Sts.) | 212-982-8200 | www.formaggio-kitchen.com

"The best of Cambridge comes to NYC" via this Essex Street Market arrival, an offshoot of a beloved Boston institution whose "cramped" stall is "easy to miss but worth looking for" given its "small but fantastic" lineup of cheeses, plus "fabulous" salumi, condiments and sandwiches; it's gained an enthusiastic following, thanks in part to its "friendly", "knowledgeable" staffers – and the "amazing samples" they hand out.

Fortunato Bros. ◐ ▤ ⊭ *Baked Goods*

| 25 | 23 | 19 | M |

Williamsburg | 289 Manhattan Ave. (Devoe St.) | Brooklyn | L to Graham Ave. | 718-387-2281

A "homey" holdover from pre-hipster days, this "full-service" Italian bakery/sidewalk cafe in Williamsburg can supply "everything your sweet tooth ever desired", ranging from a "nice selection of miniature pastries" and "always-fresh" cookies (the pignoli are "tops") to "heavenly" ricotta cheesecake, spumoni and gelato; order coffee to "give you a boost" and help stave off the sugar shock.

Franchia ◐ *Coffee/Tea*

| 24 | 23 | 22 | M |

Murray Hill | 12 Park Ave. (bet. 34th & 35th Sts.) | 6 to 33rd St. | 212-213-1001 | www.franchia.com

Murray Hill's "serene" scene, this "exotic Korean tearoom" and "healthy" restaurant is a "Zen-like" retreat serving a profusion of "unusual and delectable" teas (wild green, white, oolong, herbal, et al.) in "lovely" surroundings that mix modern simplicity with a regal ceiling mural and other ornate elements; its gift shop vends loose leaves and accessories like ceramic teasets, and the "cozy" top floor is available for bridal showers and other private affairs.

NEW Frankly Wines *Wine/Liquor*

| - | - | - | M |

TriBeCa | 66 W. Broadway (bet. Murray & Warren Sts.) | 1/2/3/A/ C to Chambers St. | 212-346-9544 | www.franklywines.com

A "frankly fabulous addition to the neighborhood" according to locals, this new TriBeCa wine boutique uncorks a "small but thoughtfully selected" range of labels highlighting small producers and wines from the Southern Hemisphere (Australia and New Zealand, Argentina and Chile, etc.); those who've discovered it give a thumbs-up to the fair prices and "perfect recommendations" from its able staff.

	QUALITY	DISPLAY	SERVICE	COST

Frank's Gourmet Market *Specialty Shop* ▽ 21 | 18 | 17 | M

Washington Heights | 807 W. 187th St. (bet. Cabrini Blvd. & Ft. Washington) | A to 190th St. | 212-795-2929

This Washington Heights grocery got its start as "a neighborhood butcher shop" nearly 60 years ago and it's since "mushroomed" into a 7,000-sq.-ft. "gourmet" market that retains a "homey atmosphere" to go with its "decent selection" of fish, meats, cheeses, produce and prepared foods; it's handy "for those who live way Uptown", but opinions vary regarding the prices (moderate vs. "outrageous").

Fraser-Morris Fine Foods *Prepared Food* ▽ 26 | 25 | 21 | VE

Carroll Gardens | 191 Columbia St. (bet. Degraw & Sackett Sts.) | Brooklyn | F/G to Carroll St. | 718-643-3507

In business since 1947, this bakery/caterer relocated from the Upper East Side to an out-of-the-way corner of Carroll Gardens a few years back, and continues to produce the *"très chere"* brownies, muffins, pies, rugalach and such that go into the gift baskets that are its specialty; it also turns out sandwiches and the like, all made on-premises, and patrons can unwind in the cafe area offering a few seats.

NEW FreeFoods *Prepared Food* ▽ 25 | 22 | 19 | E

W 40s | 18 W. 45th St. (5th Ave.) | 7 to 5th Ave. | 212-249-4529 | www.freefoodsnyc.com

Midtown office workers hail the arrival of this stylish new player on the lunchtime take-out/delivery scene providing "wonderfully fresh", "beautiful" sandwich-and-salad selections and "innovative" high-end prepared foods made from mostly organic ingredients; however, despite its moniker, the "pricey" goods here are far from free.

Fresco by Scotto on the Go *Prepared Food* 24 | 19 | 19 | E

E 50s | 40 E. 52nd St. (bet. Madison & Park Aves.) | E/V to 5th Ave./53rd St. | 212-754-2700 | www.frescoonthego.com

"Media" and "finance" types favor this family-operated Midtown take-out wing of next-door Fresco by Scotto, a provider of "excellent", "gourmet" Italiana, from salads and sandwiches to signature grilled pizzas; it's the "perfect" (albeit "pricey") quick-lunch option, plus partisans praise it as a "first-rate" caterer.

Fresh Bites ● *Prepared Food* 20 | 16 | 18 | M

W 50s | 1394 Sixth Ave. (57th St.) | N/Q/R/W to 57th St. | 212-245-3327

"Fair" prices for "decent", "healthy and quick" soups, sandwiches and such have customers walking away "satisfied" from this tiny Midtown take-out joint, a staple come lunch hour; for the zip code "the prices can't be beat", and it's also a convenient weekday option for office workers wanting a "quick bite before a stroll through Central Park."

Z FreshDirect *Major Gourmet Mkt.* 23 | 14 | 21 | M

LIC | 23-30 Borden Ave. (23rd Ave.) | Queens | 7 to Vernon Blvd. | 866-283-7374 | www.freshdirect.com

A "godsend" for "convenience", this Queens-based "online grocer" allows shoppers to browse its "pain-free" website and order an

	QUALITY	DISPLAY	SERVICE	COST

array of "surprisingly high-quality" gourmet goods for "prompt delivery" with "a click of a mouse", offered at "amazing overall value"; customers can count on the "freshest" selection of produce, deli items, "first-rate" "artisanal cheeses", "fabulous" "ready-to-bake breads", "restaurant-quality" prepared foods ("pretend you cooked"), and "reliably" "excellent cuts of meat" and seafood; now that its "growing pains" are "rapidly improving" the "addicted" declare it "sure beats schlepping."

NEW Friedman's Delicatessen ● Deli/Sandwich

| 21 | 15 | 16 | M |

Chelsea | Chelsea Mkt. | 75 Ninth Ave. (bet. 15th & 16th Sts.) | A/C/E/L to 14th St./8th Ave. | 212-929-7100 | www.friedmansdeli.com

From the owners of the Pastrami Queen comes this new Chelsea Market deli with an "old-school" vibe, where all of the usual suspects – "piled-high" sandwiches, "tasty" "real"-deal chopped liver, matzo ball soup, knishes, kreplach – are dispensed in digs bedecked with black-and-white posters of 1940s-era delis; the prices are strictly up-to-date, but jumbo portions mean you can "grab tonight's dinner and tomorrow's lunch at the same time."

Friend of a Farmer ● Baked Goods

| 21 | 19 | 18 | M |

Gramercy | 77 Irving Pl. (bet. 18th & 19th Sts.) | 4/5/6/L/N/Q/R/W to 14th St./Union Sq. | 212-477-2188 | www.friendofafarmernyc.com

Among the "wholesome" baked goods at this Gramercy Park "faux farmhouse" are "tasty muffins and pies" and "hearty scones and cakes" that seemingly "just came out of mom's oven", plus "fresh", "reliable" breads ("excellent honey whole wheat") that'll "cure what ails ya"; the less-impressed cite "overpriced" wares and call this farmer "no friend of mine", but "long waits" prove he's plenty popular.

Gail Watson Custom Cakes ▣ Baked Goods

| – | – | – | VE |

Garment District | 335 W. 38th St., 11th fl. (8th Ave.) | 212-967-9167 | 877-867-5088 | www.gailwatsoncake.com
By appointment only

Garment District–based wedding cake baker Gail Watson turns out "beautiful", elaborately crafted gâteaux decorated not only with the usual sugar flowers but also with candy sea shells, marzipan and fresh fruits; she offers bridal favors too (e.g. monogrammed cookies, custom candy trays, cast-sugar boxes holding jordan almonds), and, for those tying the knot outside of the NYC area, she sells 'cake kits' with instructions and tools to pass along to your local baker.

Garden, The Specialty Shop

| ▽ 24 | 21 | 21 | M |

Greenpoint | 921 Manhattan Ave. (Kent St.) | Brooklyn | G to Greenpoint Ave. | 718-389-6448 | www.thegardenfoodmarket.com

"A veritable oasis" in Greenpoint, this "organic market" "offers a nice range of upscale natural" products (the beer selection is a particular strength) as well as "scrumptious bakery items" and "tasty" prepared foods; "Manhattan expats" aver "you can find almost anything here", meaning there's really "no need to go to the city."

NEW Gardenia Organic *Flowers*

W Village | 526 Hudson St. (W. 10th St.) | 1 to Christopher St. | 646-688-5753 | www.gardeniaorganic.com

When you want to splurge on flowers "with a clear conscience", shoot over to this "friendly" new West Village petal peddler that claims to be the city's first organic, eco-conscious florist, creating stylish bouquets that are pesticide-free and environmentally sound right down to the recycled tissue paper they're wrapped in; there's also a selection of Fair Trade gifts such as candles and jewelry.

Garden of Eden Gourmet Market ● ▣ *Major Gourmet Mkt.*

Chelsea | 162 W. 23rd St. (bet. 6th & 7th Aves.) | 1 to 23rd St. | 212-675-6300

Union Sq | 7 E. 14th St. (bet. 5th Ave. & University Pl.) | 4/5/6/L/N/Q/R/W to 14th St./Union Sq. | 212-255-4200

W 100s | 2780 Broadway (107th St.) | 1 to 110th St. | 212-222-7300

Brooklyn Heights | 180 Montague St. (bet. Clinton & Court Sts.) | Brooklyn | 2/3/4/5/M/N/R/W to Borough Hall/Court St. | 718-222-1515

www.edengourmet.com

Paradise if you "want to avoid crowds", this gourmet market foursome fits "everything you need" in the way of "higher-end" goods into its "fairly small shops", harboring a "pretty display" of "above-average" baked goods, a cheese section with "lots of imports", "reliably high-quality produce", "exceptional" meat and poultry and an "amazing selection of hard-to-find" specialty items ("if they don't have it, you don't need it"); despite "high prices", their status as "local favorites" keeps them "hanging in there against the big boys."

Garnet Wines & Liquors ● ▣ *Wine/Liquor*

E 60s | 929 Lexington Ave. (bet. 68th & 69th Sts.) | 6 to 68th St. | 212-772-3211 | www.garnetwine.com

Still the ruby standard for "super prices" on "high- and low-end items" "from around the world", this "well-stocked" Upper East Side "staple" is often "crowded" with bargain-hunters looking for (and finding) the latest and greatest in scotches, champagne and French and Italian wines; one caveat: the staffers, while "knowledgeable", are sometimes "on the brusque side."

Gary Null's Uptown Whole Foods ● *Health Food*

W 80s | 2421 Broadway (89th St.) | 1 to 86th St. | 212-874-4000 | www.garysmarketplace.com

Not to be confused with the superstar natural supermarket chain, this more modest but still "wonderful" Upper West Side health-fooder is an "independent" market with a hands-on owner, "knowledgeable" staff and an "abundant variety" of products; still, there are some complaints about the "budget-taxing" prices, "narrow aisles" and "cramped" conditions, not to mention produce whose quality "varies."

	QUALITY	DISPLAY	SERVICE	COST

Gauchas *Prepared Food*

∇ 25	16	19	I

E 90s | 1748 First Ave. (bet. 90th & 91st Sts.) | 4/5/6 to 86th St. |
212-360-6400 | www.gauchasnyc.com

Beloved for its "flaky" empanadas, aka "fresh, wonderful" "pockets of
goodness", this Yorkville eatery/take-out shop is also applauded for its
assortment of Argentinean prepared foods including "flavorful"
steaks; locals laud it as the "next best thing to a trip to South America."

NEW Get Fresh ● *Prepared Food*

-	-	-	E

Park Slope | 370 Fifth Ave. (bet. 5th & 6th Sts.) | Brooklyn | F/M/R to
9th St./4th Ave. | 718-360-8469 | www.getfreshnyc.com

On a mission to make home-cooking easier and greener, this new
Park Slope market/meal preparation service carries a seasonally
changing array of ready-to-cook meals, including plenty of kid-
friendly options; the ingredients – humanely raised meats and
mostly organic and local produce – are prepped, measured and
boxed together with instructions in eco-friendly packaging;
N.B. delivery is free throughout Brooklyn with a $20 order (which
can be placed online), and available for a fee to Manhattan and
other parts of the city; plans are afoot for an indoor/outdoor cafe.

Giant Big Apple Beer Co. *Beer*
(fka B & E Quality Beverage)

-	-	-	M

Woodside | 32-31 57th St. (bet. Northern Blvd. & 32nd Ave.) |
Queens | G/R/V to Northern Blvd. | 212-243-6812

A veritable "beer paradise", this "wonderful", recently renamed
Woodsider "has it all" when it comes to suds, offering "everything
from kegs to hard-to-find microbrews", with a particular emphasis
on hard ciders and Belgian, German and English brews; its impressive inventory also includes soft drinks, ice and snacks, presided
over by a "pleasant" staff, and there's convenient delivery too – in
short, it's a "great source" for "party"-throwers.

Gimme! Coffee ▣✍ *Coffee/Tea*

∇ 27	22	24	I

NEW NoLita | 228 Mott St. (bet. Prince & Spring Sts.) | 6 to Spring St. |
212-226-4011 ●
Williamsburg | 495 Lorimer St. (bet. Grand & Powers Sts.) | Brooklyn |
L to Lorimer St. | 718-388-7771
www.gimmecoffee.com

"Plenty of Williamsburg hipsters" caffeinate at this "simple yet excellent coffee shop", the loftlike urban outpost of an Upstate college-
town chain that air-roasts its own beans to give you joe "of outstanding
quality" in a "great variety of blends"; they also decant "really strong
espresso" topped with "cool" crema filigree, and their global selection is available online in one- or five-pound bags; N.B. the NoLita
branch opened post-Survey.

Glaser's Bake Shop ✍ *Baked Goods*

21	16	21	I

E 80s | 1670 First Ave. (bet. 87th & 88th Sts.) | 4/5/6 to 86th St. |
212-289-2562 | www.glasersbakeshop.com

"Old Yorkville lives" at this "no-frills" "time capsule", "family-run"
since 1902 and still boasting "original tile floors and wooden display

cases" brimming with Mitteleuropean desserts that "don't break the bank"; "loyal customers" love what they consider NYC's "best black-and-whites", as well as "delicious rolls", "great Danish", butter cookies and "wonderful" apple turnovers – and find the staff's "warm" welcomes as "comforting" as the "baked treats."

Glazier Group on Location   *Caterer* | - | - | - | E |

G Village | Twenty Four Fifth | 24 Fifth Ave. (bet. 8th & 9th Sts.) | R/W to 8th St. | 212-505-8000
Seaport | Bridgewaters | 11 Fulton St. (bet. East River Piers & Seaport Plaza) | 2/3 to Fulton St. | 212-608-7400
www.theglaziergroup.com

As a "sizable" "player" in the "field of restaurant-backed catering", this Downtown outfit produces "beautifully done" events at eateries like the Strip House and Michael Jordan's The Steak House, as well as major venues like Bridgewaters and Twenty Four Fifth; matching up stylish spaces, pro service and classic American cuisine, it's considered by those in-the-know as "one of the best" in its "niche."

☑ Glorious Food   *Caterer* | 25 | 25 | 24 | VE |

E 70s | 504 E. 74th St. (bet. East River & York Ave.) | 6 to 77th St. | 212-628-2320 | www.gloriousfood.com

"They'll go over the top for you" at this "premier" UES caterer, which "knows every trick in the book" about "making an event special", from "elegant" and "tasty" cuisine to "the fanciest" presentation ("they're not called 'glorious' for nothing"); the "superb" staff includes "the best-looking waiters in town" and leaves "no detail overlooked", whether the occasion's a "dinner for 12" or a mega institutional affair, so though most "wouldn't call it a bargain", "you get what you pay for."

NEW Gnarly Vines ☽ *Wine/Liquor* | - | - | - | M |

Fort Greene | 350 Myrtle Ave. (bet. Adelphi St. & Carlton Ave.) | Brooklyn | C to Lafayette Ave. | 718-797-3183 | www.gnarlyvines.com

Those who've discovered this new Fort Greene shop are calling it a "great new" local vino source that "focuses on small producers", "wines with personality" and those from sustainably raised vineyards; owned by a "terrific guy who really knows his" stuff, it features rotating displays of artwork and regular tastings.

Godiva Chocolatier ▣ *Candy/Nuts* | 22 | 24 | 20 | E |

E 40s | Grand Central Terminal | main concourse (42nd St. & Vanderbilt Ave.) | 4/5/6/7/S to 42nd St./Grand Central | 212-808-0276
E 50s | 560 Lexington Ave. (bet. 50th & 51st Sts.) | 6 to 51st St. | 212-980-9810
E 60s | 793 Madison Ave. (67th St.) | 6 to 68th St. | 212-249-9444
Financial District | 21 Fulton St. (South St.) | J/M/Z to Fulton St. | 212-571-6965 ☽
Financial District | 33 Maiden Ln. (Nassau St.) | J/M/Z to Fulton St. | 212-840-8990
W 40s | 1460 Broadway (bet. 41st & 42nd Sts.) | 1/2/3/7/N/Q/R/S/W to 42nd St./Times Sq. | 212-840-6758

(continued)

Godiva Chocolatier

W 40s | 30 Rockefeller Plaza, concourse level (bet. 49th & 50th Sts.) | B/D/F/V to 47-50th Sts./Rockefeller Ctr. | 212-246-0346
W 50s | Shops at Columbus Circle | 10 Columbus Circle (bet. 58th & 60th Sts.) | 1/A/B/C/D to 59th St./Columbus Circle | 212-823-9462 ◗
W 50s | 52 W. 50th St. (bet. 5th & 6th Aves.) | B/D/F/V to 47-50th Sts./Rockefeller Ctr. | 212-399-1875
W 70s | 245 Columbus Ave. (bet. 71st & 72nd Sts.) | B/C to 72nd St. | 212-787-5804 ◗
800-946-3482 | www.godiva.com
Additional locations throughout the NY area

This bonbon behemoth's "reliable", "verrry smooth" morsels packed in that trademark "fancy gold box" guaranteed to "light up faces" make it a "popular" "favorite" among "mass-market" contenders; however, the less-impressed call it the "Campbell's Soup of Belgian chocolate", citing "waxy", "too-sweet" output that doesn't measure up to the city's burgeoning "boutique" producers', but even critics concede the "convenience" of its ubiquitous "golden storefronts" is hard to beat when "you need a quick gift."

Golden Fung Wong
Bakery Shop ◗⇄ *Baked Goods*

18 | 12 | 14 | I

Chinatown | 41 Mott St. (Pell St.) | 6/J/M/N/Q/R/W/Z to Canal St. | 212-267-4037

"Traditional Chinese wedding pastries", "delicious BBQ pork buns", "airy sponge cakes", mooncakes and – yes – fortune cookies have made this small Chinatown bakery a "longtime staple" for its loyal fan base; however, trendier types would like to see the "old-style" setting get an "upgrade."

Good & Plenty To Go *Prepared Food*

22 | 19 | 19 | M

W 40s | 410 W. 43rd St. (bet. 9th & 10th Aves.) | A/C/E to 42nd St./Port Authority | 212-268-4385

"The name says it all" at this "friendly", "tiny" Theater District take-out shop in the Manhattan Plaza complex, where regulars fight "maddening crowds" at lunch for the likes of bourbon-glazed ham, jambalaya, peanut-butter brownies and plenty of other "reliably good" comfort dishes; overall, it's a "real standout – if you can find it."

Gorilla Coffee ◗▱ *Coffee/Tea*

24 | 17 | 19 | I

Park Slope | 97 Fifth Ave. (Park Pl.) | Brooklyn | 2/3 to Bergen St. | 718-230-3243 | www.gorillacoffee.com

"Ggrrrrrr": if you're "looking for a robust brew", this Park Slope "neighborhood hang" doesn't monkey around as it supplies "rich, organic Fair Trade coffee" (house-roasted "in small batches") and "nuclear-powered espresso", matched with ape-pealing baked goods; the "cool employees" and "funky, relaxed" vibe are a "perfect fit" for the "requisite Brooklyn hipsters" in residence, who'd "die without" "a jolt" to "start off the day."

	QUALITY	DISPLAY	SERVICE	COST

Gorzynski Ornery Farm ⊄ *Produce* | 27 | 22 | 27 | M |

See Greenmarket; for more information, call 845-252-7570

"As good as it gets" – "from arugula" to "root veggies" – is how exuberant herbivores describe the goods from this "quintessential Greenmarket stand", where the "tremendous range" of "100% organic" produce is overseen by "genius" Upstate farmer John Gorzynski ("no 'ornery' guy"), who can advise you on "how to cook the weird vegetable you're waving" around; the offerings "may seem expensive" but for the "taste and freshness" they're "well-worth the price."

Gotham Gardens ▭ *Flowers* | ▽ 24 | 25 | 23 | E |

W 70s | 325 Amsterdam Ave. (bet. 75th & 76th Sts.) | 1/2/3 to 72nd St. | 212-877-8908 | www.gothamgardens.com

"Otherworldly" is how Upper Westsiders describe the "exquisite", "excitingly different arrangements" that "often incorporate the unexpected" at this "dependable" floral boutique; exotic plants plus "a selection of unusual objects" like imported vases, potpourri, candles, soaps and such help "make it a favorite" for gift-buyers, while brides-to-be and party-throwers can enlist full-service decor design.

Gotham Wines & Liquors ◐▭ *Wine/Liquor* | 22 | 17 | 18 | M |

W 90s | 2517 Broadway (94th St.) | 1/2/3 to 96th St. | 212-932-0990 | www.gothamwines.com

"Prices that can't be beat" keep "bargain-hunters" and others "coming back" to this Upper West Side "neighborhood" wine stop that's extolled for its offerings in the under-$15 range, as well as for its "great"variety (some 300) of kosher wines; backers believe the "inventory is worth" putting up with the somewhat "insular" service; P.S. "get on the mailing list for additional discounts."

Gourmet Garage ● *Major Gourmet Mkt.* | 20 | 17 | 15 | M |

E 60s | 301 E. 64th St. (bet. 1st & 2nd Aves.) | F to Lexington Ave./63rd St. | 212-535-6271
E 90s | 1245 Park Ave. (96th St.) | 6 to 96th St. | 212-348-5850
G Village | 117 Seventh Ave. S. (bet. Christopher & W. 10th Sts.) | 1 to Christopher St. | 212-699-5980
SoHo | 453 Broome St. (Mercer St.) | 6 to Spring St. | 212-941-5850
W 90s | 2567 Broadway (96th St.) | 1/2/3 to 96th St. | 212-663-0656
www.gourmetgarage.com

Shoppers "in a hurry" who pull in to this "solid" mini-chain discover a "less-crowded alternative" that "hits on the major categories" of "gourmet goodies" with its "interesting selection" of cheeses, "decent baked goods", "healthy" prepared foods, "creative" deli counter and even "surprisingly good coffee"; but in spite of "generally" "high quality", naysayers are "not impressed" with what they consider a "limited" lineup that "certainly isn't cheap."

Grab Specialty Foods *Specialty Shop* | ▽ 24 | 24 | 21 | M |

Park Slope | 438 Seventh Ave. (bet. 14th & 15th Sts.) | Brooklyn | F to 7th Ave. | 718-369-7595 | www.grabspecialtyfoods.com

This "lovely little shop" in the South Slope supplies the locals with artisanal cheeses and charcuterie, baked goods (including loaves from Amy's Bread and cupcakes from Baked), produce and bottled and jarred items like vinegars, oils and jams; it's no longer the only "gourmet" option in the area, but it distinguishes itself with its knowledgeable staffers who can help when "you're in a hurry and need to impress"; N.B. it's also a good choice for picking up a gift (think cheese boards, knives, picnic supplies), and does custom baskets too.

Grace's Marketplace ●☀🖃 *Major Gourmet Mkt.* | 24 | 20 | 18 | VE |

E 70s | 1237 Third Ave. (71st St.) | 6 to 68th St. | 212-737-0600 | www.gracesmarketplace.com

Lucky "locals" who "don't want to travel" "could happily spend all day" at this "friendly" Eastsider, "one of the original NYC gourmet markets" and still a "winner" whose "narrow aisles" are graced with "basically everything you could possibly need", including "highly praised" baked goods, "fresh produce", "prime meats", a "wide selection" of cheeses and "top-notch" deli items and prepared foods ("who needs to cook?"); a few fret that it's "expensive" and "too cramped for comfort", but consensus says the "excellent quality", "convenience" and "eternally cheerful service" are "totally worth it."

Gracious Home 🖃 *Cookware* | 25 | 18 | 19 | E |

E 70s | 1217-1220 Third Ave. (70th St.) | 6 to 68th St. | 212-517-6300
W 60s | 1992 Broadway (67th St.) | 1 to 66th St./Lincoln Ctr. | 212-231-7800 ●
800-338-7809 | www.gracioushome.com

"A NYC institution", this "dependable" duo is an Uptown "favorite" for its kitchen sections' "amazing array" of cookware, appliances, utensils and accessories, "basic" to "high-end", all at "un-gracious" prices that have some warning "better get a second mortgage"; service from the "knowledgeable" staff can be "spotty", and its "narrow aisles" try some surveyors' patience, but nonetheless it remains a "favorite" "one-stop" source "for almost anything"; N.B. they now charge $6.50 for delivery.

Gracious Thyme Catering *Caterer* | - | - | - | E |

Harlem | 2191 Third Ave. (bet. 119th & 120th Sts.) | 6 to 116th St. | 212-873-1965 | www.graciousthyme.com

Classic French cuisine inspires the "elegant array of dishes" from this Harlem-based "full-service caterer" and off-site event planner, whose "superb food" is "presented beautifully" enough to do justice to a reception at the Whitney or a U.N. state dinner; also "a delight" is the "extremely gracious staff", which goes all-out to turn festivities of any size into a "wonderful" thyme.

Gramercy Fish 🖃 *Seafood* | 24 | 20 | 22 | E |

Gramercy | 383 Second Ave. (bet. 22nd & 23rd Sts.) | 6 to 23rd St. | 212-213-5557

There's "always a catch" at this "terrific" Gramercy fishmonger, but of the "flavorful, succulent" variety – i.e. "sparklingly fresh" seafood and "homemade" prepared dishes; "accoutrements such as sauces and produce" and a "helpful" staff are other reasons it's a "go-to" for locals, who agree that "for a tiny place, it delivers" – but "at a high price."

	QUALITY	DISPLAY	SERVICE	COST

❷ Grandaisy Bakery *Baked Goods*   29 | 21 | 20 | M

SoHo | 73 Sullivan St. (bet. Broome & Spring Sts.) | C/E to Spring St. | 212-334-9435 ⬛

NEW W 70s | 176 W. 72nd St. (Amsterdam Ave.) | 1/2/3 to 72nd St. | 646-274-1607

www.grandaisybakery.com

It goes by a new name after an ownership split in 2007, but otherwise "nothing's changed" at this "small" SoHo Italian bakery (formerly the original Sullivan St. Bakery), whose "to-die-for" artisanal breads are voted "the best in the city"; some say "pane pugliese and filore are the two best loaves", but it's hard to pick favorites among its "unforgettable" offerings from flatbreads and focaccialike pizzas to panini and sweets; given such "fresh, wonderful" goods, no one minds much if the service "can be lacking" and the decor's "nothing fancy"; N.B. the Upper West Side outpost opened post-Survey.

Grande Harvest Wines ● *Wine/Liquor*   23 | 21 | 21 | E

E 40s | Grand Central Terminal | main concourse (42nd St. & Vanderbilt Ave.) | 4/5/6/7/S to 42nd St./Grand Central | 212-682-5855 | www.ghwines.com

Commuters browse the "attractive displays" then "grab a bottle" before boarding at this Grand Central wine boutique that's an on-the-go oenophile's "delight" given its "limited but decent" selections from France and California as well as its strong showing of single-malt scotches; the staff "impresses", but know that the "handy" location translates to "expensive" prices.

Grand Wine & Liquor ●⬛ *Wine/Liquor*   ▽ 25 | 17 | 17 | I

Astoria | 30-05 31st St. (30th Ave.) | Queens | N/W to 30th Ave. | 718-728-2520 | www.grandwl.com

"If you can't find it here, it's probably discontinued or doesn't exist" say fans of this "great" Astoria source of unusual wines from Greece, Eastern Europe, Asia and even Peru; low prices and proximity to the N train compensate nonlocals who make the trek to Queens; N.B. they deliver to Manhattan on Saturday mornings.

Great Performances *Caterer*   24 | 23 | 22 | VE

SoHo | 304 Hudson St. (Spring St.) | C/E to Spring St. | 212-727-2424 | www.greatperformances.com

A "very professional" performer after nearly 30 years in the business, this SoHo caterer/event planner is "one of the best" at staging indoor or outdoor affairs – often on an epic scale – with "attentive" service and "fantastic food"; it boasts in-house contracts with Jazz at Lincoln Center, BAM, Sotheby's and numerous other notables, though a few razz the "commercial" style of so "big an operation"; P.S. it now has its own organic farm upstate, intended to supply pristine produce to be used in its "fabulous" fare.

Greene Grape, The ● *Wine/Liquor*   24 | 23 | 24 | M

Financial District | 55 Liberty St. (bet. B'way & Nassau St.) | J/M/Z to Fulton St. | 212-406-9463

(continued)

Greene Grape, The

Fort Greene | 765 Fulton St. (bet. S. Oxford & S. Portland Sts.) | Brooklyn | C to Lafayette Ave. | 718-797-9463
www.greenegrape.com

These separately owned wine sources are run by "committed" staffers who impart advice on the "outstanding" examples of low-production labels; the larger Fort Greene original is "great", while Manhattanites rate the Financial District spot a "godsend" in an area "bereft of similar shops"; there are also "incredible" boutique spirits at both.

NEW Greene Grape

| ▽ | 24 | 21 | 21 | E |

Provisions ☕ *Specialty Shop*

Fort Greene | 753 Fulton St. (S. Portland Ave.) | Brooklyn | C to Lafayette Ave. | 718-233-2700 | www.greenegrape.com

"New in the neighborhood" but already hailed as a "great addition" to Fort Greene, this cute-as-a-button gourmet market from the owners of the Greene Grape wine store "up the block" has an eco-friendly, locavore bent, stocking a variety of "fresh", mostly organic and local produce, farmstead cheeses, fish, meat and craft beers; staffers who "know their stuff" are icing on the cake.

Z Greenmarket *Produce*

| 26 | 23 | 23 | M |

E 40s | Dag Hammarskjold Plaza | 2nd Ave. & 47th St. | 212-788-7476 | Wed., Year-round

E 80s | St. Stephens | E. 82nd St. bet. 1st. & York Aves. | 212-788-7476 | Sat., July–Nov.

E 90s | 92nd St. | 1st Ave. bet. 92nd & 93rd Sts. | 212-788-7476 | Sun., July–Nov.

E 90s | Mt. Sinai Hospital | E. 99th St. bet. Madison & Park Aves. | 212-788-7476 | Fri., July–Nov.

E Village | St. Mark's Church | 2nd Ave. & 10th St. | 212-788-7476 | Tues., May–Dec.

E Village | Tompkins Sq. | Ave. A & 7th St. | 212-788-7476 | Sun., Year-round

Financial District | Bowling Green | Battery Pl. & B'way | 212-788-7476 | Tues./Thurs., Year-round

Financial District | City Hall Park | B'way bet. Chambers & Warren Sts. | 212-788-7476 | Fri., July–Dec.

Financial District | Downtown Path | Church & Vesey Sts. | 212-788-7476 | Tues./Thurs., April–Dec.

Financial District | Greenwich St. bet. Chambers & Duane Sts. | 212-788-7476 | Wed., Apr.–Dec.; Sat., Year-round

Harlem | Harlem Hospital | Lenox Ave. bet 136th & 137th Sts. | 212-788-7476 | Thurs., July–Nov.

Murray Hill | 2nd Ave. & 33rd St. | 212-788-7476 | Sat., June–Dec.

Union Sq | Union Sq. | B'way & 17th St. | 212-788-7476 | Mon./Wed./Fri./Sat., Year-round

Inwood | Isham St. bet. Cooper St. & Seaman Ave. | 212-788-7476 | Sat., Year-round

Washington Heights | 175th St. | B'way & 175th St. | 212-788-7476 | Thurs.; June–Nov.

W 50s | Rockefeller Ctr. | 50th St. & Rockefeller Plaza | 212-788-7476 | Thur./Fri./Sat., July–Oct.

(continued)

	QUALITY	DISPLAY	SERVICE	COST

(continued)

Greenmarket

W 50s | 57th St. | 57th St. & 9th Ave. | 212-788-7476 | Wed., Apr.–Dec.; Sat., Year-round

W 60s | Tucker Sq. | Columbus Ave. & 66th St. | 212-788-7476 | Thurs./Sat., Year-round

W 70s | 77th St. | Columbus Ave. & 77th St. | 212-788-7476 | Sun., Year-round

W 90s | 97th St. | Columbus Ave. & 97th St. | 212-788-7476 | Fri., Year-round

W 100s | Columbia | B'way bet. 114th & 115th Sts. | 212-788-7476 | Thurs./Sun., Year-round

W 100s | Stranger's Gate | Central Park W. & 106th St. | 212-788-7476 | Sat., July–Nov.

W Village | Abingdon Sq. | Hudson & 12th Sts. | 212-788-7476 | Sat., Year-round

Bronx | Poe Park | Grand Concourse & 192nd St. | 212-788-7476 | Tues., July–Nov.

Bronx | Bronx Borough Hall | Grand Concourse bet. 156th & 158th Sts. | 212-788-7476 | Tues., July–Nov.

Bronx | Lincoln Hospital | Morris Ave. & 148th St. | 212-788-7476 | Tues./Fri., July–Nov.

Borough Park | 14th Ave. bet. 49th & 50th Sts. | Brooklyn | 212-788-7476 | Thurs., July–Nov.

Carroll Gardens | Carroll Park | Carroll St. bet. Court & Smith Sts. | Brooklyn | 212-788-7476 | Sun., June–Nov.

Downtown | Court & Montague Sts. | Brooklyn | 212-788-7476 | Tues./Sat., Year-round; Thurs., Apr.–Dec.

Flatbush | P.S. 139 Schoolyard | Beverly & Cortelyou Rds. | Brooklyn | 212-788-7476 | Sat., June–Nov.

Fort Greene | Fort Greene Park | Washington Park bet. Dekalb Ave. & Willoughby St. | Brooklyn | 212-788-7476 | Sat., Year-round

Greenpoint | McCarren Park | Driggs Ave. & Lorimer St. | Brooklyn | 212-788-7476 | Sat., Year-round

Park Slope | Grand Army Plaza | Prospect Park, NW entrance | Brooklyn | 212-788-7476 | Sat., Year-round

Sunset Park | Sunset Park | 4th Ave. bet. 59th & 60th Sts. | Brooklyn | 212-788-7476 | Sat., July–Nov.

Williamsburg | B'way & Havemeyer St. | Brooklyn | 212-788-7476 | Thurs., July–Nov.

Windsor Terrace | 15th St. & Prospect Park W. | Brooklyn | 212-788-7476 | Wed., May–Oct.

Astoria | 31st Ave. bet. 12th & 14th Sts. | Queens | 212-788-7476 | Wed., July–Nov.

Glendale | Atlas Park | Cooper Ave. & 80th St. | Queens | 212-788-7476 | Sat., June–Nov.

Jackson Heights | 34th Ave. bet. 77th & 78th Sts. | Queens | 212-788-7476 | Sun., May–Nov.

LIC | 48th Ave. & Vernon Blvd. | Queens | 212-788-7476 | Sat., May–Nov.

Staten Island | St. George at Borough Hall parking lot | Hyatt & St. Mark's Sts. | 212-788-7476 | Sat., May–Nov.

www.cenyc.org

"One of the best things to have happened in NYC", this "wonderful" network of markets throughout the five boroughs ("Union Square is the biggest") gives top chefs, gourmands and the "think-globally, eat-locally" set the chance to select from "flowers and fruits piled high" plus regional produce "picked that day" – all the "finest, from farmer to consumer" – as well as "fresh" meats, seafood, cheese, baked goods, jams and other "seasonal goodies"; indeed, it's a veritable "feast for the eyes and palate" – "what would NYers do without it?"

Greenwich Produce ❶ *Produce* | 25 | 23 | 20 | E |

E 40s | Grand Central Mkt. | Lexington Ave. (43rd St.) | 4/5/6/7/S to 42nd St./Grand Central | 212-490-4444

With an "extra-convenient" location in two booths at opposite ends of Grand Central Market, this produce purveyor "makes waiting for the train a pleasure" as you "pick up last-minute fruit and vegetable needs" or restock your pantry with "gourmet items" like dried nuts, mushrooms and edible flowers; sure, "prices can be high, but the quality lives up to what you pay."

Grom ❶ *Ice Cream* | 27 | 21 | 19 | E |

NEW G Village | 233 Bleecker St. (Carmine St.) | A/B/C/D/E/F/V to W. 4th St. | 212-206-1738

W 70s | 2165 Broadway (bet. 76th & 77th Sts.) | 1 to 79th St. | 646-290-7233

www.grom.it

Lines that "snake out the door" and "curve down Broadway" are the calling card of this "tiny" outpost of an Italian chain scooping "absolutely exquisite" artisanal gelati, sorbets and granitas in "flavors that pop" – perhaps because they're made on-premises with "unparalleled-quality" ingredients, such as lemons imported from Sicily and pistachios from the Piedmont; yes, it's priced like "gold", but "at least it's cheaper than airfare" to Italy; N.B. the Greenwich Village location opened post-Survey.

NEW Grove 🖃 *Flowers* | - | - | - | E |

W Village | 617 Hudson St. (bet. Jane & W. 12th Sts.) | 1/2/3 to 14th St. | 212-673-8300 | www.grovenyc.com

Fresh flowers, furniture and home decor items and a signature line of home fragrances, all under one roof, is the concept at this new West Village boutique opened by a former beauty executive; sure to be a selling point is the back 'flower bar' where customers can sit and choose from a menu of cut blooms and seasonal bouquets, then sip a cup of tea while waiting for them to be assembled.

G.S. Food Market 🗗 *Seafood* | ▽ 19 | 18 | 13 | M |

Chinatown | 250 Grand St. (Chrystie St.) | B/D to Grand St. | 212-274-0990

'G.S.' could stand for "good selection" at this Chinatown grocery/ seafood market stocking unusual fruits and veggies – durians to mangosteens – an array of fresh and frozen fin fare, noodles, sauces and sundries that make its aisles "so much fun to walk through"; prices that "beat the supermarkets" are another reason most conclude it's "worth the visit", notwithstanding the staff's limited English.

	QUALITY	DISPLAY	SERVICE	COST

Güllüoglu ▭ *Baked Goods* — — — M

Sheepshead Bay | 1985 Coney Island Ave. (bet. Ave. P & Kings Hwy.) | Brooklyn | B/Q to Kings Hwy. | 718-645-1822 | www.gulluoglubaklava.com

Straight out of Istanbul comes this Sheepshead Bay branch of a 130-plus-year-old Turkish dessert company, which specializes in "can't-be-beat" honey-drenched baklava in its many shapes and permutations; there are also savory treats like filo layered with spinach or kashkaval cheese, poppy-seed pastries and, naturally, thick Turkish coffee (by the cup only).

Gustiamo ▭ *Specialty Shop* ▽ 23 22 25 E

Bronx | 1715 W. Farms Rd. (Sheridan Expy.) | 2/5 to 174th St. | 718-860-2949 | www.gustiamo.com

"The best of the best Italian" is how surveyors sum up the inventory at this Bronx-based source for "high-quality" "gourmet products" imported from The Boot and overseen by a staff that "couldn't be nicer or more responsive"; given its out-of-the-way location, many shop via its website, whose extensive, "expensive" selection of artisanal foods and sophisticated gift baskets is browsable by category or region, from Abruzzo to the Veneto.

Guy & Gallard *Coffee/Tea* 20 17 17 M

Garment District | 1001 Sixth Ave. (bet. 37th & 38th Sts.) | 1/2/3/A/C/E to 34th St./Penn Station | 212-730-0010

Garment District | 245 W. 38th St. (bet. 7th & 8th Aves.) | A/C/E to 42nd St./Port Authority | 212-302-7588

Garment District | 339 Seventh Ave. (29th St.) | 1 to 28th St. | 212-279-7373

Garment District | 469 Seventh Ave. (bet. 35th & 36th Sts.) | 1/2/3/A/C/E to 34th St./Penn Station | 212-695-0006

Murray Hill | 120 E. 34th St. (Lexington Ave.) | 6 to 33rd St. | 212-684-3898 ●

Murray Hill | 180 Madison Ave. (34th St.) | 6 to 33rd St. | 212-725-2392

Murray Hill | 475 Park Ave. S. (bet. 31st & 32nd Sts.) | 6 to 33rd St. | 212-447-5282

www.guyandgallard.com

Granted, "there are better" coffees and teas in town, but this local chain is always there for a "quick" "caffeine jolt" if you're "grabbing early-morning" joe "to go", and it follows through with "light lunch" fare like sandwiches, salads, bagels and baked goods; naysayers are galled at the "movie-theater prices", but most maintain these guys "can definitely compete."

Häagen Dazs ● *Ice Cream* 24 18 17 M

Chinatown | 53½ Mott St. (Bayard St.) | A/C/E to Canal St. | 212-571-1970 ▱

E 60s | 1188 First Ave. (bet. 64th & 65th Sts.) | 6 to 68th St. | 212-288-5200

Garment District | Penn Station | 110 Penn Plaza (32nd St.) | 1/2/3/A/C/E to 34th St./Penn Station | 212-630-0321

NoHo | 655 Broadway (bet. Bleecker & Bond Sts.) | B/D/F/V to B'way/Lafayette St. | 212-260-8490

Seaport | Pier 17 | 89 South St. (Fulton St.) | 2/3 to Fulton St. | 212-587-5335

(continued)

Häagen Dazs
W 60s | 187 Columbus Ave. (bet. 68th & 69th Sts.) | 1 to 66th St./ Lincoln Ctr. | 212-787-0265
W 70s | 263 Amsterdam Ave. (72nd St.) | 1/2/3 to 72nd St. | 212-787-7165
W 100s | 2905 Broadway (113th St.) | 1 to 116th St. | 212-662-5265
www.haagendazs.com

A "delicious and reliable standby", this national chain's "classic", "rich" ice cream comes in "sinfully decadent" flavors that are "packed with luscious calories"; wallet-watchers, miffed by "small portions" and "not-so-friendly" service, point out that "you can buy a pint cheaper at the supermarket", but for many it's "always a treat" on a "summer day in the hot city."

Haas Company Inc. 🖾 *Cookware*

25	18	20	M

Chelsea | 11 W. 25th St. (5th Ave.) | R/W to 23rd St. | 212-242-2044
"You need it, they got it" say surveyors of this Chelsea "hidden gem" of a cookware store that's "worth seeking out" for "excellent"-quality supplies favored by "professional chefs"; it specializes in hard-to-find items as well as products by All-Clad, Kyocera and Epicurean, and is also a "great place to browse" for "bargains"; N.B. closed weekends.

Hale & Hearty Soups *Soup*

22	17	17	M

Chelsea | Chelsea Mkt. | 75 Ninth Ave. (bet. 15th & 16th Sts.) | A/ C/E/L to 14th St./8th Ave. | 212-255-2400
E 40s | 22 E. 47th St. (bet. 5th & Madison Aves.) | 4/5/6/7/S to 42nd St./Grand Central | 212-557-1900
E 40s | 466 Lexington Ave. (45th St.) | 4/5/6/7/S to 42nd St./ Grand Central | 212-599-7220
E 40s | 685 Third Ave. (bet. 43rd & 44th Sts.) | 4/5/6/7/S to 42nd St./ Grand Central | 212-681-6460
E 60s | 849 Lexington Ave. (bet. 64th & 65th Sts.) | 6 to 68th St. | 212-517-7600
Garment District | 462 Seventh Ave. (35th St.) | 1/2/3/A/C/E to 34th St./Penn Station | 212-971-0605
W 40s | 49 W. 42nd St. (bet. 5th & 6th Aves.) | 7/B/D/F/V to 42nd St./ Bryant Park | 212-575-9090
W 50s | 30 Rockefeller Plaza, dining concourse (bet. 49th & 50th Sts.) | B/D/F/V to 47-50th Sts./Rockefeller Ctr. | 212-265-2117
W 50s | 55 W. 56th St. (bet. 5th & 6th Aves.) | N/Q/R/W to 57th St. | 212-245-9200
Brooklyn Heights | 32 Court St. (Remsen St.) | Brooklyn | 2/3/4/5/ M/N/R/W to Borough Hall/Court St. | 718-596-5600
www.haleandhearty.com
Additional locations throughout the NY area

"Take stock" of the "wide variety" of "enticing" soups that "rotate often" at this "reliable" if "pricey" chain that also earns souper-latives for "fresh" salads and "unique sandwiches"; those with special diets laud the "handy ingredients lists", and, despite the "boot camp–style queue system and yelling staff", it's the "favorite stop" of many "on a cold, wintry day."

	QUALITY	DISPLAY	SERVICE	COST

Hampton Chutney
Company ◐ *Prepared Food*
23 | 18 | 19 | M

SoHo | 68 Prince St. (bet. Crosby & Lafayette Sts.) | C/E to Spring St. | 212-226-9996

W 80s | 464 Amsterdam Ave. (bet. 82nd & 83rd Sts.) | 1 to 86th St. | 212-362-5050

www.hamptonchutney.com

"Completely delicious" dosas and trademark housemade chutneys mean seats are "hard to come by" at this twosome serving "tasty" "spins" on traditional Indian offerings along with more authentic examples; "models flock" to the SoHo outpost, while the Upper West Side site tends to be "overrun with children" thanks to the store's kiddie corner.

Han Ah Reum Market ◐ *Specialty Shop*
22 | 13 | 11 | M

Garment District | 25 W. 32nd St. (bet. 5th & 6th Aves.) | B/D/F/N/Q/R/V/W to 34th St./Herald Sq. | 212-695-3283 ▣

Flushing | 141-40 Northern Blvd. (Bowne St.) | Queens | 7 to Flushing-Main St. | 718-358-0700

Flushing | 156-40 Northern Blvd. (Roosevelt Ave.) | Queens | 7 to Flushing-Main St. | 718-888-0005

Flushing | 29-02 Union St. (29th Ave.) | Queens | 7 to Flushing-Main St. | 718-445-5656

www.hanahreum.com

"There's something for everyone" at this quartet of Korean specialty markets (one in the Garment District and three in Flushing) where "just walking through" the "endless array of products, logically arranged" – it's "tops for fish", "fresh fruits and veggies" – is enough to "inspire a non-cook to start"; it's "not always user-friendly" but the "prices are right."

H & H Bagels ◐▣⌀ *Bagels*
26 | 15 | 17 | M

W 40s | 639 W. 46th St. (12th Ave.) | A/C/E to 42nd St./Port Authority | 212-595-8000

W 80s | 2239 Broadway (80th St.) | 1 to 79th St. | 212-595-8003

800-692-2435 | www.hhbagels.com

"Iconic bagels" earn these West Side "mainstays" their "well-deserved" rep as a "benchmark" for "fat", "perfectly crafted" rings with "just the right consistency" to be "addictive", served "hot from the ovens" "round the clock"; despite "sparse shops" with "no seating" and "DIY toppings", the multitudes gladly "pony up" "premium prices" (approaching "a buck" a pop) 'cause this is what "makes living in NYC a privilege"; P.S. to avoid "frustrating lines" hit the 46th Street outpost, an "easy" hop "off the West Side Highway."

H & H Midtown Bagels East ◐▣ *Bagels*
25 | 17 | 19 | I

E 80s | 1551 Second Ave. (bet. 80th & 81st Sts.) | 4/5/6 to 86th St. | 212-734-7441 | www.hhmidtownbagelseast.com

"Off-the-hook" bagels – "big and chewy" but "crisp on the outside" – are dispensed by a "friendly" crew at this 24/7 eatery/caterer, which, as the "sign out front states", has no tie to its crosstown competitor; it's a "madhouse on weekends" and some say prices are "through the roof" for the genre, but most don't mind much given its spheres rated among "the best on the UES."

Harlem Tea Room *Coffee/Tea*   25 | 23 | 23 | M

Harlem | 1793 Madison Ave. (bet. E. 117th & E. 118th Sts.) | 6 to 116 St. | 212-348-3471 | www.harlemtearoom.com

"You'll want to stay all day" at this petite tearoom, a "low-profile" "gem in Harlem" where the plush drapes and "classy" copper-top bar create a "warm vibe" for enjoying an intriguing international choice of stepped brews, with "mouthwatering" cakes and tarts on the side; to confirm it's "a real find", check out the "wonderful" spread of scones, sandwiches and desserts during Saturday afternoon's "high tea."

Harlem Vintage ●◖▣ *Wine/Liquor*   ▽ 28 | 29 | 26 | M

Harlem | 2235 Frederick Douglass Blvd. (bet. 120th & 121st Sts.) | A/B/C/D to 125th St. | 212-866-9463 | www.harlemvintage.com

"Well worth the trip Uptown", this "superior" Harlem "jewel" of a wine shop spotlights its selections in a "lovely room" and boasts a "knowledgeable" staff and "fabulous" Saturday tastings; small producers (as well as labels by vintners of color) are its specialty, and the offerings are so "wonderful", even if it had "neighborhood competition", most would still consider it "not to be missed."

Hawthorne Valley Farm *Produce*   28 | 23 | 25 | M

See Greenmarket; for more information, call 518-672-7500 ext. 250 | www.hawthornevalleyfarm.org

There's "no need to venture into Whole Foods" when this Greenmarket stall (by way of a community-supported farm in Columbia County) offers its own array of "excellent" organic and biodynamic foods, from "fresh produce" to "great dairy products" – particularly the "luscious yogurt" – grass-fed beef and pork and baked goods that are tasty, if "a little hippie-ish"; don't overlook the eight different kinds of sauerkraut and other fermented delights – their "version of kimchi is fun."

Health & Harmony ●◖▣ *Health Food*   ▽ 26 | 20 | 22 | M

W Village | 470 Hudson St. (bet. Barrow & Grove Sts.) | 1 to Christopher St. | 212-691-3036

It might be small, but this West Village health shop has an "excellent selection of healthy foods of all types", including vegan options, sugar-free baked goods and Atkins fare, though the produce section is "somewhat limited"; the "attentive" and "helpful" staff – including the resident dietician (call ahead to check his availability) – can guide you through the "wide variety of products", some of which can be hard to find elsewhere.

Health Nuts ●◖▣ *Health Food*   21 | 14 | 18 | M

E 40s | 835 Second Ave. (bet. 44th & 45th Sts.) | 4/5/6/7/S to 42nd St./ Grand Central | 212-490-2979

E 60s | 1208 Second Ave. (bet. 63rd & 64th Sts.) | F to Lexington Ave./ 63rd St. | 212-593-0116

(continued)

(continued)

Health Nuts

W 70s | 2141 Broadway (bet. 75th & 76th Sts.) | 1/2/3 to 72nd St. |
212-724-1972

W 90s | 2611 Broadway (bet. 98th & 99th Sts.) | 1/2/3 to 96th St. |
212-678-0054

Bayside | Bay Terrace | 211-35 26th Ave. (Bell Blvd.) | Queens |
718-225-8164

"Just be careful you don't knock something over" in this chain of
stuffed-to-the-gills health food markets, where you "can always find
what you need", even if it means digging through some "confusing"
displays; while some feel "produce is not its forte", most find it a "reliable" source for "competitively priced" "healthy dry goods."

Heights Chateau ● *Wine/Liquor*   25 | 24 | 23 | M

Brooklyn Heights | 123 Atlantic Ave. (bet. Clinton & Henry Sts.) |
Brooklyn | 2/3/4/5/M/N/R/W to Borough Hall/Court St. |
718-330-0963 | www.heightschateau.com

Brooklyn Heights wine enthusiasts find it easy to "treasure" this
"neighborhood" standby whose "spirited" staff dispenses "wonderful advice" on any of its 2,000 labels (plus a bountiful array of tequi-
las and single-malt scotches); not only can you expect to walk away
with the "perfect" bottle "to suit your budget", but their case discounts can make for "real bargains."

Heights Prime Meats *Meat/Poultry*   ▽ 24 | 15 | 21 | E

Brooklyn Heights | 59 Clark St. (bet. Henry & Hicks Sts.) | Brooklyn |
2/3 to Clark St. | 718-237-0133

Locals rely on this Brooklyn Heights butcher and deli for a variety of
fresh and aged prime meats, poultry (including some organic birds)
and sausages, as well as "tasty sandwiches"; overall, "you'll find
what you need" and the quality's "good across the board", so most
are willing to stomach the "$$$" prices.

Hendricks Wine & Liquors ● *Wine/Liquor*   19 | 19 | 22 | M

Bay Ridge | 7624 Third Ave. (77th St.) | Brooklyn | R to 77th St. |
718-748-1690

Since 1935, this "service-oriented" Bay Ridge boozery has offered a
"great selection" of traditional liquors, with a focus on whiskeys, co-
gnacs, bourbons and vodkas; for serious oenophiles, its "friendly"
owner scouts out hard-to-find wines and boutique vintages, with a
more general focus on bottles from LI and NY State, Greece, Spain,
Australia and South America – 3,000 labels in all, even though the
"store's not very big."

Hershey's Times Square ● 🔲 *Candy/Nuts*   18 | 23 | 15 | M

W 40s | 1593 Broadway (48th St.) | N/R/W to 49th St. | 212-581-9100 |
800-454-7737 | www.hersheys.com

Think "Hershey's theme park without the roller coasters" and you've
got this Times Square "slice of Americana" whose "cool" Vegas-like
facade featuring 3-D props, steam machines and neon threatens to
outshine the inventory of "classic" "mass-produced chocolates" (in-
cluding some "limited-edition" offerings) and "interesting gifts" in-

side; its mix of sugar-fueled kids, "tourists getting a bellyful" and "slow" service can add up to "madhouse" conditions – but nonetheless die-hards declare the overall experience "just plain fun."

Hinsch's ⌀ *Ice Cream*

| 22 | 20 | 22 | I |

Bay Ridge | 8518 Fifth Ave. (bet. 85th & 86th Sts.) | Brooklyn | R to 86th St. | 718-748-2854

"Old Brooklyn at its most authentic", this "absolute classic" of a parlor is a Bay Ridge "landmark" serving up the "freshest" ice cream in 12 flavors, "homemade" chocolates and "the best egg creams"; the "very special" ambiance and "sweet, helpful" staff make it a "great family place" and a must-stop for those who are nostalgic for the "malt shops of yore."

Holland Court Meat Market *Meat/Seafood*

| ∇ 24 | 19 | 18 | E |

E 90s | 1423 Lexington Ave. (93rd St.) | 6 to 96th St. | 212-289-8330

An Upper East Side "standby" for more than a half-century, this small, old-time butcher shop/fish market is a "good neighborhood" purveyor of "quality" seafood and fresh, cut-to-order meats (including cold cuts, sausage and other charcuterie), as well as cheeses and other delicatessen fare; the selection is somewhat "limited", however, and it can be "pricey."

Hong Keung Seafood & Meat Market *Seafood*

| 22 | 15 | 15 | I |

Chinatown | 75 Mulberry St. (bet. Bayard & Canal Sts.) | 6/J/M/N/Q/R/W/Z to Canal St. | 212-571-1445

Although the fin fare is sold without fanfare outside this unassuming Chinatown storefront, the "quality" seafood "is literally swimming" and the prices "can't be beat"; Chinese sauces, noodles, dried mushrooms and other imported dry goods are also available, and while the staff speaks mostly Cantonese, the fish are labeled in English, so if all else fails, pointing usually works.

Hong Kong Supermarket *Specialty Shop*

| 20 | 14 | 11 | I |

Chinatown | 109 E. Broadway (Pike St.) | F to E. B'way | 212-227-3388
Sunset Park | 60-23 Eighth Ave. (61st St.) | Brooklyn | N to 8th Ave. | 718-438-2288 ●
Elmhurst | 82-02 45th Ave. (B'way) | Queens | G/R/V to Elmhurst Ave. | 718-651-3838 ●
Flushing | 37-11 Main St. (bet. 37th & 38th Aves.) | Queens | 7 to Flushing-Main St. | 718-539-6868 ●

"Chock-full of every single Asian product you can imagine and some that you can't", this market mini-chain "carries all the essentials" for Eastern cooking plus "quality meats, vegetables", seafood, "condiments, nuts and all manner of scary, pickled things"; plus, "you can't beat the price", although you can expect a "chaotic", "no-frills" setup.

Hot & Crusty ● *Baked Goods*

| 15 | 15 | 15 | I |

E 40s | Grand Central Terminal | main concourse (42nd St. & Vanderbilt Ave.) | 4/5/6/7/S to 42nd St./Grand Central | 212-687-6054

(continued)

(continued)

Hot & Crusty

E 60s | 1201 Second Ave. (63rd St.) | F to Lexington Ave./63rd St. | 212-753-2542

E 80s | 1276 Lexington Ave. (bet. 86th & 87th Sts.) | 4/5/6 to 86th St. | 212-426-2111

Garment District | Penn Station | Seventh Ave. (32nd St.) | 1/2/3/ A/C/E to 34th St./Penn Station | 212-279-6450

W 80s | 2387 Broadway (bet. 87th & 88th Sts.) | 1 to 86th St. | 212-496-0632 ⊟

W 100s | 2720 Broadway (bet. 104th & 105th Sts.) | 1 to 103rd St. | 212-666-4900

www.hotandcrusty.com

"When you're hungry, they're around" shrug surveyors about this "unfortunately named" chain that "caters to the masses" with its "run-of-the-mill" baked goods, sandwiches, soups and such, fodder for "quick" and inexpensive breakfasts or lunches on the move; "boring" it may be, but "when you're running for the train" it's hard to beat.

Hot Bialys ⊟ *Bagels*

| 25 | 15 | 18 | I |

Kew Gardens | 116-63 Queens Blvd. (78th Ave.) | Queens | E/F to Kew Gardens/Union Tpke. | 718-544-0900

"Now *that's* a bialy" rave reviewers of this "unassuming" Kew Gardens veteran's "delicious" eponymous product – they're "huge and come in many varieties" – and "the bagels are good too"; the "lack of decor" may be a turnoff for some, but connoisseurs willing to "travel 15 miles" don't give it a second thought because this is "the real thing."

House of Spices ⊡ *Herbs/Spices*

| 24 | 18 | 18 | M |

Flushing | 127-40 Willets Point Blvd. (Northern Blvd.) | Queens | 7 to Shea Stadium | 718-507-4600 | www.hosindia.com

This Flushing warehouse brimming with Indian imports is a "total 'wow' when you walk in" thanks to its "fresh", fragrant selection of just about every spice "you can imagine", plus other comestibles from rice, beans and nuts to pickles, pastes, chutneys and frozen meals; much of its business is wholesale, but individuals willing to trek to its "inconvenient" industrial location are rewarded with "unique" finds at "great prices" – "if you can't find it here, you can't find it anywhere."

NEW How Sweet It Is ◗⊡ *Baked Goods*

| - | - | - | M |

LES | 157 Allen St. (bet. Rivington & Stanton Sts.) | F to 2nd Ave. | 212-777-0408 | www.howsweetitispastry.com

The aroma is "incredible" at this new LES retail bakery/cake studio, which is garnering a reputation for "gorgeously delicious sweets" baked up by its two owners, one a former pastry chef at the River Café and the other an ex-food editor at *Martha Stewart Living*; the bakery dishes out sophisticated pastries and coffee while the studio (a few doors down) creates custom gateaux for weddings and other special occasions by appointment only.

	QUALITY	DISPLAY	SERVICE	COST

Hudson Yards Catering *Caterer/Events* ▽ 24 | 21 | 22 | E

Chelsea | Hudson Yards | 640 W. 28th St., 8th fl. (bet. 11th & 12th Aves.) |
212-488-1500 | www.hycnyc.com
By appointment only

Linked to restaurateur Danny Meyer's dominion (Union Square Cafe,
Gramercy Tavern, The Modern and more), this "up-and-coming"
West Chelsea caterer takes a chef-driven tack to supply globe-
spanning cuisines matched with top-flight service; its warehouselike
HQ can accommodate guests in a private dining area (The Hudson
Room) or a massive contiguous events space (The Tunnel at the
Waterfront), and it continues to shore up its relationships with a
host of off-site corporate clients.

Hungarian Pastry Shop ●♦♥ *Baked Goods* 22 | 18 | 18 | I

W 100s | 1030 Amsterdam Ave. (111th St.) | 1 to 110th St. | 212-866-4230
"Many a Columbia student wouldn't have graduated" without the
"mile-high pastries", "top-notch hamentaschen", "heated poppy
seed strudel" and "crisp, buttery butterflies" washed down with
"unlimited cups of coffee" at this "charming" Morningside Heights
Hungarian bakery/cafe, "a neighborhood icon for decades"; still,
many maintain the eats are "secondary" to the "relaxed" old-world
vibe ("Nietzsche would love it").

Hung Chong Import ♥ *Cookware* 19 | 13 | 13 | I

Chinatown | 14 Bowery (bet. Doyers & Pell Sts.) | 6/J/M/N/Q/R/
W/Z to Canal St. | 212-349-3392
"Budget-minded" chefs in search of woks, cleavers, bamboo steam-
ers and other "authentic" Asian implements and dishware (like
restaurant-style floral serving platters and chopsticks) hit this
Chinatown kitchenware shop with an "old NYC" feel where the
"awesome selection" overcomes less-than-impressive service and
looks; thrifty types tout the sale table on the street "where you can
sometimes also buy jade or socks."

Iavarone Bros. 🖃 *Prepared Food* 25 | 24 | 22 | M

Maspeth | 6900 Grand Ave. (69th St.) | Queens | 718-639-3623
Middle Village | 75-12 Metropolitan Ave. (75th St.) | Queens | M to
Middle Vill./Metropolitan Ave. | 718-326-0510
www.ibfoods.com
When you need a "homemade dinner you don't have to make",
these family-run Italian specialty shops in Queens supply patrons
with a "great variety" of prepared foods, as well as "on-the-mark"
items "you can't always find in the city", including cheeses, pastas
and more; a "great butcher counter" featuring housemade sausages
(fresh and dry-cured) is another draw, closely followed by the "gracious service" that keeps you "coming back."

Ideal Cheese 🖃 *Cheese/Dairy* 27 | 21 | 23 | E

E 50s | 942 First Ave. (52nd St.) | 6 to 51st St. | 212-688-7579 |
800-382-0109 | www.idealcheese.com
A "popular place" in Sutton Place, this "high-grade cheesemonger" is
"sure to entice" with its "wide variety" of "excellent" fromages "from

around the world", presented with "ample tasting opportunities" by an "informed" team; it's also "ideal" for spreads and charcuterie, so expect "to go home with a bagful of goodies."

☑ Il Laboratorio del Gelato ☞🎁 *Ice Cream* | 28 | 19 | 20 | E |

LES | 95 Orchard St. (Broome & Delancy Sts.) | F/J/M/Z to Delancey/Essex Sts. | 212-343-9922 | www.laboratoriodelgelato.com

"Fantasies do come true" at this LES "shrine to frozen confections", voted No. 1 for Ice Cream in this Survey, where the "irresistible" gelato is "ambrosia" to devotees; while some find it "ridiculously expensive", virtually all agree the "fantastic, imaginative flavors" "ranging from rich to subtle" are "simply the best" and well "worth the trek Downtown", "the wait on line" and "every penny" spent.

Indiana Market & Catering *Caterer* | ▽ 26 | 25 | 27 | M |

Garment District | 333 W. 39th St., Suite 404 (bet. 8th & 9th Aves.) | 1/2/3/7/N/Q/R/S/W to 42nd St./Times Sq. | 212-736-3531 | www.indiananyc.com

"Meticulous" "attention to detail" marks this "top-notch" UWS caterer/event planner, whose "simpatico staff" is "able to flex to special needs" as they organize off-site events "from inception through execution", covering everything from venue hunting to arranging for flowers and musicians; "innovative" "culinary treats" help "transform any location into a dream party", and they top off the "enthusiastic" performance with "amazing bang for the buck."

Indian Bread Co. ● *Prepared Food* | 21 | 13 | 17 | I |

G Village | 194 Bleecker St. (bet. MacDougal St. & 6th Ave.) | A/B/C/D/E/F/V to W. 4th St. | 212-228-1909 | www.indianbreadco.com

Equally "quick" and "yummy" are the meals turned out in this Village Indian take-out/delivery champ whose "tasty" range of stuffed flatbreads, 'naanwiches' (the "perfect analogue to panini"), soups and other inexpensive "delights" suit on-the-go fans just fine; what's more, heat-seekers can get the goods "spiced up."

Insomnia Cookies ●☞ *Baked Goods* | - | - | - | M |

G Village | 50 W. Eighth St. (6th Ave.) | R/W to 8th St. | 212-673-2629 | www.insomniacookies.com

Jumbo-size cookies and brownies served warm into the wee hours – with the option of delivery – is the surefire concept behind this new Greenwich Village bakery; an outpost of a national franchise, it's strategically located in the heart of NYU country.

Integral Yoga Natural Foods ● *Health Food* | 24 | 17 | 19 | M |

W Village | 229 W. 13th St. (bet. 7th & 8th Aves.) | 1/2/3 to 14th St. | 212-243-2642 | 800-343-1735 | www.integralyoganaturalfoods.com

"Bulk buyers" get "a warm and fuzzy feeling" at this West Village health food market offering a "solid" selection of "high-quality" "loose grains, nuts", "whole spices" and more, as well as "hard-to-find" produce, prepared foods, vitamins and beauty products; though the space is "cramped", a "meditative" atmosphere prevails, thanks in part to the "relaxed, helpful" staffers, many of whom seem to have just come from a "yoga session" in the attached studio.

	QUALITY	DISPLAY	SERVICE	COST

In Vino Veritas ● *Wine/Liquor* ▽ 25 | 22 | 22 | M

E 70s | 1375 First Ave. (74th St.) | 6 to 77th St. | 212-288-0100

It's true: having occupied its spot since the repeal of Prohibition, this "cute" Upper Eastsider is one of NYC's oldest wine and liquor stores, still decked out in vintage decor featuring original stained-glass windows, Murano lamps and cast-iron grapes; comprising its "well-edited" yet "eclectic" inventory are roughly 1,200 Italian vintages, more than a few "bargains" among them, and there's a "helpful" staff on hand to offer suggestions.

Irving Farm Coffee Co. ▣ *Coffee/Tea* 22 | 20 | 19 | M

NEW **G Village** | 56 Seventh Ave. (bet. 13th & 14th Sts.) | A/C/E/L to 8th Ave./14th St. | 212-475-5200

71 Irving Place Coffee & Tea Bar ●▣ *Coffee/Tea*

Gramercy | 71 Irving Pl. (bet. 18th & 19th Sts.) | 4/5/6/L/N/Q/R/W to 14th St./Union Sq. | 212-995-5252
www.irvingfarm.com

Dubbed the "anti-Starbucks", this Gramercy "neighborhood cafe holdout" is the "perfect pit stop for a refuel" of "quality" house-roasted coffee that's a "non-bitter" winner by the cup or by the pound; its "other tempting goodies" ("breakfast snacks", panini, "tasty sweets") "do not disappoint", so it's no surprise the "folksy", "living room"-like premises are "perennially packed"; N.B. the Village branch opened post-Survey.

Is Wine ● *Wine/Liquor* 22 | 24 | 24 | M

G Village | 24 West 8th St. (bet. 5th Ave. & MacDougal St.) | R/W to 8th St. | 212-254-7800 | www.is-wine.com

This "handsome" "Adirondack lodge"-like wine store in NYU country focuses on boutique bottlings and "unique" hard-to-find vintages, most of them imports; the personable owner introduces these "unknown gems" ("many under $20") to the public via seasonal wine classes at Cooper Union and at Saturday afternoon tastings at the store.

Italian Food Center *Specialty Shop* 22 | 18 | 20 | M

Little Italy | 186 Grand St. (Mulberry St.) | 6/J/M/N/Q/R/W/Z to Canal St. | 212-925-2954

"An authentic, local-NYC experience" for more than 60 years, this Little Italy deli and specialty foods market is "an old favorite", offering "fantastic sandwiches" (made with "wonderful" house-baked breads) and other "fresh prepared foods" at "quite good" prices; in addition to hefty heros that "taste like heaven", it also stocks "all the Italian staples", including "lots of imported" items.

🆉 Italian Wine Merchants ▣ *Wine/Liquor* 27 | 24 | 25 | E

Union Sq | 108 E. 16th St. (bet. Irving Pl. & Union Sq. E.) | 4/5/6/L/N/Q/R/W to 14th St./Union Sq. | 212-473-2323 | www.italianwinemerchant.com

Restaurateur Joe Bastianich's "expertise shines through" at this Union Square "haven for the wine-obsessed" (co-owned with Mario Batali), which deals only in producers from The Boot, offering a "tremendous selection" of "top-flight" "standards" as well as "hard-to-find" "gems"; it's curated by a staff so "knowledgeable and passion-ate" you could "get your PhD in *vino Italiano*" just shopping here, and while it's "quite a treat" for "collectors" and novices too, there are a few grumbles about "paying restaurant prices at the liquor store" ("mamma mia, that's expensive").

Z Ito En ▱ *Coffee/Tea* | 28 | 27 | 25 | E |

E 60s | 822 Madison Ave. (69th St.) | 6 to 68th St. | 212-988-7111 | www.itoen.com

Ranking as the "best tea emporium in NYC", this Upper East Side "sanctuary" "has no peers" in its "superb selection" of "authentic" Japanese, Chinese and Indian leaves "both traditional" and "exotic", packaged and "treated as works of art" in a "so-civilized" "boutique" space that's also stocked with "one-of-a-kind" "accoutrements"; run by one of Japan's "premier producers" and staffed by "sophisti-cated" sorts who "can make neophytes experts", it's "very expen-sive" but "worth it" to steep in "tea as spirituality."

Z Jack's Stir Brew Coffee ▱ *Coffee/Tea* | 27 | 23 | 23 | M |

G Village | 138 W. 10th St. (bet. Greenwich Ave. & Waverly Pl.) | 1 to Christopher St. | 212-929-0821 ▱
Seaport | 222 Front St. (bet. Beekman St. & Peck Slip) | A/C to Fulton St. | 212-227-7631
www.cupajack.com

"Crunchy" types "could live at" this ultra-"cozy" Village coffeehouse, which showcases "awesome" "organic" java of the shade-grown, Fair Trade variety plus "funky teas" and baked goods including choc-olate chip cookies so addictive they "should be illegal"; its "quaint" digs and "service with a smile" all but revive the Beat scene, and the newer Seaport site may be even more "mellow and welcoming."

Z Jacques Torres Chocolate ▱ *Candy/Nuts* | 28 | 26 | 23 | E |

SoHo | 350 Hudson St. (King St.) | 1 to Houston St. | 212-414-2462
W 70s | 285 Amsterdam Ave. (bet. 73rd & 74th Sts.) | 1 to 72nd St. | 212-414-2462
Dumbo | 66 Water St. (bet. Dock & Main Sts.) | Brooklyn | A/C to High St. | 718-875-9772
www.mrchocolate.com

Follow "pied piper of chocolate" Jacques Torres to one of his "chic", "*Willy Wonka*"-worthy factories/shops – either the "quaint" Dumbo original or the "larger", sleeker West SoHo and UWS offshoots – for trademark "ooh-la-la" hot chocolate and "ecstasy-inducing" confec-tions "handmade on the spot"; the "extensive", "delightfully" dis-played selection includes treats ranging from "highbrow" "modern truffles" to "fun" chocolate-covered cornflakes and a parade of novelty shapes, ensuring "there's always something new" to sample here.

Jane Packer *Flowers* | ▽ 29 | 27 | 22 | VE |

E 50s | 328 E. 59th St. (bet. 1st & 2nd Aves.) | 4/5/6/N/R/W to 59th St./Lexington Ave. | 212-754-1731 | www.janepacker.com

"The place to buy your bouquet if you mean it" is how devotees describe the NYC operation of U.K. floral designer Jane Packer (she has other stores in London and Tokyo); formerly inside the Conran Shop, it moved into its own East 50s boutique last year, where it continues to turn out stylish, seriously expensive arrangements for individual and corporate clients; N.B. it also offers group and private flower-arranging lessons.

JAS Mart ● *Specialty Shop*
21 | 16 | 16 | M

E Village | 35 St. Marks Pl. (bet. 2nd & 3rd Aves.) | 6 to Astor Pl. | 212-420-6370
Flatiron | 34 E. 23rd St. (bet. Madison & Park Aves.) | 6 to 23rd St. | 212-387-8721
W 100s | 2847 Broadway (bet. 110th & 111th Sts.) | 1 to 110th St. | 212-866-4780

"You walk into Tokyo" when you enter one of these "small" but "well-stocked" shops that carry "all the specialties from the Land of the Rising Sun" ("from soba to rice to wild candy" options) at "hard-to-beat prices"; there's even "ready-to-eat sushi and edamame" plus plenty of "interesting" spices and ingredients to "make your Japanese meal look and taste fabulous."

Java Girl *Coffee/Tea*
24 | 23 | 23 | M

E 60s | 348 E. 66th St. (bet. 1st & 2nd Aves.) | 6 to 68th St. | 212-737-3490

Sink into "a comfy seat" at this "cute", "eclectic" East Side coffee shop, a "warm little" "place to sip" "quality brews" and munch French pastries with the "neighborhood regulars" who brag it "buries the chains"; it's also a "welcome" chance to browse for "creative bric-a-brac" or pick up some "premium beans and teas" to go.

Jefferson Market ● *Major Gourmet Mkt.*
▽ 26 | 20 | 25 | E

G Village | 450 Sixth Ave. (bet. 10th & 11th Sts.) | A/B/C/D/E/F/V to W. 4th St. | 212-533-3377

It "doesn't fancy itself too cool", but this Greenwich Village gourmet market has "managed to stick around since 1929" and still aims to "satisfy" with a mix of "staples" and "upscale treats"; highlights include "fresh", "delicious" prepared foods that are "more in the nature of comfort" fare and above all an "old-fashioned butcher" where the "very accommodating" countermen will "hook you up" with the "best-quality meat."

☑ Jeffrey's on Essex *Meat/Poultry*
25 | 20 | 27 | M

LES | Essex St. Market | 120 Essex St. (bet. Delancey & Rivington Sts.) | F/J/M/Z to Delancey/Essex Sts. | 212-475-6521 | www.jeffreysonessex.com

Regulars of this LES meat and poultry counter inside the Essex Street Market advise "always ask for" proprietor and fourth-generation butcher Jeffrey Ruhalter, who "knows exactly what he's doing" and has a "sense of humor" ("among the meats, Jeffrey is the biggest ham of them all"); the result is a side of "education" and "entertainment" to go with his "excellent-quality", "outer-borough-priced" meats – notably dry-aged beef – and ready-to-cook 'Dinner by Jeffrey' dishes; N.B. catering is a sideline.

	QUALITY	DISPLAY	SERVICE	COST

jesGORDON ⊄ Flowers

–	–	–	VE

Garment District | 242 W. 30th St., Suite 1005 (bet. 7th & 8th Aves.) | 212-229-2165 | www.jesgordon.com
By appointment only

With a client list that runs the gamut from Sarah Jessica Parker to Woody Allen, Target to Nissan, Garment District floral and event designer Jes Gordon's "fun" style also spans the spectrum from "beautiful flowers" arranged in "slightly edgy, contemporary displays" to simple vines cascading under a canvas ceiling; keep in mind that, if you really "want to spend a fortune", she crafts opulent, old world–style towering arrangements to beautify a wedding or corporate do.

Jim and Andy's ⊄ Produce

19	16	19	M

Cobble Hill | 208 Court St. (Warren St.) | Brooklyn | F/G to Bergen St. | 718-522-6034

At this "small", "old-school neighborhood" produce outfit in Cobble Hill, "there's more stuff than you'd ever think possible", from everyday varieties to "occasional great finds" like "fancy radicchio" and "beautiful endive"; make no mistake: this shop's "friendly" "father-and-son" owners "know their" vegetables and fruits.

Jive Turkey ●▣ Prepared Food

▽ 23	20	21	M

Clinton Hill | 441 Myrtle Ave. (bet. Clinton & Waverly Aves.) | Brooklyn | G to Clinton/Washington Aves. | 718-797-1688 | www.thejiveturkey.com

Your family may "fight over the leftovers" after they've tasted the "juicy" turkeys that turn up "every which way" (including the house specialty, deep-fried) at this Clinton Hill storefront; it also vends "easy" ready-to-bake birds paired with lots of "fixin's'" as well as house-baked sweets like honey-pecan pie and brownies to chase them.

Joe ▣⊄ Coffee/Tea

26	20	22	M

NEW **Chelsea** | 405 W. 23rd St. (bet. 9th & 10th Aves.) | C/E to 23rd St./8th Ave. | 212-206-0669
NEW **E 40s** | Grand Central Terminal | Graybar Passage (Lexington Ave. & 43rd St.) | 212-661-8580
E Village | 9 E. 13th St. (bet. 5th Ave. & University Pl.) | 4/5/6/L/N/Q/R/W to 14th St./Union Sq. | 212-924-7400
G Village | 141 Waverly Pl. (6th Ave.) | A/B/C/D/E/F/V to W. 4th St. | 212-924-6750
SoHo | Alessi store | 130 Greene St. (bet. Houston & Prince Sts.) | N/R to Prince St. | 212-941-7330
www.joetheartofcoffee.com

"Joe knows joe" sums up this burgeoning chain of coffeehouse "favorites", which bring a "little piece of Seattle" to NYC via "classic indie-style" setups where "superb" (and "strong") Fair Trade java is poured "with heart" by "top-notch" baristas in "quaint" boho surroundings; they're "experts at the art" of latte and cappuccino, and the original Waverly Place location sporadically serves Amy Sedaris' "to-die-for" cupcakes.

	QUALITY	DISPLAY	SERVICE	COST

☑ Joe's Dairy ⌷ *Cheese/Dairy* | 28 | 14 | 23 | I

SoHo | 156 Sullivan St. (bet. Prince & W. Houston Sts.) | 1 to Houston St. | 212-677-8780

The "undisputed" "best smoked mozzarella" going is the pride of this "quaint" SoHo old-timer, whose cheese is famed for its "smooth-as-silk" texture and "heavenly" "homemade" freshness ("get it when it's still warm"); the rest of this "tiny", "very Italian" shop's offerings are "limited", but it's "a must-visit" for "authenticity" that's also "very reasonably priced."

JoMart Chocolates 🖻 *Candy/Nuts* | 24 | 20 | 21 | M

Marine Park | 2917 Ave. R (bet. E. 29th St. & Nostrand Ave.) | Brooklyn | Q to Ave. U | 718-375-1277 | 800-471-1277 | www.jomartchocolates.com

Now a third-generation family business, this 60-plus-year-old Marine Park chocolatier produces "awesome" confections at prices that won't break the bank; party-throwers appreciate its assortment of molded favors that can suit just about any event, and if what you're looking for isn't on display, they'll make it custom.

Jonathan Flowers *Flowers* | - | - | - | E

W 50s | 36 W. 56th St. (bet. 5th & 6th Aves.) | 212-586-8414
By appointment only

"Jonathan is a creative genius!" rave reviewers of this West 50s florist/event planning outfit whose proprietor "will do exactly what you want, only better" using "the most amazing flowers" and a selection of original props like masks and feathers; better still, he'll "work with your budget" to create an event to be remembered.

Jordan's Lobster Dock *Seafood* | 23 | 13 | 17 | M

Sheepshead Bay | 1 Harkness Ave. (Belt Pkwy. & Knapp St.) | Brooklyn | 718-934-6300 | www.jordanslobsterdock.com

As "close to a Maine lobster shack" as you'll find in Brooklyn, this "no-frills" Sheepshead Bay "staple" is known for "snappy service" and "fresh", "moderately priced" crustaceans that you can have prepared "to order" or buy live "to cook at home"; it may be the "7-11 of seafood", but nonetheless for fans "it's tops."

Joyce Bakeshop *Baked Goods* | ▽ 25 | 21 | 21 | M

Prospect Heights | 646 Vanderbilt Ave. (bet. Park & Prospect Pls.) | Brooklyn | 718-623-7470 | www.joycebakeshop.com

A Prospect Heights "godsend", this "cheerful" retro-style bakery/coffee bar is locally beloved for its "excellent-quality" baked goods produced in a glass-walled kitchen that allows the telecommuting types and others parked in its front seating area a glimpse of the floury action; coffee from local roaster Gorilla goes down well with its expertly rendered goods, which include a mix of classics both American (cupcakes) and French (macarons, galettes).

Juan Valdez Café *Coffee/Tea* | 22 | 19 | 18 | I

E 40s | 480 Lexington Ave. (47th St.) | 4/5/6/7/S to 42nd St./Grand Central | 212-871-6107

(continued)

(continued)

Juan Valdez Café

E 50s | 140 E. 57th St. (bet. 3rd & Lexington Ave.) | 4/5/6/N/R/W to 59th St./Lexington Ave. | 917-289-0981
W 40s | 1451 Broadway (41st St.) | 1/2/3/7/N/Q/R/S/W to 42nd St./Times Sq. | 212-871-7515 ●
www.juanvaldez.com

"A famous name" that proves Columbia's National Federation of Coffee Growers can do "more than just exporting", these local links of a Bogota-based coffee bar chain dispense "rich, dark" Fair Trade *café* that's "guaranteed to keep you up all day"; also boasting Columbian pastries, "refreshing" sunny environs and "good prices", they may have the mule power to "challenge Starbucks."

Jubilee Marketplace ● *Major Gourmet Mkt.*

| 21 | 19 | 15 | M |

Financial District | 99 John St. (bet. Cliff & Gold Sts.) | 2/3 to Fulton St. | 212-233-0808
SoHo | 447 Broadway (bet. Grand & Howard Sts.) | 6/J/M/N/Q/R/W/Z to Canal St. | 212-966-6100
W 60s | Trump Place | 180 Riverside Blvd. (bet. 68th & 69th Sts.) | 1/2/3 to 72nd St. | 212-877-6000

Deemed "decent grocery" stops, this gourmet market trio is "well-stocked" with "varied and reasonably priced" produce, health foods, a "creative variety of prepared foods" and "quite good" meats and seafood; a less-than-jubilant few feel the offerings "could be better", but even they say they're "worth trying" as "convenient" options in underserved areas, which "definitely get extra points" for staying "open 24/7."

Junior's Restaurant ●🍴 *Baked Goods*

| 23 | 18 | 17 | M |

E 40s | Grand Central Terminal | dining concourse (42nd St. & Vanderbilt Ave.) | 4/5/6/7/S to 42nd St./Grand Central | 212-983-5257
E 40s | Grand Central Terminal | main concourse (42nd St. & Vanderbilt Ave.) | 4/5/6/7/S to 42nd St./Grand Central | 212-692-9800
W 40s | Shubert Alley | 1515 Broadway (45th St.) | 1/2/3/7/N/Q/R/S/W to 42nd St./Times Sq. | 212-302-2000
Downtown | 386 Flatbush Ave. Ext. (DeKalb Ave.) | Brooklyn | 2/3 to Grand Army Plaza | 718-852-5257
800-958-6467 | www.juniorscheesecake.com

The "heavy, creamy", "gold-standard" "classic NY–style" cheesecake at this Downtown Brooklyn "landmark" (with offshoots in Grand Central and the Theater District's Shubert Alley) is still "better than sex" according to connoisseurs; however, there are grumbles that the prices are starting to get "out of line", and as for the "glorified diner fare", surveyors say "skip" it and "eat a full slice of cake instead."

🗹 Kalustyan's 🍴 *Specialty Shop*

| 27 | 20 | 19 | M |

Gramercy | 123 Lexington Ave. (bet. 28th & 29th Sts.) | 6 to 28th St. | 212-685-3451 | www.kalustyans.com

A "huge selection of fresh spices" anchors the "mind-boggling" trove of "hard-to-find" "goodies" at this mostly Indian and Mideastern

	QUALITY	DISPLAY	SERVICE	COST

"mecca" in Gramercy, which stocks everything from "excellent" nuts, dried fruits, rice, beans and teas to "wonderful frozen canapés", fresh flatbreads and cookware; it's a favorite of "adventurous chefs" seeking "fair" prices, but its "narrow" aisles also appeal to novices who "eavesdrop on the great recipes people are shopping for", then afterwards "sate their hunger" at the moderately priced upstairs cafe.

Kam Man Food Products, Inc. ◑▤ *Specialty Shop*

21	14	10	I

Chinatown | 200 Canal St. (bet. Mott & Mulberry Sts.) | 6/J/M/N/Q/R/W/Z to Canal St. | 212-571-0330

"Where else can you find plates and bowls for $5 that look like they belong in MoMA" but at this "Chinatown institution" that's "stuffed to the gills" with "Asian foods" – "great teas", "exotic" dry goods, sweets and prepared dishes like barbecued duck – not to mention a basement collection of dishes and cookware that "keeps improving"; this "grotty" spot is strictly "do-it-yourself", though, as the "staff doesn't always speak English."

K & D Wines & Spirits ◑▤ *Wine/Liquor*

24	21	22	M

E 90s | 1366 Madison Ave. (bet. 95th & 96th Sts.) | 6 to 96th St. | 212-289-1818 | www.kdwine.com

The "global" 4,000-label wine inventory at this Carnegie Hill "staple" includes a "fairly extensive selection at all price points", from "solid everyday bottles" to "interesting red Bordeaux" and "château" bottlings; though "informed", "affable" employees will "help you find what you want", customers who care to learn more can attend happy-hour tastings on Thursdays, Fridays and Saturdays; N.B. free delivery throughout Manhattan for any purchase.

Katagiri ▤ *Specialty Shop*

23	16	16	E

E 50s | 224 E. 59th St. (bet. 2nd & 3rd Aves.) | 4/5/6/N/R/W to 59th St./Lexington Ave. | 212-755-3566 | www.katagiri.com

"Delightfully out of place" for a full century now, the "only Japanese supermarket on the Upper East Side" packs loads of "hard-to-find" grocery items into its "tiny" space; "you'll pay a bit more" than at other spots, but you can grab "tasty sushi to go" while shopping, and it's "a lifesaver when you can't get Downtown for sprouts, soy, veggies, spices" and other staples.

Katrina Parris Flowers ▤ *Flowers*

-	-	-	M

Harlem | 1844 Adam Clayton Powell Jr. Blvd. (bet. 111th & 112th Sts.) | 212-222-7030 | www.katrinaparrisflowers.com
By appointment only

A simple, elegant philosophy informs the "fabulous" creations at Katrina Parris and Mark Pinn's Uptown floral emporium, a studio space designed with an eye toward the modern; aside from catering to clients such as President Clinton, Deutsche Bank and Swarovski, this florist offers online services and "something at every price range", along with arrangements for weddings and other special events.

	QUALITY	DISPLAY	SERVICE	COST

☑ Katz's Delicatessen ●⏢ *Deli/Sandwich*   24 | 16 | 16 | M

LES | 205 E. Houston St. (Ludlow St.) | F/V to Lower East Side/2nd Ave. |
212-254-2246 | 800-446-8364 | www.katzdeli.com

"The food is so tasty at this classic" kosher-style deli (circa 1888)
that it's definitely "worth the schlep to the Lower East Side" for what
many agree is the "best corned beef and pastrami on earth" "piled
high" on "huge sandwiches" that "can feed two people" – thus making "the cost in dollars and calories a bit more reasonable"; if you
don't mind the "lack of ambiance", "long queues" or "cranky-waiter
bit", it makes for a "fun madhouse."

☑ Kee's Chocolates *Candy/Nuts*   29 | 22 | 24 | E

SoHo | 80 Thompson St. (bet. Broome & Spring Sts.) | C/E to Spring St. |
212-334-3284 | www.keeschocolates.com

"OMG!" rave reviewers of the "divine", "creative" chocolates "made
by hand on the premises" at this tiny, "hidden-away" SoHo shop – this
year voted tops in NYC for Candy – that's owned and run by "master
of flavors" Kee Ling Tong, whose "exotic" fillings, many reflecting an
Asian influence, are deemed "unforgettable"; "exquisite" product
aside, the vibe is "unpretentious" and the staff "a pleasure to talk
to", so "treat yourself" – "it's worth every penny"; N.B. it's now offering French-style macarons and various tea-flavored cupcakes.

Keith's Farm ⊘ *Produce*   28 | 25 | 25 | M

See Greenmarket; for more information, call 845-856-4955

"Go for the garlic" – "it's the best in the city and maybe anywhere" –
but the rest of the organic vegetables and herbs are also "sublime"
at this Greenmarket farm stall run by farmer-turned-author Keith
Stewart, an "intelligent and thoughtful grower" based in Orange
County, NY, whose conversations with customers over the veggie
bins can be "one of the greatest things about the market"; "prices
are high" but "totally fair" given the quality and "friendly" staff.

Kidfresh *Specialty Shop*   18 | 21 | 16 | E

E 80s | 1628 Second Ave. (bet. 84th & 85th Sts.) | 4/5/6 to 86th St. |
212-861-1141 | www.kidfresh.com

"Boy, do these guys know their racket" admire visitors to this UES
"lazy mom's" dream market created for guppy-size gourmands, who
drop their "fresh", all-natural meals-to-go (animal shaped sandwiches, chicken tenders with strawberry ketchup), lunch boxes and
other healthy edibles into carts scaled just for them; the ice cream
bar is a crowd-pleaser, as are the cooking classes for young 'uns offered in a teaching 'kidchen', so the only drawback is that parents
"gotta have large wallets" to bring their little people here; N.B. it
delivers Manhattan-wide.

Klatch Coffee Bar ⊘ *Coffee/Tea*   21 | 21 | 20 | I

Financial District | 9 Maiden Ln. (bet. B'way & Nassau St.) | J/M/Z to
Fulton St. | 212-227-7276

One of the Financial District's more "appreciated" "signs of life",
this "funky" coffee bar-cum-gallery is a "little" "oasis" that gives
"way Downtown types" access to coffee from Porto Rico, "delicious

teas" from T Salon and "tasty" breads and baked goods from Balthazar, the Little Pie Company and other foodie faves; the "cool room" is all the more so thanks to a revolving art display.

Koglin Royal Hams ●⊡ *Meat/Poultry* ∇ 24 | 21 | 19 | E

E 40s | Grand Central Mkt. | Lexington Ave. (43rd St.) | 4/5/6/7/S to 42nd St./Grand Central | 212-499-0725 | www.koglinroyalhams.com
When a "German meat craving" hits, this Euro-style charcuterie stand in Grand Central "is the perfect cure", boasting a selection of great wursts ("their frankfurters will be the star of your next barbecue") and other "long-forgotten treats" reminiscent of "once-booming Yorkville"; there are also specialties representing the rest of Europe (e.g. Italian prosciutto), as well as prepared side dishes like macaroni salad.

☒ Korin Japanese Trading Corp. ⊡ *Cookware* 28 | 23 | 23 | E

TriBeCa | 57 Warren St. (bet. Church St. & W. B'way) | 1/2/3/A/C to Chambers St. | 212-587-7021 | 800-626-2172 | www.korin.com
Slicing and dicing are elevated to an "art" at this "jewel of a store" in TriBeCa (rated No. 1 in NYC for Cookware & Supplies), a veritable "sanctuary" of "high-quality" Japanese wares, including a "fantastic" assortment of traditional "handcrafted" knives that are priced up into the thousands; if the variety seems "overwhelming", rely on the "expert" staff to "guide you through with aplomb."

☒ Kossar's Bialys ⊡✦ *Bagels* 28 | 15 | 18 | I

LES | 367 Grand St. (bet. Essex & Norfolk Sts.) | F/J/M/Z to Delancey/Essex Sts. | 212-473-4810 | 877-424-2597 | www.kossarsbialys.com
The reigning "king of the bialy world", this "landmark" (once again voted No. 1 in its category) still turns out the same "little floury clouds of love" it's been known for since 1935, standing as a slice of "living history" on the "now-hip Lower East Side"; it definitely "isn't fancy-schmancy", but its namesake goods are roundly voted "worth the schlep", especially "when hot out of the oven" – and "don't forget" it also vends "old-school bagels", bulkas and pletzels.

Krispy Kreme Doughnuts ● *Baked Goods* 19 | 16 | 15 | I

Garment District | Penn Station | Seventh Ave. (32nd St.) | 1/2/3/A/C/E to 34th St./Penn Station | 212-947-7175 | www.krispykreme.com
"Its red ['Hot Doughnuts'] light shines to us like a beacon" admit "addicts" of this national chain – now only in Penn Station – where "right before your eyes" conveyor belts "churn" out "sinful", "pillowy", "melt-in-your-mouth" doughnuts; though many maintain that the goods are "sugar overkill", even critics admit their "tasty, greasy", "sweet" goodness can help "soften hangover" woes.

🆕 Krumbs Bakery ✦ *Baked Goods* 22 | 21 | 19 | M

Clinton Hill | 154 Vanderbilt Ave. (Myrtle Ave.) | Brooklyn | G to Clinton/Washington Aves. | 718-596-5999
"Colossal cupcakes" in a "delicious range" of flavors that offer a little "something different" from the usual distinguish this Clinton Hill bakery, which loyalists claim could "give Magnolia a run for its

money"; maybe its treats are on the "decadent" side ("have some cake with that frosting"), but consensus says it's "worth the splurge."

La Bagel Delight *Bagels*   23 | 17 | 22 | I

Brooklyn Heights | 90 Court St. (bet. Livingston & Schermerhorn Sts.) | Brooklyn | A/C/F to Jay St./Borough Hall | 718-522-0520
Dumbo | 104 Front St. (Adams St.) | Brooklyn | F to York St. | 718-625-2235
Park Slope | 122 Seventh Ave. (bet. Carroll & President Sts.) | Brooklyn | B/Q to 7th Ave. | 718-398-9529
Park Slope | 252 Seventh Ave. (5th St.) | Brooklyn | F to 7th Ave. | 718-768-6107
www.labageldelight.com

"Everything a bagel should be" says it all about the "chewy, savory" hand-rolled goods turned out at this Brooklyn chain "favorite"; it's also an unpretentious source for solid salads and sandwiches, with "fast", "friendly" service that lox up fans far and wide.

La Bergamote *Baked Goods*   26 | 24 | 20 | E

Chelsea | 169 Ninth Ave. (20th St.) | C/E to 23rd St. | 212-627-9010
For "a taste of Paris on Ninth Avenue", "*vaux un detour*" to this Chelsea corner patisserie whose "impressive-looking" display cases are stocked with "works of art" from "the best croissants", brioches and Danish to "must-try" tarts and handmade truffles; it's a perfect "place to relax with coffee and real French" treats, even if service is *un peu* "uptight", so no surprise it's "extremely popular" – expect "lines out the door" at prime times.

NEW La Colombe *Coffee/Tea*   - | - | - | E

TriBeCa | 319 Church St. (Lispenard St.) | N/Q/R/W to Canal St. | 212-343-1515 | www.lacolombe.com
Now that this new TriBeCa outpost has opened, NYers no longer have to go online – or take a trip down the Turnpike – to buy coffee from Philadelphia's legendary artisanal coffee roaster, a supplier to many of NYC's top eateries (Alain Ducasse, Daniel, Jean Georges, etc.); the minimalist quarters with just a few seats offers little to distract from its expertly brewed espresso and coffee, offered along with pastries from Ceci-Cela.

Z Ladybird Bakery *Baked Goods*   28 | 23 | 23 | M

Park Slope | 1112 Eighth Ave. (bet. 11th & 12th Sts.) | Brooklyn | F to 7th Ave. | 718-499-8108 | www.ladybirdbakery.com
This tiny, "charming" original branch of Two Little Red Hens last year took on a new name to signal an ownership shakeup, but much to the relief of its faithful Park Slope following, it's still producing the same "delectable, beautiful" baked goods for which it has long been known; as ever, it's most appreciated for its artfully decorated cakes and cupcakes, "perfect for showers, engagements" and birthday parties.

Z Lady M Cake Boutique ⊟ *Baked Goods*   28 | 26 | 22 | VE

E 70s | 41 E. 78th St. (bet. Madison & Park Aves.) | 6 to 77th St. | 212-452-2222 | www.ladymconfections.com
"Combining Japanese aesthetics with French technique", this "austere" Upper East Side "high-end patisserie" is a vision of "heavenly

white chic", whose "decadent" "must-try" specialty is the mille crêpes cake (featuring impossibly "creamy and light" layers interspersed with custard), but also notable are the petits choux and chocolate sponge cake with caramel mousse; while customers should "be prepared to drop a bundle", enthusiasts M-phasize it's "worth every single penny."

Lafayette French Pastry Bakers ●⇪ Baked Goods

| 21 | 18 | 18 | M |

G Village | 26 Greenwich Ave. (bet. Charles & W. 10th Sts.) | A/B/C/D/E/F/V to W. 4th St. | 212-242-7580

You'll "gain weight just walking in" to this "good old" French bakery in Greenwich Village, an *ancien* source of "classic treats" like "delicious" crème brûlée, croissants, mille-feuille and possibly the "last surviving charlotte russe"; it's all such a "comfort" that regulars happily "overlook the occasional" service quirks.

La Guli ▣ Baked Goods

∇ | 24 | 25 | 22 | I |

Astoria | 29-15 Ditmars Blvd. (bet. 29th & 31st Sts.) | Queens | N/W to Astoria/Ditmars Blvd. | 718-728-5612

This "classic old-style Italian neighborhood bakery" (circa 1937) "can't be beat" according to adoring Astorians who adore its "fresh and delicious" baked goods ("excellent pignoli nut cookies and sfogliatelle", the 'pregnant cannoli'), gelati and ices; just as customers "who have moved away" still "come back for the treats", the "original owners" bought back this family business in 2007, and locals are hoping they'll restore all of its "original pizzazz."

☒ La Maison du Chocolat ▣ Candy/Nuts

| 29 | 28 | 23 | VE |

E 70s | 1018 Madison Ave. (bet. 78th & 79th Sts.) | 6 to 77th St. | 212-744-7117 | 800-988-5632
W 40s | 30 Rockefeller Plaza, concourse level (bet. 49th & 50th Sts.) | B/D/F/V to 47-50th Sts./Rockefeller Ctr. | 212-265-9404
www.lamaisonduchocolat.com

Just about "the best this side of Paris – or heaven" is the word on the "superb" truffles and other "fragrant, intense", "subtly flavored" chocolates imported from France and offered in "jewel"-worthy displays and packaging at this "ultra-high-end" Madison Avenue boutique and its Rock Center offshoot; it's the "Rolls-Royce" of bonbons – with "awe"-inspiring prices to match – though there are a few grumbles about service that, while "knowledgeable and efficient", can be "frosty" at times; P.S. "try the hot chocolate!" (both stores have tearooms), and check out the tastings and classes.

Lamarca ⇪ Cheese/Dairy

∇ | 26 | 17 | 20 | M |

Gramercy | 161 E. 22nd St. (3rd Ave.) | 6 to 23rd St. | 212-673-7920

"Your cheese palate" "will be rewarded" at this Gramercy shop/trattoria, which makes its mark with the "wonderful", "very fresh" fromages aged on-premises in owner Joe Lamarca's subterranean cave; it also carries a "cherce" lineup of "specialty items" to take out (including baked goods, pastas and "amazing soups"), leaving loyalists with only one lament: it's "closed on weekends."

	QUALITY	DISPLAY	SERVICE	COST

Landmark Wine & Sake ● *Wine/Liquor* ▽ 25 | 21 | 25 | M

Chelsea | 167 W. 23rd St. (bet. 6th & 7th Aves.) | 1 to 23rd St. |
212-242-2323 | www.landmarkwinesake.com

This Chelsea wine merchant offers what may well be "the largest
sake stash in Manhattan" (some 300 labels) as well as a strong
showing of soju (200) and an eccentric, "beautifully edited" selection of wines including Argentinean, French, Spanish and California
producers; "affable", "expert" employees who "know their stuff
and are willing to share" and a store layout featuring "user-
friendly displays" plus a tasting bar for sampling the wares add up
to copasetic experiences here.

Ƶ L'Arte del Gelato *Ice Cream* 27 | 21 | 24 | M

Chelsea | Chelsea Mkt. | 75 Ninth Ave. (bet. 15th & 16th Sts.) | A/
C/E/L to 14th St./8th Ave. | 212-366-0570

NEW G Village | 75 Seventh Ave. (bet. Bleecker & W. 4th Sts.) |
212-924-0803 ●⊄
www.lartedelgelato.com

The gelato hits the "top of the charts" at this Chelsea Market stand
where classics such as "heavenly" chocolate share space with "wild"
daily changing flavors, and regulars recommend "torta anything"
(upscale ice cream cakes) for parties; the "friendly" service includes
"free samples", but cognoscenti caution "if you don't buy once you
try, you'll get looks colder than the treats behind the glass"; N.B. the
Greenwich Village location opened post-Survey.

Lassen & Hennigs ● *Caterer* ▽ 22 | 21 | 23 | M

Brooklyn Heights | 114 Montague St. (bet. Henry & Hicks Sts.) |
Brooklyn | 2/3/4/5/M/N/R/W to Borough Hall/Court St. |
718-875-6272 | www.lassencatering.com

Treat your gathering to "everything from soup to nuts" from this
"neighborhood deli", a Brooklyn "Heights tradition" since 1949
that's gone "inexorably upscale" and now industriously handles "catering for business and parties"; specializing in "excellent" "homemade" baked goods and prepared foods, they reliably put together
platters that matter.

Lassi ● *Prepared Food* ▽ 21 | 13 | 20 | M

G Village | 28 Greenwich Ave. (bet. Charles & W. 10th Sts.) | 1 to
Christopher St. | 212-675-2688 | www.lassinyc.com

"Authentic" dals, "carefully prepared" curries, parathas, namesake
yogurt drinks and other traditional Indian items are the hallmark of
this Village eatery owned by a former Union Square Cafe pastry
chef; stick with takeout "unless you want to sit at a narrow counter" –
this sliver of a storefront is only six-ft. wide.

La Tropezienne ▤⊄ *Baked Goods* - | - | - | M

Harlem | 2131 First Ave. (bet. 109th & 110th Sts.) | 6 to 110th St. |
212-860-5324

A "great little secret" in East Harlem, this "homey, humble" bakery's
"classic French baked goods" – "perfect, buttery madeleines", croissants, baguettes and other "tasty" "indulgences" at prices "cheaper

than what you'll find Downtown" – have earned it a loyal local following; it's also possible to pick up sandwiches, salads and quiches, which are best taken to go given that the cafe area only seats 10.

Leaf & Bean ▭ *Coffee/Tea*   23 | 21 | 22 | M

Park Slope | 83 Seventh Ave. (bet. Berkeley Pl. & Union St.) | Brooklyn | B/Q to 7th Ave. | 718-638-5791 | 888-811-5282 | www.leafnbean.com

Park Slopers liken this "very special" "neighborhood" "staple" to a "savvy" "country store" that stocks an "impressive" selection of "wonderful coffees and teas", focusing on organic and Fair Trade blends; the shelves are "cluttered" with an "eclectic" mix of bean-related "accessories", "cool kitchen gadgets" and "kitschy" "decorative items", with an amiable and "informative" crew on hand to "help navigate" the wares.

☑ Le Dû's Wines ●▭ *Wine/Liquor*   27 | 24 | 26 | E

W Village | 600 Washington St. (bet. Leroy & Morton Sts.) | 1 to Houston St. | 212-924-6999 | www.leduwines.com

"You could walk into this store blindfolded and walk out with a winning wine every time" rave regulars of this spacious West Village "oasis" owned by Jean-Luc Le Dû, onetime sommelier at Restaurant Daniel; he "picks the best of the best" (including some "really original standouts") from "quality producers" and his staff "couldn't be more helpful" to the neophyte, while weekly in-store tastings are rated "way above average" – as are most prices.

Lee Sims Chocolates ▭ *Candy/Nuts*   ∇ 25 | 22 | 24 | M

Staten Island | 1909 Victory Blvd. (bet. Jewett Ave. & Manor Rd.) | 718-448-9276 | 800-540-4887 | www.lschocolates.com

"The quality is always there" say surveyors sweet on this SI chocolate purveyor that's a "must-stop for holiday treats" and other "delicious", "high-quality" specialty confections; its quaint quarters are "a pleasure" to visit, thanks in no small part to the "helpful" staffers and wallet-amenable prices.

Le Marais ▭ *Meat/Poultry*   26 | 21 | 19 | E

W 40s | 150 W. 46th St. (bet. 6th & 7th Aves.) | B/D/F/V to 47-50th Sts./ Rockefeller Ctr. | 212-869-0900 | www.lemarais.net

Sharing quarters with the Theater District French brasserie of the same name, this glatt kosher butcher has enthusiasts praising its "beautiful display" of meats (lamb, poultry and game) plus sausages, pâtés and such, insisting "if you didn't know they were kosher" you'd never guess; the "expensive" tabs seem to be justified by "first-rate quality" – but at these prices, can't they "at least smile"?

☑ Lemon Ice King of Corona ●▭ *Ice Cream*   27 | 15 | 18 | I

Corona | Corona Park | 52-02 108th St. (Corona & 52nd Aves.) | Queens | 7 to 103rd St. | 718-699-5133 | www.thelemonicekingofcorona.com

"Long live the King" chant the fervent fans of this Corona "treasure", where "nuttin' – I mean nothing – beats" the namesake lemon Italian ice, though there are a "zillion" other flavors to choose from too, all fabulous enough to make it "worth the wait", especially on a "hot summer night"; "may it be there forever."

⚡ LeNell's Ltd.: a Wine & Spirit Boutique ❶⌐ *Wine/Liquor*

| 27 | 24 | 26 | M |

Red Hook | 416 Van Brunt St. (bet. Coffey & Van Dyke Sts.) | Brooklyn | F/G to Smith/9th Sts. | 718-360-0838 | 877-667-6627 | www.lenells.com

In her quirky Red Hook grape-and-grain shop, Southern gal LeNell Smothers "emphasizes quality over snob appeal" as she "educates" "cocktail geeks" and others about "boutique wines" and lesser-known spirits (highlights include the extensive stock of small-cask bourbons, American whiskeys and a "wide selection of bitters"); aptly, the "funky" shop has a shabby-chic country-store ambiance, enhanced by "laid-back", "friendly" service; N.B. there are rumors that it might relocate soon.

Lenny's Bagels ⊭ *Bagels*

| 23 | 16 | 19 | I |

W 90s | 2601 Broadway (bet. 98th & 99th Sts.) | 1/2/3 to 96th St. | 212-222-0410

"Lots of varieties", including some "unusual" ones (e.g. chocolate-raisin), distinguish this Upper West Side fixture dealing in "tasty" bagels; ok, maybe its quarters "leave something to be desired" and service can "disappoint", but nonetheless carb cronies "can't resist" – especially given the bargain pricing that includes deals like "buy 12, and get another three free."

Leonard's ⌐ *Seafood*

| 26 | 23 | 24 | E |

E 70s | 1385 Third Ave. (bet. 78th & 79th Sts.) | 6 to 77th St. | 212-744-2600 | www.leonardsmarket.citysearch.com

Since 1910, locals have relied on this "family-run" Yorkville "staple" for "impeccable" fresh seafood and meats "cut to your precise order", as well as an impressive array of smoked fish, caviar and game birds; it "doesn't come cheap", but most agree that the "high quality" and "personalized" service are "worth it."

Leonidas ⌐ *Candy/Nuts*

| 26 | 24 | 23 | E |

E 50s | 485 Madison Ave. (bet. 51st & 52nd Sts.) | E/V to 5th Ave./53rd St. | 212-980-2608

Financial District | 120 Broadway (Thames St.) | J/M/Z to Broad St. | 212-766-6100

Financial District | 3 Hanover Sq. (Pearl & William Sts.) | 2/3 to Wall St. | 212-422-9600

Financial District | 74 Trinity Pl. (bet. Rector & Thames Sts.) | 1 to Rector St. | 212-233-1111

800-900-2462 | www.leonidas-chocolate.com

"Flown fresh from Belgium", the "silky" chocolates on sale at these "friendly, Euro-feeling" shops almost make it impossible to go "mass-market" again, especially when the "incredible" goods come at a relatively "fair price" for the upscale genre; the Downtown outposts share space with Manon Cafe espresso bars, where you'll "get a free" bonbon "with your perfect cappuccino" – in sum, *"très magnifique."*

	QUALITY	DISPLAY	SERVICE	COST

Le Pain Quotidien *Baked Goods*   `24` `23` `18` `M`

E 60s | 833 Lexington Ave. (bet. 63rd & 64th Sts.) | F to Lexington Ave./ 63rd St. | 212-755-5810

E 70s | 252 E. 77th St. (bet. 2nd & 3rd Aves.) | 6 to 77th St. | 212-249-8600

E 80s | 1131 Madison Ave. (bet. 84th & 85th Sts.) | 4/5/6 to 86th St. | 212-327-4900

G Village | 10 Fifth Ave. (8th St.) | R/W to 8th St. | 212-253-2324

SoHo | 100 Grand St. (Mercer St.) | 6/J/M/N/Q/R/W/Z to Canal St. | 212-625-9009

Union Sq | 38 E. 19th St. (bet. B'way & Park Ave. S.) | 4/5/6/L/N/ Q/R/W to 14th St./Union Sq. | 212-673-7900

W 50s | 922 Seventh Ave. (bet. 58th & 59th Sts.) | N/Q/R/W to 57th St. | 212-757-0775 🌑

W 60s | 60 W. 65th St. (bet. B'way & CPW) | 1 to 66th St./Lincoln Ctr. | 212-721-4001

W 70s | 50 W. 72nd St. (bet. Columbus Ave. & CPW) | B/C to 72nd St. | 212-712-9700

W 80s | 494 Amsterdam Ave. (84th St.) | 1 to 86th St. | 212-877-1200

www.painquotidien.com

Additional locations throughout the NY area

There's nothing quotidian about the "impressive" blend of "Euro style" and "substance" at these "awesome" Belgian bakeries/cafes, where "high-quality" "organic ingredients" yield "exceptional" "hearty breads" and pastries, plus "scrumptious" sandwiches, salads and soups; the "provincial" settings with "communal farm tables" lend a "convivial" feel, and while the cost "can be steep" "for a chain", most maintain the only pain here is "spotty" service.

L'Epicerie *Specialty Shop*   `22` `22` `18` `E`

Fort Greene | 270 Vanderbilt Ave. (DeKalb Ave.) | Brooklyn | G to Clinton/Washington Aves. | 718-636-1200

"Hits the mark with love and care" say supporters of this "sweet", slightly "spendy" Fort Greene "little French market", whose "limited, select" mostly organic offerings include charcuterie, cheeses, produce, meat, seafood and beyond; when you need a meal to go, there are sandwiches as well as prepared dishes like coq au vin.

Les Halles Market *Meat/Poultry*   `26` `23` `20` `E`

Gramercy | 411 Park Ave. S. (bet. 28th & 29th Sts.) | 6 to 28th St. | 212-679-4111 | www.leshalles.net

"French-style cuts, rich and red" are the main attraction at this butcher beside the famed Gramercy brasserie, closely followed by the meaty "'nasty bits' Anthony Bourdain is always talking about", and it's also a "great resource" for "incredible bread", Paris-worthy desserts and other Gallic goodies; given its proximity, you can either "try the meat" next door "before you buy", or "order, have a bite in the restaurant and pick up on the way out."

Leske's *Baked Goods*   ∇ `23` `18` `19` `I`

Bay Ridge | 7612 Fifth Ave. (bet. 76th & 77th Sts.) | Brooklyn | R to 77th St. | 718-680-2323

A "specialty Scandinavian" bakery that's "been around for years", this "Bay Ridge landmark" puts "old-fashioned" "quality" into a rep-

QUALITY | DISPLAY | SERVICE | COST

ertoire that includes "all the favorites", from Danishes and black-and-white cookies to "out-of-this-world" rye bread; its loyal clientele claims the "classic treats" are nearly "a magical experience."

ⓩ Levain Bakery ☑️⌀ *Baked Goods*   28 | 18 | 22 | E

W 70s | 167 W. 74th St. (bet. Amsterdam & Columbus Aves.) | 1/2/3 to 72nd St. | 212-874-6080 | 877-453-8246 | www.levainbakery.com

"Cookies will never be the same" after a taste of the "delectable", "softball-size" batter-bombs at this "tiny" Upper West Side bakery, where the "moist and thick" chocolate chip version is "chewy" "decadence defined" – whether to "satiate your sweet tooth" or supply your "last meal"; they also do "off-the-hook" breads, scones and pizzas, and though it's "not the cheapest", most agree it's "worth saving up for", especially since the "nice folks" in charge donate each day's unsold output to charity.

LifeThyme Natural Market ◑ *Health Food*   24 | 19 | 18 | M

G Village | 410 Sixth Ave. (bet. 8th & 9th Sts.) | A/B/C/D/E/F/V to W. 4th St. | 212-420-9099 | www.lifethymemarket.com

"Not the usual natural market", this Greenwich Villager offers a "dazzling array" of "healthy staples" and "hard-to-find items", as well as an "upstairs beauty emporium", "excellent raw foods selection", "delicious" prepared foods and "sinful" vegan desserts, plus one of the "best juice bars in Manhattan"; things can get "hectic" in its "cramped", overstuffed space, but the staff is usually "helpful."

Likitsakos ◑ *Produce*   22 | 18 | 15 | M

E 80s | 1174 Lexington Ave. (bet. 80th & 81st Sts.) | 6 to 77th St. | 212-535-4300

Upper Eastsiders praise this "wonderful" gourmet food store for its "consistent produce" but suggest that the "beautifully presented" "Greek specialty items" – "fantastic dips" ("to-die-for taramasalata"), "homemade yogurt", spanakopita – are what really "keep this market packed"; "extras" like "fresh herbs", baked goods and cheese at "reasonable prices" also help to compensate for "cramped" quarters.

Li-Lac Chocolates ☑️ *Candy/Nuts*   26 | 23 | 23 | E

E 40s | Grand Central Mkt. | Lexington Ave. (43rd St.) | 4/5/6/7/S to 42nd St./Grand Central | 212-370-4866 ◑
W Village | 40 Eighth Ave. (Jane St.) | A/B/C/D/E/F/V to W. 4th St. | 212-924-2280
866-898-2462 | www.li-lacchocolates.com

Long before "high-quality chocolate was fashionable", this "old-school" West Village "favorite" was producing "irresistable" "American-style" confections and thrilling gift-givers with its "amazing" molded shapes; some say this "old friend" "lost some of its charm" when it moved away from its "original Christopher Street" digs, and note that the city's "newer highbrow" purveyors offer "stiff competition" in its price range, but for most it's a "fantasy come true"; N.B. commuters appreciate the Grand Central outpost.

	QUALITY	DISPLAY	SERVICE	COST

Lindt Chocolate Shop 🖃 Candy/Nuts | 24 | 22 | 21 | M |

E 40s | 367 Madison Ave. (45th St.) | 7 to 5th Ave. | 212-286-1970
W 50s | 692 Fifth Ave. (54th St.) | E/V to 5th Ave./53rd St. | 212-582-3047
www.lindt.com

"Delights for chocoholics" located on prime Midtown shopping blocks, these twin outposts of the Swiss chocolate giant carry the company's full product line, from "luscious" Lindor truffles to every imaginable kind of bar, meaning "you don't have to jump a plane" to get that "truly European taste"; sourpusses dismiss its "mass-produced" goods as a "step down from" NYC's boutique "specialty shops", but most don't mind because it's "priced right" and makes for "excellent" "casual gifts."

Lioni Latticini   ▽ 29 | 17 | 21 | I |
Mozzarella Company Cheese/Dairy

Bensonhurst | 7803 15th Ave. (bet. 78th & 79th Sts.) | Brooklyn | D/M to 79th St. | 718-232-1411

"You want mozzarella, you go here" urge boosters of this Bensonhurst specialty goods and sandwich shop, where the "melt-in-your-mouth" mutz and "fresh" ricotta are delivered direct from their Jersey factory (and other cheeses are imported from The Boot itself); it's also lionized for its "yummy" pastas, Italian desserts and a "mind-boggling" list of 150 "massive" heros, each christened with a "celebrity" name.

Liqueteria ⚫ Soup   ▽ 19 | 16 | 17 | M |

E Village | 170 Second Ave. (11th St.) | L to 3rd Ave. | 212-358-0300

While this longtime "healthnik haven" in the East Village is popular for its "wonderful choices" of organic juices and smoothies and wheat-free baked goods, "if you love soups, say no more" – except maybe "mm-mm good"; just ignore the noise from the blenders and grab a seat at the counter.

Little Cupcake Bake Shop Baked Goods | 21 | 21 | 19 | M |

Bay Ridge | 9102 Third Ave. (91st St.) | Brooklyn | R to 95th St. | 718-680-4465 | www.littlecupcakebakeshop.com

"You want to eat every pretty morsel" at this "adorable" Bay Ridge cupcakery where the baked-from-scratch sweets are "beautifully displayed" and so "delish" they put other gentrified "cupcake shops to shame"; however, a few wallet-watchers note that for such "little" treats, the tab can get rather "big."

Little Pie Company 🖃 Baked Goods | 24 | 19 | 18 | M |

E 40s | Grand Central Terminal | dining concourse (42nd St. & Vanderbilt Ave.) | 4/5/6/7/S to 42nd St./Grand Central | 212-983-3538 ⚫
Meatpacking | 407 W. 14th St. (bet. 9th & 10th Aves.) | A/C/E/L to 14th St./8th Ave. | 212-414-2324
W 40s | 424 W. 43rd St. (bet. 9th & 10th Aves.) | A/C/E to 42nd St./Port Authority | 212-736-4780
www.littlepiecompany.com

"One bite and you're hooked" on the "heaven-sent" pies from this Theater District bakery (with its Grand Central and Meatpacking

District offshoots), the "all-time winner" for "perfect crusts" and "scrumptious" fillings at a "fair" price; with an "unparalleled" sour cream–apple-walnut variety that's an "irresistible" temptation to "break your diet", it's a "first choice" "for holidays" ("order in advance" on Thanksgiving), and solo sweet tooths "have to love" the "individual-size" option.

Little Piggy Market ●⊘⊜ *Specialty Shop*

| - | - | - | M |

Fort Greene | 64 Lafayette Ave. (Elliot Pl.) | Brooklyn | 718-797-0292 | www.littlepiggymarket.com

Fort Greene's popular BBQ spot Smoke Joint begat this adjacent bite-size market, where local "little piggies" savor seasonally changing, made-to-order sandwiches (e.g. pulled pork, blackened tilapia po' boys), salads and other "special" prepared foods; there are also house-baked cupcakes, pies, gelato and other sweets, as well as a smattering of high-end Southern grocery items such as artisanal hams and organic grits.

LMD Floral Events Interiors *Flowers*

| - | - | - | VE |

E Village | 437 E. 12th St. (bet. Ave. A & 1st Ave.) | L to 1st Ave. | 212-614-2734 | www.lmdfloral.com

"I wouldn't use anyone else" aver acolytes of this "inventive" East Village florist/event designer that takes old-fashioned flowers (e.g. black irises) and presents them in handmade or vintage containers; although "imaginative young" owner Lewis Miller and his team are equipped to handle high-budget events too.

☒ Lobel's Prime Meats ⊞ *Meat/Poultry*

| 29 | 25 | 27 | VE |

E 80s | 1096 Madison Ave. (bet. 82nd & 83rd Sts.) | 4/5/6 to 86th St. | 212-737-1373 | www.lobels.com

Voted No. 1 in its category in NYC, this fifth-generation family-run business on the Upper East Side is "the Rolls-Royce of butchers" – "the Cartier", the "Tiffany's" – supplying "absolutely, positively the best meat you will every buy" "anywhere on the planet", "from the hot dogs to the Châteaubriand"; "bloody high" prices are "part of the legend", but the consensus is that the "remarkable variety and quality" make it all worthwhile, so go ahead – "sell the kid, buy a steak"; N.B. prepared foods and online ordering are added bonuses.

Lobster Place ⊞ *Seafood*

| 26 | 23 | 22 | M |

Chelsea | Chelsea Mkt. | 75 Ninth Ave. (bet. 15th & 16th Sts.) | A/C/E/L to 14th St./8th Ave. | 212-255-5672

G Village | 252 Bleecker St. (bet. 6th & 7th Aves.) | A/B/C/D/E/F/V to W. 4th St. | 212-352-8063
www.lobsterplace.com

One of the city's biggest seafood suppliers, this wholesale/retail pair in the Village and Chelsea Market is a "paradise" for piscophiles, stocking an "impressive selection" of "super-fresh" offerings from the sea, including, yes, "da best" lobsters, as well as a "wonderful treasure chest" of prepared dishes; add "helpful" service and "reasonable" prices and it's easy to see why many consider it "worth a special trip."

	QUALITY	DISPLAY	SERVICE	COST

L'Olivier ▣ *Flowers* ▽ 29 | 29 | 25 | VE

Chelsea | 213 W. 14th St. (7th Ave.) | A/C/E/L to 14th St./8th Ave. |
212-255-2828
E 70s | 19 E. 76th St. (bet. 5th & Madison Aves.) | 6 to 77th St. |
212-774-7676
www.lolivier.com

A delivery of an "exquisite", "exotic arrangement" from Olivier
Giugni's UES floral shop will have your co-workers saying "wow" –
just before they "swoon with jealousy"; using a sculptural, orchid-
centered signature look, they "make masterpieces" here, some of
which can be found in NYC's toniest eateries; yes, such envy-
producing *fleurs* come at couture prices; N.B. their Chelsea seedling
focuses on events.

Lorenzo & Maria's Kitchen *Prepared Food* 25 | 24 | 21 | VE

E 80s | 1418 Third Ave. (bet. 80th & 81st Sts.) | 4/5/6 to 86th St. |
212-794-1080

At this high-end Yorkville take-out/catering "staple" (since 1978), the
gorgeous window display showcases prepared offerings that range
from meat and fish dishes to cakes, cookies and tarts; no doubt, frugal
fans "save it for special occasions", but even though it's "very expensive", the consensus is the goods "are the best you can buy."

Lorimer Street Meat Market ⊅ *Meat/Poultry* – | – | – | M

Williamsburg | 620 Lorimer St. (Skillman Ave.) | Brooklyn | L to
Lorimer St. | 718-389-2691

It moved a couple of years ago into new "across-the-street" quarters, but this meat butcher and deli in Williamsburg continues to
supply the same old-school Italian aged beef, seasonal game, sausages and prepared foods (lasagna, chicken parm, sandwiches) for
which it's long been known; "friendly, eager-to-serve" staffers help
ensure it's holding its own in a neighborhood "undergoing lots
of great changes."

Lung Moon Bakery ⊅ *Baked Goods* 19 | 16 | 14 | I

Chinatown | 83 Mulberry St. (bet. Bayard & Canal Sts.) | 6/J/M/N/
Q/R/W/Z to Canal St. | 212-349-4945

Purists who "crave the old-style" Chinese goodies are likely to land
at this veteran Chinatown bakery, a "cornerstone" for "great pastries" ("especially" the "gorgeous moon cakes") with "just the right
texture" to make you long for Hong Kong; mandarins also moon over
the pork buns, custard pie, bean cakes and "seasonal" items like
bubble tea in the summer.

Luscious Food ● *Prepared Food* ▽ 19 | 17 | 15 | M

Park Slope | 59 Fifth Ave. (bet. Bergen St. & St. Marks Ave.) | Brooklyn |
2/3 to Bergen St. | 718-398-5800 | www.lusciousbrooklyn.com

This Park Slope gourmet-to-go storefront run by two caterers is a
neighborhood source for "tasty" comfort fare – mac 'n' cheese,
meatloaf and sandwiches built on Royal Crown bakery bread – as
well as packaged items such as olive oils, pasta sauces and teas;
there are a few seats for on-site munching, but most get it to go.

QUALITY | DISPLAY | SERVICE | COST

Macy's Cellar ● ▢ *Cookware* `21` `18` `12` `M`

Garment District | 151 W. 34th St. (bet. 6th & 7th Aves.) | 1/2/3/ A/C/E to 34th St./Penn Station | 212-695-4400 | 800-456-2297 | www.macys.com

"Load up on basics" at this "chaotic" department store basement where "everything you need for the kitchen" – from cookware and cutlery to appliances and gadgets – is offered "in many trendy brands" all "in one place" and at "moderate prices" to boot; the goods get downright "cheap" on "sale days", but be warned that those can be a "jungle", with "nonexistent service" fueling the "aggravation", meaning you may end up paying for the "deals" with a "headache."

NEW Madeleine Patisserie *Baked Goods* `24` `19` `20` `M`

Chelsea | 132 W. 23rd St. (bet. 6th & 7th Aves.) | F/V to 23rd St. | 212-243-2757

"Truly a sweet spot", this "friendly neighborhood" patisserie brings a "touch of Paris" to Chelsea via its "tempting" array of French baked goods, including "amazing macarons in so many flavors" and "beautiful pastries"; its address on "bustling" 23rd Street remains an "unexpected" locale for "such a treasure"; P.S. it also excels at "inventive" custom "specialty cakes."

Madison *Baked Goods* ▽ `20` `22` `21` `E`

E 90s | 1292 Madison Ave. (bet. 91st & 92nd Sts.) | 6 to 96th St. | 212-860-1598

Formerly known as Yura, this Upper East Side bakery changed names recently after a split in ownership; the only location that remains in the hands of baker-caterer extraordinaire Yura Mohr, it continues to turn out the same high-level cakes and pastries, as well as prepared foods, for which it has long been beloved in the neighborhood.

☑ Madonia Bakery ⌘ *Baked Goods* `28` `20` `23` `I`

Bronx | 2348 Arthur Ave. (187th St.) | B/D to Fordham Rd. | 718-295-5573

An "Arthur Avenue favorite" "for many decades", this ultra-"authentic" Italian bakery is "known for" "wonderful" "specialty" breads that "can't be surpassed", with upper-crust honors going to the "excellent" olive and prosciutto loaves; add a "nice selection" of cannoli and cookies and "lots of help when needed" and it's "worth the drive" not to "miss out."

☑ Magnolia Bakery ● *Baked Goods* `23` `20` `17` `M`

NEW W 60s | 200 Columbus Ave. (69th St.) | 1 to 66th St./Lincoln Ctr. | 212-724-8101

W Village | 401 Bleecker St. (W. 11th St.) | 1 to Christopher St. | 212-462-2572

www.magnoliacupcakes.com

A "serious" "sugar rush" awaits at this "legendary" West Village bakery, a "tiny" shop "reminiscent of yesteryear" that "earns its reputation" with a "swoon"-worthy selection of "sinful" cupcakes topped with "obscenely good" "butter icing", along with "unsung stars" like "must-have" banana pudding; it's "annoying" to "fight off the tourists" and abide a "snooty" staff, but "lines out the door" prove that this "sweet" "taste of Americana" is an enduring "crowd-pleaser"; N.B. the UWS branch opened post-Survey.

Magnolia Flowers & Events *Flowers* ▽ 26 | 26 | 26 | E

W Village | 436 Hudson St. (bet. Leroy & Morton Sts.) | 1 to Houston St. | 212-243-7302 | www.magnoliaflowersandevents.com

"Outstanding flowers" from across the globe form the basis for the "fantastically beautiful arrangements" at this West Village florist that's "never a disappointment" to its celeb clientele; though "worth the $$$", they're also adept "at taking a price point and creating a very memorable" piece, making them "perfect for any celebration" – or budget; N.B. gifts and premade displays are available at their Bryant Park kiosk, open April–December.

Make My Cake *Baked Goods* 25 | 18 | 18 | M

Harlem | 121 St. Nicholas Ave. (116th St.) | 2/3 to 116th St. | 212-932-0833 ✏

Harlem | 2380 Adam Clayton Powell Blvd. (139th St.) | B/C to 135th St. | 212-234-2344

www.makemycake.com

"Just like grandma's" is the word on the Southern specialties from these Harlem bakeries, home to the "out-of-this-world" likes of red velvet cake, sweet potato cheesecake, "light, fluffy cupcakes" and a butter-cream number that'll "melt in your mouth"; whether for birthdays, weddings or catering, a visit is sure to make your day; N.B. the St. Nicholas Avenue original is a sit-down cafe while the adjunct farther Uptown is retail only.

M & I International Foods ● *Specialty Shop* 24 | 23 | 13 | M

Brighton Bch | 249 Brighton Beach Ave. (bet. Brighton 1st & Brighton 2nd Sts.) | Brooklyn | B/Q to Brighton Bch. | 718-615-1011

It's the "Russian Zabar's" rave reviewers of this big, bi-level Eastern European market that's a "bright spot in Brighton Beach" thanks to its "huge selection" spanning fresh meat and sausages, smoked fish and caviar, cheeses, imported comestibles, "delicious" prepared dishes – from chicken Kiev to pierogi and blintzes – as well as breads, cakes and other bakery items; still, keep in mind that some of its Slavic staples may "require an adventurous palate" – and a "translator" for the Cyrillic-challenged; P.S. it gets "crowded on weekends."

Manganaro Foods *Deli/Sandwich* 24 | 19 | 19 | M

Garment District | 488 Ninth Ave. (bet. 37th & 38th Sts.) | A/C/E to 42nd St./Port Authority | 212-563-5331 | 800-472-5264 | www.manganarofoods.com

"A little slice of Italy" in the shadow of the Port Authority, this grocery store/caterer/cafe "with an old-world look" is "like eating in mama's kitchen, assuming mama really knew how to cook"; the counter staff may "need to smile more", but most admit the reason you come to this "irreplaceable institution" is for "top-quality food", including "fresh meats and cheeses" and "killer sandwiches."

	QUALITY	DISPLAY	SERVICE	COST

Manganaro's Hero Boy ❷ *Deli/Sandwich* | 21 | 15 | 16 | M |

Garment District | 494 Ninth Ave. (bet. 37th & 38th Sts.) | A/C/E to 42nd St./Port Authority | 212-947-7325 | www.manganarosheroboy.com

There's "nothing like a hero, boy, to get your juices flowing" fawn fans of this "authentic" Midtown Italian deli that's been a "standby" for over 50 years for its "terrific" selection of 40-odd sandwiches ("they set the bar for six-ft.-long" babies) at "very fair prices"; though critics claim it's "nothing special", others insist it's perfect "pre–Madison Square Garden" or after a softball game.

Mangia *Prepared Food* | 24 | 23 | 17 | E |

E 40s | 16 E. 48th St. (bet. 5th & Madison Aves.) | B/D/F/V to 47-50th Sts./Rockefeller Ctr. | 212-754-7600

Financial District | Trump Bldg. | 40 Wall St. (bet. Broad & Pine Sts.) | 2/3 to Wall St. | 212-425-4040 ❷

Flatiron | 22 W. 23rd St. (bet. 5th & 6th Aves.) | N/R/W to 23rd St. | 212-647-0200 ❷

W 50s | 50 W. 57th St. (bet. 5th & 6th Aves.) | N/Q/R/W to 57th St. | 212-582-5882

www.mangiatogo.com

"Every possible food one could crave" lures lunchtime hordes to this quartet of prepared foods factories featuring "amazing" salad bars, "tasty" sandwiches and panini, pizzas and a "wonderful" array of seafood and meat dishes (cold and hot) as well as "delish" pastries; the "ridiculously expensive" tabs may be fit for "bankers", but even lowly desk jockeys pony up because the "reliable" goods are "absolutely delicious"; N.B. it specializes in office catering.

Manhattan Espresso Cafe *Coffee/Tea* | 21 | 19 | 19 | M |

E 40s | 146 E. 49th St. (bet. Lexington & 3rd Aves.) | 6 to 51st St. | 212-832-3010 | www.manhattanespressocafe.com

Midtown's tourists and desk jockeys refuel on the fly at this "total gem" of an espresso bar, a five-seater cubbyhole whose Illy brand Italian coffee makes for a flavorful shot or cuppa; they also dole out crêpes, croissants, pastries and sandwiches, "but space is limited" so plan for an express stop when the cappuccino craving strikes.

Manhattan Fruit Exchange ⊄ *Produce* | 24 | 21 | 16 | I |

Chelsea | Chelsea Mkt. | 75 Ninth Ave. (bet. 15th & 16th Sts.) | A/C/E/L to 14th St./8th Ave. | 212-989-2444

"Filled with attractive, exotic treasures" this "cash-only" Chelsea Market produce peddler is a veritable "cornucopia" of "impeccable" fruits and veggies including slews of seasonal standouts like "terrific mushrooms" and "baby vegetables galore" plus "quality nuts", candy, coffee and juices as well as "lots of fresh and dried herbs"; its "reasonable prices" help explain why it's "always bustling."

ⓩ Manhattan Fruitier ▭ *Specialty Shop* | 27 | 25 | 24 | E |

Gramercy | 105 E. 29th St. (bet. Lexington & Park Aves.) | 6 to 28th St. | 212-686-0404 | www.manhattanfruitier.com

"Discriminating" present-givers looking to "impress" find baskets brimming with "exotic fruits" "almost too lovely to eat" and other

	QUALITY	DISPLAY	SERVICE	COST

delicacies at this Gramercy Park specialist whose "stellar" composi-
tions "should be in the dictionary next to the words 'classy gift'"; the
assortments include "quality" chocolates, dried fruits, artisanal
cheeses, caviar and assorted other "luscious" "temptations" that
can be purchased in the store or through the "reliable online ordering and delivery" system – but know that while they're "oh-so-
pretty", they're also "oh-so-pricey."

Manley's Wines & Spirits ◑ *Wine/Liquor*

▽ 22	18	21	M

W Village | 35 Eighth Ave. (bet. 12th & 13th Sts.) | A/C/E/L to 14th St./
8th Ave. | 212-242-3712

"Wonderfully local", with an "attentive staff" and small-town vibe,
this West Village veteran (since 1934) proffers affordable everyday
wines and a full line of spirits; stop by during the holiday season for
some "model-train action" on tracks suspended near the ceiling.

Manna Catering *Caterer*

-	-	-	E

TriBeCa | 24 Harrison St. (bet. Greenwich & Hudson Sts.) | 1 to
Franklin St. | 212-966-3449 | www.mannacatering.com

Known for "haute kosher cuisine" so "delish" it seems heaven sent,
this TriBeCa caterer is a sensation for off-site occasions that's done
divine work for the likes of Steven Spielberg and Ronald Perelman;
with exotic presentations and worldly influences extending from the
Mideast to the Far East, this is a nosh that "grandma never made."

Mansoura ▣ *Baked Goods*

-	-	-	M

Midwood | 515 Kings Hwy. (bet. E. 2nd & 3rd Sts.) | Brooklyn | F to
Kings Hwy. | 718-645-7977 | www.mansoura.com

"It's the real thing" agree effendis at this Midwood bakery, whose
Sephardic kosher specialties are an all-but-unique taste of the Mideast
and Mediterranean; "great pastries and candies" are highlights of a
lineup that also includes confections and hors d'oeuvres, and gift
tins and catering platters present a range of appetizing samples.

Marché Madison *Prepared Food*

20	18	15	VE

E 50s | 36 E. 58th St. (bet. Madison & Park Aves.) | N/R/W to 5th Ave./
59th St. | 212-355-3366

E 70s | 931 Madison Ave. (74th St.) | 6 to 77th St. | 212-794-3360 ◑

On-the-go Eastsiders march over to this "chichi" pair that vends a
"good" variety of "fresh" fruits, veggies and prepared foods that regulars say "make your mouth water"; but alas, mad shoppers maul
"overpriced", "ok" products sold by "sullen servers."

Margaret Braun Cakes & Sugar Objects ⊘ *Baked Goods*

-	-	-	VE

W Village | 33 Bank St. (W. 4th St.) | 212-929-1582 |
www.margaretbraun.com
By appointment only

"Art that tastes delicious" is the métier of exclusive baker Margaret
Braun, whose cakes are elaborate creations on fanciful themes, lovingly crafted with baroque details that make each one "a rare thing indeed"; she's the Rembrandt of weddings and special occasions, with
a sideline in sugar sculptures that sometimes show up in movies.

	QUALITY	DISPLAY	SERVICE	COST

Margaret Palca Bakes *Baked Goods* ▽ 26 | 20 | 22 | M

Carroll Gardens | 191 Columbia St. (bet. Degraw & Sackett Sts.) | Brooklyn | 718-802-9771 | www.margaretpalcabakes.com

Rolling "the best" "buttery rugalach" around, pastry chef Margaret Palca's "fair-priced" Carroll Gardens bake shop is a modest setup with a "friendly local vibe" where dessert devotees will also find "delicious" "heart-felt", "housemade" cakes, pies, brownies and "cookies almost too beautiful to eat"; plus the ovens turn out the "amazing" bread and rolls that bolster their first-rate sandwiches to go.

Margot Pâtisserie *Baked Goods* 27 | 21 | 22 | M

W 70s | 2109 Broadway (74th St.) | 1/2/3 to 72nd St. | 212-721-0076

Francophiles nominate this West Side "hideaway" as the "perfect" patisserie since its "outstanding" pastries, tarts, cakes and baguette sandwiches are sure to make you "feel like you're back in Paris"; it's something of a "neighborhood" "secret" thanks to an "easy-to-miss" locale, and the expats "sipping coffee and eating croissants" are inclined to plead "don't tell."

Z MarieBelle's Fine Treats & 26 | 26 | 21 | E
Chocolates 🖃 *Candy/Nuts*

NEW **E 60s** | 762 Madison Ave., 2nd fl. (bet. 65th & 66th Sts.) | 6 to 68th St./Hunter College | 212-249-4588

SoHo | 484 Broome St. (bet. W. B'way & Wooster St.) | 1/A/C/E to Canal St. | 212-925-6999 | 866-925-8800
www.mariebelle.com

It's "an experience" just visiting Maribel Lieberman's "stylish" SoHo chocolate boutique (with a new UWS offshoot), a favorite among "fashionistas" for its trademark silkscreen-patterned bonbons, "delicious little works of art" that "taste as good as they look"; equally "lovely" packaging ensures they make "delightful gifts", leading most to overlook the "pricey" tabs and occasionally "self-important" service; P.S. the tearoom pours "divine" hot chocolate.

Marlow & Sons ● *Specialty Shop* 24 | 23 | 19 | E

Williamsburg | 81 Broadway (Berry St.) | Brooklyn | L to Bedford Ave. | 718-384-1441 | www.marlowandsons.com

The "most fun part of shopping" at this "adorable little" Williamsburg grocery shop, from the owners of nearby Diner, is that once you're done you can "sit down for a plate of oysters" in the cafe/wine bar "nestled in back"; it's a prized "neighborhood resource" for "impressive" (if "expensive") comestibles from biodynamic dairy products, farmstead cheeses and pasture-raised meats to small-batch honeys, imported oils and vinegars.

Marquet Patisserie *Baked Goods* 24 | 21 | 19 | M

Boerum Hill | 221 Court St. (Warren St.) | Brooklyn | F/G to Bergen St. | 718-855-1289

Fort Greene | 680 Fulton St. (S. Portland St.) | Brooklyn | G to Fulton St. | 718-596-2018 ⌀

Croissant connoisseurs tip their berets to "the light touch" at these separately owned Boerum Hill and Fort Greene bakeries, where the

	QUALITY	DISPLAY	SERVICE	COST

"excellent" "French pastries", tarts and cakes confirm the value of "attention paid to details"; they also market take-out lunches, and most "don't mind the prices" – it's still "cheaper than a ticket to Paris."

Martha's Country Bakery ● *Baked Goods* | 23 | 24 | 21 | M |

Astoria | 3621 Ditmars Blvd. (bet. 36th & 37th Sts.) | Queens | N/W to Astoria/Ditmars Blvd. | 718-545-9737
Forest Hills | 70-30 Austin St. (70th Rd.) | Queens | E/F/R/V to 71st Ave. | 718-544-0088
www.marthascountrybakery.com

It's "good to know that old-fashioned American bakeries still exist" enthuse discoverers of this Astoria pastry shop/cafe and its Forest Hills offshoot, both of which serve up "fabulous fresh pies", cakes and other "absolutely delish" "homestyle" desserts at "reasonable" prices; supporters of this "country-style", "very un-NY" duo will appreciate that a lunch menu is in the works.

Martin Bros. Wines & Spirits ● ◐ ☑ *Wine/Liquor* | 21 | 18 | 23 | M |

W 100s | 2781 Broadway (107th St.) | 1 to 110th St. | 212-222-8218 | www.martinbrotherswine.com

Upper Westsiders toast the "unpretentious, approachable" yet "knowledgeable" staffers who make this small shop near Columbia a "great neighborhood resource" for the inquisitive imbiber ("I went from a scotch greenhorn to a learned individual after a lesson from the proprietor"); its "carefully selected" stock includes not only "everyday" wines but also a "superb selection of high-dollar Cabernets" and more than 150 single-malt whiskeys.

☑ Martine's Chocolates ☑ *Candy/Nuts* | 29 | 24 | 22 | VE |

E 50s | Bloomingdale's | 1000 Third Ave., 6th fl. (59th St.) | 4/5/6/ N/R/W to 59th St./Lexington Ave. | 212-705-2347 ●
E 80s | 400 E. 82nd St. (bet. 1st & York Aves.) | 4/5/6 to 86th St. | 212-744-6289
www.martineschocolates.com

"Truly freshly made" chocolates – you can "actually see them" being prepared on premises – lure cacao-nnoisseurs to these "sweet assets" on the East Side, whose original Bloomie's location makes the perfect "shoppers' pit stop"; beyond its signature "amazing, rich" filled chocolates, there are novelty offerings "in every shape possible" (think "baseballs and Statues of Liberty") – though naturally such "high quality" comes at a steep price.

Martin's Pretzels ☑ *Baked Goods* | 27 | 18 | 24 | I |

See Greenmarket; for more information, call 315-628-4927 | www.martinspretzels.com

It's a "must for pretzel mavens" say snackers who swear by the hand-rolled, "perfectly crisped and salted" specimens cranked out by this year-round Greenmarket stalwart; the lineup includes whole pretzels, "bags of pieces" ("go for those broken ones!") and a "wonderful" whole-wheat version for the health-conscious, so "take a sample and see for yourself" – they're "great to munch on" as you stroll around "the rest of the market."

	QUALITY	DISPLAY	SERVICE	COST

Masturbakers *Baked Goods*

▽ 22 | 19 | 23 | M

E Village | Old Devil Moon | 511 E. 12th St. (bet. Aves. A & B) | L to 1st Ave. | 212-475-0476 | www.masturbakers.com

When the occasion calls for "witty" "X-rated confections", this East Village custom baker gets down and dirty with "yummy" "porno cakes" that "surprisingly taste just like mom's"; the graphic goodies are "perfect for bachelor/ette parties", but they'll turn even the tamest get-together into "an orgasmic experience" – however, if you're a soft-core sort, nonexplicit versions are also available.

Mauzone *Prepared Food*

22 | 16 | 18 | M

Flushing | 72-30 Main St. (bet. 72nd & 73rd Aves.) | Queens | 7 to Flushing-Main St. | 718-261-7723 | www.mauzonemarketplace.com

An "outstanding range" of "reasonably" priced food such as "delicious" fried chicken, kugel and all sorts of "homemade" sides send patrons back to this glatt kosher take-out champ in Flushing; N.B. the stores close early on Fridays and all day Saturdays.

Max & Mina's Homemade Inc. ●⊭ *Ice Cream*

▽ 25 | 21 | 24 | I

Flushing | 71-26 Main St. (bet. 71st Rd. & 72nd Ave.) | Queens | 7 to Flushing-Main St. | 718-793-8629

If you've ever had a craving for housemade ice cream flavored with lox, horseradish or red wine, this Queens-based kosher parlor with a penchant for wacky concoctions "is your place" (perhaps not surprisingly, the original founder, Max, was a dairy-loving biochemist with an experimental edge); less-adventuresome eaters needn't fret, because tamer flavors are available too; N.B. closes early on Friday and reopens Saturday after sundown.

Max Brenner, Chocolate by the Bald Man ▣ *Candy/Nuts*

22 | 24 | 18 | E

E Village | 141 2nd Ave. (9th St.) | R/W to 8th St. | 212-388-0030
G Village | 841 Broadway (bet. 13th & 14th Sts.) | 4/5/6/L/N/Q/ R/W to 14th St./Union Sq. | 212-388-0030
www.maxbrenner.com

One look at the "chocolate pipes running across the ceiling" and it's clear that "Willy Wonka has landed in NYC" at this Union Square outpost of an Israeli-born, "over-the-top" chain of chocolate-themed shops/cafes known for its "inventive" sweets (e.g. chocolate pizza) to make the "blood sugar soar"; "brunch is a zoo", and some consider the offerings overly "expensive" – particularly when you factor in "erratic service" and "screaming kids" – but still diehards declare "I don't care if my hair does fall out"; N.B. there's also a smaller East Village branch.

Maya Schaper Cheese & Antiques ▣ *Cheese/Dairy*

▽ 22 | 23 | 22 | E

W 60s | 106 W. 69th St. (bet. B'way & Columbus Ave.) | 1 to 66th St./ Lincoln Ctr. | 212-873-2100

Sure, it's a "strange juxtaposition", but this "quirky" Upper West Side "gem" may make you a "believer" with its "beautiful" sales dis-

	QUALITY	DISPLAY	SERVICE	COST

play of "quaint" kitchen curios side-by-side with "fabulous" from-ages, leading to "great finds" both edible and collectible; the antiques run from cheese trays to cookware and cutlery, and though the "selection could be bigger", "friendly service" ensures it's always a pleasure to "browse."

🇿 May May ⌨ *Specialty Shop*   23 | 16 | 19 | I

Chinatown | 35 Pell St. (bet. Bowery & Mott St.) | 6/J/M/N/Q/R/W/Z to Canal St. | 212-267-0733 | www.maymayfood.com
"A NYC classic" for over 40 years, this Chinatown bakery is the "frozen dim sum depot" of choice for party-throwers and others; "flaky pork buns", "fantastic sticky rice pouches" and dumplings with all manner of "fillings to choose from" are "well worth the trip" to Pell Street, as are holiday "sweets" like moon cakes and what some call "the best egg tarts in town."

Mazal Kosher Food ◑⌨ *Candy/Nuts*   17 | 13 | 17 | M

Flushing | 14901 Union Tpke. (150th St.) | Queens | 718-380-2424
Though it moved to its current Flushing quarters in 2006, this unpretentious shop has "been around forever" and continues to stock an extensive, all-kosher selection of grocery items imported from Israel; however, it's the house-specialty "wonderful kosher candy" that really keeps 'em coming back: "for the occasions when you need" kosher sweets, this is the "place to go."

Mazur's Marketplace &   20 | 17 | 18 | E
Restaurant *Meat/Poultry*

Douglaston | 254-51 Horace Harding Blvd. (Little Neck Pkwy.) | Queens | 718-428-5000 | www.mazursmarketplace.com
This full-service glatt kosher food market in Queens can be counted on for a "great selection" of edibles ("just ask if you don't see it"), including "excellent quality" butcher items, rotisserie birds, take-out prepared dishes, challah and other baked goods, fresh and smoked fish and now sushi; catering and a next-door restaurant are part of the package; N.B. closes early on Friday and all day Saturday.

Mazzola Bakery ⊘ *Baked Goods*   25 | 18 | 19 | I

Carroll Gardens | 192 Union St. (Henry St.) | Brooklyn | F/G to Carroll St. | 718-643-1719
The "bread is heaven" at this '20s-era Carroll Gardens "neighborhood bakery", a "pre-gentrification holdover" celebrated for dispensing a "delicious" assortment of specialty loaves (notably the prosciutto-packed lard variety) in an "amazingly warm environment"; and if you don't live by bread alone, they also vend "wonderful baked goods" and "excellent java."

McAdam Buy Rite ◑⌨ *Wine/Liquor*   ∇ 22 | 14 | 19 | M

Gramercy | 398 Third Ave. (bet. 28th & 29th Sts.) | 6 to 28th St. | 212-679-1224 | www.americaswineshop.com
The staff at this veteran Gramercy Park wine discounter can help you locate a particular Long Island wine (it carries more than 210), but it also stocks selections from the expected regions (California,

France, Australia) for more mainstream shoppers; regulars recommend it as a place to "find the best prices on workhorse" bottles (e.g. "cases of white for the office party"), but say it pays to go in "knowing what you want."

McCabe's Wines & Spirits ● *Wine/Liquor* | 19 | 16 | 19 | M |

E 70s | 1347 Third Ave. (77th St.) | 6 to 77th St. | 212-737-0790
At this "decent neighborhood store" on the Upper East Side, plentiful kosher wines (some 300) share the cellar with French, Australian and a growing number of German vintages, along with boutique bottlings from California; those who prefer the hard stuff can get lots of single-malts and small-batch bourbons at "fair prices", so although service gets mixed reviews, this place is "always busy."

McNulty's Tea & Coffee Co. ●⬛ *Coffee/Tea* | 27 | 22 | 23 | M |

W Village | 109 Christopher St. (bet. Bleecker & Hudson Sts.) | 1 to Christopher St. | 212-242-5351 | 800-356-5200 | www.mcnultys.com
"No one can call it trendy", but you "can't do better" for "all things good to brew" than this "old-time" (circa 1895) West Village purveyor of "fine coffees and teas", where the "superb" assortment of "exotic" blends is so wide-ranging it's "hard to pick just one"; count on "courteous" "guidance" from in-house "experts" in a milieu so "atmospheric" that "just a whiff is enough" for a "caffeine fix."

Mediterranean Foods ●⬛ *Specialty Shop* | ▽ 26 | 22 | 21 | I |

Astoria | 23-18 31st St. (bet. 23rd & 24th Aves.) | Queens | N/W to Astoria/Ditmars Blvd. | 718-721-0221
Astoria | 30-12 34th St. (30th Ave.) | Queens | N/W to 30th Ave. | 718-728-6166
The "best place for a taste of Greece" outside of the Peloponnesus is this "outstanding" Astoria market duo where the "excellent selection" comes at "bargain" prices and is presided over by a "helpful and friendly" crew; "love the choices of olives" and oil, "yogurt, orzo, spices, nuts, candies" and "other essentials" say surveyors who sigh "so many fetas, so little time."

Melange ● *Prepared Food* | 21 | 15 | 19 | I |

E 60s | 1188 First Ave. (bet. 64th & 65th Sts.) | 6 to 68th St. | 212-249-3743
E 60s | 1277 First Ave. (bet. 68th & 69th Sts.) | 6 to 68th St. | 212-535-7773
Best known for its "yummy" Middle Eastern "treats", this East Side prepared-foods open till midnight twosome has "everything you need" by way of "healthy", "gourmet" fare, whether it's hummus, falafel or the "best" halvah, all sold at a "great" price; rounding out the endorsement is a "friendly" staff always "willing to offer advice."

NEW Mercury Dime, The ●⬛ *Coffee/Tea* | - | - | - | M |

E Village | 246 E. Fifth St. (bet. 2nd & 3rd Aves.) | 6 to Astor Pl. | 212-533-3295
Mixology maestro Sasha Petraske (Milk & Honey) had planned to open a wine bar here, but after being denied a license he and his partner created this homey East Village coffeehouse instead; its ex-

pertly pulled espresso is made with esoteric (and seriously aromatic) Ethiopian unwashed beans, and there are also fresh juices, made-to-order sandwiches and free WiFi to boot.

Metro Party Rentals *Party Rentals*

| - | - | - | M |

Paterson | 188 Lafayette St. (bet. Rosa Parks Ave. & 16th St.), NJ | 973-684-4144 | 800-234-2011 | www.metropartyrentals.com
Though based in northern New Jersey, this rental enterprise serves all of the tri-state area, catering to commercial and private party-throwers and keeping them well-supplied with tables, chairs and china, not to mention customized tents and dance floors; N.B. $200 minimum charge for delivery to Manhattan.

Michael George *Flowers*

| ∇ 25 | 25 | 20 | E |

E 40s | 5 Tudor City Pl. (41st St.) | 212-883-0304 | www.mgflowers.com
By appointment only
In business for over three decades, this Tudor City florist-to-the-stars boasts a "fashion"-friendly client list including boldface names such as Tom Ford and Tommy Hilfiger; it also plans chic events, but its real "magic" can be found in its minimalist arrangements – how does it "get those tulips to stand that way"?

Michael-Towne
Wines & Spirits ● *Wine/Liquor*

| 24 | 24 | 24 | M |

Brooklyn Heights | 73 Clark St. (Henry St.) | Brooklyn | 2/3 to Clark St. | 718-875-3667
"Serving the wine snob and the peppermint-schnapps crowd with equal care", this "convenient", "pleasant and reliable" Brooklyn Heights shop offers a "wide-ranging" selection of vintages from all over the world, plus "top-shelf liquors" (especially bourbon and single-malts) and sake; "extremely helpful" service and "reasonable pricing" enhanced by generous by-the-case discounts make this "handsome" contender that much more attractive.

Michelle's Kitchen *Prepared Food*

| 18 | 17 | 17 | M |

E 90s | 1614 Third Ave. (bet. 90th & 91st Sts.) | 4/5/6 to 86th St. | 212-996-0012 | www.michelleskitchen.com
Although its hors d'oeuvres turn up at a number of off-site events, this Yorkville French-Belgian caterer also runs a "pleasant" prepared-foods shop where locals "stop by on their way home" for "upscale" sandwiches and other "homestyle" prepared dishes; critics say the offerings are "hit-or-miss", but few would argue with a place offering "quick" to-go meals in an "underserved neighborhood."

Migliorelli Farm *Produce*

| 26 | 23 | 22 | I |

See Greenmarket; for more information, call 845-757-3276
"One of the foundations" of the Greenmarket, this "go-to vendor" for fresh fruit and vegetables hauls its "lovely variety of produce", including "especially good greens" that are always "fresh and flavor-ful", from Tivoli, NY, year-round and is one of the "hardy few" still at Union Square in winter; the gilding on the lettuce leaf is that it's also one of the more "reasonably priced" stalls around.

Miho Kosuda Ltd. *Flowers*

- | - | - | VE

E 40s | 310 E. 44th St. (bet. 1st & 2nd Aves.) | 212-922-9122
By appointment only

This chic East Side florist and event planner uses only "the lushest roses and peonies" in her "stunning" pieces that have long attracted a celeb clientele (Manolo Blahnik, among others) but represent "once-in-a-lifetime splurges" for ordinary mortals; the eponymous owner creates posies that are "simple, elegant" and exhibit "just a dash of individual style", generally utilizing only one type of flower in a rainbow of hues.

Milano Gourmet *Prepared Food*

25 | 21 | 21 | M

E 80s | 1582 Third Ave. (89th St.) | 4/5/6 to 86th St. | 212-996-6681 ◐
Murray Hill | 14 E. 34th St. (bet. 5th & Madison Aves.) | 6 to 33rd St. | 212-532-1177
W 100s | 2892 Broadway (bet. 112th & 113th Sts.) | 1 to 110th St. | 212-665-9500 ◐
www.milanogourmet.com

With "great" sandwiches, the "best" cold cuts and "delicious" pastas and salads, it's no wonder the "devoted clientele" can't get enough of the Italian-accented dishes sold at these East Side–West Side markets; plus, all those "helpful" folks inside make the experience all the more *"bellissimo."*

Milk & Cookies ◐☞ *Baked Goods*

24 | 22 | 21 | M

W Village | 19 Commerce St. (bet. Bedford St. & 7th Ave.) | 1 to Christopher St. | 212-243-1640 | www.milkandcookiesbakery.com

"Pick your own dough and mix-ins" and have "custom cookies" "made fresh to order" at this "cute" West Village bakery, which will whip up an "mm-mm good" batch in about 15 minutes and serve 'em with milk from Ronnybrook Farms Dairy; they also sell premade cookies and bars along with ice cream sandwiches and shakes, so though the selection's "simple", "kids" at heart "can't resist."

Mille Fiori *Flowers*

- | - | - | VE

Chelsea | 227 W. 29th St., 2nd fl. (bet. 7th & 8th Aves.) | 212-714-2202 | www.millefioriflowers.com
By appointment only

"Recipients are always thrilled" to sign for a delivery from this "expert" Chelsea floral shop that sources "gorgeous flowers" – the Japanese peony is among their signature blooms – "made even more beautiful by their arrangements"; it specializes in weddings and corporate events, but no matter the occasion, you can expect "exquisite work" that's "worth the somewhat high prices."

❷ Minamoto Kitchoan ☞ *Candy/Nuts*

28 | 27 | 25 | E

W 40s | Swiss Center Bldg. | 608 Fifth Ave. (49th St.) | B/D/F/V to 47-50th Sts./Rockefeller Ctr. | 212-489-3747 | www.kitchoan.com

This "serene" Japanese confectionary in Midtown is "the closest you can get to Tokyo" without hopping a JAL flight, proffering "beautifully displayed", Japanese wagashi ("traditional" tea sweets) carefully crafted to resemble "perfect little pieces of art"; such "exquisite" creations make "lovely" and "unusual gifts" – thanks particularly to a staff that "takes great care in packaging" – but as some say these "dainty", costly delights are "an acquired taste", just be sure "the recipient knows how special they are."

Miss Elisabeth's Catering ⊘ Caterer — | — | — | E

E Village | 52 E. 13th St. (bet. Broadway & University Pl.) | 917-414-0512 | www.misselisabeths.com
By appointment only

Specializing in "smallish dinner parties" served at the client's home, this East Village–based caterer aims to create restaurant-quality meals employing seasonal and organic ingredients whenever possible; given the "exquisite" results and "very professional" service, surveyors say she's a "must for any special occasion."

Mister Wright ● Wine/Liquor 24 | 20 | 24 | M

E 80s | 1593 Third Ave. (bet. 89th & 90th Sts.) | 4/5/6 to 86th St. | 212-722-4564

"You can't go wrong at Mister Wright" aver admirers of this "no-attitude" Yorkville establishment where there's lots of "open space to browse" the global "variety" of "wines for the common man", though some say the layout can be "a little hard to navigate"; oenophiles "on a budget" appreciate "passionate", "helpful" staffers who "treat you with the same respect" whether you're spending "$5 or $500", toasting this longtime staple as a neighborhood "favorite."

Mona Lisa Pastry Shop ●⬤ Baked Goods 24 | 24 | 19 | M

Bay Ridge | 1476 86th St. (bet. Bay 8th St. & 15th Ave.) | Brooklyn | D/M to 18th Ave. | 718-837-9053 | www.monalisabakery.com

Patrons are all smiles when it comes to this Bay Ridge Italian bakery and cafe that has been in business for more than 90 years, specializing in "decadent desserts" (including cheesecake baked in a coal-fired brick oven), as well as savory panini and pizzas; service can be "slow" so you might as well relax and "check out the da Vinci-esque frescoed ceiling."

Mondel Chocolates ⬤ Candy/Nuts 22 | 19 | 20 | M

W 100s | 2913 Broadway (114th St.) | 1 to 116th St. | 212-864-2111 | www.mondelchocolates.com

This "old-school" "neighborhood candy joint" in Morningside Heights has supplied the Columbia crowd with quality chocolates and other sweets since the 1940s ("they've been using dark chocolate for decades"), and happily retains its "charming", "unpretentious" atmosphere; a few find its output "uninspired" and shrug the appeal must be "a nostalgia thing", but they're outvoted by boosters who say this "treasure" "should be given landmark protection."

Montague St. Bagels ●⬤ Bagels 22 | 14 | 18 | I

Brooklyn Heights | 108 Montague St. (bet. Henry & Hicks Sts.) | Brooklyn | 2/3/4/5/M/N/R/W to Borough Hall/Court St. | 718-237-2512

"Huge" (think "nuclear-size") bagels "hot" from the oven are the high point at this "reliable" Brooklyn Heights deli/take-out specialist that's also a standby for "surprisingly good" sandwiches, wraps and such; factor in "cheap" pricing and "24-hour" availability, and to many it's "as good as it gets" in the area.

Monteleone's-Cammereri's ● 🗐 *Baked Goods*

23 | 19 | 21 | M

Carroll Gardens | 355 Court St. (bet. President & Union Sts.) | Brooklyn | F/G to Carroll St. | 718-852-5600

The "marriage" "works" say those who have witnessed the merger of "two famous" decades-old "authentic Italian bakeries" into this single Carroll Gardens standout; its "classic" selection of Italian-American desserts includes "delicious" versions of "all the old favorites" ("nothing nouvelle" here), so grab a pignoli cookie and savor a taste of the "old neighborhood" in an "ever-gentrifying area."

⚡ Moore Brothers Wine Co. ● 🗐 *Wine/Liquor*

29 | 27 | 29 | M

Flatiron | 33 E. 20th St. (bet. B'way & Park Ave. S.) | 6 to 23rd St. | 212-375-1575 | 866-986-6673 | www.moorebrothersblogs.com

"Welcome to NY" – this Philadelphia-area import is voted No. 1 for Service in this Survey (and second for Quality in its category), an "elegant", bi-level, 4,000-sq.-ft. "refrigerated" Flatironer whose "limited" but "outstanding" selection of artisanal European wines from "small", independent producers are offered at "reasonable" rates; owners Greg and David Moore "take responsibility" once the bottles "leave the winery" and ensure they're "imported and stored at the right temperature", while in the shop "exceptionally knowledgeable" staffers "go out of their way to inform"; N.B. there are frequent tastings and classes.

⚡ Morrell & Co. 🗐 *Wine/Liquor*

27 | 24 | 24 | E

W 40s | 1 Rockefeller Plaza (bet. 5th & 6th Aves.) | B/D/F/V to 47-50th Sts./Rockefeller Ctr. | 212-688-9370 | 800-969-4637 | www.morrellwine.com

It's "my Midtown sommelier" coo cognoscenti who cram this "tiny" but "elegant" Rock Center retailer filled floor-to-ceiling with a "fantastic selection" of hard-to-find wines and "top-notch" spirits; enthusiasts appreciate the staff's "outstanding knowledge" – not to mention the "informative courses" and "educational catalogs" – while acknowledging hefty tabs ("you pay for what you get"); still, a minority mutters that the "high-end" inventory is matched by "high-end attitude"; N.B. services include wedding registration, consignment and the sale of futures online.

⚡ Morrell Wine Xchange ● 🗐 *Wine/Liquor*

26 | 24 | 23 | E

E 60s | 1035 Third Ave. (bet. 61st & 62nd Sts.) | 4/5/6/N/R/W to 59th St./Lexington Ave. | 212-832-1144

"Any purchase is a winner" at this "small, refined", "reliable" Eastsider (no longer affiliated with Rockefeller Center's Morrell & Co.) known for its "great" imported champagne, Cabernet and Chardonnay – though it has increased its stock of lesser-known

California boutique vintages and "might just have that bottle you can't find anywhere else"; its staffers are "accommodating" "even to customers with little expertise", which makes up for prices that, not surprisingly, "aren't cheap."

Mother Mousse ▣ Baked Goods — 26 | 21 | 23 | M

Staten Island | 2175 Hylan Blvd. (bet. Lincoln & Midland Aves.) | 718-987-4242
Staten Island | 3767 Victory Blvd. (Travis Ave.) | 718-983-8366
www.mamamousse.com

Staten Islanders "insist" the mother of all "homemade mousses" is the "creamy" variety (in numerous "rich" flavors) that this bakery duet layers into their "top-notch" "triple-decker" cakes and other "fantastic" desserts, guaranteeing "a really special treat" for birthdays, weddings or any occasion; "presentation is top-of-the-line", and "nice gift baskets" offer a sampling of their cookies and other treats.

Mother's Bake Shop ⊘ Baked Goods — 21 | 20 | 21 | I

Bronx | 548 W. 235th St. (Johnson Ave.) | 1 to 231st St. | 718-796-5676
"Mother never disappoints" say supporters of this "landmark" Jewish bakery in Riverdale, for more than a half-century a "dependable" source of "total comfort" classics like "divine" black-and-white cookies, the "world's best babka" and a plethora of "old-fashioned" cakes and pastries; "neighborhood" know-it-alls add the breads and sandwiches are a true "taste of home" too.

Mount Carmel Wine & Spirits ◑▣ Wine/Liquor — ▽ 26 | 20 | 24 | M

Bronx | 609 E. 187th St. (bet. Arthur & Hughes Aves.) | B/D to Fordham Rd. | 718-367-7833 | www.mountcarmelwines.com
"A real find off Arthur Avenue", this Bronx dealer boasts one of NYC's most "extensive selections of Italian wines", including lots of lesser-known *vini* and "specialty spirits" (including a "one-of-a-kind" lineup of grappas); "friendly staffers" provide "wonderful service" – especially during Saturday afternoon tastings – so although it makes for a "long trip" for fans from other boroughs, it's a "favorite destination"; N.B. a move to new across-the-street quarters is in the works.

Movable Feast, The Caterer — 23 | 22 | 22 | E

Park Slope | 284 Prospect Park W. (bet. 17th & 18th Sts.) | Brooklyn | 718-965-2900 | www.mfcatering.com
By appointment only

For festivities "done right", this "very experienced" Park Slope caterer/event planner has a knack for moving "out of the box" to personalize "all types of" affairs with a "comforting" start-to-finish competence that's "a dream come true"; from "memorable", "elegantly presented" food to "professional" service, Brooklynites boast it's a "class act" that's also "an amazing value"; N.B. it's the in-house caterer for Prospect Park venues including the Boathouse, Audubon Center and Picnic House.

	QUALITY	DISPLAY	SERVICE	COST

Mrs. Field's Cookies ◑ ▭ *Baked Goods* | 18 | 15 | 15 | M |

Garment District | 1 Herald Sq. (bet. 33rd & 34th Sts.) | B/D/F/N/
Q/R/V/W to 34th St./Herald Sq. | 212-967-1716
Seaport | Pier 17 | 89 South St. (Fulton St.) | 2/3 to Fulton St. |
212-587-5335
W 40s | Port Authority | 625 Eighth Ave. (bet. 40th & 41st Sts.) | A/
C/E to 42nd St./Port Authority | 212-695-1186
Elmhurst | Queens Place Mall | 8801 Queens Blvd. (bet. 55th & 56th Aves.) |
Queens | G/R/V to Grand Ave. | 718-699-0780
www.mrsfields.com

Feedback is all over the field on this "very commercial" mega-chain,
with advocates still "warm and fuzzy" on the "freshly baked",
"melty" cookies but others "unimpressed" by "cloyingly sweet",
"mass-produced" merchandise at "steep" prices; regardless, it's
"time-tested" for a "quick" "sugar high" "on the run" – even if many
have "no problem jogging past."

m2m ◑ *Specialty Shop* | 18 | 15 | 13 | I |

E Village | 55 Third Ave. (11th St.) | 6 to Astor Pl. | 212-353-2698
W 100s | 2935 Broadway (114th St.) | 1 to 110th St. |
212-280-4600

At this "handy" East Village Japanese-Korean "deli-on-steroids"
(with a smaller Morningside Heights outpost), "fresh sushi" and
other "decent", priced-right prepared foods are joined by a "wide
variety of Asian packaged goods" including sauces, condiments and
some "hard-to-find ingredients", plus plenty of crunchy-salty
"snack staples"; there are also cooking implements, gadgets and
small appliances like rice cookers, making it the perfect "pop-in"
when "you don't have time to go to Chinatown."

Mudspot ◑ ▭ ⊟ *Coffee/Tea* | 26 | 19 | 22 | I |

E Village | 307 E. Ninth St. (2nd Ave.) | 6 to Astor Pl. | 212-228-9074 |
www.mudnyc.com

Java junkies who flock to the mobile Mudtruck parked on Astor
Place can fuel up on the same "explosively strong" brew at this "laid-
back" coffeehouse, a model of "East Village hipness" defined by
"cozy", brick-lined quarters and "too-cool" service; besides a "serious" "cup o' joe", it proffers "delish" munchies ranging from baked
goods to panini and fajitas, so something's sure to hit the spot.

Murray's Bagels ◑ *Bagels* | 26 | 20 | 20 | I |

Chelsea | 242 Eighth Ave. (bet. 22nd & 23rd Sts.) | C/E to 23rd St. |
646-638-1335
G Village | 500 Sixth Ave. (bet. 12th & 13th Sts.) | F/L/V to 14th St./
6th Ave. | 212-462-2830
www.murraysbagels.com

The "golden" ratio of "crispy" outside to "chewy" inside has devotees
declaring this Chelsea–Greenwich Village twosome's "heavenly",
"generously sized", "malty" bagels some of the "best in town" – "no
question about it"; there are a few grumbles that they "don't toast",
but few grouse about the "abundance" of "fresh spreads" and
"quick-moving" staff that keeps the "lines" of noshers moving.

	QUALITY	DISPLAY	SERVICE	COST

☑ Murray's Cheese Shop ⌨ Cheese/Dairy | 28 | 25 | 25 | E |

E 40s | Grand Central Mkt. | Lexington Ave. (43rd St.) | 4/5/6/7/S to 42nd St./Grand Central | 212-922-1540 ●
G Village | 254 Bleecker St. (Cornelia St.) | A/B/C/D/E/F/V to W. 4th St. | 212-243-3289
888-692-4339 | www.murrayscheese.com

Widely considered "the gold standard of cheese in NY", this Village "wonderland" boasts an "astounding" assortment of "premium" "artisanal and seasonal" fromages "from all over the map", with "congenial" "experts" on staff dispensing advice and taste tests; it also offers an array of "accoutrements" and "tasty" prepared foods, and its "spacious" digs include "caves under the store" plus classrooms offering "a cheese education"; P.S. the small "Grand Central outpost is a godsend" for the 'burbs-bound, albeit with less exotic choices.

Murray's Sturgeon ⌨ Caviar/Smoked Fish | 27 | 19 | 22 | E |

W 80s | 2429 Broadway (bet. 89th & 90th Sts.) | 1/2/3 to 96th St. | 212-724-2650 | www.murrayssturgeon.com

Fans of "fresh smoked fish" laud this "tiny" Upper West Side "nosh heaven" for its "sublime" Nova, sturgeon and pickled herring, all sliced "to perfection" by "neighborly" countermen who "know their stuff"; it's also an "institution" for "top-notch" deli-style "Jewish staples", with "homey" "throwback" surroundings dating to 1946 that prove it's "the real deal" – so "what more could you ask?"

Myers of Keswick ⌨ Specialty Shop | 23 | 21 | 22 | M |

W Village | 634 Hudson St. (bet. Horatio & Jane Sts.) | A/C/E/L to 14th St./8th Ave. | 212-691-4194 | www.myersofkeswick.com

"Mushy peas, marmite and Molly the cat" (the store's mascot) await "homesick" Brits at this bonny "haunt" located in an Anglophilic corner of the West Village, which is "crowded as London's tube" with "old faves" that remind one there'll "always be an England"; "expats, there really is a place for treacle" in NYC, plus "fresh bangers and Scotch eggs", "great pork pies", "prawn cocktail crisps", "Bird's custard" and "all of the other 'beastly muck' from across the pond."

My Most Favorite Food ●⌨ Baked Goods | 21 | 21 | 18 | E |
(fka My Most Favorite Dessert Co.)

W 40s | 120 W. 45th St. (bet. B'way & 6th Ave.) | 1/2/3/7/N/Q/R/S/W to 42nd St./Times Sq. | 212-997-5130

"Well, certainly one of them" concur fans of the "top-notch" kosher desserts (pareve and dairy) retailed at this Midtown eatery/bakery, featuring a "fresh" selection of "decadent" cakes along with all the preferred pastries, pies, cookies and breads; it's admired for "fantastic" "quality", though the bottom line reveals this is a "pricey option."

Myzel Chocolates ⌨ Candy/Nuts | ▽ 19 | 23 | 19 | E |

W 50s | 140 W. 55th St. (bet. 6th & 7th Aves.) | N/Q/R/W to 57th St. | 212-245-4233 | www.myzels.com

"Although tiny", this Midtown sweet spot "convenient to City Center" manages to cram in dozens of "glass jars" filled with mass-market chocolates, truffles, cookies, licorice and other crowd-pleasers; satis-

QUALITY DISPLAY SERVICE COST

fied surveyors appreciate that the proprietor "will go beyond the call of duty" when it comes to creating special packages and baskets.

Naidre's ◐⇆ *Coffee/Tea* `22 | 20 | 20 | M`

Carroll Gardens | 502 Henry St. (Sackett St.) | Brooklyn | F/G to Carroll St. | 718-596-3400
Park Slope | 384 Seventh Ave. (bet. 11th & 12th Sts.) | Brooklyn | F to 7th Ave. | 718-965-7585
www.naidres.com

"Neighborhood" necessities in Park Slope and Carroll Gardens, this "friendly" coffeehouse/cafe couple plies "robust" java along with organic tea, smoothies and a home-cooking menu that offers "a lot of alternatives", from fresh pastries and breakfast fare to stout sandwiches and refreshing "vegetarian options"; the casual quarters provide some "spartan" seating, and their to-go trade is brisk.

Nancy's–Wines For Food ◑▱ *Wine/Liquor* `24 | 22 | 23 | M`

W 70s | 313 Columbus Ave. (bet. 74th & 75th Sts.) | B/C to 72nd St. | 212-877-4040 | www.nancyswines.com
The "devoted following" of Nancy Maniscalco's "terrific" UWS shop applauds her "concept" of emphasizing "food-friendly" vintages "geared to drinking every day"; they also appreciate "personalized" advice on pairings from an "enthusiastic" staff, and report that among the "offbeat selections" – including Mitteleuropean choices, rosés, armagnacs and sakes – are some "real finds at reasonable prices."

Napoli Bakery ⇆ *Baked Goods* `▽ 23 | 21 | 22 | M`

Williamsburg | 616 Metropolitan Ave. (bet. Leonard & Lorimer Sts.) | Brooklyn | G/L to Metropolitan Ave./Lorimer St. | 718-384-6945
All-Italian and "all good", this mom-and-pop bakery is an enclave of "old-school charm" in "hipster" Williamsburg that keeps its brick oven burning to supply a generous selection of "excellent" breads and focaccia; "fresh" loaves are its sole claim to fame, however, so expect a sparse stock otherwise.

Natural Frontier ◑ *Health Food* `24 | 17 | 18 | M`

E 80s | 1424 Third Ave. (bet. 80th & 81st Sts.) | 6 to 77th St. | 212-794-0922
Gramercy | 266 Third Ave. (bet. 21st & 22nd Sts.) | 6 to 23rd St. | 212-228-9133
On the Upper East Side and Gramercy Park frontiers, these natural food shops are "convenient" options for "quality" "basic health fare", and some "things you can't find elsewhere", happily at "reasonable prices"; a "knowledgeable", if "aloof", staff can guide you through the "tight aisles", and for those on the go, there's also an "organic" juice bar, salad bar and "delicious" prepared foods.

Naturally Delicious *Caterer/Events* `- | - | - | E`

Carroll Gardens | 487 Court St. (bet. Huntington & Nelson Sts.) | Brooklyn | 718-237-3727 | www.naturallydelicious.com
By appointment only
Co-owner and "brilliant cook" Loren Michelle got her start as a chef in eateries like the legendary Quilted Giraffe, so naturally the "fresh",

	QUALITY	DISPLAY	SERVICE	COST

"wonderful" fare from this Carroll Gardens caterer/event planner are "yum"-inducing and "served up in beautiful presentations"; the "accommodating" staff will handle details from venue selection to photography and music with boutique flair, though critics charge the "follow-through" can be "expensive and a bit haughty."

Nature's Gifts ● *Health Food* `21` `18` `17` `M`

E 80s | 1297 Lexington Ave. (bet. 87th & 88th Sts.) | 4/5/6 to 86th St. | 212-289-6283

E 80s | 320 E. 86th St. (bet. 1st & 2nd Aves.) | 4/5/6 to 86th St. | 212-734-8298

Upper Eastsiders head to this pair of "tiny" health food locations for "fresh and delicious" prepared foods, including Greek specialties such as moussaka, spanakopita and housemade yogurt, as well as a line of unusual baked goods like banana-pomegranate bread; there's also a great selection of cheeses, olive oils and olives.

☑ Nespresso Boutique *Coffee/Tea* `25` `27` `25` `E`

E 60s | 761 Madison Ave. (65 St.) | 6 to 68th St. | 800-562-1465 | www.nespresso.com

"Take a break between Hermès and Armani" at this "stylish" East Side boutique for upmarket caffeine fiends, the local branch of an international outfit that packages its own "perfect espressos" in "fancy" "capsules" designed for brewing by its "incredible" high-tech coffeemakers; the gourmet javas and "Rolls-Royce"-caliber machines are "sold at the site" by "hands-on" staffers, though some will settle for just a "chic" cup since that alone's "expensive" enough.

Neuchatel Chocolates ▣ *Candy/Nuts* `24` `23` `21` `VE`

E 50s | Park Ave. Plaza | 55 E. 52nd St. (bet. Madison & Park Aves.) | E/V to 5th Ave./53rd St. | 212-759-1388 | 800-597-0759 | www.neuchatelchocolates.com

A "great choice for Swiss chocolates", this quiet East Side player on the city's bonbon scene impresses with "the best truffles" and other "luscious" bites that are as "delicious" as they are "attractive"; the prices are way "expensive", but for such "mmm"-quality goods, most say it's "worth it"; N.B. the Financial District branch has closed.

Neuhaus Chocolate Boutique ▣ *Candy/Nuts* `25` `23` `22` `E`

E 40s | Grand Central Terminal | main concourse (42nd St. & Vanderbilt Ave.) | 4/5/6/7/S to 42nd St./Grand Central | 212-972-3740

E 50s | 569 Lexington Ave. (bet. 50th & 51st Sts.) | 6 to 51st St. | 212-593-0848

W 70s | 2151 Broadway (bet. 75th & 76th Sts.) | 1 to 72nd St. | 212-712-2112

www.neuhaus.be

"Belgian know-how does it again" at these "fabulous" offshoots of the Brussels-based chocolate chain, where the "high-end" truffles and other "wonderful" confections in "gorgeous displays" can easily become an "expensive" "weakness"; free samples and choose-your-own gift assortments are pluses, but what some consider an increasingly "commercial" feel and occasionally "slow" service are not.

	QUALITY	DISPLAY	SERVICE	COST

Neuman's *Caterer*
(fka Neuman & Bogdonoff)

▽ 25 | 23 | 22 | E

LES | 173 Chrystie St. (bet. Delancey & Rivington Sts.) | F/V to Lower East Side/2nd Ave. | 212-228-2444 | www.caterernyc.com

Paul Neuman's a solo act since the buyout of his former partner, Stacy Bogdonoff, but this Lower East Side caterer/event planner still "does a spectacular job" at delivering "everything you ask for and much more" in the way of "fabulous" seasonal spreads and "wonderful" off-site setups; admirers attest "you can't go wrong" with their handling of "all types of parties", and they "don't charge ridiculous prices, although they could."

New Beef King *Meat/Poultry*

- | - | - | I

Chinatown | 89 Bayard St. (bet. Mott & Mulberry Sts.) | 6/J/M/N/Q/R/W/Z to Canal St. | 212-233-6612

"Beef jerky, Chinese-style" is the specialty of this single-minded, "out-of-the-way" Chinatowner, where you won't find fresh meat, just owner Robert Yee's 10 different styles of dried and cured beef and pork, based on an old family recipe rooted in Hong Kong; initiates say the "surprisingly delicious" results are "juicy morsels" of "flavorful jerky heaven."

New Green Pea *Produce*

▽ 23 | 20 | 19 | M

Brooklyn Heights | 181 Atlantic Ave. (bet. Clinton & Court Sts.) | Brooklyn | 2/3/4/5/M/N/R/W to Borough Hall/Court St. | 718-596-4624

Bedecked with old-fashioned carts for the fruits and vegetables, this "archetype" lives up to its name, supplying Brooklyn Heights residents with "fresh", "high-quality" greens as well as a "wide selection" of condiments, herbs, dried fruits, nuts and more; considering its "reasonable prices", it's "the sort of greengrocer every neighborhood should have."

Newman & Leventhal *Caterer*

▽ 21 | 19 | 22 | E

W 80s | 45 W. 81st St. (bet. Columbus Ave. & CPW) | 212-362-9400 By appointment only

If your event "has to be kosher", "one of the top" caterers in town is this "longtime" (circa 1908) Upper West Side outfit, recognized as "true professionals" at providing "beautifully presented" feasts whether traditional or contemporary, indoors or outdoors, private or corporate; maybe their style's "a bit old-fashioned" – very up-to-date prices notwithstanding – but satisfied customers "cannot recommend them enough."

New York Beverage *Beer*

- | - | - | M

Bronx | 515 Bruckner Blvd. (bet. Austin Pl. & 149th St.) | 6 to 149th St. | 212-831-4000 | www.newyorkbeverage.com

The drinkables distributed by this Bronx beverage house aren't limited to alcohol – more than half the company's business is water, soda and juice – but for those who do want a belt with a buzz, it also stocks 300 labels of beer (domestic, German, Belgian, English and Mexican), sold by the keg or by the case, and there's hard cider too.

	QUALITY	DISPLAY	SERVICE	COST

New York Cake & Baking Distributor ☰ *Cookware*

| 24 | 13 | 12 | M |

Flatiron | 56 W. 22nd St. (bet. 5th & 6th Aves.) | F/V to 23rd St. | 212-675-2253

This Flatiron shop stocks "everything for the sweet kitchen" from cake-decorating supplies like food coloring, gum paste and sprinkles to cookie cutters, pans "in any shape", doilies and "beautiful dragées" and decorations that "pique the imagination" of "amateurs" and "professionals" alike; on the downside are a "surly" staff and a "jumbled" interior that "needs a major face-lift."

New York Wine Exchange ●◗☰ *Wine/Liquor*

| ▽ 23 | 21 | 20 | E |

Financial District | 9 Broadway (bet. Battery Pl. & Morris St.) | 4/5 to Bowling Green | 212-422-2222 | www.nywineexchange.com

Bankers and accountants are often in the red thanks to this pricey Financial District wine dealer near the Stock Exchange, whose "great selection" emphasizes California Cabernets and Merlots, ports (some 200) and a growing inventory of Hungarian whites and bottles from Uruguay, Portugal and Israel; "location, location, location" is a selling point too – way "south of Houston" this may be one of your "best" options; N.B. a full line of liquor is also available.

New York Wine Warehouse ☰ *Wine/Liquor*

| 23 | 18 | 19 | M |

LIC | 8-05 43rd Ave. (Vernon Blvd.) | Queens | E/V to 23rd St./Ely Ave. | 718-784-8776 | www.nywines.com

If you "need a '63 Fonseca port on the fly, they've got it" declare fans of this LIC vintner, a "secret resource" that will "sell, deal, auction, store, catalog and deliver" wines for knowledgeable oenophiles; its 10,000 labels make it a favorite of "wine geeks" and collectors, who can order not only by phone or fax but also via the company's website.

Nicky's Vietnamese Sandwiches ⊘ *Deli/Sandwich*

| 24 | 13 | 20 | I |

E Village | 150 E. Second St. (Ave. A) | F/V to Lower East Side/2nd Ave. | 212-388-1088 ●
Boerum Hill | 311 Atlantic Ave. (bet. Hoyt & Smith Sts.) | Brooklyn | A/C/G to Hoyt/Schermerhorn Sts. | 718-855-8838
www.nickyssandwiches.com

This "tiny, cheerful" East Villager (with an outpost in Boerum Hill) specializes in "delicate iterations of the wonderful Vietnamese *banh-mi*" sandwiches: filled with a choice of chicken or pork liver pâté plus "lightly pickled veggies", they pack "a symphony of flavor"; "perfect for a snack", the "cheap" goods also make "quite a tasty bargain."

Ninth Avenue International ☰ *Specialty Shop*

| 23 | 18 | 20 | I |

W 40s | 543 Ninth Ave. (bet. 40th & 41st Sts.) | A/C/E to 42nd St./Port Authority | 212-279-1000

"The smell alone makes you want to buy spices you've never even heard of", so it's a good thing you can procure them "by the pound" at this "adventure" of a Med mart in Hell's Kitchen; "extraordinary discoveries lurk" beyond the seasonings as well, including everything from "olives and cheese" to "various pickled vegetables" and spreads including what some consider "the best taramasalata in NYC."

Ninth Street Espresso ⊘ *Coffee/Tea* ∇ 28 | 17 | 22 | I

NEW Chelsea | Chelsea Mkt. | 75 Ninth Ave. (bet. 15th & 16th Sts.) | A/C/E/L to 8th Ave./14th St. | 212-228-2930
E Village | 700 E. Ninth St. (Ave. C) | L to 1st Ave. | 212-358-9225
www.ninthstreetespresso.com

Among "the few real" caffeine craftsmen, this "funky" East Villager (with a new Chelsea Market offshoot) combines Northern Italian inspiration with beans from Portland, OR's Stumptown Coffee Roasters to produce "excellent" espresso and variants like "true cappuccino" and "mind-blowing macchiato"; throw in baked goods from Balthazar and service from "hip" folks "who care", and "there's no point" in settling for less; N.B. a third location at 341 East 10th Street is planned for summer 2008.

Nordic Delicacies ⌑ *Specialty Shop* ∇ 28 | 18 | 23 | M

Bay Ridge | 6909 Third Ave. (bet. Bay Ridge & Ovington Aves.) | Brooklyn | R to Bay Ridge Ave. | 718-748-1874 | 800-346-6734 | www.nordicdeli.com

"One of a kind, from a bygone era" (the 1980s, actually), this "small" twentysomething "Norsk delight" "caters to the remaining Scandinavians" in Bay Ridge with "delicacies they remember from childhood"; there's "not a lot to choose from" if you're hankering for something from the Southern hemisphere, but Nordic "deli items" like pickled herring and cheeses, as well as the "canned fish, jams and sweaters", are all of "the highest quality" at prices you can afford.

#1 Farmers Market ● *Produce* 23 | 19 | 19 | M

E 50s | 1095 Second Ave. (bet. 57th & 58th Sts.) | 4/5/6/N/R/W to 59th St./Lexington Ave. | 212-688-2618
E 70s | 1458 Second Ave. (76th St.) | 6 to 77th St. | 212-396-2626

You "never know what you're going to find" at this "crowded" 24/7 Upper East Side duo where the fruits and vegetables are "always beautiful" and the cheese, olives, spreads, flowers, cookies and kosher items equally "fresh"; although a few feel that "better deals can be found" elsewhere, the markets' round-the-clock hours trump all: "'convenient' is the word."

Nusbaum & Wu Bakery ● *Baked Goods* 18 | 17 | 15 | M

W 100s | 2897 Broadway (113th St.) | 1 to 110th St. | 212-280-5344

Cookie buffs claim the signature black-and-whites are "a revelation" at this Columbia-area bakery/cafe, which otherwise woos the "students" with its "prime location" and "fair" assortment of bagels, sandwiches and deli goods; local consensus calls it "nothing amazing, but convenient" if you can "survive the crowds."

| | QUALITY | DISPLAY | SERVICE | COST |

NEW Oak & Steel ◐ *Wine/Liquor*
- | - | - | M

W 50s | 1776 Broadway (bet. 57th & 58th Sts.) | 1/A/B/C/D to 59th St./Columbus Circle | 212-262-7702 | www.oakandsteel.com

New to the Columbus Circle *vin* scene, this small, clean-lined shop boasts a succinct inventory of exclusively small-production, hand-made wines (including champagnes), plus a selection of high-end spirits; its expert staff boasts six sommeliers and a chef who's ready to address food-pairing questions.

O&CO. ▭ *Specialty Shop*
25 | 25 | 22 | E

E 40s | Grand Central Terminal | main concourse (42nd St. & Vanderbilt Ave.) | 4/5/6/7/S to 42nd St./Grand Central | 212-973-1472
G Village | 249 Bleecker St. (bet. 6th & 7th Aves.) | A/B/C/D/E/F/V to W. 4th St. | 646-230-8373
877-828-6620 | www.oliviersandco.com

The "green lemon olive oil makes your socks roll up and down" – and that's a good thing at this paean to the juice of the pitted fruit in Grand Central Station and Greenwich Village; an "amazing array" of "gorgeously packaged" "regional and infused" olive oil ("and anything made with it" or used to serve it) "tempts" "commuters" to stop in and get "educated" by "knowledgeable salespeople"; the quality is "incomparable", but, alas, so are the markups at this "olive oil lover's version of a wine tasting bar."

NEW Öko ◐⇝ *Ice Cream*
24 | 23 | 22 | M

E Village | 137 First Ave. (bet. 8th & 9th Sts.) | L to 1st Ave./14th St. | 212-228-3321
Park Slope | 152 Fifth Ave. (bet. Degraw & Douglass Sts.) | Brooklyn | R to Union St. | 718-398-3671
www.okoyogurt.com

Solar panels on the awning out front are the first clue that this Park Slope arrival (with a new East Village offshoot) isn't your usual pinkberry knockoff: from its "easy-on-the-eye" interior constructed with "green" building materials to the "biodegradable" cups and spoons, it has a seriously eco-conscious bent; "oooh, so good!" is the verdict on its "tart" fro-yo made on-premises with Greek yogurt and crowned with "assorted fruit, nut or candy toppings"; N.B. it also pours 18 kinds of organic, Fair Trade tea.

NEW Old Brooklyn Parlor ◐ *Ice Cream*
24 | 19 | 23 | M

Prospect Heights | 564 Vanderbilt Ave. (bet. Bergen & Dean Sts.) | Brooklyn | 2/3 to Bergen St. | 646-393-5712 | www.oldbrooklynparlor.com

At this new Prospect Heights ice cream parlor dispensing "egg creams, lime rickeys", malteds and other "old-fashioned" frozen treats, the "summertime lines are longer" than those for a "Disneyland ride", but the "amazing" "homemade taste" has supporters saying it's "worth" the wait; it's got the retro soda fountain look down pat, from the counter that seats six to the black-and-white "old Brooklyn" photos, but its purveyors are strictly up-to-the-minute (scoops are from Ronnybrook and coffee from Gorilla).

	QUALITY	DISPLAY	SERVICE	COST

☑ Olive's *Deli/Sandwich*

| 25 | 19 | 18 | M |

SoHo | 120 Prince St. (bet. Greene & Wooster Sts.) | N/R to Prince St. | 212-941-0111 | www.olivesnyc.com

A perfect quick lunch "stop in SoHo", this tiny storefront is known for its "addictive", super-"fresh" Med-inflected sandwiches, as well as "excellent soups", salads, scones and such, offered in appealingly "substantial portions"; it draws a "trendy crowd" – after all, "the Mac store is across the street" – despite its lack of seating and sometimes "slow service"; N.B. you can order online for local deliveries.

Olivier Cheng Catering & Events ⊭ *Caterer*

| ▽ 22 | 26 | 26 | VE |

TriBeCa | 12-16 Vestry St. (Hudson St.) | 212-625-3151 | www.ocnyc.com
By appointment only

"Olivier is an artist" coo fans of the chef and co-owner of this top-shelf TriBeCa caterer/event planner, whose superior "aesthetic sense" informs chic stagings and "sophisticated" Asian-influenced cuisine ("no rubber chicken here") while the staff's "strong feeling for flow" ensures events large and small "run smoothly"; though designer-label "pricey", it's got all the style "money can buy" and routinely sews up business with clients like Gucci and Chanel.

Olivino Wines ◑ *Wine/Liquor*

| - | - | - | M |

NEW **Bed-Stuy** | 426D Marcus Garvey Blvd. (Macon St.) | Brooklyn | C to Fulton St. | 718-249-0721

Fort Greene | 905 Fulton St. (Clinton Ave.) | Brooklyn | G to Clinton/Washington Aves. | 718-857-7952

Fort Greene's vino "connoisseurs" go to this "small", olive-green boutique to explore Katrine Pollari's "highly personal, sometimes eccentric" stock of some 350 wines; along with her signature entries from Portugal, Lebanon and South Africa, Pollari pursues unusual varietals from Germany and Austria, and will occasionally host tastings to introduce her finds; N.B. an offshoot opened recently in Bed-Stuy.

Once Upon A Tart . . . ▣ *Baked Goods*

| 25 | 22 | 19 | M |

SoHo | 135 Sullivan St. (bet. Houston & Prince Sts.) | C/E to Spring St. | 212-387-8869 | www.onceuponatart.com

Those craving "classic tarts" both sweet and savory "can't resist" the "delish" selection at this "quaint" SoHo bakery/cafe, a "welcoming" "gem" that also turns out "must-have pastries", scones, cakes and cookies and "excels at sandwiches"; with a "helpful staff" to take custom orders for events and "a few tables" on hand "for those needing instant gratification", it leaves the majority happy ever after.

One Girl Cookies ▣ *Baked Goods*

| 24 | 23 | 22 | E |

Cobble Hill | 68 Dean St. (bet. Brooklyn Bridge Blvd. & Smith St.) | Brooklyn | F/G to Bergen St. | 212-675-4996 | www.onegirlcookies.com

The "delightful" "morsels" of "yumminess" are just "the right size" for a "girlie" treat at this Cobble Hill bakery/espresso bar, which packs "high quality" into its "tiny", "aesthetically pleasing" cookies and offers them in a "warm and inviting" space; the "unsurpassed" "attention to detail" extends to their "beautifully designed" gift boxes and event favors, which come so "artfully packaged" you may even forget the "hefty prices."

131 Fish Market ⊘ Seafood | 24 | 17 | 17 | M |
Chinatown | 131 Mott St. (bet. Grand & Hester Sts.) | 6/J/M/N/Q/ R/W/Z to Canal St. | 212-925-0970
"Just about every type" of seafood – fish, lobster, crab, prawn, squid, octopus, even sea cucumber – can be found at this "awesome" Chinatown fishmonger where the "consistent" selection comes "at a moderate cost" that "always beats the supermarkets"; those in-the-know recommend "go early" to get the freshest catch.

Oppenheimer Meats, Inc. ⊟ Meat/Poultry | 26 | 18 | 24 | E |
W 90s | 2606 Broadway (bet. 98th & 99th Sts.) | 1/2/3 to 96th St. | 212-662-0246 | www.oppenheimermeats.com
A "winner" since the 1950s, this UWS butcher comes through with "memory-making" prime meats and other "quality" selections, including poultry, veal, pork, lamb, game, sausages and even fish; nostalgists note the "terrific", amiable counter folk take you "back to the good old days" when "service really meant something."

Orchard, The Specialty Shop | 27 | 23 | 22 | E |
Midwood | 1367 Coney Island Ave. (bet. Ave. J & Cary Ct.) | Brooklyn | Q to Ave. J | 718-377-1799 | 800-222-0240 | www.orchardfruit.com
Want "the best produce in Brooklyn"? – order delivery from "the gold standard" of Midwood, this kosher shop "famous for their baskets", which are "beautifully" brimming with smoked fish, chocolates, nuts and "fruit, fruit and more fruit"; yes, they deliver, but you might have to tip double because their "platters are so heavy, two people need to carry them."

Oren's Daily Roast ⊟ Coffee/Tea | 24 | 19 | 21 | M |
E 40s | Grand Central Mkt. | Lexington Ave. (43rd St.) | 4/5/6/7/S to 42nd St./Grand Central | 212-338-0014 ☾
E 40s | Grand Central Terminal | main concourse (42nd St. & Vanderbilt Ave.) | 4/5/6/7/S to 42nd St./Grand Central | 212-953-1028 ☾
E 50s | 33 E. 58th St. (bet. Madison & Park Aves.) | 4/5/6/N/R/W to 59th St./Lexington Ave. | 212-838-3345
E 70s | 1144 Lexington Ave. (bet. 79th & 80th Sts.) | 6 to 77th St. | 212-472-6830
E 70s | 985 Lexington Ave. (71st St.) | 6 to 68th St. | 212-717-3907
E 80s | 1574 First Ave. (bet. 81st & 82nd Sts.) | 6 to 77th St. | 212-737-2690
G Village | 31 Waverly Pl. (bet. Greene St. & University Pl.) | A/B/C/ D/E/F/V to W. 4th St. | 212-420-5958
Murray Hill | 434 Third Ave. (bet. 30th & 31st Sts.) | 6 to 28th St. | 212-779-1241
W 100s | 2882 Broadway (bet. 112th & 113th Sts.) | 1 to 110th St. | 212-749-8779 ☾
888-348-5400 | www.orensdailyroast.com
"Never far away when you're jonesing" for a "reliable cup", this "worthy" "local" franchise pours "flavorful" coffee that's "freshly roasted" every weekday at its Jersey facility and "impeccably

brewed" by "sweet slacker" staffers; they vend 50 blends by the pound and stock H&H bagels, Donut Planet 'nuts and baked goods from Balthazar, ensuring "you're set for the morning" and giving the megachains "a run for their money."

NEW Organic Heights *Prepared Food* `- | - | - | M`

Park Slope | 460 Bergen St. (bet. 5th & Flatbush Aves.) | Brooklyn | 2/3 to Bergen St. | 718-622-4303

The verdantly painted exterior trumpets the eco-conscious ethos of this bright new organic prepared foods/baked goods shop on the nothern edge of Park Slope; in addition to its vegan-friendly, agave-sweetened treats and organic sandwiches, salads and soups, it offers some 30 varieties of tea and Fair Trade, shade-grown coffees.

Oriental Pastry & Grocery ● ☰ *Specialty Shop* `22 | 10 | 18 | I`

Brooklyn Heights | 170 Atlantic Ave. (bet. Clinton & Court Sts.) | Brooklyn | F to Bergen St. | 718-875-7687

"Bins filled with exotic food" keep shoppers coming back to this "wonderful remnant of Little Syria" on Brooklyn Heights' Atlantic Avenue that has been in business for more than 40 years; it's the place to go when "you want raisins from Yemen", "rice from Egypt", "authentic Lebanese hummus and baba ghanoush", spices, coffee or "freshly made" Middle Eastern pastries, all "reasonably priced" and dispensed by a "caring, thoughtful" crew.

Z Original SoupMan *Soup* `23 | 16 | 15 | M`

E 40s | 4 E. 42nd St. (bet. 5th & Madison Aves.) | 4/5/6/7/S to 42nd St./Grand Central | 212-599-5900 ●

E 50s | 672 Lexington Ave. (56th St.) | E/V to Lexington Ave./53rd St. | 212-355-2521 ●

Financial District | 110 Pearl St. (Hanover Sq.) | 2/3 to Wall St. | 212-968-7687

Financial District | 97 Trinity Pl. (bet. Cedar & Thames Sts.) | 1 to Rector St. | 212-566-7400

W 40s | Rockefeller Ctr. | 37 W. 48th St. (bet. 5th & 6th Aves.) | B/D/F/V to 47-50th Sts./Rockefeller Ctr. | 212-582-7400 ●

Staten Island | 2345 Richmond Ave. (Norme Ave.) | 718-477-7687 www.originalsoupman.com

"Legendary" 'Soup Nazi' of *Seinfeld* fame Al Yeganeh may forever be a cultural "mascot", but his signature dish is "no joke" say devotees of his "divine" chicken chile and "to-die-for" seafood bisques; cynics claim "franchising ruined" his product, and yet the lines at all locations remain "long" – most agree it's "still darn good soup."

NEW Oro Bakery and Bar ● *Baked Goods* `- | - | - | M`

Little Italy | 375 Broome St. (bet. Mott & Mullberry Sts.) | 6 to Spring St. | 212-941-6368 | www.orobakerybar.com

This Little Italy newcomer has struck upon a golden combination – bakery and wine bar – and "aims to please" with its "tempting array" of French-American "goodies"; by day, it plies pastries and organic coffee at breakfast and sandwiches, quiche and such at lunch, but come evening it "stays open for mingling over wine" or sake.

	QUALITY	DISPLAY	SERVICE	COST

Orwasher's Bakery ⌂☞ *Baked Goods* | 26 | 19 | 21 | M |

E 70s | 308 E. 78th St. (bet. 1st & 2nd Aves.) | 6 to 77th St. |
212-288-6569 | www.orwashers.com

"One of the best" "old-time bakeries", this Upper East Side "original"
(founded in 1916) "can't be beat" for "traditional Jewish" loaves and
rolls that epitomize what kosher bread "is supposed to be", served
up "fresh" and "with a smile"; "stop by for the rye" and "you'll know"
why such "great stuff" is "hard not to eat before you get home."

Oslo Coffee Company ☞ *Coffee/Tea* | 20 | 17 | 17 | M |

Williamsburg | 133B Roebling St. (Metropolitan Ave.) | Brooklyn | L to
Bedford Ave. | 718-782-0332
Williamsburg | 328 Bedford Ave. (bet. 2nd & 3rd Sts.) | Brooklyn | L to
Bedford Ave. | 718-930-9520
www.oslocoffee.com

Though its name's Nordic the inspiration skews Italian at these
Williamsburg java joints, which fire up an in-house roaster to produce "awesome espresso drinks" like latte and macchiatto that "hit
the spot every time"; with "prompt and polite service" whether
you're power boosting "on the way to work" or picking up beans by
the pound, it's a "top" contender for "best coffee in the 'Burg."

Otafuku ◐☞ *Prepared Food* | ▽ 19 | 9 | 14 | I |

E Village | 236 E. Ninth St. (bet. 2nd & 3rd Aves.) | L to 3rd Ave. |
212-353-8503

The menu may be brief, but the taste is big ("yum, yum") at this "tiny"
East Villager offering just two "authentic" Japanese "street-food"
snacks, takoyaki (an octopus croquette) and okonomiyaki (pancakes
with shredded cabbage and a choice of shellfish or meat); it's a "popular" stop for nibbles on the fly, where "you can't beat the prices."

⦿ Ottomanelli & Sons ⌂ *Meat/Poultry* | 27 | 21 | 26 | E |

G Village | 285 Bleecker St. (bet. Jones St. & 7th Ave. S.) | 1 to
Christopher St. | 212-675-4217
Woodside | 61-05 Woodside Ave. (61st St.) | Queens | 7 to 61st St. |
718-651-5544

Home to possibly the "most personable butchers in the city", these
Italian "gems" owned by separate branches of the Ottomanelli clan are
the kind of "classic butcher shops" where the staff "knows its customers by name" and offers a "fabulous" selection of "highest-quality"
prime meats, including dry-aged beef, housemade sausages and an
array of game (everything from kangaroo to quail); the fact that "prices
are within reason" makes legions of longtime customers all the more
loyal; N.B. the Woodside branch has a line of kosher organic meats.

Ottomanelli Brothers ⌂ *Meat/Poultry* | 24 | 18 | 23 | E |

E 80s | 1549 York Ave. (82nd St.) | 4/5/6 to 86th St. | 212-772-7900 |
www.ottomanellibros.com
W 70s | 395 Amsterdam Ave. (79th St.) | 1 to 79th St. | 212-496-1049

This "old-school" Upper East Side butcher and its separately owned
crosstown cousin keep carnivores happy with "top-quality" cuts, including prime meats, poultry and game, alongside "excellent"

Italian-accented prepared foods (baked ziti, lasagna); factor in "value" (though still not cheap) prices and "knowledgeable, helpful" service, and surveyors ask "how can you go wrong?"; N.B. the York Avenue location offers online ordering.

☑ Ottomanelli's Prime Meats ▣▱ *Meat/Poultry*

| 27 | 19 | 22 | E |

Flushing | 190-21 Union Tpke. (bet. 189th & 190th Sts.) | Queens | 718-468-2000

"The quality is high, high, high" at this Flushing "neighborhood butcher" that sells everything from ground beef yielding "juicy, succulent burgers" ("you'll never go back to the supermarket" kind) to Kobe beef, alligator, pheasant and other "great" game; "excellent" prepared foods, including Italian specialties, are also on hand, and dispensed by a "friendly" staff.

Our Daily Bread *Baked Goods*

| 26 | 21 | 22 | M |

See Greenmarket; for more information, call 518-392-9852

Bread bingers "can't make a bad choice" when selecting from the "wide, unusual selection" of "fresh, tasty" loaves – from challah and cranberry pecan sourdough to sunflower millet flax – baked by this year-round Greenmarket vendor based in Chatham, NY; also eliciting a collective "mmm" are its "delicious fruit scones" and "fab cookies."

Out of the Kitchen ❶ *Prepared Food*

| 20 | 17 | 16 | M |

W Village | 420 Hudson St. (Leroy St.) | 1/2/3 to Houston St. | 212-242-0399 | www.outofthekitchenonline.com

A "great place to pick up" prepared "food for dinner" when you don't have time to cook, this "quality local pit stop" in the West Village earns affection with "tasty" dishes that have a "home-cooked feel"; service may be "lackadaisical" at times, but it remains a neighborhood standby nonetheless.

Ovando *Flowers*

| ▽ 28 | 28 | 25 | VE |

W Village | 337 Bleecker St. (bet. Christopher & W. 10th Sts.) | 1 to Christopher St. | 212-924-7848 | www.ovandony.com

With a "unique" aesthetic among NYC's floral shops, this "amazing" West Village store "displays its wares like no other", sporting an all-black decor scheme and "theatrical lighting" that allows its colorful blooms to be the star of the show ("if you want drama, they win the Tony"); clients also "love" the outfit's "innovative", "super-cool" designs (a European–South American fusion of styles often featuring orchids and cacti), which are admittedly "for the chic set", i.e. those that can appreciate both the arrangement's charm and price tag.

Ozzie's Coffee ❶◗▣ *Coffee/Tea*

| 19 | 16 | 16 | M |

Park Slope | 249 Fifth Ave. (Garfield Pl.) | Brooklyn | M/R to Union St. | 718-768-6868
Park Slope | 57 Seventh Ave. (Lincoln Pl.) | Brooklyn | B/Q to 7th Ave. | 718-398-6695
www.ozziescoffee.com

Maybe they're "no big deal", but for Park Slopers seeking a stress-less "place to stop" for house-roasted coffee and "snacks" this twosome awaits with a "decent" chalkboard-menu lineup delivered by a "hip staff"; the going is "very relaxed (including the service sometimes)" and the overall quality's "simply ok", but if "you have hours to kill" they're eazzy "alternatives" that also retail beans and loose teas.

Paffenroth Gardens ⊄ *Produce* | 28 | 26 | 25 | I |
See Greenmarket; for more information, call 845-258-2539
All of the produce is "fabulous" here but "superior root vegetables" ("man, those parsnips!") are the true pay dirt at this Greenmarket stand – even the potatoes actually "have taste" exclaim fans; given the farm stall's specialty, it's perhaps not surprising that service (overseen by Upstate grower Alex Paffenroth) is incredibly down-to-earth – they're "friendly" enough to make "customers feel as if they were part of a small town."

Paneantico Bakery & Café ● *Baked Goods* | 26 | 22 | 19 | M |
Bay Ridge | 9124 Third Ave. (92nd St.) | Brooklyn | R to Bay Ridge Ave./ 95th St. | 718-680-2347 | www.newyorkitalianmarket.com
Bread heads "travel for" the "gourmet" "brick-oven" loaves at this Bay Ridge Italian bakery/cafe from the Royal Crown Pastry Shop team, but it's also "noted" for pastries, the "freshest, tastiest" "specialty foods" and its bountiful sandwich board; besides being a "top-quality" "to-go" outlet, it's a "friendly" "neighborhood place" to kick back with a primo "cup of joe."

Pane d'Italia ▣⊄ *Baked Goods* | - | - | - | M |
Whitestone | 20-04 Utopia Pkwy. (20th Ave.) | Queens | 7 to Flushing-Main St. | 718-423-6260
The staff of life for scores of restaurants around the city emerges from the ovens of this Whitestone Italian bakery, whose 20-plus artisanal breads run the gamut from traditional panella and Tuscan to loaves loaded with broccoli rabe and prosciutto; it also wins the endorsement of walk-in customers who pick up their own from the front retail store.

Panya Bakery ●⊄ *Baked Goods* | 22 | 19 | 20 | I |
E Village | 10 Stuyvesant St. (9th St.) | 6 to Astor Pl. | 212-777-1930
This "sweet little" East Villager crams its "tiny" shopfront space with "quality" "Japanese baked goods" like green-tea cake and tiramisu, "cute" "pastries with interesting fillings" (including some "funky" savory items) and "fabulous" "fluffy" bread; the staff is "friendly and fast", and cognoscenti confirm the offerings taste "as delicious as they look, which is saying a lot."

NEW Papabubble ●▣ *Candy/Nuts* | ∇ 24 | 26 | 24 | E |
Little Italy | 380 Broome St. (bet. Mott & Mulberry Sts.) | 6 to Spring St. | 212-966-2599 | www.papabubble.com
Elevating candy-making to an art form, this Little Italy sugar gallery (the first U.S. branch of an Australian confectioner) features artisans on view "pulling huge gobs" of the "prettiest sugar you'll ever see" into "multicolor strands of confectionary bliss", i.e. "trendy hard candies"; the "pricey", "unusually flavored and colored" sweets are

made with fruit and herbal oils and make "excellent" gifts – especially if the recipient can appreciate "true eye candy."

NEW Papa Lima Sandwich ◑ *Deli/Sandwich*   ▽ 22 | 19 | 19 | M

Williamsburg | 362 Bedford Ave. (S. 4th St.) | Brooklyn | L to Bedford Ave. | 718-218-7720

Williamsburg gets a welcome purveyor of "absolutely delicious", "creative" sandwiches in this attractive arrival where the bread comes from Tom Cat Bakery and the ingredients from the Greenmarket or top-drawer purveyors like SF salumi standout Fra' Mani; prices may be slightly high for the zip code, but given the clean-lined space with plenty of seating and free WiFi, not to mention the "cutest chalk-boards and staff in town", most don't seem to mind.

Papa Pasquale Ravioli & Pasta Co. *Pasta*   ▽ 26 | 18 | 21 | M

Bensonhurst | 7817 15th Ave. (bet. 78th & 79th Sts.) | Brooklyn | D/M to 79th St. | 718-232-1798 | www.papapasqualeravioli.com

"For the Italian in all of us", this family-owned Bensonhurst pasta purveyor is a "must-try" according to surveyors citing the "amazing four-cheese and lobster ravioli" as standouts; manicotti, stuffed shells and such join a wide assortment of olive oils, vinegars and other imported condiments in the grocery storefront, while the "dee-lish" pastas are produced in a mini-factory in back.

NEW Paradou Marché *Deli/Sandwich*   21 | 19 | 18 | M

LES | Essex Street Mkt. | 120 Essex St. (Delancey St.) | F/J/M/Z to Essex/Delancey Sts. | 212-477-4177

The selection is "limited" but deemed "very good" by those who know this Essex Street Market takeout place, a spin-off of the veteran Meatpacking District eatery Paradou; reports are it has a flair for rustic French-Mediterannean panini, crêpes, ratatouille and fresh-made pastas.

Paramount Caviar ⌫ *Caviar*   27 | 21 | 23 | VE

LIC | 38-15 24th St. (bet. 38th & 39th Aves.) | Queens | N/W to 39th Ave. | 718-786-7747 | 800-992-2842 | www.paramountcaviar.com

It's "*the* destination" for "great caviar" enthuse eggheads about this Long Island City entrepôt, a distributor to such big names as Le Bernardin and Grace's Marketplace, whose premium stock is available to walk-ins in the adjacent showroom; owners Hossain and Amy Aimani are "nice people" who also carry gourmet goodies like foie gras and smoked fish, so "if you have the time" it's worth the hike (though they'll deliver if you call or order online).

Parisi Bakery ⌵ *Baked Goods*   23 | 16 | 21 | I

NoLita | 198 Mott St. (bet. Kenmare & Spring Sts.) | 6 to Spring St. | 212-226-6378

"Prosciutto bread straight from heaven" is one of the blessings at this long-running (since 1910) NoLita Italian bakery, a vendor of authentic homemade loaves to numerous area eateries; Frank Sinatra once was a regular, and nowadays its "great value" on sandwiches (e.g. meatball, chicken parmigiana, "the best cold cuts") keeps it way above par for takeout.

Park Avenue Liquor Shop 🖃 Wine/Liquor | 26 | 19 | 22 | E |

E 40s | 292 Madison Ave. (bet. 40th & 41st Sts.) | 4/5/6/7/S to 42nd St./Grand Central | 212-685-2442 | www.parkaveliquor.com

This venerable Midtown wine-and-liquor purveyor focuses on "excellent" "niche items", stocking "one of Gotham's deepest single-malt selections" (some 400 labels), including "whiskies you thought you'd never find", plus "rare infused spirits" and a "top-notch" showing of "interesting" old vintages (especially Burgundies and Bordeaux); however, wallet-watchers note its prices may place it in the "millionaires-only" category.

Park East Kosher Butchers & Fine Foods 🖃 Meat/Poultry | 26 | 17 | 19 | VE |

E 80s | 1623 Second Ave. (bet. 84th & 85th Sts.) | 4/5/6 to 86th St. | 212-737-9800 | www.parkeastkosher.com

Yes, "it may cost you an arm and a leg" just to buy "a rib" at this glatt kosher butcher/specialty market on the Upper East Side, but regulars swear its "cramped, bustling" store "is the place to shop" for the "highest-quality" meats, poultry and game, not to mention seafood and "tons" of prepared foods and other "goodies" to "fill your pantry, fridge and freezer"; just remember to "up the limit on your card before any visit"; N.B. it keeps Sabbath hours.

Park Natural and Organic Health Food | 22 | 19 | 21 | M |

Carroll Gardens | 350 Court St. (Union St.) | Brooklyn | F/G to Carroll St. | 718-802-1652 | www.parknatural.com

For some of the "freshest" vegetables and fruits in the area, organic-minded shoppers head for this "tidy" Carroll Gardens "health-food supermarket"; the fact that it "has everything" (including a macrobiotic section, a deli and a range of household cleaning supplies and all-natural cosmetics) and employs a "quite knowledgeable" staff ensures that the locals stay loyal.

Party Rental Ltd. Party Rentals | 22 | 20 | 22 | E |

Chelsea | 261 Fifth Ave., 16th fl. (29th St.) | 888-774-4776
Bridgehampton | 5 Tradesman Path (Butter Ln.), NY | 631-537-4477
Teterboro | 275 North St. (Green St.), NJ | 201-727-4700
888-774-4776 | www.partyrentalltd.com
By appointment only

This party rental giant is the largest of its kind in the NYC area, making their familiar truck logo – a pink hippo – all the more apt, and it has a selection to match, drawing from 325,000 sq.-ft. of warehouse space to offer more than 500 styles of linens and some 65,000 chairs ("they have everything" – except tents); dealings are "professional" but be prepared for an "expensive" bill at the end of it all, with a $500 minimum in peak season (April–June; September–December) and $350 the rest of the year.

	QUALITY	DISPLAY	SERVICE	COST

Party Time *Party Rentals*

| 20 | 9 | 14 | M |

Elmhurst | 82-33 Queens Blvd. (bet. 51st Ave. & Van Loon St.) |
Queens | F to Roosevelt Ave. | 212-682-8838 | 877-865-1122 |
www.partytimeofcourse.com

A veteran in the party rental biz, this Queens-based operation has
been stocking equipment for celebrations since 1935 and continues
to offer everything from tables and tents to hot dog carts and ice
cream wagons; however, extended track record aside, a few critics
complain that service can be iffy.

Pasanella & Son, Vintners ● *Wine/Liquor*

| ▽ 26 | 25 | 27 | E |

Seaport | 115 South St. (bet. Beekman St. & Peck Slip) | 2/3 to Fulton St. |
212-233-8383 | www.pasanellaandson.com

Set in a former fishmonger's store dating from 1839 and now boasting a 1967 Ferrari parked in the middle of the sales floor, this "fabulous" Seaport shop isn't exactly a run-of-the-mill neighborhood
wine source; instead, its "quaint and beautiful" space houses a
"well-chosen but limited selection" of "pricey" bottles (about a third
of them Italian), along with vino-related accoutrements, all overseen by a "warm", "knowledgeable" staff.

☑ Pastosa Ravioli ⌧ *Pasta*

| 26 | 20 | 21 | M |

Bronx | 3812 E. Tremont Ave. (Lamport Pl.) | 718-822-2800
Bensonhurst | 7425 New Utrecht Ave. (75th St.) | Brooklyn | D/M to
71st St. | 718-236-9615
Mill Basin | 5223 Ave. N (E. 53rd St.) | Brooklyn | 718-258-1002
Ozone Park | 132-10 Cross Bay Blvd. (Sutter Ave.) | Queens | A to
Liberty Ave. | 718-835-6240
Staten Island | 1076 Richmond Rd. (Columbus Ave.) |
718-667-2194
Staten Island | 3817 Richmond Ave. (Wilson Ave.) |
718-356-4600
Staten Island | 764 Forest Ave. (B'way) | 718-420-9000
800-727-8672 | www.pastosa.com

"Why cook, when you can go" to one of these separately owned
"traditional" Italian "pasta palaces" wonder devoted customers who
line up for the "best ravioli and manicotti" "made fresh" and "excellent sauces" to go with them, plus "delicious cold cuts" and "even
salads to take out"; it "only gets better than this in your nonna's
kitchen", so, given the relatively "cheap prices", you may as well
"buy lots and freeze some"; P.S. the Forest Avenue branch specializes in cheeses, offering more than 250 varieties.

Pastrami Queen ● *Deli/Sandwich*

| 21 | 13 | 15 | M |

E 70s | 1125 Lexington Ave. (bet. 78th & 79th Sts.) | 6 to 77th St. |
212-734-1500 | www.pastramiqueen.com

For an "excellent sandwich without all the hubbub" of other lauded
delis, head to this UES classic where the kosher fare is "not cheap, but
is worth the price" for "heaping" portions packed with "lots of flavor" –
"remember what pastrami used to taste like?"; still, those who object
to the "less-than-glamorous" setting look back nostalgically to the
Pastrami King, its former incarnation in Queens.

	QUALITY	DISPLAY	SERVICE	COST

Patel Brothers ⏺️🖃 *Specialty Shop* — 23 | 17 | 13 | I

Flushing | 42-92 Main St. (bet. Blossom & Cherry Aves.) | Queens |
7 to Flushing-Main St. | 718-661-1112
Jackson Heights | 37-27 74th St. (Northern Blvd.) | Queens | E/V to
Roosevelt Ave. | 718-898-3445
www.patelbrothersusa.com

"A mainstay of the large South Asian community in Jackson Heights"
(with a sister shop in Flushing), this is an "indispensible" stop for "authentic Indian and Pakistani stuff" – at "bargain-basement prices";
with its "dizzying array of spices, chutneys and specialty pickles", as
well as "basmati rice", "yogurts, dahls" and "indescribably shaped
vegetables" ("fresh, very fresh!"), "the store could be in Delhi."

🗹 Patisserie Claude 🚭 *Baked Goods* — 27 | 19 | 19 | M

G Village | 187 W. Fourth St. (bet. 6th & 7th Aves.) | A/B/C/D/E/F/
V to W. 4th St. | 212-255-5911

"If you can survive" Claude's "big-time" "Parisian hauteur" at this "true
French bakery" in the Village, "your palate will be enriched" by "perfect" croissants that "bring tears to your eyes"; after 25 years, the
"small" but "excellent" selection of "stunning" pastries and cookies
shows that this baker may be "mercurial", but he has "hands of gold."

**Patisserie des
Ambassades** ⏺️🖃 *Baked Goods* — 21 | 19 | 19 | M

Chelsea | 161 W. 22nd St. (bet. 6th & 7th Aves.) | 1 to 23rd St. |
212-255-5106
Harlem | 2200 Frederick Douglass Blvd. (bet. 118th & 119th Sts.) | 1 to
116th St. | 212-666-0078 🚭
www.patisseriedesambassades.com

This "oh-so-French" bakery/cafe/catering twosome in Chelsea and
Harlem is known for its "delicious", "mouthwatering" butter-licious
pastries, but it also purveys some Senegal specialties and sandwiches like grilled merguez on baguette; happily, the service is "polite and helpful", even if it can be "slow" at times.

**🗹 Payard Pâtisserie &
Bistro** ⏺️🖃 *Baked Goods* — 28 | 28 | 21 | VE

E 70s | 1032 Lexington Ave. (bet. 73rd & 74th Sts.) | 6 to 77th St. |
212-717-5252 | 877-972-9243 | www.payard.com

"Ooh-la-la", this "world-class", "oh-so-French" Upper Eastsider is
"the Louvre" of "edible art", where the "*magnifique*" pastries, cakes
and chocolates, not to mention ice cream, are "exquisitely" "handcrafted" for "a sugar rush like no other"; all that "froufrou" "indulgence" is "hard on the wallet" but equally "hard to pass up", so
"mortgage the co-op" and go; P.S. "ladies who lunch" congregate
over light bites in the neighboring cafe or a full menu in the back bistro, while Tastings by Payard provides catering.

PE & DD Seafood 🚭 *Seafood* — 28 | 23 | 28 | M

See Greenmarket; for more information, call phone number unavailable ·

"Catch them early" and you'll "go home with the best" "amazing-
quality" fresh seafood "caught that morning off of Long Island" and

trucked to the Greenmarket, making for a "pristine" selection running the gamut from various "whole fish" to "clams, mussels, oysters and scallops" to "more exotic items like eel and sea urchin"; owner Phil Karlin, a 30-year fisherman, has netted an enthusiastic school of supporters with his "knowledgeable" and "friendly" service.

☒ Penzeys Spices ● ▣ ▭ Herbs/Spices | 27 | 23 | 23 | M |

E 40s | Grand Central Mkt. | Lexington Ave. (43rd St.) | 4/5/6/7/S to 42nd St./Grand Central | 212-972-2777 | 800-741-7787 | www.penzeys.com

"Marco Polo would be proud" to see the "wonderful selection" of the "best, freshest spices and herbs" around at this Grand Central outpost of a beloved national chain, where the scents can be "intoxicating", and so can the "unbeatable" prices and quality; "so many spices, so little time to cook" sigh the fans of this "small but substantial" shop where the "knowledgeable" staff can offer tips on how to use the "unusual" and "fantastic" spice blends and rubs; N.B. there's even greater variety through its catalog/web ordering business.

Pepe Giallo To Go ● Prepared Food | 26 | 15 | 17 | I |

Chelsea | 253 10th Ave. (bet. 24th & 25th Sts.) | C/E to 23rd St. | 212-242-6055

Pepe Rosso Caffe Prepared Food

E 40s | Grand Central Terminal | dining concourse (42nd St. & Vanderbilt Ave.) | 4/5/6/7/S to 42nd St./Grand Central | 212-867-6054
E Village | 127 Ave. C (8th St.) | L to 1st Ave. | 212-529-7747 ●

Pepe Rosso Osteria ● Prepared Food

W 50s | 346 W. 52nd St. (bet. 8th & 9th Aves.) | C/E to 50th St./8th Ave. | 212-245-4585

Pepe Rosso To Go ● Prepared Food

SoHo | 149 Sullivan St. (bet. Houston & Prince Sts.) | A/B/C/D/E/F/V to W. 4th St. | 212-677-4555

Pepe Verde To Go ● Prepared Food

W Village | 559 Hudson St. (bet. Perry & W. 11th Sts.) | A/C/E/L to 14th St./8th Ave. | 212-255-2221
www.peperossotogo.com

These popular Italian storefronts prove that the "freshest" pastas can emerge from the "tiniest spaces"; overall, they "can't be beat", especially when picking up a "quick" take-home meal "on-the-go", with "unbelievably" reasonable prices as the clincher.

Perelandra Natural Food Center ● Health Food | 24 | 20 | 19 | M |

Brooklyn Heights | 175 Remsen St. (bet. Clinton & Court Sts.) | Brooklyn | 2/3/4/5/M/N/R/W to Borough Hall/Court St. | 718-855-6068 | www.perelandranatural.com

This "natural foods palace" of Brooklyn Heights has "fabulous, healthy" takeout, a "fantastic variety" of frozen goods and the "best bulk section around", not to mention "knowledgeable vitamin-counter help"; it can be "difficult to maneuver" the "cramped, tall aisles", but it's still a "very pleasant place to shop", and the smoothies, sandwiches and salads make it "a fun place for lunch" too.

	QUALITY	DISPLAY	SERVICE	COST

Pescatore Seafood ◑ 🖃 *Seafood*   25 | 25 | 22 | E

E 40s | Grand Central Mkt. | Lexington Ave. (43rd St.) | 4/5/6/7/S to 42nd St./Grand Central | 212-557-4466

The "extensive" selection of both raw and "creative" prepared fin fare at this "friendly" Grand Central booth "looks so good and tastes the same way", and commuters in need of "dinner supplies" after work appreciate its "convenience"; "helpful" service is another plus, and while it's "expensive", the "specials make it very affordable."

Petak's *Prepared Food*   23 | 20 | 19 | E

E 80s | 1246 Madison Ave. (bet. 89th & 90th Sts.) | 4/5/6 to 86th St. | 212-722-7711

Upper Eastsiders have grown accustomed to this "upscale" source for prepared foods thanks to its range of "consistent" offerings (from sandwiches to sushi) that supporters appreciate for their "high quality"; however, the less-impressed say they'd rather bypass what they see as "routine" fare served by staffers with "attitude."

Pete Milano's Discount Wine & Liquor Supermarket *Wine/Liquor*   21 | 20 | 20 | M

Staten Island | 1441 Forest Ave. (Marianne St.) | 718-447-2888

With 4,000 sq. ft., this "old reliable" Staten Islander has room to display its "excellent selection" of 4,000 vintages, including a sizable roster of reds from Spain and Argentina, plus bottlings from New Zealand and South Africa; customers can get a 10% case discount (even for mixed selections), while "average drinkers" seeking spirits will find a lineup stressing single-malts, bourbons and vodkas.

Peter's Market 🖃 *Specialty Shop*   22 | 18 | 22 | M

Bayside | 33-35 Francis Lewis Blvd. (bet. 33rd & 34th Aves.) | Queens | 718-463-4141 | www.petersmarketny.com

Four 'greats' equal near-"perfection" – as in "great service, great quality, great prices" and "great creativity" – at this Italian-style specialty shop in Bayside; Manhattanites must take the LIRR to get there, but intrepid gourmets who venture out find prime meats, cheeses, pastas, sauces and – "thank God" say locals – "endless" elegant prepared dishes, like espresso-and-anisette demi-glace pork tenderloin; N.B. it's also one of the top caterers in the borough.

Petite Abeille ◑ *Prepared Food*   22 | 19 | 19 | M

Flatiron | 44 W. 17th St. (bet. 5th & 6th Aves.) | F/V to 6th Ave. | 212-727-2989
Gramercy | 401 E. 20th St. (bet. Ave. A & 1st Ave.) | 6 to 23rd St. | 212-727-1505
TriBeCa | 134 W. Broadway (bet. Duane & Reade Sts.) | 1/A/C/E to Canal St. | 212-791-1360
W Village | 466 Hudson St. (Barrow St.) | 1 to Christopher St. | 212-741-6479 ⊘
www.petiteabeille.com

"Cute as the name", this 'little-bee' quartet of "European cafes" is a popular lunchtime stop for "excellent-value" Belgian-accented soups, salads, sandwiches and pastries; though there is seating, overly "cozy" conditions at some branches have regulars opting for takeout.

◪ Petrossian Boutique & Cafe ⊟ *Caviar/Smoked Fish*

| 28 | 27 | 25 | VE |

W 50s | 911 Seventh Ave. (bet. 57th & 58th Sts.) | N/Q/R/W to 57th St. | 212-245-2217 | 800-828-9241 | www.petrossian.com
The "Tiffany's of caviar", this "luxe" market/cafe near Carnegie Hall, an adjunct of the posh French-Continental restaurant, is the "ne plus ultra" for "all things roe" as well as "glorious" smoked fish, foie gras and "creative" housemade pastries and chocolates; "impeccable" service and "indulgent" atmospherics are de rigueur, and though it's all "absurdly priced", anyone prepared to "max out" their plastic will find this one's in a "class of its own."

Philip's Candy Shop ⊘ *Candy/Nuts*

| - | - | - | M |

Staten Island | 8 Barrett Ave. (Forest Ave.) | 718-981-0062
Although this confectioner moved to Staten Island in 2001 after 70 years in Coney Island, it still hearkens back to the "glory days" of old-school amusement-park treats, with its dreamy selection of cotton candy, caramel apples, candied popcorn, "excellent fudge" and more, all made from scratch.

Piazza Mercato ⊟ *Meat/Poultry*

| ∇ 23 | 23 | 22 | M |

Bay Ridge | 9204 Third Ave. (92nd St.) | Brooklyn | R to Bay Ridge Ave./ 95th St. | 718-513-0071 | www.piazzamercato.biz
"Bay Ridge has got the chops!" cheer boosters of this Italian specialty foods shop from the folks behind Royal Crown, where the butcher counter and its "wonderful" selection of house-cured sausages and meats is "enough to make a vegan salivate"; it also offers an expansive lineup of cheeses, as well as "absolutely delicious sandwiches" and an array of old-fashioned Boot-centric prepared dishes.

Pick a Bagel ● *Bagels*

| 20 | 18 | 18 | I |

E 70s | 1101 Lexington Ave. (77th St.) | 6 to 77th St. | 212-517-6590
E 70s | 1473 Second Ave. (bet. 76th & 77th Sts.) | 6 to 77th St. | 212-717-4662
Financial District | 102 North End Ave. (West Side Hwy.) | 1/2/3/ A/C to Chambers St. | 212-786-9200
Gramercy | 297 Third Ave. (bet. 22nd & 23rd Sts.) | 6 to 23rd St. | 212-686-1414
www.pickabageltogo.com
Its "wide variety" of offerings – including the "amazing selection of spreads and toppings" that can add up to a "real meal" – is just one reason fans flock to this bagel quartet for "doughy", "life preserver"-size orbs; the less-impressed detect "no particular pizzazz" here, but even skeptics concede it's "convenient" for a "quick carb fix."

◪ Pickle Guys, The ⊟ *Specialty Shop*

| 27 | 18 | 23 | I |

LES | 49 Essex St. (bet. Grand & Hester Sts.) | B/D to Grand St. | 212-656-9739 | www.pickleguys.com
"These guys seem to have eclipsed Gus" marvel longtime brine-lovers of this descendant of a "Lower East Side icon", where "one of

| | QUALITY | DISPLAY | SERVICE | COST |

the joys of living in NYC" is a peck of "pickles like your bubby used to make", served "straight out of the barrel" with "old-style humor"; from "full sours" and "snappy half-sours to horseradish-infused" varieties, these "fresh and flavorful" puppies will "shock a bland palate"; P.S. also "try the pickled tomatoes and celery" – "and don't forget the kraut"; closed Saturdays.

Pickles, Olives Etc. 🖃 *Specialty Shop* | 23 | 19 | 22 | M |

E 80s | 1647 First Ave. (86th St.) | 4/5/6 to 86th St. | 212-717-8966 | www.picklesandolives.com

Cuke aficionados find heaven in a half-sour and divinity in a kosher dill at this "pickle-lover's paradise", though at 20 varieties strong, it's also an "olive-lover's orgasmatron"; and given other offerings like "roasted eggplant salad with a delicious smoky flavor", regulars rate it a "wonderland" that's the perfect stop on your way to an UES dinner party ("bring something to your hosts other than wine").

Pie by the Pound ◑ *Prepared Food* | 20 | 18 | 16 | M |

E 80s | 1542 Second Ave. (bet. 80th & 81st Sts.) | 6 to 77th St. | 212-517-5017
E Village | 124 Fourth Ave. (bet. 12th & 13th Sts.) | 4/5/6/L/N/Q/R/W to 14th St./Union Sq. | 212-475-4977
www.piebythepound.com

The pizzas are "nothing like the heavy, old-school NYC" pies aver experts who've tasted the "tasty", "unique", thin-crust samplings cut up and dished out by this Downtown-Uptown duo that vends its offerings, as the name states, by the pound; while the pies may be somewhat "pricier" than the competition, the myriad options (over 40 varieties) help compensate.

Piemonte Ravioli *Pasta* | 27 | 19 | 22 | M |

Little Italy | 190 Grand St. (bet. Mott & Mulberry Sts.) | B/D to Grand St. | 212-226-0475 | www.piemonteravioli.com

"So many shapes, so many fillings, so little time!" lament loyalists of this veteran pasta shop that's deemed "worth a special trip to Little Italy"; in the biz since 1920, it offers "the best selection", including "real-deal" "fresh", "flavorful" ravioli varieties "from pumpkin to lobster" that will "make anyone look like a master chef"; there are also chocolates and other comestibles imported from the old country.

Ⓩ Pierre Marcolini 🖃 *Candy/Nuts* | 28 | 27 | 24 | VE |

E 50s | 485 Park Ave. (58th St.) | 4/5/6/N/R/W to 59th St./Lexington Ave. | 212-755-5150 | www.marcolinichocolatier.com

"Just when you thought NYC didn't need another fancy chocolatier", along came this East Side Belgian "class act" and its "phenomenal", "mmm" chocolates in "gorgeous flavors" and connoisseur-conscious formulations (e.g. "fantastic single-origin" bonbons that "provide insight into chocolate *terroir*"); yes, they're "beyond expensive", but when looking to splurge or give a gift "perfect for any occasion", most find it "well worth" the outlay to sample "Brussels' best – on Park Avenue."

	QUALITY	DISPLAY	SERVICE	COST

pinkberry ● *Ice Cream*   21 | 20 | 18 | M

Chelsea | 170 Eighth Ave. (bet. 18th & 19th Sts.) | A/C/E/L to 14th St. | 212-488-2510

E 80s | 1577 Second Ave. (82nd St.) | 4/5/6 to 86th St. | 212-861-0574

Garment District | 7 W. 32nd St. (bet. 5th & 6th Aves.) | B/D/F/N/Q/R/V/W to 34th St./Herald Sq. | 212-695-9631

NEW Gramercy | 350 Third Ave. (bet. 25th & 26th Sts.) | 6 to 28th St. | 212-685-4301

NEW G Village | 177 Bleecker St. (bet. MacDougal & Sullivan Sts.) | A/B/C/D/E/F/V to W. 4th St. | 212-477-1810

NEW G Village | 523 Sixth Ave. (bet. 13th & 14th Sts.) | 1/2/3 to 14th St. | 212-414-8429

NEW NoLita | 41 Spring St. (bet. Mott & Mulberry Sts.) | 6 to Spring St. | 212-274-8883

NEW Washington Heights | 2873 Broadway (bet. 111th & 112th Sts.) | 1 to Cathedral Pkwy./110th St. | 212-222-0195

NEW W 70s | 2041 Broadway (70th St.) | 1/2/3 to 72nd St. | 212-580-3410

NEW Flushing | 136-09 Roosevelt Ave. (Main St.) | Queens | 7 to Main St./Flushing | 718-886-7389

www.pinkberry.com

Additional locations throughout the NY area

Aka "crackberry", this "genius" LA-based fro-yo chain has gained a cult following – and inspired a multitude of imitators – with its "addictive, tart, refreshing goodness", topped with the "freshest fruit" or other "fun" offerings ("Fruity Pebbles, Cap'n Crunch") and served in "creatively designed", "mod" spaces; skeptics cite "sour taste", "lax" service and "kinda pricey" tabs, but those "insane lines" that form "no matter what the weather" speak for themselves.

Pino Prime Meats ⊕ *Meat/Poultry*   ∇ 27 | 20 | 24 | M

SoHo | 149 Sullivan St. (bet. Houston & Prince Sts.) | C/E to Spring St. | 212-475-8134

"Simply terrific" is how surveyors describe this small "old-time" family butcher in SoHo "that goes the extra mile", whether serving up prime meats, housemade sausages, salami or wild boar; if the "excellent quality" and "reasonable prices" weren't enticement enough, how could "you not love" a place where "opera is always on the radio" and owner Pino Cinquemani "is bantering in Italian with customers"?

Z Pisacane Midtown *Seafood*   28 | 19 | 26 | E

E 50s | 940 First Ave. (bet. 51st & 52nd Sts.) | 6 to 51st St. | 212-752-7560

A "devoted clientele" has "such faith" in this "reliable" East Side fishmonger that many "just ask what is fresh", and the staff "never advises wrong"; a "traditional" kind of place selling both raw and prepared offerings, it "caters to the wealthy", but hey, "these guys know their fish", and sometimes, you really do "get what you pay for."

Piu Bello ● *Ice Cream*   21 | 19 | 17 | M

Forest Hills | 70-09 Austin St. (67th Dr.) | Queens | E/F/G/R/V to Forest Hills/71st Ave. | 718-268-4400 | www.piubellogelato.com

"There's no need to go to Manhattan" for the cafe experience provided by this Forest Hills "staple" that makes you feel like "you're in

	QUALITY	DISPLAY	SERVICE	COST

Little Italy" given its Boot-erific menu of baked goods, coffee and "wonderful" gelato "in a huge array of flavors"; however, given the service that's "not very cheery or attentive", some find it best to grab your goodies "to go."

P.J. Bernstein ❶ *Deli/Sandwich*

19	13	17	M

E 70s | 1215 Third Ave. (bet. 70th & 71st Sts.) | 6 to 68th St. | 212-879-0914 | www.nydelicaterer.com

"In the [era] of dwindling delis", this "local place" on the UES is "still a standout" – even if "it ain't Katz's" – for "standard sandwiches" as well as "remarkably good borscht", chicken soup and matzo balls (it isn't strictly kosher); yes, it can feel "crowded" and "overwhelmed" at times, but "what it lacks in service, it makes up for in taste."

PJ Wine ❶ ⊟ *Wine/Liquor*

27	17	20	I

Inwood | 4898 Broadway (bet. 204th & 207th Sts.) | A to 207th St. | 212-567-5500 | www.pjwine.com

Oenophiles "in-the-know" toast the "tremendous selection" at this "warehouse-size" Inwood "find", a "supermarketlike" setup where the aisles are stocked with an "unmatched" array of wines (especially Spanish vintages) and "brand-name liquors" priced for serious "value"; for those who "don't want to hoof it" Uptown, they have a "user-friendly website" loaded with special "features" and deliver gratis "for orders over $150."

Plaza Flowers *Flowers*

25	26	22	E

E 60s | 944 Lexington Ave. (69th St.) | 6 to 68th St. | 212-472-7565

"Beautiful work but very expensive" seems to be the consensus on this "wonderful" French-style Upper East Side florist featuring *pavé*-style arrangements in which blooms are set close and level so as to seem like one; contented customers report it's a "very reliable choice" for "corporate events" and other occasions "when you want correct rather than creative."

Polux Fleuriste ⊟ *Flowers*

-	-	-	E

NoLita | 248 Mott St. (bet. Houston & Prince Sts.) | 6 to Spring St. | 212-219-9646

This quaint NoLita florist will have you humming *La vie en rose* as you appreciate owner Anouchka Levy's French-style arrangements: wild and natural, with herbs and vines scattered among the blooms; the shop also plans events and is a source for other gift items: pashmina shawls, aromatherapy, candles and teas as well as a line of semiprecious jewelry.

Porto Rico Importing Co. ⊟ *Coffee/Tea*

26	22	22	I

E Village | 40½ St. Marks Pl. (bet. 1st & 2nd Aves.) | R/W to 8th St. | 212-533-1982 | 800-453-5908

G Village | 201 Bleecker St. (bet. MacDougal St. & 6th Ave.) | A/B/C/D/E/F/V to W. 4th St. | 212-477-5421 | 800-453-5908❶

NEW LES | Essex Street Mkt. | 120 Essex St. (Delancey St.) | F/J/M/Z to Essex/Delancey Sts. | 212-477-5421

(continued)

(continued)

Porto Rico Importing Co.

SoHo | 107 Thompson St. (bet. Prince & Spring Sts.) | C/E to Spring St. | 212-966-5758 | 800-453-5908

NEW Williamsburg | 636 Grand St. (bet. Leonard St. & Manhattan Ave.) | Brooklyn | L to Lorimer St./Metropolitan Ave. | 212-477-5421
www.portorico.com

"Legions of loyal" "coffeephiles in-the-know" "worship" this 1907-vintage Village "emporium" and its sibs for their 140 "glorious" javas ("exotic", "organic and Fair Trade" types included), all "roasted to perfection" and laid out in "sacks of beans" in a "buzzing" "bazaar setting" overseen by a "spacey" but "congenial crew"; the "huge variety of teas" and "unbelievably" "gentle prices" also win support, especially since they "could charge for the smell" alone.

Poseidon Bakery *Baked Goods* 26 | 17 | 23 | I

W 40s | 629 Ninth Ave. (bet. 44th & 45th Sts.) | A/C/E to 42nd St./Port Authority | 212-757-6173

They "hand-roll their phyllo" dough "the way grandmother used to" at this "old-time" (circa 1952) Greek bakery in Hell's Kitchen, the "real deal" for "finger-lickingly sweet" pastries and "savory treats" like the "best spinach pie" around; Hellenists insist the "kind service" makes the "super-fresh" specialties "that much better" – "may they never change!"

Pour *Wine/Liquor* ∇ 21 | 25 | 25 | M

W 70s | 321 Amsterdam Ave. (75th St.) | 1/2/3 to 72nd St. | 212-501-7687 | www.pourwines.com

"Very helpful" for the dinner party set, this snug Upper West Side wine shop aims to instruct on "pairings with food", providing each vintage with a notecard that gives info on matching cuisine categories (reinforced by a color-coded tag affixed to the bottle); suppourters "love the concept" and the "offbeat" labels, even if snobs sniff at the "gimmicky" approach; P.S. its "knowledgeable" team hosts tastings Monday–Saturday at the bar in back.

Premier Cru *Wine/Liquor* ∇ 24 | 23 | 23 | E

E 80s | 1200 Madison Ave. (bet. 87th & 88th Sts.) | 4/5/6 to 86th St. | 212-534-6709 | www.premiercruwine.com

After more than doubling its dimensions, this "lovely neighborhood" wine-and-liquor boutique continues its crusade to bring first-class vinos and personalized service to its corner of the UES; its 1,200-label inventory showcases prime picks from vintners in Burgundy and California, and if some suggest it's "a little overpriced", discerning buyers are bound to encounter some "inexpensive gems" too.

Press 195 *Deli/Sandwich* ∇ 25 | 18 | 18 | I

Park Slope | 195 Fifth Ave. (bet. Sackett & Union Sts.) | Brooklyn | M/R to Union St. | 718-857-1950

Bayside | 40-11 Bell Blvd. (40th Ave.) | Queens | 718-281-1950
www.press195.com

Luring locals with "the longest list of panini options" some "have ever seen", this duo in Park Slope and Bayside boasts "delicious, sometimes inventive" pressed sandwiches plus "nice salads", a "friendly staff" and a wealth of outdoor seating at both locations; the only catch: you have to be "willing to wait."

Pret A Manger *Deli/Sandwich*   21 | 20 | 18 | M

E 40s | 205 E. 42nd St. (3rd Ave.) | 4/5/6/7/S to 42nd St./ Grand Central | 212-867-1905

E 40s | 287 Madison Ave. (bet. 40th & 41st Sts.) | 4/5/6/7/S to 42nd St./Grand Central | 212-867-0400

E 50s | 400 Park Ave. (54th St.) | E/V to Lexington Ave./53rd St. | 212-207-4101

E 50s | 630 Lexington Ave. (54th St.) | E/V to Lexington Ave./53rd St. | 646-497-0510

Financial District | 60 Broad St. (bet. Beaver St. & Exchange Pl.) | 2/3 to Wall St. | 212-825-8825

Garment District | 530 Seventh Ave. (bet. 38th & 39th Sts.) | 1/2/3/7/N/Q/R/S/W to 42nd St./Times Sq. | 646-728-0750

W 40s | 11 W. 42nd St. (bet. 5th & 6th Aves.) | 7/B/D/F/V to 42nd St./ Bryant Park | 212-997-5520

W 40s | 30 Rockefeller Plaza, concourse level (bet. 49th & 50th Sts.) | B/D/F/V to 47-50th Sts./Rockefeller Ctr. | 212-246-6944

W 50s | 135 W. 50th St. (bet. 6th & 7th Aves.) | 1 to 50th St. | 212-489-6458

W 50s | 1350 Sixth Ave. (55th St.) | N/Q/R/W to 57th St. | 212-307-6100 866-328-7738 | www.pret.com

Additional locations throughout the NY area

"The best British invasion since the Beatles", this U.K.-based chain serves up "wholesome" sandwiches and salads that are a welcome "change from the norm"; "gracious" counter folk and "crisp, clean" setups add to the experience, and while a few lament the "London prices", most say the rates are "reasonable" given the "quality."

Props for Today *Party Rentals*   20 | 22 | 23 | E

Garment District | 330 W. 34th St., 12th fl. (bet. 8th & 9th Aves.) | 1/2/3/ A/C/E to 34th St./Penn Station | 212-244-9600 | www.propsfortoday.com

Loaded with sophisticated, movie set-worthy furniture and "tons of playful props" suited to elaborate parties (with themes ranging from "Art Deco" to "Raj Period" to "Carnival"), this rental vendor draws most of its clients from TV, film and other media companies but also opens its 100,000-sq.-ft. Garment District warehouse to civilians; all agree service is "extremely helpful" – and that you'll need a movie star's salary to cover the "expensive" tab.

Z Prospect Wine Shop ●☑️🖃 *Wine/Liquor*   26 | 22 | 26 | M

Park Slope | 322 Seventh Ave. (bet. 8th & 9th Sts.) | Brooklyn | F to 7th Ave. | 718-768-1232 | www.prospectwine.com

Stocked floor-to-ceiling with a "tremendous" 1,500-strong wine selection, this Park Sloper is an "interesting" prospect for special vintages from old-world growers, premium sakes and "many organic" and biodynamic options; "fair pricing" and a "passionate staff eager to help" with "advice" and "pairing ideas" make it a "great neighborhood shop", and on seasonal Saturday afternoons "wonderful" tastings convene in the garden out back.

QUALITY DISPLAY SERVICE COST

Pumpkins Organic Market *Specialty Shop* ▽ 26 | 23 | 21 | E

Park Slope | 1302 Eighth Ave. (bet. 13th & 14th Sts.) | Brooklyn | F to 7th Ave. | 718-499-8539 | www.pumpkinsorganicmarket.com

"Surely in past decades groceries like this were common" say surveyors of this Park Sloper, a "lovely" if "limited" source of things "to buy for a picnic lunch": "fresh artisanal breads, real heavy whipping cream", "vegan chocolate cookies to die for", locally sourced produce and other "interesting organic foods", all "served with a smile"; even hard-core Manhattanites admit "it rates a trip across the river."

Quality House ☞ *Wine/Liquor* ▽ 27 | 21 | 27 | E

Murray Hill | 2 Park Ave. (bet. 32nd & 33rd Sts.) | 6 to 33rd St. | 212-532-2944 | www.qualityhousewines.com

After "three generations" in the biz, this "high-end" Murray Hill vino shop "serves clients well" with its encyclopedic French inventory, as well as stock from Italy, Germany and Australia; its owner "knows more about wine" than most and carries labels "you can't find" elsewhere, so though it can get "pricey", all agree "quality reigns here."

Quattro's Game & Poultry Farm ☞ *Meat/Poultry* 26 | 19 | 23 | M

See Greenmarket; for more information, call 845-635-2018

Fans who flock to this Dutchess County farm's Union Square Greenmarket stall on Saturdays cluck over its "superb" poultry selections, from the "best free-range chicken" to pheasant, duck and heritage holiday birds (don't forget to "special-order" "your Thanksgiving turkey and Christmas goose"), not to mention smoked varieties and sausage; loyal customers "quail at the thought of buying birds anywhere else."

Queen Ann Ravioli *Pasta* 27 | 19 | 22 | I

Bensonhurst | 7205 18th Ave. (bet. 72nd & 73rd Sts.) | Brooklyn | N to 18th Ave. | 718-256-1061

Some of the "best homemade pasta in Brooklyn" comes from this longtime "favorite" that inspires loyalists to make "the trek" to Bensonhurst, though its raviolis and other filled "great shapes" are available "in Italian markets all over the city"; it also vends sauces (meat, puttanesca or marinara), fresh mozz, prepared foods like eggplant rollatini and lasagna as well as olive oils and vinegars.

☑ Raffetto's ⌲ *Pasta* 28 | 20 | 24 | I

G Village | 144 W. Houston St. (bet. MacDougal & Sullivan Sts.) | A/B/C/D/E/F/V to W. 4th St. | 212-777-1261

"Wonderful", "crazy-fresh" pasta "cut to order on amazing jangly old machines" is what this "family-owned" Greenwich Village "institution" has been turning out for more than 100 years – and surveyors say "bless them for keeping" up the tradition; in addition to its "heavenly" ravioli and myriad other pasta varieties, it also offers "sauces, cheeses and other tasty ingredients for Italian dishes", as well as a line of prepared foods like lasagna and baked ziti, all at the "world's-best-bargain" prices; P.S. there are even a few more "contemporary" offerings – "chocolate fettuccini" anyone?

QUALITY | DISPLAY | SERVICE | COST

Rainbo's Fish at Essex St. Market ⊘ *Seafood* | 26 | 19 | 21 | M |

LES | Essex Street Market | 120 Essex St. (bet. Delancey & Rivington Sts.) |
F/J/M/Z to Delancey/Essex Sts. | 212-982-8585

This Essex Street Market fishmonger is considered a prize catch for
its standout selection of "fresh" seafood ("love that they show the
country of origin for each") and "can't-be-beat" smoked fish offered
at reasonable prices; its has a new three-seat counter for enjoying
its "great-quality" prepared foods, notably the grilled fish sandwiches, but you can grab them to go as well.

☑ Ralph's Famous Italian Ices ●⊘ *Ice Cream* | 24 | 14 | 18 | I |

Bayside | 214-13 41st Ave. (Bell Blvd.) | Queens | 718-428-4578
Floral Park | 264-21 Union Tpke. (bet. 264th & 265th Sts.) | Queens |
718-343-8724
Whitestone | 12-48 Clintonville St. (12th Rd.) | Queens | 7 to
Flushing-Main St. | 718-746-1456
Staten Island | 4212 Hylan Blvd. (bet. Armstrong & Robinson Aves.) |
718-605-5052
Staten Island | 501 Port Richmond Ave. (Catherine St.) | 718-273-3675
Staten Island | 6272 Amboy Rd. (Bloomingdale Rd.) | 718-605-8133
www.ralphsices.com

"Summer wouldn't feel like summer" without a trip to the original 1949
branch of this Staten Island institution – or one of its ever-multiplying
offspring – where "people flock" to enjoy "the best Italian ices" in the
warm-weather months and the "line spills out to the street"; there
are "so many flavors" (even no-sugar options for dieters) you'll
"want to try them all", so "buy pints for home" while you're at it.

☑ Randazzo's Seafood *Seafood* | 28 | 21 | 24 | M |

Bronx | 2327 Arthur Ave. (bet. 183rd & 187th Sts.) | B/D to Fordham Rd. |
718-367-4139

Seafood "from all over the world" at "a fraction" of Manhattan
prices, "freshness" you "can always count on" and "service with a
smile" – "what's not to like?" about this "Arthur Avenue institution"
that "continues to be fabulous"; if you're "looking for the unusual",
such as baccalà, anchovies and other Italian specialties, "this should
be where you're headed"; P.S. "try the clams at the raw bar outside."

Ready to Eat ● *Prepared Food* | ▽ 21 | 21 | 24 | M |

W Village | 525 Hudson St. (bet. Charles & W. 10th Sts.) | 1 to
Christopher St. | 212-229-1013 | www.readytoeat.net

Classic American cooking is the forte of this "affordable" Village
prepared-foods shop/caterer whose "well-packed" offerings come
in handy when cooking at home isn't an option; cornbread and
cranberry-stuffed turkey breasts, meatloaf and carrot-cream
cheesecake are popular choices, and can be eaten on-site in a
small seating area.

Rebecca Cole Design *Flowers* | - | - | - | VE |

Garment District | 247 W. 30th St. (bet. 7th & 8th Aves.) | 1/2/3/A/
C/E to 34th St/Penn Station | 212-216-9492 | www.colecreates.com

The Today Show's "fun" gardening editor is the eponymous "color
wizard" behind this Garment District florist that enlivens special

events and indoor gardens with its "breathtaking designs"; even jaded sorts who've "seen many flower arrangements" agree this pricey shop "does fabulous work" ("given only four hours notice, they came through").

Red Jacket Orchards ⌐≡⌐ Produce | 27 | 19 | 22 | M

See Greenmarket; for more information, call 315-781-2749 or 800-828-9410 | www.redjacketorchards.com

Hard-core "apple addicts" get their fix at this Finger Lakes orchard's Greenmarket stall, where the "delicious apples" in the crisp-weather months rotate to "fabulous" apricots, plums, peaches and other stone fruits in summer, and are all offered at "very fair prices"; still, it may be most beloved for its "best-on-the-planet" juices, ciders and nectars, which are also available via Fresh Direct, Fairway, Whole Foods and other markets.

NEW Red Mango ● Ice Cream | 22 | 20 | 20 | M

Chelsea | 63 W. 14th St. (bet. 5th & 6th Aves.) | 1/2/3 to 14th St. | 212-414-3009

Flatiron | 688 Sixth Ave. (bet. 21st & 22nd Sts.) | F/V to 23rd St. | 212-929-2313

G Village | 182 Bleecker St. (bet. MacDougal & Sullivan Sts.) | A/B/C/D/E/F/V to West 4th St. | 212-777-2303

W 40s | 723 Eighth Ave. (bet. 45th & 46th Sts.) | A/C/E to 42nd St./Port Authority | 212-315-0101

Flushing | 136-53 Roosevelt Ave. (Main St.) | Queens | 7 to Main St. | 718-886-1916

www.redmangousa.com

The "frozen yogurt that foodies like" is how devotees describe the goods from this member of the fro-yo fray, calling it a "great riff on the classic" stuff that's neither too "sour nor too sweet", has a "very creamy texture" and can be topped with virtually "anything"; the company "boasts of probiotic benefits", but most are more focused on the "delicious" flavor and under-the-radar "buzz" that has meant "half the lines" of the competition.

☒ Red, White & Bubbly ●⌐≡⌐ Wine/Liquor | 26 | 24 | 25 | M

Park Slope | 211-213 Fifth Ave. (bet. President & Union Sts.) | Brooklyn | M/R to Union St. | 718-636-9463 | www.redwhiteandbubbly.com

Wine lovers "would consider moving to Park Slope just to be closer" to this "wonderful shop", a "favorite" for its "attractive" layout (with a temperature-controlled room for the finer vintages), "reasonable" cost and staff of "bubbly", "no-attitude" "enthusiasts"; the frequent tastings feature "some good stuff", and owner Darrin Siegfried offers "amazingly reliable" monthly picks for 'Discovery Wines', 'Best Buys' and '4-pack' specials; N.B. their on-site classes range from Wine 101 to Advanced.

Remi to Go Prepared Food | 26 | 19 | 19 | E

W 50s | 145 W. 53rd St. (bet. 6th & 7th Aves.) | N/Q/R/W to 57th St. | 212-581-7115 | www.remi.citysearch.com

Though under separate ownership, this Midtown prepared foods/catering shop still features the same "top-notch pastas, salads" and

	QUALITY	DISPLAY	SERVICE	COST

other Italian specialties as can be found at its adjacent (but much more expensive) sister restaurant, Remi; in fact, area suits insist it's "one of the best places for a take-out lunch" around; N.B. it expanded its seating during a recent redo.

Renny & Reed *Flowers*

∇ | 28 | 25 | 23 | VE

E 50s | 505 Park Ave. (bet. 59th & 60th Sts.) | 4/5/6/N/R/W to 59th St./Lexington Ave. | 212-288-7000 | www.rennyandreed.com

Specializing in the proper English-garden style of arrangements, this tony, family-run florist in Midtown "never disappoints", delivering "creative, lovely", "beautiful bouquets" that have some supporters insisting it's among "the best NY has" to offer (just "expect to shell out"); if you can "describe it, they'll produce it", as they have for area hotels like the Essex House and Four Seasons and, on occasion, for events at the White House.

☑ Rice to Riches ◑ ☱ *Baked Goods*

23 | 26 | 21 | M

NoLita | 37 Spring St. (bet. Mott & Mulberry Sts.) | 6 to Spring St. | 212-274-0008 | www.ricetoriches.com

The "Baskin-Robbins" of "gourmet rice pudding", this "upbeat" NoLita shop specializes in just this one dessert, bringing "new pizzazz" to a heretofore humble dish with its "rich", "super-creamy" version offered in "flavors you never dared to dream of" (mascarpone with cherries, chocolate hazelnut, cheesecake, etc.) and served in "UFO-like snap-lid containers"; the "bright", "futuristic space" is a "nirvana" to "converts" who consider its "unique" concept "totally unexpected" but "brilliant" ("when are they going to franchise?").

Richard Salome Flowers ☱ *Flowers*

- | - | - | VE

E 70s | 1034 Lexington Ave. (bet. 73rd & 74th Sts.) | 6 to 77th St. | 212-988-2933 | 800-578-2621 | www.richardsalomeflowers.com

Bloom boosters say "the flowers are always fresh" at this "first-rate" Upper East Side florist and event planner that "never disappoints" with its "amazing displays", all nestled in unique containers from around the world; it's seriously pricey, but surveyors insist its cut arrangements and hand-painted silk blooms "are worth every penny."

Rick's Picks ☱ *Specialty Shop*

- | - | - | E

See Greenmarket; for more information, call 212-358-0428 | www.rickspicksnyc.com

One of the few Manhattan-based vendors you'll find at the Greenmarket, this pickle peddler uses all-natural, locally grown produce to create its bounty of small-batch briny goods, all of which are made and packed by hand; its trademark unusual flavor combos are matched with irresistibly punny names, e.g. Phat Beets, Kool Gherks, Whup Asp (pickled asparagus); N.B. its jars can be found at gourmet stores around town, and it even supplies the relish for Shake Shack's Chicago dog.

	QUALITY	DISPLAY	SERVICE	COST

Risotteria ● *Prepared Food*　　　23 | 16 | 20 | M

G Village | 270 Bleecker St. (Morton St.) | 1 to Christopher St. |
212-924-6664 | www.risotteria.com

"If you like risotto, you'll love" this sliver of a Greenwich Village
eatery/take-out shop and its many "addictively delicious" varieties
of the made-to-order signature dish; however, surveyors note
there's "much more" to be had here, including "excellent" pizza, salads and panini, and "those with food allergies" give it "a gold star"
for its gluten-free lineup.

Rita's Ices ● *Ice Cream*　　　21 | 14 | 19 | I

Staten Island | Greenridge Plaza Shopping Ctr. | 3285D Richmond Ave.
(Arthur Kill Rd.) | 718-227-7860 | www.ritasice.com

"Awesomely cool" and "a kick in the butt for old Italian ice" peddlers
is the verdict on this Pennsylvania import in Staten Island that specializes in "totally addictive" "classic summer treats" in a "large variety of flavors", with fantastically fruity ones getting frequent
shout-outs and even the sugar-free variety earning full marks
("yummy"); N.B. open April–September.

Roasting Plant ●●▣ *Coffee/Tea*　　　22 | 24 | 20 | M

LES | 81 Orchard St. (bet. Broome & Grand Sts.) | F/J/M/Z to
Delancey/Essex Sts. | 212-775-7755 | www.roastingplant.com

"Watch the beans fly around and get brewed" at this high-tech LES
"full-service coffee shop" whose "nifty tube system" "full of hoops
and loops" is operated by a 'Javabot' that grinds beans only after an
order is placed, ensuring some of the "freshest, most delicious coffee around"; if the space-age interior is rife with "hipster attitude",
happily the "friendly" service is not.

Robbins Wolfe Eventeurs *Caterer*　　　▽ 26 | 20 | 22 | VE

Meatpacking | 521 West St. (bet. Gansevoort & Horatio Sts.) |
212-924-6500 | www.robbinswolfe.com
By appointment only

A "fave of UESers and Hamptonites" and other gentry, this ultra-
upmarket caterer/event planner (with offices in the Meatpacking
District, Locust Valley and the Hamptons) does the full-service
monte on a grand scale, handling everything from invites to entertainment to theme decor for smart-set clients like Julliard and the
Rubin Museum; the food and drink is predictably top-tier, but "you
pay for the quality" and wolves in the fold growl it's "overrated."

Robert Isabell ⌘ *Flowers*　　　▽ 27 | 26 | 24 | VE

Meatpacking | 410 W. 13th St. (bet. 9th Ave. & Washington St.) |
212-645-7767
By appointment only

"When name-dropping matters", this "wonderful" florist and event
planner in the Meatpacking District delivers with "inventive, lavish,
showstopping" productions (including "stylish weddings") that you
and "your friends will always remember"; plus, the eponymous
owner "knows his flowers" too – "everything he does is tasteful" – so
when you need an arrangement, this shop is "tops."

	QUALITY	DISPLAY	SERVICE	COST

Rocco's Pastry Shop ●◐▣ *Baked Goods*   25 | 23 | 20 | M

G Village | 243 Bleecker St. (bet. Carmine & Leroy Sts.) | A/B/C/D/
E/F/V to W. 4th St. | 212-242-6031 | www.roccospastry.com

Those "looking for an authentic Italian" pastry-and-coffee "fix"
should look no further than this "cheerful" Greenwich Village
bakery/cafe, a "sinful" "sweetfest" that's "often crowded" with
natives and "tourists" alike; besides the signature "freshly made
cannoli" ("stuffed to order"), highlights of the "huge selection"
include "yummy" sfogliatelle and "real" gelato and ices for summer, and enthusiasts who "love all of it" can always "load up" at
a "reasonable price."

Rohrs, M. ●◐▣ *Coffee/Tea*   24 | 18 | 22 | M

E 80s | 310 E. 86th St. (bet. 1st & 2nd Aves.) | 4/5/6 to 86th St. |
212-396-4456 | 888-772-7647 | www.rohrs.com

It claims "a long history" dating to 1896, and this Upper East Side
"gem" remains a roaring success as a "quality purveyor" of
"smooth" house-roasted coffee in "lots of different" specialty
blends, along with a profusion of "wonderful" teas; the goods are
available online, but its homespun charm is "totally worth a trip"
and in true "old-time" style "a daily dose doesn't break the bank."

Ronaldo Maia *Flowers*   ∇ 28 | 26 | 28 | VE

E 90s | 1143 Park Ave. (bet. 91st & 92nd Sts.) | 6 to 96th St. |
212-288-1049

This Upper East Side florist attracts an upscale clientele that's simply "thrilled" with the shop's customized arrangements of "lovely
and unusual flowers" (no catalogs or mail order here); it also has a
way with topiaries and sells a streamlined selection of small gift
items, but as with the pricey blooms, you'll "pay dearly."

Ron Ben-Israel Cakes *Baked Goods*   ∇ 25 | 25 | 24 | VE

SoHo | 42 Greene St., 5th fl. (bet. Broome & Grand Sts.) | 212-625-3369 |
www.weddingcakes.com
By appointment only

"Charmer" Ron Ben-Israel's "very high-end" SoHo custom bakery
specializes in "heavenly" wedding cakes bedizened with "unbelievably real-looking sugar flowers", which may seem "too beautiful to
eat" but taste "divine" every time; it's a "rare opportunity" to com-
mission handiwork that's featured in magazine spreads, but if the
gâteaux are guaranteed to be "dazzling", "the prices are too."

NEW Roni-Sue's Chocolates ▣ *Candy/Nuts*   ∇ 23 | 21 | 27 | M

LES | Essex Street Mkt. | 120 Essex St. (bet. Delancey & Rivington Sts.) | F/J/
M/Z to Delancey/Essex Sts. | 212-260-0421 | www.roni-sue.com

"Talented and affable" confectioner Rhonda Kave, an "artiste in
chocolate", is "always inventing fascinating new flavors" and offering "free samples" at her bite-size shop "tucked away" in the Essex
Street Market; her "fabulous selection" of "handmade" bonbons
("oooh, the truffles") are often made from ingredients sourced from
the Greenmarket, like Ronnybrook Farm dairy products.

	QUALITY	DISPLAY	SERVICE	COST

☑ Ronnybrook Milk Bar *Cheese/Dairy* — 28 | 18 | 23 | M

Chelsea | Chelsea Mkt. | 75 Ninth Ave. (bet. 15th & 16th Sts.) | A/
C/E/L to 14th St./8th Ave. | 212-741-6455 | 800-772-6455 |
www.ronnybrook.com

If there were an Olympic category for "all-around best dairy", this
"wonderful family-run" farm would have to win, udders down, for its
ultrafresh line of milk, cream, butter, yogurt and "ice cream flavors
found nowhere else", all offered at its Chelsea Market storefront as
well as at the Greenmarket and in gourmet stores citywide; surveyors moo in favor of its "old-fashioned bottles" and declare its relatively "pricey" goods "worth every penny" – and "every fat gram."

NEW Root Hill Cafe *Coffee/Tea* — - | - | - | E

Park Slope | 262 Fourth Ave. (Carroll St.) | Brooklyn | R to Union St. |
718-797-0100

Tucked among the auto-body shops of Park Slope's Fourth Avenue
frontier is this new connoisseur's coffee stop that boasts an ultra-
high-end Clover coffee machine, which inspires such interest the
owners have mounted a mirror on the ceiling above it so customers
can watch the magic happen; other endearments are a roster of light
bites and a cleverly appointed, free WiFi–equipped space.

Root Stock & Quade ▭ *Flowers* — - | - | - | E

NEW **Clinton Hill** | 471 Myrtle Ave. (bet. Hall St. & Washington Ave.) |
Brooklyn | G to Clinton/Washington Aves. | 718-230-8081
Park Slope | 297 Seventh Ave. (bet. 7th & 8th Sts.) | Brooklyn | F to
7th Ave. | 718-788-8355
www.rootstockquade.com

"Lovely arrangements and quality flowers" are the deal at this
custom-only Park Slope florist (with a new Clinton Hill offshoot)
that appeals to clients like the Brooklyn Museum of Art with its
monochromatic signature style; it also sells herbs and other plants,
containers and garden furniture, puts on seasonal lectures and offers event design services.

Rosa Rosa *Flowers* — ▽ 21 | 18 | 19 | M

E 60s | 831A Lexington Ave. (bet. 63rd & 64th Sts.) | F to Lexington Ave./
63rd St. | 212-935-4706 | www.rosarosaflowers.com

The name of this Upper East Side florist says it all: it specializes in
"great deals on roses" that "always look beautiful and last longer",
perhaps because the shop receives flower shipments six days a
week; it's added orchids to its repertoire not too long ago, but acolytes admit "you don't come here for fantastic floral displays, you
come here for nice arrangements at nice prices."

Rosenthal Wine Merchant *Wine/Liquor* — ▽ 28 | 20 | 27 | E

E 80s | 318 E. 84th St. (bet. 1st & 2nd Aves.) | 4/5/6 to 86th St. |
212-249-6650

A vino vendor "of the old school", this Upper Eastsider is a showroom for "hand-picked gems" from 80 "lesser-known" "small vintners", limited to estate-bottled French, Italian and California wines
imported by Neal Rosenthal (who is not associated with the store);

	QUALITY	DISPLAY	SERVICE	COST

they "don't sell anything they don't know intimately", so a visit's sure to be "interesting" if "no bargain"; N.B. tastings are held Saturdays from 4–6 PM.

☑ Royal Crown Pastry Shop *Baked Goods* | 26 | 21 | 21 | M |

Bensonhurst | 6512 14th Ave. (bet. 65th & 66th Sts.) | Brooklyn | D/M/N to New Utrecht Ave./62nd St. | 718-234-1002 🚭
Staten Island | 1350 Hylan Blvd. (Old Town Rd.) | 718-668-0284 ◖
www.newyorkitalianmarket.com

"This is what bread should taste like" declare loyal subjects at these "brick-oven" Italian bakeries, where "classic" "crunchy" loaves "rule" and the "specialty" varieties like fig-and-walnut or chocolate rank among "the best" to be had; other crowning achievements include an "outstanding" "assortment" of pastries and "some great sandwiches" at the cafe-equipped Staten Island branch.

Royal Wine Merchants ▣ *Wine/Liquor* | – | – | – | E |

Gramercy | 25 Waterside Plaza, 2nd fl. (25th St.) | 6 to 23rd St. | 212-689-4855 | www.royalwinemerchants.com

The connoisseur is king at this citadel of oenophilia on the East River's edge (behind Bellevue Hospital Center), a French and Italian specialist that caters to the insider with meticulously chosen wines, including fine and rare vintages stored in a climate-controlled 'cellar' room; buyers in the market for a 1900 Margaux or 1961 Petrus should expect top-tier prices, but on request they fax out notices of "closeouts and specials" that can be "great for bargains."

Ruben's Empanadas *Prepared Food* | 20 | 13 | 18 | I |

E Village | 122 First Ave. (bet. 7th St. & St. Marks Pl.) | L to 1st Ave. | 212-979-0172 ◖
Financial District | 77 Pearl St. (bet. Broad St. & Hanover Sq.) | 2/3 to Wall St. | 212-361-6323
SoHo | 505 Broome St. (W. B'way) | C/E to Spring St. | 212-334-3351 ◖
Seaport | Pier 17 | 64 Fulton St. (bet. Cliff & Gold Sts.) | 2/3 to Fulton St. | 212-962-5330

An "absolute favorite" of Downtown lunchers, this storefront minichain churns out "incredibly authentic" South American–style "pockets of flavor" popular enough to require getting there "right at noon before the line is out the door"; given that it serves such "awesome" "handheld food at reasonable prices", it's "no accident they've been in business for over 30 years."

Ruby et Violette *Baked Goods* | ▽ 26 | 23 | 23 | E |

W 50s | 457 W. 50th St. (bet. 9th & 10th Aves.) | C/E to 50th St. | 212-582-6720 | 877-353-9099 | www.rubyetviolette.com

"The Cartier" of chocolate-chunk cookies, this Way West Side gourmet baker puts premium imported ingredients into every "delicious" doughy delight and offers "creative variations" infused with dozens of "fantastical" flavorings like champagne, espresso bean, jasmine and Key lime and also vends brownies and blondies; all agree these "cookies for grown-ups" are of "the best" quality, so expect a suitably adult "price tag"; N.B. it reopened recently following an extensive post-Survey renovation.

	QUALITY	DISPLAY	SERVICE	COST

☒ Russ & Daughters 🖃 Smoked Fish · 28 · 24 · 24 · E

LES | 179 E. Houston St. (bet. Allen & Orchard Sts.) | F/V to Lower East Side/
2nd Ave. | 212-475-4880 | 800-787-7229 | www.russanddaughters.com

Smoked fish like "your grandparents would remember" leads the "vaunted" lineup at this "old-world" Jewish deli "treasure" on the Lower East Side, offering "one-stop shopping" for "unbeatable" lox, sable, whitefish, caviar and "everything else" that makes for a "happy nosher"; it's also "the real deal" for "goodies" like rugalach, halvah and babka, not to mention "jewel"-like dried fruits and candy, and as for the tab, most shrug "you gotta pay" for "greatness."

Russo Mozzarella & Pasta Cheese/Dairy · 26 · 17 · 21 · M

E Village | 344 E. 11th St. (bet. 1st & 2nd Aves.) | L to 1st Ave. |
212-254-7452

Park Slope | 363 Seventh Ave. (bet. 10th & 11th Sts.) | Brooklyn | F to
7th Ave. | 718-369-2874

Rustle up "your own Italian feast" with one stop at this near-centenarian East Villager, a "neighborhood destination" that's known for "excellent", "super-fresh mozzarella" but "satisfies" with "more than just cheese" given its "real-deal" pastas, sauces and meats; the Park Slope offshoot adds housemade prepared foods, breads and desserts to the mix, and it also caters.

Ruthy's Bakery & Cafe 🖃 Baked Goods · ▽ 15 · 19 · 16 · M

Chelsea | Chelsea Mkt. | 75 Ninth Ave. (bet. 15th & 16th Sts.) | A/
C/E/L to 14th St./8th Ave. | 212-463-8800

Chelsea | Chelsea Piers | Pier 62 (Hudson River & 23rd St.) | C/E to
23rd St. | 212-336-6333

888-729-8800 | www.ruthys.com

Known for "awesome cheesecake" and rugalach, this Chelsea Market bakery/cafe (along with its Chelsea Piers satellite) also custom-designs specialty and birthday cakes, with everything available for nationwide shipping or Manhattan delivery below 96th Street; it leaves the majority "really delighted", even if a ruthless few report "mediocre" results.

Sable's Smoked Fish 🖃 Caviar/Smoked Fish · 27 · 19 · 22 · E

E 70s | 1489 Second Ave. (bet. 77th & 78th Sts.) | 6 to 77th St. |
212-249-6177 | www.sablesnyc.com

"These guys know their smoked fish" boast Upper East Side admirers of this "cramped" shop, where an able team "wins raves" for "succulent" salmon, sturgeon and caviar that'll "melt in your mouth" (and don't miss the "outstanding" lobster salad); the "solicitous countermen" are "generous" with "free taste tests" to "whet your appetite", and though "you pay a premium", it "never fails" "for top quality."

☒ Sahadi's Specialty Shop · 27 · 20 · 22 · I

Brooklyn Heights | 187 Atlantic Ave. (bet. Clinton & Court Sts.) | Brooklyn |
2/3/4/5/M/N/R/W to Borough Hall/Court St. | 718-624-4550 |
www.sahadis.com

"It's worth a trip to the County of Kings" (even on "elbow-to-elbow" weekends) to feast like a sultan on the Mideastern "gold mine" at this "phenomenal" Brooklyn Heights food "bazaar"; the "displays are not high-tech" and you gotta "run to grab a number ticket", but amid the "controlled chaos" you'll find "all sorts of goodies hidden in every corner": "vast selections" of high-quality prepared foods, cheese, chocolates, olives, teas, spices, dried fruits and nuts, rice, grains and beans, coffee, "vinegars and oils" and more – and "all at rock-bottom prices."

NEW Sakaya *Wine/Liquor* ∇ 25 | 23 | 24 | E

E Village | 324 E. Ninth St. (bet. 1st & 2nd Aves.) | L to 1st Ave. | 212-505-7253 | www.sakayanyc.com

NYC's first store dedicated to sake, this "small, beautiful" East Village boutique impresses novice and expert sippers alike with its "quite nice selection" of over 100 labels, plus a few types of shochu (a Japanese spirit similar to vodka); "excellent" service and owners who are "knowledgeable and passionate" about their subject round out the endorsement; N.B. off-premises tastings can be arranged, and classes and online ordering were just introduced.

Sal & Dom's *Baked Goods* ∇ 28 | 23 | 24 | M

Bronx | 1108 Allerton Ave. (Laconia Ave.) | 2/5 to Pelham Pkwy. | 718-515-3344 | www.salanddoms.com

"Everything Italian" and sweet seems to show up at this "standby" bakery in the Bronx's Williamsbridge area, where the "freshest" pastries, biscotti and cakes ensure "just the smell" "adds an inch to your waistline"; seasonal specialties make it "hands-down popular" "on the holidays", with the locals lining up come Christmas for their marzipan, struffoli and pastiera.

Z Salumeria Biellese ▱ *Meat/Poultry* 29 | 18 | 24 | M

Chelsea | 376-378 Eighth Ave. (29th St.) | 1/2/3/A/C/E to 34th St./Penn Station | 212-736-7376 | www.salumeriabiellese.com

This second-generation Chelsea salumeria brings out "the Italian in everyone" with its "mind-boggling" array of "super-duper sausages" (some 40 varieties) and "wonderful cured meats", both "house-made" and imported, which it supplies to the public as well as to restaurants the likes of Daniel Boulud's and Thomas Keller's; its "reasonable prices" and appealing "slice-of-the-past" milieu are other reasons to "love" this place; N.B. sells sandwiches and other prepared foods too.

Samascott Orchards *Produce* 27 | 20 | 21 | M

See Greenmarket; for more information, call 518-758-7224 | www.samascott.com

"You'll never eat a Red Delicious from the corner deli again" after sampling the "amazing assortment" of heirloom apples that are the specialty of this Kinderhook orchard's Greenmarket stand; its fruits' "endless variety" (e.g. the "juiciest" Yellow Newton Pippins) and "peerless" quality make it a standout, and it doesn't hurt that there are also "bubbling hot cider" and "mmm" doughnuts to "keep you warm" while you make your picks.

	QUALITY	DISPLAY	SERVICE	COST

S&S Cheesecake 🖼🍴 *Baked Goods*   27 | 12 | 19 | M

Bronx | 222 W. 238th St. (bet. Bailey Ave. & B'way) | 1 to 238th St. |
718-549-3888

"There is no better cheesecake" declare dessert-cart cognoscenti who "dare you to resist" the "creamy", "incredibly smooth
texture" of this Bronx bakery's output, which continues to "wow"
as the "hands-down" "finest" available; the quality justifies "a
schlep" to the frill-free "warehouse" outlet (open Monday-
Friday till 3 PM), but it's also "easy enough to find around town" at
classy eateries like Morton's.

Sandwich Planet ◑ *Deli/Sandwich*   ▽ 25 | 14 | 21 | M

Garment District | 534 Ninth Ave. (bet. 39th & 40th Sts.) | A/C/E to
42nd St./Port Authority | 212-273-9768 |
www.sandwichplanet.com

If "brilliant sandwiches made to order" send you into outer space,
head to this Garment District shop that "rewards patrons" with so
many "offbeat" options (over 100) that some surveyors just "don't
know how they do it all in such a tiny place"; given its diminutive
size, many say delivery or takeout is the "best option during lunch
hour"; P.S. the "only problem: no liquor license."

Sant Ambroeus ◑ *Ice Cream*   26 | 25 | 21 | E

E 70s | 1000 Madison Ave. (77th St.) | 6 to 77th St. |
212-570-2211
W Village | 259 W. Fourth St. (Perry St.) | 1 to Christopher St. |
212-604-9254
www.santambroeus.com

"'Sheer ambrosia' would be a better name" declare devotees who
swoon over this "high-end" Upper East Side–West Village duo's
espresso, gelato and other "real-deal" Italian "goodies"; it's all "civ-
ilized", "fresh and delicious" enough to have you thinking you're on
a "trip to Milan" – complete with "expensive" prices.

Sarabeth's 🖼 *Baked Goods*   24 | 22 | 19 | E

Chelsea | Chelsea Mkt. | 75 Ninth Ave. (bet. 15th & 16th Sts.) | A/
C/E/L to 14th St./8th Ave. | 212-989-2424
E 70s | Whitney Museum | 945 Madison Ave. (75th St.) | 6 to 77th St. |
212-570-3670
E 90s | 1295 Madison Ave. (bet. 92nd & 93rd Sts.) | 6 to 96th St. |
212-410-7335 ◑
W 80s | 423 Amsterdam Ave. (bet. 80th & 81st Sts.) | 1 to 79th St. |
212-496-6280 ◑
800-773-7378 | www.sarabeth.com

Many "well-maintained" urbanites confess they're "fools for" these
"charming" bakeries and "brunch musts", which turn out the
"freshly" minted likes of "scrumptious" scones, "marvelous muffins" and other "goodies" best paired with their "luscious" "homemade jams"; the picturesque "country kitchen" setups are a bit
"precious" atmospherically (and pricewise), but "the whole world
knows" they're "special" so "get on line early to beat the crowd"
on Sunday mornings.

	QUALITY	DISPLAY	SERVICE	COST

Sarge's Deli ●⎘ *Deli/Sandwich* | 21 | 15 | 16 | M |

Murray Hill | 548 Third Ave. (bet. 36th & 37th Sts.) | 6 to 33rd St. |
212-679-0442 | www.sargesdeli.com

"Sarge keeps his stripes!" decree devotees of this Murray Hill deli
"gem" that hits the spot with "huge sandwiches", "24/7 breakfasts"
and "chicken noodle soup when you're not feeling so great", all "at
reasonable prices"; there's "no problem finding a table" here, and
those in-the-know advise "don't come for the interior, come for the
vast menu" – better yet, take advantage of its "huge delivery area."

Savino's Quality Pasta ⌀ *Pasta* | - | - | - | I |

Williamsburg | 111 Conselyea St. (bet. Leonard St. & Manhattan Ave.) |
Brooklyn | L to Lorimer St. | 718-388-2038

This unpretentious pasta purveyor in Williamsburg is run by a multi-
generational crew of Savino family members, who produce fresh
noodles like fettuccini and pappardelle as well as frozen filled varieties, including 13 kinds of ravioli, stuffed shells and manicotti; offered alongside are ready-to-go housemade pesto or marinara
sauce, as well as a small selection of dried pastas, oils and vinegars.

Saxelby Cheesemongers *Cheese/Dairy* | ▽ 28 | 22 | 27 | M |

LES | Essex Street Mkt. | 120 Essex St. (bet. Delancey & Rivington Sts.) | F/J/
M/Z to Delancey/Essex Sts. | 212-228-8204 | www.saxelbycheese.com

"Many a new cheese lover will emerge" from this "boutique"-like
Essex Street Market stall, which honors "the finest in American-
made", "small-farm" fromages with its 30-plus "artisanal" offerings
("expect the unusual here") paired with "fresh-baked breads" from
Sullivan Street Bakery; owner Anne Saxelby is a "sweetheart" with
an "infectious" "passion for her product", so "it's impossible to
leave without something."

Ⓩ Schaller & Weber ⎘ *Meat/Poultry* | 27 | 22 | 23 | M |

E 80s | 1654 Second Ave. (bet. 85th & 86th Sts.) | 4/5/6 to 86th St. |
212-879-3047 | 800-847-4115 | www.schallerweber.com

"Blessedly unchanged" and "still the best", this "last bastion" of
"Germanic sausages" and "other Teutonic specialties" in Yorkville has
long been known for its "jaw-dropping" selection of meats, wursts and
hard-to-find imported delicacies that will have almost anyone "salivating like one of Pavlov's dogs"; even better, the "old-world charm"
extends to the "landmark"-worthy setting and "helpful" staff.

Scharffen Berger | 26 | 21 | 21 | E |
Chocolate Maker ⎘ *Candy/Nuts*

W 80s | 473 Amsterdam Ave. (bet. 82nd & 83rd Sts.) | 1 to 86th St. |
212-362-9734 | www.scharffenberger.com

Since this "pretty little" store landed on the UWS, "elite chocolate
eaters" have been thrilled to "finally" have an outlet of the San
Francisco chocolate producer "America can be proud of"; its "stunning baking products" with "to-die-for high cacao content" make for
"recipes that explode with taste" ("this is the chocolate to eat, cook
with and rub all over!"), and there are also bonbons and drinking options, considered by most to be "worth" the "boutique" prices.

	QUALITY	DISPLAY	SERVICE	COST

Schatzie's Prime Meats *Meat/Poultry*
25 | 17 | 22 | E

E 80s | 1200 Madison Ave. (bet. 87th & 88th Sts.) | 4/5/6 to 86th St. | 212-410-1555

Regulars of this UES butcher say it's worth going in "just to meet" "friendly, warm, welcoming" owner Tony Schatzie, but the main attraction is his selection of prime meats, poultry and game, any of which he's happy to custom-prepare for a customer; naturally such "quality" offerings and personal service don't come cheap, but "quick delivery and house accounts" sweeten the deal.

Schick's Bakery ▣ *Baked Goods*
20 | 14 | 14 | M

Borough Park | 4710 16th Ave. (bet. 47th & 48th Sts.) | Brooklyn | F to Ditmas Ave. | 718-436-8020 | www.schicksbakery.com

"Where else would one get cakes for Passover?" wonder faithful followers of this "traditional kosher bakery" in Borough Park, an "old standby" for a "large variety" of "heaven-blessed" bounty like mousse cakes, rugalach, krakovsky (cashew brittle) and fancy cookies; "it's all good" "even if you don't have to eat kosher", and Manhattanites can find their products stocked at Zabar's, Fairway and other markets.

Sea Breeze *Seafood*
23 | 17 | 20 | I

W 40s | 541 Ninth Ave. (40th St.) | A/C/E to 42nd St./Port Authority | 212-563-7537

A "large and tempting display" of "fresh-out-of-the-water" seafood is the catch at this third-generation family seafood market in Hell's Kitchen, where "bargain" prices mean you "won't break the bank"; the "dated, slippery locale" was renovated post-Survey, so perhaps it's no longer necessary to "hose your shoes off" before heading home.

Sea Grape Wine Shop ◑▣ *Wine/Liquor*
∇ 23 | 20 | 26 | M

W Village | 512 Hudson St. (bet. Christopher & W. 10th Sts.) | 1 to Christopher St. | 212-463-7688 | www.seagrapewines.com

"What a great wine shop!" cheer champions of this wee West Villager, known on the "neighborhood" grapevine for stocking "excellent" choices "from around the world", embracing many "lesser-known vineyards" from Languedoc to South Africa; the "very friendly" team is ever "willing to help" with "knowledgeable" suggestions, and the focus on labels under $10 is "always a pleasant" incentive to drift in.

Seaport Flowers *Flowers*
∇ 26 | 26 | 24 | E

Brooklyn Heights | 214 Hicks St. (bet. Montague & Remsen Sts.) | Brooklyn | 2/3/4/5/M/N/R/W to Borough Hall/Court St. | 718-858-6443 | www.seaportflowers.com

"The height of perfection in Brooklyn Heights", this "boutique florist" and event planner produces "artful arrangements" (laced with unique ingredients like artichokes, berries and grapes) that devotees describe as "simply ethereal" and "supremely fresh"; "talented" owner Amy Gardella "is a joy to work with" as is the "wonderful staff", but surveyors are split on price – relatively "affordable" vs. "big bucks."

	QUALITY	DISPLAY	SERVICE	COST

Sebastians Catering & Special Events *Caterer*

| - | - | - | E |

E 50s | 875 Third Ave. (bet. 52nd & 53rd Sts.) | 212-832-3880 | www.sebastians.com
By appointment only

The local branch of a Boston firm, this off-premises caterer specializes in corporate klatches and product launches for clients like Microsoft, Morgan Stanley and Pfizer, serving variations on American fare at prices accounts payable will appreciate; it also provides full event services at sites around town, and a take-out counter at its East Side HQ offers a sandwich-centric preview of the goods.

Second Helpings ● *Prepared Food*

| - | - | - | M |

Park Slope | 448 Ninth St. (7th Ave.) | Brooklyn | F to 7th Ave. | 718-965-1925 | www.secondhelpings.com

At this "health-oriented" Park Slope prepared foods shop, the emphasis is on a rotating variety of natural, mostly organic sandwiches, soups and other offerings that don't scrimp on "seasonings and creativity"; there are some meat and fish dishes on offer, but "amazing veggie" specialties (e.g. "wonderful vegan stews") are its forte, ensuring that this is "no boring health-food place."

Sedutto's ●≠ *Ice Cream*

| 24 | 16 | 18 | M |

E 70s | 1498A First Ave. (bet. 78th & 79th Sts.) | 6 to 77th St. | 212-879-9557
Staten Island | 314 New Dorp Ln. (Clawson St.) | 718-351-3344

"Unassuming, ungimmicky and unbelievably great" is how diehards describe this separately owned UES–Staten Island pair of ice cream "standbys" and their "simple flavors, large portions" and "*delizioso*" "rich and super-creamy" premium product; admirers only "wish there were more locations around the city."

Sensuous Bean, The ⬚ *Coffee/Tea*

| 25 | 21 | 23 | M |

W 70s | 66 W. 70th St. (bet. Columbus Ave. & CPW) | B/C to 72nd St. | 212-724-7725 | 800-238-6845 | www.sensuousbean.com

"Refreshingly quaint", this longtime Upper Westsider is a "tiny joint" "stuffed" with an "amazing" assortment of 150 "first-class coffees" both "native and imported", plus a 100-strong selection of teas highlighting many "unusual" artisanal leaves; the "charming" staffers offer "advice for the novice", and sensualists can throw in some gourmet chocolates or sweet stuff from Villabate.

September Wines & Spirits ● *Wine/Liquor*

| ▽ 25 | 24 | 24 | E |

LES | 100 Stanton St. (Ludlow St.) | F/V to Lower East Side/2nd Ave. | 212-388-0770 | www.septemberwines.com

A "very eclectic mix" marks this "cool", "friendly" boutique wine seller on the Lower East Side, a specialist in vintages from family-run, green-leaning producers in up-and-coming regions like Slovenia, Mexico, Morocco, Lebanon and Brazil; it holds tastings Thursday–Saturday nights, and it's also "the perfect place to pick up a bottle" en route to an international "BYOB meal"; N.B. private tastings for the home or office can also be arranged.

	QUALITY	DISPLAY	SERVICE	COST

Settepani ● ◐ ▣ *Baked Goods*   ▽ 23 | 26 | 20 | M

Harlem | 196 Lenox Ave. (120th St.) | 2/3 to 125th St. | 917-492-4806
Williamsburg | 602 Lorimer St. (bet. Conselyea St. & Skillman Ave.) |
Brooklyn | G/L to Metropolitan Ave./Lorimer St. | 718-349-6524
www.settepani.com

Supporters set store by these "authentic" Italian bakeries for a
"wide selection of breads" (old-fashioned casareccio, focaccia,
Pullman sandwich loaves) and "exquisite" dolci such as mousse
cakes, pastries and fruit tarts; the Williamsburg flagship caters to
the take-out trade while the Harlem spin-off is a full-service "godsend" even if it's "not for those in a hurry."

7th Avenue Wine &   ▽ 20 | 19 | 17 | M
Liquor Co. ● *Wine/Liquor*

Park Slope | 88 Seventh Ave. (bet. Berkeley Pl. & Union St.) | Brooklyn |
2/3 to Grand Army Plaza | 718-399-3300

There's "no snobbery" at this Park Slope vintner, just an "eclectic"
assortment of wines, with especially strong representation from
Spain and South America, as well as concentration of bourbons and
single-malts; free delivery and tastings Mondays–Thursdays are additional draws, however, "if you're looking for a bargain, keep walking."

S. Feldman Housewares *Cookware*   23 | 15 | 22 | E

E 90s | 1304 Madison Ave. (bet. 92nd & 93rd Sts.) | 4/5/6 to 86th St. |
212-289-7367 | 800-359-8558

This "solid" Upper East Side longtimer with the feel of an "old-
fashioned hardware store stocked with luxury items" services the
neighborhood with cookware and tabletop items at prices in step
with its "well-heeled" client base; service is "helpful", and though its
"crammed" quarters can be hard to navigate, for most it's still a
"treat to browse."

Shake Shack ● *Prepared Food*   25 | 15 | 15 | I

Flatiron | Madison Square Park (Madison Ave. & 23rd St.) | N/R/W to
23rd St. | 212-889-6600 | www.shakeshack.com

At this fast-food stand boasting "an unbeatable location" in
Madison Square Park, restaurateur Danny Meyer's "Missouri heritage
shows": lunchers wash down "astonishingly tasty", "juicy burgers",
"Chicago-style dawgs" and "to-die-for french fries" with "amazing"
St. Louis-style frozen custards (as well as beer or wine) – "brave"
the "insane lines" because it's "absolutely worth the wait."

Shakoor's Sweet Tooth *Baked Goods*   - | - | - | M

Bed-Stuy | 305 Halsey St. (bet. Marcus Garvey Blvd. & Throop Ave.) |
Brooklyn | C to Kingston-Throop Aves. | 718-574-2580 |
www.shakoorssweettooth.com

"Unbeatable" sweet potato cheesecake headlines a roster of many
"delicious" desserts at this Bed-Stuy bakery, whose traditional
Southern slant and "imaginative recipes" do proud by Dixie favorites
like red velvet cake, puddings, pies and cobbler; it's also worth
giving it a shake for event catering and weddings (complete with
down-home prepared foods).

	QUALITY	DISPLAY	SERVICE	COST

Shawn's Fine Wines & Spirits ● ⌷ *Wine/Liquor* ▽ 24 | 20 | 21 | M

Park Slope | 141 Seventh Ave. (bet. Carroll St. & Garfield Pl.) | Brooklyn | 2/3 to Grand Army Plaza | 718-622-7947 | www.wineaccess.com/store/shawns/

Loyal locals "like the atmosphere" at this 35-year Park Slope stalwart, whose "dark and woody interior" is the perfect accompaniment for a 1,000-strong wine lineup that's "packed with good choices" at an affordable cost; with fortes in French, Italian and Californian labels and a "very helpful" staff to point out esoteric options, its regulars report they "never bought a bad bottle" here.

☒ Sherry-Lehmann ⌷ *Wine/Liquor* 29 | 24 | 24 | E

E 60s | 505 Park Ave. (59th St.) | N/R/W to 5th Ave./59th St. | 212-838-7500 | www.sherry-lehmann.com

"Still the standard-bearer", this "classic" East Side "mecca for wine enthusiasts" maintains a "staggering inventory" ("particularly" the "amazing stock of Bordeaux") that's hailed for its "impeccable quality" and "competitive" cost "in all price ranges", though the "awesome" variety – extending to glassware and accessories – is more fully revealed via "catalog or web"; it moved post-Survey to snazzy, roomier Park Avenue digs, but it still has the same "second-to-none service" from staffers who have the "consummate knowledge" to assist everyone from the "upper crust to the regular Joe."

Silver Moon Bakery *Baked Goods* 26 | 21 | 20 | M

W 100s | 2740 Broadway (105th St.) | 1 to 103rd St. | 212-866-4717 | www.silvermoonbakery.com

The Upper West Side gets "upped a notch" by this "darling" French bakery, a "popular" stop for "killer" artisanal breads (including brioche and the "ever-fresh baguettes") plus "outstanding" "sweet treats" likes cakes and tarts; most agree it's "worth it to pay extra" for the "highest quality", and the "daunting" "weekend lines" prove it's "much needed in the neighborhood."

☒ Simchick, L. *Meat/Poultry* 28 | 19 | 25 | E

E 50s | 988 First Ave. (bet. 54th & 55th Sts.) | 6 to 51st St. | 212-888-2299

Though it relocated within the neighborhood post-Survey, this East Side butcher remains an "old-school place" where countermen "tell you how to prepare the meat you're buying" and then "ask how it turned out when you return"; it purveys "outstanding" prime cuts "worthy of the most demanding eaters" as well as ready-to-cook offerings like marinated steaks and meatloaf, but no matter what you order, "you get what you pay for" – "and that's a lot."

Sip Fine Wine ● *Wine/Liquor* ▽ 27 | 27 | 24 | M

Park Slope | 67 Fifth Ave. (bet. Prospect & St. Marks Pls.) | Brooklyn | 2/3 to Bergen St. | 718-638-6105 | www.sipfinewine.com

This "down-to-earth" little Park Slope wine shop features a "well-chosen", "well-priced" selection with a "focus on lesser-known" vintages from small producers around the globe, concentrating on Spain, France, Italy and California; the "courteous staff" is "not

	QUALITY	DISPLAY	SERVICE	COST

snobby in the least" but it "really knows its stuff", and "educational" sipping's on offer at tastings every Saturday.

67 Wines & Spirits ●🔲 Wine/Liquor

| 25 | 20 | 21 | M |

W 60s | 179 Columbus Ave. (68th St.) | 1 to 66th St./Lincoln Ctr. | 212-724-6767 | 888-671-6767 | www.67wine.com

There's "nothing to whine about" at this "lively" wine store on the Upper West Side boasting a "fantastic", "reasonably priced" inventory of "wines from around the world" (10,000-plus labels), which, following an extensive post-Survey renovation of the two-story space, can now be perused without having to "squeeze through the aisles"; "terrific tastings", "cheerful" "connoisseurs" on staff, an "unbeatable" delivery policy and an informative website make it many an oenophile's "mainstay."

Skyview Discount Wines & Liquors ●🔲 Wine/Liquor

| 26 | 19 | 24 | I |

Bronx | Skyview Shopping Ctr. | 5681 Riverdale Ave. (259th St.) | 1 to 231st St. | 718-601-8222 | www.skyviewwines.com

Observant oenophiles will find "much to choose from" at this Bronx "kosher wine nirvana", where a 500-label international inventory (including champagnes) boasts the "best assortment and prices" around and choice vintages always go "on sale for the holidays"; they also stock sakes and a full line of spirits, and Manhattanites can save themselves a schlep with the free delivery service (for orders over $150).

Slavin, M. & Sons Ltd. Seafood

| 23 | 13 | 16 | M |

Brownsville | 31 Belmont Ave. (Thatford Ave.) | Brooklyn | 3 to Sutter Ave. | 718-495-2800 | www.mslavin.com

"Fish doesn't get any fresher" than the fin fare from this seafood wholesaler that "supplies many restaurants" via its familiar fleet of trucks seen all over town; although its nearly century-old family business has evolved into a mega-operation with an online catalog boasting some 4,000 items, it still custom-cuts orders at its Brownsville plant, where it sells its products retail.

Slope Cellars ● Wine/Liquor

| 24 | 21 | 24 | M |

Park Slope | 436 Seventh Ave. (bet. 14th & 15th Sts.) | Brooklyn | F to 7th Ave. | 718-369-7307 | www.slopecellars.com

"Deservedly popular" among "connoisseurs and novices alike", this Park Slope wine seller "serves the neighborhood well" with an "excellent" assortment color-coded by price, including some very "decent" deals in the under-$10 'Cheap and Tasty' category; they're "always eager to help" with "atypical" picks "without being overbearing" and sponsor a "fun frequent buyer program" (purchase 12 bottles and the next one's 99¢) as well as biweekly tastings.

Smith & Vine ● Wine/Liquor

| 23 | 22 | 24 | M |

Cobble Hill | 268 Smith St. (bet. Degraw & Sackett Sts.) | Brooklyn | F/G to Carroll St. | 718-243-2864 | www.smithandvine.com

"Boutique but not expensive", this "charming" Smith Street vintner stocks a "fairly small" but "choice selection" of wines ranging from the high-end to numerous "surprisingly delicious" options on the

"$10-and-under table"; overseen by "the friendliest" owners who are "always ready" with "smart" suggestions, it also provides pairing ideas "for their cheese store", Stinky Bklyn, "just across the street."

Snack ◐ *Prepared Food* ▽ 27 | 13 | 16 | M

SoHo | 105 Thompson St. (bet. Prince & Spring Sts.) | C/E to Spring St. | 212-925-1040

Snack Taverna ◐ *Prepared Food*

W Village | 63 Bedford St. (Morton St.) | 1 to Houston St. | 212-929-3499
This "great hidden gem in SoHo" is known for its homemade Greek dishes including moussaka, lamb stew and savory pies, as well as sandwiches, soups and salads, which are all available for takeout or delivery; its bigger, more ambitious West Village sibling, Snack Taverna, is also an option when cooking at home isn't in the cards.

sNice ◐⋈ *Deli/Sandwich* 23 | 19 | 21 | M

W Village | 45 Eighth Ave. (bet. Horatio & Jane Sts.) | A/C/E/L to 14th St. | 212-645-0310
NEW Park Slope | 315 Fifth Ave. (bet. 2nd & 3rd Sts.) | Brooklyn | M/R to Union St. | 718-788-2121
It's herbivore heaven at this West Village shop (with a Park Slope offshoot that opened post-Survey) supplying "excellent", "creative", affordable all-veggie sandwiches, wraps and salads to a "hipster" clientele; its "pleasant" vibe, "free WiFi" and ample "space for meeting with friends" or quietly "reading Proust" has earned it a following as a "real neighborhood" standby.

Soda Shop, The ⋈ *Ice Cream* 20 | 21 | 21 | M

TriBeCa | 125 Chambers St. (bet. Charles St. & W. B'way) | 1/2/3/A/ C/E to Chambers St. | 212-571-1100 | www.sodashopnewyork.com
At this mom-and-pop TriBeCa stop tricked out in "old-fashioned" "soda shoppe" style, the "fountain classics" – "terrific" malteds, shakes, lime rickeys, etc. – are undeniably the "main attraction", though there's a full diner menu as well; "pleasant" service and "extras" like an array of "old-time candy" are reason enough to "step back in time" at this "cute throwback."

SoHo Wines & Spirits *Wine/Liquor* ▽ 21 | 20 | 20 | E

SoHo | 461 W. Broadway (bet. Houston & Prince Sts.) | N/R to Prince St. | 212-777-4332 | www.sohowines.com
"If you're in a pinch" "and need a quick bottle", this airy SoHo wine-and-liquor merchant is a safe "local bet"; the minimalist, gallery-esque space showcases 1,000 vinos (Spain and Italy being strong suits) plus some "excellent" single-malts, and though the going can get "expensive", most maintain "you get what you pay for."

Something Different Party Rental *Party Rentals* - | - | - | E

Paterson | 107-117 Pennsylvania Ave. (Iowa Ave.), NJ | 212-772-0516 | www.somethingdifferentparty.com
By appointment only
This party rental company's Manhattan showroom can double as a reception space, while its broad inventory includes hip, modern table-

QUALITY DISPLAY SERVICE COST

top wares and a full range of event furnishings, including tents, portable bars and some 100,000 chairs; it emphasizes high-tech service (delivery trucks are equipped with GPS) to satisfy corporate and private clients and handle last-minute assignments when needed.

Something Sweet ● *Baked Goods* ▽ 23 | 21 | 25 | M

E Village | 177 First Ave. (11th St.) | L to 1st Ave. | 212-533-9986
Though little-known outside the neighborhood, this sweet little East Village bakery boasts a broad selection of "really fresh" cakes, pies and pastries that would "wow" 'em in Paree; it's a modest operation, but the "homemade taste" is really something.

Soup Spot *Soup* 23 | 16 | 18 | M

Garment District | 220 W. 31st St. (bet 7th & 8th Aves.) | 1/2/3/ to Penn Station | 212-643-8623
"Talk about hitting the spot" – there's "a soup for everyone" at this standout choice for "lunch near Penn Station" ladling "varied", "hearty" selections both "traditional and creative" with flavor that "approaches homemade"; "free" samples and wallet-friendly prices are part of the bargain, but get there early because when the pots run dry, it closes for the day.

☑ Soutine ▭ *Baked Goods* 27 | 19 | 23 | E

W 70s | 104 W. 70th St. (bet. B'way & Columbus Ave.) | 1/2/3 to 72nd St. | 212-496-1450 | 888-806-2253 | www.soutine.com
It flies slightly "under the radar", but Upper Westsiders know this "small" bakery as a "rare treat" for "divine" tarte Tatin, pies and "traditional pastries" whose "sublime" "taste and texture" is an "indulgence" that's "worth the trip" from anywhere; the "excellent" staff will also arrange "outstanding specialty cakes" "made to order" for birthdays and weddings (or hors d'oeuvres), and "they deliver locally" too.

Special Attention *Caterer* - | - | - | E

LES | 325 E. Houston St. (bet. Aves. B & C) | F/V to Lower East Side/ 2nd Ave. | 212-477-4805 | www.special-attention.com
"Individualized" service proves this Lower East Side caterer's more than just a name as it "reliably" supplies "choice" menus flaunting the "quality and presentation" "guests always rave about", particularly with its Pan-Asian hors d'oeuvres; for off-premises events either "business or personal", it rises "up to and above expectations" to ensure any affair will be "most special"; N.B. for hassle-free hosting, they'll also deliver appetizer trays to your door.

Spice Corner ● *Herbs/Spices* 24 | 18 | 17 | I

Gramercy | 135 Lexington Ave. (29th St.) | 6 to 28th St. | 212-689-5182 | www.spicecorner29.com
Indian food lovers swoon as soon as they walk into this friendly, modest Indian grocery store in Gramercy Park, thanks to its heady aroma of cinnamon, cardamom, myriad curry blends, peppercorns – "if it's a spice, they have it"; also cramming the shelves are staples like beans, grains, chutneys and cookware, as well as an impressive selection of Indian sweets, all overseen by a friendly staff.

	QUALITY	DISPLAY	SERVICE	COST

Spoonbread Inc. ❶ *Caterer* ▽ 23 | 18 | 22 | M

Harlem | 366 W. 110th St. (bet. Columbus & Manhattan Aves.) | B/C to 110th St. | 212-865-0700
Harlem | 547 Lenox Ave. (bet. 137th & 138th Sts.) | 2/3 to 135th St. | 212-690-3100
www.spoonbreadinc.com

"Norma Jean [Darden] knows Southern food" testify faithful followers of this Harlem caterer, where the spread's "always fresh and delicious" whether you hanker for down-home delights like fried chicken, catfish and collards or "interesting" variations that give the cookin' a global spin; with "top-notch" service either off-site or at the soul fooders Miss Mamie's and Miss Maude's (not to mention a client base spanning Russell Simmons to Jazz at Lincoln Center), it can claim more than a spoonful of "hype."

Spruce ❶ ▣ *Flowers* ▽ 27 | 27 | 24 | E

Chelsea | 222 Eighth Ave. (bet. 21st & 22nd Sts.) | C/E to 23rd St. | 212-206-1025 | www.spruceup.com

Putting the "focus on the flowers themselves", this Chelsea florist and event planner will "make [you] want to splurge" on one of its "gorgeous, minimalist arrangements", including owner Gaige Clark's signature, a rose 'hedge' housed in a handmade crate; a "wonderful staff" adds to the charm, and if you find that the "sleek, clean" creations are "too expensive" for a personal purchase, note that they also "make for excellent gifts."

NEW Spuyten Duyvil - | - | - | M
Grocery ❶ *Specialty Shop*

Williamsburg | Bedford Mini-Mall | 218 Bedford Ave. (N. 5th St.) | Brooklyn | L to Bedford Ave. | 718-384-1520

A spin-off of Spuyten Duyvil, the Williamsburg bar renowned for its wide, esoteric beer selection, this nearby shop stocks its own 100-strong collection of "awesome, obscure" artisanal brews, arrayed on shelves lining the walls (there's a cooler too); it also squeezes into its pint-size space a few gourmet comestibles, including high-quality chocolate, as well as a selection of beer glasses.

Stage Deli ❶ ▣ *Deli/Sandwich* 21 | 17 | 17 | E

W 50s | 834 Seventh Ave. (bet. 53rd & 54th Sts.) | 1 to 50th St. | 212-245-7850 | 800-782-4369 | www.stagedeli.com

The legends live on – as menu items – at this Midtown deli that's been delivering "sky-high sandwiches" ("bring a big appetite" for the "wonderful pastrami and corned beef") and "sublime cheesecake" since the 1930s; though some call it "a tourist trap", others favor it for its "first-rate people-watching" and "great service" – "just remember that quality food takes time" (and money – "it's pricey").

Starbucks Coffee ❶ ▣ *Coffee/Tea* 18 | 18 | 17 | E

Chinatown | 241 Canal St. (Centre St.) | 6/J/M/N/Q/R/W/Z to Canal St. | 212-219-2725
E 70s | 1117 Lexington Ave. (78th St.) | 6 to 77th St. | 212-517-8476

(continued)

(continued)

Starbucks Coffee

E 90s | 1642 Third Ave. (92nd St.) | 6 to 96th St. | 212-360-0425
E Village | 13-25 Astor Pl. (Lafayette St.) | 6 to Astor Pl. | 212-982-3563
E Village | 141-143 Second Ave. (9th St.) | 6 to Astor Pl. | 212-780-0024
Harlem | 77 W. 125th St. (Lenox Ave.) | 2/3 to 125th St. | 917-492-2454
Murray Hill | 585 Second Ave. (32nd St.) | 6 to 33rd St. | 212-684-1299
SoHo | 150 Varick St. (Spring St.) | C/E to Spring St. | 646-230-9816
W 40s | 682 Ninth Ave. (47th St.) | C/E to 50th St. | 212-397-2288
W 60s | 152-154 Columbus Ave. (67th St.) | 1 to 66th St./Lincoln Ctr. | 212-721-0470
800-782-7282 | www.starbucks.com
Additional locations throughout the NY area

"How did we live without them?"; the chainzilla whose "super-charged coffee" "for the masses" sustains "global domination" still stirs up nonstop debate: backers "never tire of" an "efficient" "pick-me-up" "without risk" while contras "carp about" "too-acidic" brews "for too many bucks", but either way "you can always count on" its "omnipresence" for "easy" "web surfing and gawking."

Starwich *Deli/Sandwich*   23 | 17 | 18 | M

E 50s | 153 E. 53rd St. (bet. Lexington & 3rd Aves.) | E/V to 5th Ave./53rd St. | 212-371-7772 ◐
E 70s | 1055 Lexington Ave. (75th St.) | 6 to 77th St. | 212-585-0788 ◐
Financial District | 63 Wall St. (bet. Pearl & William Sts.) | 2/3 to Wall St. | 212-809-3200 ◐
Garment District | 72 W. 38th St. (bet. 5th & 6th Aves.) | B/D/F/N/Q/R/V/W to 34th St./Herald Sq. | 212-302-7775
W 40s | 525 W. 42nd St. (bet. 10th & 11th Aves.) | A/C/E to 42nd St./Port Authority | 212-736-9170 ◐
866-942-4864 | www.starwich.com

"Superior sandwiches" are the stars at this mini-galaxy of "upscale" 'wicheries where patrons pick from more than 100 "top-notch" in-gredients; skeptics wonder whether its "killer" product is "worth the big bucks" – yes, all those "choices" can "lead to overspending" – but the attractive eating areas and free WiFi access help balance the scales; N.B. they also do a big office catering business.

❷ Staubitz Market *Meat/Poultry*   29 | 23 | 25 | E

Cobble Hill | 222 Court St. (bet. Baltic & Warren Sts.) | Brooklyn | F/G to Bergen St. | 718-624-0014 | www.staubitz.com

"Old-world service and charm" permeate this Cobble Hill meat mar-ket, which has been in business since 1917 and is still known for its "first-rate" "hand-cut and -trimmed" prime beef and the "best spe-cialty game meats" like pheasant, venison and wild boar; "expen-sive" prices mean it's more of a "special-occasion" source for many, but most don't mind because "superb quality" has its price – there's good "reason this butcher is still around"; P.S. "avoid on days ap-proaching Christmas" unless you're "prepared to wait on line."

Steve's Authentic
Key Lime Pies *Baked Goods*

| 25 | 10 | 18 | M |

Red Hook | Pier 41 | 204-207 Van Dyke St. (bet. Conover & Ferris Sts.) | Brooklyn | F/G to Smith/9th Sts. | 718-858-5333 | 888-450-5463 | www.stevesauthentic.com

"A sliver of Key West in Red Hook", Steve Tarpin's single-item "niche" operation is "the gold standard for Key lime pie", attaining "tart and delicious" perfection with fresh-squeezed limes and a buttery graham cracker crust; the goods can be had at the main "warehouse" space (which also vends chocolate-coated "frozen pie pops"), delivered around town in a '50s panel truck or available at Zabar's and Citarella.

Stinky Bklyn *Cheese/Dairy*

| ▽ 28 | 22 | 25 | M |

Cobble Hill | 261 Smith St. (Degraw St.) | Brooklyn | F/G to Carroll St. | 718-522-7425 | www.stinkybklyn.com

Its moniker reflects a "pungent" "sense of humor", but this "high-style" fromagerie in Cobble Hill is serious when it comes to its "small but well-chosen" inventory of "wonderful" cheeses, tended by "hip" but "neighborly" types who are "always ready with a taste" and "creative" "wine pairing" suggestions from the "sister store", Smith & Vine, across the street; the "prices are reasonable", and it's also worth sniffing out for its charcuterie, as well as its classes and seminars.

Stokes Farm *Produce*

| 27 | 21 | 25 | M |

See Greenmarket; for more information, call 201-768-3931 | www.stokesfarm.com

"Excellent fresh produce" "locally grown" (in Bergen County, NJ) is the story behind this Greenmarket steady – one of the original farmers in the system from 30 years back – known especially for "beautiful big herb plants" that become herb wreaths at the holidays and a "nice mix of standard and heirloom" tomatoes; the produce bins are presided over by Ron Binaghi, "the friendly, funny emcee-owner-grocer."

◪ Stonehouse California
Olive Oil ▣ *Specialty Shop*

| 27 | 22 | 23 | E |

Seaport | 223 Front St. (Peck Slip) | 2/3/4/5/A/C to Fulton St. | 212-358-8700 | www.stonehouseoliveoil.com

At the tasting bar of this South Street Seaport outlet for a California olive grove, "you can sample the oils with bread and make a choice" from among the "delicious" selection, including flavored options like "to-die-for Persian lime" and blood orange–infused; "their bottles are beautiful enough for a collection", but don't leave them on your shelf – "they encourage you to bring them back for refills."

Stonekelly Events & Florals *Flowers*

| ▽ 25 | 24 | 19 | VE |

W 50s | 736 11th Ave. (bet. 51st & 52nd Sts.) | C/E to 50th St. | 212-245-6611 | www.stonekelly.com

Specializing in event design, this West 50s florist is "always on the money", producing "unusual work" that combines "high-quality" blooms with "flair galore" to achieve an experience that's "not your usual staid affair"; yes, it's "expensive, but it won't disappoint" – un-

	QUALITY	DISPLAY	SERVICE	COST

less you factor in service ("the flowers were beautiful, but the staff drove us crazy").

☑ Stork's Pastry Shop *Baked Goods*   `27` `22` `21` `M`

Whitestone | 12-42 150th St. (12th Rd.) | Queens | 7 to Flushing-Main St. | 718-767-9220

Giving Whitestone's sweet tooths a leg to stand on since "back in the day", this "old-school" German bakery and chocolate shop is the "real" thing for "marvelous" cookies, truffles and pastries that provide a "taste of childhood" with "no compromise in quality"; also a nest of "excellent breads" that "bring tears to" traditionalist's eyes, it's a "local" "favorite" that's always "worth the trip over the bridge."

Streit's Matzo Co. ⊖ *Baked Goods*   `25` `13` `16` `I`

LES | 148-154 Rivington St. (bet. Clinton & Suffolk Sts.) | F/J/M/Z to Delancey/Essex Sts. | 212-475-7000 | www.streitsmatzos.com

"*The* place to come for matzos" is this "old-world" Lower East Side factory, a "hole-in-the-wall" outlet and Passover "institution" that's famed for its assortment of kosher wafers with "no leavening ever" as well as "related products" like noodles and farfel; in business since 1925 and "still the same", it's the "best and least expensive" way to procure the "brand of choice" "right after it's made" – "how can you go wrong?"

Subtle Tea ▣ *Coffee/Tea*   `23` `21` `21` `M`

Murray Hill | 121 Madison Ave. (30th St.) | 6 to 28th St. | 212-481-4713 | www.subtleteastore.com

"Tea experts" brew with nuance at this "cute" Murray Hiller, which "will put a cheery buzz in your day" with some 75 "delicious" steeped pours (creative "combination blends" among them) accompanied by scones, sandwiches and cookies; the "friendly" staff is ever "ready to help" "the non-connoisseur", and the modern layout's roomy enough for a communal table plus a retail display of teapots, cups, loose leaves and bath and body sundries.

☑ Sugar Sweet Sunshine ◗ *Baked Goods*   `27` `21` `22` `I`

LES | 126 Rivington St. (bet. Essex & Norfolk Sts.) | F/J/M/Z to Delancey/Essex Sts. | 212-995-1960 | www.sugarsweetsunshine.com

Specializing in "superior cupcakes" rated tops in the genre – no mean feat in "cupcake-crazed" NYC – this "cute" Lower East Side bakery/cafe "warms you" with a "comfy" "place to sit" while sampling its trademark "little pieces of heaven" and "numerous other" "addictive" desserts like "moist cakes", cookies and bars; with a "laid-back" vibe that's as "unpretentious" as the goods are "completely fresh", it definitely hits the "sweet spot."

Sui Cheong Meat Market *Meat/Poultry*   ▽ `20` `19` `18` `I`

Chinatown | 89 Mulberry St. (Canal St.) | 6/J/M/N/Q/R/W/Z to Canal St. | 212-267-0350

Given its location, it's not surprising this C-town meat market is loaded with "all the cuts for Chinese cooking" including flank steak and pork belly (and ears and brains) in addition to such house specialties as "fine-quality roast pig and soy-sauce chickens" – you

QUALITY | DISPLAY | SERVICE | COST

even get to see "homemade won tons" prepared before your eyes; never mind that the premises could possibly use an "upgrade."

◪ Sullivan Street Bakery *Baked Goods* | 28 | 20 | 22 | M |

W 40s | 533 W. 47th St. (bet. 10th & 11th Aves.) | C/E to 50th St. | 212-265-5580 | www.sullivanstreetbakery.com

Though its original location "on Sullivan Street" is now separately owned, groupies of bread "genius" Jim Lahey can still go to the "Hell's Kitchen outpost" of this Italian bakery "mecca" and find the same "distinctive" loaves in all the "crusty, earthy" glory that makes many call them "the best, bar none"; it remains a "standard-bearer" for "classic" pane Pugliese and "slabs" of "Roman-style pizza", and if the "off-the-path location" is "a pain", it's "worth the effort" to acquire the goods that grace "many high-end" eateries and gourmet markets.

Sundaes & Cones ● *Ice Cream* | 25 | 22 | 25 | M |

E Village | 95 E. 10th St. (bet. 3rd & 4th Aves.) | 6 to Astor Pl. | 212-979-9398

Black sesame, wasabi, corn – "do these sound like ice cream flavors?" ask frequenters of this "cute" little East Village spot where a "fantastic fusion" of "great-tasting" "exotic" ingredients (and some "regular" ones to please purists) is the deal; what's more: the scoop size is "generous" and the quality "amazing."

Sunrise Mart ● *Specialty Shop* | 23 | 18 | 17 | M |

E Village | 4 Stuyvesant St., 2nd fl. (3rd Ave. & 9th St.) | 6 to Astor Pl. | 212-598-3040

SoHo | 494 Broome St. (bet. W. B'way & Wooster St.) | C/E to Spring St. | 212-219-0033

"For all things Japanese", head to these "authentic" markets that feel "just like Tokyo", down to the "tight but well-stocked quarters" (the SoHo branch is "easy to navigate" compared to the "tiny" East Village original); the duo offers "a marvelous assortment" of "hard-to-find" products and ingredients plus sushi, bento boxes and other "tasty snacks."

Superior Chocolatiers ▣ *Candy/Nuts* | ▽ 22 | 20 | 20 | M |

Staten Island | 1150 South Ave. (Lois Ln.) | 718-698-3300 | 800-698-3302 | www.supremechocolatier.com

This third-generation family chocolate business is Staten Islanders' "place to go" for well-priced "specialty chocolate for any holiday" and a downright "must-visit for Easter", given its "gigantic" selection of molded shapes; an added bonus: the factory "is a fun place to visit" when kids are in tow.

Sur La Table ▣ *Cookware* | 26 | 24 | 21 | E |

SoHo | 75 Spring St. (bet. Crosby & Lafayette Sts.) | 6 to Spring St. | 212-966-3375 | www.surlatable.com

"A veritable playground for those who cook" say those enamored of this Seattle chain's "gorgeous" SoHo outpost with a "serious" selection of pots and pans, dishes, "unusual utensils", "hard-to-find gadgets" and imported foods; a few quibble that "better deals can be had elsewhere", still, it's hard to "leave without something in hand."

	QUALITY	DISPLAY	SERVICE	COST

Surroundings ⌨ *Flowers*

| 25 | 24 | 23 | VE |

W 60s | 135 Amsterdam Ave. (W. 66th St.) | 1 to 66th St. | 212-580-8982 | 800-567-7007 | www.surroundingsflowers.com

At this "elegant" veteran florist on the Upper West Side, the "beautiful, lush", "to-die-for flower arrangements" ("perfect to send to the boss or a friend") are accompanied by "gracious, warm", "lovely service" – there's even a horticulturist on staff; most agree, however, that the shop's "really special" designs come at prices that are "on the high side."

Susan Holland & Co. Inc. *Caterer*

| – | – | – | E |

Flatiron | 142 Fifth Ave., 4th fl. (bet. 19th & 20th Sts.) | 212-807-8892 | www.susanholland.com
By appointment only

Combining "interesting" ideas with "absolute dedication to making every detail perfect", this Flatiron caterer/event planner is a master at stunning ambient strokes that lend "elegance" to any venue; they provide "outstanding" food as well as full services from location scouting to lighting, decor and entertainment, and though "so much excellence" is "expensive", the star-studded clientele couldn't be more appreciative.

Sutton Wine Shop ◑⌨ *Wine/Liquor*

| ∇ 22 | 18 | 21 | E |

E 50s | 403 E. 57th St. (1st Ave.) | 4/5/6/N/R/W to 59th St./ Lexington Ave. | 212-755-6626 | 888-369-9463

"Old-time neighborhood" appeal defines this Sutton Place vino vendor, which "stocks everything" in its tiny digs, from a 2,000-bottle inventory that's notable for Italian wines to specialty items like glassware; maybe "you can get a better deal elsewhere", but at least a staff that "waits on you hand and foot" is part of the package.

Sweet Life, The ⌨ *Candy/Nuts*

| 23 | 21 | 24 | M |

LES | 63 Hester St. (Ludlow St.) | F to E. B'way | 212-598-0092 | 800-692-6887 | www.sweetlifeny.com

"Get lost in all things candy" at this Lower East Side "delight of a little store" where the "fabulous selection" of gummies, jelly beans and "long-lost" candies, imports including dried fruits, nuts, chocolates, honeys and syrups, a "huge block of halvah that sits in the corner" and anything else "you could want that's sweet" is supplied at "mostly fair prices"; still, a minority contends the "quality has declined" since the ownership changed a few years back.

Sweet Melissa Patisserie *Baked Goods*

| 24 | 22 | 20 | E |

Cobble Hill | 276 Court St. (bet. Butler & Douglass Sts.) | Brooklyn | F/G to Bergen St. | 718-855-3410 ◑
Park Slope | 175 Seventh Ave. (bet. 1st & 2nd Sts.) | Brooklyn | F to 7th Ave. | 718-502-9153
www.sweetmelissapatisserie.com

"How sweet it is!" enthuse admirers of Melissa Murphy's "cozy", recently expanded (post-Survey) Cobble Hill patisserie and its "beautiful" Park Slope spin-off, where the "decadent", "freshly baked" French-American pastries and cakes can "compete with any fancy Manhattan" joint for "consistently high" standards (and prices); there's also a "light" cafe menu and "afternoon tea service" where the "ladies gather", and both sites boast "lovely" "back gardens" for "a true escape"; N.B. they excel at wedding and other special-occasion cakes.

Swich ● *Deli/Sandwich* ▽ 23 | 27 | 24 | E

Chelsea | 104 Eighth Ave. (15th St.) | A/C/E/L to 14th St./8th Ave. | 212-488-4800 | www.swichpressed.com

With a "very Chelsea look" – sleek, "modern" and apple-green – to draw in passersby, this panini peddler is already full at lunchtime with locals lining up for "quick" made-to-order pressed sandwiches stuffed with "quality" ingredients, like house-roasted meats and vegetables; carb-counters appreciate the option to switch ingredients from sandwich to salad.

☑ Sylvia Weinstock 26 | 26 | 25 | VE
Cakes ▤◐ *Baked Goods*

TriBeCa | 273 Church St. (Franklin St.) | 212-925-6698 | www.sylviaweinstock.com
By appointment only

"If you can dream it, Sylvia can bake it" is the promise at this "charming" TriBeCa custom baker, a designer of "spectacular" "gourmet" cakes for weddings and other occasions whose "one-of-a-kind" masterpieces are "a marvel to look at" and taste "as delicious as they are beautiful"; predictably, the craftsmanship is "off-the-charts expensive", but doesn't "every bride" "deserve the very best"?

Sympathy for the Kettle ●▤ *Coffee/Tea* ▽ 27 | 22 | 23 | M

E Village | 109 St. Marks Pl. (bet. Ave. A & 1st Ave.) | 6 to Astor Pl. | 212-979-1650 | www.sympathyforthekettle.com

Sympathizers delight in the "adorable atmosphere" of this "darling little" pink and chocolate-trimmed tea shop in the East Village; serious tea shoppers – both walk-in and online – applaud the "excellent selection" of "high-quality" house-blended teas (many of them organic and Fair Trade) and accoutrements, while the "exotic" beverage menu and pastries to go with make it a hit with lounging "laptop loners."

TableToppers ▤ *Party Rentals* - | - | - | E

Stamford | 7 Shady Ln. (High Ridge Rd.), CT | 203-329-9977
By appointment only

Table linen rentals and party planning are the forte of this upmarket enterprise headquartered in Stamford, CT; there's a "great selection" of linens (including custom-made options) that can be shipped anywhere – and the "knowledgeable" sales staff appeals to corporate and individual clients alike.

NEW Tafu ▤ *Coffee/Tea* ▽ 19 | 19 | 20 | M

E 50s | 569 Lexington Ave. (entrance on 51st St., bet. Lexington & 3rd Aves.) | 6 to 51st St. | 212-980-1310 | www.tafuny.com

Celebrating green tea in all its forms, this Japanese teahouse in East Midtown sets itself "apart from the rest" with its traditional

Japanese teahouse ambiance, "extensive" list of imported teas and creative sweets like green tea cheesecake; "great service" is icing on the cake.

Tai Pan Bakery Inc. 🚫 *Baked Goods* | 19 | 17 | 13 | I |

Chinatown | 194 Canal St. (bet. Mott & Mulberry Sts.) | 6/J/M/N/Q/R/W/Z to Canal St. | 212-732-2222 ●
Flushing | 37-25 Main St. (bet. 37th & 38th Aves.) | Queens | 7 to Flushing-Main St. | 718-461-8668
Flushing | 42-05B Main St. (Maple St.) | Queens | 7 to Flushing-Main St. | 718-460-8787
888-919-8282

An "unbelievable selection" awaits at these "chaotic" Flushing and Chinatown bakery "favorites", which present a panoply of "double-yummy" pastries "both sweet and savory" along with "freshly baked buns", sandwiches, cakes and plenty more; maybe they're "madhouses" with "lousy service" and "waits in line", but the "unbeatable" prices make for a "poor man's heaven."

🅉 Takashimaya Floral Boutique *Flowers* | 28 | 28 | 23 | VE |

E 50s | Takashimaya | 693 Fifth Ave., 6th fl. (bet. 55th & 56th Sts.) | E/V to 5th Ave./53rd St. | 212-350-0111

"Make a statement" with an "exotic", "exquisite" custom floral arrangement from this "Japanese eden" set within the eponymous Fifth Avenue department store; it's a "lovely place to linger and look" (the "hushed setting" is "almost museumlike") at "amazing", "unusual blooms" of "transporting beauty", but although the "presentation is suitably Zen", the prices are "totally indulgent."

Tal Bagels *Bagels* | 23 | 19 | 18 | M |

E 50s | 977 First Ave. (54th St.) | E/V to Lexington Ave./53rd St. | 212-753-9080 ●🚫
E 80s | 1228 Lexington Ave. (83rd St.) | 4/5/6 to 86th St. | 212-717-2080 🚫
E 80s | 333 E. 86th St. (bet. 1st & 2nd Aves.) | 4/5/6 to 86th St. | 212-427-6811 ●🚫
W 90s | 2446 Broadway (bet. 90th & 91st Sts.) | 1/2/3 to 96th St. | 212-712-0171 ●

"Chewy", "yeasty" rounds and a "terrific" "spread selection" add up to "bagel bliss" for boosters of this "old school"–style quartet that's also appreciated for its "wonderful lox" dispensed by "gifted slicers who work with surgical precision"; though the goods come with "high prices", "quick-as-a-wink" service compensates.

Tamarind Tea Room ● *Coffee/Tea* | 24 | 21 | 22 | M |

Flatiron | 41 E. 22nd St. (Park Ave. S.) | N/R/W to 23rd St. | 212-674-7400 | www.tamarinde22.com

A small, well-edited selection of "exotic teas" makes for a "lovely" experience at this "cozy" tearoom in the Flatiron District; while the Indian "snacks and sweets" prepared by the "fabulous chefs" at the same-named "sister restaurant next door" can provide "an interesting alternative to the traditional afternoon tea", some of the usual accompaniments are offered, including fruit tarts and pound cake.

	QUALITY	DISPLAY	SERVICE	COST

Tan My My 🥡 *Seafood* ▽ 22 | 16 | 13 | I

Chinatown | 253-249 Grand St. (bet. Bowery & Chrystie St.) | B/D to Grand St. | 212-966-7837

Considered a "good-value champion" offering some of the "freshest" fish in town, this Chinatown seafood emporium stands out from the competition by offering some "fancy stuff that no one else carries" – which can "drive up the bill" warn wallet-watchers; meats and produce are also on offer.

Tanoreen *Prepared Food* ▽ 24 | 19 | 21 | I

Bay Ridge | 7704 Third Ave. (77th St.) | Brooklyn | R to 77th St. | 718-748-5600 | www.tanoreen.com

For "tasty Mediterranean food" that you can "eat in or take home", head to this "really cheap" Bay Ridge restaurant/caterer serving up a variety of appetizers and entrees featuring eggplant plus "amazing lamb", kebabs, salads, rice and stuffed grape leaves; those in-the-know advise "don't leave without trying the hummus" – and then "buy extra to eat throughout the week"; N.B. a move to roomier nearby digs at 7523 Third Avenue is planned for summer 2008.

Tarallucci e Vino ◑ *Baked Goods* ▽ 24 | 22 | 20 | M

E Village | 163 First Ave. (10th St.) | L to 1st Ave. | 212-388-1190

Flatiron | 15 E. 18th St. (bet. B'way & 5th Ave.) | 4/5/6/L/N/Q/R/W to 14th St./Union Sq. | 212-228-5400
www.tarallucievino.net

Discerning shoppers salute these "authentic Italian" bakery/cafes for their "fresh", "wonderful coffee and pastries" and equally "delicious" panini, not to mention their rainbow of gelato varieties; the "East Village original" is "a bit more down home" and retail-oriented, while the flashier Flatiron offshoot is an eatery/enoteca that's always a stylish stop for light fare and "a great glass of wine."

Target ◑ 🖳 *Cookware* 17 | 15 | 11 | I

Bronx | 40 W. 225th St. (I-87) | 1 to 225th St./Marble Hill | 718-733-7199

Prospect Heights | Atlantic Terminal Mall | 139 Flatbush Ave. (Atlantic Ave.) | Brooklyn | D/M/N/R to Pacific St. | 718-290-1109

Starrett City | Gateway Ctr. | 519 Gateway Dr. (Erskine St.) | Brooklyn | 718-235-6032

College Point | 135-05 20th Ave. (Whitestone Expwy., exit 15) | Queens | 718-661-4346

Elmhurst | 8801 Queens Blvd. (55th Ave.) | Queens | G/R/V to Grand Ave. | 718-760-5656
800-440-0680 | www.target.com

"If only they had one in Manhattan" sigh city-dwellers who still "schlep" to the outer-borough outposts of this "nifty" "big-box" retailer for "quirky", "well-designed" kitchen supplies that are not only "stylish", but "a great value" to boot; a jaded few maintain that its "limited stock", only "passable service" and "lines, lines, lines" "do not make for pleasant shopping experiences."

	QUALITY	DISPLAY	SERVICE	COST

Tarzian West *Cookware*

22	15	18	M

Park Slope | 194 Seventh Ave. (2nd St.) | Brooklyn | F to 7th Ave. |
718-788-4213

"Absolutely packed with kitchen goodness" (as well as Brooklynites "with strollers"), this Park Slope standby makes the most of its "small" space by crowding in "almost too much merchandise" from pots and pans to appliances and gadgets; it changed hands post-Survey, so perhaps the new owners will address complaints that it's "overpriced", with service "that leaves a lot to be desired."

Tastebud's Natural Foods *Health Food*

22	21	21	M

Staten Island | 1807 Hylan Blvd. (Buel Ave.) | 718-351-8693

The main point of attraction at this diminutive health food store is that it's "one of the few natural shops on Staten Island", but nonetheless hyperbolic shoppers applaud its selection of wheat-gluten-free products as the "best in all of NYC"; there's also an organic juice bar and a respectable selection of vegan foods.

Taste Caterers *Caterer*

∇ 22	26	22	E

W Village | 113 Horatio St. (bet. Washington & West Sts.) |
212-255-8571 | www.tastecaterers.com
By appointment only

Good taste marks the boutique talents of this West Village caterer and event planner, an off-site specialist known for "elegant displays" of "exquisite" Eclectic eats from a creative kitchen that favors seasonal ingredients and gourmet flourishes; with "courteous servers" and an "accommodating" staff to handle venue prep and logistics, it's "worth every penny" for quality suited to heads of state, museums and bigwig fashion designers.

Tastings by Payard ● *Caterer/Events*

∇ 27	24	23	VE

E 70s | 1032 Lexington Ave. (bet. 73rd & 74th Sts.) | 212-744-4422 |
www.tastingsnyc.com
By appointment only

Connoisseurs claim you "can't get nicer French catering" than at this affiliate of the East Side patisserie powerhouse Payard, which takes its signature elegance off-premises with "great displays" of haute bistro fare and "amazing" dessert spreads showcasing "the most gorgeous and delicious" cakes and pastries; its full-service planners tailor events on an intimate scale, and the effect's as decorous as it is dearly priced.

Tea Box, The *Coffee/Tea*

27	24	22	E

E 50s | Takashimaya | 693 Fifth Ave., lower level (bet. 54th & 55th Sts.) | E/V to 5th Ave./53rd St. | 212-350-0100 | 800-753-2038

"Hidden" in the basement of Takashimaya, Midtown's "swanky" Japanese department store, is this "wonderful" tea shop proffering some 40 varieties of "high-quality" loose leaves (green, black and herbal), plus "superb accoutrements", presented in "rarefied" displays; the adjacent "Zen-like" tearoom makes a "lovely" "getaway from the Fifth Avenue bustle", but just keep in mind that the "exquisite" afternoon tea here requires more than a little "dough."

	QUALITY	DISPLAY	SERVICE	COST

Tea Lounge ◐ *Coffee/Tea* | 21 | 19 | 19 | M |

Cobble Hill | 254 Court St. (Kane St.) | Brooklyn | F/G to Bergen St. | 718-624-5683 ⊟
Park Slope | 837 Union St. (bet. 6th & 7th Aves.) | Brooklyn | B/Q to 7th Ave. | 718-789-2762
www.tealoungeny.com

Stroller-pushers and other "fans of the leafy brew" flock to these Park Slope–Cobble Hill teahouses with a "bohemian graduate-student feel", where loungers sip and surf free WiFi, "people-watch" or just "curl up" on the "ratty-but-comfy sofas and read" into the wee hours; they're known for their deep selection of tea as well as just "ok" coffee, but Union Street also offers a full bar – and with "all those screaming kids" you just may "need a drink."

Teitel Brothers ⊟ *Specialty Shop* | 26 | 18 | 21 | I |

Bronx | 2372 Arthur Ave. (E. 186th St.) | B/D to Fordham Rd. | 718-733-9400 | 800-850-7055 | www.teitelbros.com

This "landmark store in Bronx's Little Italy" is "worth the trip to Arthur Avenue" for "great deals" on imported "delicacies from the old country", most notably its "fabulous cheeses", olive oils, cured meats and sausages; sure, it's "no-frills" with a "very straightforward staff", but for many that's just "part of its charm."

Tempo Presto ◐⊄ *Deli/Sandwich* | ▽ 23 | 18 | 19 | M |

Park Slope | 254 Fifth Ave. (bet. Carroll St. & Garfield Pl.) | Brooklyn | M/R to Union St. | 718-636-8899 | www.tempobrooklyn.com

The take-out/catering arm of the Mediterranean eatery Tempo, this next-door storefront offers Park Slopers "something a little special for takeout"; the highlights here are "excellent twists on the usual panini" and non-pressed sandwiches (the TBLT is "a favorite"), as well as "housemade" gelato and baked goodies that range from cupcakes to wedding cakes.

⧖ Ten Ren Tea & Ginseng Co. ⊟ *Coffee/Tea* | 25 | 19 | 19 | M |

Chinatown | 75 Mott St. (bet. Bayard & Canal Sts.) | 6/J/M/N/Q/R/W/Z to Canal St. | 212-349-2286 | 800-292-2049
Chinatown | 79 Mott St. (bet. Bayard & Canal Sts.) | 6/J/M/N/Q/R/W/Z to Canal St. | 212-732-7178 ◐⊟
SoHo | 138 Lafayette St. (Howard St.) | 6/J/M/N/Q/R/W/Z to Canal St. | 212-343-8098
Sunset Park | 5817 Eighth Ave. (bet. 58th & 59th Sts.) | Brooklyn | N to 8th Ave. | 718-853-0660
Elmhurst | 83-28 Broadway (Dongan Ave.) | Queens | R to Elmhurst Ave. | 718-205-0861
Flushing | 135-18 Roosevelt Ave. (bet. Main & Prince Sts.) | Queens | 7 to Flushing-Main St. | 718-461-9305
www.tenrenusa.com

It's "heaven for tea lovers" at this "must-stop" Chinatown vet (75 Mott Street) known for its "excellent selection" of "premium" leaves imported from Taiwan and China, as well as elegant tea sets and accessories, though the "frosty" staff presiding over it all is deemed less than divine; prices range from "medium to outta-site expensive" "depending on quality", but even the most rarefied blend is way "cheaper than a trip to Shanghai"; N.B. all other locations are bubble tea bars dispensing tapioca pearl drinks and snacks.

Ⓩ Terence Conran Shop 🍴 *Cookware* | 25 | 26 | 19 | E |

E 50s | Bridgemarket, The | 407 E. 59th St. (1st Ave.) | 4/5/6/N/R/W to 59th St./Lexington Ave. | 212-755-9079 | www.conranusa.com
"If you love modern", Sir Terence Conran's "beautiful" emporium of "luxurious" housewares is "utopia" with "stylish" imported finds that are "not always practical" though they sure "look good"; if some find it "overpriced", its setting – a bi-level "glass oasis" at the foot of the Queensboro Bridge – means it's a "delight" just to "window shop."

Terhune Orchards 🎏 *Produce* | 27 | 22 | 25 | M |

See Greenmarket; for more information, call phone number unavailable
At this Greenmarket fruit stand "you watch the seasons" go "from peaches and apricots to pears and apples", all arriving from its Upstate orchard in Salt Point; it's "the real deal in freshness" according to fruit fans who also cite "pies, pies, pies" as a draw, and say that some items may be "costly", but the "excellent" products are "worth it" – especially given the "service with extra cheer."

Terrace Bagels ●🎏 *Bagels* | 25 | 18 | 22 | I |

Windsor Terrace | 224 Prospect Park W. (Windsor Pl.) | Brooklyn | F to 15th St. | 718-768-3943
Some of the "best bagels in Brooklyn" come from this Windsor Terrace storefront whose "fresh", "cooked-the-right-way" rounds are "the kind you can eat plain and not think twice about it"; "terrific" service offsets the "crowded" conditions and "waits" on weekends; N.B. a post-Survey renovation may outdate the above ratings.

Terranova Bakery 🎏 *Baked Goods* | 26 | 15 | 20 | I |

Bronx | 691 E. 187th St. (bet. Beaumont & Cambreleng Aves.) | B/D to Fordham Rd. | 718-733-3827 | www.terranovabakery.com
If "Arthur Avenue is the best choice for Italian" "staples", one of the strip's standouts is this bakery "throwback" and its "fresh and authentic" output, especially "hearty rustic" breads like the "wonderful" *pane di casa*; given other fortes like focaccia and housemade pasta, fans of the quality and prices advise "if you're in the neighborhood" "make a beeline" for it.

Ⓩ Teuscher Chocolates of Switzerland 🍬 *Candy/Nuts* | 27 | 26 | 22 | VE |

E 40s | 620 Fifth Ave. (bet. 49th & 50th Sts.) | B/D/F/V to 47-50th Sts./ Rockefeller Ctr. | 212-246-4416
E 60s | 25 E. 61st St. (bet. Madison & Park Aves.) | N/R/W to 5th Ave./ 59th St. | 212-751-8482
800-554-0924 | www.teuscher-newyork.com
"Just the name makes one's mouth water" say devotees of this "elegant" East Side pair of Swiss chocolate boutiques, who rave most about the "dreamy", "heavenly" champagne truffles that you can eat and then "die happy"; the price suggests these "outrageously good" confections and their "gorgeous packaging" "flew first class from Geneva", but don't expect top-flight service from the "haughty" staff.

	QUALITY	DISPLAY	SERVICE	COST

Thalia Kitchen ● *Prepared Food*   21 | 18 | 20 | M

W 50s | 828 Eighth Ave. (50th St.) | C/E to 50th St. | 212-399-4443 | www.restaurantthalia.com

For "fresh, memorable" entrees, "well-prepared sandwiches", "high-quality salads" and "rather tasty" baked goods and desserts, head to this Theater District take-out storefront located around the corner from parent eatery Thalia; yes, it's tiny – "blink and you'll miss it" – but it's "worth" seeking out en route to a Broadway show.

Think Coffee ● *Coffee/Tea*   23 | 19 | 19 | M

G Village | 248 Mercer St. (bet. 3rd & 4th Sts.) | 6 to Bleecker St. | 212-228-6226

NEW **NoHo** | 1 Bleecker St. (Bowery) | 6 to Bleecker St. | 212-533-3366 www.thinkcoffeenyc.com

"Lots of" organic and Free Trade coffee options and hordes of "NYU students" set the scene at this Greenwich Village coffeehouse and "hangout" ("free wireless"), where sippers can enjoy "a relaxing cup" on the "comfy couches and chairs" while reading a book or having a "Craig's List missed connections" moment; snacks are available too, but whatever you order, "don't expect to get in and out quickly"; N.B. a Bleecker Street branch opened post-Survey.

Thomas Preti Caterers *Caterer*   ∇ 23 | 25 | 22 | E

Murray Hill | 146 E. 37th St. (Lexington Ave.) | 212-764-3188 | www.thomaspreti.com
By appointment only

With its combo of "down-to-earth" flexibility and "top restaurant quality", this off-premises caterer/event planner based in Murray Hill goes "beyond expectations" in furnishing "delicious" food and "friendly service", whether for private gatherings or big-box galas; "amazing attention" goes into Preti-fying both cuisine and backdrop to suit the occasion, so count on a performance guests "will complement for years."

3-Corner Field Farm ▣ *Cheese/Dairy*   27 | 22 | 25 | E

See Greenmarket; for more information, call 518-854-9695 | www.dairysheepfarm.com

"Sheep's-milk yogurt and excellent merguez" are only two of the "extensive" uses this Adirondacks farm dedicated to 'the complete sheep' finds for its "well-cared-for" hormone- and drug-free livestock: "succulent lamb", "amazing mutton", half a dozen "terrific" cheeses and even yarn, sheepskin and pet food; the "gracious", "dedicated" owners provide "cheerful service", and as for the "high prices", surveyors say the "quality" makes up for 'em.

3 Guys from Brooklyn ● *Produce*   23 | 19 | 15 | I

Bay Ridge | 6502 Ft. Hamilton Pkwy. (65th St.) | Brooklyn | N to Fort Hamilton Pkwy. | 718-748-8340

"Who'da thunk" a "fabulous smorgasbord of fruits and vegetables" ("some quite unusual") could be found "in the heart of Brooklyn", but this "dirt-cheap" Bay Ridge market proves it's possible; happily it's open 24/7, but "steel your nerves" on weekends when "the place gets overwhelmed" with seekers of "produce bargains" considered some of the "best in the city."

Three Tarts ☒ *Baked Goods* | ▽ 22 | 21 | 21 | M |

Chelsea | 164 Ninth Ave. (20th St.) | C/E to 23rd St. | 212-462-4392 | www.3tarts.com

"Bite-sized pieces of ecstasy" await at this "little sweets" boutique in Chelsea, which does a "delicious" job with the eponymous "nibbles" ("a must-taste") as well as an uncommon lineup of truffles, parfaits (sold in optional stemware), petits fours and more; also a gift shop tarted up with ceramics, housewares and artisanal honeys, it's "a bit pricey" but "definitely worth" a "stop to get something for the road."

Times Square Bagels ◗ *Bagels* | 19 | 15 | 17 | M |

W 40s | 200 W. 44th St. (bet. B'way & 8th Ave.) | 1/2/3/7/N/Q/R/S/W to 42nd St./Times Sq. | 212-997-7300

Amid the "hustle and bustle" of Times Square resides this handy "pit stop" for "light, fluffy" bagels and bialys on the go; while it gets demerits for relatively hefty tabs (chalk it up to the "tourist-trap" locale), regulars rate the "flavorful" offerings more than "worth it" – "long lines" notwithstanding.

Tinto Fino ◗ *Wine/Liquor* | - | - | - | M |

E Village | 85 First Ave. (bet. 5th & 6th Sts.) | L to 1st Ave. | 212-254-0850 | www.tintofino.com

Named for (and scarcely larger than) a premium grape of Spain, this East Village "tiny treasure" of a wine "boutique" from a co-owner of the eatery Tía Pol aims to catch a rising trend by specializing in Spanish imports, offering a multiregional overview spanning familiar Riojas to a novel spotlight on sherries; but the "string-bean" space holds only 150 *botellas*, leading partialists to pray they can "build up their selections" and find "room to display more."

Tiny's Giant Sandwich Shop ◗☒ *Deli/Sandwich* | 22 | 18 | 20 | I |

LES | 129 Rivington St. (bet. Essex & Norfolk Sts.) | F/J/M/Z to Delancey/Essex Sts. | 212-982-1690 | www.tinysgiant.com

The "tastes are big" at this Lower Eastsider turning out a "staggering variety" of "giant" sandwiches, "generous salads" and such; just as the name covers the spectrum, so do the offerings from hot roast beef for carnivores to Big Mack Daddy veggie burgers for the meat-averse.

Tisserie *Baked Goods* | 20 | 22 | 16 | M |

NEW **SoHo** | DKNY | 420 W. Broadway (bet. Prince & Spring Sts.) | C/E to Spring St. | 646-613-8996

Union Sq | 857 Broadway (E. 17th St.) | 4/5/6/L/N/R/Q/W to 14th St./Union Sq. | 212-463-0850 ◗ ☒

www.tisserie.com

Run by a Paris-trained Venezuelan chef and his brother, this "large and bustling" Union Square patisserie/cafe showcases a "wide range" of "decadent" French pastries and desserts that incorporate some "super" "Latin variations" like "out-of-this-world" dulce de leche and "intense" South American chocolate; also serving up sandwiches, "great quiche" and even "vegan soups", it's "a godsend" for the area even if the crowds make the going "kind of slow"; N.B. a second location opened post-Survey inside the DKNY store in SoHo.

❱ Titan Foods ◐▣ *Specialty Shop*   26 | 22 | 20 | I

Astoria | 2556 31st St. (bet. Astoria Blvd. & 28th Ave.) | Queens | N/W to 30th Ave. | 718-626-7771 | www.titanfood.com

When you can't "afford a flight to Athens", this "granddaddy of Greek supermarkets" in Astoria is "the next best thing", offering an array of specialties and "imported items", including "delicious cheeses", "to-die-for olives" and "exceptional baked goods", all at "the best prices"; if the "authentic products" aren't enough to make you feel like you're "back in the homeland", there's "even Greek music" on the sound system.

Todaro Brothers ◐▣ *Specialty Shop*   24 | 21 | 21 | E

Murray Hill | 555 Second Ave. (bet. 30th & 31st Sts.) | 6 to 33rd St. | 212-532-0633 | 877-472-2767 | www.todarobros.com

Murray Hill residents "depend on" this family-owned "blast from the past", an "old-world Italian" gourmet store stocking an "excellent selection of fresh fruits, vegetables, meats, cheeses", fish, pastas and olive oils as well as "wonderful prepared foods" and sandwiches, all "squeezed into a relatively small space"; plus, there's a "friendly" staff that "knows exactly what it's talking about"; P.S. claustrophobes are advised to "avoid Sunday afternoons."

Tops Wines & Spirits ◐ *Wine/Liquor*   ▽ 23 | 15 | 21 | I

Marine Park | 2816 Ave. U (E. 28th St.) | Brooklyn | Q to Ave. U | 718-648-7590 | www.topswines.com

This "popular" Marine Park grape-and-grain store is considered tops on its turf for a "wide range of wines", unsurprising given the "huge" stock of 4,000 labels that spans price points "from cheap to very expensive" and highlights a "large selection of kosher" and Australian vintages; for those who need an assist with the wares, owner "Jeff's recommendations" are "very helpful."

❱ Trader Joe's ◐ *Major Gourmet Mkt.*   24 | 19 | 21 | I

Union Sq | 142 E. 14th St. (bet. 3rd & 4th Aves.) | 4/5/6/L/N/Q/R/W to 14th St./Union Sq. | 212-529-4612

NEW **Rego Park** | 90-30 Metropolitan Ave. (Woodhaven Blvd.) | Queens | M to Metropolitan Ave. | 718-275-1791
www.traderjoes.com

"Finally", Manhattanites "can afford to eat better" thanks to these "happening" Union Square–Rego Park gourmet grocers, links in a "cheery" Cali-based chain that "beats the pants off of ritzier competitors" with its selection offering "lots of organic, natural choices" (including "excellent house" labels that taste "better than name brands"), all at "really fair prices"; trading in the "well-displayed" likes of "reliable" produce, "wonderful frozen meals" with "ethnic" twists, "excellent meats", "fantastic" cheeses and much more, it's "truly all it's cracked up to be" as a "mecca" the multitudes "can't re-

	QUALITY	DISPLAY	SERVICE	COST

sist", resulting in prime-time "lines longer than the Nile" and wide-spread appeals for "more locations, please!"

Trader Joe's Wine Shop ◗ *Wine/Liquor* | 19 | 19 | 20 | I |

Union Sq | 138 E. 14th St. (bet. Irving Pl. & Union Sq. E.) | 4/5/6/L/N/Q/R/W to 14th St./Union Sq. | 212-529-6326 | www.traderjoes.com

A "lifesaver for the budget-conscious", this Union Square megamart's "welcome" vino annex is "perfect for stocking up" on a "serviceable selection" of "very decent" vintages (with "the occasional jewel" thrown in) at "unbeatable prices", typified by the celebrated "two-buck chuck", which goes for $2.99; snoots scoff at oenology "for beginners" that's "cheap for a reason", but it's "handy" "for a quick fix" and where else can you "walk away with a case" and still "feel rich"?

Tribeca Treats ▣ *Baked Goods* | ▽ 27 | 25 | 25 | M |

TriBeCa | 94 Reade St. (bet. Church St. & W. B'way) | 1/2/3/A/C to Chambers St. | 212-571-0500 | www.tribecatreats.com

Relatively new to the TriBeCa sweet scene, this "stylish" bakery treats its patrons to a "fantastic" confection selection including cookies, "handmade" chocolates "to die for" and many flavors of "amazing" cakes in sizes ranging from "beautiful cupcakes" on up; it already has a rep as a "reliable" place to indulge or "pick up a gift", with the "sweetest" staff standing by to "make you feel welcome"; N.B. they also take orders for wedding and birthday packages.

Tribeca Wine Merchants ▣ *Wine/Liquor* | 23 | 19 | 20 | E |

TriBeCa | 40 Hudson St. (bet. Duane & Thomas Sts.) | 1/2/3/A/C to Chambers St. | 212-393-1400

An "up-and-comer" on the TriBeCa scene, this boutique's wines tend to "eclectic", carefully curated choices showcasing "harder-to-find varieties", with a concentration on Burgundies and smaller vineyards in California and Oregon; it may seem "a bit expensive" to "unfortunates who eschewed Wall Street" careers, but there's a value-oriented $10-$20 rack too, not to mention "great" tastings on Saturdays.

Trois Pommes Patisserie ▣ *Baked Goods* | 23 | 21 | 18 | E |

Park Slope | 260 Fifth Ave. (bet. Carroll St. & Garfield Pl.) | Brooklyn | M/R to Union St. | 718-230-3119 | www.troispommespatisserie.com

A former Union Square Cafe pastry chef opened this "lovely" patisserie along Park Slope's Fifth Avenue strip, where she whips up "delicious" small-batch cakes, pies and ice cream in a neighborhood that suddenly seems awash in high-caliber baked goods; the "easy-on-the-eyes" space has a few seats for on-site snacking, as well as an open kitchen that allows patrons to watch the magic happen.

Truffette ▣ *Specialty Shop* | - | - | - | E |

E Village | 104 Ave. B (bet. 6th & 7th Sts.) | 6 to Astor Pl. | 212-505-5813 | www.sos-chefs.com

Discerning foodies depend on this East Village gourmet store that supplies some of the city's top restaurants with all manner of luxury imported and domestic foodstuffs like imported oils, vanilla beans, flavored salts and "the freshest" exotic products and spices; to top it all off, it also features "potentially the best mushrooms in town", including year-round and seasonal choices; N.B. its wholesale business is known as SOS Chefs.

Trunzo Bros. ⊑ᵉ *Specialty Shop* ▽ 25 | 20 | 21 | M

Bensonhurst | 6802 18th Ave. (68th St.) | Brooklyn | N to 18th Ave. | 718-331-2111 | www.trunzobros.com

For over 30 years, this Bensonhurst market has been the place "to go in the neighborhood" for "meat, pastas, produce, sandwiches", breads and housemade sausages and mozzarella, along with imported "Italian specialties" like cheeses, olive oils and sweets; so whether you're assembling an indulgent gift basket or arranging a catered lunch, this is "a great place."

T Salon ⊑ᵉ *Coffee/Tea* 26 | 24 | 21 | E

Chelsea | Chelsea Mkt. | 75 Ninth Ave. (bet. 15th & 16th Sts.) | A/C/E/L to 14th St./8th Ave. | 212-243-2259 | 888-358-0506 | www.tsalon.com

"Tea snobs" trek to this "relaxing" alternative to "the usual coffee bars" inside Chelsea Market, where owner Miriam Novalle (she "has raised sipping tea to an art form") and her "knowledgeable help" allow you to "sample and smell" their "amazing selection" of over 400 "unusual" blends; its "elegant", roomy space features a bar/cafe area in addition to the retail space up front.

Tuck Shop ● *Prepared Food* 20 | 16 | 17 | I

E Village | 68 E. First St. (bet. 1st & 2nd Aves.) | F/V to Lower East Side/2nd Ave. | 212-979-5200 | www.tuckshopnyc.com

Anyone craving "a touch of Australia in the East Village" can tuck into a "perfect bite on-the-go" at this bakery proffering "authentic meat pies" – ranging from "classic" ground beef to more modern varieties – and "other Aussie treats" such as beer and wine; N.B. they also do catering and feature a selection of groceries from Down Under.

☒ Two for the Pot ⊑ᵉ⊭ *Coffee/Tea* 27 | 20 | 25 | M

Brooklyn Heights | 200 Clinton St. (bet. Atlantic Ave. & State St.) | Brooklyn | 2/3/4/5/M/N/R/W to Borough Hall/Court St. | 718-855-8173

"You never know what treat you'll find" among the jars, tins and boxes steeply stacked in this old-fashioned Brooklyn Heights emporium, from a "wide range of coffees" and "unusual teas" to herbs and spices, pantry items and equipment; the "genial owner" "loves his store and it shows" in the "knowledgeable", "wonderfully friendly" service and the "well-chosen" stock – he really does "seem to have everything" – just "look around and ask lots of questions."

☒ Two Little Red Hens *Baked Goods* 26 | 22 | 22 | E

E 80s | 1652 Second Ave. (bet. 85th & 86th Sts.) | 4/5/6 to 86th St. | 212-452-0476 | www.twolittleredhens.com

"Cure any sweet craving" at this Upper East Side bakery/cafe, a "favorite local" "pit stop" for "killer" specialties like the "feather-light" cakes and cupcakes ("a gift from the gods"), "first-rate" tarts and other "habit-forming" goodies; the "homey" quarters and "lovely staff" have "small-town" charm, and though some cluck it "could be cheaper", there's "no substitute" for "perfection"; N.B. the original branch in Park Slope now operates under the name Lady Bird Bakery.

Umanoff & Parsons 🖃🖅 *Baked Goods* | 24 | – | 17 | M |

Bronx | 1704 Boone Ave. (bet. E. 173rd & 174th Sts.) | 2/5 to 174th St. | 212-219-2240 | www.umanoffparsons.com

Its status as a wholesaler to upscale restaurants proves "you can't go wrong" with this bakery's "wide array" of "wonderful" (and kosher) cakes, pies and tarts, "true works of art" featuring the likes of "the best mud cake ever"; it's "not the easiest shopping" – everything is sold over the counter right "in their factory", which is temporarily located in the Bronx – but the "excellent value" is "well worth" "the hassle"; N.B. it's expected to move into a permanent home at 121st Street and Park Avenue in summer 2008.

Uncle Louie G ➊🖅 *Ice Cream* | 20 | 14 | 17 | I |

W 80s | 2259 Broadway (bet. 80th & 81st Sts.) | 1 to 79th St. | 212-721-2818
Bronx | 3760 E. Tremont Ave. (Randall Ave.) | 718-822-1492
Park Slope | 321 Seventh Ave. (bet. 8th & 9th Sts.) | Brooklyn | F to 7th Ave. | 718-965-4237
Park Slope | 741 Union St. (bet. 5th & 6th Aves.) | Brooklyn | M/R to Union St. | 718-623-6668
Prospect Heights | 157 Prospect Park SW (bet. Seeley & Vanderbilt Sts.) | Brooklyn | F to Fort Hamilton Pkwy. | 718-438-9282
Astoria | 38-02 Broadway (38th St.) | Queens | G/R/V to Steinway St. | 718-728-4454
Forest Hills | 72-73 Austin St. (67th Dr.) | Queens | E/F/G/R/V to Forest Hills/71st Ave. | 718-897-7855
Howard Bch | 158-08 Cross Bay Blvd. (158th Ave.) | Queens | A to Howard Bch./JFK Airport | 718-677-9551
Kew Gardens | 68-46 Main St. (68th Dr.) | Queens | 718-544-7256
Staten Island | 30 Giffords Ln. (bet. Baltimore St. & Brower Ct.) | 718-605-0056
www.unclelouieg.com
Additional locations throughout the NY area

On a hot summer day in Gotham "you can't argue with Louie G's", nothing-fancy franchises scooping "sure-to-please", all-kosher ices and ice creams throughout the five boroughs ("they're just good, they don't have to be cool"); "success speaks for itself", as evidenced by the "long lines", although some surveyors are wary of those "Day-Glo colors" and find the flavors "entirely too artificial"; N.B. closed in winter.

Union Market ➊◐🖃 *Major Gourmet Mkt.* | ▽ 26 | 23 | 23 | M |

NEW **Park Slope** | 402 Seventh Ave. (bet. 12th & 13th Sts.) | Brooklyn | F to 7th Ave. | 718-499-4026
Park Slope | 754-756 Union St. (6th Ave.) | Brooklyn | 2/3 to Grand Army Plaza | 718-230-5152
www.unionmarket.com

It's "perfect for Park Slope" say neighbors of this gourmet market stocking "some really delicious finds", including "breads from the best bakeries", an "amazing cheese section", a "wide selection of specialty items" and prepared foods, "beautiful meat and fish" and "quality produce" that makes it the "place to shop in the summer"; "beautifully laid out" and overseen by "very helpful" staffers, it unites "yuppie" types into a "steady" clientele; N.B. the Seventh Avenue branch opened post-Survey.

Union Square Wines & Spirits ● □ *Wine/Liquor*

| 25 | 23 | 21 | E |

Union Sq | 140 Fourth Ave. (13th St.) | 4/5/6/L/N/Q/R/W to 14th St./ Union Sq. | 212-675-8100 | www.unionsquarewines.com

This Union Square temple of oenophilia ensconced in a "tremendous space" augments it "fabulous variety" of vinos with a roomy bar for tastings with the "innovation of the year": a "high-tech" "enomatic" "tasting apparatus" that allows "savvy sippers" to sample among 50 bottles using a refillable "wine card"; with a "courteous" and "trustworthy" staff and "frequent sales and specials" to help quell gripes about "inflated prices", it's "a winner" that "should be a tourist attraction."

United Meat Market *Meat/Poultry*

| 26 | 19 | 24 | M |

Windsor Terrace | 219 Prospect Park W. (bet. 16th St. & Windsor Pl.) | Brooklyn | F to 15th St. | 718-768-7227

An "out-of-the-way gem" and "a godsend in the land of vanishing butcher shops", this "traditional" Italian meat and specialty foods shop – a "perfect staple" in Windsor Terrace – has gone slightly "upscale" in recent years to "adjust to the needs" of the area's "new population"; in addition to its fresh beef, pork, chicken and game spanning the spectrum from "everyday" to "specialty cut", there are imported vinegars and oils, cheeses, salumi and a host of prepared traditional dishes (lasagnas, roast chickens, "meatballs in sauce") that locals call the "answer to takeout."

UN Wine Exchange ● *Wine/Liquor*

| 22 | 17 | 22 | M |

E 40s | 885 First Ave. (bet. 49th & 50th Sts.) | 6 to 51st St. | 212-829-7200

Sited two blocks from the U.N., this offshoot of the New York Wine Exchange clan is packed to the rafters with a cellarlike showing of wines, offering a diplomatic choice of 4,000 labels traversing the range from California Cabernets to small producers in Australia, Chile, Italy and Spain; it also deserves recognition for its "accommodating" staff and generous tasting schedule (Monday–Saturday from 5–8 PM).

Urban Organic ● *Produce*

| ▽ 22 | 8 | 17 | M |

Park Slope | 240 Sixth St. (bet. 3rd & 4th Aves.) | Brooklyn | 718-499-4321 | www.urbanorganic.com
By appointment only

The name may sound like an oxymoron, but this "fabulous" Park Slope outfit appeals to busy urbanites with the convenience of weekly or bi-weekly "home-delivered organic fruits and veggies" plus breads, spices, dairy and soy products; it can be "pricey", however, and some say service "has its ups and downs"; N.B. there's a $25 lifetime membership fee.

	QUALITY	DISPLAY	SERVICE	COST

NEW Urban Rustic Market ◐ *Specialty Shop* — — — E

Williamsburg | 236 N. 12th St. (Driggs Ave.) | Brooklyn | L to Bedford Ave. | 718-388-9444 | www.urbanrusticnyc.com

From the owners of Williamsburg's Lodge comes this nearby market where organic, "locally produced and grown items" are the focus, from grass-fed meats and farmstead cheeses to housemade sandwiches and fresh-squeezed juices; clad in Adirondack wood shelves and counters, it looks like an old general store, but one in which even the produce is "labeled by origin" (e.g. "turnips from a quaint farm in New Hampshire").

Uva Wines ◐ *Wine/Liquor*   ▽ 24 | 19 | 25 | M

Williamsburg | 199 Bedford Ave. (N. 6th St.) | Brooklyn | L to Bedford Ave. | 718-963-3939 | www.uvawines.com

Spike your vino shopping "with a dollop of hip" at this Williamsburg shop, whose "small" size belies a "high-quality" lineup of expertly picked vintages (organics and biodynamics from global sources among them) that may be the "yuppiest wine selection in the 'Burg"; expect a "helpful", "knowledgeable" staff and under-$20 pricing that promises "an outstanding bottle for not a lot of money"; N.B. tastings are held Wednesdays and Saturdays.

Varsano's ▤ *Candy/Nuts*   ▽ 26 | 21 | 26 | E

G Village | 172 W. Fourth St. (bet. 6th & 7th Aves.) | A/B/C/D/E/F/V to W. 4th St. | 212-352-1171 | 800-414-4718 | www.varsanos.com

The recent move across the street to more visible digs has been a good thing according to surveyors who say this little-known "find" of a candy emporium in the West Village is "getting better and better"; its "superb" selection of "old-fashioned" handmade chocolates, caramel-smothered pretzel rods, s'mores, chocolate-covered potato chips and other decadent delights present so many choices, the "patient service" offered by the counter-folk is all the more welcome.

Veniero's ◐▤ *Baked Goods*   25 | 22 | 19 | M

E Village | 342 E. 11th St. (bet. 1st & 2nd Aves.) | L to 1st Ave. | 212-674-7070 | www.venierospastry.com

"You'll want one of everything" from the "mouthwatering display" of "classic Italian pastries" at this "legendary" East Village bakery, a survivor from "bygone days" (established 1894) that still "will wow you" with an "endless" selection of "delectable desserts" like "luscious" cannoli and "cheesecakes made to perfection"; the "touristy" milieu "can get hectic" and "the lines can be interminable", but given such "irresistible" quality at "moderate prices", traditionalists insist "you gotta go."

Vere ▤ *Candy/Nuts*   ▽ 29 | 19 | 23 | E

Flatiron | 12 W. 27th St., 6th fl. (B'way) | N/R to 28th St. | 866-410-8373 | www.veregoods.com

Chocolate for those who don't like it too sweet is the forte of this high-end confectioner that uses no refined sugar in its "oh-my-God" "wonderful" bars, bonbons, truffles and brownies, making them instead with fructose and agave nectar, as well as "outstanding quality" organic, Fair Trade, 75%-cacao chocolate; while it has no storefront, it opens its Flatiron factory to retail shoppers on Fridays, when free samples are given out.

NEW Very Berry ● *Ice Cream* | 20 | 17 | 18 | M |

E Village | 34½ St. Marks Pl. (bet. 2nd & 3rd Aves.) | 6 to Astor Pl. | 212-387-7959

A "fun place" with "delightful selections", this East Village arrival to the city's ever-growing "pinkberry clone" culture is winning a local following for its frozen yogurt "without the lines and attitude"; it offers four flavors that can be topped with fruit and chocolate, leading boosters to rate it a "berry delicious" contender overall.

Vestry Wines ● ▭ *Wine/Liquor* | - | - | - | M |

TriBeCa | 65 Vestry St. (Washington St.) | 1 to Canal St. | 212-810-2899 | www.vestrywines.com

Birch wood frames the modern interior of this "classy" way-West TriBeCa wine store, lending warmth to the attractive space and inspiring lingering amid its selection of some 600 labels, the bulk of which are from small producers in California, France and Italy; the accomplished staff is equally welcoming, and, perhaps best of all, offers daily tastings at the bar; N.B. customers can rate wines, take notes and track purchases on the store's website.

Vesuvio Bakery *Prepared Food* | 23 | 19 | 19 | M |

SoHo | 160 Prince St. (bet. Thompson St. & W. B'way) | N/R to Prince St. | 212-925-8248

"Step back in time" at this "old-world" Italian bakery, a SoHo "treasure" that's "retained its charm" (and its 1920s-era facade); although it offers the same "wonderful" breads, biscotti and pastries, it's "expanded the options to include lovely sandwiches", salads and other "treats"; the only downside: it "can run out of popular items."

Viet-Nam Bánh Mì So #1 ⊘ *Deli/Sandwich* | 23 | 9 | 15 | I |

Chinatown | 369 Broome St. (Mott St.) | 6/J/M/N/Q/R/W/Z to Canal St. | 212-219-8341

"Makes you grateful you live in NYC" say surveyors of this Vietnamese deli in Chinatown specializing in "truly superb" and "totally cheap" *banh mi* sandwiches "cheerfully" prepared with "fresh ingredients"; whether you opt for pork, chicken or vegan varieties, regulars advise: "get it spicy – with peppers" and wash it down with fresh sugarcane juice or an iced coffee with condensed milk.

Ζ Villabate Pasticceria & Bakery ● *Baked Goods* | 28 | 24 | 22 | M |

Bensonhurst | 7117 18th Ave. (bet. 71st & 72nd Sts.) | Brooklyn | N to 18th Ave. | 718-331-8430 | www.villabate.net

Behold "the Italian baker's art" in its "colorful" glory at this "quintessential Brooklyn bakery" in Bensonhurst, where the display cases present a "gorgeous" abundance of the "wonderful pastries and cakes" that "Sicilian dreams" are made of, including "extraordinary cassata", marzipan and rice balls crafted to "perfection" (and "don't forget the cannoli"); "traditional" breads and summertime gelati further confirm it's "the best bet around", so "be prepared for long lines during the holidays."

Vincent's Meat Market ☐ *Meat/Poultry*   27 | 21 | 23 | M

Bronx | 2374 Arthur Ave. (bet. E. 186th & E. 187th Sts.) | B/D to Fordham Rd. | 718-295-9048

"Yeah, Bronx!" – "Vincent's is the tops" crow champions of this circa-1954 Arthur Avenue Italian butcher shop, where the meaty goods (baby lambs among them) hang in the window and the plentiful offerings include prime beef, housemade sausages, chicken and veal rollatini and lots of game; while you're at this "culinary destination" you can also grab imported pastas, cheese and dry goods.

Ⓩ Vino ◑☐ *Wine/Liquor*   28 | 25 | 25 | E

Gramercy | 121 E. 27th St. (bet. Lexington & Park Aves.) | 6 to 28th St. | 212-725-6516 | www.vinosite.com

Take "a tour of the wine regions of Italy" at this Gramercy store devoted to producers from The Boot, where the "lovely" stock (70% of it poured at the companion eatery, I Trulli) is "well-grouped" geographically and tended by staffers who "know their stuff"; it features "little-known" finds plus numerous "aperitivos and digestivos", and is a "must-stop" even if pricing skews "a touch high."

VinoVino ◑ *Wine/Liquor*   ▽ 25 | 21 | 21 | E

TriBeCa | 211 W. Broadway (bet. Franklin & White Sts.) | 1 to Franklin St. | 212-925-8510 | www.vinovino.net

Oenophiles in-the-know "love love" this tasteful TriBeCa two-in-one, a lofty space that unites a Euro-style enoteca with a glassed-off retail display of some 250 "great wines" "matched with knowledgeable service", with a focus on smaller Spanish and Italian estate growers; the wine bar offers a chance to sample the wares by the glass, and tastings are held Thursday through Saturday evenings; P.S. it's "good for private parties" too.

Vintage New York ◑☐ *Wine/Liquor*   23 | 24 | 24 | M

SoHo | 482 Broome St. (Wooster St.) | 1/A/C/E to Canal St. | 212-226-9463

W 90s | 2492 Broadway (bet. 92nd & 93rd Sts.) | 1/2/3 to 96th St. | 212-721-9999
www.vintagenewyork.com

Out to prove Eastern labels can "rival the highly touted Californians", this SoHo–Upper West Side duo showcases a "terrific selection" of solely "Empire State wines", with "virtually every NY State vineyard represented", from "all over the Finger Lakes, Hudson Valley and the North Fork of Long Island"; you also "gotta love the tasting bars" (sample five vinos for $15) and array of chocolates, artisanal cheeses and other comestibles, which likewise originate in-state.

Violet Hill Farm *Meat/Poultry*   29 | 19 | 29 | E

See Greenmarket; for more information, call 845-439-8040 | vilothillarabians.tripod.com/violethillfarm

"Great goat, heavenly hens and beautiful bacon" are among the standouts at this Sullivan County farm's Greenmarket stall considered one of the "best-of-class in so many categories": "heirloom" pork that's "the platonic ideal of porkiness", "amazing lamb", "great" chicken and rabbits, "many varieties of sausages" and possibly the "best eggs in the market"; to top it all off, staffers are "incredibly knowledgeable" and will "tailor their advice to how adventurous you are feeling" – so go ahead, "taste the difference."

☑ Vosges Haut Chocolat 🖃 *Candy/Nuts* | 26 | 26 | 22 | E |

NEW **E 80s** | 1100 Madison Ave. (bet. 82nd & 83rd Sts.) | 4/5/6 to 86th St. | 212-717-2929
SoHo | 132 Spring St. (bet. Greene & Wooster Sts.) | C/E to Spring St. | 212-625-2929
888-301-9866 | www.vosgeschocolate.com

"The finest choco-centric adventure in NY" is how hip chocolate-lovers sum up this "fabulous – and fabulously expensive" SoHo-UES pair of boutiques that has earned a reputation for its bonbons boasting "wild twists of flavor" like curry and horseradish as well as for its "beautiful purple packaging" and "gorgeous" environs; traditionalists sneer "it's trying too hard" and, needless to say, it's "not a place for people who like Hershey's."

VSF *Flowers* | ▽ 29 | 27 | 25 | VE |

W Village | 204 W. 10th St. (bet. Bleecker & W. 4th Sts.) | 1 to Christopher St. | 212-206-7236 | www.vsfnyc.com

"Outstanding in every way", this "spectacular" floral shop in the West Village is the source for "unusual blooms" brought together in arrangements that are "always fabulous, never stilted"; they call their look 'Flemish-garden style', which translates to "universally appealing" products perfect for events or for sending "to favorite clients"; the only drawback seems to be pricing levels that mean its blooms are as expensive "as they are lovely."

Warehouse Wines & Spirits ● *Wine/Liquor* | 22 | 15 | 18 | I |

G Village | 735 Broadway (bet. 8th St. & Waverly Pl.) | R/W to 8th St. | 212-982-7770

"Looks like a warehouse, costs like a warehouse" is the lowdown on this "massive" Village resource for the "everyday drinker", where it's "worth braving the crowds" to score "some incredible buys" on wines ("if you know what you want" and "choose carefully") as well as "brand liquors"; downsides include "minimal service" and packs of party-hearty "college students", but "the financially strapped" will "typically save a few bucks."

☑ Westerly Natural Market ● 🖃 *Health Food* | 25 | 17 | 20 | M |

W 50s | 913 Eighth Ave. (bet. 54th & 55th Sts.) | 1/A/B/C/D to 59th St./ Columbus Circle | 212-586-5262 | www.westerlynaturalmarket.com

Attention all "granolaheads": this "awesome" Hell's Kitchen health food oasis is "a wonderland of natural foods", with "top-notch organic" fruits and vegetables, a "great bulk-foods section" and myriad grocery items stocked to the ceiling; the service is "warm and welcoming" and its digs "clean and bright" (even if its "very tight aisles" are "cramped"), while prices are "surprisingly reasonable", especially for office workers looking for "delicious" healthy lunches" from the well-priced back prepared foods area.

Westside Market ●⊟ *Major Gourmet Mkt.* ▽ 21 | 19 | 17 | M |

Chelsea | 77 Seventh Ave. (bet. 15th & 14th Sts.) | 1/2/3 to 14th St. | 212-807-7771

W 70s | 2171 Broadway (bet. 76th & 77th Sts.) | 1/2/3 to 79th St. | 212-595-2536

NEW **W 100s** | 2840 Broadway (bet. 110th & 111th Sts.) | 1 to Cathedral Pkwy./110th St. | 212-222-3367
www.wmarketnyc.com

Though "nothing fancy", this longtime gourmet-market fixture is a "real UWS sleeper" that joins with its Chelsea offshoot to offer "all the basics" "for a fair price", including "fresh" produce, "excellent" prepared foods and a "surprisingly wide variety" of cheeses, specialty items, dry goods, deli and more; it's "better than your average" "neighborhood spot", and the original's 24/7 hours makes it a welcome "after-hours alternative" (the Chelsea store closes at midnight).

West Side Wine ● *Wine/Liquor* 24 | 23 | 24 | M |

W 80s | 481 Columbus Ave. (83rd St.) | 1 to 86th St. | 212-874-2900 | www.westsidewine.com

Overseen by "well-traveled" owner Andy Besch ("author of *The Wine Guy*"), this "charming" Upper Westsider boasts "one of the best selections of moderately priced" bottles around (mixed with some "premium" picks), all "displayed properly" and tended by a "superb" staff; it aims to make "interesting" sipping affordable, and neophytes who "don't know the difference between a Cabernet and a cabaret" can "trust them" for "lots of great tips."

Whole Earth Bakery ●⊅ *Baked Goods* 21 | 18 | 19 | M |

E Village | 130 St. Marks Pl. (bet. Ave. A & 1st Ave.) | 6 to Astor Pl. | 212-677-7597

Proof that "wholesome" fare can be "great tasting too", this congenial East Village bakery and juice bar is a vegetarian/vegan "haven" whose organic output includes pastries, brownies and flourless cakes; savories like tofu pizzas, quiche and sandwiches also figure, and their made-to-order wedding cakes will get any marriage off to a healthy start.

☑ Whole Foods 26 | 25 | 21 | E |
Market ●⊟ *Major Gourmet Mkt.*

Chelsea | 250 Seventh Ave. (24th St.) | 1 to 23rd St. | 212-924-5969

LES | 95 E. Houston St. (Bowery) | F/V to Lower East Side/2nd Ave. | 212-420-1320

Union Sq | 40 E. 14th St. (bet. B'way & University Pl.) | 4/5/6/L/N/Q/R/W to 14th St./Union Sq. | 212-673-5388

W 50s | Shops at Columbus Circle | 10 Columbus Circle (bet. 58th & 60th Sts.) | 1/A/B/C/D to 59th St./Columbus Circle | 212-823-9600

888-746-7936 | www.wholefoodsmarket.com

We'd be "wholly lost without them" say New Yorkers who "can't remember life without" these "bright", "well-organized" "shopping arenas", branches of a Texas franchise whose Chelsea flagship and "overwhelming" Columbus Circle and Union Square sites are hailed as the "ultimate" "all-in-one" "health and natural food" sources, featuring "lip-smacking" baked goods, a "sensational display" of "super-fresh" produce, a "dizzying" "smorgasbord" of prepared foods, tons of "interesting" coffees, "incredible" "upscale" cheeses, "wonderful organic meats and poultry" and "stunning seafood"; in sum, it's just about the "best game in town"; N.B. the Lower East Side store opened post-Survey and includes a full-service eatery, Rustica Minardi Osteria.

'wichcraft   *Deli/Sandwich* | 24 | 19 | 18 | E |

Chelsea | 269 Eleventh Ave. (bet. 27th & 28th Sts.) | C/E to 23rd St. | 212-780-0577

NEW **E 40s** | 245 Park Ave. (47th St.) | 6 to 51st St. | 212-780-0577

E 40s | 555 Fifth Ave. (bet. 45th & 46th Sts.) | B/D/F/V to 47-50th Sts./ Rockefeller Ctr. | 212-780-0577

Flatiron | 11 E. 20th St. (bet. B'way & 5th Ave.) | 4/5/6/L/N/Q/R/ W to 14th St./Union Sq. | 212-780-0577 ◗

G Village | 60 E. Eighth St. (Mercer St.) | R/W to 8th St. | 212-780-0577

Murray Hill | Equinox | 1 Park Ave. (33rd St.) | 6 to 33rd St. | 212-780-0577 ◗

SoHo | 568 Broadway (Prince St.) | N/R to Prince St. | 212-334-2065

TriBeCa | 397 Greenwich St. (Beach St.) | 1 to Franklin St. | 212-780-0577 ◗

W 40s | Bryant Park | Sixth Ave. (bet. 40th & 42nd Sts.) | 7/B/D/F/ V to 42nd St./Bryant Park | 212-780-0577

NEW **W 50s** | 1 Rockefeller Plaza (on 50th St., bet. 5th & 6th Aves.) | B/D/F/V to 47th-50th Sts./Rockefeller Ctr. | 212-780-0577

866-942-4272 | www.wichcraftnyc.com

Additional locations throughout the NY area

"Genius" Tom Colicchio (of Craft and *Top Chef* fame) casts his spell ever-wider with the proliferating branches of this chain dispensing "ridiculously good" sandwiches along with "delicious soups and salads" and sweets including "unbelievable cupcakes"; its strippeddown digs (most with seating) "feel very of-the-moment" while service is "courteous", but "the sun may set while you wait in line" – and "geez, those prices."

Wild Edibles ◑▣ *Seafood* | 26 | 25 | 22 | E |

E 40s | Grand Central Mkt. | Lexington Ave. (43rd St.) | 4/5/6/7/S to 42nd St./Grand Central | 212-687-4255

Murray Hill | 535 Third Ave. (bet. 35th & 36th Sts.) | 6 to 33rd St. | 212-213-8552

www.wildedibles.com

"If the fish were any fresher, it would be in the ocean" gush groupies of this "superb", "high-end" East Side pair that's "got it all" – a "wide selection" of "usual and unusual catches" "nicely displayed", a "wonderful" staff and "tasty", "well-prepared" dishes; it's "wildly expensive", but many are "willing to pay" for the "excellent quality."

	QUALITY	DISPLAY	SERVICE	COST

William Greenberg Jr.

25	20	20	VE

Desserts ⬛ *Baked Goods*

E 80s | 1100 Madison Ave. (bet. 82nd & 83rd Sts.) | 4/5/6 to 86th St. | 212-744-0304 | 800-255-8278 | www.wmgreenbergdesserts.com

"Blow your budget and your diet" at this "benchmark" Jewish bakery, an "Upper East Side tradition" dating back to 1946 for "old-fashioned" "treats" so "hard to resist" they deserve their own "support group", including such standouts as "the ultimate" schnecken, babka, "black-and-whites" and "special-occasion cakes"; though you'll need to "take out a mortgage" to pay, this is "quality you can't get at a lower price" even if some sense a "slide" "since the Greenberg family sold."

☑ William Poll ⬛ *Prepared Food*

26	23	24	VE

E 70s | 1051 Lexington Ave. (75th St.) | 6 to 77th St. | 212-288-0501 | 800-951-7655 | www.williampoll.com

"When you want to make that special impression", try this "top-of-the-line" prepared-foods shop that's been a "dependably dependable" Upper East Side "mainstay" for two generations courtesy of its "exquisite offerings" – from the sandwiches and house-smoked fish to the "amazing" homemade chips and dips; add in "always impeccable service" and "the prices seem almost reasonable."

Williamson Calvert ⊘ *Caterer*

-	-	-	VE

Prospect Heights | 150 St. Marks Ave. (Carlton Ave.) | Brooklyn | B/Q to 7th Ave. | 718-956-5633 | www.williamsoncalvert.com

Missoni, MoMA and Annie Leibovitz are just a few of the high-profile clients who've secured the catering and event-planning services of this high-end, Brooklyn-based, "lovely-to-work-with" outfit favored by big guns in the arts, entertainment and publishing fields; chef Bryan Calvert provides a range of market-driven New American menu options, while partner and veteran producer Deborah Williamson oversees all areas of event production.

☑ Williams-Sonoma ⬛ *Cookware*

27	27	23	E

Chelsea | 110 Seventh Ave. (bet. 16th & 17th Sts.) | 1 to 18th St. | 212-633-2203

E 50s | 121 E. 59th St. (bet. Lexington & Park Aves.) | 4/5/6/N/R/W to 59th St./Lexington Ave. | 917-369-1131

E 80s | 1175 Madison Ave. (86th St.) | 4/5/6 to 86th St. | 212-289-6832

W 50s | Shops at Columbus Circle | 10 Columbus Circle (bet. 58th & 60th Sts.) | 1/A/B/C/D to 59th St./Columbus Circle | 212-823-9750 ◐ 800-541-2233 | www.williams-sonoma.com

This "superior-quality" chain – for some the "standard-bearer" of kitchenware shops – "makes you think NYers actually cook" with its "tempting" "high-end" displays of pots and pans, cutlery and small appliances, as well as "preppy" color-coordinated utensils and cleaning supplies, not to mention baking supplies, specialty oils, vinegars, sauces and cookbooks; "tasting demos", "free samples" and "fab service" mean it's always "fun to shop", despite prices that some say verge on the "ridiculous."

	QUALITY	DISPLAY	SERVICE	COST

Windfall Farms ⊘ *Produce* — 27 | 21 | 21 | E

See Greenmarket; for more information, call 845-457-5988 | www.windfallfarms.com

Fanciers of arugula and "unique" greens "found nowhere else" count on this Montgomery, NY, producer's year-round Greenmarket stall in Union Square to supply them with "amazingly fresh, flavorful" "specialty" lettuces and edible leaves of all sorts; "they care for their lettuces" and other goods "as if they came from Tiffany's" – and "the price reflects this", which makes some surveyors wonder just who's reaping a windfall, but to the majority it's well "worth it."

Windsor Florist ▣ *Flowers* — ∇ 24 | 19 | 19 | E

E 70s | 1118 Lexington Ave. (78th St.) | 6 to 77th St. | 212-734-4540

E 70s | 1382 Second Ave. (71st St.) | 6 to 68th St. | 212-734-4524

800-234-3761 | www.thewindsorflorist.com

With two locations on the Upper East Side, this veteran florist (in business since 1936) emphasizes fresh, handpicked flowers over mod, sculptural blooms; although some surveyors suggest the simple style is "boring", most appreciate them as "good neighborhood florists" adept at handling events, weddings and home arrangements too.

W.I.N.E. ◑ *Wine/Liquor* — ∇ 21 | 16 | 19 | E

E 80s | Eli's Manhattan | 1415 Third Ave. (80th St.) | 6 to 77th St. | 212-717-1999 | www.elizabar.com

Prices are "far more gentle" than "the rest of Eli Zabar's empire" at this petite annex to Eli's Manhattan on the Upper East Side, which carries a "small selection" of boutique wines chosen in part for affordability; the "first-rate" staffers "know their stock" well enough to dispense "valuable" tips, and even those who find it "underwhelming" acknowledge it's "convenient" in this underserved neighborhood.

Wine & Spirit Co. of Forest Hills ◑ *Wine/Liquor* — ∇ 22 | 15 | 19 | M

Forest Hills | 72-09 Austin St. (71st Ave.) | Queens | R/V to 67th Ave. | 718-575-2700

The always "friendly atmosphere" is certain to elevate spirits at this largish "local store" on a "bustling" Forest Hills thoroughfare, known in the neighborhood for a broad selection of grape and grain that features "some unusual finds" and $15–$25 "bargains" in its 2,000-label vino department; also specializing in kosher vintages, it has a resilient rep as "the only good wine shop" in the vicinity.

Winesby.com ▣ *Wine/Liquor* — - | - | - | M

G Village | 23 Jones St. (bet. Bleecker & W. 4th Sts.) | A/B/C/D/E/F/V to W. 4th St. | 212-242-5144 | www.winesby.com

This tiny Greenwich Village shop "makes it easy to try wines" without venturing far from home since better than half of its trade is online or by phone (with Manhattan delivery within two hours); focused on Italian and French labels in the $10–$100 range, the inventory is limited but lovingly chosen by the "super-friendly" owner; N.B. they'll arrange next-day delivery for bottles they don't have on hand.

	QUALITY	DISPLAY	SERVICE	COST

Wine Therapy ●□ Wine/Liquor   ▽ 25 | 22 | 24 | M

NoLita | 171 Elizabeth St. (Spring St.) | 6 to Spring St. | 212-625-2999 |
www.winetherapynyc.com

Providing "just the sort of therapy NYers should have", this "unpretentious" NoLita vintner-in-miniature is run by a couple who spun it off from the adjacent hair salon, using their "wine smarts" to showcase boutique labels from small European vineyards; given its "strong nose" for style, those who attend the Saturday tastings should be in fashionable company.

Winfield-Flynn Ltd. ●□ Wine/Liquor   ▽ 23 | 18 | 21 | M

Murray Hill | 558 Third Ave. (37th St.) | 6 to 33rd St. | 212-679-4455 |
800-364-8918 | www.winfieldflynn.com

"A cut above" "your average wine shop", this longtime Murray Hill entry wins over the "neighborhood" with its "fair prices" and willingness to embellish its global lineup with "lesser-known" labels; with savvy staffers to offer "pretty dead-on" recommendations, it's "a good compromise" between low- and high-end venues that loyalists come back to "constantly."

WK Trading Inc. ⊘ Produce   23 | 17 | 15 | I
(fka WK Vegetable Co.)

Chinatown | 124-126 Mott St. (bet. Grand & Hester Sts.) | 6/J/M/
N/Q/R/W/Z to Canal St. | 212-334-4603

A "maze" of "very fresh" produce at "terrific prices" awaits those who can navigate the overstuffed ailes at this Chinatown wholesaler and retailer that's "well worth the effort when you're searching for that rare ingredient"; "don't expect a lot of personal attention", but what's lacking in service is made up for by the dream combo of "high quality and low prices."

World of Nuts & Chocolates ● Candy/Nuts   15 | 14 | 14 | M

E 40s | 847 Second Ave. (45th St.) | 4/5/6/7/S to 42nd St./
Grand Central | 212-490-7112

E 60s | 1293 First Ave. (bet. 69th & 70th Sts.) | 6 to 68th St. |
212-717-5393

E 70s | 1113 Lexington Ave. (bet. 77th & 78th Sts.) | 6 to 77th St. |
212-717-5622

G Village | 9 E. Eighth St. (bet. 5th Ave. & Univeristy Pl.) | R/W to 8th St. |
212-375-9004

Murray Hill | 529 Third Ave. (35th St.) | 6 to 33rd St. | 212-696-9264

W 50s | 1363 Sixth Ave. (55th St.) | B/D/F/V to 47-50th Sts./
Rockefeller Ctr. | 212-956-9322

W 50s | 352 W. 57th St. (bet. 8th & 9th Aves.) | 1/A/B/C/D to 59th St./
Columbus Circle | 212-262-4220

W 70s | 2194 Broadway (bet. 77th & 78th Sts.) | 1 to 79th St. |
212-769-1006

Seemingly everywhere, these "handy, reliable" bulk candy stores offer sugar addicts an "adequate" "chocolate or nut fix" for "not a lot of money"; "convenience" and "selection" are the "selling points" here – more so than quality, which respondents say "varies", citing occasional encounters with "stale" product.

	QUALITY	DISPLAY	SERVICE	COST

Yoghurt Place, The ⊄ *Cheese/Dairy* ▽ 23 | 19 | 21 | M

SoHo | 71 Sullivan St. (bet. Broome & Spring Sts.) | C/E to Spring St. | 212-219-3500

Elmhurst | 77-20 21st Ave. (77th St.) | Queens | N/W to Astoria/ Ditmars Blvd. | 718-777-5303

Creamy "Greek-style" Kesso yogurt churned out by Vea Kessissoglou's Elmhurst milk plant and retailer is likened to a "delicious" "gift from the Olympian gods", and its SoHo "snack" shack adds smoothies, desserts and savory pastries to the lineup; Hellenists insist anything "so tasty" for "only a few bucks" qualifies as a "must-try."

NEW **Yogurtland** ● *Ice Cream* - | - | - | M

W Village | 267 Bleecker St. (Morton St.) | A/B/C/D/E/F/V to W. 4th St. | 212-206-1824 | www.yogurt-land.com

The first NYC branch of a California-based fro-yo chain, this vivid-hued West Village contender sets itself apart from the pack by offering its yogurt on a self-serve basis (you pay by the weight of your cup, 30¢ per ounce); it features 16 rotating flavors and some 30 toppings, from fresh fruit to sweetened breakfast cereal and candy.

Yolato ● *Ice Cream* 20 | 17 | 17 | M

Chelsea | 168 W. 27th St. (bet. 6th & 7th Aves.) | 1 to 28th St. | 212-366-5960

NEW **E 40s** | 125 Park Ave. (bet. 41st & 42nd Sts.) | 4/5/6/S to 42nd St./Grand Central | 212-922-1169

W 80s | 2286 Broadway (W. 82nd St.) | 1/9 to 79th St. | 212-580-1635 www.yolato.com

"Frozen yogurt meets gelato" is the idea behind this mini-chain whose "creamy, indulgent" product is either "to-die-for-good" or just "ok", depending on who you ask; you can "try as many samples as you want" as you scan the selection of more than 100 flavors, or pick up a custom fro-yo cake (order two days in advance).

Yonah Schimmel 23 | 11 | 16 | I
Knish Bakery ▣ *Baked Goods*

LES | 137 E. Houston St. (bet. 1st & 2nd Aves.) | F/V to Lower East Side/ 2nd Ave. | 212-477-2858 | www.yonahschimmel.com

A "one-of-a-kind" "old-world noshery", this Lower East Side bakery has "been around since Jonah" (well, since 1910) and "still holds its own" with "perfectly textured" "handmade knishes" in 20 "knock-out" variations – not to mention "killer" kugel and blintzes – chased with egg creams and lime rickeys; the "grumpy service" and "time-warp" setup are "the real thing", and both loyalists and moviegoers at the nearby Sunshine Cinemas "hope they last forever."

Yorkshire Wines & Spirits ●▣ *Wine/Liquor* 23 | 18 | 22 | M

E 80s | 1646 First Ave. (85th St.) | 4/5/6 to 86th St. | 212-717-5100 | www.yorkshirewines.com

"Wines for all budgets and tastes" are the hallmark of this 25-year Yorkville vet, where the "wide selection" concentrates on California, France and Italy and provides those on "moderate" budgets with

	QUALITY	DISPLAY	SERVICE	COST

plenty to choose from; enthusiasts are equally impressed with a floor team that "goes out of its way to be helpful."

Yorkville Meat Emporium *Meat/Poultry* ▽ 23 | 16 | 18 | M

E 80s | 1560 Second Ave. (81st St.) | 4/5/6 to 86th St. | 212-628-5147 | www.hungarianmeatmarket.com

At this "last bastion" of the "Magyar butchers" on the Upper East Side, you can expect to find "great Hungarian sausages", pork products of all kinds and, of course, "paprika galore" – not to mention take-home portions of authentic goulash, Eastern European breads (and beers), and house-baked strudels, linzertortes and the like.

Yuno's Farm ⊘ *Produce* 29 | 27 | 28 | M

See Greenmarket; for more information, call 609-723-3753

"If Martha Stewart had a farm stand" it wouldn't be any more "gorgeous" than this Bordentown, NJ, grower's Greenmarket stall, where the "top-quality" lettuces and greens and other "impeccably fresh, top-notch" produce are so "beautifully displayed", "people take pictures"; among the offerings are some unusual vegetables ("amaze your friends with the latest before they're in expensive shops"), all of which happily "taste as good as they look."

🅉 Zabar's ▣ *Major Gourmet Mkt.* 27 | 21 | 20 | M

W 80s | 2245 Broadway (bet. 80th & 81st Sts.) | 1 to 79th St. | 212-787-2000 | www.zabars.com

"The one and only" – voted NYC's No. 1 Major Gourmet Market – this "thriving" Upper West Side "landmark" is a "multipurpose" "gourmet's delight" renowned as a "quintessential" source of "absolutely the best" smoked fish ("a line worth waiting in") that also boasts "delectable" baked goods "galore", an "exhaustive cheese counter", "yummy prepared foods", a "gold-standard" deli, an "amazing selection" of specialty items, "fab coffee", candy and nuts and "great deals" upstairs on "a jumble" of cookware "you never knew you wanted"; the "gruff" salespeople and "chaotic" conditions "are all part of the charm" for "savvy" shoppers who also commend the "very competitive" pricing – so "accept no substitutes", and try to avoid getting hit by the customers using carts as bumper cars.

Zaitzeff ● *Prepared Food* ▽ 28 | 18 | 22 | M

Financial District | 72 Nassau St. (John St.) | J/M/Z to Fulton St. | 212-571-7272 | www.zaitzeffnyc.com

An "undiscovered killer burger joint down among Wall Street's towers", this eat-in/take-out shop specializes in "fresh", hormone-free ground sirloin and Kobe beef patties served on "the best Portuguese muffin rolls" with skillet-cooked fries and organic coffee on the side; for some, "the eats can't be beat" – ditto the "cool, fun staff."

Zarela Catering *Caterer/Events* ▽ 24 | 20 | 23 | E

E 50s | 953 Second Ave. (bet. 50th & 51st Sts.) | 6 to 51st St. | 212-644-6740 | www.zarela.com

Amigos affirm the catering arm of Zarela Martinez's East Side cantina "does the best job" around at supplying all the fixings "for a fun

Mexican event", with "awesome" regional cuisine laid out as lavishly or casually as you like; their crew can either set up at the restaurant or convert any corporate or private locale into an "authentic" fiesta.

Zaro's Bread Basket 🖃 *Baked Goods* | 17 | 17 | 15 | M |

E 40s | Grand Central Mkt. | Lexington Ave. (43rd St.) | 4/5/6/7/S to 42nd St./Grand Central | 212-292-0160 | 877-692-2531 | www.zaro.com ●
Flatiron | 920 Broadway (bet. 20th & 21st Sts.) | R/W to 23rd St. | 212-260-5327
Garment District | Penn Station | 501 Seventh Ave. (32nd St.) | 1/2/3/A/C/E to 34th St./Penn Station | 212-575-7031 | 877-692-2531 | www.zaro.com ●
W 40s | Port Authority | 625 Eighth Ave. (bet. 40th & 41st Sts.) | A/C/E to 42nd St./Port Authority | 212-292-0185 | 877-692-2531 | www.zaro.com ●

These "mass-market" bakery franchises supply the "transit hubs" with a "large selection" of breads, bagels, cookies and such, making for a "quick and easy" "commuters' crutch"; the goods are just "decent" and the "mall-ish" setups get "a bit frenetic", but they're "always there" when you're "making a dash" and "convenience is key."

Zeytuna ●🖃 *Major Gourmet Mkt.* | ▽ 23 | 21 | 16 | M |

Financial District | 59 Maiden Ln. (William St.) | J/M/Z to Fulton St. | 212-742-2436 | www.zeytunamarket.com

Locals and lunchers are attuned to this Financial District gourmet market as their "best choice" for "tasty" sandwiches and Turkish-accented prepared foods (with ample seating to enjoy them in), along with "excellent produce", a "wide variety of cheeses", "delicious" baked goods and a "decent range" of meats; paupers protest the "Wall Street prices", but it remains "one of the few" options in the area.

🅉 Zezé *Flowers* | 29 | 28 | 28 | VE |

E 50s | 938 First Ave. (bet. 51st & 52nd Sts.) | 6 to 51st St. | 212-753-7767 | www.zezeflowers.com

"Whatever the season, whatever the flowers, you're the winner" at this East 50s "florist to the stars" – rated Best Overall in this Survey – where the "low-key shop" is a dramatic contrast to the "spectacular arrangements" made from "unusual" blooms (including lots of orchids "so exquisite" they would please "Persephone herself"); the staff even "takes the time to talk with you about the recipient to try to capture the perfect mood", and although perfection "will cost you", it's "worth every last penny."

Zibetto Espresso Bar ⌾ *Coffee/Tea* | ▽ 26 | 21 | 24 | M |

W 50s | 1385 Sixth Ave. (bet. 56th & 57th Sts.) | F to 57th St.

Maybe it's "no longer a secret", but this connoisseur's espresso stop still "seems undiscovered somehow", pulling "wow"-quality shots ("with some charming foam art to boot") in an unlikely West 50s location; its "caffeinated wonderfulness" comes in a sliver of a space that feels "perfectly European in every way" from the stand-up marble counter, Italian sodas and biscotti to the "chic barista who remembers you with a sly, knowing nod the minute you walk in."

	QUALITY	DISPLAY	SERVICE	COST

`NEW` Zucker's Bagels & Smoked Fish *Bagels*

| 22 | 18 | 18 | M |

TriBeCa | 146 Chambers St. (W. B'way) | 1/2/3/A/C to Chambers St. | 212-608-5844

"A welcome addition to bagel-starved Downtown", this "friendly" TriBeCa arrival from a Murray's Bagels partner has been reeling 'em in from day one with "fresh, tasty" hand-rolled rounds and "delish" smoked fish and spreads (notably "sable like buttah"); if a few feel it's "still working out kinks", most find it keeps "getting better and better."

ZuZu's Petals *Flowers*

| ▽ 26 | 27 | 24 | M |

Park Slope | 158A Berkeley Pl. (bet. 6th & 7th Aves.) | Brooklyn | B/Q to 7th Ave. | 718-636-2022

Park Slope | 374 Fifth Ave. (bet. 5th & 6th Sts.) | Brooklyn | F/M/R to 4th Ave./9th St. | 718-638-0918

This "longtime favorite" with two Park Slope locations has been offering "personalized service" for over 30 years, creating "beautiful arrangements" from "unusual, high-quality flowers, plants and ceramics"; the always-fresh stock (they don't even use refrigeration) is accompanied by a selection of linens, pottery, soaps and other gift items; N.B. in summer, purchase your annuals and perennials from Fifth Avenue's back garden.

Party Sites

The capacity (cap) and maximum capacity (max cap) – for multiple spaces – figures below are only guidelines. Call ahead for pricing, and remember that most sites will negotiate.

Museums & Other Spaces

Alger House | *rooms: 1 | cap: 125*
G Village | 45 Downing St. (bet. Bedford & 7th Ave. S.) | 212-627-8838 | www.algerhouse.com

Altman Building | *rooms: 2 | max cap: 1000*
Chelsea | 135 W. 18th St. (bet. 6th & 7th Aves.) | 212-741-3400 | www.altmanbldg.com

**American Museum
of Natural History** | *rooms: 45 | max cap: 3000*
W 70s | 79th St. & CPW | 212-769-5350 | www.amnh.org

Americas Society | *rooms: 3 | max cap: 120*
E 60s | 680 Park Ave. (68th St.) | 212-249-8950 | www.americas-society.org

Angel Orensanz Foundation | *rooms: 1 | cap: 550*
LES | 172 Norfolk St. (bet. E. Houston & Stanton Sts.) | 212-529-7194 | www.orensanz.org

Art Farm, The | *rooms: 1 | cap: 35*
E 90s | 419 E. 91st St. (bet. 1st & York Aves.) | 212-410-3117 | www.theartfarms.org

Astra | *rooms: 1 | cap: 300*
E 50s | 979 Third Ave., 14th fl. (bet. 58th & 59th Sts.) | 212-644-9394 | www.charliepalmer.com

Bateaux New York | *rooms: 2 | max cap: 300*
Chelsea | Chelsea Piers | Pier 62 (West Side Hwy.) | 212-352-1366 | www.bateauxnewyork.com

Boylan Studios | *rooms: 3 | max cap: 850*
Chelsea | 601 W. 26th St. (11th Ave.) | 212-924-7550 | www.boylanstudios.com

Bridgewaters | *rooms: 3 | max cap: 3500*
Seaport | 11 Fulton St. (bet. East River Piers & Seaport Plaza) | 212-608-7400 | www.theglaziergroup.com

Bronx Zoo | *rooms: 4 | max cap: 750*
Bronx | 2300 Southern Blvd. (Fordham Rd.) | 718-220-5076 | www.bronxzoo.com

**Brooklyn Botanic Garden,
Palm House** | *rooms: 1 | cap: 300*
Prospect Heights | 1000 Washington Ave. (Montgomery St.) | Brooklyn | 718-398-2400 | www.palmhouse.com

Brooklyn Museum of Art | *rooms: 6 | max cap: 1000*
Prospect Heights | 200 Eastern Pkwy. (Washington Ave.) | Brooklyn | 718-638-5000 | www.brooklynmuseum.org

Carnegie Hall Dining Rooms | *rooms: 4* | *max cap: 600*
W 50s | 154 W. 57th St. (bet. 6th & 7th Aves.) | 212-903-9770 |
www.carnegiehall.org

Center for Architecture | *rooms: 3* | *max cap: 500*
G Village | 536 LaGuardia Pl. (Bleecker St.) | 212-683-0023 |
www.aiany.org

Central Park Wildlife Center | *rooms: 4* | *max cap: 1200*
E 60s | 830 Fifth Ave. (bet. 64th & 65th Sts.) | 212-439-6509 |
www.wcs.org

Central Park Zoo | *rooms: 5* | *max cap: 1200*
E 60s | 830 Fifth Ave. (64th St.) | 212-439-6509 |
www.centralparkzoo.com

Chelsea Piers Lighthouse | *rooms: 1* | *cap: 800*
Chelsea | Chelsea Piers | Pier 61 (bet. 23rd St. & West Side Hwy.) |
212-336-6144 | www.piersixty.com

Chelsea Piers, Pier 60 | *rooms: 1* | *cap: 2000*
Chelsea | Chelsea Piers | Pier 60 (bet. 23rd St. & West Side Hwy.) |
212-336-6144 | www.piersixty.com

Children's Museum
of Manhattan | *rooms: 7* | *max cap: 1200*
W 80s | 212 W. 83rd St. (bet. Amsterdam Ave. & B'way) | 212-721-1223 |
www.cmom.org

Cooper Classics Collection, The | *rooms: 2* | *max cap: 400*
G Village | 137 Perry St. (bet. Greenwich & Washington Sts.) |
212-929-3909 | www.cooperclassiccars.com

Council on Foreign Relations: Peterson Hall/
Harold Pratt House | *rooms: 6* | *max cap: 300*
E 60s | 58 E. 68th St. (bet. Madison & Park Aves.) | 212-434-9576 |
www.prattmansion.com

Culinary Loft | *rooms: 1* | *cap: 70*
SoHo | 515 Broadway, Suite 5A (bet. Broome & Spring Sts.) |
212-431-7425 | www.culinaryloft.com

Dance New Amsterdam | *rooms: 6* | *max cap: 500*
TriBeCa | 280 Broadway, Suite 5A (bet. Chambers & Reade Sts.) |
212-625-8369 | www.dnadance.org

Delegates Dining Room | *rooms: 6* | *max cap: 800*
E 40s | United Nations | 1st Ave. & 46th St. | 212-963-7625 |
www.aramark-un.com

Dia Art Foundation | *rooms: 1* | *cap: 450*
Chelsea | 535 W. 22nd St., 4th fl. (bet. 10th & 11th Aves.) | 212-989-5566 |
www.diaart.org

Downtown Community
Television Center | *rooms: 2* | *max cap: 280*
Financial District | 87 Lafayette St. (bet. Walker & White Sts.) |
212-966-4510 | www.dctvny.org

Drawing Center | *rooms: 1* | *cap: 250*
SoHo | 35 Wooster St. (bet. Broome & Grand Sts.) | 212-219-2166 |
www.drawingcenter.org

Drive In Studios | *rooms: 3* | *max cap: 1200*
Chelsea | 443 W. 18th St. (bet. 9th & 10th Aves.) | 212-645-2244 |
www.driveinstudios.com

Elevated Acre | *rooms: 1* | *cap: 1000*
Financial District | 55 Water St. (bet. Coenties Slip E. & Hanover Sq.) |
212-963-7099 | www.elevatedacre.com

Ellis Island
Immigration Museum | *rooms: 5* | *max cap: 2000*
Ellis Island | Ellis Island | 212-344-0996 | www.ellisisland.com

Explorers Club | *rooms: 3* | *max cap: 300*
E 70s | 46 E. 70th St. (bet. Madison & Park Aves.) | 212-628-8383 |
www.manhattaneventsny.com

Eyebeam | *rooms: 1* | *cap: 624*
Chelsea | 540 W. 21st St. (bet. 10th & 11th Aves.) | 212-937-6581 |
www.eyebeam.org

40/40 Club | *rooms: 6* | *max cap: 730*
Chelsea | 6 W. 25th St. (bet. B'way & 5th Ave.) | 212-989-0040 |
www.the4040club.com

Foundry, The | *rooms: 1* | *cap: 200*
LIC | 42-38 Ninth St. (bet. 43rd Ave. & Queens Plaza S.) | Queens |
718-786-7776 | www.thefoundry.info

Frick Collection | *rooms: 3* | *max cap: 350*
E 70s | 1 E. 70th St. (5th Ave.) | 212-288-0700 | www.frick.org

Georgian Suite | *rooms: 1* | *cap: 120*
E 70s | 1A E. 77th St. (5th Ave.) | 212-734-1468

Glorious Food | *rooms: 1* | *cap: 125*
E 70s | 522 E. 74th St. (bet. FDR Dr. & York Ave.) |
212-628-2320

Grand Central Terminal,
Northeast Balcony | *rooms: 1* | *cap: 200*
E 40s | 42nd St. & Park Ave. | 212-340-3404 |
www.grandcentralterminal.com

Grand Central Terminal,
Vanderbilt Hall | *rooms: 1* | *cap: 1300*
E 40s | 42nd St. & Park Ave. | 212-340-3404 |
www.grandcentralterminal.com

House of the Redeemer | *rooms: 3* | *max cap: 100*
E 90s | 7 E. 95th St. (bet. 5th & Madison Aves.) | 212-289-0399 |
www.houseoftheredeemer.org

Hudson Yards Catering | *rooms: 2* | *max cap: 1500*
Chelsea | Hudson Yards | 640 W. 28th St., 8th fl. (bet. 11th Ave. &
West Side Hwy.) | 212-488-1500 | www.hycnyc.com

Industria | *rooms: 9* | *max cap: 1000*
G Village | 775 Washington St. (bet. Jane & W. 12th Sts.) | 212-366-1114 |
www.industrianyc.com

Institute of Culinary Education, The | *rooms: 4* | *max cap: 40*
Chelsea | 50 W. 23rd St. (bet. 5th & 6th Aves.) | 212-847-0707 |
www.iceculinary.com

Intrepid Sea-Air-Space Museum | *rooms: 10* | *max cap: 5000*
Chelsea | Pier 86 (46th St. & 12th Ave.) | 212-957-7342 |
www.intrepidmuseum.org

Italian Wine Merchants | *rooms: 2* | *max cap: 125*
Union Sq | 108 E. 16th St. (bet. Irving Pl. & Union Sq. E.) | 212-473-2323 |
www.italianwinemerchant.com

Landmark on the Park | *rooms: 11* | *max cap: 600*
W 70s | 160 Central Park W. (bet. 75th & 76th Sts.) | 212-595-8410 |
www.landmarkonthepark.org

Loft 11 | *rooms: 5* | *max cap: 300*
Garment District | 336 W. 37th St. (bet. 8th & 9th Aves.) | 212-871-0940 |
www.loft11.com

Lotus Space | *rooms: 1* | *cap: 500*
Chelsea | 122 W. 26th St. (bet. 6th & 7th Aves.) | 212-463-9961 |
www.lotusspacenyc.com

Lower East Side
Tenement Museum | *rooms: 2* | *max cap: 75*
LES | 91 Orchard St. (Broome St.) | 212-431-0233 |
www.tenement.org

Madame Tussaud's | *rooms: 3* | *max cap: 1200*
W 40s | 234 W. 42nd St. (bet. 7th & 8th Aves.) | 212-512-9611 |
www.madame-tussauds.com

Manhattan Center Studios | *rooms: 3* | *max cap: 3500*
Garment District | 311 W. 34th St. (bet. 8th & 9th Aves.) | 212-279-7740 |
www.mcstudios.com

Manhattan Penthouse
on Fifth Avenue | *rooms: 1* | *cap: 250*
Flatiron | 80 Fifth Ave., 17th fl. (bet. 13th & 14th Sts.) | 212-627-8838 |
www.manhattanpentouse.com

Merchant's House Museum | *rooms: 3* | *max cap: 100*
G Village | 29 E. Fourth St. (bet. Bowery & Lafayette St.) | 212-777-1089 |
www.merchantshouse.org

Metropolitan Museum of Art | *rooms: 4* | *max cap: 800*
E 80s | 1000 Fifth Ave. (82nd St.) | 212-570-3773 |
www.metmuseum.org

Metropolitan Pavilion | *rooms: 4* | *max cap: 1500*
Flatiron | 125 W. 18th St. (bet. 6th & 7th Aves.) | 212-463-0071 |
www.metropolitanevents.com

Michelson Studio | *rooms: 1* | *cap: 350*
G Village | 163 Bank St. (bet. Washington St. & West Side Hwy.) |
212-633-1111 | www.michelsonstudio.com

Milk Studios | *rooms: 3* | *max cap: 650*
Chelsea | 450 W. 15th St., 1st fl. (bet. 9th & 10th Aves.) | 212-645-2797 |
www.milkstudios.com

Morgan Library & Museum | *rooms: 8* | *max cap: 800*
Murray Hill | 225 Madison Ave. (bet. 36th & 37th Sts.) | 212-685-0008 |
www.morganlibrary.org

Morrell Tasting Room | *rooms: 1* | *cap: 90*
E 60s | Morell & Co. | 729 Seventh Ave. (bet. 48th & 49th Sts.) |
212-688-9370 | www.morrellwine.com

Morris-Jumel Mansion | *rooms: 3* | *max cap: 100*
Harlem | 65 Jumel Terrace (bet. 160th & 162nd Sts.) | 212-923-8008 |
www.morrisjumel.org

**Mount Vernon Hotel, Museum & Garden and the
Abigail Adams Smith Auditorium** | *rooms: 5* | *max cap: 240*
E 60s | 417-421 E. 61st St. (bet. 1st & York Aves.) | 212-838-7225 |
www.mvhm.org

Museum of Jewish Heritage | *rooms: 2* | *max cap: 1000*
Financial District | Battery Park City | 36 Battery Pl. (Little West St.) |
646-437-4206 | www.mjhnyc.org

Museum of the City of New York | *rooms: 3* | *max cap: 500*
E 90s | 1220 Fifth Ave. (103rd St.) | 212-534-1672, ext. 3309 |
www.mcny.org

Nansen Park/A Taste of Honey | *rooms: 3* | *max cap: 900*
Staten Island | 3465 Victory Blvd. (Signs Rd.) | 718-983-0464 |
www.tasteofhoney.com

National Academy Museum | *rooms: 3* | *max cap: 200*
E 80s | 1083 Fifth Ave. (bet. 89th & 90th Sts.) | 212-369-4880 |
www.nationalacademy.org

**National Museum of the
American Indian** | *rooms: 9* | *max cap: 1500*
Financial District | 1 Bowling Green (State St.) | 212-514-3820 |
www.americanindian.si.edu

NBC Experience Store | *rooms: 1* | *cap: 500*
W 40s | 30 Rockefeller Plaza (bet. 49th & 50th Sts.) | 212-262-7700 |
www.nbcstore.com

New York Academy of Sciences | *rooms: 4* | *max cap: 300*
Financial District | 7 World Trade Center | 250 Greenwich St. (bet. Barclay &
Vesey Sts.) | 212-838-0230 | www.nyas.org/hostanevent

New York Aquarium | *rooms: 7* | *max cap: 5000*
Coney Island | 602 Surf Ave. (W. 8th St.) | Brooklyn | 718-265-3427 |
www.nyaquarium.com

New York Botanical Garden | *rooms: 1* | *cap: 450*
Bronx | Southern Blvd. & 200th St. | 718-220-0300 |
www.abigailkirsch.com

New York City Bar Association | *rooms: 12* | *max cap: 450*
W 40s | 42 W. 44th St. (bet. 5th & 6th Aves.) | 212-382-6637 |
www.nycbar.org

New York City Fire Museum | *rooms: 1* | *cap: 300*
SoHo | 278 Spring St. (bet. Hudson & Varick Sts.) | 212-691-1303 |
www.nycfiremuseum.org

New-York Historical Society | *rooms: 1* | *cap: 500*
W 70s | 2 W. 77th St. (CPW) | 212-873-3466 |
www.nyhistory.org

New York Public Library | *rooms: 4* | *max cap: 750*
E 40s | Fifth Ave. & 42nd St. | 212-930-0730 |
www.nypl.org/spacerental

New York State Theater | *rooms: 1* | *cap: 1000*
W 60s | 20 Lincoln Ctr. (62nd St.) | 212-870-5567

91 – The Upper Crust | *rooms: 2* | *max cap: 200*
G Village | 91 Horatio St. (bet. Washington St. & West Side Hwy.) |
212-691-4570 | www.theuppercrust.com

Pasanella & Son, Vintners | *rooms: 1* | *cap: 250*
Seaport | 115 South St. (bet. Beekman St. & Peck Slip) | 212-233-8383 |
www.pasanellaandson.com

Picnic House in Prospect Park | *rooms: 1* | *cap: 220*
Park Slope | 95 Prospect Park W. (5th St.) | Brooklyn | 718-287-6215 |
www.prospectpark.org

Pratt Mansions | *rooms: 2* | *max cap: 150*
E 80s | 1027 Fifth Ave. (bet. 83rd & 84th Sts.) | 212-744-4486, ext. 173 |
www.prattmansions.org

Puck Building | *rooms: 2* | *max cap: 1400*
SoHo | 295 Lafayette St. (Houston St.) | 212-274-8900 |
www.thepuckbuilding.com

Radio City Music Hall | *rooms: 15* | *max cap: 5900*
W 50s | 1260 Sixth Ave. (bet. 50th & 51st Sts.) | 212-465-6106 |
www.radiocity.com

Reception House | *rooms: 3* | *max cap: 250*
Flushing | 167-17 Northern Blvd. (167th St.) | Queens | 718-463-1600 |
www.receptionhouse.com

Scandinavia House | *rooms: 6* | *max cap: 175*
Murray Hill | 58 Park Ave. (bet. 37th & 38th Sts.) | 212-879-9779 |
www.scandinaviahouse.org

632 on Hudson | *rooms: 1* | *cap: 175*
W Village | 632 Hudson St. (Horatio St.) | 212-620-7631 |
www.632onhudson.com

Skylight | *rooms: 1* | *cap: 1000*
G Village | 275 Hudson St. (Spring St.) | 212-367-3730 |
www.skylightnyc.com

Sky Studios | *rooms: 2* | *max cap: 300*
G Village | 704A Broadway (bet. 4th St. & Washington Pl.) |
212-533-3030 | www.skystudios.com

South Oxford Space | *rooms: 1* | *cap: 74*
Brooklyn Heights | 138 S. Oxford St. (bet. Atlantic Ave. & Fulton St.) |
Brooklyn | 718-398-3078 | www.offbroadwayonline.com

Spirit Cruises | *rooms: 1* | *cap: 600*
Chelsea | Chelsea Piers | Pier 61 (23rd St. & West Side Hwy.) |
212-727-2789 | www.spiritcruises.com

Splashlight Studios | *rooms: 1* | *cap: 500*
Garment District | 529-535 W. 35th St. (bet. 10th & 11th Aves.) |
212-268-7247 | www.splashlightstudios.com

St. Bartholomew's Church | *rooms: 5* | *max cap: 350*
E 50s | 109 E. 50th St. (Park Ave.) | 212-378-0254 |
www.stbarts.org

Sun Factory | *rooms: 1* | *cap: 200*
TriBeCa | 394 Broadway (Walker St.) | 212-965-1213 |
www.sunfactory.com

Toys "R" Us Times Square | *rooms: 2* | *max cap: 300*
W 40s | 1514 Broadway (44th St.) | 646-366-8800 |
www.toysrustimessquare.com

Tribeca Rooftop | *rooms: 1* | *cap: 400*
TriBeCa | 2 Desbrosses St. (bet. Greenwich & Hudson Sts.) |
212-625-2600 | www.tribec.com

Ukrainian Institute of America | *rooms: 3* | *max cap: 250*
E 70s | 2 E. 79th St. (bet. 5th & Madison Aves.) | 212-288-8660 |
www.ukrainianinstitute.org

Union Ballroom | *rooms: 1* | *cap: 200*
W 100s | 3041 Broadway (121st St.) | 212-280-1345 |
www.showstoppersny.com

Union Square Ballroom | *rooms: 2* | *max cap: 475*
Union Sq | 27 Union Sq. W. (bet. 15th & 16th Sts.) | 212-645-1802 |
www.unionsquareballroom.com

Union Square Wines & Spirits | *rooms: 1* | *cap: 60*
Union Sq | 140 Fourth Ave. (13th St.) | 212-675-8100 |
www.unionsquarewines.com

Villa Barone | *rooms: 2* | *max cap: 600*
Bronx | 737 Throgs Neck Expwy. (bet. Philip & Randall Aves.) |
718-892-3500 | www.villabaronemanor.com

Vintage New York | *rooms: 2* | *max cap: 85*
SoHo | 482 Broome St. (Wooster St.) | 212-226-9463 |
www.vintagenewyork.com

Wave Hill | *rooms: 1* | *cap: 180*
Bronx | 675 W. 252nd St. (enter on W. 249th St. at Independence Ave.) |
718-549-3200 | www.wavehill.org

Westside Loft | *rooms: 1* | *cap: 450*
Garment District | 336 W. 37th St., 6th fl. (bet. 8th & 9th Aves.) |
212-871-0940 | www.thewestsideloft.com

Whitney Museum | *rooms: 5* | *max cap: 500*
E 70s | 945 Madison Ave. (bet. 74th & 75th Sts.) | 212-570-3600, ext. 388 |
www.whitney.org

World Financial Center:
Winter Garden & Plaza | *rooms: 2* | *max cap: 1800*
Financial District | 250 Vesey St. (North End Ave.) | 212-417-7143 |
www.rentals.worldfinancialcenter.com

World Yacht | *rooms: 4* | *max cap: 500*
W 40s | Pier 81 (41st St. & West Side Hwy.) | 212-630-8800 |
www.worldyacht.com

Hotels

Alex Hotel | *rooms: 1* | *cap: 50*
E 40s | 205 E. 45th St. (3rd Ave.) | 212-850-6302 |
www.thealexhotel.com

Algonquin | *rooms: 4* | *max cap: 150*
W 40s | 59 W. 44th St. (bet. 5th & 6th Aves.) | 212-840-6800 |
www.algonquinhotel.com

Beekman Tower | *rooms: 2* | *max cap: 100*
E 40s | 3 Mitchell Pl. (49th St.) | 212-355-7300 |
www.thebeekmanhotel.com

Bryant Park | *rooms: 2* | *max cap: 300*
W 40s | 40 W. 40th St. (bet. 5th & 6th Aves.) | 212-869-0100 |
www.bryantparkhotel.com

Carlton | *rooms: 7* | *max cap: 175*
Gramercy | 88 Madison Ave. (bet. 28th & 29th Sts.) | 212-532-4100 |
www.carltonhotelny.com

Carlyle | *rooms: 2* | *max cap: 500*
E 70s | 35 E. 76th St. (Madison Ave.) | 212-570-7106 |
www.thecarlyle.com

Crowne Plaza Manhattan | *rooms: 34* | *max cap: 700*
W 50s | 1605 Broadway (bet. 48th & 49th Sts.) | 212-977-4000 |
www.manhattan.crowneplaza.com

DoubleTree Guest Suites | *rooms: 6* | *max cap: 200*
W 40s | 1568 Broadway (47th St.) | 212-719-1600 |
www.nyc.doubletreehotels.com

Dream Hotel | *rooms: 4* | *max cap: 300*
W 50s | 210 W. 55th St. (bet. B'way & 7th Ave.) | 212-974-1934 |
www.dreamny.com

Flatotel | *rooms: 4* | *max cap: 400*
W 50s | 135 W. 52nd St. (bet. 6th & 7th Aves.) | 212-887-9515 |
www.flatotel.com

Gansevoort | *rooms: 4* | *max cap: 250*
Meatpacking | 18 Ninth Ave. (13th St.) | 212-206-6700 |
www.hotelgansevoort.com

Giraffe | *rooms: 1* | *cap: 60*
Gramercy | 365 Park Ave. S. (26th St.) | 212-685-7700 |
www.hotelgiraffe.com

Grand Hyatt New York | *rooms: 25 | max cap: 1700*
E 40s | 109 E. 42nd St. (Park Ave.) | 646-213-6640 |
www.hyatt.com

Helmsley Park Lane | *rooms: 10 | max cap: 400*
W 50s | 36 Central Park S. (bet. 5th & 6th Aves.) | 212-521-6203 |
www.helmsleyparklane.com

Hilton New York and Towers | *rooms: 53 | max cap: 3300*
W 50s | 1335 Sixth Ave. (bet. 53rd & 54th Sts.) | 212-261-5790 |
www.hilton.com

Hotel on Rivington, The | *rooms: 4 | max cap: 125*
LES | 107 Rivington St. (bet. Essex & Ludlow Sts.) | 212-475-2600 |
www.hotelonrivington.com

Hudson Hotel | *rooms: 8 | max cap: 300*
W 50s | 356 W. 58th St. (bet. 8th & 9th Aves.) | 212-554-6309 |
www.morganshotelgroup.com

Inn at Irving Place | *rooms: 3 | max cap: 55*
(aka Lady Mendl's)
Union Sq | 56 Irving Pl. (bet. 17th & 18th Sts.) | 212-533-4466 |
www.innatirving.com

Inter-Continental, Barclay NY | *rooms: 18 | max cap: 320*
E 40s | 111 E. 48th St. (bet. Lexington & Park Aves.) | 212-906-3124 |
www.interconti.com

Jumeirah Essex House | *rooms: 12 | max cap: 500*
W 50s | 160 Central Park S. (bet. 6th & 7th Aves.) | 212-484-5144 |
www.jumeirahessexhouse.com

Kitano, The | *rooms: 1 | cap: 146*
Murray Hill | 66 Park Ave. (38th St.) | 212-885-7017 |
www.kitano.com

Le Parker Meridien | *rooms: 9 | max cap: 800*
W 50s | 118 W. 57th St. (bet. 6th & 7th Aves.) | 212-708-7450 |
www.parkermeridien.com

Library Hotel | *rooms: 1 | cap: 75*
E 40s | 299 Madison Ave. (41st St.) | 212-983-4500 |
www.libraryhotel.com

Loews Regency | *rooms: 3 | max cap: 200*
E 60s | 540 Park Ave. (61st St.) | 212-759-4100 |
www.loewsregency.com

Lowell, The | *rooms: 1 | cap: 75*
E 60s | 28 E. 63rd St. (bet. Madison & Park Aves.) | 212-605-6825 |
www.lowellhotel.com

Mandarin Oriental | *rooms: 3 | max cap: 900*
W 60s | Time Warner Ctr. | 80 Columbus Circle (60th St.) |
212-805-8800 | www.mandarinoriental.com

Maritime Hotel, The | *rooms: 9 | max cap: 2450*
Chelsea | 363 W. 16th St. (bet. 8th & 9th Aves.) | 212-242-4300 |
www.themaritimehotel.com

Marriott Financial Center | *rooms: 13* | *max cap: 450*
Financial District | 85 West St. (Albany St.) | 212-266-6145 |
www.nymarriottfinancialcenter.com

Millennium Broadway | *rooms: 15* | *max cap: 730*
W 40s | 145 W. 44th St. (bet. B'way & 6th Ave.) | 212-789-7546 |
www.millenniumhotels.com

Millennium UN Plaza | *rooms: 7* | *max cap: 300*
E 40s | 1 United Nations Plaza (1st Ave. & 44th St.) | 212-758-1234 |
www.millenniumhotels.com/unplaza

Morgans | *rooms: 3* | *max cap: 75*
Murray Hill | 237 Madison Ave. (bet. 37th & 38th Aves.) |
212-686-0300 | www.morganshotelgroup.com

Muse, The | *rooms: 4* | *max cap: 100*
W 40s | 130 W. 46th St. (bet. 6th & 7th Aves.) | 212-485-2400 |
www.themusehotel.com

New York Marriott Marquis | *rooms: 58* | *max cap: 2800*
W 40s | 1535 Broadway (bet. 45th & 46th Sts.) | 212-398-1900 |
www.marriott.com

New York Palace | *rooms: 13* | *max cap: 300*
E 50s | 455 Madison Ave. (bet. 50th & 51st Sts.) | 212-303-7766 |
www.newyorkpalace.com

Night Hotel | *rooms: 1* | *cap: 150*
W 40s | 132 W. 45th St. (bet. 6th & 7th Aves.) | 212-835-9600 |
www.nighthotelny.com

Omni Berkshire Place | *rooms: 10* | *max cap: 120*
E 50s | 21 E. 52nd St. (bet. 5th & Madison Aves.) | 212-754-5090 |
www.omnihotels.com

Paramount | *rooms: 1* | *cap: 75*
W 40s | 235 W. 46th St. (bet. B'way & 8th Ave.) | 212-764-5500 |
www.nycparamount.com

Peninsula, The | *rooms: 6* | *max cap: 150*
E 50s | 700 Fifth Ave. (55th St.) | 212-903-3072 |
www.peninsula.com

Pierre, The | *rooms: 6* | *max cap: 1200*
E 60s | 2 E. 61st St. (5th Ave.) | 212-940-8111 |
www.fourseasons.com

Plaza Athénée | *rooms: 4* | *max cap: 150*
E 60s | 37 E. 64th St. (bet. Madison & Park Aves.) | 212-606-4663 |
www.plaza-athenee.com

Plaza Hotel, The | *rooms: 10* | *max cap: 1200*
W 50s | 768 Fifth Ave. (bet. 58th & 59th Sts.) | 212-549-0550 |
www.theplaza.com

Ritz-Carlton, Battery Park | *rooms: 10* | *max cap: 500*
Financial District | 2 West St. (bet. Battery Pl. & South St.) |
917-790-2400 | www.ritzcarlton.com

Ritz-Carlton, Central Park | *rooms: 3* | *max cap: 155*
W 50s | 50 Central Park S. (bet. 5th & 6th Aves.) | 212-308-9100 |
www.ritzcarlton.com

70 Park Avenue | *rooms: 3* | *max cap: 100*
Murray Hill | 70 Park Ave. (38th St.) | 212-973-2400 |
www.70parkave.com

60 Thompson | *rooms: 3* | *max cap: 150*
SoHo | 60 Thompson St. (bet. Broome & Spring Sts.) |
212-431-0400 | www.60thompson.com

Soho Grand | *rooms: 7* | *max cap: 350*
SoHo | 310 W. Broadway (bet. Canal & Grand Sts.) | 212-519-6666 |
www.sohogrand.com

St. Regis | *rooms: 15* | *max cap: 220*
E 50s | 2 E. 55th St. (bet. 5th & Madison Aves.) | 212-339-6776 |
www.stregis.com

Tribeca Grand | *rooms: 6* | *max cap: 400*
TriBeCa | 2 Sixth Ave. (Church St.) | 212-519-6666 |
www.tribecagrand.com

Waldorf-Astoria | *rooms: 40* | *max cap: 1500*
E 40s | 301 Park Ave. (bet. 49th & 50th Sts.) | 212-872-4700 |
www.waldorf.com

Westin Times Square | *rooms: 40* | *max cap: 330*
W 40s | 270 W. 43rd St. (8th Ave.) | 212-201-2700 |
www.westinny.com

W New York | *rooms: 12* | *max cap: 500*
E 50s | 541 Lexington Ave. (bet. 49th & 50th Sts.) | 212-755-1200 |
www.whotels.com

W The Court | *rooms: 8* | *max cap: 100*
Murray Hill | 130 E. 39th St. (Lexington Ave.) | 212-592-8820 |
www.whotels.com

W Times Square | *rooms: 6* | *max cap: 150*
W 40s | 1567 Broadway (47th St.) | 212-930-7404 |
www.whotels.com

W Union Square | *rooms: 6* | *max cap: 500*
Union Sq | 201 Park Ave. S. (17th St.) | 917-534-5900 |
www.whotels.com

Nightclubs/Bars

For additional listings, see Zagat NYC Nightlife.

APT | *rooms: 2* | *max cap: 300*
Meatpacking | 419 W. 13th St. (bet. 9th Ave. & Washington St.) |
212-414-4245 | www.aptwebsite.com

Aspen | *rooms: 3* | *max cap: 350*
Flatiron | 30 W. 22nd St. (bet. 5th & 6th Aves.) | 212-645-5040 |
www.aspen-nyc.com

Blue Owl | *rooms: 3* | *max cap: 120*
E Village | 196 Second Ave. (bet. 12th & 13th Sts.) | 212-505-2583 |
www.blueowlnyc.com

BLVD | *rooms: 4* | *max cap: 1500*
SoHo | 199 Bowery St. (Spring St.) | 212-982-7767 |
www.blvdnyc.com

Bowlmor | *rooms: 1* | *cap: 600*
G Village | 110 University Pl. (bet. 12th & 13th Sts.) | 212-255-8188 |
www.bowlmor.com

Bubble Lounge | *rooms: 2* | *max cap: 300*
TriBeCa | 228 W. Broadway (bet. Franklin & White Sts.) | 212-431-3433 |
www.bubblelounge.com

Buddha Bar | *rooms: 1* | *cap: 1000*
Meatpacking | 25 Little W. 12th St. (bet. 9th Ave. & Washington St.) |
212-647-7315 | www.buddhabarnyc.com

Butter | *rooms: 2* | *max cap: 300*
G Village | 415 Lafayette St. (bet. Astor Pl. & 4th St.) | 212-253-2828 |
www.butterrestaurant.com

Campbell Apartment, The | *rooms: 1* | *cap: 125*
E 40s | Grand Central Terminal | 15 Vanderbilt Ave. (bet. 42nd &
43rd Sts.) | 212-980-9476 | www.hospitalityholdings.com

Canal Room | *rooms: 1* | *cap: 450*
SoHo | 285 W. Broadway (Canal St.) | 212-941-8100, ext. 104 |
www.canalroom.com

Capitale | *rooms: 3* | *max cap: 1500*
SoHo | 130 Bowery (bet. Broome & Grand Sts.) | 212-334-5500 |
www.capitaleny.com

Carnegie Club | *rooms: 2* | *max cap: 150*
W 50s | 156 W. 56th St. (bet. 6th & 7th Aves.) | 212-957-9676 |
www.hospitalityholdings.com

Cotton Club | *rooms: 1* | *cap: 175*
Harlem | 656 W. 125th St. (12th Ave.) | 212-663-7980 |
www.cottonclub-newyork.com

Delancey, The | *rooms: 5* | *max cap: 700*
LES | 168 Delancey St. (bet. Attorney & Clinton Sts.) | 212-254-9920 |
www.thedelancey.com

Duvet | *rooms: 2* | *max cap: 1200*
Flatiron | 45 W. 21st St. (bet. 5th & 6th Aves.) | 212-989-2121 |
www.duvetny.com

Flûte
rooms: 2 | *max cap: 125*
Gramercy | 40 E. 20th St. (bet. B'way & Park Ave. S.) |
212-529-7870
rooms: 1 | *cap: 100*
W 50s | 205 W. 54th St. (bet. B'way & 7th Ave.) | 212-265-5169
www.flutebar.com

Glass | *rooms: 1* | *cap: 150*
Chelsea | 287 10th Ave. (bet. 26th & 27th Sts.) | 212-904-1580 |
www.glassloungenyc.com

Happy Ending | *rooms: 2* | *max cap: 250*
E Village | 302 Broome St. (bet. Eldridge & Forsythe Sts.) | 212-334-9676 |
www.happyendinglounge.com

Latitude | *rooms: 4* | *max cap: 300*
W 40s | 783 Eighth Ave. (bet. 47th & 48th Sts.) | 212-245-3034 |
www.latitudebarnyc.com

Madame X | *rooms: 2* | *max cap: 150*
G Village | 94 W. Houston St. (bet. La Guardia Pl. & Thompson St.) |
917-568-9069 | www.madamex.com

Mercury Lounge | *rooms: 1* | *cap: 250*
LES | 217 E. Houston St. (bet. Essex & Ludlow Sts.) | 212-260-4700 |
www.mercuryloungenyc.com

Nikki Midtown | *rooms: 2* | *max cap: 450*
E 50s | 151 E. 50th St. (bet. Lexington & 3rd Aves.) | 212-753-1144 |
www.nikkibeach.com

Pink Elephant | *rooms: 1* | *cap: 360*
Chelsea | 527 W. 27th St. (bet. 10th & 11th Aves.) | 212-463-0000 |
www.pinkelephantclub.com

PM | *rooms: 1* | *cap: 475*
G Village | 50 Gansevoort St. (bet. Greenwich & Washington Sts.) |
212-255-6676 | www.pmloungenyc.com

Pressure | *rooms: 6* | *max cap: 600*
G Village | 110 University Pl., 5th fl. (bet. 12th & 13th Sts.) |
212-255-8188 | www.pressurenyc.com

Providence/Triumph Room | *rooms: 3* | *max cap: 1200*
W 50s | 311 W. 57th St. (bet. 8th & 9th Aves.) | 212-505-7400 |
www.providencenyc.com

PS 450 | *rooms: 3* | *max cap: 350*
Murray Hill | 450 Park Ave. S. (bet. 30th & 31st Sts.) | 212-532-7474 |
www.ps450.com

Roseland Ballroom | *rooms: 1* | *cap: 2500*
W 50s | 239 W. 52nd St. (bet. B'way & 8th Ave.) | 212-489-8350 |
www.roselandballroom.com

S.O.B.'s | *rooms: 2* | *max cap: 400*
SoHo | 204 Varick St. (Houston St.) | 212-645-2577 |
www.sobs.com

Spice Market | *rooms: 4* | *max cap: 222*
Meatpacking | 403 W. 13th St. (9th Ave.) | 212-675-2322 |
www.jean-georges.com

Spy Bar | *rooms: 2* | *max cap: 700*
Flatiron | 17 W. 19th St. (bet. 5th & 6th Aves.) | 212-352-2001 |
www.spyclubnyc.com

Stone Rose | *rooms: 2* | *max cap: 500*
W 50s | Time Warner Ctr. | 10 Columbus Circle, 4th fl. (59th St.) |
212-750-6361 | www.mocbars.com

T New York | *rooms: 3* | *max cap: 750*
W 50s | 240 W. 52nd St. (bet. B'way & 8th Ave.) | 212-489-7656 |
www.tnewyorkcity.com

Tonic Times Square | *rooms: 3* | *max cap: 500*
W 40s | 727 Seventh Ave. (bet. 48th & 49th Sts.) | 212-382-1059 |
www.thetonicbar.com

230 Fifth | *rooms: 5* | *max cap: 1200*
Chelsea | 230 Fifth Ave., penthouse (bet. 26th & 27th Sts.) |
212-725-4300 | www.230fifthave.com

Webster Hall | *rooms: 5* | *max cap: 3000*
E Village | 125 E. 11th St. (bet. 3rd & 4th Aves.) | 212-353-1600 |
www.websterhall.com

World Bar, The | *rooms: 1* | *cap: 100*
E 40s | Trump World Tower | 845 United Nations Plaza (48th St.) |
212-980-9476 | www.hospitalityholdings.com

Private Clubs

Members only, or nonmembers with sponsorship

Branch | *rooms: 1* | *cap: 400*
E 50s | 226 E. 54th St. (3rd Ave.) | 212-688-5577 |
www.branchny.com

National Arts Club, The | *rooms: 7* | *max cap: 300*
Gramercy | 15 Gramercy Park S. (Irving Pl.) | 212-475-3424 |
www.nationalartsclub.org

Players Club | *rooms: 4* | *max cap: 350*
Union Sq | 16 Gramercy Park S. (Irving Pl.) | 212-475-6116 |
www.theplayersnyc.org

Williams Club | *rooms: 8* | *max cap: 150*
Murray Hill | 24 E. 39th St. (Madison Ave.) | 212-697-5300 |
www.williamsclub.org

Yale Club | *rooms: 11* | *max cap: 400*
E 40s | 50 Vanderbilt Ave. (bet. 44th & 45th Sts.) | 212-716-2122 |
www.yaleclubnyc.org

Restaurants

For additional listings, see Zagat NYC Restaurants.

Alto | *rooms: 2* | *max cap: 24*
E 50s | 11 E. 53rd St. (bet. 5th & Madison Aves.) | 212-308-1099 |
www.altorestaurant.com | Northern Italian

American Girl Place Cafe | *rooms: 2* | *max cap: 40*
E 40s | 609 Fifth Ave. (49th St.) | 212-371-2220 |
www.americangirlplace.com | American

PARTY SITES - RESTAURANTS

Arium | *rooms: 1* | *cap: 65*
Meatpacking | 31 Little W. 12th St. (bet. 9th & Washington Sts.) | 212-463-8630 | www.ariumnyc.com | British

Bar Americain | *rooms: 1* | *cap: 50*
W 50s | 152 W. 52nd St. (bet. 6th & 7th Aves.) | 212-265-9700 | www.baramericain.com | American

Barbetta | *rooms: 4* | *max cap: 140*
W 40s | 321 W. 46th St. (bet. 8th & 9th Aves.) | 212-246-9171 | www.barbettarestaurant.com | Italian

Bar Boulud | *rooms: 3* | *max cap: 70*
W 60s | 1900 Broadway (bet. 63rd & 64th Sts.) | 212-595-0303 | www.danielnyc.com | French

Battery Gardens | *rooms: 2* | *max cap: 250*
Financial District | Battery Park (opp. 17 State St.) | 212-809-5508 | www.batterygardens.com | American/Continental

Bayard's | *rooms: 9* | *max cap: 1000*
Financial District | 1 Hanover Sq. (bet. Pearl & Stone Sts.) | 212-514-9454 | www.bayards.com | American

Beacon | *rooms: 1* | *cap: 100*
W 50s | 25 W. 56th St. (bet. 5th & 6th Aves.) | 212-332-0500 | www.beaconnyc.com | New American

Becco | *rooms: 3* | *max cap: 110*
W 40s | 355 W. 46th St. (bet. 8th & 9th Aves.) | 212-397-7597 | www.becconyc.com | Northern Italian

Benoit | *rooms: 2* | *max cap: 60*
W 50s | 60 W. 55th St. (bet. 5th & 6th Aves.) | 646-943-7373 | www.benoitny.com | French

Bill's Gay '90s | *rooms: 2* | *max cap: 100*
E 50s | 57 E. 54th St. (bet. Madison & Park Aves.) | 212-355-0243 | www.billsnyc.com | American

BLT Fish | *rooms: 1* | *cap: 65*
Flatiron | 21 W. 17th St. (bet. 5th & 6th Aves.) | 212-691-8888 | www.bltfish.com | Seafood

BLT Prime | *rooms: 2* | *max cap: 250*
Gramercy | 111 E. 22nd St. (bet. Lexington Ave. & Park Ave. S.) | 212-995-8500 | www.bltprime.com | New American

BLT Steak | *rooms: 1* | *cap: 22*
E 50s | 106 E. 57th St. (Park Ave.) | 212-752-7470 | www.bltsteak.com | New American/Steakhouse

Blue Fin | *rooms: 3* | *max cap: 195*
W 40s | 1567 Broadway (bet. 47th & 48th Sts.) | 212-918-1400 | www.brguestrestaurants.com | Seafood

Blue Hill | *rooms: 2* | *max cap: 60*
G Village | 75 Washington Pl. (bet. 6th Ave. & Washington Sq. W.) | 212-539-1776 | www.bluehillfarm.com | New American

Blue Smoke | *rooms: 2* | *max cap: 480*
Gramercy | 116 E. 27th St. (bet. Lexington & Park Aves.) | 212-447-7733 |
www.bluesmoke.com | BBQ

Blue Water Grill | *rooms: 3* | *max cap: 300*
Union Sq | 31 Union Sq. W. (16th St.) | 212-331-0323 |
www.brguestrestaurants.com | Seafood

Bottega del Vino | *rooms: 3* | *max cap: 193*
E 50s | 7 E. 59th St. (bet. 5th & Madison Aves.) | 212-223-3028 |
www.bottegadelvinonyc.com | Italian

Brasserie Julien | *rooms: 1* | *cap: 120*
E 80s | 1422 Third Ave. (bet. 80th & 81st Sts.) | 212-744-6327 |
www.brasseriejulien.com | French Brasserie

Brasserie Ruhlmann | *rooms: 1* | *cap: 280*
W 50s | 45 Rockefeller Plaza (bet. 5th & 6th Aves.) | 212-974-2020 |
www.brasserieruhlmann.com | French Brasserie

Bryant Park Grill/Cafe | *rooms: 4* | *max cap: 2000*
W 40s | 25 W. 40th St. (bet. 5th & 6th Aves.) | 212-206-8815 |
www.arkrestaurants.com | American

Bubba Gump Shrimp Co. | *rooms: 1* | *cap: 360*
W 40s | 1501 Broadway (44th St.) | 212-391-7100 |
www.bubbagump.com | Seafood

Buddakan | *rooms: 4* | *max cap: 700*
Chelsea | 75 Ninth Ave. (bet. 15th & 16th Sts.) | 212-989-6699 |
www.buddakannyc.com | Asian Fusion/Chinese

Butterfield 8 | *rooms: 2* | *max cap: 250*
Murray Hill | 5 E. 38th St. (bet. 5th & Madison Aves.) | 212-679-0646 |
www.butterfield8nyc.com | American

Cafe Fiorello | *rooms: 2* | *max cap: 220*
W 60s | 1900 Broadway (63rd St.) | 212-265-0100 |
www.thefiremangroup.com | Italian

Calle Ocho | *rooms: 1* | *cap: 325*
W 80s | 446 Columbus Ave. (bet. 81st & 82nd Sts.) | 212-873-5025 |
www.calleochonyc.com | Pan-Latin

Cellini | *rooms: 2* | *max cap: 100*
E 50s | 65 E. 54th St. (bet. Madison & Park Aves.) | 212-751-1555 |
www.cellinirestaurant.com | Northern Italian

Central Park Boathouse | *rooms: 1* | *cap: 1500*
E 70s | Central Park | E. 72nd St. (Central Park Dr. N.) | 212-517-2233 |
www.thecentralparkboathouse.com | New American

Chinatown Brasserie | *rooms: 2* | *max cap: 168*
NoHo | 380 Lafayette St. (Great Jones St.) | 212-533-7000 |
www.chinatownbrasserie.com | Chinese

Chin Chin | *rooms: 2* | *max cap: 80*
SoHo | 216 E. 49th St. (bet. 2nd & 3rd Aves.) | 212-888-4555 |
Chinese

PARTY SITES – RESTAURANTS

Cipriani Dolci | *rooms: 1* | *cap: 850*
E 40s | Grand Central | West Balcony (42nd St. & Vanderbilt Ave.) |
212-499-0599 | www.cipriani.com | Italian

City Hall | *rooms: 3* | *max cap: 415*
TriBeCa | 131 Duane St. (bet. Church St. & W. B'way) | 212-964-4118 |
www.cityhallnewyork.com | American

Compass | *rooms: 3* | *max cap: 165*
W 50s | 208 W. 70th St. (bet. Amsterdam & West End Aves.) |
212-875-8600 | www.compassrestaurant.com | New American

Cowgirl | *rooms: 3* | *max cap: 135*
G Village | 519 Hudson St. (10th St.) | 212-633-1133 |
www.cowgirlnyc.com | Southwestern

Craftsteak | *rooms: 1* | *cap: 300*
Chelsea | 85 10th Ave. (bet. 15th & 16th Sts.) | 212-400-6699 |
www.craftsteaknyc.com | Seafood/Steakhouse

Cub Room | *rooms: 3* | *max cap: 168*
SoHo | 131 Sullivan St. (Prince St.) | 212-677-4100 | www.cubroom.com |
New American

Daniel | *rooms: 2* | *max cap: 250*
E 50s | 60 E. 65th St. (bet. Madison & Park Aves.) | 212-933-5261 |
www.danielnyc.com | French

davidburke & donatella | *rooms: 1* | *cap: 110*
E 60s | 133 E. 61st St. (bet. Lexington & Park Aves.) | 212-813-2121 |
www.dbdrestaurant.com | New American

Del Frisco's | *rooms: 5* | *max cap: 75*
W 40s | 1221 Sixth Ave. (49th St.) | 212-575-5129 |
www.delfriscos.com | Steakhouse

Del Posto | *rooms: 5* | *max cap: 1200*
Chelsea | 85 10th Ave. (bet. 15th & 16th Sts.) | 646-278-0800 |
Italian

Dos Caminos
rooms: 1 | *cap: 50*
E 50s | 825 Third Ave. (50th St.) | 212-336-5400
rooms: 3 | *max cap: 300*
Gramercy | 373 Park Ave. S. (bet. 26th & 27th Sts.) | 212-294-1000
rooms: 1 | *max cap: 100*
G Village | 475 W. Broadway (Houston St.) | 212-277-4300
ww.brguestrestaurants.com | Mexican

Eleven Madison Park | *rooms: 2* | *max cap: 50*
Gramercy | 11 Madison Ave. (24th St.) | 212-889-0905 |
www.elevenmadisonpark.com | New French

Eli's Vinegar Factory | *rooms: 1* | *cap: 180*
E 90s | 431 E. 91st St. (bet. 1st & York Aves.) | 212-987-0885 |
www.elizabar.com | American

Elmo | *rooms: 1* | *cap: 100*
Chelsea | 156 Seventh Ave. (bet. 19th & 20th Sts.) | 212-337-8000 |
www.elmorestaurant.com | New American

EN Japanese Brasserie | *rooms: 2* | *max cap: 300*
W Village | 435 Hudson St. (Leroy St.) | 212-647-9196 |
www.enjb.com | Japanese

ESPN Zone | *rooms: 6* | *max cap: 1070*
W 40s | 1472 Broadway (42nd St.) | 212-921-3776 |
www.espnzone.com | American

Felidia | *rooms: 1* | *cap: 65*
E 50s | 243 E. 58th St. (bet. 2nd & 3rd Aves.) | 212-758-1479 |
www.lidiasitaly.com | Italian

Fiamma | *rooms: 1* | *cap: 80*
SoHo | 206 Spring St. (bet. 6th Ave. & Sullivan St.) | 212-653-0100 |
www.brguestrestaurants.com | Italian

FireBird | *rooms: 6* | *max cap: 325*
W 40s | 365 W. 46th St. (bet. 8th & 9th Aves.) | 212-586-0244 |
www.firebirdrestaurant.com | Russian

5 Ninth | *rooms: 1* | *cap: 250*
G Village | 5 Ninth Ave. (bet. Gansevoort & Little W. 12th Sts.) |
212-929-9460 | www.fiveninth.com | Eclectic

Four Seasons | *rooms: 3* | *max cap: 350*
E 50s | 99 E. 52nd St. (bet. Lexington & Park Aves.) | 212-754-9494 |
www.fourseasonsrestaurant.com | Continental

Fraunces Tavern | *rooms: 3* | *max cap: 350*
Financial District | 54 Pearl St. (Broad St.) | 212-968-9689 |
www.frauncestavern.com | American

Fred's at Barneys NY | *rooms: 2* | *max cap: 60*
E 60s | 660 Madison Ave., 9th fl. (bet. 60th & 61st Sts.) |
212-833-2207 | Northern Italian

Freemans | *rooms: 1* | *cap: 150*
LES | Freeman Alley (off Rivington St., bet. Bowery &
Chrystie St.) | 212-420-0012 | www.freemansrestaurant.com |
New American

Fresco by Scotto | *rooms: 2* | *max cap: 45*
E 50s | 34 E. 52nd St. (bet. Madison & Park Aves.) | 212-935-3434 |
www.frescobyscotto.com | Italian

FROG | *rooms: 1* | *cap: 110*
SoHo | 71 Spring St. (bet. Crosby & Lafayette Sts.) | 212-966-5050 |
www.frognyc.com | French

Gabriel's | *rooms: 2* | *max cap: 45*
W 60s | 11 W. 60th St. (B'way) | 212-956-4600 |
www.gabrielsbarandrest.com | Northern Italian

Geisha | *rooms: 2* | *max cap: 40*
E 60s | 33 E. 61st St. (bet. Madison & Park Aves.) | 212-813-1113 |
www.geisharestaurant.com | Japanese/Seafood

Giovanni's Atrium | *rooms: 3* | *max cap: 275*
Financial District | 100 Washington St. (Rector St.) | 212-513-4133 |
www.giovannisatriumnyc.com | Italian

Girasole | *rooms: 1* | *cap: 40*
E 80s | 151 E. 82nd St. (bet. Lexington & 3rd Aves.) | 212-772-6690 | Italian

Golden Unicorn | *rooms: 3* | *max cap: 300*
Chinatown | 18 E. Broadway (Catherine St.) | 212-941-0911 | Chinese

Gramercy Tavern | *rooms: 1* | *cap: 22*
Flatiron | 42 E. 20th St. (bet. B'way & Park Ave. S.) | 212-477-0777 | www.gramercytavern.com | American

Grayz | *rooms: 5* | *max cap: 100*
W 50s | 13-15 W. 54th St. (bet. 5th & 6th Aves.) | 212-262-4600 | www.grayz.net | Eclectic

Guastavino's | *rooms: 1* | *cap: 2200*
E 50s | 409 E. 59th St. (bet. 1st & York Aves.) | 212-980-2711 | www.guastavinos.com | New American

Harrison, The | *rooms: 2* | *max cap: 40*
TriBeCa | 355 Greenwich St. (Harrison St.) | 212-274-9310 | www.theharrison.com | American

Highline | *rooms: 3* | *max cap: 390*
Meatpacking | 835 Washington St. (Little W. 12th St.) | 212-243-3339 | www.nychighline.com | Thai

Ici | *rooms: 3* | *max cap: 140*
Fort Greene | 246 DeKalb Ave. (bet. Clermont & Vanderbilt Aves.) | Brooklyn | 718-789-2778 | www.icirestaurant.com | American

Il Buco | *rooms: 2* | *max cap: 100*
NoHo | 47 Bond St. (bet. Bowery & Lafayette St.) | 212-533-1932 | www.ilbuco.com | Italian/Mediterranean

Insieme | *rooms: 1* | *cap: 32*
W 50s | Michelangelo Hotel, The | 777 Seventh Ave. (bet. 50th & 51st Sts.) | 212-582-1310 | www.restaurantinsieme.com | Italian

I Trulli | *rooms: 4* | *max cap: 160*
Gramercy | 122 E. 27th St. (bet. Lexington Ave. & Park Ave. S.) | 212-481-7372 | www.itrulli.com | Southern Italian

Jean Georges | *rooms: 1* | *cap: 35*
W 60s | Trump Int'l Hotel | 1 Central Park W. (bet. 60th & 61st Sts.) | 212-299-3900 | www.jean-georges.com | New French

Keens Steakhouse | *rooms: 4* | *max cap: 500*
Garment District | 72 W. 36th St. (bet. 5th & 6th Aves.) | 212-268-5056 | www.keens.com | Steakhouse

Kelley & Ping | *rooms: 2* | *max cap: 80*
E Village | 325 Bowery (www.casadistile.com) | 212-979-7866 x201 | www.eatrice.com | Pan-Asian

La Esquina | *rooms: 2* | *max cap: 70*
Little Italy | 114 Kenmare St. (bet. Cleveland Pl. & Lafayette St.) | 646-613-7100 | www.esquinanyc.com | Mexican

La Grenouille | *rooms: 1* | *cap: 70*
E 50s | 3 E. 52nd St. (bet. 5th & Madison Aves.) | 212-752-0652 |
www.la-grenouille.com | French

Landmarc | *rooms: 2* | *max cap: 125*
W 60s | 10 Columbus Circle, 3rd fl. (60th St.) | 212-823-6123 |
www.landmarc-restaurant.com | French Bistro

Le Bernardin | *rooms: 2* | *max cap: 130*
W 50s | 155 W. 51st St. (bet. 6th & 7th Aves.) | 212-554-1108 |
www.le-bernardin.com | French/Seafood

Le Cirque | *rooms: 2* | *max cap: 240*
E 50s | One Beacon Court | 151 E. 58th St. (bet. Lexington & 3rd Aves.) |
212-405-5094 | www.lecirque.com | French

Le Perigord | *rooms: 1* | *cap: 140*
E 50s | 405 E. 52nd St. (bet. FDR Dr. & 1st Ave.) | 212-755-6244 |
www.leperigord.com | French

Lupa | *rooms: 1* | *cap: 35*
G Village | 170 Thompson St. (bet. Bleecker & Houston Sts.) |
212-982-5089 | www.luparestaurant.com | Italian

Megu | *rooms: 3* | *max cap: 600*
TriBeCa | 62 Thomas St. (bet. Church St. & W. B'way) | 212-964-7777 |
www.megunyc.com | Japanese

Megu Midtown | *rooms: 1* | *cap: 175*
E 40s | Trump World Tower | 845 United Nations Plaza (1st Ave. &
47th St.) | 212-644-0777 | www.megunyc.com | Japanese

Metrazur | *rooms: 1* | *cap: 600*
E 40s | Grand Central Terminal | East Balcony (42nd St. & Park Ave.) |
212-687-4750 | www.metrazur.com | New American

**Michael Jordan's
The Steak House NYC** | *rooms: 1* | *cap: 500*
E 50s | Grand Central Terminal | West Balcony (42nd St. &
Vanderbilt Ave.) | 212-608-7400 | www.theglaziergroup.com |
Steakhouse

Mickey Mantle's | *rooms: 3* | *max cap: 300*
W 50s | 42 Central Park S. (bet. 5th & 6th Aves.) | 212-688-7777 |
www.mickeymantles.com | American

Modern, The | *rooms: 1* | *cap: 80*
W 50s | Museum of Modern Art | 9 W. 53rd St. (bet. 5th & 6th Aves.) |
212-408-6641 | www.themodernnyc.com | New American/New French

Monkey Bar | *rooms: 1* | *cap: 200*
E 50s | 60 E. 54th St. (bet. Madison & Park Aves.) | 212-608-7400 |
www.theglaziergroup.com | American

Moran's Chelsea | *rooms: 4* | *max cap: 500*
Chelsea | 146 10th Ave. (19th St.) | 212-627-3030 |
www.moranschelsea.com | Seafood/Steakhouse

Morimoto | *rooms: 2* | *max cap: 350*
Chelsea | 88 10th Ave. (16th St.) | 212-989-8883 |
www.morimotonyc.com | Japanese

Mr. Chow Tribeca | *rooms: 1* | *cap: 250*
TriBeCa | 121 Hudson St. (N. Moore St.) | 212-965-9500 |
www.mrchow.com | Chinese

Nobu | *rooms: 1* | *cap: 220*
TriBeCa | 105 Hudson St. (Franklin St.) | 212-219-8095 |
www.myriadrestaurantgroup.com | Japanese/Peruvian

Nobu 57 | *rooms: 1* | *cap: 300*
W 50s | 40 W. 57th St. (bet. 5th & 6th Aves.) | 212-757-3000 |
www.myriadrestaurantgroup.com | Japanese/Peruvian

Oceana | *rooms: 2* | *max cap: 60*
E 50s | 55 E. 54th St. (bet. Madison & Park Aves.) | 212-759-5941 |
www.oceanarestaurant.com | Seafood

Ocean Grill | *rooms: 2* | *max cap: 150*
W 70s | 384 Columbus Ave. (bet. 78th & 79th Sts.) | 212-579-2300 |
www.brguestrestaurants.com | Seafood

One | *rooms: 1* | *cap: 50*
Meatpacking | 1 Little W. 12th St. (Gansevoort St.) | 212-255-9717 |
www.onelw12.com | Eclectic

One if by Land, Two if by Sea | *rooms: 2* | *max cap: 140*
G Village | 17 Barrow St. (bet. 7th Ave. S. & W. 4th St.) | 646-496-6433 |
www.oneifbyland.com | New American

Opia | *rooms: 3* | *max cap: 400*
E 50s | 130 E. 57th St. (Lexington Ave.) | 212-688-3939 |
www.opiarestaurant.com | French

Park, The | *rooms: 5* | *max cap: 1200*
Chelsea | 118 10th Ave. (bet. 17th & 18th Sts.) | 212-352-3313 |
www.theparknyc.com | Mediterranean

Patroon | *rooms: 6* | *max cap: 100*
E 40s | 160 E. 46th St. (bet. Lexington & 3rd Aves.) | 212-883-7373 |
www.patroonrestaurant.com | American

Periyali | *rooms: 1* | *cap: 50*
Flatiron | 35 W. 20th St. (bet. 5th & 6th Aves.) | 212-463-7890 |
www.periyali.com | Greek

Per Se | *rooms: 2* | *max cap: 60*
W 60s | Time Warner Ctr. | 10 Columbus Circle, 4th fl. (60th St.) |
212-823-9335 | www.perseny.com | French/New American

Picholine | *rooms: 2* | *max cap: 24*
W 60s | 35 W. 64th St. (bet. B'way & CPW) | 212-724-8585 |
www.picholinenyc.com | French/Mediterranean

Pop Burger
rooms: 2 | *max cap: 300*
E 50s | 14 E. 58th St. (bet. 5th & Madison Aves.) | 212-991-6644
rooms: 1 | *cap: 250*
Meatpacking | 58-60 Ninth Ave. (bet. 14th & 15th Sts.) |
212-414-8686
www.popburger.com | American

PARTY SITES - RESTAURANTS

Primavera | *rooms: 1* | *cap: 50*
E 80s | 1578 First Ave. (82nd St.) | 212-861-8608 |
www.primaveranyc.com | Northern Italian

Prune | *rooms: 1* | *cap: 30*
E Village | 54 E. First St. (bet. 1st & 2nd Aves.) | 212-677-6221 |
www.prunerestaurant.com | New American

Public | *rooms: 1* | *cap: 120*
NoLita | 210 Elizabeth St. (bet. Prince & Spring Sts.) | 212-343-7011 |
www.public-nyc.com | Eclectic

Quality Meats | *rooms: 1* | *cap: 40*
W 50s | 57 W. 58th St. (bet. 5th & 6th Aves.) | 212-371-7777 |
www.qualitymeatsnyc.com | New American/Steakhouse

Rainbow Room | *rooms: 7* | *max cap: 600*
E 40s | 30 Rockefeller Plaza (bet. 49th & 50th Sts.) | 212-632-5000 |
www.rainbowroom.com | Continental/Italian

Redeye Grill | *rooms: 3* | *max cap: 400*
W 50s | 890 Seventh Ave. (bet. 56th & 57th Sts.) | 212-265-0100 |
www.thefiremangroup.com | New American/Seafood

Remi | *rooms: 3* | *max cap: 1000*
W 50s | 145 W. 53rd St. (bet. 6th & 7th Aves.) | 212-581-4242 |
Northern Italian

River Café | *rooms: 1* | *cap: 125*
Dumbo | 1 Water St. (bet. Furman & Old Fulton Sts.) | Brooklyn |
718-522-5200 | www.rivercafe.com | American

Rosa Mexicano | *rooms: 2* | *max cap: 300*
W 60s | 61 Columbus Ave. (62nd St.) | 212-977-7700 |
www.rosamexicano.com | Mexican

**Rosie O'Grady's
Manhattan Club** | *rooms: 4* | *max cap: 300*
W 50s | 800 Seventh Ave. (52nd St.) | 212-582-2975 |
www.rosieogradys.com | Italian/Steakhouse

Ruby Foo's
rooms: 1 | *cap: 300*
W 40s | 1626 Broadway (49th St.) | 212-489-5600
rooms: 2 | *max cap: 350*
W 70s | 2182 Broadway (77th St.) | 212-724-6700
www.brguestrestaurants.com | Asian

Shun Lee Palace | *rooms: 1* | *cap: 30*
E 50s | 155 E. 55th St. (bet. Lexington & 3rd Aves.) | 212-371-8844 |
www.shunleepalace.com | Chinese

Smith & Wollensky | *rooms: 4* | *max cap: 200*
E 40s | 201 E. 49th St. (3rd Ave.) | 212-753-1530 |
www.smithandwollensky.com | Steakhouse

Spotted Pig | *rooms: 1* | *cap: 100*
W Village | 314 W. 11th St. (Greenwich St.) | 212-620-0393 |
www.thespottedpig.com | British/Modern European

subscribe to ZAGAT.com

Stanton Social | rooms: 1 | cap: 120
LES | 99 Stanton St. (bet. Ludlow & Orchard Sts.) | 212-995-0099 | www.thestantonsocial.com | Eclectic

SushiSamba
rooms: 3 | max cap: 180
Flatiron | 245 Park Ave. S. (bet. 19th & 20th Sts.) | 212-475-9377
rooms: 3 | max cap: 270
G Village | 87 Seventh Ave. S. (bet. Bleecker & W. 4th Sts.) | 212-691-7885
www.sushisamba.com | Brazilian/Japanese

Tabla | rooms: 2 | max cap: 210
Gramercy | 11 Madison Ave. (25th St.) | 212-889-0667 | www.tablany.com | American/Indian

Taj II | rooms: 2 | max cap: 350
Flatiron | 48 W. 21st St. (bet. 5th & 6th Aves.) | 212-620-3033 | www.tajlounge.com | New American

Tao | rooms: 4 | max cap: 500
E 50s | 42 E. 58th St. (bet. Madison & Park Aves.) | 212-399-3097 | www.taorestaurant.com | Pan-Asian

Tavern on the Green | rooms: 6 | max cap: 2500
W 60s | Central Park W. (bet. 66th & 67th Sts.) | 212-873-4111 | www.tavernonthegreen.com | American

Terrace in the Sky | rooms: 2 | max cap: 450
W 100s | 400 W. 119th St. (bet. Amsterdam Ave. & Morningside Dr.) | 212-666-9490 | www.terraceinthesky.com | French/Mediterranean

Thalassa | rooms: 3 | max cap: 450
TriBeCa | 179 Franklin St. (bet. Greenwich & Hudson Sts.) | 212-941-7661 | www.thalassanyc.com | Greek/Seafood

Tocqueville | rooms: 2 | max cap: 74
Union Sq | 1 E. 15th St. (bet. 5th Ave. & Union Sq. W.) | 212-647-1515 | www.tocquevillerestaurant.com | New American/New French

Trattoria Dell'Arte | rooms: 5 | max cap: 275
W 50s | 900 Seventh Ave. (bet. 56th & 57th Sts.) | 212-245-9800 | www.trattoriadellarte.com | Northern Italian

Tribeca Grill | rooms: 2 | max cap: 160
TriBeCa | 375 Greenwich St. (Franklin St.) | 212-941-3905 | www.myriadrestaurantgroup.com | New American

Twenty Four Fifth | rooms: 1 | cap: 500
G Village | 24 Fifth Ave. (bet. 9th & 10th Sts.) | 212-505-8000 | www.theglaziergroup.com | French

21 Club | rooms: 10 | max cap: 150
W 50s | 21 W. 52nd St. (bet. 5th & 6th Aves.) | 212-582-1400 | www.21club.com | American

Wallsé | rooms: 2 | max cap: 75
G Village | 344 W. 11th St. (Washington St.) | 212-352-2300 | www.wallse.com | Austrian

Water Club | *rooms: 3* | *max cap: 1000*
Murray Hill | 500 E. 30th St. (East River, enter via E. 23rd St.) |
212-545-1155 | www.thewaterclub.com | American

Water's Edge | *rooms: 3* | *max cap: 400*
LIC | 44th Dr. (East River & Vernon Blvd.) | Queens | 718-482-0033 |
www.watersedgenyc.com | New American/Seafood

Zarela | *rooms: 2* | *max cap: 160*
E 50s | 953 Second Ave. (bet. 50th & 51st Sts.) | 212-644-6740 |
www.zarela.com | Mexican

NYC SOURCES INDEXES

Special Features

Listings cover the best in each category and include source names, locations and Quality ratings. ⚡ indicates places with the highest ratings, popularity and importance.

BAGELS & BIALYS

⚡ Absolute Bagels | **W 100s** — 26
Bagel Bob's | **multi.** — 22
Bagel Buffet | **G Vill** — 17
Bagel Hole | **Park Slope** — 22
Bagel Oasis | **Fresh Meadows** — 26
Bagels & Co. | **multi.** — 22
Bagels on Sq. | **G Vill** — 21
Bagelworks | **E 60s** — 23
⚡ Barney Greengrass | **W 80s** — 27
Bergen Bagels | **Boerum Hill** — 22
Corner Bagel | **E 80s** — 22
Corrado | **multi.** — 21
Daniel's Bagels | **Murray Hill** — 24
David's Bagels | **multi.** — 23
East Side Bagel | **E 70s** — 21
⚡ Eli's Manhattan | **E 80s** — 25
Eli's Vinegar | **E 90s** — 25
Ess-a-Bagel | **multi.** — 26
Good & Plenty | **W 40s** — 22
Gourmet Garage | **multi.** — 20
H & H Bagels | **multi.** — 26
⚡ Kossar's | **LES** — 28
La Bagel | **multi.** — 23
Lenny's | **W 90s** — 23
Montague St. | **Bklyn Hts** — 22
Murray's Bagels | **multi.** — 26
Murray's Sturgeon | **W 80s** — 27
Oren's/Roast | **E 50s** — 24
Pick a Bagel | **multi.** — 20
Tal Bagels | **multi.** — 23
Terrace Bagels | **Windsor Terr** — 25
Times Sq. Bagels | **W 40s** — 19
Yonah Schimmel | **LES** — 23
⚡ Zabar's | **W 80s** — 27
NEW Zucker's Bagels | **TriBeCa** — 22

BAKED GOODS

(See also Bagels & Bialys, Cakes & Cupcakes, Cookies, Pies/Tarts)
Addeo Bakery | **Bronx** — 27
⚡ Agata/Valentina | **E 70s** — 26

Ah Wong Bakery | **Chinatown** — 20
⚡ Almondine | **Dumbo** — 28
NEW Amai Tea | **Gramercy** — 20
Amish Market | **multi.** — 23
⚡ Amy's Bread | **multi.** — 26
Andre's | **multi.** — 23
Andrew & Alan's | **SI** — 22
Arte/Corner | **W 70s** — 24
Artuso Pastry | **Bronx** — 26
Au Bon Pain | **multi.** — 16
Baked | **Red Hook** — 25
Baked Ideas | **SoHo** — -
⚡ Balducci's | **W 60s** — 25
Balthazar Bakery | **SoHo** — 27
Barbarini | **Financial** — -
Baskin-Robbins | **multi.** — 17
NEW Batch | **G Vill** — -
Bay Ridge Bake | **Bay Ridge** — 25
⚡ Bazzini | **TriBeCa** — 27
Beard Papa | **multi.** — 24
⚡ Bedford Cheese | **W'burg** — 27
Betty Bakery | **Boerum Hill** — 23
⚡ Bierkraft | **Park Slope** — 28
Bijoux Doux | **Boerum Hill** — -
Billy's Bakery | **Chelsea** — 25
Birdbath/Build Green | **multi.** — 23
⚡ Black Hound | **E Vill** — 26
⚡ Blue Apron | **Park Slope** — 27
⚡ Blue Ribbon Mkt. | **G Vill** — 28
Boerum Hill Food | **Boerum Hill** — 22
Bonsignour | **W Vill** — 26
⚡ Bouchon Bakery | **W 60s** — 27
⚡ Bouley Bakery | **TriBeCa** — 27
Brasil Coffee | **LIC** — 21
Bread Alone | **Boiceville** — 27
Bread Stuy | **Bed-Stuy** — -
Bruno Bakery | **G Vill** — 23
Bruno/Ravioli | **multi.** — 24
Buttercup | **multi.** — 23
Caffé Roma | **L Italy** — 23

Caffe' Simpatico/Ruthy's | **Chelsea**	15
Cake Chef | **SI**	22
Cakeline | **Rockaway Bch**	-
☑ Cake Man | **Ft Greene**	26
Cakes 'N Shapes | **W 50s**	22
Caputo Bakery | **Carroll Gdns**	23
Carrot Top | **Wash. Hts**	23
Carry On Tea | **W Vill**	23
CBK Cookies | **E 80s**	23
Ceci-Cela | **L Italy**	24
Cheeks Bakery | **W'burg**	-
Cheryl Kleinman | **Boerum Hill**	28
NEW ChikaLicious Puddin' | **E Vill**	24
Choc-Oh! | **Bay Ridge**	25
Chocolate Bar | **W 50s**	26
Chocolate Room | **Park Slope**	25
Choice Mkt. | **Clinton Hill**	23
Cipriani | **E 40s**	26
☑ Citarella | **multi.**	26
☑ City Bakery | **Flatiron**	25
Clinton St. | **LES**	26
Cobblestone | **Carroll Gdns**	21
☑ Colette's | **W Vill**	29
Colson | **Park Slope**	25
Confetti | **W 80s**	24
Conn. Muffin | **multi.**	17
Corner Café | **E 90s**	-
Corrado | **multi.**	21
Così | **multi.**	18
Court Pastry | **Cobble Hill**	25
Cousin John's | **Park Slope**	21
Creative Cakes | **E 70s**	25
Crumbs | **multi.**	22
Damascus Bakery | **Bklyn Hts**	25
☑ Dean/DeLuca | **multi.**	27
Delillo Pastry | **Bronx**	26
DeRobertis | **E Vill**	22
☑ Dessert Delivery | **E 50s**	28
Di Fiore Marquet | **G Vill**	-
☑ Doughnut Plant | **LES**	26
Downtown Atlantic | **Boerum Hill**	21
Duane Pk. | **TriBeCa**	26
DUB Pies | **Windsor Terr**	24
☑ E.A.T. | **E 80s**	25

Egg Custard King | **Chinatown**	21
Egidio Pastry | **Bronx**	24
Eileen's Cheesecake | **NoLita**	26
Eleni's Cookies | **Chelsea**	22
☑ Eli's Manhattan | **E 80s**	25
Eli's Vinegar | **E 90s**	25
Fabiane's | **W'burg**	-
☑ Fairway | **multi.**	26
Fat Witch | **Chelsea**	25
Fay Da | **multi.**	19
Ferrara Cafe | **L Italy**	22
Financier | **Financial**	27
Fortunato Bros. | **W'burg**	25
Fraser-Morris | **Carroll Gdns**	26
☑ FreshDirect | **LIC**	23
Friend/Farmer | **Gramercy**	21
Gail Watson | **Garment**	-
Garden | **Greenpt**	24
Garden of Eden | **multi.**	24
Glaser's Bake | **E 80s**	21
Golden Fung | **Chinatown**	18
Good & Plenty | **W 40s**	22
Gourmet Garage | **multi.**	20
Grab Specialty | **Park Slope**	24
Grace's Mktpl. | **E 70s**	24
☑ Grandaisy Bakery | **multi.**	29
☑ Greenmarket | **multi.**	26
Güllüoglu | **Sheepshead**	-
Hot/Crusty | **multi.**	15
NEW How Sweet It Is | **LES**	-
Hungarian Pastry | **W 100s**	22
Insomnia Cookies | **G Vill**	-
Joyce Bake | **Prospect Hts**	25
Junior's | **multi.**	23
Kidfresh | **E 80s**	18
NEW Krumbs | **Clinton Hill**	22
La Bergamote | **Chelsea**	26
☑ Ladybird Bakery | **Park Slope**	28
Lafayette | **G Vill**	21
La Guli | **Astoria**	24
Lassen/Hennigs | **Bklyn Hts**	22
L'Epicerie | **Ft Greene**	22
Leske's | **Bay Ridge**	23
☑ Levain Bakery | **W 70s**	28

Little Cupcake	**Bay Ridge**	21	Pumpkins	**Park Slope**	26
Little Pie	**multi.**	24	☑ Rice/Riches	**NoLita**	23
Little Piggy	**Ft Greene**	–	Rocco's Pastry	**G Vill**	25
Lorenzo/Maria's	**E 80s**	25	Ron Ben-Israel	**SoHo**	25
Lung Moon	**Chinatown**	19	☑ Royal Crown	**multi.**	26
NEW Madeleine	**Chelsea**	24	Ruby/Violette	**W 50s**	26
☑ Madonia Bakery	**Bronx**	28	Sal & Dom's	**Bronx**	28
☑ Magnolia Bakery	**multi.**	23	S&S Cheesecake	**Bronx**	27
Make My Cake	**Harlem**	25	Sarabeth's	**multi.**	24
M & I Foods	**Brighton Bch**	24	Schick's Bakery	**Borough Pk**	20
Mangia	**Flatiron**	24	Settepani	**multi.**	23
Mansoura	**Midwood**	–	Shakoor's Sweet	**Bed-Stuy**	–
Margaret Braun	**W Vill**	–	Silver Moon	**W 100s**	26
Margaret Palca	**Carroll Gdns**	26	Something Sweet	**E Vill**	23
Margot Pâtisserie	**W 70s**	27	☑ Soutine	**W 70s**	27
Marquet Patiss.	**multi.**	24	Steve's/Pies	**Red Hook**	25
Martha's Bakery	**Astoria**	23	☑ Stork's Pastry	**Whitestone**	27
Martin's Pretzels	**Theresa**	27	Streit's Matzo	**LES**	25
Masturbakers	**E Vill**	22	☑ Sugar Sweet	**LES**	27
Max Brenner	**multi.**	22	☑ Sullivan St. Bakery	**W 40s**	28
☑ May May	**Chinatown**	23	Sweet Melissa	**multi.**	24
Mazzola Bakery	**Carroll Gdns**	25	☑ Sylvia Weinstock	**TriBeCa**	26
Milk & Cookies	**W Vill**	24	NEW Tafu	**E 50s**	19
Mona Lisa Pastry	**Bay Ridge**	24	Tai Pan Bakery	**multi.**	19
Mother Mousse	**SI**	26	Tempo Presto	**Park Slope**	23
Mother's Bake	**Bronx**	21	Terranova	**Bronx**	26
Mrs. Field's	**multi.**	18	Three Tarts	**Chelsea**	22
My Most/Food	**W 40s**	21	Tisserie	**Union Sq**	20
Napoli Bakery	**W'burg**	23	☑ Titan Foods	**Astoria**	26
Nusbaum & Wu	**W 100s**	18	Todaro Bros.	**Murray Hill**	24
Once Upon/Tart	**SoHo**	25	Tribeca Treats	**TriBeCa**	27
One Girl	**Cobble Hill**	24	Trois Pommes	**Park Slope**	23
Oriental Pastry	**Bklyn Hts**	22	Trunzo Bros.	**Bensonhurst**	25
NEW Oro Bakery	**L Italy**	–	☑ Two Little Red	**E 80s**	26
Orwasher's	**E 70s**	26	Umanoff/Parsons	**Bronx**	24
Our Daily Bread	**Chatham**	26	Union Market	**Park Slope**	26
Paneantico	**Bay Ridge**	26	NEW Urban Rustic	**W'burg**	–
Pane d'Italia	**Whitestone**	–	Veniero's	**E Vill**	25
Panya Bakery	**E Vill**	22	Vesuvio	**SoHo**	23
Parisi Bakery	**NoLita**	23	☑ Villabate	**Bensonhurst**	28
☑ Patisserie Claude	**G Vill**	27	☑ Vosges	**SoHo**	26
Patisserie des Ambassades	**multi.**	21	Whole Earth	**E Vill**	21
☑ Payard	**E 70s**	28	☑ Whole Foods	**multi.**	26
☑ Petrossian	**W 50s**	28	William Greenberg	**E 80s**	25
Poseidon	**W 40s**	26	Yonah Schimmel	**LES**	23

Zabar's | **W 80s**	27
Zaro's Bread | **multi.**	17
Zeytuna | **Financial**	23

BEER SPECIALISTS

American Beer | **Cobble Hill**	26
Z Bierkraft | **Park Slope**	28
BJ's Wholesale | **multi.**	17
Dual Specialty | **E Vill**	22
Eagle Provisions | **Park Slope**	24
East Coast Beer | **Sunset Pk**	22
Z FreshDirect | **LIC**	23
Garden | **Greenpt**	-
Giant Big Apple | **Woodside**	-
Gourmet Garage | **multi.**	20
Grace's Mktpl. | **E 70s**	24
NEW Greene Grape Provisions | **Ft Greene**	24
New York Bev. | **Bronx**	-
NEW Spuyten/Grocery | **W'burg**	-
Z Whole Foods | **Chelsea**	26

BREAD

Addeo Bakery | **Bronx**	27
Z Amy's Bread | **multi.**	26
Balthazar Bakery | **SoHo**	27
Z Bedford Cheese | **W'burg**	27
Z Blue Apron | **Park Slope**	27
Z Blue Ribbon Mkt. | **G Vill**	28
Z Bouchon Bakery | **W 60s**	27
Z Bouley Bakery | **TriBeCa**	27
Bread Alone | **Boiceville**	27
Bread Stuy | **Bed-Stuy**	-
Caputo Bakery | **Carroll Gdns**	23
Cheeks Bakery | **W'burg**	-
Corrado | **multi.**	21
Damascus Bakery | **Bklyn Hts**	25
Z Dean/DeLuca | **multi.**	27
Z E.A.T. | **E 80s**	25
Z Eli's Manhattan | **E 80s**	25
Eli's Vinegar | **E 90s**	25
Z Fairway | **Red Hook**	26
Grab Specialty | **Park Slope**	24
Z Grandaisy Bakery | **multi.**	29
Z Greenmarket | **multi.**	26
L'Epicerie | **Ft Greene**	22
Leske's | **Bay Ridge**	23

Z Levain Bakery | **W 70s**	28
Z Madonia Bakery | **Bronx**	28
M & I Foods | **Brighton Bch**	24
Mazzola Bakery | **Carroll Gdns**	25
Mother's Bake | **Bronx**	21
Napoli Bakery | **W'burg**	23
Orwasher's | **E 70s**	26
Our Daily Bread | **Chatham**	26
Paneantico | **Bay Ridge**	26
Pane d'Italia | **Whitestone**	-
Panya Bakery | **E Vill**	22
Parisi Bakery | **NoLita**	23
Z Royal Crown | **multi.**	26
Settepani | **multi.**	23
Z Sullivan St. Bakery | **W 40s**	28
Terranova | **Bronx**	26
Trunzo Bros. | **Bensonhurst**	25
Union Market | **Park Slope**	26
Vesuvio | **SoHo**	23
Z Villabate | **Bensonhurst**	28
Z Whole Foods | **multi.**	26

CAKES & CUPCAKES

(See also Wedding Cakes)

Z Agata/Valentina | **E 70s**	26
Ah Wong Bakery | **Chinatown**	20
Z Amy's Bread | **multi.**	26
Andre's | **multi.**	23
Andrew & Alan's | **SI**	22
Artuso Pastry | **Bronx**	26
Z Balducci's | **W 60s**	25
Balthazar Bakery | **SoHo**	27
Baskin-Robbins | **multi.**	17
NEW Batch | **G Vill**	-
Bay Ridge Bake | **Bay Ridge**	25
Betty Bakery | **Boerum Hill**	23
Bijoux Doux | **Boerum Hill**	-
Billy's Bakery | **Chelsea**	25
Z Black Hound | **E Vill**	26
Bread Stuy | **Bed-Stuy**	-
Bruno Bakery | **G Vill**	23
Buttercup | **E 50s**	23
Caffé Roma | **L Italy**	23
Caffe' Simpatico/Ruthy's | **Chelsea**	15
Cake Chef | **SI**	22
Cakeline | **Rockaway Bch**	-

🄩 Cake Man | **Ft Greene**	26
Cakes 'N Shapes | **W 50s**	22
Carrot Top | **Wash. Hts**	23
Ceci-Cela | **L Italy**	24
Cheeks Bakery | **W'burg**	–
Cheryl Kleinman | **Boerum Hill**	28
NEW ChikaLicious Puddin' | **E Vill**	24
Cipriani | **E 40s**	26
🄩 Citarella | **multi.**	26
🄩 Colette's | **W Vill**	29
Confetti | **W 80s**	24
Court Pastry | **Cobble Hill**	25
Creative Cakes | **E 70s**	25
Crumbs | **multi.**	22
🄩 Dean/DeLuca | **multi.**	27
Delillo Pastry | **Bronx**	26
DeRobertis | **E Vill**	22
🄩 Dessert Delivery | **E 50s**	28
Duane Pk. | **TriBeCa**	26
🄩 E.A.T. | **E 80s**	25
Egidio Pastry | **Bronx**	24
Eileen's Cheesecake | **NoLita**	26
🄩 Eli's Manhattan | **E 80s**	25
Eli's Vinegar | **E 90s**	25
Fabiane's | **W'burg**	–
Ferrara Cafe | **L Italy**	22
Financier | **Financial**	27
Gail Watson | **Garment**	–
Glaser's Bake | **E 80s**	21
Grace's Mktpl. | **E 70s**	24
NEW How Sweet It Is | **LES**	–
Hungarian Pastry | **W 100s**	22
Joyce Bake | **Prospect Hts**	25
NEW Krumbs | **Clinton Hill**	22
La Bergamote | **Chelsea**	26
🄩 Ladybird Bakery | **Park Slope**	28
Lafayette | **G Vill**	21
Little Cupcake | **Bay Ridge**	21
Little Pie | **multi.**	24
Lung Moon | **Chinatown**	19
NEW Madeleine | **Chelsea**	24
🄩 Magnolia Bakery | **W 60s**	23
Make My Cake | **Harlem**	25
Margaret Braun | **W Vill**	–

Margaret Palca | **Carroll Gdns**	26
Margot Pâtisserie | **W 70s**	27
Marquet Patiss. | **Ft Greene**	24
Martha's Bakery | **Astoria**	23
Masturbakers | **E Vill**	22
Monteleone's | **Carroll Gdns**	23
Mother Mousse | **SI**	26
Mother's Bake | **Bronx**	21
My Most/Food | **W 40s**	21
NEW Oro Bakery | **L Italy**	–
Paneantico | **Bay Ridge**	26
Panya Bakery | **E Vill**	22
🄩 Patisserie Claude | **G Vill**	27
🄩 Payard | **E 70s**	28
Rocco's Pastry | **G Vill**	25
Ron Ben-Israel | **SoHo**	25
🄩 Royal Crown | **multi.**	26
Sal & Dom's | **Bronx**	28
S&S Cheesecake | **Bronx**	27
Sarabeth's | **multi.**	24
Schick's Bakery | **Borough Pk**	20
Settepani | **multi.**	23
Shakoor's Sweet | **Bed-Stuy**	–
Silver Moon | **W 100s**	26
Something Sweet | **E Vill**	23
🄩 Soutine | **W 70s**	27
🄩 Stork's Pastry | **Whitestone**	27
🄩 Sugar Sweet | **LES**	27
Sweet Melissa | **multi.**	24
🄩 Sylvia Weinstock | **TriBeCa**	26
Tai Pan Bakery | **multi.**	19
Tempo Presto | **Park Slope**	23
Tisserie | **Union Sq**	20
Tribeca Treats | **TriBeCa**	27
🄩 Two Little Red | **E 80s**	26
Veniero's | **E Vill**	25
🄩 Villabate | **Bensonhurst**	28
🄩 Vosges | **SoHo**	26
Whole Earth | **E Vill**	21
🄩 Whole Foods | **multi.**	26
William Greenberg | **E 80s**	25
🄩 Zabar's | **W 80s**	27

CANDY & NUTS

Aji Ichiban | **multi.**	21
Andrew & Alan's | **SI**	22

Australian Home. | **multi.**	23
Z Balducci's | **W 60s**	25
Z Bazzini | **TriBeCa**	27
Z Bierkraft | **Park Slope**	28
Z Black Hound | **E Vill**	26
Z Blue Apron | **Park Slope**	27
Bruno Bakery | **G Vill**	23
Charbonnel/Walker | **E 40s**	22
Chelsea Baskets | **Chelsea**	24
Choc-Oh! | **Bay Ridge**	25
Chocolate Bar | **W 50s**	26
Chocolate Girl | **Park Slope**	23
Chocolate Room | **Park Slope**	25
Chocolat Moderne | **Chelsea**	26
Christopher Norman | **Financial**	23
Z Citarella | **multi.**	26
Cocoa Bar | **multi.**	26
Z Dean/DeLuca | **multi.**	27
Debauve/Gallais | **E 60s**	27
Z Divalicious | **L Italy**	24
Z Dylan's Candy | **E 60s**	21
Economy Candy | **LES**	24
Eggers Ice Cream | **SI**	25
Z Eli's Manhattan | **E 80s**	25
Eli's Vinegar | **E 90s**	25
Evelyn's Choc. | **Financial**	25
Z Fairway | **Red Hook**	26
Fifth Ave. Choc. | **multi.**	20
Z FreshDirect | **LIC**	23
Godiva | **multi.**	22
Grab Specialty | **Park Slope**	24
Gustiamo | **Bronx**	23
Hershey's | **W 40s**	18
Hinsch's | **Bay Ridge**	22
Z Jacques Torres | **multi.**	28
JoMart Choc. | **Marine Pk**	24
Z Kalustyan's | **Gramercy**	27
Z Kee's Choc. | **SoHo**	29
Z La Maison/Choc. | **multi.**	29
Lee Sims Choc. | **SI**	25
Leonidas | **multi.**	26
L'Epicerie | **Ft Greene**	22
Li-Lac Choc. | **multi.**	26
Lindt | **multi.**	24
Z Manhattan Fruitier | **Gramercy**	27

Z MarieBelle's | **multi.**	26
Z Martine's | **multi.**	29
Mazal Kosher | **Flushing**	17
Z Minamoto | **W 40s**	28
Mondel Choc. | **W 100s**	22
m2m | **E Vill**	18
Neuchatel Choc. | **E 50s**	24
Neuhaus Choc. | **multi.**	25
NEW Papabubble | **L Italy**	24
Z Payard | **E 70s**	28
Z Petrossian | **W 50s**	28
Philip's Candy | **SI**	–
Z Pierre Marcolini | **E 50s**	28
NEW Roni-Sue's | **LES**	23
Z Russ & Daughters | **LES**	28
Z Sahadi's | **Bklyn Hts**	27
Scharffen Berger | **W 80s**	26
NEW Spuyten/Grocery | **W'burg**	–
Z Stork's Pastry | **Whitestone**	27
Superior Choc. | **SI**	22
Sweet Melissa | **multi.**	24
Z Teuscher Choc. | **E 40s**	27
Z Trader Joe's | **Rego Pk**	24
Tribeca Treats | **TriBeCa**	27
Varsano's | **G Vill**	26
Vere | **Flatiron**	29
Z Vosges | **multi.**	26
Z Whole Foods | **multi.**	26
World of Nuts | **multi.**	15
Z Zabar's | **W 80s**	27

CARRIAGE TRADE

Z Abigail Kirsch | **multi.**	26
Acker Merrall | **W 70s**	26
Z Agata/Valentina | **E 70s**	26
Z Alessi | **SoHo**	27
Z Balducci's | **W 60s**	25
Z Belle Fleur | **Flatiron**	28
Butterfield Mkt. | **E 70s**	23
Cakeline | **Rockaway Bch**	–
Castle/Pierpont | **Garment**	24
Caviar Russe | **E 50s**	26
CBK Cookies | **E 80s**	23
Z Citarella | **multi.**	26
Z Dean/DeLuca | **multi.**	27
Debauve/Gallais | **E 60s**	27

Ẑ Eli's Manhattan | **E 80s**	25
Eli's Vinegar | **E 90s**	25
Feast/Fêtes | **E 60s**	27
Fellan Florist | **E 60s**	24
Ẑ Glorious Food | **E 70s**	25
Grace's Mktpl. | **E 70s**	24
Holland Ct. | **E 90s**	24
Ẑ Ito En | **E 60s**	28
Jane Packer | **E 50s**	29
Ẑ Lady M | **E 70s**	28
Ẑ La Maison/Choc. | **multi.**	29
Ẑ Lobel's Meats | **E 80s**	29
L'Olivier | **E 70s**	29
Lorenzo/Maria's | **E 80s**	25
Ẑ Manhattan Fruitier | **Gramercy**	27
Marché Madison | **multi.**	20
Margaret Braun | **W Vill**	-
Ẑ MarieBelle's | **SoHo**	26
Miho Kosuda | **E 40s**	-
Ẑ Morrell & Co. | **W 40s**	27
New York/Warehse. | **LIC**	23
O&CO. | **multi.**	25
Ẑ Payard | **E 70s**	28
Ẑ Petrossian | **W 50s**	28
Ẑ Pierre Marcolini | **E 50s**	28
Renny/Reed | **E 50s**	28
Richard Salome | **E 70s**	-
Robert Isabell | **Meatpacking**	27
Ronaldo Maia | **E 90s**	28
Ron Ben-Israel | **SoHo**	25
Ẑ Sherry-Lehmann | **E 60s**	29
Susan Holland | **Flatiron**	-
Ẑ Sylvia Weinstock | **TriBeCa**	26
Ẑ Takashimaya | **E 50s**	28
Tea Box | **E 50s**	27
Ẑ Teuscher Choc. | **multi.**	27
Ẑ Vosges | **SoHo**	26
Wild Edibles | **E 40s**	26
William Greenberg | **E 80s**	25
Ẑ William Poll | **E 70s**	26

CATERERS

(See also Event Planners and Office Catering)

Ẑ Abigail Kirsch | **multi.**	26
Ẑ Agata/Valentina | **E 70s**	26

Areo Rist. | **Bay Ridge**	21
Artie's Deli | **W 80s**	21
Ben's Kosher | **multi.**	21
Between/Bread | **W 50s**	21
Blue Smoke | **Gramercy**	25
Boerum Hill Food | **Boerum Hill**	22
Bottega/Via | **E 70s**	25
Butterfield Mkt. | **E 70s**	23
Caffe' Simpatico/Ruthy's | **Chelsea**	15
Callahan | **Garment**	-
Call Cuisine | **E 50s**	24
Ẑ Carnegie Deli | **W 50s**	23
Carol's Cafe | **SI**	-
Carve | **W 40s**	23
Catering/Rest. Assoc. | **Garment**	20
Catering Co. | **Chelsea**	-
Ceriello | **multi.**	24
Certé | **W 50s**	26
Charles/Sally | **Park Slope**	25
Chef & Co. | **Flatiron**	25
Ẑ Citarella | **multi.**	26
Ẑ City Bakery | **Flatiron**	25
Ẑ Cleaver Co. | **Chelsea**	25
Creative Edge | **W Vill**	25
Cucina | **E 40s**	21
Cucina Vivolo | **E 70s**	23
David Burke | **E 50s**	23
David Ziff | **E 90s**	22
Ẑ Dean/DeLuca | **multi.**	27
Deli Masters | **Fresh Meadows**	21
Delmonico | **multi.**	21
Devon/Blakely | **multi.**	22
Dishes | **E 40s**	24
Durso's Pasta | **Flushing**	26
Ẑ E.A.T. | **E 80s**	25
Eli's Vinegar | **E 90s**	25
Ẑ Fairway | **Red Hook**	26
Family Store | **Bay Ridge**	-
F&B | **Chelsea**	20
Feast/Fêtes | **E 60s**	27
Financier | **Financial**	27
Fine/Schapiro | **W 70s**	20
Food/Thought | **Chelsea**	21
Fraser-Morris | **Carroll Gdns**	26

subscribe to ZAGAT.com

Fresco/Scotto | **E 50s**	24
Garden of Eden | **multi.**	24
Good & Plenty | **W 40s**	22
Grace's Mktpl. | **E 70s**	24
Great Performances | **SoHo**	24
Iavarone Bros. | **Maspeth**	25
Indiana Mkt. | **Garment**	26
Italian Food | **L Italy**	22
∅ Jeffrey's | **LES**	25
∅ Katz's Deli | **LES**	24
Lassen/Hennigs | **Bklyn Hts**	22
Lorenzo/Maria's | **E 80s**	25
Luscious Food | **Park Slope**	19
Manganaro Foods | **Garment**	24
Mangia | **multi.**	24
Mansoura | **Midwood**	-
Mazur's | **Douglaston**	20
Miss Elisabeth's | **E Vill**	-
Movable Feast | **Park Slope**	23
Nordic Delicacies | **Bay Ridge**	28
Olivier Cheng | **TriBeCa**	22
Patisserie des Ambassades | **multi.**	21
∅ Payard | **E 70s**	28
Petak's | **E 80s**	23
Peter's Mkt. | **Bayside**	22
Pret A Manger | **multi.**	21
Ready to Eat | **W Vill**	21
Remi | **W 50s**	26
Risotteria | **G Vill**	23
Robbins Wolfe | **Meatpacking**	26
Russo Mozzarella | **Park Slope**	26
Sandwich Planet | **Garment**	25
Sebastians | **E 50s**	-
Second Helpings | **Park Slope**	-
Shakoor's Sweet | **Bed-Stuy**	-
Snack | **SoHo**	27
Special Attention | **LES**	-
Spoonbread | **Harlem**	23
Starwich | **multi.**	23
Susan Holland | **Flatiron**	-
Taste Caterers | **W Vill**	22
Tastings/Payard | **E 70s**	27
Thomas Preti | **Murray Hill**	23
Trunzo Bros. | **Bensonhurst**	25
∅ Whole Foods | **multi.**	26

Wild Edibles | **multi.**	26
∅ William Poll | **E 70s**	26
Williamson Cal. | **Prospect Hts**	-
Zeytuna | **Financial**	23

CAVIAR & SMOKED FISH

Acme Fish | **Greenpt**	24
∅ Agata/Valentina | **E 70s**	26
∅ Balducci's | **W 60s**	25
∅ Barney Greengrass | **W 80s**	27
∅ Blue Apron | **Park Slope**	27
Blue Moon Fish | **Mattituck**	29
Caviar Russe | **E 50s**	26
∅ Citarella | **multi.**	26
∅ Dean/DeLuca | **multi.**	27
∅ E.A.T. | **E 80s**	25
∅ Eli's Manhattan | **E 80s**	25
Eli's Vinegar | **E 90s**	25
∅ Fairway | **multi.**	26
∅ FreshDirect | **LIC**	23
Grace's Mktpl. | **E 70s**	24
Gustiamo | **Bronx**	23
Leonard's | **E 70s**	26
M & I Foods | **Brighton Bch**	24
Murray's Sturgeon | **W 80s**	27
Orchard | **Midwood**	27
Paramount Caviar | **LIC**	27
∅ Petrossian | **W 50s**	28
∅ Russ & Daughters | **LES**	28
Sable's Smoked | **E 70s**	27
Todaro Bros. | **Murray Hill**	24
∅ Trader Joe's | **Rego Pk**	24
Truffette | **E Vill**	-
Union Market | **Park Slope**	26
NEW Urban Rustic | **W'burg**	-
∅ Whole Foods | **multi.**	26
Wild Edibles | **multi.**	26
∅ William Poll | **E 70s**	26
∅ Zabar's | **W 80s**	27
Zeytuna | **Financial**	23
NEW Zucker's Bagels | **TriBeCa**	22

CHARCUTERIE

∅ Agata/Valentina | **E 70s**	26
∅ Balducci's | **W 60s**	25
Bari Pork | **multi.**	24

☑ Bedford Cheese | W'burg	27
Belfiore Meats | SI	25
☑ Blue Apron | Park Slope	27
BuonItalia | Chelsea	26
☑ Calabria Pork | Bronx	28
Ceriello | multi.	24
Cheese/World | Forest Hills	25
Christos Steak | Astoria	23
☑ Citarella | multi.	26
☑ Dean/DeLuca | multi.	27
☑ Despaña | multi.	27
☑ DiPalo Dairy | L Italy	29
Durso's Pasta | Flushing	26
Eagle Provisions | Park Slope	24
☑ East Vill. Meat | E Vill	28
☑ Eli's Manhattan | E 80s	25
Eli's Vinegar | E 90s	25
Empire Market | College Pt	16
Esposito Meat | Garment	25
Esposito's Pork | Carroll Gdns	26
☑ Faicco's Pork | multi.	28
☑ Fairway | multi.	26
Foragers Mkt. | Dumbo	22
Formaggio Essex | LES	26
Grab Specialty | Park Slope	24
Grace's Mktpl. | E 70s	24
Heights Meats | Bklyn Hts	24
Iavarone Bros. | multi.	25
Italian Food | L Italy	22
Koglin Hams | E 40s	24
L'Epicerie | Ft Greene	22
Les Halles | Gramercy	26
☑ Murray's Cheese | G Vill	28
☑ Ottomanelli & Sons | multi.	27
Ottomanelli Bros. | multi.	24
☑ Ottomanelli's Meats | Flushing	27
Peter's Mkt. | Bayside	22
☑ Petrossian | W 50s	28
Piazza Mercato | Bay Ridge	23
☑ Salumeria | Chelsea	29
☑ Schaller/Weber | E 80s	27
☑ Simchick | E 50s	28
Stinky Bklyn | Cobble Hill	28
Todaro Bros. | Murray Hill	24
Trunzo Bros. | Bensonhurst	25

United Meat | Windsor Terr	26
NEW Urban Rustic | W'burg	-
☑ Whole Foods | multi.	26
Yorkville Meat | E 80s	23
☑ Zabar's | W 80s	27
Zeytuna | Financial	23

CHEESE & DAIRY

☑ Agata/Valentina | E 70s	26
Albert & Sons | E 60s	26
Alleva Dairy | L Italy	27
Amish Market | multi.	23
☑ Artisanal | multi.	28
☑ Balducci's | W 60s	25
☑ Bazzini | TriBeCa	27
☑ Bedford Cheese | W'burg	27
☑ Bierkraft | Park Slope	28
☑ Blue Apron | Park Slope	27
☑ Blue Ribbon Mkt. | G Vill	28
BuonItalia | Chelsea	26
Butterfield Mkt. | E 70s	23
Calandra Cheese | Bronx	26
Casa Della | Bronx	29
Cheese/World | Forest Hills	25
☑ Citarella | multi.	26
Cobblestone | Carroll Gdns	21
☑ Coluccio/Sons | Borough Pk	28
Commodities Mkt. | E Vill	25
Costco | multi.	21
☑ D'Amico | Carroll Gdns	27
☑ Dean/DeLuca | multi.	27
☑ Despaña | multi.	27
☑ DiPalo Dairy | L Italy	29
Durso's Pasta | Flushing	26
☑ D'Vine | Park Slope	25
East Vill. Cheese | E Vill	22
☑ E.A.T. | E 80s	25
☑ Eli's Manhattan | E 80s	25
Eli's Vinegar | E 90s	25
☑ Fairway | multi.	26
Foragers Mkt. | Dumbo	22
Formaggio Essex | LES	26
☑ FreshDirect | LIC	23
Garden of Eden | multi.	24
Gourmet Garage | multi.	20
Grab Specialty | Park Slope	24

Grace's Mktpl. | **E 70s**	24
Z Greenmarket | **multi.**	26
Gustiamo | **Bronx**	23
Hawthorne Farm | **Ghent**	28
Iavarone Bros. | **Maspeth**	25
Ideal Cheese | **E 50s**	27
Italian Food | **L Italy**	22
Jefferson Mkt. | **G Vill**	26
Z Joe's Dairy | **SoHo**	28
Lamarca | **Gramercy**	26
L'Epicerie | **Ft Greene**	22
Lioni Latticini | **Bensonhurst**	29
M & I Foods | **Brighton Bch**	24
Maya Schaper | **W 60s**	22
Mediterranean | **Astoria**	26
Z Murray's Cheese | **multi.**	28
Ninth Ave. Int'l | **W 40s**	23
Nordic Delicacies | **Bay Ridge**	28
Z Pastosa Ravioli | **multi.**	26
Peter's Mkt. | **Bayside**	22
Piazza Mercato | **Bay Ridge**	23
Pumpkins | **Park Slope**	26
Z Ronnybrook | **Chelsea**	28
Russo Mozzarella | **multi.**	26
Z Sahadi's | **Bklyn Hts**	27
Saxelby Cheese | **LES**	28
Z Staubitz Mkt. | **Cobble Hill**	29
Stinky Bklyn | **Cobble Hill**	28
3-Corner Farm | **Shushan**	27
Z Titan Foods | **Astoria**	26
Todaro Bros. | **Murray Hill**	24
Z Trader Joe's | **multi.**	24
Trunzo Bros. | **Bensonhurst**	25
Union Market | **Park Slope**	26
United Meat | **Windsor Terr**	26
NEW Urban Rustic | **W'burg**	-
Westside Mkt. | **multi.**	21
Z Whole Foods | **multi.**	26
Yoghurt Place | **multi.**	23
Z Zabar's | **W 80s**	27
Zeytuna | **Financial**	23

CLASSES

(Call for details)

Z Alessi | **SoHo**	27
Z Artisanal | **multi.**	28

Astor Wines | **NoHo**	25
Z Balducci's | **Chelsea**	25
Bloomingdale's | **E 50s**	24
Brooklyn Kitchen | **W'burg**	23
Bruno Bakery | **G Vill**	23
Carol's Cafe | **SI**	-
CBK Cookies | **E 80s**	26
Choc-Oh! | **Bay Ridge**	25
Z Colette's | **W Vill**	29
Confetti | **W 80s**	24
Garden of Eden | **Bklyn Hts**	24
Gourmet Garage | **W 90s**	20
JoMart Choc. | **Marine Pk**	24
Kidfresh | **E 80s**	18
Make My Cake | **Harlem**	25
Margaret Palca | **Carroll Gdns**	26
Z Moore Bros. | **Flatiron**	29
One Girl | **Cobble Hill**	24
Pumpkins | **Park Slope**	26
Stinky Bklyn | **Cobble Hill**	28
Z Sullivan St. Bakery | **W 40s**	28
Sur La Table | **SoHo**	26

COFFEE & TEA

Z **NEW** Abraço Espresso | **E Vill**	27
Z Agata/Valentina | **E 70s**	26
Z Alessi | **SoHo**	27
Alice's Tea | **multi.**	24
NEW Amai Tea | **Gramercy**	20
Amish Market | **multi.**	23
Z Balducci's | **W 60s**	25
Z Bazzini | **TriBeCa**	27
Bell Bates | **TriBeCa**	24
Z Blue Apron | **Park Slope**	27
NEW Blue Marble | **multi.**	24
Boerum Hill Food | **Boerum Hill**	22
Z Bouchon Bakery | **W 60s**	27
Brasil Coffee | **multi.**	21
BuonItalia | **Chelsea**	26
Café Grumpy | **multi.**	26
Cafe Regular | **Park Slope**	24
Carry On Tea | **W Vill**	23
Chelsea Baskets | **Chelsea**	24
Chocolate Bar | **W 50s**	26
Z Citarella | **multi.**	26

Cocoa Bar | **multi.**	26
Conn. Muffin | **multi.**	17
☑ D'Amico | **Carroll Gdns**	27
☑ Dean/DeLuca | **multi.**	27
Dual Specialty | **E Vill**	22
Dynasty Supermkt. | **Chinatown**	19
NEW El Beit | **W'burg**	–
☑ Eli's Manhattan | **E 80s**	25
Eli's Vinegar | **E 90s**	25
Empire Coffee | **W 40s**	23
☑ Fairway | **multi.**	26
Family Store | **Bay Ridge**	–
Fika | **W 50s**	22
Franchia | **Murray Hill**	24
☑ FreshDirect | **LIC**	23
Gimme! Coffee | **multi.**	27
Gorilla Coffee | **Park Slope**	24
Gourmet Garage | **multi.**	20
Gustiamo | **Bronx**	23
Guy/Gallard | **multi.**	20
Harlem Tea | **Harlem**	25
Hungarian Pastry | **W 100s**	22
Iavarone Bros. | **MiddlE Vill**	25
Irving Farm/71 | **multi.**	22
☑ Ito En | **E 60s**	28
☑ Jack's Stir Brew | **G Vill**	27
Java Girl | **E 60s**	24
Jefferson Mkt. | **G Vill**	26
Joe | **multi.**	26
Joyce Bake | **Prospect Hts**	25
Juan Valdez | **multi.**	22
☑ Kalustyan's | **Gramercy**	27
Katagiri | **E 50s**	23
Klatch Coffee | **Financial**	21
Leaf/Bean | **Park Slope**	23
Le Pain Quotidien | **W 70s**	24
L'Epicerie | **Ft Greene**	22
Manhattan Espresso | **E 40s**	21
McNulty's Tea | **W Vill**	27
NEW Mercury Dime | **E Vill**	–
Mudspot | **E Vill**	26
Myers/Keswick | **W Vill**	23
Naidre's | **multi.**	22
☑ Nespresso | **E 60s**	25
Ninth Ave. Int'l | **W 40s**	23

Ninth St. Espresso | **multi.**	28
NEW Öko | **Park Slope**	24
Oslo Coffee | **W'burg**	20
Ozzie's Coffee | **Park Slope**	19
Paneantico | **Bay Ridge**	26
Porto Rico | **multi.**	26
Roasting Plant | **LES**	22
Rohrs | **E 80s**	24
NEW Root Hill | **Park Slope**	–
☑ Sahadi's | **Bklyn Hts**	27
Sensuous Bean | **W 70s**	25
Starbucks | **multi.**	18
Subtle Tea | **Murray Hill**	23
NEW Tafu | **E 50s**	19
Tamarind Tea | **Flatiron**	24
Tarallucci e Vino | **multi.**	24
Tea Box | **E 50s**	27
Tea Lounge | **multi.**	21
☑ Ten Ren Tea | **multi.**	25
Think Coffee | **multi.**	23
Tisserie | **SoHo**	20
Todaro Bros. | **Murray Hill**	24
☑ Trader Joe's | **Rego Pk**	24
☑ Two for the Pot | **Bklyn Hts**	27
Union Market | **Park Slope**	26
☑ Whole Foods | **multi.**	26
☑ Zabar's | **W 80s**	27
Zeytuna | **Financial**	23
Zibetto Espresso | **W 50s**	26

COOKIES

☑ Agata/Valentina | **E 70s**	26
NEW Amai Tea | **Gramercy**	20
☑ Amy's Bread | **multi.**	26
Andre's | **multi.**	23
Andrew & Alan's | **SI**	22
Baked Ideas | **SoHo**	–
☑ Balducci's | **W 60s**	25
Balthazar Bakery | **SoHo**	27
NEW Batch | **G Vill**	–
Betty Bakery | **Boerum Hill**	23
Bijoux Doux | **Boerum Hill**	–
☑ Black Hound | **E Vill**	26
☑ Bouchon Bakery | **W 60s**	27
Bread Alone | **Boiceville**	27
Bruno Bakery | **G Vill**	23

Caffé Roma | **L Italy** — 23

Caffe' Simpatico/Ruthy's | **Chelsea** — 15

Cake Chef | **SI** — 22

🄩 Cake Man | **Ft Greene** — 26

Carry On Tea | **W Vill** — 23

CBK Cookies | **E 80s** — 23

Ceci-Cela | **L Italy** — 24

Cheeks Bakery | **W'burg** — -

Choc-Oh! | **Bay Ridge** — 25

🄩 Citarella | **multi.** — 26

🄩 City Bakery | **Flatiron** — 25

Court Pastry | **Cobble Hill** — 25

Crumbs | **multi.** — 22

🄩 Dean/DeLuca | **multi.** — 27

Delillo Pastry | **Bronx** — 26

DeRobertis | **E Vill** — 22

🄩 Dessert Delivery | **E 50s** — 28

Duane Pk. | **TriBeCa** — 26

🄩 E.A.T. | **E 80s** — 25

Eleni's Cookies | **Chelsea** — 22

🄩 Eli's Manhattan | **E 80s** — 25

Eli's Vinegar | **E 90s** — 25

Ferrara Cafe | **L Italy** — 22

Financier | **Financial** — 27

Fortunato Bros. | **W'burg** — 25

Good & Plenty | **W 40s** — 22

Grace's Mktpl. | **E 70s** — 24

Hungarian Pastry | **W 100s** — 22

Insomnia Cookies | **G Vill** — -

Joyce Bake | **Prospect Hts** — 25

La Bergamote | **Chelsea** — 26

🄩 Ladybird Bakery | **Park Slope** — 28

Leske's | **Bay Ridge** — 23

🄩 Levain Bakery | **W 70s** — 28

Little Pie | **multi.** — 24

NEW Madeleine | **Chelsea** — 24

🄩 Madonia Bakery | **Bronx** — 28

🄩 Magnolia Bakery | **W Vill** — 23

Mansoura | **Midwood** — -

Margaret Palca | **Carroll Gdns** — 26

Margot Pâtisserie | **W 70s** — 27

Milk & Cookies | **W Vill** — 24

Monteleone's | **Carroll Gdns** — 23

Mother Mousse | **SI** — 26

Mother's Bake | **Bronx** — 21

Mrs. Field's | **multi.** — 18

My Most/Food | **W 40s** — 21

Nusbaum & Wu | **W 100s** — 18

One Girl | **Cobble Hill** — 24

NEW Oro Bakery | **L Italy** — -

Panya Bakery | **E Vill** — 22

🄩 Patisserie Claude | **G Vill** — 27

🄩 Payard | **E 70s** — 28

Rocco's Pastry | **G Vill** — 25

Ruby/Violette | **W 50s** — 26

Sal & Dom's | **Bronx** — 28

Sarabeth's | **multi.** — 24

Schick's Bakery | **Borough Pk** — 20

Settepani | **multi.** — 23

Silver Moon | **W 100s** — 26

Something Sweet | **E Vill** — 23

🄩 Soutine | **W 70s** — 27

🄩 Stork's Pastry | **Whitestone** — 27

Sweet Melissa | **multi.** — 24

Todaro Bros. | **Murray Hill** — 24

🄩 Two Little Red | **E 80s** — 26

Veniero's | **E Vill** — 25

Whole Earth | **E Vill** — 21

🄩 Whole Foods | **multi.** — 26

William Greenberg | **E 80s** — 25

COOKWARE & SUPPLIES

🄩 Alessi | **SoHo** — 27

NEW applewares | **Park Slope** — 24

Bed Bath/Beyond | **multi.** — 20

BJ's Wholesale | **multi.** — 17

Bloomingdale's | **E 50s** — 24

Bowery Kitchen | **Chelsea** — 22

Broadway Pan. | **G Vill** — 26

Brooklyn Kitchen | **W'burg** — 23

Choc-Oh! | **Bay Ridge** — 25

Cook's Companion | **Bklyn Hts** — 26

Costco | **Sunset Pk** — 21

Crate/Barrel | **multi.** — 22

🄩 Dean/DeLuca | **SoHo** — 27

Gracious Home | **multi.** — 25

Hung Chong | **Chinatown** — 19

Kam Man | **Chinatown** — 21

🄩 Korin | **TriBeCa** — 28

Macy's Cellar | **Garment** — 21

Maya Schaper | **W 60s**	22
O&CO. | **G Vill**	25
S. Feldman | **E 90s**	23
Sunrise Mart | **E Vill**	23
Sur La Table | **SoHo**	26
Target | **multi.**	17
Tarzian West | **Park Slope**	22
Z Terence Conran | **E 50s**	25
Z Williams-Sonoma | **multi.**	27

DELIS & SANDWICHES

Z Agata/Valentina | **E 70s**	26
Z Amy's Bread | **multi.**	26
Artie's Deli | **W 80s**	21
Baked | **Red Hook**	25
Z Balducci's | **W 60s**	25
Bánh Mì Saigon | **Chinatown**	25
Barbarini | **Financial**	-
Belfiore Meats | **SI**	25
Bell Bates | **TriBeCa**	24
Ben's Best | **Rego Pk**	23
Ben's Kosher | **multi.**	21
Berger's | **Murray Hill**	21
Between/Bread | **W 50s**	21
Z Bierkraft | **Park Slope**	28
Bottega/Via | **E 70s**	25
Bottino | **Chelsea**	22
Z Bouchon Bakery | **W 60s**	27
Z Bouley Bakery | **TriBeCa**	27
Bread Stuy | **Bed-Stuy**	-
BuonItalia | **Chelsea**	26
Butterfield Mkt. | **E 70s**	23
Café Habana | **NoLita**	24
Call Cuisine | **E 50s**	24
Z Carnegie Deli | **W 50s**	23
Carve | **W 40s**	23
Choice Mkt. | **Clinton Hill**	23
Colson | **Park Slope**	25
Così | **multi.**	18
Z D'Amico | **Carroll Gdns**	27
Deli Masters | **Fresh Meadows**	21
Delmonico | **multi.**	21
Z D'Vine | **Park Slope**	25
Eagle Provisions | **Park Slope**	24
Z E.A.T. | **E 80s**	25
Eisenberg's Sandwich | **Flatiron**	20

Z Eli's Manhattan | **E 80s**	25
Eli's Vinegar | **E 90s**	25
Esposito's Pork | **Carroll Gdns**	26
Z Fairway | **Red Hook**	26
Fika | **W 50s**	22
Financier | **Financial**	27
Fine/Schapiro | **W 70s**	20
Foragers Mkt. | **Dumbo**	22
Fraser-Morris | **Carroll Gdns**	26
Fresco/Scotto | **E 50s**	24
NEW Friedman's Deli | **Chelsea**	21
Garden of Eden | **multi.**	24
Good & Plenty | **W 40s**	22
Grace's Mktpl. | **E 70s**	24
Z Grandaisy Bakery | **SoHo**	29
Guy/Gallard | **multi.**	20
Health Nuts | **multi.**	21
Heights Meats | **Bklyn Hts**	24
Iavarone Bros. | **Maspeth**	25
Italian Food | **L Italy**	22
Z Kalustyan's | **Gramercy**	27
Z Katz's Deli | **LES**	24
Lassen/Hennigs | **Bklyn Hts**	22
Le Pain Quotidien | **multi.**	24
L'Epicerie | **Ft Greene**	22
Lioni Latticini | **Bensonhurst**	29
Little Piggy | **Ft Greene**	-
Manganaro Foods | **Garment**	24
Manganaro's Hero | **Garment**	21
Mangia | **multi.**	24
Milano Gourmet | **multi.**	25
Z Murray's Cheese | **G Vill**	28
Naidre's | **multi.**	22
Nicky's Viet. | **multi.**	24
Z Olive's | **SoHo**	25
Paneantico | **Bay Ridge**	26
NEW Papa Lima | **W'burg**	-
NEW Paradou Marché | **LES**	21
Parisi Bakery | **NoLita**	23
Pastrami Queen | **E 70s**	21
Petak's | **E 80s**	23
Peter's Mkt. | **Bayside**	22
P.J. Bernstein | **E 70s**	19
Press 195 | **multi.**	25
Pret A Manger | **multi.**	21

Russo Mozzarella | **Park Slope**	26
☑ Salumeria | **Chelsea**	29
Sandwich Planet | **Garment**	25
Sarge's Deli | **Murray Hill**	21
Silver Moon | **W 100s**	26
sNice | **multi.**	23
Starwich | **multi.**	23
Swich | **Chelsea**	23
Tempo Presto | **Park Slope**	23
Todaro Bros. | **Murray Hill**	24
Trunzo Bros. | **Bensonhurst**	25
NEW Urban Rustic | **W'burg**	-
Viet-Nam Bánh | **Chinatown**	23
☑ Whole Foods | **LES**	26
'wichcraft | **multi.**	24
☑ William Poll | **E 70s**	26
☑ Zabar's | **W 80s**	27
Zeytuna | **Financial**	23

DRIED FRUIT

Aji Ichiban | **multi.**	21
☑ Balducci's | **W 60s**	25
☑ Bazzini | **TriBeCa**	27
Bell Bates | **TriBeCa**	24
☑ Citarella | **multi.**	26
Commodities Mkt. | **E Vill**	25
☑ Dean/DeLuca | **multi.**	27
Dual Specialty | **E Vill**	22
☑ D'Vine | **Park Slope**	25
Economy Candy | **LES**	24
☑ Eli's Manhattan | **E 80s**	25
Eli's Vinegar | **E 90s**	25
☑ Fairway | **Red Hook**	26
Gourmet Garage | **multi.**	20
Greenwich Produce | **E 40s**	25
Gustiamo | **Bronx**	23
☑ Kalustyan's | **Gramercy**	27
Manhattan Fruit Ex. | **Chelsea**	24
Mazal Kosher | **Flushing**	17
New Green Pea | **Bklyn Hts**	23
Orchard | **Midwood**	27
Patel Bros. | **Jackson Hts**	23
☑ Russ & Daughters | **LES**	28
☑ Sahadi's | **Bklyn Hts**	27
Sweet Life | **LES**	23

Truffette | **E Vill**	-
☑ Zabar's | **W 80s**	27

EVENT PLANNERS

Banchet Flowers | **Meatpacking**	-
Callahan | **Garment**	-
Castle/Pierpont | **Garment**	24
Chestnuts | **TriBeCa**	-
☑ Cleaver Co. | **Chelsea**	25
Colin Cowie | **SoHo**	28
David Stark | **Carroll Gdns**	-
Gracious Thyme | **Harlem**	-
jesGORDON | **Garment**	-
Jonathan Flowers | **W 50s**	-
L'Olivier | **multi.**	29
Miho Kosuda | **E 40s**	-
Movable Feast | **Park Slope**	23
Naturally Delic. | **Carroll Gdns**	-
Olivier Cheng | **TriBeCa**	22
Renny/Reed | **E 50s**	28
Robert Isabell | **Meatpacking**	27
Susan Holland | **Flatiron**	-
TableToppers | **Stamford**	-
Taste Caterers | **W Vill**	22
Tempo Presto | **Park Slope**	23

EXOTIC PRODUCE

☑ Agata/Valentina | **E 70s**	26
☑ Dean/DeLuca | **E 80s**	27
☑ Eli's Manhattan | **E 80s**	25
Eli's Vinegar | **E 90s**	25
☑ Fairway | **multi.**	26
Garden of Eden | **multi.**	24
Grace's Mktpl. | **E 70s**	24
Greenwich Produce | **E 40s**	25
Hong Kong | **multi.**	20
Jim/Andy's | **Cobble Hill**	19
Katagiri | **E 50s**	23
Keith's Farm | **Westtown**	28
Likitsakos | **E 80s**	22
Manhattan Fruit Ex. | **Chelsea**	24
Marché Madison | **E 70s**	20
Perelandra | **Bklyn Hts**	24
3 Guys/Brooklyn | **Bay Ridge**	23
Truffette | **E Vill**	-
Zeytuna | **Financial**	23

FLOWERS

Academy Floral	**W 100s**	23
Anthony Gdn.	**E 70s**	−
Antony Todd	**E Vill**	−
Ariston	**multi.**	27
Banchet Flowers	**Meatpacking**	−
⊠ Belle Fleur	**Flatiron**	28
Big Apple Florist	**E 40s**	24
⊠ Bloom	**E 50s**	27
Blue Water	**SoHo**	−
Castle/Pierpont	**Garment**	24
Chestnuts	**TriBeCa**	−
Dahlia	**multi.**	26
⊠ Dean/DeLuca	**multi.**	27
⊠ Eli's Manhattan	**E 80s**	25
Eli's Vinegar	**E 90s**	25
Elizabeth Ryan	**LES**	28
Fellan Florist	**E 60s**	24
Floralies	**E 50s**	26
Flowers/Reuven	**Garment**	27
Flowers/World	**multi.**	28
NEW Gardenia Organic	**W Vill**	−
Gotham Gdns.	**W 70s**	24
⊠ Greenmarket	**multi.**	26
NEW Grové	**W Vill**	−
Jane Packer	**E 50s**	29
Jonathan Flowers	**W 50s**	−
Katrina Parris	**Harlem**	−
LMD Floral	**E Vill**	−
L'Olivier	**E 70s**	29
Magnolia Flowers	**W Vill**	26
Michael George	**E 40s**	25
Miho Kosuda	**E 40s**	−
Mille Fiori	**Chelsea**	−
Ovando	**W Vill**	28
Plaza Flowers	**E 60s**	25
Polux Fleuriste	**NoLita**	−
Renny/Reed	**E 50s**	28
Richard Salome	**E 70s**	−
Robert Isabell	**Meatpacking**	27
Ronaldo Maia	**E 90s**	28
Root Stock	**Park Slope**	−
Rosa Rosa	**E 60s**	21
Seaport Flowers	**Bklyn Hts**	26
Stonekelly	**W 50s**	25

Surroundings	**W 60s**	25
⊠ Takashimaya	**E 50s**	28
VSF	**W Vill**	29
⊠ Whole Foods	**multi.**	26
Windsor Florist	**E 70s**	24
⊠ Zezé	**E 50s**	29
ZuZu's Petals	**Park Slope**	26

GAME

(May need prior notice)

⊠ Agata/Valentina	**E 70s**	26
Albert & Sons	**E 60s**	26
⊠ Balducci's	**W 60s**	25
Biancardi Meats	**Bronx**	27
⊠ Citarella	**multi.**	26
⊠ Dean/DeLuca	**multi.**	27
Eagle Provisions	**Park Slope**	24
⊠ Eli's Manhattan	**E 80s**	25
Eli's Vinegar	**E 90s**	25
Empire Market	**College Pt**	16
Esposito Meat	**Garment**	25
⊠ Florence Meat	**G Vill**	29
Grace's Mktpl.	**E 70s**	24
NEW Greene Grape Provisions	**Ft Greene**	24
Heights Meats	**Bklyn Hts**	24
Holland Ct.	**E 90s**	24
Iavarone Bros.	**Maspeth**	25
Le Marais	**W 40s**	26
Leonard's	**E 70s**	26
Les Halles	**Gramercy**	26
⊠ Lobel's Meats	**E 80s**	29
Mazur's	**Douglaston**	20
Oppenheimer	**W 90s**	26
⊠ Ottomanelli & Sons	**multi.**	27
Ottomanelli Bros.	**multi.**	24
⊠ Ottomanelli's Meats	**Flushing**	27
Peter's Mkt.	**Bayside**	22
Pino Meats	**SoHo**	27
Quattro's	**Pleasant Valley**	26
⊠ Schaller/Weber	**E 80s**	27
Schatzie's Meats	**E 80s**	25
⊠ Simchick	**E 50s**	28
Vincent's Meat	**Bronx**	27
⊠ Whole Foods	**multi.**	26

GIFT BASKETS

(All Mail Order index entries as well as most candy and flower shops, plus the following standouts)

NYC SOURCES

SPECIAL FEATURES

Z Zabar's | **W 80s**	27
Zeytuna | **Financial**	23
Z Zezé | **E 50s**	29

GIFT IDEAS

(See also Gift Baskets)

Z Alessi | **SoHo**	27
Alice's Tea | **W 70s**	24
NEW Amai Tea | **Gramercy**	20
NEW applewares | **Park Slope**	24
Z Bazzini | **TriBeCa**	27
Bloomingdale's | **E 50s**	24
Broadway Pan. | **G Vill**	26
Z Dean/DeLuca | **SoHo**	27
NEW Grove | **W Vill**	-
Z Ito En | **E 60s**	28
Z Korin | **TriBeCa**	28
Leaf/Bean | **Park Slope**	23
Z MarieBelle's | **SoHo**	26
Maya Schaper | **W 60s**	22
Z Minamoto | **W 40s**	28
Nordic Delicacies | **Bay Ridge**	28
Ronaldo Maia | **E 90s**	28
Z Takashimaya | **E 50s**	28
Tea Box | **E 50s**	27
Z Terence Conran | **E 50s**	25
Z Williams-Sonoma | **multi.**	27

GINGERBREAD HOUSES

Amish Market | **W 40s**	23
Z Bazzini | **TriBeCa**	27
Bruno Bakery | **G Vill**	23
Caffe' Simpatico/Ruthy's | **Chelsea**	15
Z Citarella | **multi.**	26
Z Dean/DeLuca | **multi.**	27
Egidio Pastry | **Bronx**	24
Garden of Eden | **multi.**	24
Z Ladybird Bakery | **Park Slope**	28
Todaro Bros. | **Murray Hill**	24
Z Two Little Red | **E 80s**	26

GREENMARKET

(See p. 111 for locations)

Berkshire Berries	27
Berried Treasures	28
Beth's Farm	27
Blue Moon Fish	29
Bread Alone	27
Bulich Mushroom	29
Cato Farm	27
Cherry Ln.	28
DiPaola Turkey	27
Eckerton Hill	26
Flying Pigs	28
Gorzynski/Farm	27
Z Greenmarket	26
Hawthorne Farm	28
Keith's Farm	28
Martin's Pretzels	27
Migliorelli Farm	26
NEW Oro Bakery	-
Our Daily Bread	26
Paffenroth	28
PE & DD	28
Quattro's	26
Red Jacket	27
Rick's Picks	-
Z Ronnybrook	28
Samascott	27
Stokes Farm	27
Terhune Orchards	27
3-Corner Farm	27
Violet Hill	29
Windfall Farms	27
Yuno's Farm	29

HARD-TO-FIND INGREDIENTS

Z Agata/Valentina | **E 70s**	26
Angelica's Herbs | **E Vill**	23
Aphrodisia | **G Vill**	26
Asia Market | **Chinatown**	21
Z Balducci's | **W 60s**	25
Z Bangkok Grocery | **Chinatown**	27
Z Citarella | **multi.**	26
Z Dean/DeLuca | **multi.**	27
Dual Specialty | **E Vill**	22
Z Eli's Manhattan | **E 80s**	25
Eli's Vinegar | **E 90s**	25
Z Fairway | **multi.**	26
Foods/India | **Murray Hill**	23
Grace's Mktpl. | **E 70s**	24
Z Greenmarket | **Financial**	26

Han Ah Reum | **multi.**	22
Hong Keung | **Chinatown**	22
JAS Mart | **W 100s**	21
☑ Kalustyan's | **Gramercy**	27
Kam Man | **Chinatown**	21
Katagiri | **E 50s**	23
m2m | **multi.**	18
Ninth Ave. Int'l | **W 40s**	23
Nordic Delicacies | **Bay Ridge**	28
Patel Bros. | **multi.**	23
☑ Sahadi's | **Bklyn Hts**	27
Spice Corner | **Gramercy**	24
Sunrise Mart | **E Vill**	23
Teitel Bros. | **Bronx**	26
☑ Titan Foods | **Astoria**	26
Truffette | **E Vill**	-
☑ Two for the Pot | **Bklyn Hts**	27
☑ Whole Foods | **Chelsea**	26
☑ Zabar's | **W 80s**	27

HEALTH & NATURAL FOODS

(See also Organic)

A Matter/Health | **E 70s**	21
BabyCakes | **LES**	24
Back/Land | **Park Slope**	23
Bell Bates | **TriBeCa**	24
Better Burger | **Murray Hill**	19
Birdbath/Build Green | **E Vill**	23
Commodities Mkt. | **E Vill**	25
☑ Fairway | **multi.**	26
Foragers Mkt. | **Dumbo**	22
☑ FreshDirect | **LIC**	23
Gary Null's | **W 80s**	25
Health/Harmony | **W Vill**	26
Health Nuts | **multi.**	21
Integral Yoga | **W Vill**	24
Le Pain Quotidien | **E 60s**	24
LifeThyme Mkt. | **G Vill**	24
Natural Frontier | **multi.**	24
Nature's Gifts | **E 80s**	21
Park Natural | **Carroll Gdns**	22
Perelandra | **Bklyn Hts**	24
Pumpkins | **Park Slope**	26
Second Helpings | **Park Slope**	-
Tastebud's | **SI**	22

☑ Trader Joe's | **Rego Pk**	24
NEW Urban Rustic | **W'burg**	-
☑ Westerly Natural | **W 50s**	25
Whole Earth | **E Vill**	21
☑ Whole Foods | **multi.**	26

HERBS & SPICES

Angelica's Herbs | **E Vill**	23
Aphrodisia | **G Vill**	26
Asia Market | **Chinatown**	21
Bell Bates | **TriBeCa**	24
Commodities Mkt. | **E Vill**	25
☑ Dean/DeLuca | **multi.**	27
Dual Specialty | **E Vill**	22
☑ D'Vine | **Park Slope**	25
Dynasty Supermkt. | **Chinatown**	19
☑ Fairway | **Red Hook**	26
Family Store | **Bay Ridge**	-
Foods/India | **Murray Hill**	23
House of Spices | **Flushing**	24
☑ Kalustyan's | **Gramercy**	27
New Green Pea | **Bklyn Hts**	23
Ninth Ave. Int'l | **W 40s**	23
Patel Bros. | **Jackson Hts**	23
☑ Penzeys Spices | **E 40s**	27
☑ Sahadi's | **Bklyn Hts**	27
Spice Corner | **Gramercy**	24
☑ Trader Joe's | **Rego Pk**	24
Truffette | **E Vill**	-
☑ Two for the Pot | **Bklyn Hts**	27
☑ Zabar's | **W 80s**	27

HISTORIC INTEREST

(Year opened)

1820 | Acker Merrall | **W 70s**	26
1886 | Bazzini | **TriBeCa**	27
1886 | Bloomingdale's | **E 50s**	24
1888 | Katz's Deli | **LES**	24
1890 | Esposito Meat | **Garment**	25
1890 | Yonah Schimmel | **LES**	23
1892 | Alleva Dairy | **L Italy**	27
1892 | Ferrara Cafe | **L Italy**	22
1893 | Manganaro Foods | **Garment**	24
1894 | Veniero's | **E Vill**	25
1895 | McNulty's Tea | **W Vill**	27
1896 | Rohrs | **E 80s**	24

1898	Sahadi's	Bklyn Hts	27
1900	Faicco's Pork	multi.	28
1900	Ottomanelli Bros.	E 80s	24
1900	Paffenroth	Warwick	28
1900	Samascott	Kinderhook	27
1900	Sea Breeze	W 40s	23
1902	Glaser's Bake	E 80s	21
1902	Macy's Cellar	Garment	21
1904	Caputo Bakery	Carroll Gdns	23
1904	DeRobertis	E Vill	22
1906	Raffetto's	G Vill	28
1907	Katagiri	E 50s	23
1907	Porto Rico	multi.	26
1908	Anopoli Ice Cream	Bay Ridge	22
1908	Barney Greengrass	W 80s	27
1908	Empire Coffee	W 40s	23
1908	Newman/Leventhal	W 80s	21
1908	Russo Mozzarella	E Vill	26
1910	Academy Floral	W 100s	23
1910	Eddie's Sweet	Forest Hills	25
1910	Leonard's	E 70s	26
1910	Parisi Bakery	NoLita	23
1910	Pisacane	E 50s	28
1911	Superior Choc.	SI	22
1912	Egidio Pastry	Bronx	24
1914	Russ & Daughters	LES	28
1915	Butterfield Mkt.	E 70s	23
1915	Cosenza's Fish	Bronx	27
1915	Teitel Bros.	Bronx	26
1916	Orwasher's	E 70s	26
1917	Staubitz Mkt.	Cobble Hill	29
1917	Todaro Bros.	Murray Hill	24
1918	Balducci's	Chelsea	25
1918	Caffé Roma	L Italy	23
1918	Madonia Bakery	Bronx	28
1918	Mona Lisa Pastry	Bay Ridge	24
1920	Piemonte Ravioli	L Italy	27
1920	Slavin	Brownsville	23
1920	Vesuvio	SoHo	23
1921	Empire Market	College Pt	16
1921	Fong Inn	Chinatown	18
1921	William Poll	E 70s	26
1922	Casa Della	Bronx	29
1922	Esposito's Pork	Carroll Gdns	26
1923	Jeffrey's	LES	25
1923	Li-Lac Choc.	multi.	26
1923	Poseidon	W 40s	26
1924	Hinsch's	Bay Ridge	22
1925	County Chair	Mt. Vernon	–
1925	Delillo Pastry	Bronx	26
1925	DiPalo Dairy	L Italy	29
1925	Joe's Dairy	SoHo	28
1925	Randazzo's	Bronx	28
1925	Salumeria	Chelsea	29
1925	Streit's Matzo	LES	25
1927	Fellan Florist	E 60s	24
1927	Fine/Schapiro	W 70s	20
1927	Iavarone Bros.	multi.	25
1927	Mazzola Bakery	Carroll Gdns	25
1929	Addeo Bakery	Bronx	27
1929	Eisenberg's Sandwich	Flatiron	20
1929	Jefferson Mkt.	G Vill	26
1929	Lafayette	G Vill	21
1929	S. Feldman	E 90s	23
1930	Damascus Bakery	Bklyn Hts	25
1930	Philip's Candy	SI	–
1931	Zabar's	W 80s	27
1932	Biancardi Meats	Bronx	27
1932	Quality Hse.	Murray Hill	27
1933	Eggers Ice Cream	SI	25
1933	In Vino	E 70s	25
1933	Migliorelli Farm	Tivoli	26
1933	Sutton Wine	E 50s	22
1934	Carnegie Deli	W 50s	23
1934	Columbus Wine	W 50s	22
1934	Economy Candy	LES	24
1934	Famous Wines	Financial	22
1934	Manley's Wines	W Vill	22
1934	Park Ave. Liquor	E 40s	26
1934	Sherry-Lehmann	E 60s	29
1935	Borgatti's	Bronx	29
1935	Hendricks Wine	Bay Ridge	19

1935	K & D Wines	**E 90s** 24	1948	Court Pastry	**Cobble Hill** 25
1935	Kossar's	**LES** 28	1948	D'Amico	**Carroll Gdns** 21
1935	McAdam	**Gramercy** 22	1948	Frank's Gourmet	
1935	Mount Carmel	**Bronx** 26	**Wash. Hts**
1935	Ottomanelli & Sons	27	1948	Morrell & Co.	**W 40s** 27
G Vill	1948	Winfield-Flynn	23
1935	Party Time	**Elmhurst** 20	**Murray Hill**
1936	Florence Meat	**G Vill** 29	1948	Yorkville Meat	**E 80s** 23
1936	Windsor Florist	**E 70s** 24	1949	Bari Equipment	**LES** 24
1937	La Guli	**Astoria** 24	1949	Fischer Bros.	**W 70s** 27
1937	Schaller/Weber	**E 80s** 27	1949	Lassen/Hennigs	22
1937	Stage Deli	**W 50s** 21	**Bklyn Hts**
1938	Jordan's Lobster	23	1949	Ralph's/Ices	**SI** 24
Sheepshead	1950	Deli Masters	21
1940	Beekman Mktpl.	**E 40s** 22	**Fresh Meadows**
1940	Haas Co.	**Chelsea** 25	1950	Junior's	**multi.** 23
1940	Holland Ct.	**E 90s** 24	1950	Lee Sims Choc.	**SI** 25
1940	Murray's Cheese	**G Vill** 28	1950	Leske's	**Bay Ridge** 23
1941	Italian Food	**L Italy** 22	1950	Mauzone	**Flushing** 22
1941	Pete Milano's	**SI** 21	1950	Stork's Pastry	27
1941	Ronnybrook	**Chelsea** 28	**Whitestone**
1941	Sedutto's	**SI** 24	1950	United Meat	26
1941	67 Wines	**W 60s** 25	**Windsor Terr**
1941	Tops Wines	**Marine Pk** 23	1951	DiPaola Turkey	**Hamilton** 27
1943	Mondel Choc.	**W 100s** 22	1951	Flowers/World	**Financial** 28
1943	Schick's Bakery	20	1952	Berger's	**Murray Hill** 21
Borough Pk	1952	Calandra Cheese	**Bronx** 26
1944	Kalustyan's	**Gramercy** 27	1952	Cheese/World	25
1944	Lemon Ice	**Corona** 27	**Forest Hills**
1944	Quattro's	**Pleasant Valley** 26	1954	Abbey Rent	**Bayside** –
1945	Bulich Mushroom	**Catskill** 29	1954	Acme Fish	**Greenpt** 24
1945	Cherry Ln.	**Bridgeton** 28	1954	Ideal Cheese	**E 50s** 27
1945	Terhune Orchards	27	1954	Lobel's Meats	**E 80s** 29
Salt Pt	1954	Mother's Bake	**Bronx** 21
1946	Artuso Pastry	**Bronx** 26	1954	Oppenheimer	**W 90s** 26
1946	Baskin-Robbins	**multi.** 17	1954	Vincent's Meat	**Bronx** 27
1946	JoMart Choc.	**Marine Pk** 24	1955	Orchard	**Midwood** 27
1946	Murray's Sturgeon	**W 80s** 27	1956	Manganaro's Hero	21
1946	William Greenberg	**E 80s** 25	**Garment**
1947	American Beer	26	1956	Sal & Dom's	**Bronx** 28
Cobble Hill	1956	SoHo Wines	**SoHo** 21
1947	Astor Wines	**NoHo** 25	1956	Williams-Sonoma	27
1947	Atlas Party	**Mt. Vernon** 23	**Chelsea**
1947	Ben's Best	**Rego Pk** 23	1957	Beekman Liquors	**E 40s** 24
1947	Fraser-Morris	26	1958	Cassinelli Food	**Astoria** 25
Carroll Gdns	1958	Red Jacket	**Geneva** 27

HORS D'OEUVRES

Ⓩ Agata/Valentina | **E 70s** — 26

Ⓩ Balducci's | **W 60s** — 25

Between/Bread | **W 50s** — 21

BJ's Wholesale | **multi.** — 17

Butterfield Mkt. | **E 70s** — 23

Call Cuisine | **E 50s** — 24

Ⓩ Carnegie Deli | **W 50s** — 23

Ceriello | **multi.** — 24

Certé | **W 50s** — 26

Ⓩ Citarella | **multi.** — 26

Ⓩ Dean/DeLuca | **multi.** — 27

Dishes | **E 40s** — 24

Dumpling Man | **E Vill** — 20

Ⓩ E.A.T. | **E 80s** — 25

Eli's Vinegar | **E 90s** — 25

Ⓩ Fairway | **multi.** — 26

Family Store | **Bay Ridge** — -

Gourmet Garage | **multi.** — 20

Grace's Mktpl. | **E 70s** — 24

Italian Food | **L Italy** — 22

Likitsakos | **E 80s** — 22

Mangia | **multi.** — 24

Mansoura | **Midwood** — -

Marché Madison | **E 70s** — 20

Ⓩ May May | **Chinatown** — 23

Nordic Delicacies | **Bay Ridge** — 28

Once Upon/Tart | **SoHo** — 25

Petak's | **E 80s** — 23

Peter's Mkt. | **Bayside** — 22

Ⓩ Petrossian | **W 50s** — 28

Piazza Mercato | **Bay Ridge** — 23

Remi | **W 50s** — 26

Ⓩ Soutine | **W 70s** — 27

Special Attention | **LES** — -

Todaro Bros. | **Murray Hill** — 24

Ⓩ Trader Joe's | **multi.** — 24

Wild Edibles | **E 40s** — 26

Ⓩ William Poll | **E 70s** — 26

Ⓩ Zabar's | **W 80s** — 27

ICE CREAM & FROZEN YOGURT

Anopoli Ice Cream | **Bay Ridge** — 22

Australian Home. | **E Vill** — 23

Baskin-Robbins | **multi.** — 17

Ⓩ Bazzini | **TriBeCa** — 27

Ben & Jerry's | **multi.** — 24

NEW Blue Marble | **multi.** — 24

Blue Pig | **Bklyn Hts** — 21

Bottega/Via | **multi.** — 25

Brooklyn Ice Cream | **multi.** — 25

Bruno Bakery | **G Vill** — 23

Chinatown Ice Cream | **Chinatown** — 25

Chocolate Girl | **Park Slope** — 23

Ciao Bella | **multi.** — 25

Cold Stone | **multi.** — 20

Colson | **Park Slope** — 25

Cones | **G Vill** — 26

Ⓩ Dylan's Candy | **E 60s** — 21

East Vill. Ice Cream | **E Vill** — 22

Eddie's Sweet | **Forest Hills** — 25

Eggers Ice Cream | **SI** — 25

NEW /eks/ | **multi.** — -

Emack/Bolio | **multi.** — 25

Ferrara Cafe | **L Italy** — 22

Financier | **Financial** — 27

NEW Flurt | **Gramercy** — 21

Fortunato Bros. | **W'burg** — 25

Grom | **W 70s** — 27

Häagen Dazs | **multi.** — 24

Hinsch's | **Bay Ridge** — 22

Ⓩ Il Laboratorio | **LES** — 28

La Guli | **Astoria** — 24

Ⓩ L'Arte del Gelato | **multi.** — 27

Ⓩ Lemon Ice | **Corona** — 27

Little Piggy | **Ft Greene** — -

Max & Mina's | **Flushing** — 25

NEW Öko | **multi.** — 24

NEW Old Brooklyn Parlor | **Prospect Hts** — 24

Ⓩ Payard | **E 70s** — 28

pinkberry | **multi.** — 21

Piu Bello | **Forest Hills** — 21

Ⓩ Ralph's/Ices | **multi.** — 24

NEW Red Mango | **multi.** — 22

Rita's Ices | **SI** — 21

Rocco's Pastry | **G Vill** — 25

Ⓩ Ronnybrook | **Chelsea** — 28

Sant Ambroeus | **multi.** — 26

Sedutto's | **multi.** — 24

Shake Shack | **Flatiron**	25
Soda Shop | **TriBeCa**	20
Sundaes & Cones | **E Vill**	25
Tarallucci e Vino | **Flatiron**	24
Tempo Presto | **Park Slope**	23
Uncle Louie | **multi.**	20
NEW Very Berry | **E Vill**	20
☑ Villabate | **Bensonhurst**	28
☑ Vosges | **SoHo**	26
NEW Yogurtland | **W Vill**	–
Yolato | **multi.**	20

KOSHER

Andre's | **multi.**	23
Bagels & Co. | **multi.**	22
Ben's Best | **Rego Pk**	23
Ben's Kosher | **multi.**	21
Brasil Coffee | **Murray Hill**	21
Buttercup | **W 70s**	23
Chocolate Girl | **Park Slope**	23
Crumbs | **multi.**	22
Deli Masters | **Fresh Meadows**	21
☑ Dessert Delivery | **E 50s**	28
Fifth Ave. Choc. | **multi.**	20
Fine/Schapiro | **W 70s**	20
Fischer Bros. | **W 70s**	27
Foremost Caterers | **Moonachie**	24
H & H Bagels | **multi.**	26
H & H Midtown | **E 80s**	25
☑ Kossar's | **LES**	28
Le Marais | **W 40s**	26
☑ Magnolia Bakery | **W 60s**	23
Manna Catering | **TriBeCa**	–
Mansoura | **Midwood**	–
Mauzone | **Flushing**	22
Max & Mina's | **Flushing**	25
Mazal Kosher | **Flushing**	17
Mazur's | **Douglaston**	20
Mother's Bake | **Bronx**	21
My Most/Food | **W 40s**	21
Newman/Leventhal | **W 80s**	21
Orchard | **Midwood**	27
Orwasher's | **E 70s**	26
Park E. Kosher | **E 80s**	26
Pastrami Queen | **E 70s**	21
☑ Pickle Guys | **LES**	27

Schick's Bakery | **Borough Pk**	20
Streit's Matzo | **LES**	25
Uncle Louie | **multi.**	20
William Greenberg | **E 80s**	25

MAJOR GOURMET MARKETS

☑ Agata/Valentina | **E 70s**	26
Amish Market | **multi.**	23
☑ Balducci's | **multi.**	25
BJ's Wholesale | **Starrett City**	17
☑ Citarella | **multi.**	26
Costco | **multi.**	21
☑ Dean/DeLuca | **multi.**	27
☑ Eli's Manhattan | **E 80s**	25
Eli's Vinegar | **E 90s**	25
☑ Fairway | **multi.**	26
Food Emporium | **multi.**	16
☑ FreshDirect | **LIC**	23
Garden of Eden | **multi.**	24
Gourmet Garage | **multi.**	20
Grace's Mktpl. | **E 70s**	24
Jefferson Mkt. | **G Vill**	26
Jubilee | **Financial**	21
☑ Trader Joe's | **multi.**	24
Union Market | **Park Slope**	26
Westside Mkt. | **W 100s**	21
☑ Whole Foods | **multi.**	26
☑ Zabar's | **W 80s**	27
Zeytuna | **Financial**	23

MEAT & POULTRY

☑ Agata/Valentina | **E 70s**	26
Albert & Sons | **E 60s**	26
Astoria Meat | **Astoria**	25
☑ Balducci's | **W 60s**	25
Bari Pork | **multi.**	24
Bayard St. | **multi.**	23
☑ Bazzini | **TriBeCa**	27
Beekman Mktpl. | **E 40s**	22
Belfiore Meats | **SI**	25
Biancardi Meats | **Bronx**	27
☑ Calabria Pork | **Bronx**	28
Ceriello | **multi.**	24
Christos Steak | **Astoria**	23
☑ Citarella | **multi.**	26

Costco | **multi.**	21
☑ Dean/DeLuca | **multi.**	27
Deluxe Food | **Chinatown**	21
Dynasty Supermkt. | **Chinatown**	19
Eagle Provisions | **Park Slope**	24
☑ East Vill. Meat | **E Vill**	28
☑ Eli's Manhattan | **E 80s**	25
Eli's Vinegar | **E 90s**	25
Empire Market | **College Pt**	16
Esposito Meat | **Garment**	25
Esposito's Pork | **Carroll Gdns**	26
Euro Shop | **Sunnyside**	–
☑ Faicco's Pork | **multi.**	28
☑ Fairway | **multi.**	26
Fischer Bros. | **W 70s**	27
☑ Florence Meat | **G Vill**	29
☑ FreshDirect | **LIC**	23
Garden | **Greenpt**	24
Garden of Eden | **multi.**	24
Grace's Mktpl. | **E 70s**	24
NEW Greene Grape Provisions | **Ft Greene**	24
☑ Greenmarket | **multi.**	26
G.S. Food | **Chinatown**	19
Hawthorne Farm | **Ghent**	28
Heights Meats | **Bklyn Hts**	24
Holland Ct. | **E 90s**	24
Iavarone Bros. | **Maspeth**	25
☑ Jeffrey's | **LES**	25
Jubilee | **multi.**	21
Koglin Hams | **E 40s**	24
Le Marais | **W 40s**	26
Leonard's | **E 70s**	26
L'Epicerie | **Ft Greene**	22
Les Halles | **Gramercy**	26
☑ Lobel's Meats | **E 80s**	29
Lorimer St. Meat | **W'burg**	–
M & I Foods | **Brighton Bch**	24
Mazur's | **Douglaston**	20
New Beef | **Chinatown**	–
Oppenheimer | **W 90s**	26
☑ Ottomanelli & Sons | **multi.**	27
Ottomanelli Bros. | **multi.**	24
☑ Ottomanelli's Meats | **Flushing**	27
Papa Pasquale | **Bensonhurst**	26

Park E. Kosher | **E 80s**	26
Peter's Mkt. | **Bayside**	22
Piazza Mercato | **Bay Ridge**	23
Pino Meats | **SoHo**	27
Quattro's | **Pleasant Valley**	26
☑ Salumeria | **Chelsea**	29
☑ Schaller/Weber | **E 80s**	27
Schatzie's Meats | **E 80s**	25
☑ Simchick | **E 50s**	28
☑ Staubitz Mkt. | **Cobble Hill**	29
Sui Cheong Meat | **Chinatown**	20
Sunrise Mart | **E Vill**	23
Tan My My | **Chinatown**	22
3-Corner Farm | **Shushan**	27
Todaro Bros. | **Murray Hill**	24
☑ Trader Joe's | **Rego Pk**	24
Union Market | **Park Slope**	26
NEW Urban Rustic | **W'burg**	–
Vincent's Meat | **Bronx**	27
☑ Whole Foods | **multi.**	26
Yorkville Meat | **E 80s**	23
☑ Zabar's | **W 80s**	27
Zeytuna | **Financial**	23

NOTEWORTHY NEWCOMERS

☑ Abraço Espresso | **E Vill**	27
Amai Tea | **Gramercy**	20
applewares | **Park Slope**	24
Batch | **G Vill**	–
Berrywild | **Murray Hill**	22
Blue Marble | **multi.**	24
ChikaLicious Puddin' | **E Vill**	24
D.O.C. Wine | **W'burg**	22
/eks/ | **multi.**	–
El Beit | **W'burg**	–
Flurt | **Gramercy**	21
Frankly Wines | **TriBeCa**	–
FreeFoods | **W 40s**	25
Friedman's Deli | **Chelsea**	21
Gardenia Organic | **W Vill**	–
Get Fresh | **Park Slope**	–
Gnarly Vines | **Ft Greene**	–
Greene Grape Provisions | **Ft Greene**	24
Grove | **W Vill**	–

How Sweet It Is | **LES**	-_
Krumbs | **Clinton Hill**	22
La Colombe | **TriBeCa**	-_
Madeleine | **Chelsea**	24
Mercury Dime | **E Vill**	-_
Oak & Steel | **W 50s**	-_
Öko | **multi.**	24
Old Brooklyn Parlor | **Prospect Hts**	24
Organic Heights | **Park Slope**	-_
Oro Bakery | **L Italy**	-_
Papabubble | **L Italy**	24
Papa Lima | **W'burg**	22
Paradou Marché | **LES**	21
Red Mango | **multi.**	22
Roni-Sue's | **LES**	23
Root Hill | **Park Slope**	-_
Sakaya | **E Vill**	25
Spuyten/Grocery | **W'burg**	-_
Tafu | **E 50s**	19
Think Coffee | **NoHo**	23
Urban Rustic | **W'burg**	-_
Very Berry | **E Vill**	20
Yogurtland | **W Vill**	-_
Zucker's Bagels | **TriBeCa**	22

OFFBEAT

Aji Ichiban | **Chinatown**	21
Beard Papa | **multi.**	24
Z Cake Man | **Ft Greene**	26
Cakes 'N Shapes | **W 50s**	22
Choux Factory | **multi.**	23
Dale & Thomas | **W 40s**	23
Z Divalicious | **L Italy**	24
Z Doughnut Plant | **LES**	26
DUB Pies | **Carroll Gdns**	24
Empire Market | **College Pt**	16
Insomnia Cookies | **G Vill**	-_
Jim/Andy's | **Cobble Hill**	19
Kidfresh | **E 80s**	18
Z Kossar's | **LES**	28
Z LeNell's | **Red Hook**	27
Mansoura | **Midwood**	-_
Masturbakers | **E Vill**	22
Max & Mina's | **Flushing**	25
Max Brenner | **multi.**	22
Maya Schaper | **W 60s**	22

Z May May | **Chinatown**	23
Myers/Keswick | **W Vill**	23
Otafuku | **E Vill**	19
NEW Papabubble | **L Italy**	24
Paramount Caviar | **LIC**	27
Z Rice/Riches | **NoLita**	23
Rick's Picks | **LES**	-_
Winesby | **G Vill**	-_

OFFICE CATERING

(All caterers and delis, plus the
following standouts)

Z Agata/Valentina | **E 70s**	26
Alice's Tea | **multi.**	24
Arte/Corner | **W 70s**	24
Arthur Ave. | **Bronx**	24
Z Balducci's | **Chelsea**	25
Balthazar Bakery | **SoHo**	27
Barbarini | **Financial**	-_
Bari Pork | **multi.**	24
Z Barney Greengrass | **W 80s**	27
Z Bazzini | **TriBeCa**	27
Beekman Mktpl. | **E 40s**	22
Belfiore Meats | **SI**	25
Between/Bread | **W 50s**	21
Boerum Hill Food | **Boerum Hill**	22
Bonsignour | **W Vill**	26
Bottino | **Chelsea**	22
Z Bouchon Bakery | **W 60s**	27
Z Bouley Bakery | **TriBeCa**	27
BuonItalia | **Chelsea**	26
Butterfield Mkt. | **E 70s**	23
Call Cuisine | **E 50s**	24
Carmine's | **multi.**	23
Carve | **W 40s**	23
Ceriello | **multi.**	24
Certé | **W 50s**	26
Cipriani | **E 40s**	26
Z Citarella | **multi.**	26
Z City Bakery | **Flatiron**	25
Clinton St. | **LES**	26
Cobblestone | **Carroll Gdns**	21
Cucina | **multi.**	21
Cucina Vivolo | **multi.**	23
Z Dean/DeLuca | **multi.**	27
Delmonico | **multi.**	21

Dishes	multi.	24
☑ E.A.T.	E 80s	25
☑ Eli's Manhattan	E 80s	25
Eli's Vinegar	E 90s	25
☑ Fairway	multi.	26
Family Store	Bay Ridge	–
F&B	Chelsea	20
Financier	Financial	27
Fresco/Scotto	E 50s	24
Garden of Eden	multi.	24
Good & Plenty	W 40s	22
Grace's Mktpl.	E 70s	24
Hale/Hearty	multi.	22
Iavarone Bros.	Maspeth	25
Indian Bread	G Vill	21
Italian Food	L Italy	22
☑ Katz's Deli	LES	24
Le Pain Quotidien	multi.	24
Lorenzo/Maria's	E 80s	25
Luscious Food	Park Slope	19
Madison	E 90s	20
Mangia	multi.	24
Mansoura	Midwood	–
Marché Madison	E 70s	20
Melange	E 60s	21
Milano Gourmet	multi.	25
Out/Kitchen	W Vill	20
☑ Payard	E 70s	28
Petak's	E 80s	23
Petite Abeille	multi.	22
Pret A Manger	multi.	21
Ready to Eat	W Vill	21
Remi	W 50s	26
Risotteria	G Vill	23
☑ Salumeria	Chelsea	29
Sandwich Planet	Garment	25
Sebastians	E 50s	–
Snack	SoHo	27
Starwich	multi.	23
Sweet Melissa	Park Slope	24
Swich	Chelsea	23
Tisserie	Union Sq	20
Todaro Bros.	Murray Hill	24
☑ Whole Foods	multi.	26
Wild Edibles	multi.	26

☑ Zabar's	W 80s	27
Zeytuna	Financial	23

ONE-STOP SHOPPING

☑ Agata/Valentina	E 70s	26
Amish Market	multi.	23
☑ Balducci's	W 60s	25
☑ Bazzini	TriBeCa	27
BJ's Wholesale	multi.	17
☑ Citarella	multi.	26
Costco	multi.	21
☑ Dean/DeLuca	multi.	27
Delmonico	multi.	21
☑ Eli's Manhattan	E 80s	25
Eli's Vinegar	E 90s	25
☑ Fairway	multi.	26
Food Emporium	multi.	16
☑ FreshDirect	LIC	23
Garden	Greenpt	24
Garden of Eden	multi.	24
Gary Null's	W 80s	25
Gourmet Garage	multi.	20
Grace's Mktpl.	E 70s	24
NEW Greene Grape Provisions	Ft Greene	24
Gustiamo	Bronx	23
Hong Keung	Chinatown	22
Jefferson Mkt.	G Vill	26
Jubilee	Financial	21
Kam Man	Chinatown	21
LifeThyme Mkt.	G Vill	24
M & I Foods	Brighton Bch	24
Patel Bros.	multi.	23
Perelandra	Bklyn Hts	24
Sunrise Mart	E Vill	23
☑ Titan Foods	Astoria	26
Todaro Bros.	Murray Hill	24
☑ Trader Joe's	Union Sq	24
Union Market	Park Slope	26
☑ Whole Foods	multi.	26
☑ Zabar's	W 80s	27
Zeytuna	Financial	23

OPEN LATE

BAGELS & BIALYS

☑ Absolute Bagels	W 100s	26
Daniel's Bagels	Murray Hill	24

East Side Bagel | E 70s — 21
Ess-a-Bagel | multi. — 26
H & H Bagels | multi. — 26
H & H Midtown | E 80s — 25
Murray's Bagels | G Vill — 26
Pick a Bagel | multi. — 20
Tal Bagels | multi. — 23
Times Sq. Bagels | W 40s — 19

BAKED GOODS

🅩 Amy's Bread | multi. — 26
Au Bon Pain | multi. — 16
Balthazar Bakery | SoHo — 27
Billy's Bakery | Chelsea — 25
🅩 Black Hound | E Vill — 26
Bruno Bakery | G Vill — 23
Buttercup | E 50s — 23
Carrot Top | Wash. Hts — 23
Clinton St. | LES — 26
Crumbs | multi. — 22
Eileen's Cheesecake | NoLita — 26
Fabiane's | W'burg — -
Ferrara Cafe | L Italy — 22
Financier | Financial — 27
Hungarian Pastry | W 100s — 22
Junior's | multi. — 23
Little Pie | E 40s — 24
Mrs. Field's | Seaport — 18
Nusbaum & Wu | W 100s — 18
🅩 Payard | E 70s — 28
🅩 Rice/Riches | NoLita — 23
Rocco's Pastry | G Vill — 25
Sarabeth's | multi. — 24
🅩 Sugar Sweet | LES — 27
Sweet Melissa | Cobble Hill — 24
Tai Pan Bakery | Chinatown — 19
Veniero's | E Vill — 25

CANDY & NUTS

🅩 Dylan's Candy | E 60s — 21
Godiva | Financial — 22
World of Nuts | multi. — 15

CHEESE & DAIRY

🅩 Artisanal | Murray Hill — 28
🅩 Bedford Cheese | W'burg — 27

COFFEE & TEA

Brasil Coffee | LIC — 21
Carry On Tea | W Vill — 23
Doma | W Vill — 25
Franchia | Murray Hill — 24
Gorilla Coffee | Park Slope — 24
Juan Valdez | W 40s — 22
Mudspot | E Vill — 26
Naidre's | multi. — 22
Ozzie's Coffee | Park Slope — 19
Tea Lounge | Park Slope — 21

DELIS & SANDWICHES

🅩 Carnegie Deli | W 50s — 23
Così | multi. — 18
🅩 Katz's Deli | LES — 24
Nicky's Viet. | E Vill — 24
Tiny's Giant | LES — 22

HEALTH & NATURAL FOODS

Gary Null's | W 80s — 25
Health/Harmony | W Vill — 26
Health Nuts | multi. — 21
Integral Yoga | W Vill — 24
LifeThyme Mkt. | G Vill — 24

ICE CREAM

Australian Home. | E Vill — 23
Baskin-Robbins | multi. — 17
Ben & Jerry's | multi. — 24
Brooklyn Ice Cream | Dumbo — 25
Chinatown Ice Cream | Chinatown — 25
Cold Stone | multi. — 20
Cones | G Vill — 26
Emack/Bolio | W 70s — 25
Häagen Dazs | multi. — 24
🅩 Lemon Ice | Corona — 27
Sant Ambroeus | multi. — 26
Sedutto's | multi. — 24

MEAT, POULTRY & GAME

Christos Steak | Astoria — 23

PREPARED FOODS

A Salt/Battery | W Vill — 22
Better Burger | multi. — 19
Café Habana | NoLita — 24
Cafe Spice | E 40s — 19

Carmine's	**multi.**	23
Cozy Soup	**G Vill**	17
F&B	**Chelsea**	20
Hampton Chutney	**SoHo**	23
Milano Gourmet	**W 100s**	25
Otafuku	**E Vill**	19
Petite Abeille	**multi.**	22
Pie/Pound	**E Vill**	20
Risotteria	**G Vill**	23
Snack	**SoHo**	27
Starwich	**Financial**	23
Tuck Shop	**E Vill**	20
Zaitzeff	**Financial**	28

PRODUCE

Annie's	**E 80s**	21
Likitsakos	**E 80s**	22
#1 Farmers Mkt.	**multi.**	23

SOUPS

⚡ Original SoupMan	**multi.**	23

SPECIALTY SHOPS

Ceriello	**E 40s**	24
Dale & Thomas	**W 40s**	23
Delmonico	**multi.**	21
Han Ah Reum	**multi.**	22
JAS Mart	**multi.**	21
Kam Man	**Chinatown**	21
Marlow	**W'burg**	24
m2m	**W 100s**	18
Patel Bros.	**multi.**	23
Sunrise Mart	**multi.**	23
Todaro Bros.	**Murray Hill**	24

WINES, BEER & LIQUOR

Astor Wines	**NoHo**	25
Beacon Wines	**W 70s**	21
⚡ Bierkraft	**Park Slope**	28
De Vino	**LES**	25
Greene Grape	**Financial**	24
Is Wine	**G Vill**	22
⚡ Le Dû's Wines	**W Vill**	27
Manley's Wines	**W Vill**	22
Nancy's-Wines	**W 70s**	24
New York/Exchange	**Financial**	23
Pasanella	**Seaport**	26
Sea Grape	**W Vill**	23
Sept. Wines	**LES**	25

Wine Therapy	**NoLita**	25
Winfield-Flynn	**Murray Hill**	23

OPEN SUNDAY

(Except for liquor stores, butchers and fish markets, most places are open Sunday; here are some sources in those hard-to-find categories)

Acker Merrall	**W 70s**	26
Ambassador Wine	**E 50s**	24
Astor Wines	**NoHo**	25
Bacchus Wine	**W 70s**	19
Bari Pork	**multi.**	24
Bayard St.	**multi.**	23
Beacon Wines	**W 70s**	21
Belfiore Meats	**SI**	25
Best Cellars	**multi.**	21
⚡ Bierkraft	**Park Slope**	28
Blanc & Rouge	**Dumbo**	25
Brooklyn Liquors	**Sunset Pk**	23
Chambers Wines	**TriBeCa**	26
Chelsea Wine	**Chelsea**	23
Christos Steak	**Astoria**	23
Columbus Wine	**W 50s**	22
Crossroads	**Union Sq**	25
⚡ Crush Wine	**E 50s**	26
De Vino	**LES**	25
Discovery Wines	**E Vill**	22
Eagle Provisions	**Park Slope**	24
Embassy Wines	**E 60s**	19
Empire Market	**College Pt**	16
Esposito's Pork	**Carroll Gdns**	26
⚡ Faicco's Pork	**multi.**	28
Garnet Wines	**E 60s**	24
Gotham Wines	**W 90s**	22
Gramercy Fish	**Gramercy**	24
Grande Harvest	**E 40s**	23
Greene Grape	**multi.**	24
G.S. Food	**Chinatown**	19
Harlem Vintage	**Harlem**	28
Hong Keung	**Chinatown**	22
Iavarone Bros.	**multi.**	25
Is Wine	**G Vill**	22
Jordan's Lobster	**Sheepshead**	23
Koglin Hams	**E 40s**	24
Le Marais	**W 40s**	26

LeNell's	**Red Hook**	27
Leonard's	**E 70s**	26
Les Halles	**Gramercy**	26
Lobster Pl.	**Chelsea**	26
Manley's Wines	**W Vill**	22
Mazur's	**Douglaston**	20
McAdam	**Gramercy**	22
McCabe's Wines	**E 70s**	19
Mister Wright	**E 80s**	24
Morrell & Co.	**E 60s**	26
Mount Carmel	**Bronx**	26
Nancy's–Wines	**W 70s**	24
New Beef	**Chinatown**	–
Ottomanelli Bros.	**multi.**	24
Park E. Kosher	**E 80s**	26
Pescatore	**E 40s**	25
Piazza Mercato	**Bay Ridge**	23
Premier Cru	**E 80s**	24
Prospect Wine	**Park Slope**	26
Quattro's	**Pleasant Valley**	26
Red/White	**Park Slope**	26
Sea Grape	**W Vill**	23
67 Wines	**W 60s**	25
Slavin	**Brownsville**	23
Slope Cellars	**Park Slope**	24
Smith & Vine	**Cobble Hill**	23
Sui Cheong Meat	**Chinatown**	20
Sutton Wine	**E 50s**	22
Union Sq. Wines	**Union Sq**	25
Uva	**W'burg**	24
Vino	**Gramercy**	28
Vintage NY	**multi.**	23
Warehouse Wines	**G Vill**	22
Wild Edibles	**multi.**	26
W.I.N.E.	**E 80s**	21
Winfield-Flynn	**Murray Hill**	23
Yorkshire Wines	**E 80s**	23
Yorkville Meat	**E 80s**	23

ORGANIC

Albert & Sons	**E 60s**	26
A Matter/Health	**E 70s**	21
Amish Market	**multi.**	23
Amy's Bread	**W 40s**	26
Aphrodisia	**G Vill**	26
Appellation	**Chelsea**	25

Arte/Corner	**W 70s**	24
BabyCakes	**LES**	24
Back/Land	**Park Slope**	23
NEW Batch	**G Vill**	–
Beekman Mktpl.	**E 40s**	22
Bell Bates	**TriBeCa**	24
Bierkraft	**Park Slope**	28
Birdbath/Build Green	**multi.**	23
NEW Blue Marble	**multi.**	24
Boerum Hill Food	**Boerum Hill**	22
Bouchon Bakery	**W 60s**	27
Bread Alone	**Boiceville**	27
City Bakery	**Flatiron**	25
Cleaver Co.	**Chelsea**	25
Commodities Mkt.	**E Vill**	25
Discovery Wines	**E Vill**	22
NEW D.O.C. Wine	**W'burg**	22
Earthmatters	**LES**	21
NEW /eks/	**multi.**	–
Empire Market	**College Pt**	16
Fabiane's	**W'burg**	–
Fairway	**multi.**	26
Foragers Mkt.	**Dumbo**	22
Frank's Gourmet	**Wash. Hts**	21
NEW FreeFoods	**W 40s**	25
FreshDirect	**LIC**	23
Garden	**Greenpt**	24
NEW Gardenia Organic	**W Vill**	–
Gary Null's	**W 80s**	25
NEW Get Fresh	**Park Slope**	–
Gorilla Coffee	**Park Slope**	24
Gourmet Garage	**multi.**	20
Hawthorne Farm	**Ghent**	28
Health/Harmony	**W Vill**	26
Health Nuts	**multi.**	21
Holland Ct.	**E 90s**	24
Integral Yoga	**W Vill**	24
Irving Farm/71	**G Vill**	22
Jack's Stir Brew	**multi.**	27
Jubilee	**SoHo**	21
Keith's Farm	**Westtown**	28
Kidfresh	**E 80s**	18
Leaf/Bean	**Park Slope**	23
Le Pain Quotidien	**multi.**	24
L'Epicerie	**Ft Greene**	22

LifeThyme Mkt.	**G Vill**	24
Liqueteria	**E Vill**	19
Marlow	**W'burg**	24
Milk & Cookies	**W Vill**	24
Natural Frontier	**multi.**	24
Ninth St. Espresso	**Chelsea**	28
Nordic Delicacies	**Bay Ridge**	28
NEW Oak & Steel	**W 50s**	-
NEW Öko	**multi.**	24
Oppenheimer	**W 90s**	26
Orchard	**Midwood**	27
NEW Oro Bakery	**L Italy**	-
Z Ottomanelli & Sons	**G Vill**	27
Ottomanelli Bros.	**E 80s**	24
Ozzie's Coffee	**Park Slope**	19
Park Natural	**Carroll Gdns**	22
Pino Meats	**SoHo**	27
Porto Rico	**multi.**	26
Z Prospect Wine	**Park Slope**	26
Pumpkins	**Park Slope**	26
Roasting Plant	**LES**	22
Z Ronnybrook	**Chelsea**	28
Second Helpings	**Park Slope**	-
Sensuous Bean	**W 70s**	25
Starwich	**multi.**	23
Tastebud's	**SI**	22
Tea Lounge	**multi.**	21
Tempo Presto	**Park Slope**	23
Think Coffee	**G Vill**	23
Union Market	**Park Slope**	26
Urban Organic	**Park Slope**	22
NEW Urban Rustic	**W'burg**	-
Uva	**W'burg**	24
Z Westerly Natural	**W 50s**	25
Whole Earth	**E Vill**	21
Z Whole Foods	**multi.**	26
Zeytuna	**Financial**	23

PARTY RENTALS

Abbey Rent	**Bayside**	-
Z Atlas Party	**Mt. Vernon**	23
Broadway Party	**multi.**	19
County Chair	**Mt. Vernon**	-
Metro Party	**Paterson**	-
Party Rental	**multi.**	22
Party Time	**Elmhurst**	20

Props/Today	**Garment**	20
Something Different	**Paterson**	-
TableToppers	**Stamford**	-

PASTAS

Z Agata/Valentina	**E 70s**	26
Arte/Corner	**W 70s**	24
Z Balducci's	**W 60s**	25
Z Bazzini	**TriBeCa**	27
Z Borgatti's	**Bronx**	29
Bruno/Ravioli	**multi.**	24
Cassinelli Food	**Astoria**	25
Ceriello	**multi.**	24
Z Citarella	**multi.**	26
Z Coluccio/Sons	**Borough Pk**	28
Z Dean/DeLuca	**multi.**	27
Z DiPalo Dairy	**L Italy**	29
Durso's Pasta	**Flushing**	26
Z Eli's Manhattan	**E 80s**	25
Eli's Vinegar	**E 90s**	25
Z Fairway	**multi.**	26
Z FreshDirect	**LIC**	23
Gourmet Garage	**multi.**	20
Grace's Mktpl.	**E 70s**	24
Gustiamo	**Bronx**	23
Iavarone Bros.	**multi.**	25
Italian Food	**L Italy**	22
Lioni Latticini	**Bensonhurst**	29
Z Murray's Cheese	**G Vill**	28
Papa Pasquale	**Bensonhurst**	26
Z Pastosa Ravioli	**multi.**	26
Peter's Mkt.	**Bayside**	22
Piemonte Ravioli	**L Italy**	27
Queen Ann	**Bensonhurst**	27
Z Raffetto's	**G Vill**	28
Russo Mozzarella	**multi.**	26
Savino's Pasta	**W'burg**	-
Todaro Bros.	**Murray Hill**	24
Z Trader Joe's	**Rego Pk**	24
Trunzo Bros.	**Bensonhurst**	25
Z Whole Foods	**multi.**	26
Z Zabar's	**W 80s**	27

PICNICS

Between/Bread	**W 50s**	21
Z Citarella	**multi.**	26

Z Dean/DeLuca | **multi.** 27

Z Eli's Manhattan | **E 80s** 25

Eli's Vinegar | **E 90s** 25

Garden of Eden | **multi.** 24

Good & Plenty | **W 40s** 22

Grace's Mktpl. | **E 70s** 24

Great Performances | **SoHo** 24

Lassen/Hennigs | **Bklyn Hts** 22

Movable Feast | **Park Slope** 23

Todaro Bros. | **Murray Hill** 24

Wild Edibles | **Murray Hill** 26

PIES/TARTS

Ah Wong Bakery | **Chinatown** 20

Andre's | **multi.** 23

Balthazar Bakery | **SoHo** 27

NEW Batch | **G Vill** -

Bay Ridge Bake | **Bay Ridge** 25

Z Black Hound | **E Vill** 26

Z Bouchon Bakery | **W 60s** 27

Bread Alone | **Boiceville** 27

Buttercup | **E 50s** 23

Caffe' Simpatico/Ruthy's | **Chelsea** 15

Cake Chef | **SI** 22

Ceci-Cela | **L Italy** 24

Z Citarella | **multi.** 26

Z City Bakery | **Flatiron** 25

Colson | **Park Slope** 25

Z Dean/DeLuca | **multi.** 27

Delillo Pastry | **Bronx** 26

Z Dessert Delivery | **E 50s** 28

Duane Pk. | **TriBeCa** 26

Egidio Pastry | **Bronx** 24

Fabiane's | **W'burg** -

Z Fairway | **multi.** 26

Financier | **Financial** 27

Friend/Farmer | **Gramercy** 21

Glaser's Bake | **E 80s** 21

Grace's Mktpl. | **E 70s** 24

NEW How Sweet It Is | **LES** -

Hungarian Pastry | **W 100s** 22

Joyce Bake | **Prospect Hts** 25

La Bergamote | **Chelsea** 26

Z Ladybird Bakery | **Park Slope** 28

La Guli | **Astoria** 24

Little Pie | **multi.** 24

Z Magnolia Bakery | **W Vill** 23

Margaret Palca | **Carroll Gdns** 26

Margot Pâtisserie | **W 70s** 27

Marquet Patiss. | **multi.** 24

Martha's Bakery | **Astoria** 23

My Most/Food | **W 40s** 21

Once Upon/Tart | **SoHo** 25

NEW Oro Bakery | **L Italy** -

Panya Bakery | **E Vill** 22

Z Patisserie Claude | **G Vill** 27

Z Payard | **E 70s** 28

Z Petrossian | **W 50s** 28

Sarabeth's | **multi.** 24

Settepani | **multi.** 23

Shakoor's Sweet | **Bed-Stuy** -

Silver Moon | **W 100s** 26

Z Soutine | **W 70s** 27

Steve's/Pies | **Red Hook** 25

Z Stork's Pastry | **Whitestone** 27

Z Sugar Sweet | **LES** 27

Sweet Melissa | **multi.** 24

Three Tarts | **Chelsea** 22

Trois Pommes | **Park Slope** 23

Z Two Little Red | **E 80s** 26

Umanoff/Parsons | **Bronx** 24

Veniero's | **E Vill** 25

William Greenberg | **E 80s** 25

PREPARED FOODS

(See also Delis & Sandwiches and Soups)

Z Agata/Valentina | **E 70s** 26

Arte/Corner | **W 70s** 24

A Salt/Battery | **W Vill** 22

Z Balducci's | **W 60s** 25

Barbarini | **Financial** -

Bari Pork | **multi.** 24

Z Bazzini | **TriBeCa** 27

Belfiore Meats | **SI** 25

Bell Bates | **TriBeCa** 24

Better Burger | **multi.** 19

Between/Bread | **W 50s** 21

Boerum Hill Food | **Boerum Hill** 22

Bonsignour | **W Vill** 26

Bottega/Via | **E 70s** 25

NYC SOURCES | SPECIAL FEATURES

☑ Bouchon Bakery | **W 60s**	27	Flor/Mayo | **multi.**	23
BuonItalia | **Chelsea**	26	Fraser-Morris | **Carroll Gdns**	26
Busy Chef | **Bklyn Hts**	21	NEW FreeFoods | **W 40s**	25
Butterfield Mkt. | **E 70s**	23	Fresco/Scotto | **E 50s**	24
Café Habana | **NoLita**	24	Fresh Bites | **W 50s**	20
Cafe Spice | **E 40s**	19	Garden | **Greenpt**	24
Call Cuisine | **E 50s**	24	Garden of Eden | **multi.**	24
Carmine's | **multi.**	23	Gary Null's | **W 80s**	25
Carry On Tea | **W Vill**	23	Gauchas | **E 90s**	25
Choice Mkt. | **Clinton Hill**	23	NEW Get Fresh | **Park Slope**	–
Christie's | **Prospect Hts**	21	Good & Plenty | **W 40s**	22
☑ Citarella | **multi.**	26	Gourmet Garage | **multi.**	20
☑ City Bakery | **Flatiron**	25	Grace's Mktpl. | **E 70s**	24
☑ Cleaver Co. | **Chelsea**	25	Gramercy Fish | **Gramercy**	24
Clinton St. | **LES**	26	Hampton Chutney | **multi.**	23
Cobblestone | **Carroll Gdns**	21	Health Nuts | **multi.**	21
Commodities Mkt. | **E Vill**	25	Heights Meats | **Bklyn Hts**	24
Corner Café | **E 90s**	–	Iavarone Bros. | **Maspeth**	25
Così | **multi.**	18	Indian Bread | **G Vill**	21
Costco | **Sunset Pk**	21	Integral Yoga | **W Vill**	24
Cozy Soup | **G Vill**	17	Italian Food | **L Italy**	22
Cucina | **multi.**	21	JAS Mart | **multi.**	21
Daisy May's | **W 40s**	24	Jefferson Mkt. | **G Vill**	26
☑ Dean/DeLuca | **multi.**	27	Jive Turkey | **Clinton Hill**	23
Delmonico | **multi.**	21	Jubilee | **multi.**	21
Devon/Blakely | **multi.**	22	☑ Kalustyan's | **Gramercy**	27
Di Fiore Marquet | **G Vill**	–	Kam Man | **Chinatown**	21
Dirty Bird | **W Vill**	20	Katagiri | **E 50s**	23
Dishes | **multi.**	24	Kidfresh | **E 80s**	18
DUB Pies | **Carroll Gdns**	24	Lassen/Hennigs | **Bklyn Hts**	22
Dumpling Man | **E Vill**	20	Leonard's | **E 70s**	26
Durso's Pasta | **Flushing**	26	Le Pain Quotidien | **W 70s**	24
☑ D'Vine | **Park Slope**	25	L'Epicerie | **Ft Greene**	22
☑ E.A.T. | **E 80s**	25	LifeThyme Mkt. | **G Vill**	24
☑ Eli's Manhattan | **E 80s**	25	Likitsakos | **E 80s**	22
Eli's Vinegar | **E 90s**	25	Little Piggy | **Ft Greene**	–
Esposito's Pork | **Carroll Gdns**	26	☑ Lobel's Meats | **E 80s**	29
Euro Shop | **Sunnyside**	–	Lobster Pl. | **Chelsea**	26
☑ Faicco's Pork | **multi.**	28	Lorenzo/Maria's | **E 80s**	25
☑ Fairway | **multi.**	26	Lorimer St. Meat | **W'burg**	–
Family Store | **Bay Ridge**	–	Luscious Food | **Park Slope**	19
F&B | **Chelsea**	20	Madison | **E 90s**	20
Fifth Ave. Epicure | **Flatiron**	19	M & I Foods | **Brighton Bch**	24
Financier | **Financial**	27	Manganaro Foods | **Garment**	24
First Ave. Pierogi | **E Vill**	25	Mangia | **multi.**	24

Marché Madison	E 50s	20
Mauzone	Flushing	22
Max Brenner	multi.	22
Z May May	Chinatown	23
Mazur's	Douglaston	20
Melange	E 60s	21
Michelle's Kitchen	E 90s	18
Milano Gourmet	multi.	25
Myers/Keswick	W Vill	23
Natural Frontier	multi.	24
Ninth Ave. Int'l	W 40s	23
Z Olive's	SoHo	25
NEW Organic Heights	Park Slope	–
Ottomanelli Bros.	multi.	24
Z Ottomanelli's Meats	Flushing	27
Paneantico	Bay Ridge	26
Park E. Kosher	E 80s	26
Pepe	multi.	26
Perelandra	Bklyn Hts	24
Pescatore	E 40s	25
Petak's	E 80s	23
Peter's Mkt.	Bayside	22
Petite Abeille	multi.	22
Piazza Mercato	Bay Ridge	23
Pie/Pound	E Vill	20
Press 195	multi.	25
Pret A Manger	multi.	21
Queen Ann	Bensonhurst	27
Ready to Eat	W Vill	21
Remi	W 50s	26
Risotteria	G Vill	23
Ruben's	multi.	20
Russo Mozzarella	Park Slope	26
Z Sahadi's	Bklyn Hts	27
Sandwich Planet	Garment	25
Z Schaller/Weber	E 80s	27
Second Helpings	Park Slope	–
Shake Shack	Flatiron	25
Snack	multi.	27
Sunrise Mart	multi.	23
Sweet Melissa	multi.	24
Tanoreen	Bay Ridge	24
Tastebud's	SI	22
Thalia Kitchen	W 50s	21
Tiny's Giant	LES	22
Tisserie	Union Sq	20
Todaro Bros.	Murray Hill	24
Z Trader Joe's	Rego Pk	24
Tuck Shop	E Vill	20
Union Market	Park Slope	26
United Meat	Windsor Terr	26
NEW Urban Rustic	W'burg	–
Westside Mkt.	multi.	21
Z Whole Foods	multi.	26
Wild Edibles	multi.	26
Z William Poll	E 70s	26
Yonah Schimmel	LES	23
Z Zabar's	W 80s	27
Zaitzeff	Financial	28
Zeytuna	Financial	23

PRODUCE

Z Agata/Valentina	E 70s	26
Amish Market	multi.	23
Annie's	E 80s	21
Asia Market	Chinatown	21
Z Balducci's	W 60s	25
Z Bazzini	TriBeCa	27
Bell Bates	TriBeCa	24
Berried Treasures	Roscoe	28
Bulich Mushroom	Catskill	29
Butterfield Mkt.	E 70s	23
Cherry Ln.	Bridgeton	28
Z Citarella	multi.	26
Commodities Mkt.	E Vill	25
Costco	multi.	21
Z Dean/DeLuca	E 80s	27
Dynasty Supermkt.	Chinatown	19
Z E.A.T.	E 80s	25
Eckerton Hill	Hamburg	26
Z Eli's Manhattan	E 80s	25
Eli's Vinegar	E 90s	25
Z Fairway	multi.	26
Foragers Mkt.	Dumbo	22
Z FreshDirect	LIC	23
Garden	Greenpt	24
Garden of Eden	multi.	24
Gary Null's	W 80s	25
Gourmet Garage	multi.	20
Grace's Mktpl.	E 70s	24

NEW Greene Grape Provisions | **Ft Greene**	24
🅉 Greenmarket | **multi.**	26
Greenwich Produce | **E 40s**	25
Hawthorne Farm | **Ghent**	28
Health/Harmony | **W Vill**	26
Health Nuts | **multi.**	21
Hong Kong | **multi.**	20
Integral Yoga | **W Vill**	24
Jefferson Mkt. | **G Vill**	26
Jim/Andy's | **Cobble Hill**	19
Katagiri | **E 50s**	23
Keith's Farm | **Westtown**	28
LifeThyme Mkt. | **G Vill**	24
Likitsakos | **E 80s**	22
Manhattan Fruit Ex. | **Chelsea**	24
🅉 Manhattan Fruitier | **Gramercy**	27
Marché Madison | **E 70s**	20
Migliorelli Farm | **Tivoli**	26
Natural Frontier | **multi.**	24
Nature's Gifts | **E 80s**	21
New Green Pea | **Bklyn Hts**	23
#1 Farmers Mkt. | **multi.**	23
Orchard | **Midwood**	27
Paffenroth | **Warwick**	28
Park Natural | **Carroll Gdns**	22
Perelandra | **Bklyn Hts**	24
Pumpkins | **Park Slope**	26
Red Jacket | **Geneva**	27
Samascott | **Kinderhook**	27
Tan My My | **Chinatown**	22
Terhune Orchards | **Salt Pt**	27
3 Guys/Brooklyn | **Bay Ridge**	23
🅉 Trader Joe's | **multi.**	24
Truffette | **E Vill**	-
Trunzo Bros. | **Bensonhurst**	25
Union Market | **Park Slope**	26
Urban Organic | **Park Slope**	22
Westside Mkt. | **multi.**	21
🅉 Whole Foods | **multi.**	26
Windfall Farms | **Montgomery**	27
WK Trading | **Chinatown**	23
Yuno's Farm | **Bordentown**	29
🅉 Zabar's | **W 80s**	27
Zeytuna | **Financial**	23

SEAFOOD

🅉 Agata/Valentina | **E 70s**	26
Amish Market | **multi.**	23
Asia Market | **Chinatown**	21
🅉 Balducci's | **W 60s**	25
Blue Moon Fish | **Mattituck**	29
🅉 Citarella | **multi.**	26
Cosenza's Fish | **Bronx**	27
Costco | **multi.**	21
🅉 Dean/DeLuca | **multi.**	27
🅉 Dorian's Seafood | **E 80s**	25
Dynasty Supermkt. | **Chinatown**	19
🅉 Eli's Manhattan | **E 80s**	25
Eli's Vinegar | **E 90s**	25
🅉 Fairway | **multi.**	26
Fish Tales | **Cobble Hill**	25
🅉 FreshDirect | **LIC**	23
Garden of Eden | **multi.**	24
Gourmet Garage | **multi.**	20
Grace's Mktpl. | **E 70s**	24
Gramercy Fish | **Gramercy**	24
NEW Greene Grape Provisions | **Ft Greene**	24
🅉 Greenmarket | **multi.**	26
G.S. Food | **Chinatown**	19
Holland Ct. | **E 90s**	24
Hong Kong | **multi.**	20
Jefferson Mkt. | **G Vill**	26
Jordan's Lobster | **Sheepshead**	23
Jubilee | **multi.**	21
Leonard's | **E 70s**	26
L'Epicerie | **Ft Greene**	22
Lobster Pl. | **multi.**	26
131 Fish Mkt. | **Chinatown**	24
Pescatore | **E 40s**	25
🅉 Pisacane | **E 50s**	28
Rainbo's Fish | **LES**	26
🅉 Randazzo's | **Bronx**	28
Sea Breeze | **W 40s**	23
Slavin | **Brownsville**	23
Sunrise Mart | **multi.**	23
Tan My My | **Chinatown**	22
Todaro Bros. | **Murray Hill**	24
🅉 Trader Joe's | **Rego Pk**	24
Union Market | **Park Slope**	26

Whole Foods	**multi.**	26
Wild Edibles	**multi.**	26
Zeytuna	**Financial**	23

SOUPS

Z Agata/Valentina	**E 70s**	26
Z Balducci's	**W 60s**	25
Z Bazzini	**TriBeCa**	27
Cipriani	**E 40s**	26
Z Citarella	**multi.**	26
Cozy Soup	**G Vill**	17
Z Dean/DeLuca	**multi.**	27
Dishes	**multi.**	24
Z Eli's Manhattan	**E 80s**	25
Fabiane's	**W'burg**	-
Z Fairway	**multi.**	26
Fashion Soup	**W 40s**	22
Fifth Ave. Epicure	**Flatiron**	19
Financier	**Financial**	27
Good & Plenty	**W 40s**	22
Grace's Mktpl.	**E 70s**	24
Hale/Hearty	**multi.**	22
Iavarone Bros.	**Maspeth**	25
Jefferson Mkt.	**G Vill**	26
Le Pain Quotidien	**multi.**	24
Likitsakos	**E 80s**	22
Liqueteria	**E Vill**	19
Marquet Patiss.	**Ft Greene**	24
Z Olive's	**SoHo**	25
Z Original SoupMan	**multi.**	23
Z Pisacane	**E 50s**	28
Soup Spot	**Garment**	23
Todaro Bros.	**Murray Hill**	24
Z Westerly Natural	**W 50s**	25
Z Whole Foods	**multi.**	26
Z Zabar's	**W 80s**	27

SPECIALTY SHOPS

Asia Market	**Chinatown**	21
Z Bangkok Grocery	**Chinatown**	27
Basket Shop	**Borough Pk**	23
Beth's Farm	**Stuyvesant Falls**	27
Z Blue Apron	**Park Slope**	27
BuonItalia	**Chelsea**	26
Butterfield Mkt.	**E 70s**	23
Ceriello	**multi.**	24

Chelsea Baskets	**Chelsea**	24
Cobblestone	**Carroll Gdns**	21
Z Coluccio/Sons	**Borough Pk**	28
Dale & Thomas	**W 40s**	23
Delmonico	**multi.**	21
Deluxe Food	**Chinatown**	21
Z Despaña	**multi.**	27
Z D'Vine	**Park Slope**	25
Dynasty Supermkt.	**Chinatown**	19
Euro Shop	**Sunnyside**	-
Family Store	**Bay Ridge**	-
Fong Inn	**Chinatown**	18
Foragers Mkt.	**Dumbo**	22
Frank's Gourmet	**Wash. Hts**	21
Garden	**Greenpt**	24
Grab Specialty	**Park Slope**	24
NEW Greene Grape Provisions	**Ft Greene**	24
Gustiamo	**Bronx**	23
Han Ah Reum	**multi.**	22
Hong Kong	**multi.**	20
Italian Food	**L Italy**	22
JAS Mart	**multi.**	21
Z Kalustyan's	**Gramercy**	27
Kam Man	**Chinatown**	21
Katagiri	**E 50s**	23
Kidfresh	**E 80s**	18
L'Epicerie	**Ft Greene**	22
Little Piggy	**Ft Greene**	-
M & I Foods	**Brighton Bch**	24
Z Manhattan Fruitier	**Gramercy**	27
Marlow	**W'burg**	24
Z May May	**Chinatown**	23
Mediterranean	**Astoria**	26
m2m	**multi.**	18
Myers/Keswick	**W Vill**	23
Ninth Ave. Int'l	**W 40s**	23
Nordic Delicacies	**Bay Ridge**	28
O&CO.	**multi.**	25
Orchard	**Midwood**	27
Oriental Pastry	**Bklyn Hts**	22
Patel Bros.	**multi.**	23
Peter's Mkt.	**Bayside**	22
Z Pickle Guys	**LES**	27
Pickles/Olives	**E 80s**	23

Pumpkins | **Park Slope**	26
🅩 Sahadi's | **Bklyn Hts**	27
NEW Spuyten/Grocery | **W'burg**	–
🅩 Stonehouse | **Seaport**	27
Sunrise Mart | **multi.**	23
Teitel Bros. | **Bronx**	26
🅩 Titan Foods | **Astoria**	26
Todaro Bros. | **Murray Hill**	24
Truffette | **E Vill**	–
Trunzo Bros. | **Bensonhurst**	25
NEW Urban Rustic | **W'burg**	–

TRENDY

🅩 **NEW** Abraço Espresso | **E Vill**	27
🅩 Alessi | **SoHo**	27
🅩 Artisanal | **Murray Hill**	28
Baked | **Red Hook**	25
Balthazar Bakery | **SoHo**	27
NEW Batch | **G Vill**	–
Billy's Bakery | **Chelsea**	25
NEW Blue Marble | **multi.**	24
🅩 Bouchon Bakery | **W 60s**	27
Cheeks Bakery | **W'burg**	–
NEW ChikaLicious Puddin' | **E Vill**	24
Chocolate Room | **Park Slope**	25
🅩 City Bakery | **Flatiron**	25
Colson | **Park Slope**	25
Cones | **G Vill**	26
🅩 Dylan's Candy | **E 60s**	21
NEW El Beit | **W'burg**	–
Falai Panetteria | **LES**	27
🅩 FreshDirect | **LIC**	23
Gimme! Coffee | **W'burg**	27
Gorilla Coffee | **Park Slope**	24
Grom | **multi.**	27
🅩 Il Laboratorio | **LES**	28
🅩 Jacques Torres | **Dumbo**	28
Le Pain Quotidien | **multi.**	24
🅩 Magnolia Bakery | **W Vill**	23
🅩 MarieBelle's | **SoHo**	26
Marlow | **W'burg**	24
NEW Mercury Dime | **E Vill**	–
🅩 Moore Bros. | **Flatiron**	29
Mudspot | **E Vill**	26
🅩 Murray's Cheese | **multi.**	28
Ovando | **W Vill**	28

Pasanella | **Seaport**	26
🅩 Pierre Marcolini | **E 50s**	28
pinkberry | **multi.**	21
🅩 Red/White | **Park Slope**	26
Roasting Plant | **LES**	22
Shake Shack | **Flatiron**	25
🅩 Sullivan St. Bakery | **W 40s**	28
Sweet Melissa | **Cobble Hill**	24
🅩 Terence Conran | **E 50s**	25
🅩 Trader Joe's | **Union Sq**	24
🅩 Vosges | **SoHo**	26
🅩 Whole Foods | **multi.**	26

WEDDING CAKES

Andrew & Alan's | **SI**	22
Artuso Pastry | **Bronx**	26
Balthazar Bakery | **SoHo**	27
Bay Ridge Bake | **Bay Ridge**	25
Betty Bakery | **Boerum Hill**	23
Bijoux Doux | **Boerum Hill**	–
Buttercup | **E 50s**	23
Caffé Roma | **L Italy**	23
Cake Chef | **SI**	22
Cakeline | **Rockaway Bch**	–
🅩 Cake Man | **Ft Greene**	26
Ceci-Cela | **L Italy**	24
Cheryl Kleinman | **Boerum Hill**	28
🅩 Citarella | **multi.**	26
🅩 Colette's | **W Vill**	29
Confetti | **W 80s**	24
Creative Cakes | **E 70s**	25
Delillo Pastry | **Bronx**	26
🅩 Dessert Delivery | **E 50s**	28
Fabiane's | **W'burg**	–
Financier | **Financial**	27
Gail Watson | **Garment**	–
NEW How Sweet It Is | **LES**	–
Hungarian Pastry | **W 100s**	22
La Bergamote | **Chelsea**	26
🅩 Ladybird Bakery | **Park Slope**	28
Lafayette | **G Vill**	21
Margaret Braun | **W Vill**	–
Margot Pâtisserie | **W 70s**	27
Mother Mousse | **SI**	26
My Most/Food | **W 40s**	21
Paneantico | **Bay Ridge**	26

Panya Bakery | **E Vill**	22
🔒 Patisserie Claude | **G Vill**	27
🔒 Payard | **E 70s**	28
Rocco's Pastry | **G Vill**	25
Ron Ben-Israel | **SoHo**	25
🔒 Royal Crown | **multi.**	26
Sal & Dom's | **Bronx**	28
Schick's Bakery | **Borough Pk**	20
Settepani | **multi.**	23
Shakoor's Sweet | **Bed-Stuy**	–
Silver Moon | **W 100s**	26
Something Sweet | **E Vill**	23
🔒 Soutine | **W 70s**	27
🔒 Stork's Pastry | **Whitestone**	27
Sweet Melissa | **multi.**	24
🔒 Sylvia Weinstock | **TriBeCa**	26
Tempo Presto | **Park Slope**	23
Tribeca Treats | **TriBeCa**	27
🔒 Two Little Red | **E 80s**	26
Veniero's | **E Vill**	25
🔒 Villabate | **Bensonhurst**	28
🔒 Vosges | **SoHo**	26
Whole Earth | **E Vill**	21
William Greenberg | **E 80s**	25

WINES & LIQUOR

(* Open Sunday)

Acker Merrall* | **W 70s**	26
Ackerson, T.B. | **Ditmas Pk**	–
Ambassador Wine* | **E 50s**	24
Appellation | **Chelsea**	25
Astor Wines* | **NoHo**	25
Bacchus Wine* | **W 70s**	19
Beacon Wines* | **W 70s**	21
Beekman Liquors | **E 40s**	24
Best Cellars* | **multi.**	21
Big Nose | **Park Slope**	24
Blanc & Rouge* | **Dumbo**	25
🔒 Bottlerocket | **Flatiron**	26
Bottle Shoppe | **W'burg**	–
Bowery & Vine | **LES**	–
Brooklyn Liquors* | **Sunset Pk**	23
🔒 Burgundy | **Chelsea**	29
Cellar 72 | **E 70s**	26
Chambers Wines* | **TriBeCa**	26
Chelsea Wine* | **Chelsea**	23

Columbus Wine* | **W 50s**	22
Crossroads* | **Union Sq**	25
🔒 Crush Wine* | **E 50s**	26
Discovery Wines* | **E Vill**	22
NEW D.O.C. Wine | **W'burg**	19
Embassy Wines* | **E 60s**	19
Famous Wines | **Financial**	22
Fermented | **Prospect Hts**	22
First Ave. Wines | **Gramercy**	23
NEW Frankly Wines | **TriBeCa**	–
🔒 FreshDirect* | **LIC**	23
Garnet Wines* | **E 60s**	24
NEW Gnarly Vines | **Ft Greene**	–
Gotham Wines* | **W 90s**	22
Grande Harvest* | **E 40s**	23
Grand Wine | **Astoria**	25
Greene Grape* | **multi.**	24
Harlem Vintage* | **Harlem**	28
Heights Chateau | **Bklyn Hts**	25
Hendricks Wine | **Bay Ridge**	19
In Vino | **E 70s**	25
Is Wine* | **G Vill**	22
🔒 Italian Wine | **Union Sq**	27
K & D Wines | **E 90s**	24
Landmark Wine | **Chelsea**	25
🔒 Le Dû's Wines | **W Vill**	27
🔒 LeNell's* | **Red Hook**	27
Manley's Wines* | **W Vill**	22
Martin Bros. | **W 100s**	21
McAdam* | **Gramercy**	22
McCabe's Wines* | **E 70s**	19
Michael-Towne | **Bklyn Hts**	24
Mister Wright* | **E 80s**	24
🔒 Moore Bros. | **Flatiron**	29
🔒 Morrell & Co. | **W 40s**	27
Mount Carmel* | **Bronx**	26
Nancy's-Wines* | **W 70s**	24
New York/Exchange | **Financial**	23
New York/Warehse. | **LIC**	23
NEW Oak & Steel | **W 50s**	–
Olivino Wines | **multi.**	–
Park Ave. Liquor | **E 40s**	26
Pasanella | **Seaport**	26
Pete Milano's | **SI**	21
PJ Wine | **Inwood**	27

Pour | **W 70s**	21	Tinto Fino | **E Vill**	-
Premier Cru* | **E 80s**	24	Tops Wines | **Marine Pk**	23
☑ Prospect Wine* | **Park Slope**	26	☑ Trader Joe's | **Union Sq**	24
Quality Hse. | **Murray Hill**	27	Trader Joe's Wine | **Union Sq**	19
☑ Red/White* | **Park Slope**	26	Tribeca Wine | **TriBeCa**	23
Rosenthal Wine | **E 80s**	28	Union Sq. Wines* | **Union Sq**	25
Royal Wine | **Gramercy**	-	UN Wine | **E 40s**	22
NEW Sakaya | **E Vill**	25	Uva* | **W'burg**	24
Sea Grape* | **W Vill**	23	Vestry Wines | **TriBeCa**	-
Sept. Wines | **LES**	25	☑ Vino* | **Gramercy**	28
7th Ave. Wine | **Park Slope**	20	VinoVino | **TriBeCa**	25
Shawn's Wines | **Park Slope**	24	Vintage NY* | **multi.**	23
☑ Sherry-Lehmann | **E 60s**	29	Warehouse Wines* | **G Vill**	22
Sip | **Park Slope**	27	West Side Wine | **W 80s**	24
67 Wines* | **W 60s**	25	W.I.N.E.* | **E 80s**	21
Skyview Wines | **Bronx**	26	Wine & Spirit | **Forest Hills**	22
Slope Cellars* | **Park Slope**	24	Winesby | **G Vill**	-
Smith & Vine* | **Cobble Hill**	23	Wine Therapy | **NoLita**	25
SoHo Wines | **SoHo**	21	Winfield-Flynn* | **Murray Hill**	23
Sutton Wine* | **E 50s**	22	Yorkshire Wines* | **E 80s**	23

Ethnic Focus

Listings cover the best in each category and include source names, categories and Quality ratings. **Z** indicates places with the highest ratings, popularity and importance.

AMERICAN

NEW Amai Tea | *Baked Gds.*	20
Andrew & Alan's | *Baked Gds.*	22
Better Burger | *Prepared*	19
Between/Bread | *Caterer*	21
Z Blue Apron | *Spec. Shop*	27
Bread Alone | *Baked Gds.*	27
Busy Chef | *Prepared*	21
Buttercup | *Baked Gds.*	23
Carrot Top | *Baked Gds.*	23
Chocolate Room | *Candy/Nuts*	25
Z City Bakery | *Baked Gds.*	25
Cousin John's | *Baked Gds.*	21
Cozy Soup | *Prepared*	17
Crumbs | *Baked Gds.*	22
David Burke | *Caterer/Events*	23
Devon/Blakely | *Prepared*	22
Eddie's Sweet | *Ice Cream*	25
Emack/Bolio | *Ice Cream*	25
Fraser-Morris | *Prepared*	26
Friend/Farmer | *Baked Gds.*	21
Good & Plenty | *Prepared*	22
Gracious Thyme | *Caterer*	-
Great Performances | *Caterer*	24
Hinsch's | *Ice Cream*	22
NEW How Sweet It Is | *Baked Goods*	-
Indiana Mkt. | *Caterer*	26
Z Jacques Torres | *Candy/Nuts*	28
Joyce Bake | *Baked Gds.*	25
Junior's | *Baked Gds.*	23
Z Ladybird Bakery | *Baked Gds.*	28
Little Pie | *Baked Gds.*	24
Luscious Food | *Prepared*	19
Madison | *Baked Gds.*	20
Z Magnolia Bakery | *Baked Gds.*	23
Martha's Bakery | *Baked Gds.*	23
Mondel Choc. | *Candy/Nuts*	22
Naidre's | *Coffee/Tea*	22
Naturally Delic. | *Caterer/Events*	-
Neuman's | *Caterer*	25

Z Olive's | *Deli/Sandwich*	25
One Girl | *Baked Gds.*	24
Out/Kitchen | *Prepared*	20
NEW Papa Lima | *Deli/Sandwich*	22
Rick's Picks | *Spec. Shop*	-
Z Ronnybrook | *Cheese/Dairy*	28
Sandwich Planet | *Deli/Sandwich*	25
Sarabeth's | *Baked Gds.*	24
Saxelby Cheese | *Cheese/Dairy*	28
Shake Shack | *Prepared*	25
NEW Spuyten/Grocery | *Spec. Shop*	-
Starwich | *Deli/Sandwich*	23
Sweet Melissa | *Baked Gds.*	24
Tempo Presto | *Deli/Sandwich*	23
Thalia Kitchen | *Prepared*	21
Think Coffee | *Coffee/Tea*	23
Trois Pommes | *Baked Gds.*	23
Z Two Little Red | *Baked Gds.*	26
Vintage NY | *Wine/Liquor*	23
'wichcraft | *Deli/Sandwich*	24
Williamson Cal. | *Caterer*	-
Zaitzeff | *Prepared*	28

ARGENTINEAN

Gauchas | *Prepared*	25
Ruben's | *Prepared*	20

ASIAN

(See also Chinese, Japanese, Korean, Thai and Vietnamese)

Aji Ichiban | *Candy/Nuts*	21
Cafe Spice | *Prepared*	19
Chinatown Ice Cream | *Ice Cream*	25
Dual Specialty | *Herbs/Spices*	22
Foods/India | *Herbs/Spices*	23
Franchia | *Coffee/Tea*	24
Hampton Chutney | *Prepared*	23
Indian Bread | *Prepared*	21
Z Kalustyan's | *Spec. Shop*	27
Z Kee's Choc. | *Candy/Nuts*	29
Lassi | *Prepared*	21

Patel Bros. | *Spec. Shop*	23
Spice Corner | *Herbs/Spices*	24
Tamarind Tea | *Coffee/Tea*	24

AUSTRALIAN

DUB Pies | *Prepared*	24
Tuck Shop | *Prepared*	20

BELGIAN

Colson | *Baked Gds.*	25
Leonidas | *Candy/Nuts*	26
Le Pain Quotidien | *Baked Gds.*	24
☑ Martine's | *Candy/Nuts*	29
Michelle's Kitchen | *Prepared*	18
Neuhaus Choc. | *Candy/Nuts*	25
Petite Abeille | *Prepared*	22
☑ Pierre Marcolini | *Candy/Nuts*	28

BRAZILIAN

Brasil Coffee | *Coffee/Tea*	21

CARIBBEAN

Christie's | *Prepared*	21

CHINESE

Ah Wong Bakery | *Baked Gds.*	20
Asia Market | *Spec. Shop*	21
Bayard St. | *Meat/Poultry*	23
Deluxe Food | *Spec. Shop*	21
Dumpling Man | *Prepared*	20
Dynasty Supermkt. | *Spec. Shop*	19
Egg Custard King | *Baked Gds.*	21
Fay Da | *Baked Gds.*	19
Flor/Mayo | *Prepared*	23
Fong Inn | *Spec. Shop*	18
Golden Fung | *Baked Gds.*	18
Hong Keung | *Seafood*	22
Hong Kong | *Spec. Shop*	20
☑ Ito En | *Coffee/Tea*	28
Kam Man | *Spec. Shop*	21
Lung Moon | *Baked Gds.*	19
☑ May May | *Spec. Shop*	23
New Beef | *Meat/Poultry*	-
Sui Cheong Meat | *Meat/Poultry*	20
Tai Pan Bakery | *Baked Gds.*	19
☑ Ten Ren Tea | *Coffee/Tea*	25

CUBAN

Café Habana | *Prepared*	24

ECLECTIC

(Most caterers and prepared food shops offer a variety of cuisines)

☑ Abigail Kirsch | *Caterer*	26
☑ Artisanal | *Cheese/Dairy*	28
☑ Balducci's | *Maj. Gourmet*	25
☑ Bottlerocket | *Wine/Liquor*	26
Butterfield Mkt. | *Spec. Shop*	23
Call Cuisine | *Prepared*	24
Certé | *Caterer/Events*	26
Cheese/World | *Cheese/Dairy*	25
Chocolate Room | *Candy/Nuts*	25
☑ Citarella | *Maj. Gourmet*	26
Cosenza's Fish | *Seafood*	27
David Ziff | *Caterer*	22
Delmonico | *Spec. Shop*	21
Dishes | *Prepared*	24
☑ D'Vine | *Spec. Shop*	25
☑ Dylan's Candy | *Candy/Nuts*	21
East Coast Beer | *Beer*	22
East Vill. Cheese | *Cheese/Dairy*	22
Elizabeth Ryan | *Flowers*	28
Fabiane's | *Baked Gds.*	-
☑ Fairway | *Maj. Gourmet*	26
F&B | *Prepared*	20
Fish Tales | *Seafood*	25
Floralies | *Flowers*	26
Flowers/World | *Flowers*	28
Food Emporium | *Maj. Gourmet*	16
Food/Thought | *Prepared*	21
Foragers Mkt. | *Spec. Shop*	22
Frank's Gourmet | *Spec. Shop*	21
☑ FreshDirect | *Maj. Gourmet*	23
Garden of Eden | *Maj. Gourmet*	24
Good & Plenty | *Prepared*	22
Gotham Gdns. | *Flowers*	24
Gracious Thyme | *Caterer*	-
NEW Greene Grape Provisions | *Spec. Shop*	24
Ideal Cheese | *Cheese/Dairy*	27
☑ Jeffrey's | *Meat/Poultry*	25
Jubilee | *Maj. Gourmet*	21
☑ Kalustyan's | *Spec. Shop*	27
Klatch Coffee | *Coffee/Tea*	21
Lassen/Hennigs | *Caterer*	22
Luscious Food | *Prepared*	19

Manna Catering | *Caterer* — ⌐

Max Brenner | *Candy/Nuts* 22

Maya Schaper | *Cheese/Dairy* 22

Mille Fiori | *Flowers* — ⌐

Miss Elisabeth's | *Caterer* — ⌐

Movable Feast | *Caterer* 23

Myzel Choc. | *Candy/Nuts* 19

Natural Frontier | *Health* 24

Naturally Delic. | *Caterer/Events* — ⌐

Z Nespresso | *Coffee/Tea* 25

Neuman's | *Caterer* 25

Once Upon/Tart | *Baked Gds.* 25

Orchard | *Spec. Shop* 27

Paneantico | *Baked Gds.* 26

Porto Rico | *Coffee/Tea* 26

Pumpkins | *Spec. Shop* 26

Ready to Eat | *Prepared* 21

Robbins Wolfe | *Caterer* 26

NEW Root Hill | *Coffee/Tea* — ⌐

Root Stock | *Flowers* — ⌐

Second Helpings | *Prepared* — ⌐

Susan Holland | *Caterer* — ⌐

Sweet Life | *Candy/Nuts* 23

Swich | *Deli/Sandwich* 23

Taste Caterers | *Caterer* 22

Tea Lounge | *Coffee/Tea* 21

Truffette | *Spec. Shop* — ⌐

NEW Urban Rustic | *Spec. Shop* — ⌐

ENGLISH

A Salt/Battery | *Prepared* 22

Carry On Tea | *Coffee/Tea* 23

Charbonnel/Walker | *Candy/Nuts* 22

Myers/Keswick | *Spec. Shop* 23

Pret A Manger | *Deli/Sandwich* 21

FRENCH

Balthazar Bakery | *Baked Gds.* 27

Bonsignour | *Prepared* 26

Z Bouchon Bakery | *Baked Gds.* 27

Z Bouley Bakery | *Baked Gds.* 27

Z Burgundy | *Wine/Liquor* 29

Caputo Bakery | *Baked Gds.* 23

Ceci-Cela | *Baked Gds.* 24

Colson | *Baked Gds.* 25

Debauve/Gallais | *Candy/Nuts* 27

Duane Pk. | *Baked Gds.* 26

Feast/Fêtes | *Caterer* 27

Financier | *Baked Gds.* 27

Z Jacques Torres | *Candy/Nuts* 28

Joyce Bake | *Baked Gds.* 25

La Bergamote | *Baked Gds.* 26

Lafayette | *Baked Gds.* 21

Z La Maison/Choc. | *Candy/Nuts* 29

La Tropezienne | *Baked Gds.* — ⌐

Le Marais | *Meat/Poultry* 26

Le Pain Quotidien | *Baked Gds.* 24

L'Epicerie | *Spec. Shop* 22

Les Halles | *Meat/Poultry* 26

NEW Madeleine | *Baked Gds.* 24

Margot Pâtisserie | *Baked Gds.* 27

Marquet Patiss. | *Baked Gds.* 24

Michelle's Kitchen | *Prepared* 18

NEW Oro Bakery | *Baked Gds.* — ⌐

Z Patisserie Claude | *Baked Gds.* 27

Patisserie des Ambassades | 21
Baked Gds.

Z Payard | *Baked Gds.* 28

Z Petrossian | *Caviar/Smoked Fish* 28

Polux Fleuriste | *Flowers* — ⌐

Royal Wine | *Wine/Liquor* — ⌐

Silver Moon | *Baked Gds.* 26

Sweet Melissa | *Baked Gds.* 24

Tastings/Payard | *Caterer/Events* 27

Tisserie | *Baked Gds.* 20

Trois Pommes | *Baked Gds.* 23

Williamson Cal. | *Caterer* — ⌐

GERMAN/AUSTRIAN

Andrew & Alan's | *Baked Gds.* 22

Duane Pk. | *Baked Gds.* 26

Empire Market | *Meat/Poultry* 16

Koglin Hams | *Meat/Poultry* 24

Oppenheimer | *Meat/Poultry* 26

Z Schaller/Weber | *Meat/Poultry* 27

Z Stork's Pastry | *Baked Gds.* 27

GREEK

Z Artopolis | *Baked Gds.* 28

Christos Steak | *Meat/Poultry* 23

Likitsakos | *Produce* 22

Mediterranean | *Spec. Shop* 26

Nature's Gifts | *Health* 21

Ninth Ave. Int'l | *Spec. Shop* 23

Poseidon | *Baked Gds.* 26

Snack | *Prepared* 27

☑ Titan Foods | *Spec. Shop* 26

HUNGARIAN

Andre's | *Baked Gds.* 23

Euro Shop | *Spec. Shop* -

Hungarian Pastry | *Baked Gds.* 22

Yorkville Meat | *Meat/Poultry* 23

INDIAN

Cafe Spice | *Prepared* 19

Dual Specialty | *Herbs/Spices* 22

Foods/India | *Herbs/Spices* 23

Hampton Chutney | *Prepared* 23

Indian Bread | *Prepared* 21

☑ Ito En | *Coffee/Tea* 28

☑ Kalustyan's | *Spec. Shop* 27

Lassi | *Prepared* 21

Patel Bros. | *Spec. Shop* 23

Spice Corner | *Herbs/Spices* 24

Tamarind Tea | *Coffee/Tea* 24

ISRAELI

Mazal Kosher | *Candy/Nuts* 17

ITALIAN

Addeo Bakery | *Baked Gds.* 27

☑ Agata/Valentina | *Maj. Gourmet* 26

☑ Alessi | *Cookware* 27

Alidoro | *Deli/Sandwich* 27

Alleva Dairy | *Cheese/Dairy* 27

Andrew & Alan's | *Baked Gds.* 22

Areo Rist. | *Caterer* 21

Arte/Corner | *Baked Gds.* 24

Arthur Ave. | *Caterer* 24

Artuso Pastry | *Baked Gds.* 26

☑ Balducci's | *Maj. Gourmet* 25

Barbarini | *Prepared* -

Bari Pork | *Meat/Poultry* 24

Belfiore Meats | *Meat/Poultry* 25

Biancardi Meats | *Meat/Poultry* 27

☑ Borgatti's | *Pasta* 29

Bottega/Via | *Prepared* 25

Bottino | *Prepared* 22

Bruno Bakery | *Baked Gds.* 23

Bruno/Ravioli | *Pasta* 24

BuonItalia | *Spec. Shop* 26

Caffé Roma | *Baked Gds.* 23

☑ Calabria Pork | *Meat/Poultry* 28

Calandra Cheese | *Cheese/Dairy* 26

Caputo Bakery | *Baked Gds.* 23

Carmine's | *Prepared* 23

Carol's Cafe | *Caterer* -

Casa Della | *Cheese/Dairy* 29

Cassinelli Food | *Pasta* 25

Ceriello | *Spec. Shop* 24

Ciao Bella | *Ice Cream* 25

Cipriani | *Baked Gds.* 26

☑ Coluccio/Sons | *Spec. Shop* 28

Cosenza's Fish | *Seafood* 27

Court Pastry | *Baked Gds.* 25

Cucina Vivolo | *Prepared* 23

☑ D'Amico | *Coffee/Tea* 27

Delillo Pastry | *Baked Gds.* 26

DeRobertis | *Baked Gds.* 22

☑ DiPalo Dairy | *Cheese/Dairy* 29

Durso's Pasta | *Pasta* 26

Egidio Pastry | *Baked Gds.* 24

Esposito Meat | *Meat/Poultry* 25

Esposito's Pork | *Meat/Poultry* 26

☑ Faicco's Pork | *Meat/Poultry* 28

Falai Panetteria | *Baked Gds.* 27

Fay Da | *Baked Gds.* 19

Ferrara Cafe | *Baked Gds.* 22

☑ Florence Meat | *Meat/Poultry* 29

Fortunato Bros. | *Baked Gds.* 25

Fresco/Scotto | *Prepared* 24

☑ Grandaisy Bakery | *Baked Gds.* 29

Grom | *Ice Cream* 27

Gustiamo | *Spec. Shop* 23

Iavarone Bros. | *Prepared* 25

☑ Il Laboratorio | *Ice Cream* 28

Italian Food | *Spec. Shop* 22

☑ Italian Wine | *Wine/Liquor* 27

☑ Joe's Dairy | *Cheese/Dairy* 28

La Guli | *Baked Gds.* 24

Lamarca | *Cheese/Dairy* 26

☑ L'Arte del Gelato | *Ice Cream* 21

☑ Lemon Ice | *Ice Cream* 27

Lioni Latticini | *Cheese/Dairy* 29

Lorimer St. Meat | *Meat/Poultry* -

🄩 Madonia Bakery | *Baked Gds.* 28

Manganaro Foods | *Deli/Sandwich* 24

Manganaro's Hero | *Deli/Sandwich* 21

Mangia | *Prepared* 24

Mazzola Bakery | *Baked Gds.* 25

Milano Gourmet | *Prepared* 25

Mona Lisa Pastry | *Baked Gds.* 24

Monteleone's | *Baked Gds.* 23

Mount Carmel | *Wine/Liquor* 26

Napoli Bakery | *Baked Gds.* 23

🄩 Ottomanelli & Sons | 27
  Meat/Poultry

Ottomanelli Bros. | *Meat/Poultry* 24

🄩 Ottomanelli's Meats | 27
  Meat/Poultry

Paneantico | *Baked Gds.* 26

Pane d'Italia | *Baked Gds.* -

Papa Pasquale | *Pasta* 26

Parisi Bakery | *Baked Gds.* 23

🄩 Pastosa Ravioli | *Pasta* 26

Pepe | *Prepared* 26

Peter's Mkt. | *Spec. Shop* 22

Piazza Mercato | *Meat/Poultry* 23

Pie/Pound | *Prepared* 20

Piemonte Ravioli | *Pasta* 27

Pino Meats | *Meat/Poultry* 27

Piu Bello | *Ice Cream* 21

Porto Rico | *Coffee/Tea* 26

Queen Ann | *Pasta* 27

🄩 Raffetto's | *Pasta* 28

🄩 Ralph's/Ices | *Ice Cream* 24

🄩 Randazzo's | *Seafood* 28

Remi | *Prepared* 26

Risotteria | *Prepared* 23

Rita's Ices | *Ice Cream* 21

Rocco's Pastry | *Baked Gds.* 25

🄩 Royal Crown | *Baked Gds.* 26

Royal Wine | *Wine/Liquor* -

Russo Mozzarella | *Cheese/Dairy* 26

Sal & Dom's | *Baked Gds.* 28

🄩 Salumeria | *Meat/Poultry* 29

Sant Ambroeus | *Ice Cream* 26

Savino's Pasta | *Pasta* -

Settepani | *Baked Gds.* 23

🄩 Sullivan St. Bakery | *Baked Gds.* 28

Tarallucci e Vino | *Baked Gds.* 24

Teitel Bros. | *Spec. Shop* 26

Tempo Presto | *Deli/Sandwich* 23

Terrace Bagels | *Bagels* 25

Terranova | *Baked Gds.* 26

Todaro Bros. | *Spec. Shop* 24

Trunzo Bros. | *Spec. Shop* 25

United Meat | *Meat/Poultry* 26

Veniero's | *Baked Gds.* 25

Vesuvio | *Prepared* 23

🄩 Villabate | *Baked Gds.* 28

Vincent's Meat | *Meat/Poultry* 27

🄩 Vino | *Wine/Liquor* 28

Zibetto Espresso | *Coffee/Tea* 26

JAPANESE

🆕 Amai Tea | *Baked Gds.* 20

Beard Papa | *Baked Gds.* 24

Han Ah Reum | *Spec. Shop* 22

🄩 Ito En | *Coffee/Tea* 28

JAS Mart | *Spec. Shop* 21

Katagiri | *Spec. Shop* 23

Landmark Wine | *Wine/Liquor* 25

🄩 Minamoto | *Candy/Nuts* 28

m2m | *Spec. Shop* 18

Otafuku | *Prepared* 19

Panya Bakery | *Baked Gds.* 22

🆕 Sakaya | *Wine/Liquor* 25

Sunrise Mart | *Spec. Shop* 23

🆕 Tafu | *Coffee/Tea* 19

🄩 Takashimaya | *Flowers* 28

Tea Box | *Coffee/Tea* 27

JEWISH

Acme Fish | *Caviar/Smoked Fish* 24

Artie's Deli | *Deli/Sandwich* 21

Bagels & Co. | *Bagels* 22

🄩 Barney Greengrass | 27
  Caviar/Smoked Fish

Ben's Best | *Deli/Sandwich* 23

Ben's Kosher | *Deli/Sandwich* 21

Berger's | *Deli/Sandwich* 21

🄩 Carnegie Deli | *Deli/Sandwich* 23

Deli Masters | *Deli/Sandwich* 21

Eisenberg's Sandwich | 20
  Deli/Sandwich

Fine/Schapiro | *Deli/Sandwich* 20
Fischer Bros. | *Meat/Poultry* 27
Foremost Caterers | *Caterer* 24
Ⓩ Katz's Deli | *Deli/Sandwich* 24
Ⓩ Kossar's | *Bagels* 28
Mansoura | *Baked Gds.* –
Mauzone | *Prepared* 22
Mazur's | *Meat/Poultry* 20
Mother's Bake | *Baked Gds.* 21
Murray's Sturgeon | 27
  Caviar/Smoked Fish
#1 Farmers Mkt. | *Produce* 23
Oppenheimer | *Meat/Poultry* 26
Orwasher's | *Baked Gds.* 26
Park E. Kosher | *Meat/Poultry* 26
Pastrami Queen | *Deli/Sandwich* 21
Ⓩ Pickle Guys | *Spec. Shop* 27
P.J. Bernstein | *Deli/Sandwich* 19
Ⓩ Russ & Daughters | 28
  Smoked Fish
Sarge's Deli | *Deli/Sandwich* 21
Schick's Bakery | *Baked Gds.* 20
Stage Deli | *Deli/Sandwich* 21
Streit's Matzo | *Baked Gds.* 25
William Greenberg | *Baked Gds.* 25
Yonah Schimmel | *Baked Gds.* 23
NEW Zucker's Bagels | *Bagels* 22

KOREAN

Han Ah Reum | *Spec. Shop* 22
m2m | *Spec. Shop* 18

MEDITERRANEAN

Ⓩ Artopolis | *Baked Gds.* 28
Caffe' Simpatico/Ruthy's | 15
  Baked Gds.
Cucina | *Prepared* 21
Good & Plenty | *Prepared* 22
Mangia | *Prepared* 24
Melange | *Prepared* 21
Ninth Ave. Int'l | *Spec. Shop* 23
O&CO. | *Spec. Shop* 25
Tanoreen | *Prepared* 24
Tempo Presto | *Deli/Sandwich* 23
Todaro Bros. | *Spec. Shop* 24
Zeytuna | *Maj. Gourmet* 23

MEXICAN/TEX-MEX

Café Habana | *Prepared* 24
Ⓩ Kalustyan's | *Spec. Shop* 27
Zarela | *Caterer/Events* 24

MIDDLE EASTERN

Damascus Bakery | *Baked Gds.* 25
Ⓩ D'Vine | *Spec. Shop* 25
Family Store | *Spec. Shop* –
Ⓩ Kalustyan's | *Spec. Shop* 27
Mansoura | *Baked Gds.* –
Melange | *Prepared* 21
#1 Farmers Mkt. | *Produce* 23
Oriental Pastry | *Spec. Shop* 22
Ⓩ Sahadi's | *Spec. Shop* 27
Snack | *Prepared* 27
Spice Corner | *Herbs/Spices* 24
Tanoreen | *Prepared* 24
Yoghurt Place | *Cheese/Dairy* 23

POLISH

Eagle Provisions | 24
  Meat/Poultry
Ⓩ East Vill. Meat | 28
  Meat/Poultry

RUSSIAN

Caviar Russe | *Caviar* 26
M & I Foods | *Spec. Shop* 24
Ⓩ Petrossian | *Caviar/Smoked* 28
  Fish

SCANDINAVIAN

Fika | *Coffee/Tea* 22
Leske's | *Baked Gds.* 23
Nordic Delicacies | *Spec. Shop* 28

SOUTH AMERICAN

Brasil Coffee | *Coffee/Tea* 21
Flor/Mayo | *Prepared* 23
Juan Valdez | *Coffee/Tea* 22
Ruben's | *Prepared* 20

SOUTHERN/SOUL FOOD

Blue Smoke | *Caterer* 25
Ⓩ Cake Man | *Baked Gds.* 26
Daisy May's | *Prepared* 24
Dirty Bird | *Prepared* 20
Make My Cake | *Baked Gds.* 25

Shakoor's Sweet | *Baked Gds.* ⊐

Spoonbread | *Caterer* 23⏌

SPANISH

�... Despaña | *Spec. Shop* 27⏌

Tinto Fino | *Wine/Liquor* ⊐

SWISS

Lindt | *Candy/Nuts* 24⏌

Neuchatel Choc. | *Candy/Nuts* 24⏌

🗹 Teuscher Choc. | *Candy/Nuts* 27⏌

THAI

Asia Market | *Spec. Shop* 21⏌

🗹 Bangkok Grocery | *Spec. Shop* 27⏌

TURKISH

Güllüoglu | *Baked Gds.* ⊐

Zeytuna | *Maj. Gourmet* 23⏌

UKRAINIAN

Astoria Meat | *Meat/Poultry* 25⏌

🗹 East Vill. Meat | 28⏌
   Meat/Poultry

First Ave. Pierogi | *Prepared* 25⏌

VEGETARIAN

(Most prepared food shops and health food stores offer vegetarian options, including these standouts)

A Matter/Health | *Health* 21⏌

Back/Land | *Health* 23⏌

Bell Bates | *Health* 24⏌

🗹 City Bakery | *Baked Gds.* 25⏌

🗹 Fairway | *Maj. Gourmet* 26⏌

Gary Null's | *Health* 25⏌

Health Nuts | *Health* 21⏌

Integral Yoga | *Health* 24⏌

LifeThyme Mkt. | *Health* 24⏌

Second Helpings | *Prepared* ⊐

Silver Moon | *Baked Gds.* 26⏌

sNice | *Deli/Sandwich* 23⏌

Tastebud's | *Health* 22⏌

Urban Organic | *Produce* 22⏌

Whole Earth | *Baked Gds.* 21⏌

VIETNAMESE

Bánh Mì Saigon | *Deli/Sandwich* 25⏌

Nicky's Viet. | *Deli/Sandwich* 24⏌

Viet-Nam Bánh | *Deli/Sandwich* 23⏌

Locations

Includes source names, categories and Quality ratings. ⚡ indicates places with the highest ratings, popularity and importance.

Manhattan

CHELSEA

(24th to 30th Sts., west of 5th; 14th to 24th Sts., west of 6th)

⚡ Abigail Kirsch	*Caterer*	26
⚡ Amy's Bread	*Baked Gds.*	26
Appellation	*Wine/Liquor*	25
Ariston	*Flowers*	27
⚡ Balducci's	*Maj. Gourmet*	25
Baskin-Robbins	*Ice Cream*	17
Bed Bath/Beyond	*Cookware*	20
Better Burger	*Prepared*	19
Billy's Bakery	*Baked Gds.*	25
Bottino	*Prepared*	22
Bowery Kitchen	*Cookware*	22
BuonItalia	*Spec. Shop*	26
⚡ Burgundy	*Wine/Liquor*	29
Café Grumpy	*Coffee/Tea*	26
Caffe' Simpatico/Ruthy's	*Baked Gds.*	15
Catering Co.	*Events*	-
Chelsea Baskets	*Spec. Shop*	24
Chelsea Wine	*Wine/Liquor*	23
Chocolat Moderne	*Candy/Nuts*	26
⚡ Cleaver Co.	*Caterer/Events*	25
David Beahm	*Flowers*	-
Eleni's Cookies	*Baked Gds.*	22
F&B	*Prepared*	20
Fat Witch	*Baked Gds.*	25
Food/Thought	*Prepared*	21
NEW Friedman's Deli	*Deli/Sandwich*	21
Garden of Eden	*Maj. Gourmet*	24
Haas Co.	*Cookware*	25
Hale/Hearty	*Soup*	22
Hudson Yards	*Caterer/Events*	24
Joe	*Coffee/Tea*	26
La Bergamote	*Baked Gds.*	26
Landmark Wine	*Wine/Liquor*	25
⚡ L'Arte del Gelato	*Ice Cream*	27
Lobster Pl.	*Seafood*	26
L'Olivier	*Flowers*	29

NEW Madeleine	*Baked Gds.*	24
Manhattan Fruit Ex.	*Produce*	24
Mille Fiori	*Flowers*	-
Murray's Bagels	*Bagels*	26
Ninth St. Espresso	*Coffee/Tea*	28
Party Rental	*Party Rent.*	22
Patisserie des Ambassades	*Baked Gds.*	21
Pepe	*Prepared*	26
pinkberry	*Ice Cream*	21
NEW Red Mango	*Ice Cream*	22
⚡ Ronnybrook	*Cheese/Dairy*	28
⚡ Salumeria	*Meat/Poultry*	29
Sarabeth's	*Baked Gds.*	24
Spruce	*Flowers*	27
Swich	*Deli/Sandwich*	23
Three Tarts	*Baked Gds.*	22
T Salon	*Coffee/Tea*	26
Westside Mkt.	*Maj. Gourmet*	21
⚡ Whole Foods	*Maj. Gourmet*	26
'wichcraft	*Deli/Sandwich*	24
⚡ Williams-Sonoma	*Cookware*	27
Yolato	*Ice Cream*	20

CHINATOWN

(Canal to Pearl Sts., east of B'way)

Ah Wong Bakery	*Baked Gds.*	20
Aji Ichiban	*Candy/Nuts*	21
Asia Market	*Spec. Shop*	21
⚡ Bangkok Grocery	*Spec. Shop*	27
Bánh Mì Saigon	*Deli/Sandwich*	25
Bayard St.	*Meat/Poultry*	23
Chinatown Ice Cream	*Ice Cream*	25
Deluxe Food	*Spec. Shop*	21
Dynasty Supermkt.	*Spec. Shop*	19
Egg Custard King	*Baked Gds.*	21
Fay Da	*Baked Gds.*	19
Fong Inn	*Spec. Shop*	18
Golden Fung	*Baked Gds.*	18
G.S. Food	*Seafood*	19
Häagen Dazs	*Ice Cream*	24
Hong Keung	*Seafood*	22

Hong Kong | *Spec. Shop*	20
Hung Chong | *Cookware*	19
Kam Man | *Spec. Shop*	21
Lung Moon | *Baked Gds.*	19
☑ May May | *Spec. Shop*	23
New Beef | *Meat/Poultry*	-
131 Fish Mkt. | *Seafood*	24
Starbucks | *Coffee/Tea*	18
Sui Cheong Meat | *Meat/Poultry*	20
Tai Pan Bakery | *Baked Gds.*	19
Tan My My | *Seafood*	22
☑ Ten Ren Tea | *Coffee/Tea*	25
Viet-Nam Bánh | *Deli/Sandwich*	23
WK Trading | *Produce*	23

EAST 40s

Amish Market | *Maj. Gourmet*	23
Ariston | *Flowers*	27
Au Bon Pain | *Baked Gds.*	16
Beard Papa | *Baked Gds.*	24
Beekman Liquors | *Wine/Liquor*	24
Beekman Mktpl. | *Meat/Poultry*	22
Ben & Jerry's | *Ice Cream*	24
Big Apple Florist | *Flowers*	24
Cafe Spice | *Prepared*	19
Ceriello | *Spec. Shop*	24
Charbonnel/Walker | *Candy/Nuts*	22
Choux Factory | *Baked Gds.*	23
Ciao Bella | *Ice Cream*	25
Cipriani | *Baked Gds.*	26
Corrado | *Baked Gds.*	21
Cucina | *Prepared*	21
Dahlia | *Flowers*	26
Delmonico | *Spec. Shop*	21
Devon/Blakely | *Prepared*	22
Dishes | *Prepared*	24
Fifth Ave. Choc. | *Candy/Nuts*	20
Godiva | *Candy/Nuts*	22
Grande Harvest | *Wine/Liquor*	23
Greenwich Produce | *Produce*	25
Hale/Hearty | *Soup*	22
Health Nuts | *Health*	21
Hot/Crusty | *Baked Gds.*	15
Joe | *Coffee/Tea*	26
Juan Valdez | *Coffee/Tea*	22
Junior's | *Baked Gds.*	23

Koglin Hams | *Meat/Poultry*	24
Li-Lac Choc. | *Candy/Nuts*	26
Lindt | *Candy/Nuts*	24
Little Pie | *Baked Gds.*	24
Mangia | *Prepared*	24
Manhattan Espresso | *Coffee/Tea*	21
Michael George | *Flowers*	25
Miho Kosuda | *Flowers*	-
☑ Murray's Cheese | *Cheese/Dairy*	28
Neuhaus Choc. | *Candy/Nuts*	25
O&CO. | *Spec. Shop*	25
Oren's/Roast | *Coffee/Tea*	24
☑ Original SoupMan | *Soup*	23
Park Ave. Liquor | *Wine/Liquor*	26
☑ Penzeys Spices | *Herbs/Spices*	27
Pepe | *Prepared*	26
Pescatore | *Seafood*	25
Pret A Manger | *Deli/Sandwich*	21
☑ Teuscher Choc. | *Candy/Nuts*	27
UN Wine | *Wine/Liquor*	22
'wichcraft | *Deli/Sandwich*	24
Wild Edibles | *Seafood*	26
World of Nuts | *Candy/Nuts*	15
Yolato | *Ice Cream*	20
Zaro's Bread | *Baked Gds.*	17

EAST 50s

Ambassador Wine | *Wine/Liquor*	24
☑ Bloom | *Flowers*	27
Bloomingdale's | *Cookware*	24
Bottega/Via | *Prepared*	25
Buttercup | *Baked Gds.*	23
Call Cuisine | *Prepared*	24
Caviar Russe | *Caviar*	26
Così | *Deli/Sandwich*	18
Crate/Barrel | *Cookware*	22
☑ Crush Wine | *Wine/Liquor*	26
Cucina Vivolo | *Prepared*	23
David Burke | *Caterer/Events*	23
Delmonico | *Spec. Shop*	21
☑ Dessert Delivery | *Baked Gds.*	28
Devon/Blakely | *Prepared*	22
Dishes | *Prepared*	24
Edible Arrangements | *Caterer*	22
Ess-a-Bagel | *Bagels*	26

Fifth Ave. Choc. | *Candy/Nuts* 20
Floralies | *Flowers* 26
Food Emporium | *Maj. Gourmet* 16
Fresco/Scotto | *Prepared* 24
Godiva | *Candy/Nuts* 22
Ideal Cheese | *Cheese/Dairy* 27
Jane Packer | *Flowers* 29
Juan Valdez | *Coffee/Tea* 22
Katagiri | *Spec. Shop* 23
Leonidas | *Candy/Nuts* 26
Marché Madison | *Prepared* 20
Z Martine's | *Candy/Nuts* 29
Neuchatel Choc. | *Candy/Nuts* 24
Neuhaus Choc. | *Candy/Nuts* 25
#1 Farmers Mkt. | *Produce* 23
Oren's/Roast | *Coffee/Tea* 24
Z Original SoupMan | *Soup* 23
Z Pierre Marcolini | *Candy/Nuts* 28
Z Pisacane | *Seafood* 28
Pret A Manger | *Deli/Sandwich* 21
Renny/Reed | *Flowers* 28
Sebastians | *Caterer* -
Z Simchick | *Meat/Poultry* 28
Starwich | *Deli/Sandwich* 23
Sutton Wine | *Wine/Liquor* 22
NEW Tafu | *Coffee/Tea* 19
Z Takashimaya | *Flowers* 28
Tal Bagels | *Bagels* 23
Tea Box | *Coffee/Tea* 27
Z Terence Conran | *Cookware* 25
Z Williams-Sonoma | *Cookware* 27
Zarela | *Caterer/Events* 24
Z Zezé | *Flowers* 29

EAST 60s

Albert & Sons | *Meat/Poultry* 26
Alice's Tea | *Coffee/Tea* 24
Bagelworks | *Bagels* 23
Baskin-Robbins | *Ice Cream* 17
Bed Bath/Beyond | *Cookware* 20
Debauve/Gallais | *Candy/Nuts* 27
Z Dylan's Candy | *Candy/Nuts* 21
Embassy Wines | *Wine/Liquor* 19
Feast/Fêtes | *Caterer* 27
Fellan Florist | *Flowers* 24
Food Emporium | *Maj. Gourmet* 16

Garnet Wines | *Wine/Liquor* 24
Godiva | *Candy/Nuts* 22
Gourmet Garage | *Maj. Gourmet* 20
Häagen Dazs | *Ice Cream* 24
Hale/Hearty | *Soup* 22
Health Nuts | *Health* 21
Hot/Crusty | *Baked Gds.* 15
Z Ito En | *Coffee/Tea* 28
Java Girl | *Coffee/Tea* 24
Le Pain Quotidien | *Baked Gds.* 24
Z MarieBelle's | *Candy/Nuts* 26
Melange | *Prepared* 21
Z Morrell & Co. | *Wine/Liquor* 26
Z Nespresso | *Coffee/Tea* 25
Plaza Flowers | *Flowers* 25
Rosa Rosa | *Flowers* 21
Z Sherry-Lehmann | *Wine/Liquor* 29
Z Teuscher Choc. | *Candy/Nuts* 27
World of Nuts | *Candy/Nuts* 15

EAST 70s

Z Agata/Valentina | 26
   Maj. Gourmet
A Matter/Health | *Health* 21
Anthony Gdn. | *Flowers* -
Bagels & Co. | *Bagels* 22
Bottega/Via | *Prepared* 25
Butterfield Mkt. | *Spec. Shop* 23
Cellar 72 | *Wine/Liquor* 26
Z Citarella | *Maj. Gourmet* 26
Corrado | *Baked Gds.* 21
Creative Cakes | *Baked Gds.* 25
Crumbs | *Baked Gds.* 22
Cucina Vivolo | *Prepared* 23
East Side Bagel | *Bagels* 21
Z Glorious Food | *Caterer* 25
Grace's Mktpl. | *Maj. Gourmet* 24
Gracious Home | *Cookware* 25
In Vino | *Wine/Liquor* 25
Z Lady M | *Baked Gds.* 28
Z La Maison/Choc. | *Candy/Nuts* 29
Leonard's | *Seafood* 26
Le Pain Quotidien | *Baked Gds.* 24
L'Olivier | *Flowers* 29
Marché Madison | *Prepared* 20
McCabe's Wines | *Wine/Liquor* 19

#1 Farmers Mkt.	*Produce*	23
Oren's/Roast	*Coffee/Tea*	24
Orwasher's	*Baked Gds.*	26
Pastrami Queen	*Deli/Sandwich*	21
Z Payard	*Baked Gds.*	28
Pick a Bagel	*Bagels*	20
P.J. Bernstein	*Deli/Sandwich*	19
Richard Salome	*Flowers*	-
Sable's Smoked	*Caviar/Smoked Fish*	27
Sant Ambroeus	*Ice Cream*	26
Sarabeth's	*Baked Gds.*	24
Sedutto's	*Ice Cream*	24
Starbucks	*Coffee/Tea*	18
Starwich	*Deli/Sandwich*	23
Tastings/Payard	*Caterer/Events*	27
Z William Poll	*Prepared*	26
Windsor Florist	*Flowers*	24
World of Nuts	*Candy/Nuts*	15

EAST 80s

Alice's Tea	*Coffee/Tea*	24
Andre's	*Baked Gds.*	23
Annie's	*Produce*	21
Bagel Bob's	*Bagels*	22
Best Cellars	*Wine/Liquor*	21
CBK Cookies	*Baked Gds.*	23
Choux Factory	*Baked Gds.*	23
Cold Stone	*Ice Cream*	20
Corner Bagel	*Bagels*	22
Z Dean/DeLuca	*Maj. Gourmet*	27
Z Dorian's Seafood	*Seafood*	25
Z E.A.T.	*Prepared*	25
Z Eli's Manhattan	*Maj. Gourmet*	25
Emack/Bolio	*Ice Cream*	25
Food Emporium	*Maj. Gourmet*	16
Glaser's Bake	*Baked Gds.*	21
H & H Midtown	*Bagels*	25
Hot/Crusty	*Baked Gds.*	15
Kidfresh	*Spec. Shop*	18
Le Pain Quotidien	*Baked Gds.*	24
Likitsakos	*Produce*	22
Z Lobel's Meats	*Meat/Poultry*	29
Lorenzo/Maria's	*Prepared*	25
Z Martine's	*Candy/Nuts*	29
Milano Gourmet	*Prepared*	25

Mister Wright	*Wine/Liquor*	24
Natural Frontier	*Health*	24
Nature's Gifts	*Health*	21
Oren's/Roast	*Coffee/Tea*	24
Ottomanelli Bros.	*Meat/Poultry*	24
Park E. Kosher	*Meat/Poultry*	26
Petak's	*Prepared*	23
Pickles/Olives	*Spec. Shop*	23
Pie/Pound	*Prepared*	20
pinkberry	*Ice Cream*	21
Premier Cru	*Wine/Liquor*	24
Rohrs	*Coffee/Tea*	24
Rosenthal Wine	*Wine/Liquor*	28
Z Schaller/Weber	*Meat/Poultry*	27
Schatzie's Meats	*Meat/Poultry*	25
Tal Bagels	*Bagels*	23
Z Two Little Red	*Baked Gds.*	26
Z Vosges	*Candy/Nuts*	26
William Greenberg	*Baked Gds.*	25
Z Williams-Sonoma	*Cookware*	27
W.I.N.E.	*Wine/Liquor*	21
Yorkshire Wines	*Wine/Liquor*	23
Yorkville Meat	*Meat/Poultry*	23

EAST 90s & 100s

(90th to 110th Sts.)

Ciao Bella	*Ice Cream*	25
Corner Café	*Deli/Sandwich*	-
Corrado	*Baked Gds.*	21
David Ziff	*Caterer*	22
Eli's Vinegar	*Maj. Gourmet*	25
Gauchas	*Prepared*	25
Gourmet Garage	*Maj. Gourmet*	20
Holland Ct.	*Meat/Seafood*	24
K & D Wines	*Wine/Liquor*	24
Madison	*Baked Gds.*	20
Michelle's Kitchen	*Prepared*	18
Ronaldo Maia	*Flowers*	28
Sarabeth's	*Baked Gds.*	24
S. Feldman	*Cookware*	23
Starbucks	*Coffee/Tea*	18

EAST VILLAGE

(14th to Houston Sts., east of B'way, excluding NoHo)

Z NEW Abraço Espresso	*Coffee/Tea*	27
Angelica's Herbs	*Herbs/Spices*	23

Antony Todd | *Events/Flowers*	–
Australian Home. | *Ice Cream*	23
Beard Papa | *Baked Gds.*	24
Ben & Jerry's | *Ice Cream*	24
Birdbath/Build Green | *Baked Gds.*	23
❷ Black Hound | *Baked Gds.*	26
Blue Meadow | *Flowers*	–
NEW ChikaLicious Puddin' | *Baked Gds.*	24
Commodities Mkt. | *Health*	25
David's Bagels | *Bagels*	23
DeRobertis | *Baked Gds.*	22
Discovery Wines | *Wine/Liquor*	22
Dual Specialty | *Herbs/Spices*	22
Dumpling Man | *Prepared*	20
East Vill. Cheese | *Cheese/Dairy*	22
East Vill. Ice Cream | *Ice Cream*	22
❷ East Vill. Meat | *Meat/Poultry*	28
NEW /eks/ | *Ice Cream*	–
First Ave. Pierogi | *Prepared*	25
JAS Mart | *Spec. Shop*	21
Joe | *Coffee/Tea*	26
Liqueteria | *Soup*	19
LMD Floral | *Flowers*	–
Masturbakers | *Baked Gds.*	22
Max Brenner | *Candy/Nuts*	22
NEW Mercury Dime | *Coffee/Tea*	–
Miss Elisabeth's | *Caterer*	–
m2m | *Spec. Shop*	18
Mudspot | *Coffee/Tea*	26
Nicky's Viet. | *Deli/Sandwich*	24
Ninth St. Espresso | *Coffee/Tea*	28
NEW Öko | *Ice Cream*	24
Otafuku | *Prepared*	19
Panya Bakery | *Baked Gds.*	22
Pepe | *Prepared*	26
Pie/Pound | *Prepared*	20
Porto Rico | *Coffee/Tea*	26
Ruben's | *Prepared*	20
Russo Mozzarella | *Cheese/Dairy*	26
NEW Sakaya | *Wine/Liquor*	25
Something Sweet | *Baked Gds.*	23
Starbucks | *Coffee/Tea*	18
Sundaes & Cones | *Ice Cream*	25
Sunrise Mart | *Spec. Shop*	23

Sympathy | *Coffee/Tea*	27
Tarallucci e Vino | *Baked Gds.*	24
Tinto Fino | *Wine/Liquor*	–
Truffette | *Spec. Shop*	–
Tuck Shop | *Prepared*	20
Veniero's | *Baked Gds.*	25
NEW Very Berry | *Ice Cream*	20
Whole Earth | *Baked Gds.*	21

FINANCIAL DISTRICT

(South of Murray St.)

Amish Market | *Maj. Gourmet*	23
Au Bon Pain | *Baked Gds.*	16
Barbarini | *Prepared*	–
Christopher Norman | *Candy/Nuts*	23
Ciao Bella | *Ice Cream*	25
Così | *Deli/Sandwich*	18
Crumbs | *Baked Gds.*	22
❷ Dean/DeLuca | *Maj. Gourmet*	27
Evelyn's Choc. | *Candy/Nuts*	25
Famous Wines | *Wine/Liquor*	22
Fifth Ave. Choc. | *Candy/Nuts*	20
Financier | *Baked Gds.*	27
Flowers/World | *Flowers*	28
Godiva | *Candy/Nuts*	22
Greene Grape | *Wine/Liquor*	24
Jubilee | *Maj. Gourmet*	21
Klatch Coffee | *Coffee/Tea*	21
Leonidas | *Candy/Nuts*	26
Mangia | *Prepared*	24
New York/Exchange | *Wine/Liquor*	23
❷ Original SoupMan | *Soup*	23
Pick a Bagel | *Bagels*	20
Pret A Manger | *Deli/Sandwich*	21
Ruben's | *Prepared*	20
Starwich | *Deli/Sandwich*	23
Zaitzeff | *Prepared*	28
Zeytuna | *Maj. Gourmet*	23

FLATIRON DISTRICT

(14th to 24th Sts., 6th Ave. to Park
Ave. S., excluding Union Sq.)

Baskin-Robbins | *Ice Cream*	17
❷ Belle Fleur | *Flowers*	28
❷ Bottlerocket | *Wine/Liquor*	26
Chef & Co. | *Caterer/Events*	25
❷ City Bakery | *Baked Gds.*	25

Casa/Cupcake	*Baked Gds.*	22
Eisenberg's Sandwich	*Deli/Sandwich*	20
Fifth Ave. Epicure	*Prepared*	19
JAS Mart	*Spec. Shop*	21
Mangia	*Prepared*	24
🆉 Moore Bros.	*Wine/Liquor*	29
New York Cake	*Cookware*	24
Petite Abeille	*Prepared*	22
NEW Red Mango	*Ice Cream*	22
Shake Shack	*Prepared*	25
Susan Holland	*Caterer*	-
Tamarind Tea	*Coffee/Tea*	24
Tarallucci e Vino	*Baked Gds.*	29
Vere	*Candy/Nuts*	29
'wichcraft	*Deli/Sandwich*	24
Zaro's Bread	*Baked Gds.*	17

GARMENT DISTRICT
(30th to 40th Sts., west of 5th)

🆉 Artisanal	*Cheese/Dairy*	28
Au Bon Pain	*Baked Gds.*	16
Ben & Jerry's	*Ice Cream*	24
Ben's Kosher	*Deli/Sandwich*	21
Callahan	*Caterer/Events*	-
Castle/Pierpont	*Flowers*	24
Catering/Rest. Assoc.	*Caterer*	20
Cucina	*Prepared*	21
Esposito Meat	*Meat/Poultry*	25
Flowers/Reuven	*Flowers*	27
Gail Watson	*Baked Gds.*	-
Guy/Gallard	*Coffee/Tea*	20
Häagen Dazs	*Ice Cream*	24
Hale/Hearty	*Soup*	22
Han Ah Reum	*Spec. Shop*	22
Hot/Crusty	*Baked Gds.*	15
Indiana Mkt.	*Caterer*	26
jesGORDON	*Flowers*	-
Krispy Kreme	*Baked Gds.*	19
Macy's Cellar	*Cookware*	21
Manganaro Foods	*Deli/Sandwich*	24
Manganaro's Hero	*Deli/Sandwich*	21
Mrs. Field's	*Baked Gds.*	18
pinkberry	*Ice Cream*	21
Pret A Manger	*Deli/Sandwich*	21

Props/Today	*Party Rent.*	20
Rebecca Cole	*Flowers*	-
Sandwich Planet	*Deli/Sandwich*	25
Soup Spot	*Soup*	23
Starwich	*Deli/Sandwich*	23
Zaro's Bread	*Baked Gds.*	17

GRAMERCY PARK
(24th to 30th Sts., east of 5th; 14th to 24th Sts., east of Park)

NEW Amai Tea	*Baked Gds.*	20
Baskin-Robbins	*Ice Cream*	17
Blue Smoke	*Caterer*	25
Bruno/Ravioli	*Pasta*	24
Così	*Deli/Sandwich*	18
David's Bagels	*Bagels*	23
Ess-a-Bagel	*Bagels*	26
First Ave. Wines	*Wine/Liquor*	23
NEW Flurt	*Ice Cream*	21
Friend/Farmer	*Baked Gds.*	21
Gramercy Fish	*Seafood*	24
Irving Farm/71	*Coffee/Tea*	22
🆉 Kalustyan's	*Spec. Shop*	27
Lamarca	*Cheese/Dairy*	26
Les Halles	*Meat/Poultry*	26
🆉 Manhattan Fruitier	*Spec. Shop*	27
McAdam	*Wine/Liquor*	22
Natural Frontier	*Health*	24
Petite Abeille	*Prepared*	22
Pick a Bagel	*Bagels*	20
pinkberry	*Ice Cream*	21
Royal Wine	*Wine/Liquor*	-
Spice Corner	*Herbs/Spices*	24
🆉 Vino	*Wine/Liquor*	28

GREENMARKET
(See p. 111 for locations)

Berkshire Berries	*Produce*	27
Berried Treasures	*Produce*	28
Beth's Farm	*Spec. Shop*	27
Blue Moon Fish	*Seafood*	29
Bread Alone	*Baked Gds.*	27
Bulich Mushroom	*Produce*	29
Cato Farm	*Cheese/Dairy*	27
Cherry Ln.	*Produce*	28
DiPaola Turkey	*Meat/Poultry*	27
Eckerton Hill	*Produce*	26

Flying Pigs | *Meat/Poultry* 28

Gorzynski/Farm | *Produce* 27

Hawthorne Farm | *Produce* 28

Keith's Farm | *Produce* 28

Martin's Pretzels | *Baked Gds.* 27

Migliorelli Farm | *Produce* 26

Our Daily Bread | *Baked Gds.* 26

Paffenroth | *Produce* 28

PE & DD | *Seafood* 28

Quattro's | *Meat/Poultry* 26

Red Jacket | *Produce* 27

Rick's Picks | *Spec. Shop* -

Samascott | *Produce* 27

Stokes Farm | *Produce* 27

Terhune Orchards | *Produce* 27

3-Corner Farm | *Cheese/Dairy* 27

Violet Hill | *Meat/Poultry* 29

Windfall Farms | *Produce* 27

Yuno's Farm | *Produce* 29

GREENWICH VILLAGE

(Houston to 14th Sts., west of
B'way, east of 7th Ave. S.)

Z Amy's Bread | *Baked Gds.* 26

Anstice Carroll | *Caterer/Events* 26

Aphrodisia | *Herbs/Spices* 26

Au Bon Pain | *Baked Gds.* 16

Australian Home. | *Ice Cream* 23

Bagel Bob's | *Bagels* 22

Bagel Buffet | *Bagels* 17

Bagels on Sq. | *Bagels* 21

NEW Batch | *Baked Gds.* -

Birdbath/Build Green | *Baked Gds.* 23

Z Blue Ribbon Mkt. | *Baked Gds.* 28

Broadway Pan. | *Cookware* 26

Bruno Bakery | *Baked Gds.* 23

Z Citarella | *Maj. Gourmet* 26

Cold Stone | *Ice Cream* 20

Cones | *Ice Cream* 26

Così | *Deli/Sandwich* 18

Cozy Soup | *Prepared* 17

Crumbs | *Baked Gds.* 22

Z Dean/DeLuca | *Maj. Gourmet* 27

Di Fiore Marquet | *Baked Gds.* -

Edible Arrangements | *Caterer* 22

Z Faicco's Pork | *Meat/Poultry* 28

Z Florence Meat | *Meat/Poultry* 29

Glazier Group | *Caterer* -

Gourmet Garage | *Maj. Gourmet* 20

Grom | *Ice Cream* 27

Indian Bread | *Prepared* 21

Insomnia Cookies | *Baked Gds.* -

Irving Farm/71 | *Coffee/Tea* 22

Is Wine | *Wine/Liquor* 22

Z Jack's Stir Brew | *Coffee/Tea* 27

Jefferson Mkt. | *Maj. Gourmet* 26

Joe | *Coffee/Tea* 26

Lafayette | *Baked Gds.* 21

Z L'Arte del Gelato | *Ice Cream* 27

Lassi | *Prepared* 21

Le Pain Quotidien | *Baked Gds.* 24

LifeThyme Mkt. | *Health* 24

Lobster Pl. | *Seafood* 26

Max Brenner | *Candy/Nuts* 22

Murray's Bagels | *Bagels* 26

Z Murray's Cheese | *Cheese/Dairy* 28

O&CO. | *Spec. Shop* 25

Oren's/Roast | *Coffee/Tea* 24

Z Ottomanelli & Sons | *Meat/Poultry* 27

Z Patisserie Claude | *Baked Gds.* 27

pinkberry | *Ice Cream* 21

Porto Rico | *Coffee/Tea* 26

Z Raffetto's | *Pasta* 28

NEW Red Mango | *Ice Cream* 22

Risotteria | *Prepared* 23

Rocco's Pastry | *Baked Gds.* 25

Think Coffee | *Coffee/Tea* 23

Varsano's | *Candy/Nuts* 26

Warehouse Wines | *Wine/Liquor* 22

'wichcraft | *Deli/Sandwich* 24

Winesby | *Wine/Liquor* -

World of Nuts | *Candy/Nuts* 15

HARLEM/EAST HARLEM

(110th to 157th Sts., excluding
Columbia U. area)

Z Citarella | *Maj. Gourmet* 26

Z Fairway | *Maj. Gourmet* 26

Gracious Thyme | *Caterer* -

Harlem Tea | *Coffee/Tea* 25

Harlem Vintage | *Wine/Liquor* 28

Katrina Parris | *Flowers* — | —

La Tropezienne | *Baked Gds.* — | —

Make My Cake | *Baked Gds.* 25 |

Patisserie des Ambassades | 21 |
Baked Gds.

Settepani | *Baked Gds.* 23 |

Spoonbread | *Caterer* 23 |

Starbucks | *Coffee/Tea* 18 |

LITTLE ITALY

(Canal to Kenmare Sts., Bowery to Lafayette St.)

Aji Ichiban | *Candy/Nuts* 21 |

Alleva Dairy | *Cheese/Dairy* 27 |

Bayard St. | *Meat/Poultry* 23 |

Caffé Roma | *Baked Gds.* 23 |

Ceci-Cela | *Baked Gds.* 24 |

Ⓩ Despaña | *Spec. Shop* 27 |

Ⓩ DiPalo Dairy | *Cheese/Dairy* 29 |

Ⓩ Divalicious | *Candy/Nuts* 24 |

Ferrara Cafe | *Baked Gds.* 22 |

Italian Food | *Spec. Shop* 22 |

NEW Oro Bakery | *Baked Gds.* — |

NEW Papabubble | *Candy/Nuts* 24 |

Piemonte Ravioli | *Pasta* 27 |

LOWER EAST SIDE

(Houston to Canal Sts., east of Bowery)

BabyCakes | *Baked Gds.* 24 |

Bari Equipment | *Cookware* 24 |

Bowery & Vine | *Wine/Liquor* — |

Bowery Kitchen | *Cookware* 22 |

Clinton St. | *Baked Gds.* 26 |

Cocoa Bar | *Candy/Nuts* 26 |

De Vino | *Wine/Liquor* 25 |

Ⓩ Doughnut Plant | *Baked Gds.* 26 |

Earthmatters | *Health* 21 |

Economy Candy | *Candy/Nuts* 24 |

Elizabeth Ryan | *Flowers* 28 |

Falai Panetteria | *Baked Gds.* 27 |

Formaggio Essex | *Cheese/Dairy* 26 |

NEW How Sweet It Is | — |
Baked Goods

Ⓩ Il Laboratorio | *Ice Cream* 28 |

Ⓩ Jeffrey's | *Meat/Poultry* 25 |

Ⓩ Katz's Deli | *Deli/Sandwich* 24 |

Ⓩ Kossar's | *Bagels* 28 |

Neuman's | *Caterer* 25 |

NEW Paradou Marché | 21 |
Deli/Sandwich

Ⓩ Pickle Guys | *Spec. Shop* 27 |

Porto Rico | *Coffee/Tea* 26 |

Rainbo's Fish | *Seafood* 26 |

Roasting Plant | *Coffee/Tea* 22 |

NEW Roni-Sue's | *Candy/Nuts* 23 |

Ⓩ Russ & Daughters | *Smoked Fish* 28 |

Saxelby Cheese | *Cheese/Dairy* 28 |

Sépt. Wines | *Wine/Liquor* 25 |

Special Attention | *Caterer* — |

Streit's Matzo | *Baked Gds.* 25 |

Ⓩ Sugar Sweet | *Baked Gds.* 27 |

Sweet Life | *Candy/Nuts* 23 |

Tiny's Giant | *Deli/Sandwich* 22 |

Ⓩ Whole Foods | *Maj. Gourmet* 26 |

Yonah Schimmel | *Baked Gds.* 23 |

MEATPACKING DISTRICT

(Gansevoort to 15th Sts., west of 9th Ave.)

Banchet Flowers | *Flowers* — |

Little Pie | *Baked Gds.* 24 |

Robbins Wolfe | *Caterer* 26 |

Robert Isabell | *Flowers* 27 |

MURRAY HILL

(30th to 40th Sts., east of 5th)

Ⓩ Artisanal | *Cheese/Dairy* 28 |

Baskin-Robbins | *Ice Cream* 17 |

Berger's | *Deli/Sandwich* 21 |

NEW Berrywild | *Ice Cream* 22 |

Better Burger | *Prepared* 19 |

Brasil Coffee | *Coffee/Tea* 21 |

Così | *Deli/Sandwich* 18 |

Daniel's Bagels | *Bagels* 24 |

Ⓩ Dean/DeLuca | *Maj. Gourmet* 27 |

Food Emporium | *Maj. Gourmet* 16 |

Foods/India | *Herbs/Spices* 23 |

Franchia | *Coffee/Tea* 24 |

Guy/Gallard | *Coffee/Tea* 20 |

Milano Gourmet | *Prepared* 25 |

Oren's/Roast | *Coffee/Tea* 24 |

Quality Hse. | *Wine/Liquor* 27 |

Sarge's Deli | *Deli/Sandwich* 21 |

Starbucks | *Coffee/Tea* 18 |

Subtle Tea	*Coffee/Tea*	23
Thomas Preti	*Caterer*	23
Todaro Bros.	*Spec. Shop*	24
'wichcraft	*Deli/Sandwich*	24
Wild Edibles	*Seafood*	26
Winfield-Flynn	*Wine/Liquor*	23
World of Nuts	*Candy/Nuts*	15

NOHO

(Houston to 4th Sts., Bowery to B'way)

Astor Wines	*Wine/Liquor*	25
Au Bon Pain	*Baked Gds.*	16
Crate/Barrel	*Cookware*	22
Häagen Dazs	*Ice Cream*	24
Think Coffee	*Coffee/Tea*	23

NOLITA

(Houston to Kenmare Sts., Bowery to Lafayette St.)

Café Habana	*Prepared*	24
Ciao Bella	*Ice Cream*	25
Eileen's Cheesecake	*Baked Gds.*	26
Gimme! Coffee	*Coffee/Tea*	27
Parisi Bakery	*Baked Gds.*	23
pinkberry	*Ice Cream*	21
Polux Fleuriste	*Flowers*	-
☑ Rice/Riches	*Baked Gds.*	23
Wine Therapy	*Wine/Liquor*	25

SOHO

(Canal to Houston Sts., west of Lafayette St.)

☑ Alessi	*Cookware*	27
Alidoro	*Deli/Sandwich*	27
Baked Ideas	*Baked Gds.*	-
Balthazar Bakery	*Baked Gds.*	27
Blue Water	*Flowers*	-
Colin Cowie	*Events*	28
☑ Dean/DeLuca	*Maj. Gourmet*	27
Emack/Bolio	*Ice Cream*	25
Gourmet Garage	*Maj. Gourmet*	20
☑ Grandaisy Bakery	*Baked Gds.*	29
Great Performances	*Caterer*	24
Hampton Chutney	*Prepared*	23
☑ Jacques Torres	*Candy/Nuts*	28
Joe	*Coffee/Tea*	26
☑ Joe's Dairy	*Cheese/Dairy*	28
Jubilee	*Maj. Gourmet*	21

☑ Kee's Choc.	*Candy/Nuts*	29
Le Pain Quotidien	*Baked Gds.*	24
☑ MarieBelle's	*Candy/Nuts*	26
☑ Olive's	*Deli/Sandwich*	25
Once Upon/Tart	*Baked Gds.*	25
Pepe	*Prepared*	26
Pino Meats	*Meat/Poultry*	27
Porto Rico	*Coffee/Tea*	26
Ron Ben-Israel	*Baked Gds.*	25
Ruben's	*Prepared*	20
Snack	*Prepared*	27
SoHo Wines	*Wine/Liquor*	21
Starbucks	*Coffee/Tea*	18
Sunrise Mart	*Spec. Shop*	23
Sur La Table	*Cookware*	26
☑ Ten Ren Tea	*Coffee/Tea*	25
Tisserie	*Baked Gds.*	20
Vesuvio	*Prepared*	23
Vintage NY	*Wine/Liquor*	23
☑ Vosges	*Candy/Nuts*	26
'wichcraft	*Deli/Sandwich*	24
Yoghurt Place	*Cheese/Dairy*	23

SOUTH STREET SEAPORT

Glazier Group	*Caterer*	-
Häagen Dazs	*Ice Cream*	24
☑ Jack's Stir Brew	*Coffee/Tea*	27
Mrs. Field's	*Baked Gds.*	18
Pasanella	*Wine/Liquor*	26
Ruben's	*Prepared*	20
☑ Stonehouse	*Spec. Shop*	27

TRIBECA

(Canal to Murray Sts., west of B'way)

Baskin-Robbins	*Ice Cream*	17
☑ Bazzini	*Maj. Gourmet*	27
Bed Bath/Beyond	*Cookware*	20
Bell Bates	*Health*	24
☑ Bouley Bakery	*Baked Gds.*	27
Chambers Wines	*Wine/Liquor*	26
Chestnuts	*Flowers*	-
Duane Pk.	*Baked Gds.*	26
Food Emporium	*Maj. Gourmet*	16
NEW Frankly Wines	*Wine/Liquor*	-
☑ Korin	*Cookware*	28

NEW La Colombe | *Coffee/Tea* -
Manna Catering | *Caterer* -
Olivier Cheng | *Caterer* 22
Petite Abeille | *Prepared* 22
Soda Shop | *Ice Cream* 20
Z Sylvia Weinstock | *Baked Gds.* 26
Tribeca Treats | *Baked Gds.* 27
Tribeca Wine | *Wine/Liquor* 23
Vestry Wines | *Wine/Liquor* -
VinoVino | *Wine/Liquor* 25
'wichcraft | *Deli/Sandwich* 24
NEW Zucker's Bagels | *Bagels* 22

UNION SQUARE

(14th to 17th Sts., 5th Ave. to
Union Sq. E.)
Au Bon Pain | *Baked Gds.* 16
Broadway Party | *Party Rent.* 19
Crossroads | *Wine/Liquor* 25
Food Emporium | *Maj. Gourmet* 16
Garden of Eden | *Maj. Gourmet* 24
Z Italian Wine | *Wine/Liquor* 27
Le Pain Quotidien | *Baked Gds.* 24
Tisserie | *Baked Gds.* 20
Z Trader Joe's | *Maj. Gourmet* 24
Trader Joe's Wine | *Wine/Liquor* 19
Union Sq. Wines | *Wine/Liquor* 25
Z Whole Foods | *Maj. Gourmet* 26

WASHINGTON HTS./INWOOD

(North of W. 157th St.)
Carrot Top | *Baked Gds.* 23
Frank's Gourmet | *Spec. Shop* 21
pinkberry | *Ice Cream* 21
PJ Wine | *Wine/Liquor* 27

WEST 40s

Amish Market | *Maj. Gourmet* 23
Z Amy's Bread | *Baked Gds.* 26
Ben & Jerry's | *Ice Cream* 24
Better Burger | *Prepared* 19
Carmine's | *Prepared* 23
Carve | *Deli/Sandwich* 23
Casa/Cupcake | *Baked Gds.* 22
Cold Stone | *Ice Cream* 20
Così | *Deli/Sandwich* 18
Crumbs | *Baked Gds.* 22

Cucina | *Prepared* 21
Dahlia | *Flowers* 26
Daisy May's | *Prepared* 24
Dale & Thomas | *Spec. Shop* 23
Z Dean/DeLuca | *Maj. Gourmet* 27
Empire Coffee | *Coffee/Tea* 23
Fashion Soup | *Soup* 22
Food Emporium | *Maj. Gourmet* 16
NEW FreeFoods | *Prepared* 25
Godiva | *Candy/Nuts* 22
Good & Plenty | *Prepared* 22
Hale/Hearty | *Soup* 22
H & H Bagels | *Bagels* 26
Hershey's | *Candy/Nuts* 18
Juan Valdez | *Coffee/Tea* 22
Junior's | *Baked Gds.* 23
Z La Maison/Choc. | *Candy/Nuts* 29
Le Marais | *Meat/Poultry* 26
Little Pie | *Baked Gds.* 24
Z Minamoto | *Candy/Nuts* 28
Z Morrell & Co. | *Wine/Liquor* 27
Mrs. Field's | *Baked Gds.* 18
My Most/Food | *Baked Gds.* 21
Ninth Ave. Int'l | *Spec. Shop* 23
Z Original SoupMan | *Soup* 23
Poseidon | *Baked Gds.* 26
Pret A Manger | *Deli/Sandwich* 21
NEW Red Mango | *Ice Cream* 22
Sea Breeze | *Seafood* 23
Starbucks | *Coffee/Tea* 18
Starwich | *Deli/Sandwich* 23
Z Sullivan St. Bakery | 28
  Baked Gds.
Times Sq. Bagels | *Bagels* 19
'wichcraft | *Deli/Sandwich* 24
Zaro's Bread | *Baked Gds.* 17

WEST 50s

Au Bon Pain | *Baked Gds.* 16
Between/Bread | *Caterer* 21
Cakes 'N Shapes | *Baked Gds.* 22
Z Carnegie Deli | *Deli/Sandwich* 23
Certé | *Caterer/Events* 26
Chocolate Bar | *Candy/Nuts* 26
Cold Stone | *Ice Cream* 20
Columbus Wine | *Wine/Liquor* 22

Così | *Deli/Sandwich* — 18

Ꮓ Dean/DeLuca | *Maj. Gourmet* — 27

Fika | *Coffee/Tea* — 22

Flowers/World | *Flowers* — 28

Fresh Bites | *Prepared* — 20

Godiva | *Candy/Nuts* — 22

Hale/Hearty | *Soup* — 22

Jonathan Flowers | *Flowers* — –

Le Pain Quotidien | *Baked Gds.* — 24

Lindt | *Candy/Nuts* — 24

Mangia | *Prepared* — 24

Myzel Choc. | *Candy/Nuts* — 19

NEW Oak & Steel | *Wine/Liquor* — –

Pepe | *Prepared* — 26

Ꮓ Petrossian | — 28
    Caviar/Smoked Fish

Pret A Manger | *Deli/Sandwich* — 21

Remi | *Prepared* — 26

Ruby/Violette | *Baked Gds.* — 26

Stage Deli | *Deli/Sandwich* — 21

Stonekelly | *Flowers* — 25

Thalia Kitchen | *Prepared* — 21

Ꮓ Westerly Natural | *Health* — 25

Ꮓ Whole Foods | *Maj. Gourmet* — 26

'wichcraft | *Deli/Sandwich* — 24

Ꮓ Williams-Sonoma | *Cookware* — 27

World of Nuts | *Candy/Nuts* — 15

Zibetto Espresso | *Coffee/Tea* — 26

WEST 60s

Ꮓ Balducci's | *Maj. Gourmet* — 25

Bed Bath/Beyond | *Cookware* — 20

Ꮓ Bouchon Bakery | *Baked Gds.* — 27

Food Emporium | *Maj. Gourmet* — 16

Gracious Home | *Cookware* — 25

Häagen Dazs | *Ice Cream* — 24

Jubilee | *Maj. Gourmet* — 21

Le Pain Quotidien | *Baked Gds.* — 24

Ꮓ Magnolia Bakery | *Baked Gds.* — 23

Maya Schaper | *Cheese/Dairy* — 22

67 Wines | *Wine/Liquor* — 25

Starbucks | *Coffee/Tea* — 18

Surroundings | *Flowers* — 25

WEST 70s

Acker Merrall | *Wine/Liquor* — 26

Alice's Tea | *Coffee/Tea* — 24

Arte/Corner | *Baked Gds.* — 24

Bacchus Wine | *Wine/Liquor* — 19

Bagels & Co. | *Bagels* — 22

Beacon Wines | *Wine/Liquor* — 21

Beard Papa | *Baked Gds.* — 24

Bruno/Ravioli | *Pasta* — 24

Buttercup | *Baked Gds.* — 23

Ꮓ Citarella | *Maj. Gourmet* — 26

Cold Stone | *Ice Cream* — 20

Così | *Deli/Sandwich* — 18

Crumbs | *Baked Gds.* — 22

Emack/Bolio | *Ice Cream* — 25

Ꮓ Fairway | *Maj. Gourmet* — 26

Fine/Schapiro | *Deli/Sandwich* — 20

Fischer Bros. | *Meat/Poultry* — 27

Godiva | *Candy/Nuts* — 22

Gotham Gdns. | *Flowers* — 24

Ꮓ Grandaisy Bakery | *Baked Gds.* — 29

Grom | *Ice Cream* — 27

Häagen Dazs | *Ice Cream* — 24

Health Nuts | *Health* — 21

Ꮓ Jacques Torres | *Candy/Nuts* — 28

Le Pain Quotidien | *Baked Gds.* — 24

Ꮓ Levain Bakery | *Baked Gds.* — 28

Margot Pâtisserie | *Baked Gds.* — 27

Nancy's-Wines | *Wine/Liquor* — 24

Neuhaus Choc. | *Candy/Nuts* — 25

Ottomanelli Bros. | *Meat/Poultry* — 24

pinkberry | *Ice Cream* — 21

Pour | *Wine/Liquor* — 21

Sensuous Bean | *Coffee/Tea* — 25

Ꮓ Soutine | *Baked Gds.* — 27

Westside Mkt. | *Maj. Gourmet* — 21

World of Nuts | *Candy/Nuts* — 15

WEST 80s

Artie's Deli | *Deli/Sandwich* — 21

Ꮓ Barney Greengrass | — 27
    Caviar/Smoked Fish

Best Cellars | *Wine/Liquor* — 21

Confetti | *Baked Gds.* — 24

Flor/Mayo | *Prepared* — 23

Gary Null's | *Health* — 25

Hampton Chutney | *Prepared* — 23

H & H Bagels | *Bagels* — 26

Hot/Crusty | *Baked Gds.* — 15

Le Pain Quotidien | *Baked Gds.* 24

Murray's Sturgeon | 27
  Caviar/Smoked Fish

Newman/Leventhal | *Caterer* 21

Sarabeth's | *Baked Gds.* 24

Scharffen Berger | *Candy/Nuts* 26

Uncle Louie | *Ice Cream* 20

West Side Wine | *Wine/Liquor* 24

Yolato | *Ice Cream* 20

Ⓩ Zabar's | *Maj. Gourmet* 27

WEST 90s

Carmine's | *Prepared* 23

Food Emporium | *Maj. Gourmet* 16

Gotham Wines | *Wine/Liquor* 22

Gourmet Garage | *Maj. Gourmet* 20

Health Nuts | *Health* 21

Lenny's | *Bagels* 23

Oppenheimer | *Meat/Poultry* 26

Tal Bagels | *Bagels* 23

Vintage NY | *Wine/Liquor* 23

WEST 100s

(See also Harlem/East Harlem)

Ⓩ Absolute Bagels | *Bagels* 26

Academy Floral | *Flowers* 23

Ben & Jerry's | *Ice Cream* 24

Edible Arrangements | *Caterer* 22

Flor/Mayo | *Prepared* 23

Garden of Eden | *Maj. Gourmet* 24

Häagen Dazs | *Ice Cream* 24

Hot/Crusty | *Baked Gds.* 15

Hungarian Pastry | *Baked Gds.* 22

JAS Mart | *Spec. Shop* 21

Martin Bros. | *Wine/Liquor* 21

Milano Gourmet | *Prepared* 25

Mondel Choc. | *Candy/Nuts* 22

m2m | *Spec. Shop* 18

Nusbaum & Wu | *Baked Gds.* 18

Oren's/Roast | *Coffee/Tea* 24

Silver Moon | *Baked Gds.* 26

Westside Mkt. | *Maj. Gourmet* 21

WEST VILLAGE

(Houston to 14th Sts., west of 7th Ave. S., excluding Meatpacking District)

A Salt/Battery | *Prepared* 22

Bonsignour | *Prepared* 26

Carry On Tea | *Coffee/Tea* 23

Ⓩ Colette's | *Baked Gds.* 29

Creative Edge | *Caterer* 25

Dirty Bird | *Prepared* 20

Doma | *Coffee/Tea* 25

NEW Gardenia Organic | *Flowers* -

NEW Grove | *Flowers* -

Health/Harmony | *Health* 26

Integral Yoga | *Health* 24

Ⓩ Le Dû's Wines | *Wine/Liquor* 27

Li-Lac Choc. | *Candy/Nuts* 26

Ⓩ Magnolia Bakery | *Baked Gds.* 23

Magnolia Flowers | *Flowers* 26

Manley's Wines | *Wine/Liquor* 22

Margaret Braun | *Baked Gds.* -

McNulty's Tea | *Coffee/Tea* 27

Milk & Cookies | *Baked Gds.* 24

Myers/Keswick | *Spec. Shop* 23

Out/Kitchen | *Prepared* 20

Ovando | *Flowers* 28

Pepe | *Prepared* 26

Petite Abeille | *Prepared* 22

Ready to Eat | *Prepared* 21

Sant Ambroeus | *Ice Cream* 26

Sea Grape | *Wine/Liquor* 23

Snack | *Prepared* 27

sNice | *Deli/Sandwich* 23

Taste Caterers | *Caterer* 22

VSF | *Flowers* 29

NEW Yogurtland | *Ice Cream* -

Bronx

Ⓩ Abigail Kirsch | *Caterer* 26

Addeo Bakery | *Baked Gds.* 27

Arthur Ave. | *Caterer* 24

Artuso Pastry | *Baked Gds.* 26

Biancardi Meats | *Meat/Poultry* 27

Ⓩ Borgatti's | *Pasta* 29

Ⓩ Calabria Pork | *Meat/Poultry* 28

Calandra Cheese | *Cheese/Dairy* 26

Casa Della | *Cheese/Dairy* 29

Cosenza's Fish | *Seafood* 27

Delillo Pastry | *Baked Gds.* 26

Edible Arrangements | *Caterer* 22

Egidio Pastry | *Baked Gds.* 24

Gustiamo	*Spec. Shop*	23
☑ Madonia Bakery	*Baked Gds.*	28
Mother's Bake	*Baked Gds.*	21
Mount Carmel	*Wine/Liquor*	26
New York Bev.	*Beer*	-
☑ Pastosa Ravioli	*Pasta*	26
☑ Randazzo's	*Seafood*	28
Sal & Dom's	*Baked Gds.*	28
S&S Cheesecake	*Baked Gds.*	27
Skyview Wines	*Wine/Liquor*	26
Target	*Cookware*	17
Teitel Bros.	*Spec. Shop*	26
Terranova	*Baked Gds.*	26
Umanoff/Parsons	*Baked Gds.*	24
Uncle Louie	*Ice Cream*	20
Vincent's Meat	*Meat/Poultry*	27

Brooklyn

BAY RIDGE

Anopoli Ice Cream	*Ice Cream*	22
Areo Rist.	*Caterer*	21
Bay Ridge Bake	*Baked Gds.*	25
Choc-Oh!	*Candy/Nuts*	25
☑ Faicco's Pork	*Meat/Poultry*	28
Family Store	*Spec. Shop*	-
Hendricks Wine	*Wine/Liquor*	19
Hinsch's	*Ice Cream*	22
Leske's	*Baked Gds.*	23
Little Cupcake	*Baked Gds.*	21
Mona Lisa Pastry	*Baked Gds.*	24
Nordic Delicacies	*Spec. Shop*	28
Paneantico	*Baked Gds.*	26
Piazza Mercato	*Meat/Poultry*	23
Tanoreen	*Prepared*	24
3 Guys/Brooklyn	*Produce*	23

BEDFORD-STUYVESANT

Bread Stuy	*Baked Gds.*	-
Olivino Wines	*Wine/Liquor*	-
Shakoor's Sweet	*Baked Gds.*	-

BENSONHURST

Bari Pork	*Meat/Poultry*	24
Lioni Latticini	*Cheese/Dairy*	29
Papa Pasquale	*Pasta*	26
☑ Pastosa Ravioli	*Pasta*	26

Queen Ann	*Pasta*	27
☑ Royal Crown	*Baked Gds.*	26
Trunzo Bros.	*Spec. Shop*	25
☑ Villabate	*Baked Gds.*	28

BOERUM HILL

Bergen Bagels	*Bagels*	22
Betty Bakery	*Baked Gds.*	23
Bijoux Doux	*Baked Gds.*	-
NEW Blue Marble	*Ice Cream*	24
Boerum Hill Food	*Prepared*	22
Cheryl Kleinman	*Baked Gds.*	28
Downtown Atlantic	*Prepared*	21
Marquet Patiss.	*Baked Gds.*	24
Nicky's Viet.	*Deli/Sandwich*	24

BOROUGH PARK

Basket Shop	*Spec. Shop*	23
☑ Coluccio/Sons	*Spec. Shop*	28
Schick's Bakery	*Baked Gds.*	20

BRIGHTON BEACH

M & I Foods	*Spec. Shop*	24

BROOKLYN HEIGHTS

Blue Pig	*Ice Cream*	21
Busy Chef	*Prepared*	21
Conn. Muffin	*Baked Gds.*	17
Cook's Companion	*Cookware*	26
Damascus Bakery	*Baked Gds.*	25
Garden of Eden	*Maj. Gourmet*	24
Hale/Hearty	*Soup*	22
Heights Chateau	*Wine/Liquor*	25
Heights Meats	*Meat/Poultry*	24
La Bagel	*Bagels*	23
Lassen/Hennigs	*Caterer*	22
Michael-Towne	*Wine/Liquor*	24
Montague St.	*Bagels*	22
New Green Pea	*Produce*	23
Oriental Pastry	*Spec. Shop*	22
Perelandra	*Health*	24
☑ Sahadi's	*Spec. Shop*	27
Seaport Flowers	*Flowers*	26
☑ Two for the Pot	*Coffee/Tea*	27

BROWNSVILLLE

Slavin	*Seafood*	23

CANARSIE

Bed Bath/Beyond | *Cookware*   20

CARROLL GARDENS

Caputo Bakery | *Baked Gds.*   23
Cobblestone | *Spec. Shop*   21
Ⓩ D'Amico | *Coffee/Tea*   27
David Stark | *Caterer/Events*   –
DUB Pies | *Prepared*   24
Esposito's Pork | *Meat/Poultry*   26
Fraser-Morris | *Prepared*   26
Margaret Palca | *Baked Gds.*   26
Mazzola Bakery | *Baked Gds.*   25
Monteleone's | *Baked Gds.*   23
Naidre's | *Coffee/Tea*   22
Naturally Delic. | *Caterer/Events*   –
Park Natural | *Health*   22

CLINTON HILL

Choice Mkt. | *Prepared*   23
Jive Turkey | *Prepared*   23
NEW Krumbs | *Baked Gds.*   22
Root Stock | *Flowers*   –

COBBLE HILL

American Beer | *Beer*   26
Court Pastry | *Baked Gds.*   25
Fish Tales | *Seafood*   25
Jim/Andy's | *Produce*   19
One Girl | *Baked Gds.*   24
Smith & Vine | *Wine/Liquor*   23
Ⓩ Staubitz Mkt. | *Meat/Poultry*   29
Stinky Bklyn | *Cheese/Dairy*   28
Sweet Melissa | *Baked Gds.*   24
Tea Lounge | *Coffee/Tea*   21

DITMAS PARK

Ackerson, T.B. | *Wine/Liquor*   –
Conn. Muffin | *Baked Gds.*   17

DOWNTOWN

Au Bon Pain | *Baked Gds.*   16
Cold Stone | *Ice Cream*   20
Junior's | *Baked Gds.*   23

DUMBO

Ⓩ Almondine | *Baked Gds.*   28
Blanc & Rouge | *Wine/Liquor*   25
Brooklyn Ice Cream | *Ice Cream*   25

Foragers Mkt. | *Spec. Shop*   22
Ⓩ Jacques Torres | *Candy/Nuts*   28
La Bagel | *Bagels*   23

FORT GREENE

Ⓩ Cake Man | *Baked Gds.*   26
Conn. Muffin | *Baked Gds.*   17
NEW Gnarly Vines | *Wine/Liquor*   –
Greene Grape | *Wine/Liquor*   24
NEW Greene Grape Provisions | *Spec. Shop*   24
L'Epicerie | *Spec. Shop*   22
Little Piggy | *Spec. Shop*   –
Marquet Patiss. | *Baked Gds.*   24
Olivino Wines | *Wine/Liquor*   –

GRAVESEND

Bari Pork | *Meat/Poultry*   24

GREENPOINT

Acme Fish | *Caviar/Smoked Fish*   24
Baskin-Robbins | *Ice Cream*   17
Brooklyn Ice Cream | *Ice Cream*   25
Café Grumpy | *Coffee/Tea*   26
Garden | *Spec. Shop*   24

KINGS PLAZA/ MARINE PARK

JoMart Choc. | *Candy/Nuts*   24
Tops Wines | *Wine/Liquor*   23

MIDWOOD

Mansoura | *Baked Gds.*   –
Orchard | *Spec. Shop*   27

MILL BASIN

Ⓩ Pastosa Ravioli | *Pasta*   26

PARK SLOPE

NEW applewares | *Cookware*   24
Back/Land | *Health*   23
Bagel Hole | *Bagels*   22
Ⓩ Bierkraft | *Beer*   28
Big Nose | *Wine/Liquor*   24
Ⓩ Blue Apron | *Spec. Shop*   27
Cafe Regular | *Coffee/Tea*   24
Charles/Sally | *Caterer/Events*   25
Chocolate Girl | *Candy/Nuts*   23
Chocolate Room | *Candy/Nuts*   25
Cocoa Bar | *Candy/Nuts*   26

Colson | *Baked Gds.* — 25
Conn. Muffin | *Baked Gds.* — 17
Cousin John's | *Baked Gds.* — 21
Z D'Vine | *Spec. Shop* — 25
Eagle Provisions | *Meat/Poultry* — 24
Edible Arrangements | *Caterer* — 22
NEW Get Fresh | *Prepared* — -
NEW Gorilla Coffee | *Coffee/Tea* — 24
Grab Specialty | *Spec. Shop* — 24
La Bagel | *Bagels* — 23
Z Ladybird Bakery | *Baked Gds.* — 28
Leaf/Bean | *Coffee/Tea* — 23
Luscious Food | *Prepared* — 19
Movable Feast | *Caterer* — 23
Naidre's | *Coffee/Tea* — 22
NEW Öko | *Ice Cream* — 24
NEW Organic Heights | *Prepared* — -
Ozzie's Coffee | *Coffee/Tea* — 19
Press 195 | *Deli/Sandwich* — 25
Z Prospect Wine | *Wine/Liquor* — 26
Pumpkins | *Spec. Shop* — 26
Z Red/White | *Wine/Liquor* — 26
NEW Root Hill | *Coffee/Tea* — -
Root Stock | *Flowers* — -
Russo Mozzarella | *Cheese/Dairy* — 26
Second Helpings | *Prepared* — -
7th Ave. Wine | *Wine/Liquor* — 20
Shawn's Wines | *Wine/Liquor* — 24
Sip | *Wine/Liquor* — 27
Slope Cellars | *Wine/Liquor* — 24
sNice | *Deli/Sandwich* — 23
Sweet Melissa | *Baked Gds.* — 24
Tarzian West | *Cookware* — 22
Tea Lounge | *Coffee/Tea* — 21
Tempo Presto | *Deli/Sandwich* — 23
Trois Pommes | *Baked Gds.* — 23
Uncle Louie | *Ice Cream* — 20
Union Market | *Maj. Gourmet* — 26
Urban Organic | *Produce* — 22
ZuZu's Petals | *Flowers* — 26

PROSPECT HEIGHTS

NEW Blue Marble | *Ice Cream* — 24
Christie's | *Prepared* — 21
Fermented | *Wine/Liquor* — 22
Joyce Bake | *Baked Gds.* — 25

NEW Old Brooklyn Parlor | *Ice Cream* — 24
Target | *Cookware* — 17
Uncle Louie | *Ice Cream* — 20
Williamson Cal. | *Caterer* — -

RED HOOK

Baked | *Baked Gds.* — 25
Z Fairway | *Maj. Gourmet* — 26
Z LeNell's | *Wine/Liquor* — 27
Steve's/Pies | *Baked Gds.* — 25

SHEEPSHEAD BAY

Edible Arrangements | *Caterer* — 22
Güllüoglu | *Baked Gds.* — -
Jordan's Lobster | *Seafood* — 23

STARRETT CITY

BJ's Wholesale | *Maj. Gourmet* — 17
Target | *Cookware* — 17

SUNSET PARK

Brooklyn Liquors | *Wine/Liquor* — 23
Costco | *Maj. Gourmet* — 21
East Coast Beer | *Beer* — 22
Hong Kong | *Spec. Shop* — 20
Z Ten Ren Tea | *Coffee/Tea* — 25

WILLIAMSBURG

Z Bedford Cheese | *Cheese/Dairy* — 27
Bottle Shoppe | *Wine/Liquor* — -
Broadway Party | *Party Rent.* — 19
Brooklyn Kitchen | *Cookware* — 23
Cheeks Bakery | *Baked Gds.* — -
NEW D.O.C. Wine | *Wine/Liquor* — 22
Edible Arrangements | *Caterer* — 22
NEW /eks/ | *Ice Cream* — -
NEW El Beit | *Coffee/Tea* — -
Fabiane's | *Baked Gds.* — -
Fortunato Bros. | *Baked Gds.* — 25
Gimme! Coffee | *Coffee/Tea* — 27
Lorimer St. Meat | *Meat/Poultry* — -
Marlow | *Spec. Shop* — 24
Napoli Bakery | *Baked Gds.* — 23
Oslo Coffee | *Coffee/Tea* — 20
NEW Papa Lima | *Deli/Sandwich* — 22
Porto Rico | *Coffee/Tea* — 26
Savino's Pasta | *Pasta* — -
Settepani | *Baked Gds.* — 23

NEW Spuyten/Grocery | *Spec. Shop*	–
NEW Urban Rustic | *Spec. Shop*	–
Uva | *Wine/Liquor*	24

WINDSOR TERRACE

DUB Pies | *Prepared*	24
Terrace Bagels | *Bagels*	25
United Meat | *Meat/Poultry*	26

Queens

ASTORIA

Z Artopolis | *Baked Gds.*	28
Astoria Meat | *Meat/Poultry*	25
Cassinelli Food | *Pasta*	25
Christos Steak | *Meat/Poultry*	23
Cold Stone | *Ice Cream*	20
Costco | *Maj. Gourmet*	21
Grand Wine | *Wine/Liquor*	25
La Guli | *Baked Gds.*	24
Martha's Bakery | *Baked Gds.*	23
Mediterranean | *Spec. Shop*	26
Z Titan Foods | *Spec. Shop*	26
Uncle Louie | *Ice Cream*	20

BAYSIDE

Abbey Rent | *Party Rent.*	–
Ben's Kosher | *Deli/Sandwich*	21
Edible Arrangements | *Caterer*	22
Health Nuts | *Health*	21
Peter's Mkt. | *Spec. Shop*	22
Press 195 | *Deli/Sandwich*	25
Z Ralph's/Ices | *Ice Cream*	24

COLLEGE POINT

BJ's Wholesale | *Maj. Gourmet*	17
Empire Market | *Meat/Poultry*	16
Target | *Cookware*	17

CORONA

| Z Lemon Ice \| *Ice Cream* | 27 |

DOUGLASTON

| Ceriello \| *Spec. Shop* | 24 |
| Mazur's \| *Meat/Poultry* | 20 |

ELMHURST

| Bed Bath/Beyond \| *Cookware* | 20 |
| Cold Stone \| *Ice Cream* | 20 |

Fay Da | *Baked Gds.*	19
Hong Kong | *Spec. Shop*	20
Mrs. Field's | *Baked Gds.*	18
Party Time | *Party Rent.*	20
Target | *Cookware*	17
Z Ten Ren Tea | *Coffee/Tea*	25
Yoghurt Place | *Cheese/Dairy*	23

FLORAL PARK

| Z Ralph's/Ices \| *Ice Cream* | 24 |

FLUSHING

Durso's Pasta | *Pasta*	26
Fay Da | *Baked Gds.*	19
Han Ah Reum | *Spec. Shop*	22
Hong Kong | *Spec. Shop*	20
House of Spices | *Herbs/Spices*	24
Mauzone | *Prepared*	22
Max & Mina's | *Ice Cream*	25
Mazal Kosher | *Candy/Nuts*	17
Z Ottomanelli's Meats | *Meat/Poultry*	27
Patel Bros. | *Spec. Shop*	23
pinkberry | *Ice Cream*	21
NEW Red Mango | *Ice Cream*	22
Tai Pan Bakery | *Baked Gds.*	19
Z Ten Ren Tea | *Coffee/Tea*	25

FOREST HILLS

Andre's | *Baked Gds.*	23
Cheese/World | *Cheese/Dairy*	25
Eddie's Sweet | *Ice Cream*	25
Edible Arrangements | *Caterer*	22
Martha's Bakery | *Baked Gds.*	23
Piu Bello | *Ice Cream*	21
Uncle Louie | *Ice Cream*	20
Wine & Spirit | *Wine/Liquor*	22

FRESH MEADOWS

Bagel Oasis | *Bagels*	26
Cold Stone | *Ice Cream*	20
Deli Masters | *Deli/Sandwich*	21

GLENDALE

| Amish Market \| *Maj. Gourmet* | 23 |
| Dahlia \| *Flowers* | 26 |

HILLCREST

| Bagels & Co. \| *Bagels* | 22 |

HOWARD BEACH

Uncle Louie | *Ice Cream*   20

JACKSON HEIGHTS

Ⓩ Despaña | *Spec. Shop*   27

Patel Bros. | *Spec. Shop*   23

KEW GARDENS

Hot Bialys | *Bagels*   25

Uncle Louie | *Ice Cream*   20

LONG ISLAND CITY

Brasil Coffee | *Coffee/Tea*   21

Ⓩ FreshDirect | *Maj. Gourmet*   23

New York/Warehse. | 23
  Wine/Liquor

Paramount Caviar | *Caviar*   27

MASPETH

Iavarone Bros. | *Prepared*   25

MIDDLE VILLAGE

BJ's Wholesale | *Maj. Gourmet*   17

Iavarone Bros. | *Prepared*   25

OZONE PARK

Ⓩ Pastosa Ravioli | *Pasta*   26

REGO PARK

Bed Bath/Beyond | *Cookware*   20

Ben's Best | *Deli/Sandwich*   23

Ⓩ Trader Joe's | *Maj. Gourmet*   24

ROCKAWAY BEACH

Cakeline | *Baked Gds.*   -

SUNNYSIDE

Euro Shop | *Spec. Shop*   -

WHITESTONE

Pane d'Italia | *Baked Gds.*   -

Ⓩ Ralph's/Ices | *Ice Cream*   24

Ⓩ Stork's Pastry | *Baked Gds.*   27

WOODSIDE

Giant Big Apple | *Beer*   -

Ⓩ Ottomanelli & Sons | 27
  Meat/Poultry

Staten Island

Andrew & Alan's | *Baked Gds.*   22

Bari Pork | *Meat/Poultry*   24

Bed Bath/Beyond | *Cookware*   20

Belfiore Meats | *Meat/Poultry*   25

Cake Chef | *Baked Gds.*   22

Carol's Cafe | *Caterer*   -

Costco | *Maj. Gourmet*   21

Edible Arrangements | *Caterer*   22

Eggers Ice Cream | *Ice Cream*   25

Lee Sims Choc. | *Candy/Nuts*   25

Mother Mousse | *Baked Gds.*   26

Ⓩ Original SoupMan | *Soup*   23

Ⓩ Pastosa Ravioli | *Pasta*   26

Pete Milano's | *Wine/Liquor*   21

Philip's Candy | *Candy/Nuts*   -

Ⓩ Ralph's/Ices | *Ice Cream*   24

Rita's Ices | *Ice Cream*   21

Ⓩ Royal Crown | *Baked Gds.*   26

Sedutto's | *Ice Cream*   24

Superior Choc. | *Candy/Nuts*   22

Tastebud's | *Health*   22

Uncle Louie | *Ice Cream*   20

Out of Town

Ⓩ Abigail Kirsch | *Caterer*   26

Ⓩ Atlas Party | *Party Rent.*   23

County Chair | *Party Rent.*   -

Foremost Caterers | *Caterer*   24

Metro Party | *Party Rent.*   -

Party Rental | *Party Rent.*   22

Something Different | *Party Rent.*   -

TableToppers | *Party Rent.*   -

Mail Order

Listings cover the best in each category and include source names and Quality ratings. ⚡ indicates places with the highest ratings, popularity and importance.

BAGELS & BIALYS

Bagel Oasis	26
Bagels & Co.	22
Ess-a-Bagel	26
H & H Bagels	26
H & H Midtown	25
⚡ Kossar's	28
Montague St.	22

BAKED GOODS

NEW Amai Tea	20
Andre's	23
Andrew & Alan's	22
BabyCakes	24
Baked	25
Baked Ideas	-
⚡ Black Hound	26
Bread Alone	27
Bruno Bakery	23
Caffe' Simpatico/Ruthy's	15
Caputo Bakery	23
CBK Cookies	23
Cipriani	26
Damascus Bakery	25
Delillo Pastry	26
DeRobertis	22
⚡ Dessert Delivery	28
Egidio Pastry	24
Eileen's Cheesecake	26
Eleni's Cookies	22
Falai Panetteria	27
Fat Witch	25
Ferrara Cafe	22
Fortunato Bros.	25
Gail Watson	-
⚡ Grandaisy Bakery	29
Güllüoglu	-
NEW How Sweet It Is	-
Insomnia Cookies	-
Junior's	23
⚡ Lady M	28
La Guli	24

La Tropezienne	-
⚡ Levain Bakery	28
Little Pie	24
Mansoura	-
Martin's Pretzels	27
Milk & Cookies	24
Mona Lisa Pastry	24
Monteleone's	23
Mother Mousse	26
Mrs. Field's	18
My Most/Food	21
Once Upon/Tart	25
One Girl	24
Orwasher's	26
Pane d'Italia	-
Patisserie des Ambassades	21
⚡ Payard	28
⚡ Rice/Riches	23
Rocco's Pastry	25
S&S Cheesecake	27
Sarabeth's	24
Schick's Bakery	20
Settepani	23
⚡ Soutine	27
⚡ Sylvia Weinstock	26
Three Tarts	22
Tisserie	20
Tribeca Treats	27
Trois Pommes	23
Umanoff/Parsons	24
Veniero's	25
William Greenberg	25
Yonah Schimmel	23
Zaro's Bread	17

CANDY & NUTS

Aji Ichiban	21
Chocolate Bar	26
Chocolate Room	25
Chocolat Moderne	26
Christopher Norman	23

Debauve/Gallais	27
Z Dylan's Candy	21
Economy Candy	24
Evelyn's Choc.	25
Fifth Ave. Choc.	20
Godiva	22
Hershey's	18
Z Jacques Torres	28
JoMart Choc.	24
Z La Maison/Choc.	29
Lee Sims Choc.	25
Leonidas	26
Li-Lac Choc.	26
Lindt	24
Z MarieBelle's	26
Z Martine's	29
Max Brenner	22
Mazal Kosher	17
Z Minamoto	28
Mondel Choc.	22
Myzel Choc.	19
Neuchatel Choc.	24
Neuhaus Choc.	25
NEW Papabubble	24
Z Pierre Marcolini	28
NEW Roni-Sue's	23
Scharffen Berger	26
Superior Choc.	22
Sweet Life	23
Z Teuscher Choc.	27
Varsano's	26
Vere	29
Z Vosges	26

CAVIAR & SMOKED FISH

Z Barney Greengrass	27
Caviar Russe	26
Murray's Sturgeon	27
Paramount Caviar	27
Z Petrossian	28
Z Russ & Daughters	28
Sable's Smoked	27

CHEESE & DAIRY

Alleva Dairy	27
Z Artisanal	28
Z Bedford Cheese	27
Cato Farm	27
Ideal Cheese	27
Maya Schaper	22
Z Murray's Cheese	28

COFFEE & TEA

Brasil Coffee	21
Carry On Tea	23
Z D'Amico	27
Empire Coffee	23
Gimme! Coffee	27
Gorilla Coffee	24
Irving Farm/71	22
Z Ito En	28
Z Jack's Stir Brew	27
Joe	26
Leaf/Bean	23
McNulty's Tea	27
Mudspot	26
Oren's/Roast	24
Ozzie's Coffee	19
Porto Rico	26
Roasting Plant	22
Rohrs	24
Sensuous Bean	25
Starbucks	18
Subtle Tea	23
Sympathy	27
NEW Tafu	19
Z Ten Ren Tea	25
T Salon	26
Z Two for the Pot	27

COOKWARE & SUPPLIES

Z Alessi	27
Bed Bath/Beyond	20
Bloomingdale's	24
Bowery Kitchen	22
Broadway Pan.	26
Brooklyn Kitchen	23
Crate/Barrel	22
Gracious Home	25
Haas Co.	25
Z Korin	28
Macy's Cellar	21
New York Cake	24

Sur La Table	26
Target	17
Z Terence Conran	25
Z Williams-Sonoma	27

DRIED FRUIT

Aji Ichiban	21
Z Balducci's	25
Z Bazzini	27
Z Citarella	26
Z Dean/DeLuca	27
Economy Candy	24
Z Eli's Manhattan	25
Eli's Vinegar	25
Gustiamo	23
Z Kalustyan's	27
Mazal Kosher	17
Patel Bros.	23
Z Russ & Daughters	28
Sweet Life	23
Truffette	-
Z Zabar's	27

FLOWERS

Academy Floral	23
Ariston	27
Banchet Flowers	-
Big Apple Florist	24
Fellan Florist	24
Flowers/World	28
Gotham Gdns.	24
NEW Grove	-
Katrina Parris	-
L'Olivier	29
Polux Fleuriste	-
Richard Salome	-
Root Stock	-
Spruce	27
Surroundings	25
Windsor Florist	24

HEALTH & NATURAL FOODS

A Matter/Health	21
Health/Harmony	26
Health Nuts	21
Z Westerly Natural	25

HERBS & SPICES

House of Spices	24
Z Penzeys Spices	27

MEAT, POULTRY & GAME

Albert & Sons	26
Beekman Mktpl.	22
Z Calabria Pork	28
Z East Vill. Meat	28
Fischer Bros.	27
Z Florence Meat	29
Iavarone Bros.	25
Koglin Hams	24
Le Marais	26
Z Lobel's Meats	29
New Beef	-
Oppenheimer	26
Z Ottomanelli & Sons	27
Ottomanelli Bros.	24
Z Ottomanelli's Meats	27
Park E. Kosher	26
Piazza Mercato	23
Quattro's	26
Z Salumeria	29
Z Schaller/Weber	27
Vincent's Meat	27

PARTY RENTALS

TableToppers	-

PASTAS

Durso's Pasta	26
Iavarone Bros.	25
Z Pastosa Ravioli	26

PRODUCE

Berkshire Berries	27
Red Jacket	27

SEAFOOD

Z Dorian's Seafood	25
Gramercy Fish	24
Leonard's	26
Lobster Pl.	26
Pescatore	25
Wild Edibles	26

SPECIALTY SHOPS

Beth's Farm	27
BuonItalia	26

Butterfield Mkt.	23	Columbus Wine	22
Ceriello	24	Crossroads	25
Chelsea Baskets	24	Z Crush Wine	26
Dale & Thomas	23	Discovery Wines	22
Z Despaña	27	Embassy Wines	19
Euro Shop	–	Famous Wines	22
Foragers Mkt.	22	Fermented	22
Gustiamo	23	Garnet Wines	24
Han Ah Reum	22	Gotham Wines	22
Z Kalustyan's	27	Grand Wine	25
Kam Man	21	Harlem Vintage	28
Katagiri	23	Z Italian Wine	27
Z Manhattan Fruitier	27	K & D Wines	24
Z May May	23	Z Le Dû's Wines	27
Mediterranean	26	Z LeNell's	27
Myers/Keswick	23	Martin Bros.	21
Ninth Ave. Int'l	23	McAdam	22
Nordic Delicacies	28	Z Moore Bros.	29
O&CO.	25	Z Morrell & Co.	27
Oriental Pastry	22	Mount Carmel	26
Patel Bros.	23	Nancy's–Wines	24
Peter's Mkt.	22	New York/Exchange	23
Z Pickle Guys	27	New York/Warehse.	23
Pickles/Olives	23	Park Ave. Liquor	26
Z Stonehouse	27	PJ Wine	27
Teitel Bros.	26	Z Prospect Wine	26
Z Titan Foods	26	Quality Hse.	27
Todaro Bros.	24	Z Red/White	26
Truffette	–	Royal Wine	–
Trunzo Bros.	25	Sea Grape	23

WINES & LIQUOR

Acker Merrall	26	Shawn's Wines	24
Appellation	25	Z Sherry-Lehmann	29
Astor Wines	25	67 Wines	25
Bacchus Wine	19	Skyview Wines	26
Beacon Wines	21	Sutton Wine	22
Beekman Liquors	24	Tribeca Wine	23
Best Cellars	21	Union Sq. Wines	25
Big Nose	24	Vestry Wines	–
Blanc & Rouge	25	Z Vino	28
Z Burgundy	29	Vintage NY	23
Cellar 72	26	Winesby	–
Chambers Wines	26	Wine Therapy	25
Chelsea Wine	23	Winfield-Flynn	23
		Yorkshire Wines	23

ONLINE SOURCES

Best Overall

Averaging Quality, Display & Service ratings.

26 Recchiuti Confections
Browne Trading
Zingerman's
Burdick, L.A.
Cheese/Beverly Hills

25 Upton Tea Imports
Fine Stationery
King Arthur Flour
Cowgirl Creamery
American Spoon

Top Quality Ratings

29 Enstrom's
Hudson/Foie Gras
Upton Tea Imports

28 La Colombe
Cowgirl Creamery

Mighty Leaf
Salumi Armandino
Fante's Kitchen
Zingerman's
Fran's Chocolates

BY CATEGORY

BAKED GOODS
28 Zingerman's
27 Burdick, L.A.
26 Dancing Deer Baking
25 Big Island Candies
24 Boudin Bakery

CANDY
29 Enstrom's
28 Fran's Chocolates
Recchiuti Confections
Fran's Chocolates
27 Burdick, L.A.
25 Bridgewater Chocolate

CAVIAR/SMOKED FISH
28 Browne Trading
Pike Place Fish
26 Di Bruno Bros.
igourmet.com
24 Tsar Nicoulai

CHARCUTERIE
28 Salumi Armandino
Zingerman's
D'Artagnan
26 Di Bruno Bros.
Ferrari, A.G.

CHEESE/DAIRY
28 Cowgirl Creamery
Zingerman's
Cheese/Beverly Hills

26 Di Bruno Bros.
25 Artisan Made-NE

COFFEE/TEA
29 Upton Tea Imports
28 La Colombe
Mighty Leaf
Fortnum & Mason
27 Illy

COOKWARE/SUPPLIES
28 Fante's Kitchen
King Arthur Flour
27 CutleryAndMore
26 Surfas
Cooking Enthusiast

FLOWERS
25 Calyx & Corolla
23 Martha Stewart
22 Hallmark
ProFlowers

GIFT BASKETS
28 Zingerman's
Fran's Chocolates
Cheese/Beverly Hills
Fortnum & Mason
27 American Spoon

HERBS/SPICES
27 Spice House
26 La Tienda

Surfas
Adriana's Caravan
24 ChefShop

MEAT, POULTRY & GAME

29 Hudson/Foie Gras
28 Niman Ranch
D'Artagnan
27 Neuske's
Allen Brothers

PARTY ACCESSORIES

26 Fine Stationery
25 Paper Source
24 Amazon.com
22 Hallmark
21 Illuminations

PASTAS, GRAINS & BEANS

28 King Arthur Flour
27 Bob's Red Mill
26 Surfas
Ferrari, A.G.
24 Amazon.com
ChefShop.com

PRODUCE, NUTS & DRIED FRUIT

27 Bob's Red Mill
24 Cushman Fruit
NapaStyle
ChefShop
Hadley Fruit

SEAFOOD

28 Browne Trading
Pike Place Fish
26 igourmet.com
23 Lobster Gram
Sea Bear

SPECIALTY ITEMS

28 Zingerman's
27 American Spoon
Stonewall Kitchen
La Tienda
26 Ferrari, A.G.

WINES/LIQUOR

28 D. Sokolin
27 Wally's Wine
26 K&L Wine
Zachy's
Wine Library

Top Display Ratings

26 Fine Stationery
Burdick, L.A.
25 Recchiuti Confections
Calyx & Corolla
Stonewall Kitchen

24 NapaStyle
Cookies By Design
Plum Party
Browne Trading
Di Bruno Bros.

Top Service Ratings

26 La Tienda
Zingerman's
Browne Trading
Recchiuti Confections
25 Upton Tea Imports

Niman Ranch
Cheese/Beverly Hills
King Arthur Flour
Fante's Kitchen
American Spoon

ONLINE SOURCES DIRECTORY

Adriana's Caravan *Herbs/Spices*

| 26 | 20 | 21 | M |

www.adrianascaravan.com | 800-316-0820

A "virtual magic blanket" of seasonings, this purveyor – still "missed" as a former inhabitant of Grand Central – proffers a "terrific" selection of herbs and spices, from everyday staples to "obscure finds", as well as a cornucopia of condiments (e.g. more than 30 hot sauces, organized by zing); "helpful descriptions" of the products are handy, especially in the absence of photos, and "excellent customer service" is also available via e-mail or phone; P.S. rated one of the "best values around", it really becomes a bargain when you buy in bulk (discounts apply for orders by the case as well as those over $200).

Allen Brothers *Meat/Poultry*

| 27 | 23 | 24 | VE |

www.allenbrothers.com | 800-957-0111

"Other steaks pale in comparison" to the "first-rate", "perfectly trimmed" prime specimens from this online arm of a circa-1893 Chicago butcher and supplier to "top steakhouses", whose "memorable" meats include Wagyu beef, pork, lamb, sausages and burgers, and there's also game, seafood and prepared foods; its goods are considered by most to be "worth every cent" of their "way-expensive" prices, not least because they arrive "on time" and "in excellent shape"; P.S. its many gift assortments "blow recipients away."

Amazon.com *Cookware/Specialty Shop*

| 24 | 21 | 23 | M |

www.amazon.com

This "clearinghouse for vendors of all shapes and sizes" has become the site to "check before buying" anywhere else due to "highly competitive pricing" (especially with "free shipping" on many items), an "easy-to-use" setup and the "convenience" of shopping a "gigantic selection" of "cook's gear" as well as "gourmet wares" like coffee, tea, chocolates, meat, seafood, cheese, pasta, caviar and charcuterie; sure, delivery's "not flawless", "top-quality products" aren't always available and customer service is "hard to reach" (good luck "trying to find an 800 number" if you need it), but "if you know what you want" you'll most likely get "a deal."

American Spoon Foods *Specialty Shop*

| 27 | 24 | 25 | E |

www.spoon.com | 800-222-5886

Find "heaven in a jar" at this online home of Michigan's "favorite" condiment specialist, where "sour cherry"-lovers and others shop for "top-of-the-heap" artisanal jams, preserves and fruit spreads, as well as "simple", "delicious" savories including salsas, dressings and sauces, all ordered from an easy-to-browse list; its sweet gift boxes are "pricey but special" ideas for food enthusiasts, particularly since voters assure you can "count on the quality."

Artisan Made-Northeast *Cheese/Dairy*

| 25 | 18 | 21 | E |

www.artisanmade-ne.com

Say "cheese" – this site carries the best of Northeastern-produced handcrafted foods, including 80-plus varieties of "delicious" farmstead fromages, some "undiscovered" gems among them, that are as "fresh" as they are "expensive", and there are also other Yankee-made offerings like "delicious" chocolates, jams and sauces; though aesthetes pan its overall look as "one-dimensional", all appreciate the "ease of ordering" and navigation, as well as special services like pairing advice from sommelier Sally Camm, which make this "the place" for artisanal treats.

Big Island Candies *Candy/Nuts*

| 25 | 21 | 22 | M |

www.bigislandcandies.com | 800-935-5510

It's easy to get "hooked on" the "delicious" candies, cookies and such produced by "Hawaii's premier" confectioner, according to "big fans" of its "decadent" signatures like macadamia-studded nut clusters and "divine chocolate-dipped shortbread", as well as newer offerings including truffles with exotic flavorings (hibiscus, yuzu); factor in "beautiful" packaging and numerous gift basket options and you've got the makings of a "wonderful" present; N.B. the altar-bound can work with a wedding specialist to create perfectly packaged favors.

Bob's Red Mill *Grains/Beans*

| 27 | 21 | 22 | M |

www.bobsredmill.com | 800-349-2173

This "old-time company" has "made the jump to the Internet" with aplomb according to surveyors "impressed" with its "marvel-ous" selection of some 400 "natural" whole grains, flours, beans, nuts, dried fruit, baking mixes, hot cereals and more (many of them organic); its website allows for browsing in several ways, has fun features like a short video in which founder Bob Moore takes viewers through the production process as well as recipes and other useful items; P.S. insiders suggest "buy in bulk" as "shipping can be expensive."

Boudin Bakery *Baked Goods*

| 24 | 20 | 20 | M |

www.boudinbakery.com | 800-992-1849

For a slice of San Francisco "delivered right to your door", it's hard to beat the online adjunct of this historic (since 1849) bakery whose selection of the "best sourdough" maybe "isn't tremendous", but it's "tremendous-quality" according to aficionados of its specialty breads and accompaniments, including seasonal ones (e.g. bunny-shaped loaves for Easter); there are also basket and club options for gift-givers, all baked-to-order and sent out the same day, though some say such special handling can add up to a lot of dough ("ship-ping costs are high").

Bridgewater Chocolate *Candy/Nuts*

| 25 | 24 | 22 | VE |

www.bridgewaterchocolate.com | 800-888-8742

"Wow", this tony confectioner's "fabulous" classic American sweets like toffee, caramels, truffles and turtles are "habit"-forming, and packaged prettily enough to make them "perfect for gift-giving"; its website is a pleasure to browse thanks to mouthwa-tering photographs showing each item as it will look upon arrival, and though it's seriously pricey, surveyors say if you're in the mood to "splurge" – "go for it."

Browne Trading Co. *Caviar*   28 | 24 | 26 | E

www.brownetrading.com | 800-944-7848

"When only the best will do" fish finatics turn to this Maine-based, family-run company that's been supplying high-end restaurants (e.g. NYC's Le Bernardin) with impeccable fresh catch, as well as smoked seafood and caviar "to die for", for generations; sure, it's "expensive", but to loyalists it's "worth every penny", especially when you factor in the "unparalleled service" and a website that's "great to shop" and boasts detailed product explanations, serving guidelines and recipes; N.B. it also vends a select assortment of oils, vinegars, salts and such.

Burdick, L.A., Handmade Chocolates *Candy/Nuts*   27 | 26 | 24 | E

www.burdickchocolate.com | 800-229-2419

Gift-givers looking to "spoil someone they love" turn to this online arm of a veteran New Hampshire "chocolate heaven", whose "tiny treasures" are "expensive" but deemed "worth every darn penny" since they're "handmade in the European style" with "quality" ingredients; among the "ethereal confections" are ganache-filled bonbons, trademark "adorable chocolate mice" ("how can you resist?") and a line of Swiss pastries, available in numerous favor and gift assortments; "very good service" and reliable delivery that has everything "arriving fresh and lovely" are icing on the cake.

Calyx & Corolla *Flowers*   25 | 25 | 23 | VE

www.calyxandcorolla.com | 800-800-7788

This petal peddler's cut flowers, arrangements and plants are "fresh" and "gorgeous" enough to make "the giver look good", while its "reliable" speedy delivery can allow even "guys with the worst foresight" to come off like a "Casanova"; the "quality" is voted better and the "designs more exotic" and "upscale-feeling" than the "other big online" players, and while it can be hard to choose among its "impressive" array of options, customers can always look to the "top-notch customer service" for guidance, but just keep in mind that "beauty doesn't come cheap" here.

Cheese Store of Beverly Hills *Cheese/Dairy*   28 | 24 | 25 | E

www.cheesestorebh.com | 800-547-1515

Fromage fans "bow to" this online extension of a Los Angeles "mecca" for "top-notch" artisanal cheeses, citing a "wonderful" 600-strong lactic inventory boasting "fabulous freshness and variety" – from "stinky to smooth and sweet" – and there are also wine, oils, vinegars, salts, caviar and truffles (in season); gift baskets are a strong suit, as is "excellent service", so never mind if a few detect a slight, well, "cheesy" feel to this somewhat basic site.

Chefs *Cookware*   25 | 21 | 21 | M

www.chefscatalog.com | 800-884-2433

A "toque above" many online cookware stores, this mega-site purveys all the "kitchen tools" that "serious cooks" and "wannabe chefs" could ever want, plus lots of fun "not-so-essential" gadgets, offered in an "attractive" format that makes shopping simple (search by brand or category, or check out the recipe section for inspiration); the service is generally considered solid and prices "reasonable", though the savvy suggest "hold out for sales" and "free shipping offers" and you really "can get some deals"; N.B. it offers wedding registry services too.

ChefShop.com *Specialty Shop*

| 24 | 20 | 22 | E |

www.chefshop.com | 800-596-0885

"Half the fun is exploring" the somewhat "weird" assortment of culinary "treats" (prawn chutney, anyone?) available at this online specialty store whose "fabulous, quality products" include everything from fresh meat, salami, seafood and produce to herbs and spices, grains, beans, pastas and baking supplies; shopping is generally an "excellent experience" due to "fast, accurate service" and a wealth of "information" and recipes provided on the site, though a befuddled few feel its convoluted layout is "in need of simplification."

Chef's Resource *Cookware*

| 25 | 21 | 22 | E |

www.chefsresource.com | 866-765-2433

"Most everything you need for your kitchen" can be found through this "easy-to-deal-with" online cookware specialist, whose "amazing", well-laid-out selection spans cookware, cutlery, small appliances and every imaginable tool and gadget, plus grilling equipment, kitchen furniture and a smattering of gourmet foodstuffs like condiments, vinegars and oils; though perspectives differ on the prices ("good" vs. "there are better elsewhere"), no one complains about the "outstanding" variety of offerings that are seemingly "never on backorder."

Cookies By Design *Baked Goods*

| 21 | 24 | 22 | E |

www.cookiesbydesign.com | 888-882-6654

"Cookies that get noticed" are the forte of this online outfit whose "cute" "colorful" signature baked treat comes in "all shapes and designs" imaginable, making for "pretty arrangements" that are "fun to send as gifts" – and "easy" too considering that the options are organized by occasion (baby shower, anniversary, housewarming, recital, etc.) and can also be "customized"; yes, it'll cost you "a lot of dough", but "people just love getting them."

Cooking.com *Cookware*

| 24 | 21 | 21 | M |

www.cooking.com | 800-663-8810

"If they don't have it, it might not exist" say worshipers of this online "mecca" of "all things kitchen-related" vending "name-brand" consumer goods at "a fraction of the cost of department stores" – and sending out "frequent free-shipping offers" that can make for real "bargains"; shoppers appreciate its "helpful" customer-written product reviews and the fact that it "redirects you to other sources if it doesn't stock an item"; other pluses like "discussion boards", recipes, "fantastic customer service" and "prompt shipping" have most praising it as an all-around "reliable resource."

	QUALITY	DISPLAY	SERVICE	COST

Cooking Enthusiast *Cookware*
26 | 20 | 23 | E

www.cutlery.com | 800-792-6650

"Real chefs and wannabes" alike "love" this "first stop for kitchen supplies", which is known foremost for its "excellent selection of knives", but also offers a range of high-end cookware, "hard-to-find gadgets", tableware and a selection of specialty foods (oils and vinegars, condiments, etc.); wallet-watchers note it's "sometimes higher-priced than its competitors", but its overall "quality", including "excellent service" and an easy-to-navigate site featuring "nice notes on equipment", tip the scales in its favor.

Cowgirl Creamery *Cheese/Dairy*
28 | 23 | 24 | E

www.cowgirlcreamery.com | 866-433-7834

Founded a decade ago by a pair of former chefs, this Point Reyes Station, CA, "cheese heaven" is now recognized as "one of America's finest" producers of "distinctive, delicious" artisanal fromages, but it also imports "wonderful" varieties from France and around the world, adding up to an overall "fantastic" (if "expensive") lineup; "online ordering is easy" thanks to the helpful info provided in its 'library of cheese', as well as by its "sharp customer service reps", and since "they know how to ship" it's sure to arrive as fresh as when it left the cave.

Cushman Fruit Co. *Produce*
24 | 19 | 24 | M

www.honeybell.com | 800-776-7575

"Get your bib ready" for the "drippy" goodness of this longtime family-run Florida fruit seller's signature offering: "sweet, super-juicy, utterly delicious" honeybells, a tangerine-grapefruit hybrid available for only a few weeks in January ("you haven't lived until you've had" one); though few find fault with the "premium" goods – including various kinds of citrus and other fruits, plus sweets and gift baskets – surveyors say these "courteous" folks "stand behind their product" and will "replace it if it's not satisfactory."

CutleryAndMore *Cookware*
27 | 22 | 23 | M

www.cutleryandmore.com | 800-650-9866

Not surprisingly, this "well-organized", no-nonsense web "favorite" is particularly "great for its namesake" product, offering "good deals" on hundreds of "high-quality" knives, cleavers, shears, scissors and sharpeners, though it also stocks a vast array of cookware and tools, as well as tough-to-find small appliance replacement parts; users report a "good shopping experience" overall, with "prompt service", low shipping costs and "well-packaged" products that "arrive in a timely fashion."

Dancing Deer Baking Co. *Baked Goods*
26 | 22 | 22 | E

www.dancingdeer.com | 888-699-3337

"Wonderful" baked goods "worth violating your diet" over ("particularly the cookies") are on offer via the "user-friendly" site of this "Boston institution" known for its "natural", "high-quality" ingredients and "good-looking packages" that make it a "go-to for gifts";

QUALITY DISPLAY SERVICE COST

"great service" and "fast shipping" are other appeals, and though the "delicious" products are "pricey", "community"-minded customers say it's "worth it" considering that the "company gives back" a portion of its profits to charity.

D'Artagnan *Meat/Poultry* | 28 | 22 | 24 | E |

www.dartagnan.com | 800-327-8246

The "freshest game you can get without a bird dog" is the word on the "exquisite" products from Ariane Daguin's "wonderful", renowned New Jersey–based site, from signature "to-die-for" foie gras and other "hard-to-find duck specialties" (pâtés, sausages, smoked delicacies) to organic poultry and "delicious" delicacies like truffles and mushrooms, many "from Perigord"; "whatever they do" is "just the best" approve its legions of fans, who appreciate the "hassle-free" service and "terrific" online recipes, and note that while the goods are predictably "expensive", it's "worth the extravagance."

Di Bruno Bros. *Cheese/Dairy* | 26 | 24 | 24 | E |

www.dibruno.com | 888-322-4337

If you can't shop in person at this circa-1939 "Philly institution" of an Italian market (aka "the house of cheese"), its "great online system" is the next best thing, boasting "some of the best" formaggio around – 500 or so varieties, browsable by type or country of origin – as well as "top-quality" charcuterie, caviar and smoked fish, olives, Boot-centric specialty ingredients, kitchenware and "excellent gift baskets"; reviewers report it can be "less expensive" than other "upscale" members of the genre, though there are a few grumbles about "hefty shipping and handling" fees.

D. Sokolin *Wine/Liquor* | 28 | 19 | 23 | E |

www.sokolin.com | 800-946-3947

A favorite of collectors and other deep-pocketed oenophiles, this Hamptons-based online wine merchant (the progeny of a NYC shop founded in 1934) boasts an astounding 100,000-label selection, including many "not readily available locally", with an emphasis on Bordeaux, Burgundy and fine and rare vintages; buyers "certainly feel confident" in purchasing, particularly when guided by the "professional, knowledgeable" staff, though naturally they "pay dearly" for the privilege – not to mention the "killer shipping fees"; N.B. it also sells futures and offers private storage services.

Enstrom's *Candy/Nuts* | 29 | 21 | 24 | M |

www.enstrom.com | 800-367-8766

"World-class toffee" worth "breaking your caps" for is the "unparalleled" signature sweet that has surveyors serenading this Colorado-based confectioner as the "hands-down best" on the web, though it also produces "love-'em" chocolate truffles, chews, fudge and even sugar-free bonbons; shopping is simple given the "great gift" options and "very helpful" customer service, and though it can get "pricey when shipping is added into the equation", "addicts" "order anyway" because it's "that good."

ONLINE SOURCES

| | QUALITY | DISPLAY | SERVICE | COST |

Ethnic Grocer *Specialty Shop*   23 | 18 | 22 | M
www.ethnicgrocer.com | 630-860-1733
"Hard-to-find ingredients are now easy to find" thanks to this
"unique" website that stocks a "wide, international" array of specialty
food items that definitely "aren't at the local grocery store"; explore
the "accessible and informative" homepage for "inspiration",
browsing products organized by country and type, or hit the "terrific" 'cooking school' section supplying "reliable" recipes from "any
number of cultures and cuisines" – just "keep this one bookmarked."

Fante's Kitchen *Cookware*   28 | 20 | 25 | M
www.fantes.com | 800-443-2683
"This is where to find the kitchen tools you didn't know you needed"
say shoppers smitten with this online arm of a circa-1906 Philly
cookware store that "has the stock", from basics to more "unusual
items", with a particular emphasis on baking equipment and "specialty Italian stuff"; all appreciate the "reasonable prices", pro customer service (they "know more about cooking than some chefs")
as well as the "helpful" online product info – now if only they'd give
the website "a little updating."

Ferrari, A.G., Foods *Specialty Shop*   26 | 22 | 21 | E
www.agferrari.com | 877-878-2783
"If you don't live close to an Italian store, don't worry" – there's always this Northern California–based purveyor's "helpful" site offering "well-chosen", "high-quality" (and "costly") artisanal goods
from The Boot, including cheeses, charcuterie, pastas, wines and
lots of specialty food items; customers can search by product type
or region, and there are also "nicely packaged gift baskets" and a
lengthy recipes section.

Fine Stationery *Party Accessories*   26 | 26 | 24 | E
www.finestationery.com | 888-808-3463
Offering "the biggest selection of the best" paper goods out
there, this online stationer is considered a "top-notch" source for
"beautiful, unique" custom invitations of all kinds; its easy-to-
browse website organizes products based on occasion, and orders
are "shipped quickly", making it ideal for "weddings, parties and
baby announcements", though some feel the personalization process "isn't the most user-friendly" and "prices are higher" than
some of the competition.

Fortnum & Mason *Coffee/Tea*   28 | 23 | 23 | E
www.fortnumandmason-usa.com | 877-533-2636
The U.S. site for this venerable, nearly 300-year-old Piccadilly
Circus purveyor of "fine British teas and coffees" and traditional
"English" snacks "never disappoints", supplying Anglophiles and expats with "superb" loose leaves and beans, as well as biscuits, jams
and other "upscale" tea-time treats, plus "wonderful gift baskets";
maybe "it's not quite like enjoying the store with its coat-and-tailed
staff" (and it "doesn't have the full selection" either), but admirers

QUALITY | DISPLAY | SERVICE | COST

appreciate that delivery is "prompt", and as for the "slightly numbing" prices – it's still "cheaper than a trip to London."

Fran's Chocolates *Candy/Nuts*
28 | 23 | 23 | E

www.franschocolates.com | 800-422-3726

Though she's "best known for her salted caramels", it's hard to pass up any of Seattle confectioner Fran Bigelow's "sinfully delicious" confections, given that the "great chocolate" bars and "fantastic" truffles in "luxurious", big-bowed gift boxes tempt anyone browsing her "easy-to-navigate" website; happily for the "addicted", delivery is "quick", though "high prices" make its "to-die-for" morsels an expensive "vice."

Hadley Fruit Orchards *Candy/Nuts*
24 | 18 | 20 | M

www.hadleyfruitorchards.com | 800-854-5655

Maybe "it's not as much fun as going there in person" but visits to this online arm of an "old reliable" Banning, CA, fruit grower are rewarded with products that "look good and taste even better", including dates (notably "great" Medjools), dried fruits and nuts; gift-givers can choose from a variety of assortment options, and there are also "yummy" trail mixes, leaving most to marvel "how do you not find something here?"

Hallmark *Flowers*
22 | 21 | 21 | M

www.hallmarkflowers.com | 800-425-5627

This mega-brand known for its "thoughtful" cards adds "better-than-you'd-expect" flowers and plants to its roster of "consistently good products", presenting them on an "easy-to-use" site offering several ways to search arrangements (occasion, type, price), a helpful 'learn about' section full of flower facts and tips, and a "free e-card" area; recipients say its blooms "last a long time", and the "Hallmark card" included with deliveries is "a nice touch"; N.B. party-throwers should note it's also a source for invitations.

Harney & Sons *Coffee/Tea*
27 | 24 | 23 | M

www.harney.com | 888-427-6398

"Tea freaks" frequent this "favorite site" – the online extension of a "family-run" Millerton, NY, shop – for its "wonderful" selection of "very fine, full-flavored teas" that span the spectrum from "staples" to "innovative" blends, and there are also "terrific" accessories; the loose leaves and sachets come "well-packaged" in adorable tins, which lend themselves naturally to a "wide variety" of "great gift" sets, while "reasonable prices" and the company's general "dedication to customers" seal the deal – just "beware the seduction" factor lest you end up with "a cabinetful."

Harry & David *Gift Baskets*
23 | 23 | 22 | E

www.harryanddavid.com | 877-322-1200

"Always appreciated" "offerings for the hard-to-shop-for" have crowned this Oregon-based business the "king of gift baskets", boasting an "easy-to-manage" website where "classic" selections that "everyone loves getting" – trademark "amazing, juicy pears best eaten with a bib" or "over-the-top" towers of treats – are easily purchased and "reliably" delivered (but if there's a problem, "customer service bends over backwards" to make it right); there are grumbles about "very costly" prices and "extra fees for everything", but the majority maintains "dependability" is "worth paying for."

Hudson Valley Foie Gras *Meat/Poultry* | 29 | 22 | 24 | VE |
www.hudsonvalleyfoiegras.com | 877-289-3643

"The source for fresh foie gras" is this "dependable duck" dealer whose products are rated the "best you can get in the U.S.", perhaps because all stages of production, from breeding to packaging, happen on its 20-acre farm in Ferndale, NY; in addition to its signature "to-die-for" whole goose livers, there are terrines, pâtés and fresh duck breasts and more, and its site boasts appealing extras like recipes and travelogues from cofounder Michael Ginor; P.S. naturally it's "expensive", but given the "very-best" quality most maintain it's "worth every penny."

igourmet.com *Gift Baskets* | 26 | 21 | 23 | E |
www.igourmet.com | 877-446-8763

"You'll reorder often" say supporters of this "lifesaver" of a site, where you can "make a gift basket out of anything you choose" – or order à la carte just for yourself – selecting from an "astounding" array of "delicacies" "from a wide range of countries", including "*très magnifique* cheeses"; some say the "amazing" number of options can make shopping here a "bit cumbersome" until "you get used to it", but the relatively "moderate prices" given the "luxury" genre make it a "great resource", as do the "helpful service" and "prompt shipping."

Illuminations *Party Accessories* | 21 | 21 | 19 | M |
www.illuminations.com | 800-621-2998

Some of the "best scents in the biz" can be found at this "no-hassles" site for "reasonably priced" candles and related "imaginative" accessories and "decorative items", including votives, tealights and tapers perfect for party-throwers; "new items" are added "all the time" and there are "lots of online specials and sales", making it a boon for "bargain-hunters."

Illy *Coffee/Tea* | 27 | 23 | 21 | E |
www.illyusa.com | 877-469-4559

"*Bellissimo!*" – bring "real Italian espresso" and other "rich-tasting roasts and blends" "to your home" via this famous Trieste-based purveyor's "modern" U.S. site, which, in addition to its "delicious", "pricey" beans, offers "good espresso machines" and coffeemakers with "top-notch design and function" (and they can be had "cheaply" if you sign up for regular coffee deliveries); if "shipping can be spotty", at least "the quality is consistent"; P.S. "love the limited-edition espresso cup" collections designed by well-known artists.

Intelligentsia Coffee *Coffee/Tea* | 27 | 20 | 23 | M |
www.intelligentsiacoffee.com | 888-945-9786

"Deli coffee it ain't" quip patrons of this informative online offshoot of a Chicago-based coffee retailer that offers a reasonably priced

QUALITY DISPLAY SERVICE COST

"wide variety of Fair Trade coffee and tea", including everything from Charlie Trotter's house blend to "green beans for home-roasters", and it also vends loose leaf and chai teas and all the necessary brewing apparatus; its "consistent" "telephone voicemail system", along with a staff that "fills orders quickly", have many applauding it as "the coffee company to end all arguments."

K&L Wine Merchants *Wine/Liquor*   26 | 19 | 21 | M

www.klwines.com | 877-559-4637

Ok, maybe it "isn't too sexy", but "who needs style when you have substance?" pose partisans of this web adjunct of a "favorite" San Francisco Bay Area wine purveyor, which imparts seriously "detailed" information about its "terrific selection" strong on California, Bordeaux and Burgundy producers (including "high-end" and hard-to-find vintages); its "competitive prices", "quality" goods "received in pristine condition" and "great e-mail and phone service" have most toasting it as an "Internet sensation"; P.S. "make sure to sign up for" their "amusing, informative" newsletter.

Karl Ehmer *Meat/Poultry*   25 | 19 | 23 | M

www.karlehmer.com | 800-487-5275

"*Sehr gut!*" cry enthusiasts of this unpretentious online market whose "old-world bratwurst and Westphalian and assorted cold cuts" trace their roots back to Mr. Ehmer's first butcher shop in NYC (founded in 1932); since his products are "hard to find in local stores", this website is prized for its offerings from *senfgurken* pickles, red cabbage and spaetzle to, of course, those "wondrous sausages" and other "German-style meats" that are simply "the very, very best."

King Arthur Flour/   28 | 23 | 25 | M
The Baker's Catalogue *Grains/Beans*

www.bakerscatalogue.com | 800-827-6836

This online arm of a 200-year-old New England flour "mecca" offers a "fantastic", "high-quality" selection spanning "everything for your baking needs", from the "best flours", mixes and "fine ingredients" to "hard-to-find accoutrements"; the company is known for its "excellent customer service", which extends to its website in the form of "good recipes, advice" and "technical information" about the products, making it "a must if you bake" – and "if you don't, you will after visiting."

La Colombe *Coffee/Tea*   28 | 20 | 22 | E

www.lacolombe.com | 800-563-0860

It's admired as "one of the best roasters in the business", and this favorite of coffee connoisseurs – "Philly's best-known!" – sells its five "rich" blends, poured in many of the country's "finest restaurants" (e.g. Jean-Georges Vongerichten's), through its attractive and easy-to-use website; yes, such "superb" products will run you a lot of beans, but at least the flat-rate shipping fee for its "fast delivery" is "reasonable"; N.B. it opened a retail store and coffee shop in TriBeCa recently.

	QUALITY	DISPLAY	SERVICE	COST

La Tienda *Specialty Shop*

26 | 22 | 26 | M

www.tienda.com | 800-710-4304

"*The* place" on the web for "authentic Spanish foods", this "excellent" purveyor's "wonderful", "well-displayed, expansive selection" of imports boasts everything from artisanal chorizo, *jamon* and cheeses to olives, nuts, grains, spices, cookware and wine, including many "otherwise hard-to-find" offerings; the crowning touches are "fair prices", top-drawer service and reliable delivery that ensures the goods arrive "in a timely fashion."

Lobster Gram *Seafood*

23 | 22 | 24 | E

www.livelob.com | 800-548-3562

"It's the original and still the best" say crustacean-lovers of this Maine monolith offering what may be "the best Internet deal for" live lobsters and frozen tails, as well as shrimp, scallops and clambakes, not to mention prepared foods like "soups and bisques to-die-for"; its site is "easy to navigate" and the service people are "great to work with", leading connoisseurs to cheer "you can't go wrong"; P.S. those "succulent" bugs make "great gifts", especially as "all the tools down to bibs and wipes" are included.

Martha Stewart for 1-800-flowers.com *Flowers*

23 | 23 | 20 | E

(fka MarthaStewartFlowers.com)

www.1800flowers.com | 800-462-7842

The domestic doyenne herself "must be on the shipping floor" because the "beautiful, fresh", "clever" arrangements from this online florist "all come out" with "that signature Martha touch"; its handy site allowing customers to "upgrade the vase" and "see what it will look like with selected flowers", not to mention "quick service", means most find it "worth" the somewhat "expensive" rates; N.B. a post-Survey merger with 1-800-flowers.com may outdate the above ratings.

Mighty Leaf *Coffee/Tea*

28 | 23 | 23 | E

www.mightyleaf.com | 877-698-5323

Though it's the top-"quality" hand-blended teas that win this San Francisco outfit its customers' unflagging loyalty ("Mighty Leaf, I love you"), what draws the most comments are its "wonderful" "netted fabric" teabags that "don't impart extra flavor" to the brew and are "pretty" to boot; the "amazing", largely organic selection spans green, black, white and herbal varieties, including "unusual" blends, arrayed on a site that's "easy-to-navigate" and backed by "great", "knowledgeable" service, which for most offsets the somewhat steep prices; N.B. there are also accessories like teapots as well as gift assortments.

Molinari & Sons *Charcuterie*

25 | 18 | 20 | M

www.molinarisalame.com

"Beautiful, authentic salumi" is the specialty of this 100-year-old family-owned San Francisco business that sells its coppa and other dry-cured meats, as well as cooked cold cuts, via a straightforward website; prices are happily "reasonable", "ordering is easy" and de-

	QUALITY	DISPLAY	SERVICE	COST

livery "on-time", making this the next best thing to living "down the street" from the store – "if you like salami, this is the place."

NapaStyle *Specialty Shop*
www.napastyle.com | 866-766-1600

| 24 | 24 | 22 | E |

Have "a piece of Wine Country delivered to your home" via chef Michael Chiarello's website that "really shows off the Napa lifestyle" while peddling an "extensive" array of "high-quality food products" – cheeses, oils, vinegars, seasonings, chocolates, specialty cookware – plus wine from Chiarello's own vineyard; it's a "great source for gifts", though price-watchers note that aside from its many "unique" offerings, you can "find the same items on other sites cheaper" – or avoid the "dazzling prices" by "waiting for a sale."

Neuske's *Meat/Poultry*
www.nueskes.com | 800-392-2266

| 27 | 24 | 24 | E |

When you're "achin' for bacon" this 75-year-old Wisconsin purveyor's applewood-smoked version is considered by connoisseurs the "absolute best anywhere", and through its no-nonsense website it also peddles a range of other "fantastic" "pig"-centric products, as well as beef, chicken, game, cheeses and various gift assortments; while a finicky few object to its site's "mass-market" feel, all appreciate its "great customer service."

Niman Ranch *Meat/Poultry*
www.nimanranch.com | 866-808-0340

| 28 | 22 | 25 | E |

"You can taste the humane treatment in every bite" claim conscientious carnivores partial to this "excellent" purveyor's "top-of-the-line" all-natural meats, including "tender, flavorful" traditionally and sustainably raised pork, beef and lamb from independent family farms; beyond the "can't-go-wrong" quality of its offerings, customers also appreciate the "great website", virtually "unequalled service" and "fastest delivery" – "these are good people."

Paper Source *Party Accessories*
www.paper-source.com | 888-727-3711

| 25 | 22 | 23 | M |

Among "the best there is in paper and invites", including "lovely" handmade products "no other store" carries, this web dealer's "fantastic selection" and many customization options make it ideal for parties and weddings; there's "friendly service if you have questions", "everything comes as-ordered" and delivery is "quick", and savvy shoppers note "if you buy in bulk, it's really cheap."

Peet's Coffee & Tea *Coffee/Tea*
www.peets.com | 800-999-2132

| 26 | 22 | 23 | M |

"Before Starbucks there was" this Bay Area–based chain beloved by legions of "Peetniks" for its "top-notch", "strong", "flavorful" coffees in a variety of "excellent" roasts, available to those who "don't live near a store" via an "easy-to-use" website; "addicts" appreciate that its "amazing beans" and "delicious" leaves ("they take their teas as seriously as their coffees") are "reasonably priced", "lovingly shipped" and "delivered on time" – "these people rock!"

Pike Place Fish Market *Seafood*   28 | 23 | 24 | E
www.pikeplacefish.com | 800-542-7732

The next best thing to "going in person", this web counterpart to Seattle's "famous" Pike Place Market is "the place to go for salmon of any type", as well as other Pacific Northwest specialties including Dungeness crabs, halibut and "incredible" smoked Copper River king salmon; "you can't get any fresher" according to fin fans who appreciate that its well-packed goods "come fast", and though they concede it's "expensive" – "you get what you pay for."

Plum Party *Party Accessories*   23 | 24 | 21 | M
www.plumparty.com | 800-227-0314

"*Très* cute" with "the perfect accessories for all occasions", this stylish site is a "fun, inspirational" place to find "terrific party supplies, decorations and special favors" according to enthusiastic hosts who note it could "save you hours of in-person shopping"; handily it "lets you search by theme or occasion", but just know "it's dangerous" – "everything is so nifty, you want to buy it all."

ProFlowers *Flowers*   22 | 20 | 22 | M
www.proflowers.com | 800-580-2913

"Always on time", this online florist "consistently" provides the "freshest flowers around" according to legions of fanciers who say its "beautiful", "classy arrangements", "long-lasting blooms" and "reasonable prices" add up to solid "bang for your buck"; "excellent customer service" and "reliable" delivery that has the goods "arriving in great shape" are other endearments; P.S. it extends "special offers to regular customers."

Recchiuti Confections *Candy/Nuts*   28 | 25 | 26 | VE
www.recchiuti.com | 800-500-3396

Approaching "chocolate perfection", Michael Recchiuti's "wonderful", "beautifully balanced" bonbons and other confections (including "exquisite fleur de sel caramels") tend toward "inventive and adventurous flavors" and "fantastic" shapes; though a few lament that the "website has a slim" lineup compared to Recchiuti's San Francisco store, the majority finds "outstanding quality and selection" that "put other more well-known chocolatiers to shame" – and that are "worth the outrageous cost"; P.S. sign up for the "great monthly newsletter."

Republic of Tea *Coffee/Tea*   25 | 23 | 22 | M
www.republicoftea.com | 800-298-4832

"Tea as a fine art form" is the aspiration of this company run by "people passionate on the subject", whose "huge selection" of "exotic", "high-quality", "wonderfully packaged" leaves are backed by "environmental and health commitments" that "make you feel good buying from them"; though its products are now "widely available in stores", insiders recommend its "beautiful website" as "the place" to shop the "full array of wares" (including "pretty accessories"), and say "buying in bulk" will get you the "best value."

	QUALITY	DISPLAY	SERVICE	COST

Salumi Armandino *Charcuterie*

| 28 | 20 | 23 | E |

www.salumicuredmeats.com | 877-223-0813

"Mario's dad is the best cured-meat maker in the world" declare devotees of Armandino Batali and his Seattle salumeria, whose website allows the rest of the country a shot at his "crazy-good" Italian-style products showcasing the "pig in all its glory"; the "exquisite, complex" offerings include about a dozen varieties of salami and other cured meats, all made traditionally by hand, so perhaps it's not surprising that the "prices are kind of high" and "they seem to be out of stock of certain things often" – most don't mind because the "quality is unparalled."

SeaBear Wild Salmon *Seafood*

| 23 | 19 | 23 | E |

www.seabear.com | 800-645-3474

"Excellent" Copper River salmon is the mainstay of this Washington State fishery and its straightforward website, but it also provides a "very good selection" of other fresh seafood (halibut, king crab), house-smoked wild salmon (packed with its patented 'gold seal pouch', which requires no refrigeration until opened) as well as prepared dishes like ready-to-eat fish and chowders; some carp about "expensive" prices, but all appreciate that "shipments are prompt"; N.B. it also offers cedar wraps, planks and other grilling accessories.

See's Candies *Candy/Nuts*

| 24 | 21 | 23 | M |

www.sees.com | 800-347-7337

"You don't have to go to California" to get the "scrumptious" chocolates, peanut brittle, scotch mallows and other "old-fashioned" confections that this "classic West Coast wonder" has long been beloved for, thanks to its "reliable" online counterpart; "the site is very easy to navigate", making it "very simple to purchase items for gifts" while prices "won't break the bank", adding up to "amazing value" – "nothing beats it!"

Spice House, The *Herbs/Spices*

| 27 | 21 | 23 | M |

www.thespicehouse.com | 800-972-8496

Voted "easily the best" spice and herb purveyor – "online and off", this family-owned Chicago merchant boasts an "everything-under-the-sun" lineup of seasonings "from all over the world", which arrive "quick" and "super-fresh"; its site's wealth of product information and features like online forums, not to mention "knowledgeable" service folk who "help you sort through the differences of hundreds" of products, add up to "great shopping experiences", with "good" prices to seal the deal.

Stonewall Kitchen *Specialty Shop*

| 27 | 25 | 24 | E |

www.stonewallkitchen.com | 800-826-1752

"Delicious" jams, jellies, sauces and condiments with a "homey" look and taste are the stock in trade of this New England outfit whose "great website" allows easy access to the full line of its "now ubiquitous" array of "high-quality" products, many with "unusual" flavor combinations; it offers many assortments "perfect for gifting", and there are also "tasty marinades" and premade baking mixtures that allow novice cooks and the pressed-for-time to "fake it" in style, all of which leads lauders to take in stride the "pricey" rates.

Surfas *Cookware*
26 | 18 | 19 | M

www.surfasonline.com | 866-799-4770

When on the hunt for "those harder-to-find items", savvy surfas turn to this moderately priced online annex to "the best kitchen supply store in LA", a "chef's nirvana" of "commercial"-quality cookware and accessories from pots and pans and cutlery to small appliances, "gizmos" and baking supplies, not to mention "interesting foodstuffs" including beans, grains, herbs, spices and more; "if it exists, they have it", however, some say the website itself "could use some improvement", and ditto the service.

Tsar Nicoulai *Caviar*
24 | 19 | 21 | VE

www.tsarnicoulai.com | 800-952-2842

"At last, domestic caviar that competes with the imports" cheer connoisseurs of this San Francisco–based purveyor best known for its "fresh, fabulous" farmed Californian Estate Osetra, though it also offers "elegant" eggs from Russia, Romania and Iran; its products are worthy of any "imperial feast", and a guilt-free one too considering that they're all sustainably sourced; N.B. it also offers the requisite accessories (mother-of-pearl spoons, etc.) as well as triple-smoked sturgeon and an array of gift assortments.

Upton Tea Imports *Coffee/Tea*
29 | 23 | 25 | M

www.uptontea.com | 800-234-8327

It "sets the standard for online tea purveyors" rave reviewers of this "fabulous" Massachusetts-based outfit that caters to the "complete fanatic" with its "superb" 400-plus selection of "quality" loose leaves "from all over the world", plus teapots, kettles and other accessories, all at "great prices"; its "easy site" allows browsing by product type (black, green, herbal, etc.) or by country of origin and provides a wealth of info on all things tea, while its "prompt" delivery and "reliable" service cinch its standing as "the best of the best."

Wally's Wine & Spirits *Wine/Liquor*
27 | 23 | 23 | E

www.wallywine.com | 888-992-5597

Everything's "easy in Wally world" according to devotees of this LA wine store and its nimble site allowing shoppers access to its "vast" (9,000 labels) "well-considered selection" of wines and spirits – "rare and hard-to-find items are no problem for them" – and its extensive "gourmet food" offerings including cheeses and charcuterie; its "helpful" customer service and delivery that gets it there "well-packed and quick" win kudos, though even "loyal Wallyites" note that while "some great prices can be had", it's "generally on the expensive side."

Whole Latte Love *Coffee/Tea*
24 | 21 | 24 | M

www.wholelattelove.com | 888-411-5282

"These guys are serious about their coffee!" rave reviewers of this connoisseur's source covering the "whole gamut of brewing needs" – from a "wide selection" of high-quality beans to "top-of-the-line espresso machines" and every imaginable tool and accessory in between; its "very competitive prices" and "exceptional" "personalized" service are other virtues, while the "easily navigable" site itself wins praise for its "helpful and objective pre-purchase advice" (including "in-depth product reviews") and "video demonstrations"; N.B. it also stocks tea and related accoutrements.

Wine.com *Wine/Liquor*   21 | 20 | 20 | M
www.wine.com | 800-592-5870

It's known as "the original" online wine store and it's "still one of the best" say admirers of this "easy-to-use" site whose 10,000-strong selection tends toward "mass-market" labels but includes "some harder-to-find" bottlings too; "fair prices" (augmented with frequent "shipping promotions") and a convenient array of gift options are points in its favor, but nonetheless a critical contingent claiming that it succeeds "by name alone" dismisses its offerings as "serviceable, but not memorable."

Wine Library *Wine/Liquor*   26 | 22 | 24 | M
www.winelibrary.com | 888-980-9463

An oenophile "could get lost for hours" browsing this "wacky" "wine-lover's heaven" of a site, the online counterpart of a legendary New Jersey store, whose "wide", "well-rounded" selection, "good prices" and "fast delivery" make it one of the "best on the web" – "if you can't find something to your liking here, give up!"; it's also appreciated for its "informative format" with features like the "must-see" Wine TV daily video blog hosted by the owner (he's "a nut").

Zachy's *Wine/Liquor*   26 | 21 | 23 | E
www.zachys.com | 866-922-4971

This "exemplary" Westchester wine store and its "amazing website" boast a "huge" (5,000 labels) selection in "all price brackets", though it's particularly known for its "high-end" vintages (especially Bordeaux, Californian and Italian producers), as well as for its "excellent" futures and online auctions; it's a "pleasure to order from them" say surveyors who appreciate that the inventory is "well-displayed" and easy to browse, while the service is "efficient and helpful", and though there are complaints about "costly" prices, connoisseurs shrug "you get what you pay for."

Zingerman's *Specialty Shop*   28 | 23 | 26 | E
www.zingermans.com | 888-636-8162

The "personality and flair" of Ann Arbor's beloved landmark, widely considered the "best deli outside of NYC", extend to its "terrific website", whose "entertaining writing" and "cute illustrations" help "make you feel like you're in the store" browsing its "zingy" array of artisanal products including "unbeatable" breads, olive oils, cheeses, charcuterie and myriad "unique treats"; also a forte are "fun" gift baskets perfect "for the foodie", which most say "arrive in great shape", but "if there's a problem", the "nice" staff will "cheerfully solve it" – "who could want more?"

ONLINE SOURCES
INDEXES

Special Features

Listings cover the best in each category and include Quality ratings.

BAKED GOODS

Big Island Candies	25
Boudin Bakery	24
Burdick, L.A.	27
Cookies By Design	21
Cooking.com	24
Dancing Deer Baking	26
Ethnic Grocer	23
igourmet.com	26
Zingerman's	28

CANDY

Amazon.com	24
Artisan Made-NE	25
Big Island Candies	25
Bridgewater Chocolate	25
Burdick, L.A.	27
ChefShop.com	24
Cooking.com	24
Enstrom's	29
Ethnic Grocer	23
Fortnum & Mason	28
Fran's Chocolates	28
Hadley Fruit	24
igourmet.com	26
La Tienda	26
NapaStyle	24
Recchiuti Confections	28
Republic of Tea	25
See's Candies	24
Surfas	26
Zingerman's	28

CAVIAR & SMOKED FISH

Amazon.com	24
Browne Trading	28
Cooking.com	24
Di Bruno Bros.	26
igourmet.com	26
Pike Place Fish	28
SeaBear Wild Salmon	23
Tsar Nicoulai	24
Wally's Wine	27

CHARCUTERIE

Amazon.com	24
ChefShop.com	24
D'Artagnan	28
Di Bruno Bros.	26
Ferrari, A.G.	26
igourmet.com	26
Karl Ehmer	25
Molinari & Sons	25
NapaStyle	24
Salumi Armandino	28
Wally's Wine	27
Zingerman's	28

CHEESE & DAIRY

Amazon.com	24
Artisan Made-NE	25
Cheese/Beverly Hills	28
Cooking.com	24
Cowgirl Creamery	28
Di Bruno Bros.	26
Ferrari, A.G.	26
igourmet.com	26
La Tienda	26
NapaStyle	24
Wally's Wine	27
Zingerman's	28

COFFEE & TEA

Amazon.com	24
Cooking Enthusiast	26
Di Bruno Bros.	26
Ethnic Grocer	23
Ferrari, A.G.	26
Fortnum & Mason	28
Harney & Sons	27
igourmet.com	26
Illy	27
Intelligentsia Coffee	27
La Colombe	28
Mighty Leaf	28
Peet's Coffee	26
Republic of Tea	25
Upton Tea Imports	29
Whole Latte Love	24

COOKWARE & SUPPLIES

Amazon.com	24
Chefs	25
Chef's Resource	25

subscribe to ZAGAT.com

ONLINE SOURCES

SPECIAL FEATURES

PRODUCE

ChefShop.com	24
Cushman Fruit	24
Hadley Fruit	24
Harry & David	23
igourmet.com	26

SEAFOOD

Allen Brothers	27
Amazon.com	24
Browne Trading	28
ChefShop.com	24
igourmet.com	26
Lobster Gram	23
Pike Place Fish	28
SeaBear Wild Salmon	23

SPECIALTY ITEMS

Amazon.com	24
American Spoon	27
Browne Trading	28
Cheese/Beverly Hills	28
Chefs	25
ChefShop.com	24
Chef's Resource	25
Cooking.com	24
Cooking Enthusiast	26
D'Artagnan	28
Di Bruno Bros.	26
Ethnic Grocer	23
Fante's Kitchen	28
Ferrari, A.G.	26
Fortnum & Mason	28
Hadley Fruit	24
Hudson/Foie Gras	29
igourmet.com	26
La Tienda	26
NapaStyle	24
Stonewall Kitchen	27
Surfas	26
Wally's Wine	27
Wine.com	21
Zingerman's	28

WINES & LIQUOR

D. Sokolin	28
Ferrari, A.G.	26
K&L Wine	26
La Tienda	26
NapaStyle	24
Wally's Wine	27
Wine.com	21
Wine Library	26
Zachy's	26